Honda CBF125

Service and Repair Manual

by Phil Mather

Models covered

CBF125M9	2009
CBF125MA	2010
CBF125MB	2011 to 2012
CBF125MD	2013 to 2014

(5540-216-5AN1)

ABCDE
FGHIJ
KLMNO
PQ

© Haynes Publishing 2014

A book in the Haynes Service and Repair Manual Series

All rights reserved. No part of this book may be reproduced or transmitted in any form or by any means, electronic or mechanical, including photocopying, recording or by any information storage or retrieval system, without permission in writing from the copyright holder.

ISBN: 978 0 85733 941 6

Printed in the USA

Haynes Publishing
Sparkford, Yeovil, Somerset BA22 7JJ, England

Haynes North America, Inc
859 Lawrence Drive, Newbury Park, California 91320, USA

Printed using 33-lb Resolute Book 65 4.0 from Resolute Forest Products Calhoun, TN mill. Resolute is a member of World Wildlife Fund's Climate Savers programme committed to significantly reducing GHG emissions. This paper uses 50% less wood fibre than traditional offset. The Calhoun Mill is certified to the following sustainable forest management and chain of custody standards: SFI, PEFC and FSC Controlled Wood.

Contents

LIVING WITH YOUR HONDA CBF125

Introduction
The Birth of a Dream	Page	0•4
Acknowledgements	Page	0•8
About this manual	Page	0•8
Model development	Page	0•9
Bike Spec	Page	0•9
Identification numbers	Page	0•10
Buying spare parts	Page	0•11
Safety first!	Page	0•12

Pre-ride checks
Engine oil level	Page	0•13
Front brake fluid level	Page	0•14
Suspension, steering and drive chain	Page	0•14
Tyres	Page	0•15
Legal and safety checks	Page	0•15

MAINTENANCE

Routine maintenance and servicing
Specifications	Page	1•2
Lubricants and fluids	Page	1•2
Maintenance schedule	Page	1•3
Component locations	Page	1•4
Maintenance procedures	Page	1•5

Contents

REPAIRS AND OVERHAUL

Engine, transmission and associated systems

Engine, clutch and transmission	Page	**2•1**
Ignition	Page	**3•1**
Engine management system	Page	**4•1**

Chassis components

Frame and suspension	Page	**5•1**
Brakes, wheels and final drive	Page	**6•1**
Bodywork	Page	**7•1**

Electrical system

Page **8•1**

Wiring diagram

Page **8•20**

REFERENCE

Tools and Workshop Tips	Page	**REF•2**
Security	Page	**REF•20**
Lubricants and fluids	Page	**REF•23**
Conversion factors	Page	**REF•26**
MOT Test Checks	Page	**REF•27**
Storage	Page	**REF•32**
Fault Finding	Page	**REF•35**
Technical Terms Explained	Page	**REF•44**

Index

Page **REF•48**

Introduction

The Birth of a Dream

by Julian Ryder

There is no better example of the Japanese post-war industrial miracle than Honda. Like other companies which have become household names, it started with one man's vision. In this case the man was the 40-year old Soichiro Honda who had sold his piston-ring manufacturing business to Toyota in 1945 and was happily spending the proceeds on prolonged parties for his friends. However, the difficulties of getting around in the chaos of post-war Japan irked Honda, so when he came across a job lot of generator engines he realised that here was a way of getting people mobile again at low cost.

A 12 by 18-foot shack in Hamamatsu became his first bike factory, fitting the generator motors into pushbikes. Before long he'd used up all 500 generator motors and started manufacturing his own engine, known as the 'chimney', either because of the elongated cylinder head or the smoky exhaust or perhaps both. The chimney made all of half a horsepower from its 50 cc engine but it was a major success and became the Honda A-type.

Less than two years after he'd set up in Hamamatsu, Soichiro Honda founded the Honda Motor Company in September 1948. By then, the A-type had been developed into the 90 cc B-type engine, which Mr Honda decided deserved its own chassis not a bicycle frame. Honda was about to become Japan's first post-war manufacturer of complete motorcycles. In August 1949 the first prototype was ready. With an output of three horsepower, the 98 cc D-type was still a simple two-stroke but it had a two-speed transmission and most importantly a pressed steel frame with telescopic forks and hard tail rear end. The frame was almost triangular in profile with the top rail going in a straight line from the massively braced steering head to the rear axle. Legend has it that after the D-type's first tests the entire workforce went for a drink to celebrate and try and think of a name for the bike. One man broke one of those silences you get when people are thinking, exclaiming 'This is like a dream!' 'That's it!' shouted Honda, and so the Honda Dream was christened.

Honda C70 and C90 OHV-engined models

'This is like a dream!' 'That's it' shouted Honda

Mr Honda was a brilliant, intuitive engineer and designer but he did not bother himself with the marketing side of his business. With hindsight, it is possible to see that employing Takeo Fujisawa who would both sort out the home market and plan the eventual expansion into overseas markets was a masterstroke. He arrived in October 1949 and in 1950 was made Sales Director. Another vital new name was Kiyoshi Kawashima, who along with Honda himself, designed the company's first four-stroke after Kawashima had told them that the four-stroke opposition to Honda's two-strokes sounded nicer and therefore sold better. The result of that statement was the overhead-valve 148 cc E-type which first ran in July 1951 just two months after the first drawings were made. Kawashima was made a director of the Honda Company at 34 years old.

The E-type was a massive success, over 32,000 were made in 1953 alone, a feat of mass-production that was astounding by the standards of the day given the relative complexity of the machine. But Honda's lifelong pursuit of technical innovation sometimes distracted him from commercial reality. Fujisawa pointed out that they were in danger of ignoring their core business, the motorised bicycles that still formed Japan's main means of transport. In May 1952 the F-type Cub appeared, another two-stroke despite the top men's reservations. You could buy a complete machine or just the motor to attach to your own bicycle. The result was certainly distinctive, a white fuel tank with a circular profile went just below and behind the saddle on the left of the bike, and the motor with its horizontal cylinder and bright red cover just below the rear axle on the same side of the bike. This was the machine that turned Honda into the biggest bike maker in Japan with 70% of the market for bolt-on bicycle motors, the F-type was also the first Honda to be exported. Next came the machine that would turn Honda into the biggest motorcycle manufacturer in the world.

The C100 Super Cub was a typically audacious piece of Honda engineering and marketing. For the first time, but not the last, Honda invented a completely new type of motorcycle, although the term 'scooterette' was coined to describe the new bike which had many of the characteristics of a scooter but the large wheels, and therefore stability, of a motorcycle. The first one was sold in August 1958, fifteen years later over nine-million of them were on the roads of the world. If ever a machine can be said to have brought mobility to the masses it is the Super Cub. If you add in the electric starter that was added for the C102 model of 1961, the design of the Super Cub has remained substantially unchanged ever since, testament to how right Honda got it first time. The Super Cub made Honda the world's biggest manufacturer after just two years of production.

The CB250N Super Dream became a favorite with UK learner riders of the late seventies and early eighties

Honda's export drive started in earnest in 1957 when Britain and Holland got their first bikes, America got just two bikes the next year. By 1962 Honda had half the American market with 65,000 sales. But Soichiro Honda had already travelled abroad to Europe and the USA, making a special

The GL1000 introduced in 1975, was the first in Honda's line of GoldWings

Introduction

Carl Fogarty in action at the Suzuka 8 Hour on the RC45

An early CB750 Four

point of going to the Isle of Man TT, then the most important race in the GP calendar. He realised that no matter how advanced his products were, only racing success would convince overseas markets for whom 'Made in Japan' still meant cheap and nasty. It took five years from Soichiro Honda's first visit to the Island before his bikes were ready for the TT. In 1959 the factory entered five riders in the 125 class. They did not have a massive impact on the event being benevolently regarded as a curiosity, but sixth, seventh and eighth were good enough for the team prize. The bikes were off the pace but they were well engineered and very reliable.

The TT was the only time the West saw the Hondas in '59, but they came back for more the following year with the first of a generation of bikes which shaped the future of motorcycling – the double-overhead-cam four-cylinder 250. It was fast and reliable – it revved to 14,000 rpm – but didn't handle anywhere near as well as the opposition. However, Honda had now signed up non-Japanese riders to lead their challenge. The first win didn't come until 1962 (Aussie Tom Phillis in the Spanish 125 GP) and was followed up with a world-shaking performance at the TT. Twenty-one year old Mike Hailwood won both 125 and 250 cc TTs and Hondas filled the top five positions in both races. Soichiro Honda's master plan was starting to come to fruition, Hailwood and Honda won the 1961 250 cc World Championship. Next year Honda won three titles. The other Japanese factories fought back and inspired Honda to produce some of the most fascinating racers ever seen: the awesome six-cylinder 250, the five-cylinder 125, and the 500 four with which the immortal Hailwood battled Agostini and the MV Agusta.

When Honda pulled out of racing in '67 they had won sixteen rider's titles, eighteen manufacturer's titles, and 137 GPs, including 18 TTs, and introduced the concept of the modern works team to motorcycle racing. Sales success followed racing victory as Soichiro Honda had predicted, but only because the products advanced as rapidly as the racing machinery. The Hondas that came to Britain in the early '60s were incredibly sophisticated. They had overhead cams where the British bikes had pushrods, they had electric starters when the Brits relied on the kickstart, they had 12V electrics when even the biggest British bike used a 6V system. There seemed no end to the technical wizardry. It wasn't that the technology itself was so amazing but just like that first E-type, it was the fact that Honda could mass-produce it more reliably than the lower-tech competition that was so astonishing.

When in 1968 the first four-cylinder CB750 road bike arrived the world of motorcycling changed for ever, they even had to invent a new word for it, 'Superbike'. Honda raced again with the CB750 at Daytona and won the

World Endurance title with a prototype DOHC version that became the CB900 roadster. There was the six-cylinder CBX, the CX500T – the world's first turbocharged production bike, they invented the full-dress tourer with the GoldWing, and came back to GPs with the revolutionary oval-pistoned NR500 four-stroke, a much-misunderstood bike that was more a rolling experimental laboratory than a racer. Just to show their versatility Honda also came up with the weird CX500 shaft-drive V-twin, a rugged workhorse that powered a new industry, the courier companies that oiled the wheels of commerce in London and other big cities.

It was true, though, that Mr Honda was not keen on two-strokes – early motocross engines had to be explained away to him as lawnmower motors! However, in 1982 Honda raced the NS500, an agile three-cylinder lightweight against the big four-cylinder opposition in 500 GPs. The bike won in its first year and in '83 took the world title for Freddie Spencer. In four-stroke racing the V4 layout took over from the straight four, dominating TT, F1 and Endurance championships with the RVF750, the nearest thing ever built to a Formula 1 car on wheels. And when Superbike arrived Honda were ready with the RC30. On the roads the VFR V4 became an instant classic while the CBR600 invented another new class of bike on its way to becoming a best-seller. The V4 road bikes had problems to start with but the VFR750 sold world-wide over its lifetime while the VFR400 became a massive commercial success and cult bike in Japan. The original RC30 won the first two World Superbike Championships is 1988 and '89, but Honda had to wait until 1997 to win it again with the RC45, the last of the V4 roadsters. In Grands Prix, the NSR500 V4 two-stroke superseded the NS triple and became the benchmark racing machine of the '90s. Mick Doohan secured his place in history by winning five World Championships in consecutive years on it.

In yet another example of Honda inventing a new class of motorcycle, they came up with the astounding CBR900RR FireBlade, a bike with the punch of a 1000 cc motor in a package the size and weight of a 750. It became a cult bike as well as a best seller, and with judicious redesigns continues to give much more recent designs a run for their money.

When it became apparent that the high-tech V4 motor of the RC45 was too expensive to produce, Honda looked to a V-twin engine to power its flagship for the first time. Typically, the VTR1000 FireStorm was a much more rideable machine than its opposition and once accepted by the market formed the basis of the next generation of Superbike racer, the VTR-SP-1.

One of Mr Honda's mottos was that technology would solve the customers' problems, and no company has embraced cutting-edge technology more firmly than Honda. In fact Honda often developed new technology, especially in the fields of materials science and metallurgy. The embodiment of that was the NR750, a bike that was misunderstood nearly as much as the original NR500 racer. This limited-edition technological tour-de-force embodied many of Soichiro Honda's ideals. It used the latest techniques and materials in every component, from the oval piston, 32-valve V4 motor to the titanium coating on the windscreen, it was – as Mr Honda would have wanted – the best it could possibly be. A fitting memorial to the man who has shaped the motorcycle industry and motorcycles as we know them today.

A Little Gem

Any new 125cc Honda has an awful lot to live up to. The now venerable CG125 was around from 1976 to 2008. Several generations of rider started on the perky little air-cooled OHV single that was one of Honda's biggest sellers for many years. Although there may have been more glamorous alternatives, the CG was always popular because it was a typical Honda of its day: smart, easy to ride and bullet proof.

The CX500 – Honda's first V-Twin and a favorite choice of dispatch riders

The VFR400R was a cult bike in Japan and a popular grey import in the UK

Introduction

The 2009 CBF125M9

Of course the main target market for the CG was learner riders, but they were also bought by a lot of big-bike riders for use as commuters because the bike had the feel of a 'proper' motorcycle. Solidity of build also meant that even the most ham-fisted of learners couldn't damage the CG enough to prevent most of them retaining a better than average percentage of their value.

That is some legacy for the next generation 125cc Honda single to live up to. It arrived in 2009 and was called the CBF125. Inevitably, the old engine with its carburettor and pushrod-operated overhead valves wasn't up to meeting modern emissions standards, so the CBF's engine got fuel injection and an overhead cam. The CBF is made by Honda's subsidiary plant in India.

The Japanese-made two-stroke 125s had died out because of emissions legislation, leaving just Aprilia making the only stroker option left for learners. The new generation of four-stroke Japanese-manufactured learner bikes were designed not just for a cleaner world, but for a poorer one too. As soon as the credit crunch hit the financial markets, Japan inc was planning new motorcycles to meet the situation they realized would arrive. It's no coincidence that in 2011 we heard about 250cc bikes from Honda and Suzuki announced with much emphasis on price and fuel economy. The CBF125 covers those bases, too.

Like its ancestor the CG125, it isn't just going to be bought by learner riders. Showroom price is suitably low, and running costs should be minimal. While Honda claims an eyebrow-raising fuel economy rate of over 160 miles per gallon using the World Motorcycle Test Cycle, in the real world the figure is going to be over 100. It's a full-size motorcycle and, with the possible exception of the rear drum brake and twin rear shocks, shows no evidence of being built down to a price. Like the old CG, the CBF125 is going to be an appealing proposition to big-city commuters and those for whom cost is a major factor. What's not to like?

Acknowledgements

Our thanks are due to Bransons Motorcycles of Yeovil who supplied the machine featured in the illustrations throughout this manual. We would also like to thank NGK Spark Plugs (UK) Ltd for supplying the colour spark plug condition photographs, the Avon Rubber Company for supplying information on tyre fitting and Draper Tools Ltd for some of the workshop tools shown.

Thanks are also due to Julian Ryder who wrote the introduction 'The Birth of a Dream' and to Honda (UK) Ltd. who supplied model photographs.

About this Manual

The aim of this manual is to help you get the best value from your motorcycle. It can do so in several ways. It can help you decide what work must be done, even if you choose to have it done by a dealer; it provides information and procedures for routine maintenance and servicing; and it offers diagnostic and repair procedures to follow when trouble occurs.

We hope you use the manual to tackle the work yourself. For many simpler jobs, doing it yourself may be quicker than arranging an appointment to get the motorcycle into a dealer and making the trips to leave it and pick it up. More importantly, a lot of money can be saved by avoiding the expense the shop must pass on to you to cover its labour and overhead costs. An added benefit is the sense of satisfaction and accomplishment that you feel after doing the job yourself.

References to the left or right side of the motorcycle assume you are sitting on the seat, facing forward.

We take great pride in the accuracy of information given in this manual, but motorcycle manufacturers make alterations and design changes during the production run of a particular motorcycle of which they do not inform us. No liability can be accepted by the authors or publishers for loss, damage or injury caused by any errors in, or omissions from, the information given.

Illegal copying

It is the policy of Haynes Publishing to actively protect its Copyrights and Trade Marks. Legal action will be taken against anyone who unlawfully copies the cover or contents of this Manual. This includes all forms of unauthorised copying including digital, mechanical, and electronic in any form. Authorisation from Haynes Publishing will only be provided expressly and in writing. Illegal copying will also be reported to the appropriate statutory authorities.

Model development and bike spec

CBF125M9 2009 model

Introduced in 2009, the CBF125 is powered by an air-cooled, fuel injected single cylinder engine. The valves are operated by a pair of rockers and a single overhead camshaft, chain driven from the left-hand side of the crankshaft. The crankcases divide vertically.

The clutch is a conventional, cable operated, multi-plate unit and the gearbox is 5-speed. Drive to the rear wheel is by chain and sprockets.

The fuel delivery system features an externally mounted pump located on the left-hand side of the machine. A fuel level sensor is located inside the fuel tank. A fully transistorised electronic system ignites the mixture. The fuel and ignition systems and jointly controlled by an engine control module to ensure the engine runs at optimum efficiency under all riding conditions. A catalytic converter is incorporated in the exhaust system.

The engine unit forms an integral part of the all-steel, open loop frame. Front suspension is by conventional, oil-damped telescopic forks. Rear suspension is by box-section swingarm with pre-load adjustable twin shock absorbers.

The front brake is a single, 240 mm hydraulically operated disc, the rear brake is a rod operated 130 mm drum. Wheels are six-spoke cast aluminium with tubeless tyres.

The half-fairing houses a single headlight and the instrument cluster is located behind a short windshield. Separate rider and passenger seats are fitted

CBF125MA 2010 model

There were no changes from the 2009 model.

CBF125MB 2011 and 2012 model

A tachometer was added to the instrument cluster in 2011 entailing a revised layout of the instruments and warning lights.

CBF125MD 2013 and 2014

A small belly fairing was fitted, colour matched to the tank and main bodywork. Also a passenger heel guard was fitted to the top of the silencer heat shield and the fairing graphics were revised.

Dimensions and weights

Overall length	1955 mm
Overall width	760 mm
Overall height	1110 mm
Wheelbase	1270 mm
Seat height	879 mm
Ground clearance	173 mm
Weight (with fuel and oil)	128 kg
Maximum weight (with passenger and luggage)	180 kg

Engine

Type	Single cylinder four-stroke
Capacity	125 cc
Bore	52.4 mm
Stroke	57.8 mm
Compression ratio	9.2 to 1
Cooling system	Air-cooled
Clutch	Wet multi-plate
Transmission	Five-speed constant mesh
Final drive	Chain and sprockets
Camshaft	SOHC, chain-driven
Fuel system	Fuel injection
Ignition system	Digital transistorised with electronic advance

Chassis

Frame type	Steel open loop
Rake	25° 55'
Trail	89 mm
Fuel tank capacity	13 litres
Front suspension	
Type	30 mm oil-damped telescopic forks (non-adjustable)
Travel	103.4 mm
Rear suspension	
Type	Twin shock absorbers (pre-load adjustable), box-section swingarm
Travel (at axle)	87.3 mm
Wheels	17 inch six-spoke alloys
Tyres	
Front	80/100-17 MC (46P)
Rear	100/90-17 MC (55P)
Front brake	Single 240 mm disc with twin piston sliding caliper
Rear brake	130 mm drum

0•10 Identification numbers

Frame and engine numbers

The frame serial number is stamped into the right-hand side of the steering head. The engine number is stamped into the crankcase on the left-hand side. Both of these numbers should be recorded and kept in a safe place so they can be given to law enforcement officials in the event of a theft.

There is also a VIN (vehicle identification number) plate on the left-hand side of the front frame downtube and a colour code label on the right-hand side of the frame below the steering head.

The fuel injector throttle body has an ID number stamped into the body.

The frame serial number, engine serial number, and colour code should also be kept in a handy place (such as with your driver's licence) so they are always available when purchasing or ordering parts for your machine.

Models are identified by their model code suffix (e.g. M9). The model code or production year is printed on the colour code label.

Model	Production year
CBF125M9	2009
CBF125MA	2010
CBF125MB	2011 and 2012
CBF125MD	2013 and 2014

The colour code label is on the right-hand side of the frame below the steering head

The frame number is stamped into the right-hand side of the steering head

Identification numbers 0•11

Buying spare parts

Once you have found all the identification numbers, record them for reference when buying parts. Since the manufacturers change specifications, parts and vendors (companies that manufacture various components on the machine), providing the ID numbers is the only way to be reasonably sure that you are buying the correct parts.

Whenever possible, take the worn part to the dealer so direct comparison with the new component can be made. Along the trail from the manufacturer to the parts shelf, there are numerous places that the part can end up with the wrong number or be listed incorrectly.

The two places to purchase new parts for your motorcycle – the franchised or main dealer and the parts/accessories store – differ in the type of parts they carry. While dealers can obtain every single genuine part for your motorcycle, the accessory store is usually limited to normal high wear items such as chains and sprockets, brake pads, spark plugs and cables.

Used parts can be obtained from breakers yards for roughly half the price of new ones, but you can't always be sure of what you're getting. Once again, take your worn part to the breaker for direct comparison, or when ordering by mail order make sure that you can return it if you are not happy.

Whether buying new, used or rebuilt parts, the best course is to deal directly with someone who specialises in your particular make.

The VIN plate is on the left-hand side of the frame front downtube

The engine number is stamped into the left-hand side of the crankcase

Safety First!

Professional mechanics are trained in safe working procedures. However enthusiastic you may be about getting on with the job at hand, take the time to ensure that your safety is not put at risk. A moment's lack of attention can result in an accident, as can failure to observe simple precautions.

There will always be new ways of having accidents, and the following is not a comprehensive list of all dangers; it is intended rather to make you aware of the risks and to encourage a safe approach to all work you carry out on your bike.

Asbestos

● Certain friction, insulating, sealing and other products - such as brake pads, clutch linings, gaskets, etc. - contain asbestos. Extreme care must be taken to avoid inhalation of dust from such products since it is hazardous to health. If in doubt, assume that they do contain asbestos.

Fire

● Remember at all times that petrol is highly flammable. Never smoke or have any kind of naked flame around, when working on the vehicle. But the risk does not end there - a spark caused by an electrical short-circuit, by two metal surfaces contacting each other, by careless use of tools, or even by static electricity built up in your body under certain conditions, can ignite petrol vapour, which in a confined space is highly explosive. Never use petrol as a cleaning solvent. Use an approved safety solvent.

● Always disconnect the battery earth terminal before working on any part of the fuel or electrical system, and never risk spilling fuel on to a hot engine or exhaust.

● It is recommended that a fire extinguisher of a type suitable for fuel and electrical fires is kept handy in the garage or workplace at all times. Never try to extinguish a fuel or electrical fire with water.

Fumes

● Certain fumes are highly toxic and can quickly cause unconsciousness and even death if inhaled to any extent. Petrol vapour comes into this category, as do the vapours from certain solvents such as trichloro-ethylene. Any draining or pouring of such volatile fluids should be done in a well ventilated area.

● When using cleaning fluids and solvents, read the instructions carefully. Never use materials from unmarked containers - they may give off poisonous vapours.

● Never run the engine of a motor vehicle in an enclosed space such as a garage. Exhaust fumes contain carbon monoxide which is extremely poisonous; if you need to run the engine, always do so in the open air or at least have the rear of the vehicle outside the workplace.

The battery

● Never cause a spark, or allow a naked light near the vehicle's battery. It will normally be giving off a certain amount of hydrogen gas, which is highly explosive.

● Always disconnect the battery ground (earth) terminal before working on the fuel or electrical systems (except where noted).

● If possible, loosen the filler plugs or cover when charging the battery from an external source. Do not charge at an excessive rate or the battery may burst.

● Take care when topping up, cleaning or carrying the battery. The acid electrolyte, evenwhen diluted, is very corrosive and should not be allowed to contact the eyes or skin. Always wear rubber gloves and goggles or a face shield. If you ever need to prepare electrolyte yourself, always add the acid slowly to the water; never add the water to the acid.

Electricity

● When using an electric power tool, inspection light etc., always ensure that the appliance is correctly connected to its plug and that, where necessary, it is properly grounded (earthed). Do not use such appliances in damp conditions and, again, beware of creating a spark or applying excessive heat in the vicinity of fuel or fuel vapour. Also ensure that the appliances meet national safety standards.

● A severe electric shock can result from touching certain parts of the electrical system, such as the spark plug wires (HT leads), when the engine is running or being cranked, particularly if components are damp or the insulation is defective. Where an electronic ignition system is used, the secondary (HT) voltage is much higher and could prove fatal.

Remember...

✗ **Don't** start the engine without first ascertaining that the transmission is in neutral.

✗ **Don't** suddenly remove the pressure cap from a hot cooling system - cover it with a cloth and release the pressure gradually first, or you may get scalded by escaping coolant.

✗ **Don't** attempt to drain oil until you are sure it has cooled sufficiently to avoid scalding you.

✗ **Don't** grasp any part of the engine or exhaust system without first ascertaining that it is cool enough not to burn you.

✗ **Don't** allow brake fluid or antifreeze to contact the machine's paintwork or plastic components.

✗ **Don't** siphon toxic liquids such as fuel, hydraulic fluid or antifreeze by mouth, or allow them to remain on your skin.

✗ **Don't** inhale dust - it may be injurious to health (see Asbestos heading).

✗ **Don't** allow any spilled oil or grease to remain on the floor - wipe it up right away, before someone slips on it.

✗ **Don't** use ill-fitting spanners or other tools which may slip and cause injury.

✗ **Don't** lift a heavy component which may be beyond your capability - get assistance.

✗ **Don't** rush to finish a job or take unverified short cuts.

✗ **Don't** allow children or animals in or around an unattended vehicle.

✗ **Don't** inflate a tyre above the recommended pressure. Apart from overstressing the carcass, in extreme cases the tyre may blow off forcibly.

✔ **Do** ensure that the machine is supported securely at all times. This is especially important when the machine is blocked up to aid wheel or fork removal.

✔ **Do** take care when attempting to loosen a stubborn nut or bolt. It is generally better to pull on a spanner, rather than push, so that if you slip, you fall away from the machine rather than onto it.

✔ **Do** wear eye protection when using power tools such as drill, sander, bench grinder etc.

✔ **Do** use a barrier cream on your hands prior to undertaking dirty jobs - it will protect your skin from infection as well as making the dirt easier to remove afterwards; but make sure your hands aren't left slippery. Note that long-term contact with used engine oil can be a health hazard.

✔ **Do** keep loose clothing (cuffs, ties etc. and long hair) well out of the way of moving mechanical parts.

✔ **Do** remove rings, wristwatch etc., before working on the vehicle - especially the electrical system.

✔ **Do** keep your work area tidy - it is only too easy to fall over articles left lying around.

✔ **Do** exercise caution when compressing springs for removal or installation. Ensure that the tension is applied and released in a controlled manner, using suitable tools which preclude the possibility of the spring escaping violently.

✔ **Do** ensure that any lifting tackle used has a safe working load rating adequate for the job.

✔ **Do** get someone to check periodically that all is well, when working alone on the vehicle.

✔ **Do** carry out work in a logical sequence and check that everything is correctly assembled and tightened afterwards.

✔ **Do** remember that your vehicle's safety affects that of yourself and others. If in doubt on any point, get professional advice.

● If in spite of following these precautions, you are unfortunate enough to injure yourself, seek medical attention as soon as possible.

Pre-ride checks

Note: *These Pre-ride checks are outlined in your owner's manual and should be performed every time you ride the machine.*

Engine oil level

Before you start:

✔ Start the engine and let it idle for 3 to 5 minutes.
Caution: Do not run the engine in an enclosed space such as a garage or workshop.
✔ Stop the engine and support the motorcycle on the centrestand on level ground. Allow it to stand for a few minutes for the oil level to stabilise.
✔ The oil level is measured using a dipstick attached to the filler cap that screws into the cover on the right-hand side of the engine. Wipe the area around the filler cap clean before unscrewing it from the cover.

Bike care:

● If you have to add oil frequently, check the engine joints, oil seals and gaskets for oil leakage. If not, the engine could be burning oil, in which case there will be white smoke coming out of the exhaust (see *Fault Finding*).

The correct oil:

● Modern, high-revving engines place great demands on their oil. It is very important that the correct oil for your bike is used.
● Always top up with a good quality motorcycle oil of the specified type and viscosity and do not overfill the engine. Do not use engine oil designed for car use.
Caution: Do not use chemical additives or oils labelled 'ENERGY CONSERVING' – such additives or oils could cause clutch slip.

Oil type	API grade SG or higher
Oil viscosity	SAE 10W-30 or 10W-40

1 Unscrew the filler cap (arrowed), withdraw the dipstick and wipe it clean.

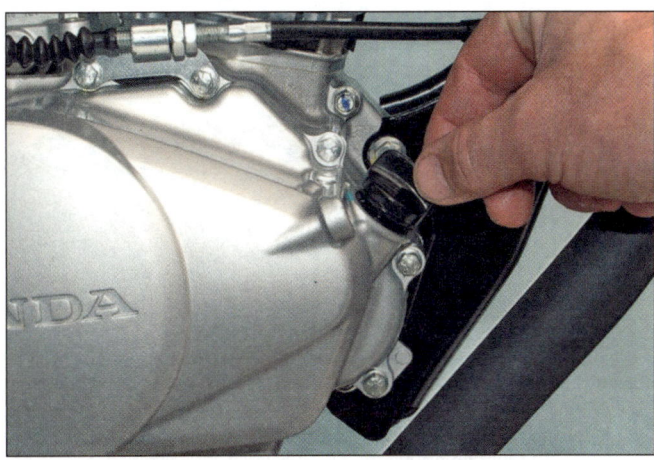

2 Insert the dipstick into its hole and rest the filler cap on the cover, but do not screw it in.

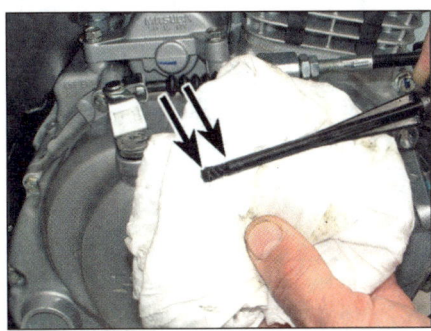

3 Withdraw the dipstick – the oil level should lie between the upper and lower level lines (arrowed) on the dipstick.

4 If the level is on or below the lower line, top-up with the recommended grade and type of oil to the upper line. **Do not overfill.** If necessary, drain off any excess (see Chapter 1).

5 On completion, make sure the O-ring (arrowed) on the filler cap is in good condition and properly seated. Fit a new one if necessary and smear it with oil. Install the cap securely.

Pre-ride checks

Front brake fluid level

Before you start:
✔ The front brake fluid reservoir is on the right-hand handlebar.
✔ Make sure you have a supply of DOT 4 brake fluid.
✔ Wrap a rag around the reservoir being worked on to ensure that any spillage does not come into contact with painted surfaces.

Bike care:
● The fluid in the front brake master cylinder reservoir will drop as the brake pads wear down. If the fluid level is low check the brake pads for wear (see Chapter 1), and replace them with new ones if necessary (see Chapter 6).
● If the fluid reservoir requires repeated topping-up there is a leak somewhere in the system, which must be investigated immediately.
● Check for signs of fluid leakage from the brake hose and/or brake system components – if found, rectify immediately (see Chapter 6).
● Check the operation of the brake before taking the machine on the road; if there is evidence of air in the system (spongy feel to the lever, it must be bled out (see Chapter 6).

> **Warning:** Brake hydraulic fluid can harm your eyes and damage painted surfaces, so use extreme caution when handling and pouring it and cover surrounding surfaces with rag. Do not use fluid that has been standing open for some time, as it is hygroscopic (absorbs moisture from the air) which can cause a dangerous loss of braking effectiveness.

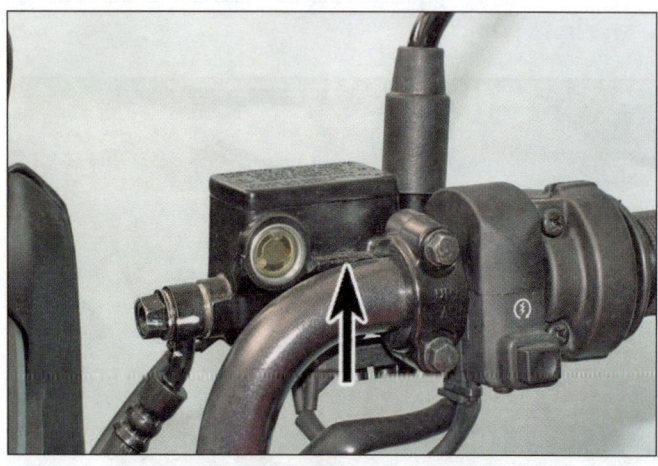

1 With the bike on its sidestand set the handlebars so the reservoir is level and check the fluid level through the window in the reservoir body – it must be above the LOWER level line (arrowed).

2 If the level is on or below the LOWER line, undo the two reservoir cover screws (arrowed) and remove the cover, diaphragm plate and diaphragm.

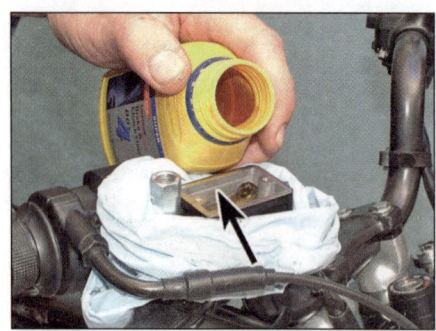

3 Top up with new clean DOT 4 brake fluid, until the level is up to the UPPER line (arrowed) on the inside of the reservoir. Do not overfill and take care to avoid spills (see **Warning** above).

4 Wipe any moisture off the diaphragm with a paper towel.

5 Ensure that the diaphragm is correctly seated before installing the plate and cover. Secure the reservoir cover with its screws.

Suspension, steering and drive chain

Suspension and Steering:
● Check that the front and rear suspension operates smoothly without binding (see Chapter 1).
● Check that the steering moves smoothly from lock-to-lock.

Drive chain:
● Check that the chain isn't too loose or too tight, and adjust it if necessary (see Chapter 1).
● If the chain looks dry, lubricate it (see Chapter 1).

Pre-ride checks

Tyres

Tyre care:
- Check the tyres carefully for cuts, tears, embedded nails or other sharp objects and excessive wear. Operation of the motorcycle with excessively worn tyres is extremely hazardous, as traction and handling are directly affected.
- Check the condition of the tyre valve and ensure the dust cap is in place.
- Pick out any stones or nails which may have become embedded in the tyre tread. If left, they will eventually penetrate through the casing and cause a puncture.
- If tyre damage is apparent, or unexplained loss of pressure is experienced, seek the advice of a tyre fitting specialist without delay.

Tyre tread depth:
- At the time of writing UK law requires that tread depth must be at least 1 mm over 3/4 of the tread breadth all the way around the tyre, with no bald patches. Many riders, however, consider 2 mm tread depth minimum to be a safer limit. Honda recommend a minimum of 1.5 mm on the front and 2 mm on the rear. Refer to the tyre tread legislation in your country.
- Many tyres now incorporate wear indicators in the tread. Identify the location marking on the tyre sidewall to locate the indicator bar and replace the tyre if the tread has worn down to the bar.

The correct pressures:
- The tyres must be checked when **cold**, not immediately after riding. Note that incorrect tyre pressures will cause abnormal tread wear and unsafe handling. Low tyre pressures may cause the tyre to slip on the rim or come off.
- Use an accurate pressure gauge. Many forecourt gauges are wildly inaccurate. If you buy your own, spend as much as you can justify on a quality gauge.
- Proper air pressure will increase tyre life and provide maximum stability and ride comfort.

Loading	Front	Rear
Rider only	25 psi (1.75 Bar)	29 psi (2.0 Bar)
Rider with passenger	25 psi (1.75 Bar)	33 psi (2.25 Bar)

1 Remove the dust cap from the valve and do not forget to fit it after checking the pressure.

2 Check the tyre pressures when the tyres are cold.

3 Measure tread depth at the centre of the tyre using a depth gauge.

4 Tyre tread wear indicator (A) and its location marking (B) on the edge or sidewall (according to manufacturer).

Legal and safety

Lighting and signalling:
- Take a minute to check that the headlight, tail light, brake light, instrument lights and turn signals all work correctly.
- Check that the horn sounds when the button is pressed.
- A working speedometer, graduated in mph, is a statutory requirement in the UK

Safety:
- Check that the throttle grip rotates smoothly when opened and snaps shut when released, in all steering positions. Also check for the correct amount of freeplay (see Chapter 1).
- Check that the brake lever and pedal, clutch lever and gearchange lever operate smoothly. Lubricate them at the specified intervals or when necessary (see Chapter 1).
- Check that the engine shuts off when the kill switch is operated. Check the starter interlock circuit (see Chapter 1).
- Check that sidestand and centrestand return springs hold the stand up securely when retracted.

Fuel:
- This may seem obvious, but check that you have enough fuel to complete your journey. If you notice signs of fuel leakage – rectify the cause immediately.
- Ensure you always use unleaded fuel, minimum 91 RON (Research Octane Number).

0•16 Notes

Chapter 1
Routine maintenance and servicing

Contents

	Section number
Air filter	19
Battery	see Chapter 8
Brake fluid level	see *Pre-ride checks*
Brakes and brake system	2
Cable lubrication	11
Clutch cable	5
Crankcase breather	9
Drive chain and sprockets	1
Engine oil change	7
Engine oil strainer and filter	18
Engine oil level	see *Pre-ride checks*
Engine wear assessment	see Chapter 2

	Section number
Fuel system	8
Idle speed	10
Nuts and bolts	17
Sidestand and starter safety circuit	12
Stand and lever pivots lubrication	13
Spark plug	4
Steering head bearings	16
Suspension	14
Throttle cable	3
Tyres	see *Pre-ride checks*
Valve clearances	6
Wheels and wheel bearings	15

Degrees of difficulty

| **Easy,** suitable for novice with little experience | | **Fairly easy,** suitable for beginner with some experience | | **Fairly difficult,** suitable for competent DIY mechanic | | **Difficult,** suitable for experienced DIY mechanic |  | **Very difficult,** suitable for expert DIY or professional |  |

1•2 Specifications

Engine
Spark plug type
  Standard
    NGK CPR7EA-9
    Bosch UR6DC
  Extended high speed
    NGK CPR8EA-9
    Bosch UR5DC
  Electrode gap .... 0.8 to 0.9 mm
Engine idle speed .... 1500 ± 100 rpm
Valve clearances (COLD engine)
  Intake valve .... 0.08 mm ± 0.02 mm
  Exhaust valve .... 0.12 mm ± 0.02 mm

Cycle parts
Clutch cable freeplay .... 10 to 20 mm at lever end
Drive chain slack .... 15 to 25 mm
Rear brake pedal freeplay .... 20 to 30 mm
Steering head bearing pre-load .... 0.6 to 0.9 kgf (5.6 to 8.9 N)
Throttle cable freeplay .... 2 to 6 mm at twistgrip flange

Lubricants and fluids
Engine oil type and viscosity .... SAE 10W-30 or 10W-40 motorcycle oil, API grade SG or higher
Engine oil capacity
  Oil change .... 0.9 litres
  Following engine overhaul .... 1.1 litres
Brake fluid .... DOT 4
Drive chain .... SAE 80 or 90 gear oil or aerosol chain lubricant suitable for O-ring chains
Steering head bearings .... Multi-purpose grease with EP2 rating
Bearing seal lips .... Multi-purpose grease
Gearchange lever/rear brake pedal/footrest pivots .... Multi-purpose grease
Clutch lever pivot .... Multi-purpose grease
Stand pivots .... Multi-purpose grease
Throttle twistgrip .... Silicone grease
Front brake lever pivot and piston tip .... Silicone grease
Front brake caliper slider pins .... Silicone grease
Cables .... Aerosol cable lubricant

Torque settings
Alternator cover centre cap .... 15 Nm
Engine oil drain plug .... 30 Nm
Rear axle nut .... 54 Nm
Spark plug .... 16 Nm
Timing inspection cap .... 10 Nm
Valve adjuster locknut .... 14 Nm

Maintenance schedule 1•3

Pre-ride
☐ The Pre-ride checks described at the beginning of this manual should be performed at every maintenance interval listed below.

After the initial 600 miles (1000 km)
Note: *This check is usually performed by a Honda dealer after the first 600 miles (1000 km) from new. Thereafter, maintenance is carried out according to the following intervals of the schedule.*

Every 600 miles (1000 km)
☐ Check, adjust, clean and lubricate the drive chain (Section 1)

Every 2500 miles (4000 km) or 6 months
☐ Check the brakes and brake system (Section 2)
☐ Check and adjust the throttle cable (Section 3)
☐ Check the spark plug (Section 4)
☐ Check and adjust the clutch cable (Section 5)
☐ Check and adjust the valve clearances (Section 6)
☐ Change the engine oil (Section 7)
☐ Check the fuel system (Section 8)
☐ Clean the crankcase breather (Section 9)
☐ Check the engine idle speed (Section 10)
☐ Lubricate the clutch and throttle cables (Section 11)
☐ Check the sidestand and starter safety circuit (Section 12)
☐ Lubricate the handlebar lever pivots, gearchange lever, brake pedal and stand pivots (Section 13)
☐ Check the front and rear suspension (Section 14)
☐ Check the condition of the wheels and wheel bearings (Section 15)
☐ Check the steering head bearings (Section 16)
☐ Check the headlight aim (Chapter 8)

Every 5000 miles (8000 km) or 12 months
Carry out all the items under the 2500 mile (4000 km) check, plus the following:
☐ Fit new spark plug (Section 4)
☐ Check the tightness of all nuts, bolts and fasteners (Section 17)

Every 7500 miles (12,000 km) or 18 months
Carry out all the items under the 2500 mile (4000 km) check, plus the following:
☐ Clean the engine oil strainer and centrifugal filter (Section 18)
☐ Fit a new air filter element* (Section 19)
*****Note:** *If the machine is continually ridden in wet or dusty conditions, the filter should be changed more frequently.*

Every 2 years
☐ Change the front brake fluid (Chapter 6)

Non-scheduled maintenance
☐ Check the battery (Chapter 8)
☐ Lubricate the swingarm pivot bolt (Chapter 5)
☐ Lubricate the steering head bearings (Chapter 5)
☐ Change the front fork oil (Chapter 5)

1•4 Component locations

Component locations on the right-hand side

1 Rear shock absorber pre-load adjuster
2 Crankcase breather hose
3 Clutch cable adjuster
4 Spark plug
5 Throttle cable adjuster
6 Front brake fluid reservoir
7 Front fork oil seal
8 Front brake pads
9 Engine oil filler cap/dipstick
10 Engine oil centrifugal filter
11 Engine oil strainer
12 Rear brake light switch adjuster
13 Rear brake pedal freeplay adjuster
14 Drive chain adjuster

Component locations on the left-hand side

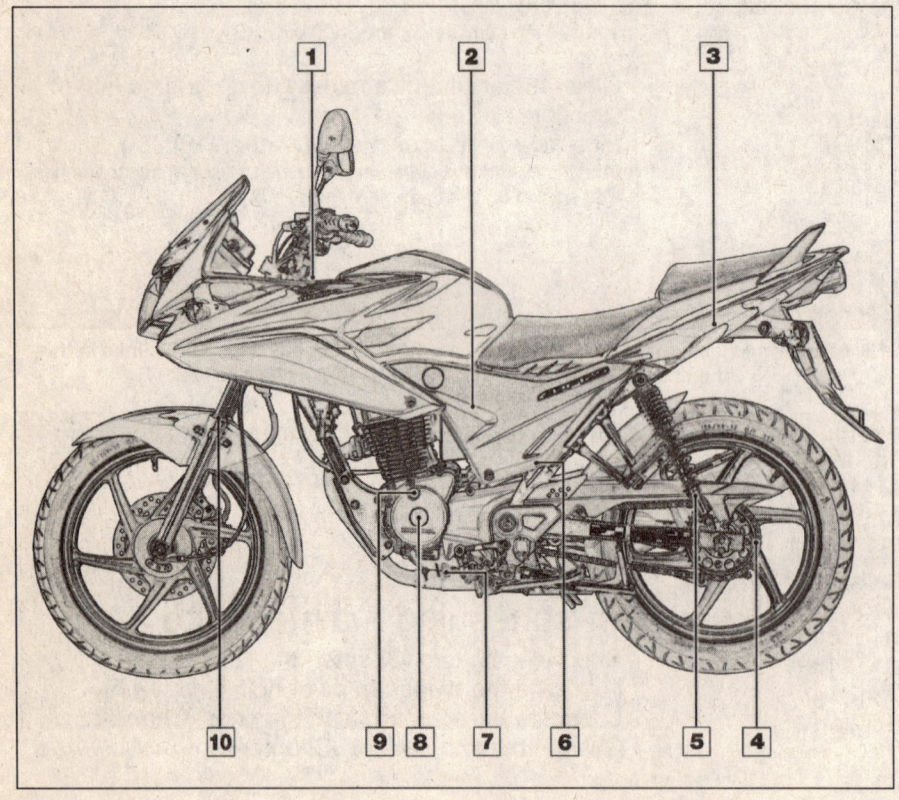

1 Steering head bearing adjuster
2 Air filter
3 Battery
4 Drive chain adjuster
5 Rear shock absorber pre-load adjuster
6 Air filter housing drain plug
7 Engine oil drain plug
8 Centre cap (for engine turning)
9 Timing inspection cap
10 Fork oil seal

Introduction 1•5

1 This Chapter is designed to help the home mechanic maintain his/her motorcycle for safety, economy, long life and peak performance.
2 Deciding where to start or plug into the routine maintenance schedule depends on several factors. If your motorcycle has been maintained according to the warranty standards and has just come out of warranty, start routine maintenance as it coincides with the next mileage or calendar interval. If you have owned the machine for some time but have never performed any maintenance on it, start at the nearest interval and include some additional procedures to ensure that nothing important is overlooked. If you have just had a major engine overhaul, then start the maintenance routine from the beginning. If you have a used machine and have no knowledge of its history or maintenance record, combine all the checks into one large service initially and then settle into the specified maintenance schedule.
3 Before beginning any maintenance or repair, the machine should be cleaned thoroughly, especially around the oil drain plug, valve cover, body panels, drive chain, suspension, wheels, etc. Cleaning will help ensure that dirt does not contaminate the engine and will allow you to detect wear and damage that could otherwise easily go unnoticed.
4 Certain maintenance information is sometimes printed on labels attached to the motorcycle. If the information on the labels differs from that included here, use the information on the label.

1 Drive chain and sprockets

Check, adjust, clean and lubricate the chain

Check chain slack

1 A neglected drive chain won't last long and will quickly damage the sprockets. Routine chain adjustment and lubrication isn't difficult and will ensure maximum chain and sprocket life.
2 To check the chain, support the bike on its centrestand and shift the transmission into neutral.
3 Hold a ruler midway between the two sprockets, then push up on the bottom run of the chain and measure the slack (see illustration). Compare your measurement to that listed in this Chapter's Specifications. As the chain stretches with wear, periodic adjustment will be necessary (see below).
4 Since the chain will rarely wear evenly, roll the bike forward so that another section of chain can be checked – having an assistant to do this makes the task a lot easier. Do this several times to check the entire length of chain, and mark the tightest spot.
Caution: Riding the bike with excess slack in the chain could lead to damage.
5 In some cases, where lubrication has been neglected, corrosion and dirt may cause the links to bind and kink, which effectively shortens the chain's length and makes it tight (see illustration). Thoroughly clean and work free any such links, then highlight them with a dab of paint. Take the bike for a ride.
6 After the bike has been ridden, repeat the measurement for slack in the highlighted area. If the chain has kinked again and is still tight, replace it with a new one (see Chapter 6). A rusty, kinked or worn chain will damage the sprockets and can damage transmission bearings. If in any doubt as to the condition of a chain, it is far better to install a new one than risk damage to other components and possible injury to yourself.
7 Check the entire length of the chain for damaged rollers, loose links and pins, and missing O-rings and replace it with a new one if necessary. Note: Never install a new chain on old sprockets, and never use the old chain if you install new sprockets – replace the chain and sprockets as a set.

Adjust chain slack

8 Move the bike so that the chain is positioned with the tightest point at the centre of its bottom run, then support the bike on its centrestand.
9 Loosen the rear axle nut (see illustration).
10 Loosen the locknut on the left and right-hand chain adjusters (see illustration). Turn both adjuster nuts evenly and a little at a time until the amount of freeplay specified at the beginning of the Chapter is obtained at the centre of the bottom run of the chain (see illustration 1.3). If the chain was slack, turn the adjuster nuts clockwise; if the chain was tight turn them anti-clockwise, then move the wheel forwards in the swingarm to take up the gap between the nuts and the swingarm end caps.
11 Following adjustment, check that the chain adjusters are in the same position on both sides by ensuring that the same number of index marks are visible through both axle slots (see illustration).
12 If the adjustment is not the same on both

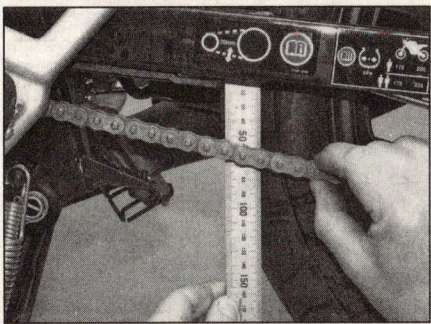

1.3 Measuring slack on the bottom run of the chain

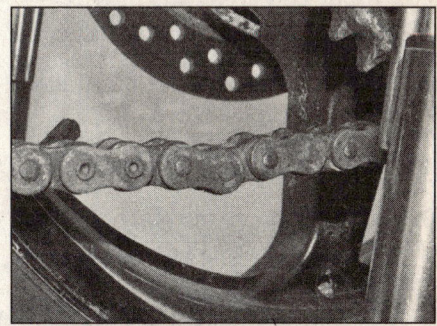

1.5 Neglect has caused the links in this chain to kink

1.9 Loosen the rear axle nut (arrowed)

1.10 Locknut (A) and chain adjuster nut (B)

1.11 Adjustment index marks (arrowed)

Routine maintenance and servicing

1.13 Check the alignment of the double-headed arrow with the wear decal (arrowed)

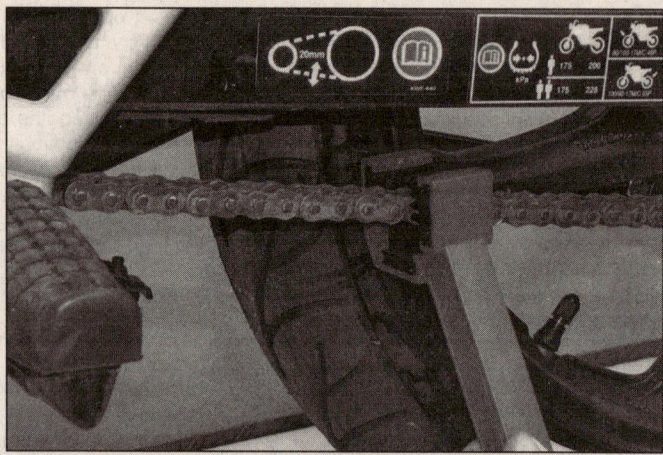

1.16 Using a special chain cleaning brush

sides the rear wheel will be out of alignment with the front (see *Wheel alignment* in Chapter 6). If there is a difference in the positions of the chain adjusters, adjust one so that its position is exactly the same as the other, then check the chain freeplay again and readjust if necessary.

13 Also check the alignment of the double-headed arrow on the adjustment marker with the wear decal on the left-hand side of the swingarm **(see illustration)**. When the arrow meets the red REPLACE CHAIN zone, the drive chain has stretched excessively and a new one must be fitted (see Chapter 6).

14 When adjustment is complete, counter-hold the adjuster nuts to prevent them turning and tighten the locknuts **(see illustration 1.10)**. Tighten the axle nut to the torque setting specified at the beginning of this Chapter. Recheck the chain adjustment as above.

15 Check the adjustment of the rear brake (see Section 2).

Clean and lubricate the chain

16 Clean the chain using a dedicated aerosol cleaner that will not damage the O-rings, or paraffin (kerosene), using a soft brush to work out any dirt **(see illustration)**. Wipe the cleaner off the chain and allow it to dry, using compressed air if available. If the chain is excessively dirty, follow the procedure in Chapter 6 to remove it from the machine and allow it to soak in the paraffin or solvent.

Caution: Don't use petrol (gasoline), an unsuitable solvent or other cleaning fluids which might damage the internal sealing properties of the chain. Don't use high-pressure water to clean the chain. The entire process shouldn't take longer than ten minutes, otherwise the O-rings could be damaged.

17 The best time to lubricate the chain is after the motorcycle has been ridden. When the chain is warm, the lubricant will penetrate the joints between the sideplates better than when cold. **Note:** *Honda specifies SAE 80 or 90 gear oil or an aerosol chain lube that it is suitable for O-ring (sealed) chains; do not use any other chain lubricants – the solvents could damage the chain's sealing rings.* Apply the lubricant to the area where the sideplates overlap – not the middle of the rollers **(see illustration)**.

 **Apply the lubricant to the top of the lower chain run, so centrifugal force will work the oil into the chain when the bike is moving. After applying the lubricant, let it soak in a few minutes before wiping off any excess.**

Warning: Take care not to get any lubricant on the tyre or wheel rim. If any of the lubricant inadvertently contacts them, clean it off thoroughly using a suitable solvent or dedicated brake cleaner before riding the machine.

Check sprocket and chain slider wear

18 Remove the front sprocket cover (see Chapter 6).

19 Check the teeth on the front and the rear sprockets for wear **(see illustration)**. If the sprocket teeth are worn excessively, replace the chain and both sprockets with a new set.

20 Inspect the drive chain slider on the front of the swingarm for excessive wear and damage and replace it with a new one if necessary (see Chapter 5).

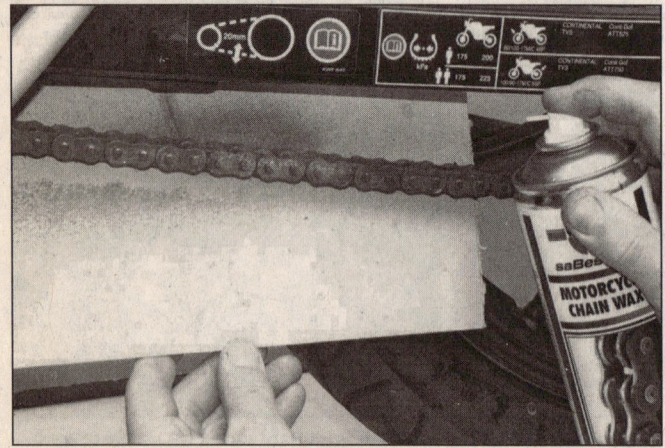

1.17 Apply the lubricant to the point where the sideplates overlap

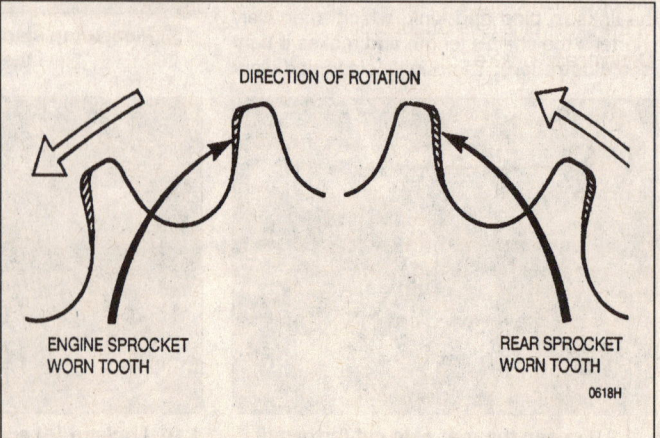

1.19 Check the sprockets in the area indicated

Routine maintenance and servicing

2.1a Check brake pad wear in the direction shown

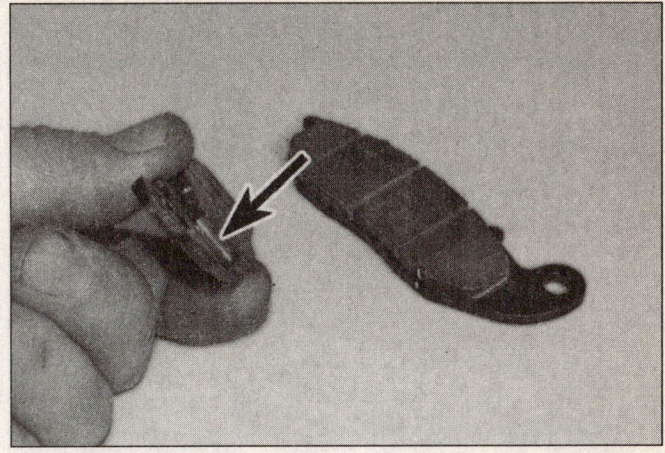

2.1b Location of the wear indicator line (arrowed)

2 Brakes and brake system

Brake wear check

Disc front brake

1 Each brake pad has wear indicator lines in the friction material. The indicator lines should be visible by looking at the edges of the friction material **(see illustrations)**. **Note:** *Some after-market pads may use different indicators to those on the original equipment.*
2 If the indicators aren't visible due to an accumulation of road dirt or brake dust, or if you are in doubt as to the amount of friction material remaining, remove the pads for inspection (see Chapter 6). Honda doesn't specify a minimum thickness for the friction material, but anything less than 2 mm should be considered worn to the service limit and new pads should be fitted.
3 If either pad is excessively worn, check the brake disc for scoring and wear (see Chapter 6). If the pads appear to be wearing unevenly, disassemble the caliper and check the operation of the pistons and the condition of the slider pins (see Chapter 6).

Drum rear brake

4 Check the rear brake pedal freeplay and compare the result with the specification at the beginning of this Chapter **(see illustration)**; measure the distance from the pedal tip when at rest to the pedal tip with the brake applied. To adjust the freeplay, turn the nut on the end of the brake rod – turn the nut clockwise to reduce freeplay and anti-clockwise to increase it **(see illustration)**. Ensure that the curved end of the nut is seated correctly against the brake arm trunnion.
5 Support the bike on the centrestand with the rear wheel off the ground. Rotate the wheel by hand and ensure the rear brake is not binding. If it is, either there is insufficient freeplay in the pedal, the brake actuating cam is binding or the brake linings have worn unevenly – follow the procedure in Chapter 6 to check the condition of the rear brake.
6 To check the brake shoe linings for wear, have an assistant apply the brake and check the position of the wear indicator on the brake arm **(see illustration)**. If the indicator aligns with the reference mark on the brake plate the linings are worn to the service limit and new brake shoes must be fitted (see Chapter 6).

Brake system check

7 Check the brake lever and pedal for loose fixings, improper or rough action, excessive play, bends, and other damage. Replace any damaged parts with new ones (see Chapter 5). Clean and lubricate the lever and pedal pivots if their action is stiff or rough (see Section 13). If the lever action is spongy, bleed the brake (see Chapter 6).
8 Make sure all brake fasteners, caliper bolts and banjo union bolts are tight (see *Torque settings* at the beginning of Chapter 6). Look for leaks at the hose unions and check for cracks in the hose **(see illustration)**; check potential areas, such as around the steering head and suspension, for hose wear. Refer to Chapter 6 for brake hose renewal details. Check that there is no sign of leakage from the caliper and master cylinder - any signs of

2.4a Press the pedal down to check the freeplay

2.4b Turn the nut (arrowed) to adjust brake pedal freeplay

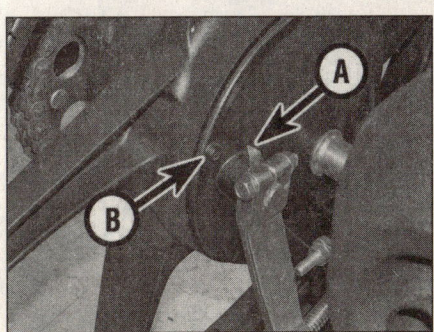

2.6 Wear indicator (A) and reference mark (B)

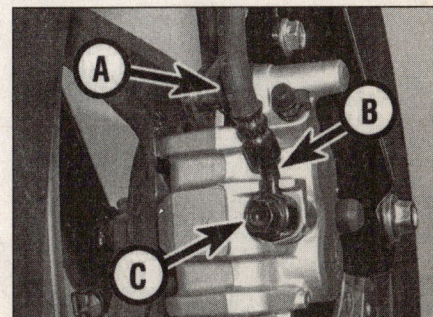

2.8 Brake hose (A), banjo union (B) and banjo bolt (C)

1•8 Routine maintenance and servicing

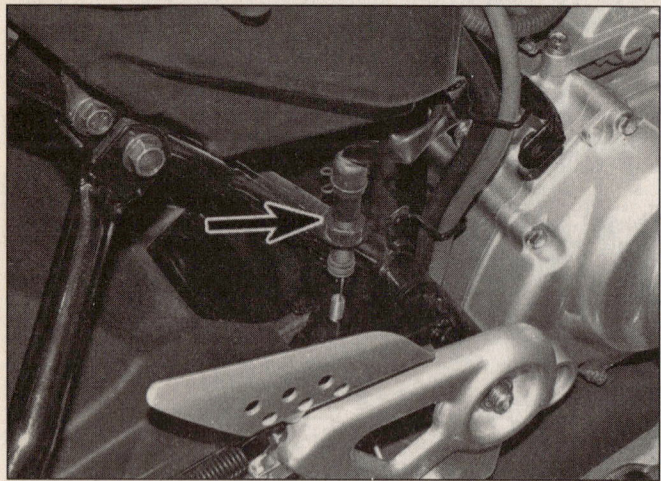

2.10 Location of the rear brake light switch (arrowed)

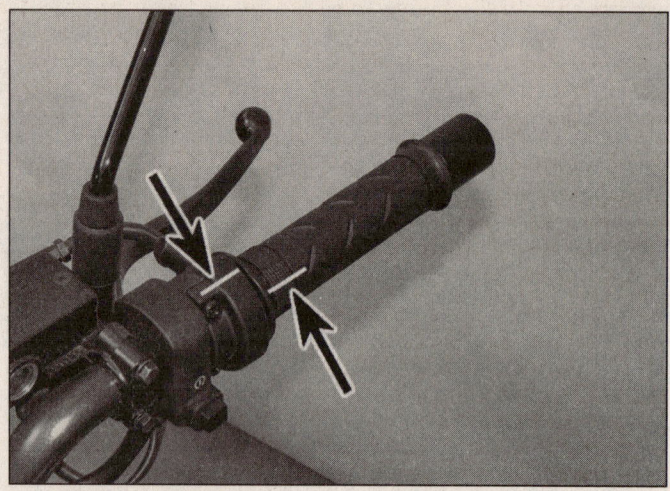

3.5 Throttle cable freeplay is measured in terms of twistgrip rotation

fluid seepage indicate failed caliper piston or master cylinder piston seals (see Chapter 6 for overhaul details).

9 Make sure the brake light operates when the front brake lever is pulled in. The front brake light switch is located on the underside of the lever bracket. The switch is not adjustable – if it fails to operate properly, check it (see Chapter 8).

10 Make sure the brake light is activated after about 10 mm of pedal travel and just before the rear brake takes effect. The switch is located behind the right-hand side panel **(see illustration)**. If adjustment is necessary, first remove the side panel (see Chapter 7). Hold the switch and turn the adjuster in the retaining bracket. If the brake light comes on too late, turn the adjuster clockwise. If the brake light comes on too soon or is permanently on, turn the adjuster anti-clockwise. If the switch doesn't operate the brake light, check the bulb, the switch and the circuit (see Chapter 8).

Brake fluid change

11 Change the brake fluid every two years or whenever a master cylinder or caliper overhaul is carried out. Refer to Chapter 6 for details. Ensure that all the old fluid is pumped from the system and that the level in the fluid reservoir is checked and the brakes tested before riding the motorcycle.

3 Throttle cable

Check

1 Make sure the throttle twistgrip rotates smoothly and freely from fully closed to fully open with the front wheel turned at various angles. The twistgrip should return automatically from fully open to fully closed when released.

2 If the throttle sticks, this is probably due to a cable fault. Remove the cable (see Chapter 4) and lubricate it (see Section 11). Check that the inner cable slides freely in the outer cable. If not, replace the cable with a new one.

3 With the cable removed, check that the twistgrip turns smoothly around the handlebar – dirt combined with a lack of lubrication can cause the action to be stiff. Remove, clean and lightly grease the twistgrip pulley and the inside of the twistgrip housing if necessary (see Chapter 5, Section 5).

4 Install the lubricated or new cable, making sure it is correctly routed (see Chapter 4). If this fails to improve the operation of the throttle, the fault could be with the pulley on the throttle body. Remove the right-hand side panel and check the action of the throttle pulley (see Chapter 4).

Adjust

5 With the throttle operating smoothly, check for a small amount of freeplay in the cable, measured in terms of the amount of twistgrip rotation before the throttle pulley begins to turn **(see illustration)**. Compare the result with the specification at the beginning of this Chapter.

6 Initial cable adjustment is made at the lower end of the cable when it is installed (see Chapter 4). Further adjustment, when required, is made at the handlebar end as follows.

7 Pull back the boot to expose the cable adjuster **(see illustration)**.

8 Loosen the adjuster locknut, then screw the adjuster in or out as required to obtain the correct amount of cable freeplay. Tighten the locknut on completion and don't forget to install the boot over the adjuster.

9 If the cable cannot be adjusted as specified, use the adjuster at the lower end. If both adjusters are fully extended, replace the cable with a new one (see Chapter 4).

⚠ **Warning: Turn the handlebars all the way through their travel with the engine idling. Idle speed should not change. If it does, the cables may be routed incorrectly. Correct this condition before riding the bike.**

4 Spark plug

Removal

1 Make sure your spark plug socket is the correct size (16 mm hex) before attempting to remove the plug – a suitable one is supplied in the motorcycle's tool kit which is stored under the seat.

2 Pull the cap off the spark plug **(see illustration)**.

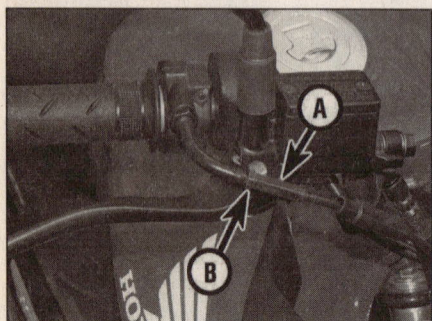

3.7 Throttle cable adjuster (A) and locknut (B)

4.2 Pull the cap off the spark plug

Routine maintenance and servicing 1•9

4.4a Using the plug socket from the bike's toolkit . . .

4.4b . . . to unscrew the spark plug

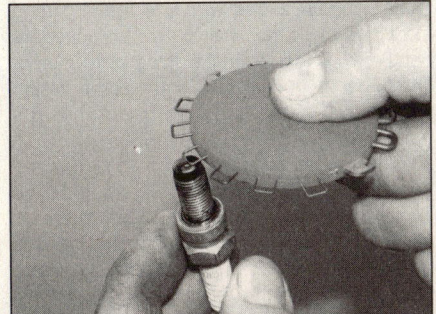

4.7a Using a wire type gauge to measure the spark plug gap

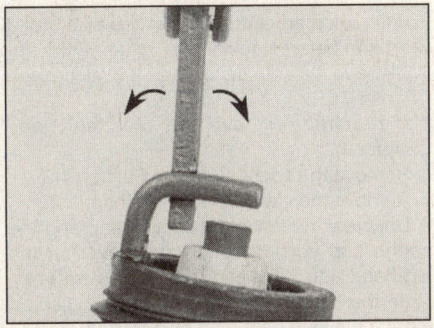

4.7b Bend the side electrode to adjust the gap

3 Clean the area around the base of the plug to prevent any dirt falling into the engine.
4 Unscrew and remove the plug from the cylinder head **(see illustrations)**.

Check

5 Make sure the plug is the correct type and heat range as specified at the beginning of this Chapter.
6 Look for excessive deposits and evidence of a cracked or chipped insulator around the centre electrode. Compare your spark plug to the colour spark plug reading chart on the inside rear cover. Inspect the ceramic insulator body for cracks and other damage. Check the threads and the sealing washer.
7 Clean the plug with a wire brush. Examine the tips of the electrodes; if a tip has rounded off, the plug is worn. Measure the gap between the two electrodes using a feeler gauge or a wire type gauge **(see illustration)**. The gap should be as given in the specifications at the beginning of this Chapter – if necessary adjust the gap by bending the side electrode **(see illustration)**.
8 If the plug is worn or damaged, or if any deposits cannot be cleaned off, renew it. A new spark plug should be fitted at the specified service interval.

Installation

9 Always install the correct type and heat range of spark plug for your machine (see *Specifications* at the beginning of this Chapter).
10 Check the gap between the electrodes (see Step 7) and make sure the sealing washer is in place on the plug.
11 Thread the plug into the cylinder head until the washer seats. Since the cylinder head is made of aluminium, which is soft and easily damaged, thread the plug as far as possible by hand **(see illustration)**. Once the plug is finger-tight, the job can be finished with the spark plug socket **(see illustration 4.4a and b)**.
12 If a torque wrench is available, tighten the spark plug to the torque setting specified at the beginning of this Chapter. Otherwise, tighten it according the instructions on the box – generally if a new plug is being used, tighten it by 1/2 a turn after the washer has seated, and if the old plug is being reused, tighten it by 1/8 to 1/4 turn after the washer has seated. Do not over-tighten the spark plug.
13 Fit the spark plug cap, making sure it locates correctly onto the plug **(see illustration 4.2)**.

> **HAYNES HINT** *Stripped plug threads in the cylinder head can be repaired with a Heli-Coil thread insert – see the Reference section at the end of the manual.*

5 Clutch cable

1 Check that the clutch lever operates smoothly and easily.
2 If the clutch lever operation is heavy or stiff, remove the cable (see Chapter 2) and lubricate it (see Section 11). If the cable is still stiff, replace it with a new one. Install the lubricated or new cable (see Chapter 2).
3 With the cable operating smoothly, check that it is correctly adjusted. Periodic adjustment is necessary to compensate for wear in the clutch plates and stretch of the cable. Check the amount of freeplay at the clutch lever ball end by pulling lightly on the lever until resistance is felt **(see illustration)**. Compare the result with the specification

4.11 Thread the plug in by hand to avoid cross-threading

5.3 Measure clutch lever freeplay as shown

1•10 Routine maintenance and servicing

5.4a Location of the clutch cable adjuster

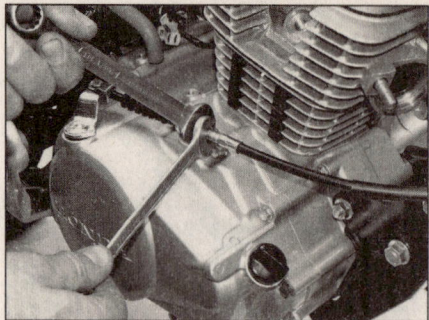

5.4b Hold the adjuster nut and tighten the locknut on completion

at the beginning of this Chapter. If required, adjust the cable as follows.

4 Cable adjustment is made at the lower end of the cable – the adjuster is located in a bracket above the cover on the right-hand side of the engine **(see illustrations)**. Loosen the adjuster locknut, then turn the adjuster nut until the specified amount of freeplay is obtained at the lever. Tighten the locknut on completion.

6 Valve clearances

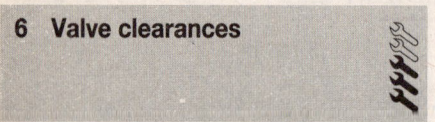

Special tool: *A set of feeler gauges is necessary for this job (see Step 10).*
1 The engine must be completely cool for this maintenance procedure, so let the bike stand overnight before beginning.
2 Remove the side panels and the fairing (see Chapter 7).
3 If required, remove the fuel tank (see Chapter 4).
4 Remove the spark plug (see Section 4).
5 Remove the valve cover (see Chapter 2).
6 Unscrew the timing inspection cap and the centre cap from the alternator cover on the left-hand side of the engine **(see illustrations)**. Note the location of the O-rings and discard them if they are damaged or distorted.
7 To check the valve clearances the engine must be turned to position the piston at top dead centre (TDC) on its compression stroke – at this point both valves will be closed. The engine can be turned using a suitable socket on the alternator nut **(see illustration 6.8a)**.

8 Turn the engine anti-clockwise until the line next to the T mark on the alternator rotor aligns with the static timing mark – the notch in the timing inspection hole **(see illustration)**. The piston should now be at TDC. Check for a small amount of freeplay in both rocker arms i.e. they are not in direct contact with the valve stems **(see illustration)**. Check that the index lines on the camshaft sprocket are parallel with the mating surface of the head **(see illustration)**.
9 If the exhaust rocker arm is in contact with the valve stem the piston is TDC on its exhaust stroke. Turn the engine anti-clockwise one full turn (360°) until the line next to the T mark again aligns with the static timing mark and the index lines on the sprocket are parallel with the mating surface of the head. The piston is now at TDC on its compression stroke and there should be freeplay in the rockers.
10 Check the valve clearance by inserting a feeler gauge of the same thickness as the correct valve clearance (see *Specifications* at the beginning of this Chapter) in the gap between the rocker arm and the valve stem **(see illustration)**. The intake valve is on the back of the cylinder head and the exhaust valve is on the front. If the clearance is correct, the gauge should be a firm sliding fit – you should feel a slight drag when you pull the gauge out. **Note:** *The intake and exhaust valve clearances are different.*
11 If the clearance is either too large or too small, slacken the locknut on the adjuster in

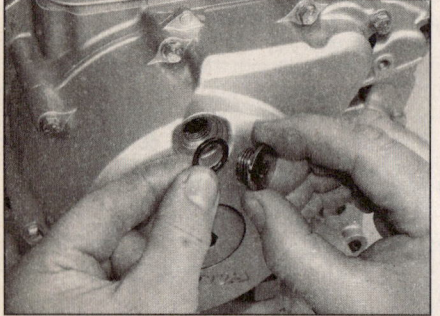

6.6a Unscrew the timing inspection cap . . .

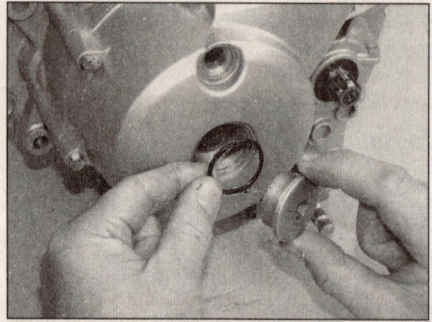

6.6b . . . and the centre cap from the cover

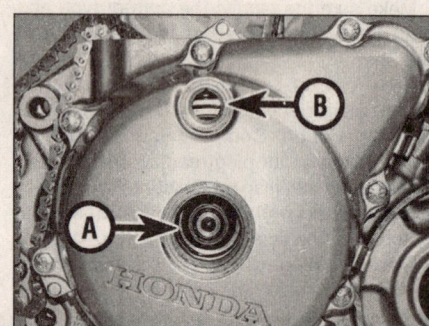

6.8a Alternator nut (A). Static timing mark (B)

6.8b Check for freeplay in both rocker arms (arrowed)

6.8c Index lines (arrowed) must be parallel with mating surface

6.10 Checking the valve clearance with a feeler gauge

Routine maintenance and servicing

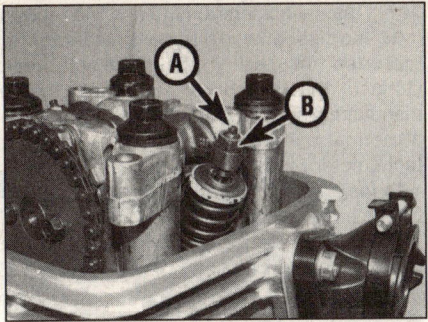

6.11a Rocker arm adjuster (A) and locknut (B)

6.11b Tighten the locknut on completion

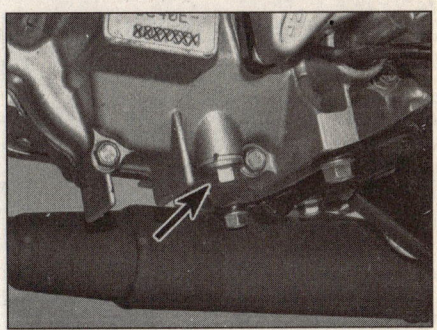

7.3 Location of the oil drain plug (arrowed)

the rocker arm **(see illustration)**. Turn the adjuster until the gap is as specified, then hold the adjuster still and tighten the locknut **(see illustration)**. Recheck the clearance after tightening the locknut.

12 When the clearances are correct install the valve cover (see Chapter 2)

13 Install the timing inspection cap and the centre cap using new O-rings if required. Smear the O-rings with engine oil and tighten the caps to the torque settings specified at the beginning of this Chapter.

14 Install the remaining components in the reverse order of removal.

7 Engine oil change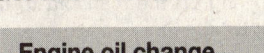

> ⚠ **Warning:** Be careful when draining the oil, as the exhaust pipe, the engine, and the oil itself can cause severe burns.

1 Regular oil changes are the single most important maintenance procedure you can perform. The oil not only lubricates the internal parts of the engine, transmission and clutch, but it also acts as a coolant, a cleaner, a sealant, and a protector. Because of these demands, the oil takes a terrific amount of abuse and should be replaced as specified with new oil of the recommended grade and type.

2 Before changing the oil, warm up the engine so the oil will drain easily. Support the bike on its centrestand on level ground.

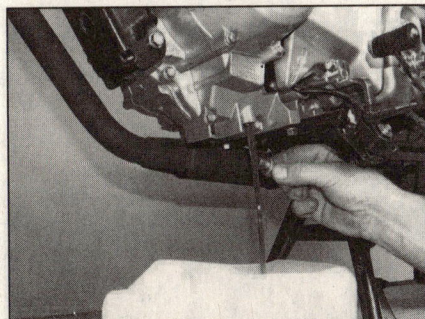

7.5a Drain the oil into a suitable tray

3 Position a drain tray below the engine – the oil drain plug is on the underside of the engine on the left-hand side **(see illustration)**.

4 Unscrew the oil filler cap to vent the crankcase and to act as a reminder that there is no oil in the engine (see **Pre-ride checks**).

5 Unscrew the drain plug and allow the oil to drain into the tray **(see illustration)**. Note the location of the sealing washer on the drain plug and discard it as a new one must be fitted – you may have to cut the old one off **(see illustration)**.

> **HAYNES HINT** To help determine whether any abnormal or excessive engine wear is occurring, place a strainer between the engine and the drain tray so that any debris in the oil is filtered out and can be examined. If there are flakes or chips of metal in the oil or on the drain plug magnet, then something is drastically wrong internally and the engine will have to be disassembled for inspection and repair. If there are pieces of fibre-like material in the oil, the clutch is wearing excessively and should be checked.

6 When the oil has completely drained, install the drain plug using a new sealing washer and tighten it to the torque setting specified at the beginning of this Chapter. Do not overtighten it as the threads in the crankcase are easily damaged.

7 Refill the engine to the correct level using

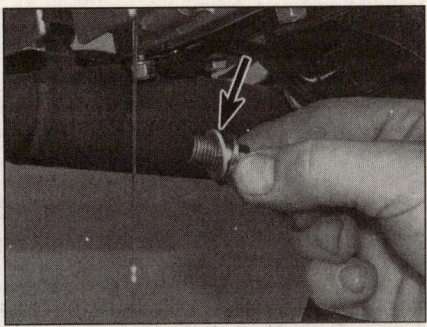

7.5b Note the sealing washer (arrowed)

the recommended grade and type of oil (see **Specifications**). **Note:** *At the specified service interval, remove and clean the oil strainer and centrifugal filter before refilling the engine (see Section 18).* Check the condition of the O-ring on the oil filler cap and renew it if necessary. Install the filler cap securely.

8 Start the engine and let it run for two or three minutes. Shut it off, wait a few minutes, then check the oil level. If necessary, add more oil to bring it up to the correct level.

9 Check around the drain plug for leaks.

10 The old oil drained from the engine cannot be re-used and should be disposed of properly. Check with your local refuse disposal company, disposal facility or environmental agency to see whether they will accept the used oil for recycling. Don't pour used oil into drains or onto the ground.

Note: It is illegal and anti-social to dump oil down the drain. To find the location of your local oil recycling bank in the UK, call 08708 506 506 or visit www.oilbankline.org.uk

8 Fuel system

> ⚠ **Warning:** Petrol (gasoline) is extremely flammable, so take extra precautions when you work on any part of the fuel system. Don't smoke or allow open flames or bare light bulbs near the work area, and don't work in a garage where a natural gas-type appliance is present. If you spill any fuel on your skin, rinse it off immediately with soap and water. When you perform any kind of work on the fuel system, wear safety glasses and have a fire extinguisher suitable for a Class B type fire (flammable liquids) on hand.

1 Remove the left and right-hand side panels to access the fuel hoses and system components (see Chapter 7).

2 Examine the tank, the fuel pump, the fuel

1•12 Routine maintenance and servicing

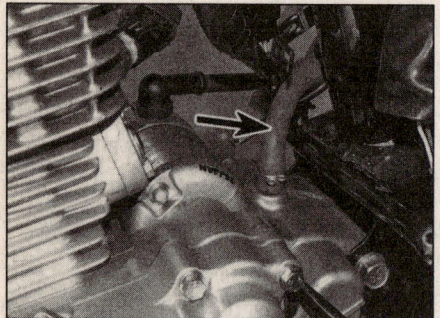

9.2 Check the crankcase breather hose

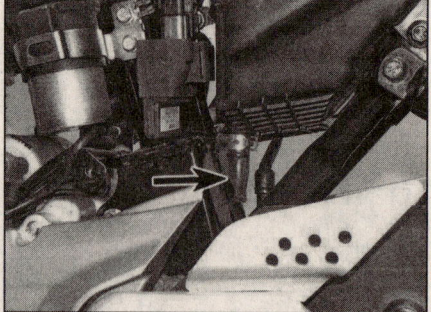

9.3 Location of the drain plug (arrowed)

hose, the fuel vapour hose and the tank breather hoses for damage and deterioration.

3 Replace any hose that is cracked or deteriorated with a new one. Where appropriate, secure each new hose to its unions using new clips. In particular check that there are no leaks from the fuel hose unions.

4 The fuel is delivered under pressure from the pump to the fuel injector. The snap-fit unions on both ends of the delivery hose contain seals that should be renewed whenever the hose is disconnected. If there are signs of fuel leakage, renew the seals (see Chapter 4).

5 Check the general condition of the throttle cable (see Section 3), the fuel pump and the engine management system wiring connectors (see Chapter 4).

6 Inspect the area around the fuel injector for signs of fuel leakage. If there are any leaks, remove the injector and fit new seals (see Chapter 4).

7 No separate fuel filter is fitted. If fuel flow is thought to be poor, check the fuel pump pressure and delivery (see Chapter 4).

9 Crankcase breather

1 Remove the left and right-hand side panels for access (see Chapter 7).
2 Examine the crankcase breather hose between the top rear of the engine unit and the bottom of the air filter housing **(see illustration)**. If the hose is cracked or deteriorated replace it with a new one. Place some rag underneath the air filter housing to catch any residual oil before disconnecting the hose. Secure the new hose to its unions using new clips.
3 Check the air filter housing drain plug on the left-hand side of the housing **(see illustration)**. If water or oil is visible inside the plug, release the clip and pull the plug off. Drain any liquid into a suitable container and clean the plug with suitable solvent. Ensure the plug is clipped firmly in position on installation.

10 Idle speed

Check

Special tool: *On M9 and MA models a test tachometer is necessary for this job (see Step 3).*

1 The idle speed (engine running with the throttle twistgrip closed) should be checked with the engine at normal operating temperature.
2 The idle speed is controlled by the idle air control valve (IACV) – a fault with the valve should be indicated by a fuel injection system fault code (see Chapter 4 for details).
3 If no fault is indicated, an accurate assessment of the idle speed can be made with a test tachometer on M9 and MA models (MB models onward have a tachometer included in the instrument cluster). Connect the tachometer according to the manufacturer's instructions. With the engine at normal operating temperature, note the tachometer reading and compare the result with the specification at the beginning of this Chapter.
4 If the idle speed is incorrect examine the possible causes as follows.

Possible causes

5 Check the operation of the throttle twistgrip and cable, and check for the correct amount of freeplay in the throttle cable (see Section 3).
6 Check the spark plug and spark plug gap (see Section 4).
7 Examine the air cleaner element (see Section 19) – the element can become clogged if the machine is ridden in extremely wet or dusty conditions.
8 If the problem persists, there could be an air leak in the intake manifold between the throttle body and the cylinder head. Check that the clamp securing the throttle body is tightened correctly (see Chapter 4). Check the gasket and O-ring on the manifold-to-head joint (see Chapter 2).

11 Cable lubrication

Special tool: *A cable lubricating adapter is necessary for this procedure (see Step 3).*

1 Cable lubrication not only ensures smooth operation of the cable, but also prevents wear and deters corrosion.
2 Disconnect the cable at its upper end – see Chapter 2 for the clutch cable removal procedure and Chapter 4 for the throttle cable.
3 Attach the pressure adapter and aerosol cable lube **(see illustrations)**. Apply the lubricant – if the adapter leaks, check the installation of the cable and ensure the adapter is tightened securely.

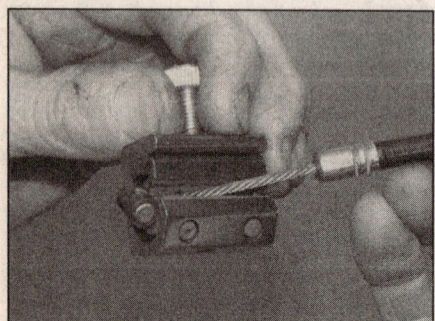

11.3a Fitting the adapter onto the inner cable

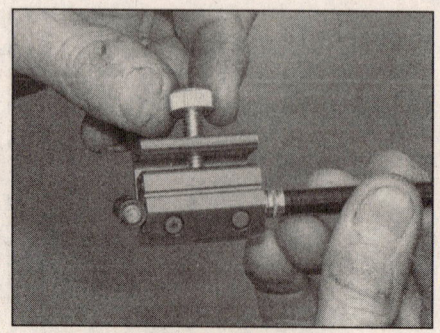

11.3b Ensure the adapter grips the inner and outer cables firmly

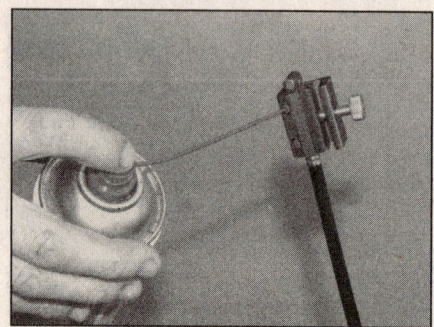

11.3c Connect the can of cable lubricant to the adapter

Routine maintenance and servicing 1•13

12.1 Examine the sidestand springs (arrowed) for damage

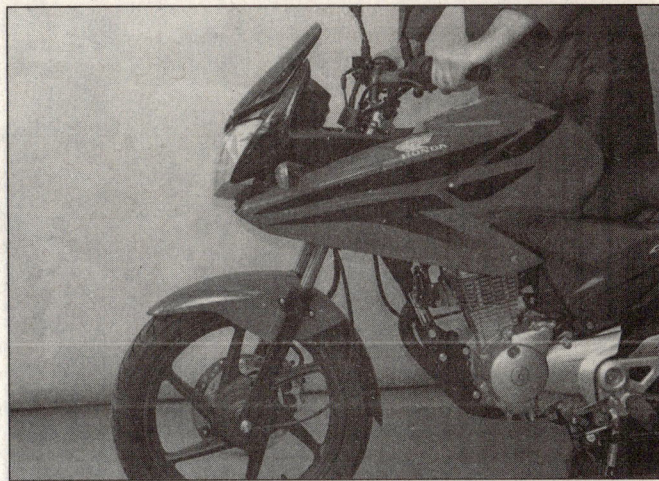

14.1 Checking the operation of the front suspension

4 On completion, check the operation of the cable and adjust the freeplay as specified – see Sections 3 (throttle cable) and 5 (clutch cable).

12 Sidestand and starter safety circuit

1 Check the stand springs – there are two, one inside the other – for damage and distortion **(see illustration)**. The springs must be capable of retracting the stand fully and holding it retracted when the motorcycle is in use. If a spring is sagged or broken it must be replaced with a new one (see Chapter 5).
2 Lubricate the stand pivot regularly (see Section 13).
3 Check the stand and its mount for bends and cracks. Stands can often be repaired by welding.
4 Check the operation of the starter safety circuit as follows:
● Make sure the transmission is in neutral, then retract the stand and start the engine. Pull in the clutch lever and select a gear. Extend the sidestand. The engine should stop as the sidestand is extended. Turn the ignition OFF.
● Make sure the transmission is in neutral and the sidestand is down, then start the engine. Pull the clutch lever in and select a gear. The engine should stop.
● Check that when the sidestand is down the engine can only be started if the transmission is in neutral.
● Check that when the sidestand is up and the transmission is in gear the engine can only be started if the clutch lever is pulled in.
5 If the circuit does not operate as described, check the neutral switch, sidestand switch, clutch switch, starter circuit diode, and the circuit wiring between them (see Chapter 8).

13 Stand and lever pivots lubrication

1 Since the components of a motorcycle are exposed to the elements, they should be checked and lubricated periodically to ensure safe and trouble-free operation.
2 The clutch and brake lever pivots, footrest pivots, brake pedal and gearchange lever linkages and stand pivots should be cleaned, inspected and lubricated. In order for the lubricant to be applied where it will do the most good, the component should be disassembled (see Chapter 5).
3 The lubricant recommended by Honda for each application is listed at the beginning of this Chapter. If a dry-film aerosol lubricant is used, it can be applied to the pivot joint gaps and will usually work its way into the areas where friction occurs, so less disassembly of the component is needed (however if the pivot area is dirty it is better to do so and clean off all corrosion, dirt and old lubricant first).
4 If motor oil or light grease is being used, apply it sparingly as it may attract dirt (which could cause the controls to bind or wear at an accelerated rate).

14 Suspension

Note: *The suspension components must be maintained in top operating condition to ensure rider safety. Loose, worn or damaged suspension parts decrease the motorcycle's stability and control.*

Front suspension check

1 While standing alongside the motorcycle, apply the front brake and push on the handlebars to compress the forks several times **(see illustration)**. See if they move up-and-down smoothly without binding. If binding is felt, the forks should be disassembled and inspected (see Chapter 5).
2 Inspect the surface of the fork inner tubes for scratches, corrosion and pitting which will cause premature seal failure **(see illustration)**. Minor blemishes can be polished out, but if the damage is excessive, new tubes should be installed (see Chapter 5).
3 Carefully lever up the dust seals using a flat-bladed screwdriver and inspect the area around the top of the fork seals. If oil leaks are evident, the fork seals must be replaced with new ones (see Chapter 5). If there is evidence of corrosion between the seal retaining ring and its groove in the fork outer tube, spray the area with a penetrative lubricant, otherwise the ring will be difficult to remove when required. Press the dust seals back into the tops of the fork outer tubes on completion.
4 Check the tightness of all suspension nuts and bolts to be sure none have worked loose, referring to the torque settings specified at the beginning of Chapter 5.
5 The front forks are not adjustable. If the suspension action is poor it may be necessary to change the fork oil or renew the fork springs (see Chapter 5).

14.2 Damage to the surface of the fork tubes (arrowed) will cause seal failure

Routine maintenance and servicing

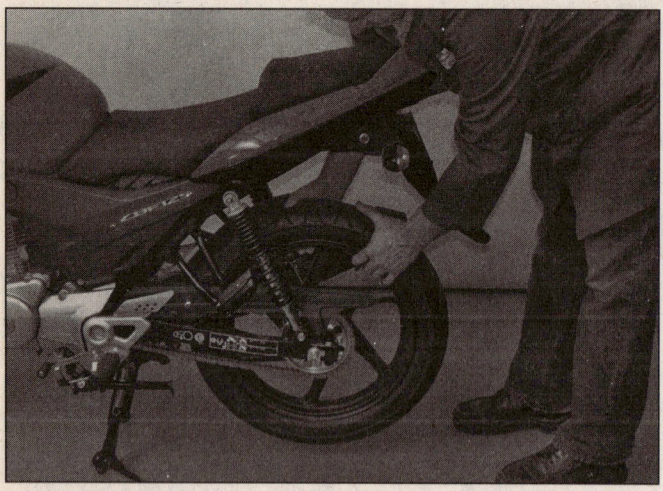

14.9 Checking for play in the rear shock mountings

14.10 Checking for play in the swingarm

Front fork oil change

6 Although there is no specified service interval for changing the fork oil, note that the oil will degrade over a period of time and lose its damping qualities. Follow the procedure Chapter 5 to change the fork oil. The forks do not need to be completely disassembled to change the oil.

Rear suspension check

7 Inspect the rear shock absorbers for fluid leaks and tightness of the mountings. If leakage is found, the shocks must be renewed – always renew the rear shocks as a pair (see Chapter 5).
8 With the aid of an assistant to support the bike, compress the rear suspension several times. It should move up-and-down freely without binding. If any binding is felt, the worn or faulty component must be identified and checked (see Chapter 5). The problem could be caused by the shock absorbers or the swingarm components.
9 Support the motorcycle on its centrestand with the rear wheel is off the ground. Grasp the top of the rear wheel and pull it upwards – there should be no discernible freeplay before the shock absorbers begin to compress (see illustration). Any freeplay indicates worn springs or shock absorber mountings.

Individual components are not available – if necessary, new shock absorbers will have to be fitted (see Chapter 5).
10 Grasp the rear of the swingarm and rock it from side-to-side – there should be no discernible movement (see illustration). If there's a little movement or a slight clicking can be heard, check the tightness of the swingarm pivot bolt, referring to the torque setting specified at the beginning of Chapter 5. If there is still movement with the pivot bolt tightened correctly, either the swingarm bushes or the pivot bolt are worn. **Note:** *The swingarm pivots on rubber bushes – these are a maintenance-free item.*
11 To make an accurate assessment of the swingarm bushes, first remove the rear wheel (see Chapter 6). Remove the lower shock mounting bolts and secure the shocks clear of the swingarm (see Chapter 5).
12 Grasp the rear of the swingarm with one hand and place your other hand at the junction of the swingarm and the frame. Try to move the rear of the swingarm from side-to-side. Any wear (play) in the bushes should be felt as forwards-and-backwards movement between the swingarm and the frame at the front.
13 Next, move the swingarm up and down through its full travel. It should move freely, without any binding or rough spots.
14 If the swingarm does not move freely,

or if the bushes appear to be worn, follow the procedure in Chapter 5 to remove the swingarm and inspect the components. Honda do not list swingarm bushes separately from the swingarm.

Rear suspension adjustment

15 The rear shock absorbers are adjustable for spring pre-load. Adjustment is made using a suitable C-spanner (one is provided in the bike's toolkit) to turn the spring seat on the bottom of the shock absorber.
16 There are three pre-load positions. Position 1 is the softest setting, position 3 is the hardest (see illustration). The standard setting is position 2.
17 Align the setting required on the spring seat cam with the stop on the lower end of the shock – to increase the pre-load, turn the spring seat clockwise; to decrease the pre-load, turn the spring seat anti-clockwise (see illustration). Do not attempt to turn the spring seat directly from setting 3 to setting 1. **Note:** *Always ensure both shock absorber pre-load adjusters are set to the same position.*

15 Wheels and wheel bearings

General

1 Check that any wheel balance weights are fixed firmly to the wheel rims. If there are signs that a weight has fallen off, have the wheel rebalanced by a motorcycle tyre specialist.
2 Check the wheel runout and front/rear wheel alignment as described in Chapter 6.

Cast wheels

3 Cast wheels are virtually maintenance free, but they should be kept clean and checked periodically for cracks and other damage.

14.16 Location of the cam on the spring seat – pre-load position 2 (arrowed)

14.17 Adjusting the pre-load with a C-spanner

Routine maintenance and servicing

15.6a Checking for play in the front wheel bearings

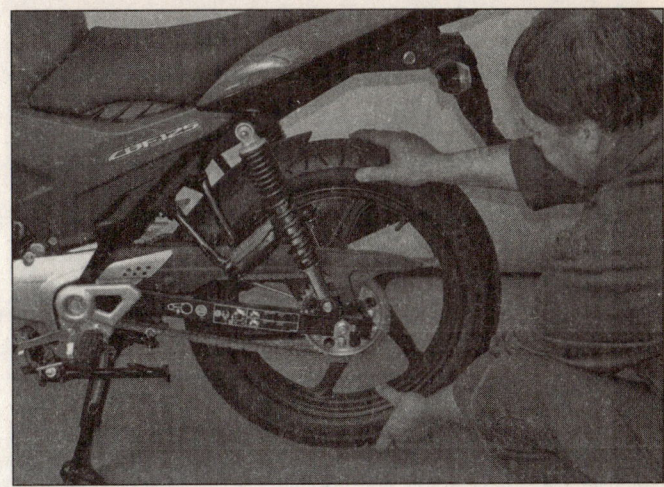

15.6b Checking for play in the rear wheel bearings

Look very closely for dents in the area where the tyre bead contacts the rim. Dents in this area may prevent complete sealing of the tyre against the rim, which leads to deflation of the tyre over a period of time.

4 If damage is evident, or if runout in either direction is excessive, the wheel will have to be renewed. Never attempt to repair a damaged cast alloy wheel.

Wheel bearings

5 Wheel bearings will wear over a considerable mileage and should be checked periodically to avoid handling problems.

6 Support the motorcycle on the centrestand so that the wheel being examined is off the ground. Always make sure that the bike is properly supported and secure. Check for any play in the bearings by pushing and pulling the wheel against the hub (see illustrations). Also rotate the wheel and check that it turns smoothly and without any grating noises.

7 If any play is detected in the hub, or if the wheel does not rotate smoothly (and this is not due to brake or transmission drag), remove the wheel and inspect the bearings for wear or damage (see Chapter 6).

16 Steering head bearings

Freeplay check and adjustment

1 Steering head bearings can become dented, rough or loose during normal use of the machine. In extreme cases, worn or loose steering head bearings can cause steering wobble – a condition that is potentially dangerous.

Check

2 Place the motorcycle on its centrestand and raise the front wheel off the ground using a support under the engine. Always make sure that the motorcycle is properly supported and secure.

3 Point the front wheel straight-ahead and slowly move the handlebars from lock to lock. Any dents or roughness in the bearing races will be felt and if the bearings are too tight the bars will not move smoothly and freely. If the bearings are damaged they should be replaced with new ones (see Chapter 5). If the bearings are too tight, they should be adjusted (see below).

4 Next, grasp the bottom of the forks and try to move them forwards and backwards (see illustration). Any looseness or freeplay in the steering head bearings will be felt as front-to-rear movement of the forks. If play is felt, adjust the bearings (see below).

Caution: *Do not pull and push the forks too hard – a gentle movement is all that is needed.*

Adjustment

Special tool: *A C-spanner will be required to locate in the notches of the bearing adjuster nut (see Step 8).*

5 Remove the fairing (see Chapter 7). Remove the fuel tank (see Chapter 4). If required, displace the handlebars (see Chapter 5).

6 Loosen the steering stem nut and both fork clamp bolts in the bottom yoke (see illustrations).

7 Raise the front wheel off the ground (see Step 2).

8 Using a C-spanner (the rear shock spring pre-load adjuster spanner in the bike's toolkit is ideal), turn the adjuster clockwise to tighten the head bearings or anti-clockwise to loosen them (see illustration 16.6a). Move the adjuster a small amount at a time, then check the freeplay before making further adjustments. The object is to set the

16.4 Checking for play in the steering head bearings

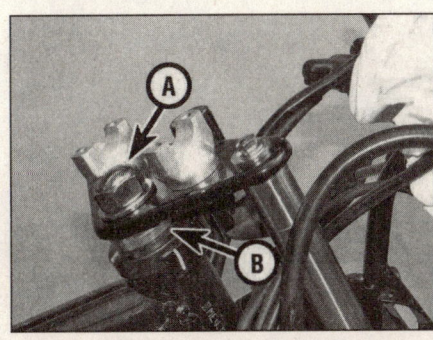

16.6a Steering stem nut (A). Bearing adjuster (B)

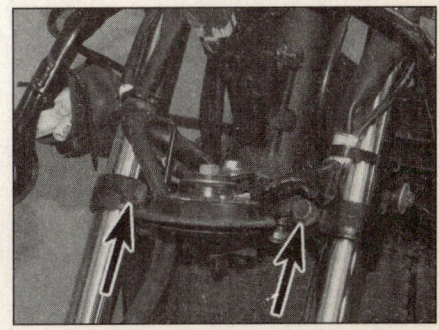

16.6b Bottom yoke fork clamp bolts

Routine maintenance and servicing

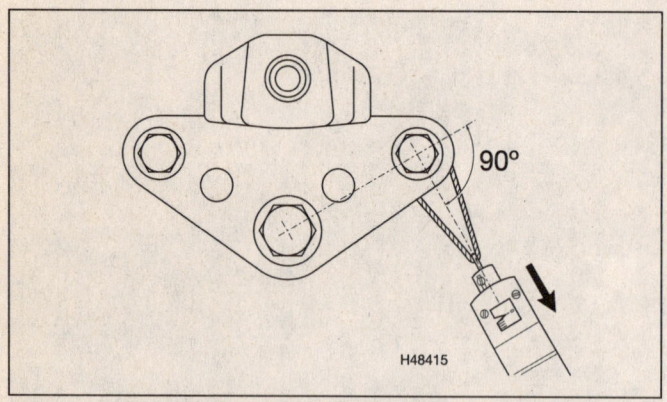

16.12 Set-up for checking the bearing pre-load

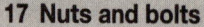

18.3 Draw out the oil strainer

adjuster so that any freeplay in the bearings is removed, not to tighten it so that the steering does not move freely from side-to-side.
Caution: Take great care not to apply excessive pressure because this will cause premature failure of the bearings.
9 Once the bearings seem to be correctly adjusted, turn the steering from lock to lock several times to settle the bearings, then recheck the adjustment.
10 If the bearings cannot be correctly adjusted, disassemble the steering head and check the bearings and races for wear (see Chapter 5).
11 With the bearings correctly adjusted, tighten the steering stem nut, then the fork clamp bolts, to the torque settings specified at the beginning of Chapter 5 **(see illustration 16.6a and b)**.
12 If a spring balance is available, check the pre-load as follows. Attach one end of a spring balance to one of the fork inner tubes, midway between the top and bottom yokes. With the steering pointing straight-ahead, hold the spring balance at right angles to a line between the steering stem and the fork leg and pull **(see illustration)**. Note the reading at which the steering starts to turn and compare the result to the specification for steering head bearing pre-load at the beginning of this Chapter. If the result is below the minimum value specified, the steering head bearings are too loose. If the result is higher than the maximum value specified, the bearings are too tight. If required, readjust the bearings (see Steps 6 to 9).

13 Install the remaining components in the reverse order of removal.

Lubrication
14 Although there is no specified service interval for lubricating the steering head bearings, note that any grease will gradually disperse or harden, allowing accelerated wear and the ingress of dirt and water. Periodically remove the steering stem and clean and re-grease the bearings (see Chapter 5).

17 Nuts and bolts

1 Since vibration of the machine tends to loosen fasteners, all nuts, bolts, screws, etc. should be periodically checked for proper tightness.
2 Pay particular attention to the following, referring to the relevant Chapter:
● Exhaust system bolts/nuts
● Engine mounting bolts
● Engine oil drain bolt
● Spark plug
● Front axle nut
● Rear axle nut
● Rear brake torque arm nut and split pin
● Front sprocket bolts and rear sprocket nuts
● Handlebar clamp bolts
● Lever and pedal bolts
● Brake caliper and master cylinder mounting bolts

● Brake hose banjo bolts and caliper bleed valve
● Brake disc bolts
● Front fork clamp bolts (bottom yoke)
● Front fork top bolts
● Steering stem nut
● Swingarm pivot bolt nut
● Shock absorber mounting bolts/nuts
● Footrest bolts
● Sidestand and centrestand pivot bolts
3 If a torque wrench is available, use it together with the torque settings given at the beginning of the relevant Chapters.

18 Engine oil strainer and filter

⚠️ **Warning: Be careful when draining the oil, as the exhaust pipe, the engine, and the oil itself can cause severe burns.**

1 Follow the procedure in Section 7 to drain the engine oil.

Oil strainer
2 Position a drain tray below the engine to catch any residual oil and remove the right-hand engine cover and gasket (see Chapter 2, Section 14).
3 Pull the oil strainer out from its recess in the crankcase, noting how it fits **(see illustration)**.
4 Wash the strainer element carefully in a suitable solvent and inspect the mesh for damage. If the element is damaged fit a new one. If there are flakes or chips of metal in the strainer, then something is drastically wrong internally and the engine will have to be disassembled for inspection and repair.
5 Wipe any residual oil out of the strainer housing with a clean cloth, then install the strainer narrow edge first.

Oil centrifugal filter
6 Undo the screws securing the oil filter rotor cover and remove the cover and gasket **(see illustrations)**. Discard the gasket as a new one must be fitted.
7 Clean the inside of the filter rotor and cover with a suitable solvent and a clean cloth.

18.6a Undo the screws (arrowed) . . .

18.6b . . . and remove the cover and gasket

Routine maintenance and servicing 1•17

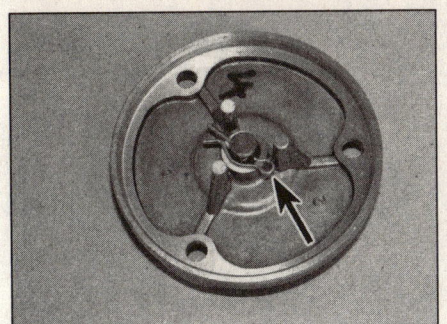
18.8a Remove the R-clip (arrowed)...

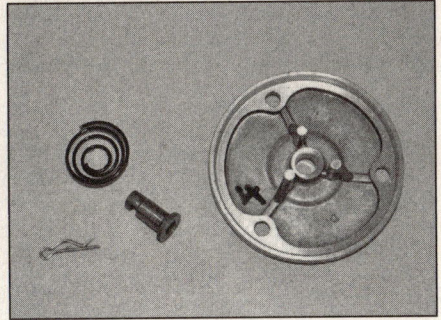
18.8b ...and remove the valve and spring

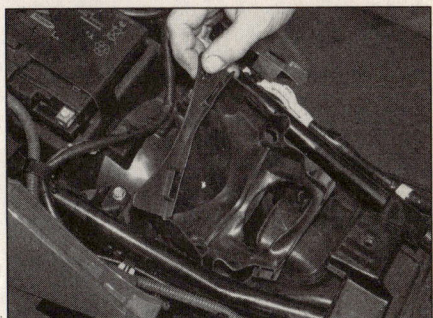
19.2 Remove the rubber cover

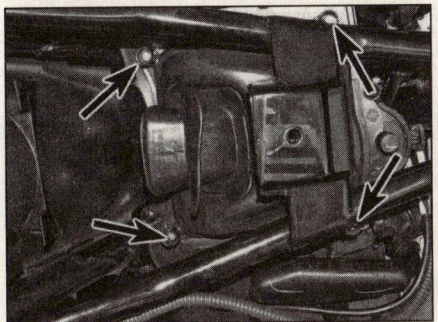
19.3a Undo the screws (arrowed)...

19.3b ...and lift off the filter cover

19.4 Lift out the air filter element

8 Depress the oil valve in the cover and remove the R-clip, then remove the valve and spring, noting how it fits (see illustrations).
9 Clean the valve with a suitable solvent and blow compressed air through it to ensure it is clear.
10 Lubricate the valve with clean engine oil, then install the spring and valve in the cover and secure them with the R-clip. Check that the valve slides freely in the cover.
11 Fit a new gasket onto the cover, then install the cover and tighten the screws securely.
12 Fit a new gasket and install the right-hand engine cover (see Chapter 2).
13 Follow the procedure in Section 7 to refill the engine oil.

19 Air filter
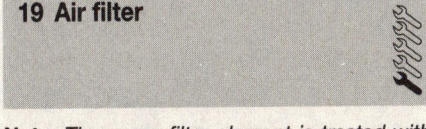

Note: *The paper filter element is treated with a dust adhesive and cannot be cleaned. If the machine is continually ridden in wet or dusty conditions, the filter should be changed more frequently.*

1 Remove the seats and the left-hand side panel (see Chapter 7).
2 Lift out the rubber cover, noting how it fits (see illustration).
3 Undo the screws securing the filter cover and lift it off (see illustrations).
4 Lift out the filter element, noting how it fits (see illustration).
5 Clean the inside of the filter cover.
6 Note the location of the filter inside the filter housing – if required, follow the procedure in Chapter 4 to remove the filter housing and clean it.
7 Release the clip securing the filter housing drain and pull off the drain (see illustration 9.3). Wipe out any oil or moisture with a clean cloth, then install the drain and secure it with the clip.
8 Install the new filter element, making sure it is properly seated, then fit the cover and secure it with its screws (see illustrations 19.4, 3b and a).
9 Fit the rubber cover, then install the seats and side panel.

1•18 Notes

Chapter 2
Engine, clutch and transmission

Contents

	Section number		Section number
Alternator	see Chapter 8	General information	1
Cam chain tensioner	7	Idle speed	see Chapter 1
Cam chain, tensioner blade and guide blade	20	Neutral switch	see Chapter 8
Camshaft and rocker arms	8	Oil change, filter and strainer	see Chapter 1
Clutch	15	Oil level check	see Pre-ride checks
Clutch cable	16	Oil pump	14
Clutch check	see Chapter 1	Piston	12
Component access	2	Piston rings	13
Crankcases and bearings	22	Primary drive gear	18
Crankcase separation and reassembly	21	Running-in procedure	27
Crankshaft and connecting rod	23	Selector drum and forks	24
Cylinder	11	Spark plug	see Chapter 1
Cylinder head and valve overhaul	10	Starter clutch and gears	19
Cylinder head removal and installation	9	Starter motor	see Chapter 8
Engine overhaul – general information	5	Transmission shaft overhaul	26
Engine removal and installation	4	Transmission shafts and bearings	25
Engine wear assessment	3	Valve clearance check and adjustment	see Chapter 1
Gearchange mechanism	17	Valve cover	6

Degrees of difficulty

Easy, suitable for novice with little experience	Fairly easy, suitable for beginner with some experience	Fairly difficult, suitable for competent DIY mechanic	Difficult, suitable for experienced DIY mechanic	Very difficult, suitable for expert DIY or professional

Specifications

General
Type	Four-stroke single cylinder
Capacity	125 cc
Bore	52.4 mm
Stroke	57.8 mm
Compression ratio	9.2 to 1
Cylinder compression	185 psi (13.0 Bar) @ 800 rpm
Cooling system	Air-cooled
Lubrication	Wet sump, trochoid pump
Clutch	Wet multi-plate
Transmission	Five-speed constant mesh
Final drive	Chain

Camshaft and followers

Intake lobe height
  Standard... 33.268 to 33.508 mm
Exhaust lobe height
  Standard... 33.018 to 33.258 mm
Rocker arm bore diameter
  Standard... 10.000 to 10.015 mm
  Service limit (max)... 10.10 mm
Rocker arm shaft diameter
  Standard... 9.972 to 9.987 mm
  Service limit (min)... 9.91 mm
Rocker arm-to-shaft clearance
  Standard... 0.013 to 0.043 mm
  Service limit (max)... 0.10 mm

Cylinder head

Warpage (max)... 0.05 mm

Valves, guides and springs

Valve clearances.. see Chapter 1
Stem diameter
  Intake valve
    Standard.. 4.975 to 4.990 mm
    Service limit (min)...................................... 4.920 mm
  Exhaust valve
    Standard.. 4.955 to 4.970 mm
    Service limit (min)...................................... 4.90 mm
Guide bore diameter – intake and exhaust valves
  Standard... 5.000 to 5.012 mm
  Service limit (max)... 5.040 mm
Stem to guide clearance
  Intake valve
    Standard.. 0.010 to 0.037 mm
    Service limit... 0.070 mm
  Exhaust valve
    Standard.. 0.030 to 0.057 mm
    Service limit... 0.090 mm
Seat width – intake and exhaust valves
  Standard... 0.90 to 1.10 mm
  Service limit (max)... 1.50 mm
Valve spring free length
  Standard
    CBF125M9 and MA models............................. 37.78 mm
    CBF125MB models onward
      Inner spring.. 37.30 mm
      Outer spring....................................... 35.95 mm

Cylinder

Bore
  Standard... 52.400 to 52.410 mm
  Service limit (max)... 52.50 mm
Ovality (out-of-round) (max).................................. 0.10 mm
Taper (max)... 0.10 mm
Warpage (max)... 0.10 mm

Piston

Piston diameter (see text)
  Standard... 52.370 to 52.390 mm
  Service limit (min)... 52.300 mm
Piston-to-bore clearance
  Standard... 0.010 to 0.040 mm
  Service limit.. 0.10 mm
Oversize pistons.. +0.25, +0.50, +0.75, +1.0 mm
Piston pin diameter
  Standard... 12.994 to 13.000 mm
  Service limit (min)... 12.98 mm

Engine, clutch and transmission

Piston (continued)
Piston pin bore diameter in piston
   Standard .... 13.002 to 13.008 mm
   Service limit (max) .... 13.03 mm
Piston-to-piston pin clearance
   Standard .... 0.002 to 0.014 mm
   Service limit .... 0.04 mm

Piston rings
Ring end gap (installed)
  Top ring
    Standard .... 0.10 to 0.25 mm
    Service limit (max) .... 0.40 mm
  Second ring
    Standard .... 0.30 to 0.45 mm
    Service limit (max) .... 0.60 mm
  Oil ring side-rail
    Standard .... 0.20 to 0.70 mm
    Service limit (max) .... 0.85 mm
Ring-to-groove clearance
  Top ring
    Standard .... 0.030 to 0.065 mm
    Service limit (max) .... 0.100 mm
  Second ring
    Standard .... 0.015 to 0.050 mm
    Service limit (max) .... 0.090 mm

Starter clutch
Driven gear hub OD
   Standard .... 45.660 to 45.673 mm

Clutch
Friction plates 5
Plain plates 4
Friction plate thickness
   Standard .... 2.92 to 3.08 mm
   Service limit (min) .... 2.80 mm
Plain plate warpage (max) .... 0.20 mm
Spring free length
   Standard .... 39.0 mm
Clutch housing centre ID
   Standard .... 23.000 to 23.021 mm
   Service limit (min) .... 23.080 mm
Clutch sleeve OD
   Standard .... 22.959 to 22.980 mm
   Service limit (min) .... 22.930 mm
Clutch housing-to-sleeve clearance .... 0.020 to 0.062 mm
Clutch sleeve ID
   Standard .... 16.991 to 17.009 mm
   Service limit (max) .... 17.040 mm
Input shaft OD at clutch sleeve
   Standard .... 16.996 to 16.984 mm
   Service limit (max) .... 16.950 mm
Clutch sleeve-to-input shaft clearance .... 0.007 to 0.043 mm

Oil pump
Inner rotor tip-to-outer rotor clearance
   Standard .... 0.15 mm
   Service limit (max) .... 0.20 mm
Outer rotor-to-body clearance
   Standard .... 0.15 to 0.21 mm
   Service limit (max) .... 0.26 mm
Rotor end-float
   Standard .... 0.05 to 0.10 mm
   Service limit (max) .... 0.15 mm

Crankshaft
Runout (max) .... 0.030 mm

Connecting rod
Small-end internal diameter
   Standard.. 13.016 to 13.034 mm
   Service limit (max)... 13.050 mm
Small-end-to-piston pin clearance
   Standard.. 0.016 to 0.040 mm
   Service limit... 0.070 mm
Big-end side clearance
   Standard.. 0.10 to 0.35 mm
   Service limit (max)... 0.80 mm
Big-end radial clearance
   Standard.. 0.008 mm
   Service limit (max)... 0.050 mm

Selector drum and forks
Selector fork end thickness .... 4.93 to 5.00 mm
Selector fork bore ID .... 10.000 to 10.018 mm
Selector fork shaft OD .... 9.986 to 9.995 mm
Selector drum left-hand journal OD .... 23.959 to 23.980 mm
Selector drum right-hand journal OD .... 20.959 to 20.980 mm
Selector drum left-hand bearing ID .... 24.000 to 24.033 mm
Selector drum right-hand bearing ID .... 21.000 to 21.021 mm
Selector drum journal-to-bearing clearance
   Left-hand... 0.020 to 0.074 mm
   Right-hand.. 0.020 to 0.062 mm

Transmission
Gear ratios (no. of teeth)
   Primary reduction... 3.350 to 1 (67/20T)
   Final reduction
      UK/Europe models .... 2.625 to 1 (42/16T)
      France only .... 2.687 to 1 (43/16T)
   1st gear.. 3.076 to 1 (40/13T)
   2nd gear.. 1.944 to 1 (35/18T)
   3rd gear.. 1.473 to 1 (28/19T)
   4th gear.. 1.190 to 1 (25/21T)
   5th gear.. 1.038 to 1 (27/26T)
Input shaft
   4th gear ID... 20.000 to 20.018 mm
   Shaft OD at 4th gear position................................. 19.968 to 19.980 mm
   4th gear-to-shaft clearance................................... 0.020 to 0.050 mm
   5th gear ID... 17.000 to 17.018 mm
   Shaft OD at 5th gear position................................. 16.968 to 16.980 mm
   5th gear-to-shaft clearance................................... 0.020 to 0.050 mm
Output shaft
   1st gear ID... 20.500 to 20.521 mm
   1st gear bush OD.. 20.459 to 20.480 mm
   1st gear-to-bush clearance.................................... 0.020 to 0.062 mm
   2nd gear ID... 23.020 to 23.041 mm
   2nd gear bush OD.. 22.984 to 23.005 mm
   2nd gear-to-bush clearance.................................... 0.015 to 0.057 mm
   3rd gear ID... 23.025 to 23.046 mm
   3rd gear bush OD.. 22.984 to 23.005 mm
   3rd gear-to-bush clearance.................................... 0.020 to 0.062 mm
   1st gear bush ID.. 17.000 to 17.018 mm
   Shaft OD at 1st gear bush position............................ 16.966 to 16.984 mm
   1st gear bush-to-shaft clearance.............................. 0.016 to 0.052 mm
   2nd gear bush ID.. 20.020 to 20.041 mm
   Shaft OD at 2nd gear bush position............................ 19.978 to 19.989 mm
   2nd gear bush-to-shaft clearance.............................. 0.031 to 0.063 mm
   3rd gear bush ID.. 20.020 to 20.041 mm
   Shaft OD at 3rd gear bush position............................ 19.979 to 20.000 mm
   3rd gear bush-to-shaft clearance.............................. 0.020 to 0.062 mm
Oil seals
   Installed depth... 0.5 to 1.0 mm

Torque settings

Alternator rotor centre nut	74 Nm
Cam chain tensioner cap screw	4 Nm
Camshaft holder sleeve nuts	32 Nm
Camshaft sprocket bolts	9 Nm
Centrifugal oil filter rotor nut	64 Nm
Clutch centre nut	74 Nm
Clutch spring bolts	12 Nm
Crankcase bolts	12 Nm
Cylinder head bolts	12 Nm
Cylinder head cover bolts	10 Nm
Cylinder studs	11 Nm
Engine mounting bolt nuts	
Front engine mounting bolts	34 Nm
Front mounting bracket bolts	54 Nm
Rear mounting bolts	54 Nm
Engine oil temperature sensor	14 Nm
Front sprocket bolts	12 Nm
Gearchange cam centre bolt	12 Nm
Gearchange stopper arm bolt	12 Nm
Intake manifold bolts	12 Nm
Main bearing retainer bolts	10 Nm
Main bearing sprung retainer bolt	10 Nm
Oil pump bolts	12 Nm
Oxygen sensor	25 Nm
Rocker shaft retainer bolts	5 Nm
Starter clutch housing bolts	16 Nm
Transmission shaft bearing retainer plate bolts	10 Nm
Valve cover bolts	10 Nm

1 General information

The engine is an air-cooled single cylinder built in unit construction with the gearbox. The two valves in the cylinder head are operated by rocker arms actuated by a single overhead camshaft which is chain driven off the left-hand side of the crankshaft.

The crankcase incorporates a wet sump, pressure-fed lubrication system which uses a twin rotor trochoidal oil pump that is gear-driven off the primary drive gear on the right-hand end of the crankshaft. Oil is filtered by a centrifugal filter located on the right-hand end of the crankshaft and by a strainer in the bottom of the crankcase. The crankcase divides vertically.

The alternator rotor is mounted on the left-hand end of the crankshaft and the alternator stator and crankshaft position sensor (part of the ignition system) are located inside the left-hand engine cover. The starter motor is located on top of the crankcases behind the cylinder.

Power from the crankshaft is transferred to the transmission via the clutch. The clutch is of the wet, multi-plate type and is gear-driven off the crankshaft. The clutch is operated by cable. The transmission is a five-speed constant-mesh unit. Final drive to the rear wheel is by chain and sprockets.

2 Component access

Operations possible with the engine in the frame

The components and assemblies listed below can be removed without having to remove the engine from the frame. If however, a number of areas require attention at the same time, removal of the engine is recommended.

   Valve cover
   Cam chain tensioner
   Camshaft and rocker arms
   Cylinder head
   Cylinder and piston
   Starter motor (see Chapter 8)
   Oil pump and filter
   Clutch
   Gearchange mechanism
   Starter clutch and gears
   Cam chain, tensioner and guide blades

Operations requiring engine removal

It is necessary to remove the engine from the frame to gain access to the following components.

   Crankshaft, connecting rod and bearings
   Transmission shafts and bearings
   Selector drum and forks

3 Engine wear assessment

Cylinder compression check

Special tool: *A compression gauge with a suitable adapter is required for this test (see Step 4).*

1 Poor engine performance, exhaust smoke, heavy oil consumption and poor starting are indications of low compression. This may be caused by leaking valve stem seals, incorrect valve clearances, a leaking head gasket, or worn piston, rings and/or cylinder bore.

2 Before you start, make sure the valve clearances are correctly set (see Chapter 1).

3 Run the engine until it reaches normal

2•6 Engine, clutch and transmission

3.4 Compression check set-up

3.11 Location of the oil bleed bolt (arrowed)

operating temperature, then turn it off and remove the spark plug (see Chapter 1).

⚠️ **Warning: Take care not to burn your hands on the hot components.**

4 Fit the adaptor and compression gauge into the spark plug hole **(see illustration)**.
5 Ensure the transmission is in neutral, then turn the ignition ON and open the throttle fully. Crank the engine over on the starter motor for a few seconds until the gauge reading stabilises and take a note of the reading. Turn the ignition OFF.
6 Compare the reading obtained with that for cylinder compression in *Specifications* at the beginning of this Chapter.
7 If the reading is below the figure specified, inject a small quantity of engine oil into the spark plug hole with a pump-type oil can – this will temporarily seal the piston rings. Repeat the compression test. If the result shows a noticeable increase in pressure this confirms that the cylinder bore, piston or rings are worn (see Sections 11 to 13). If there is no change in the reading, the cylinder head gasket or valves are leaking (see Sections 9 and 10).
8 Although unlikely with the use of modern fuels, a high compression reading indicates excessive carbon deposits in the combustion chamber. Remove the cylinder head and clean all carbon off the piston, head and valves (see Sections 9, 10 and 12).
9 Remove the test equipment, install the spark plug and reconnect the plug cap.

Engine oil circulation

10 No provision is made for checking the engine oil pressure, however a simple check can be made to confirm oil circulation. This is especially important after a top-end or complete engine overhaul.
11 Remove the right-hand side panel (see Chapter 7) to access the oil bleed bolt on the rear of the valve cover **(see illustration)**.
12 Unscrew the bleed bolt, then tighten the bolt finger-tight. Have some rag ready to catch any expelled oil.
13 Start the engine and carefully unscrew the bolt – oil should be expelled as it is pumped up to the camshaft oil feed. Tighten the bolt securely.
14 If no oil is pumped out of the bleed hole, first remove the valve cover and check the condition of the oil passage O-ring. If the O-ring is good, check the oil strainer and filter (see Chapter 1) and the operation of the oil pump (see Section 14).

4 Engine removal and installation

Caution: *The engine is heavy. Engine removal and installation should be carried out with the aid of an assistant; personal injury or damage could occur if the engine falls or is dropped.*

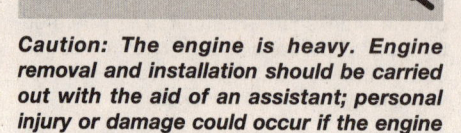

Special tools: *A motorcycle jack or trolley jack will be required to support the engine.*

1 Support the bike securely in an upright position using the centrestand. Work can be made easier by raising the machine to a comfortable working height on an hydraulic ramp or a suitable platform.
2 During the removal procedure, make a careful note of the routing of all cables, wiring and hoses and of any ties, clips or clamps that secure or guide them, so everything can be returned to its original location. Keep nuts, bolts and washers with the parts they secure.

Removal

3 Remove the seats, side panels, fairing panel, and on MD models onward the belly fairing and its mounting bracket (see Chapter 7).
4 Disconnect the negative (-) lead from the battery (see Chapter 8).
5 If required, remove the fuel tank (see Chapter 4).
6 Remove the exhaust system (see Chapter 4).
7 Disconnect the lower end of the clutch cable from the actuating arm and secure the cable clear of the engine unit (see Section 16).
8 Remove the front sprocket cover and chain guide (see Chapter 6).
9 Undo the pinch bolt securing the gearchange arm and draw the arm off the shaft, noting the alignment of the arm to the shaft (see Chapter 5, Section 3).
10 Remove the front sprocket (see Chapter 6). Rest the drive chain over the chain slider on the swingarm.
11 Trace the wiring from the sidestand switch and disconnect it at the connector (see Chapter 8). Feed the wiring back to the switch. Undo the bolts securing the sidestand bracket to the underside of the crankcase and remove the assembly (see Chapter 5).
12 If the engine is dirty, particularly around its mountings, clean it thoroughly before starting any major dismantling. This will make work much easier and rule out the possibility of dirt falling into some vital component.
13 Drain the engine oil (see Chapter 1).
14 Remove the throttle body assembly (see Chapter 4). Plug the engine intake manifold with clean rag.
15 Locate the alternator, crankshaft position (CKP) sensor and neutral switch wiring connectors and disconnect them **(see illustration)**. Secure the loom side of the wiring clear of the engine.
16 Disconnect the spark plug cap.
17 Disconnect the engine oil temperature sensor and oxygen sensor wiring connectors **(see illustrations)**.

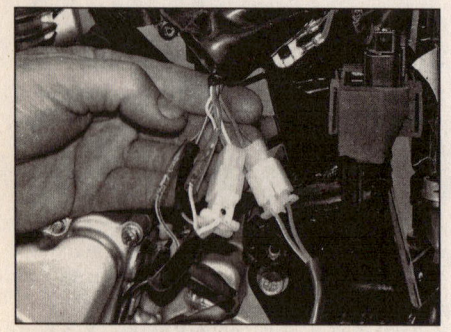

4.15 Locate the connectors inside the wiring boot

4.17a Engine oil temperature sensor ...

4.17b ... and oxygen sensor wiring connectors (arrowed)

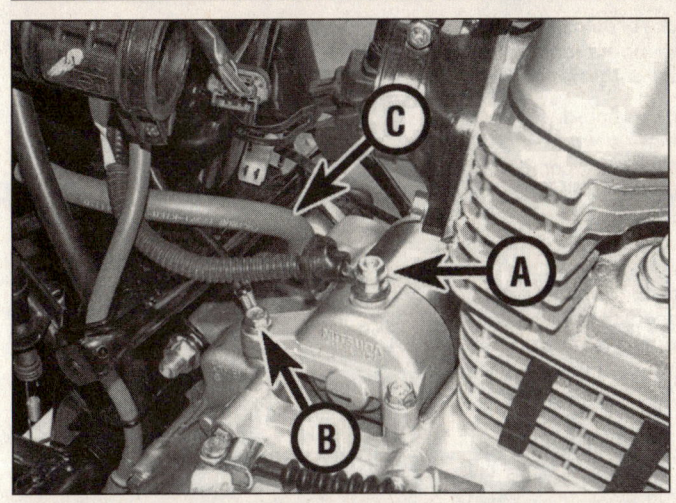

Engine, clutch and transmission 2•7

4.18 Starter motor terminal lead (A), earth (ground) lead (B) and crankcase breather hose (C)

4.20a Undo the nuts and bolts (arrowed) . . .

18 Disconnect the starter motor terminal lead, undo the bolt securing the earth (ground) lead to the rear of the crankcase and detach the crankcase breather hose from its union on the crankcase **(see illustration)**.

19 At this point, position an hydraulic or mechanical jack under the engine with a block of wood between the jack head and crankcase. Make sure the jack is centrally positioned so the engine will not topple in any direction when the last mounting bolt is removed. Take the weight of the engine on the jack.

20 Undo the nuts on the front engine mounting bolts and remove the front engine mounting bracket **(see illustrations)**.

21 Undo the nuts on the rear engine mounting bolts **(see illustration)**.

22 Make sure the engine is properly supported on the jack and have an assistant support it as well. Check that all wiring, cables and hoses are disconnected and clear of the engine.

23 Withdraw the rear mounting bolts and manoeuvre the engine unit out of the frame towards the right-hand side **(see illustrations)**.

Installation

24 Clean the threads of the engine mounting bolts.

25 With the aid of an assistant, lift the engine unit into position and support it on the jack. Ensure no wires, cables or hoses are trapped between the engine and the frame.

26 Align the bolt holes and slide the rear engine mounting bolts through from the left-hand side **(see illustrations 4.23a and b)**. Tighten the nuts finger-tight. **Note:** *All nuts and bolts should be installed finger-tight to begin with.*

27 Install the front mounting bracket, slide the bolts through from the left-hand side and tighten the nuts finger-tight **(see illustration)**.

28 Once the engine unit, frame and front mounting bracket are correctly aligned,

4.20b . . . and remove the front mounting bracket

4.21 Location of the rear engine mounting bolts (arrowed)

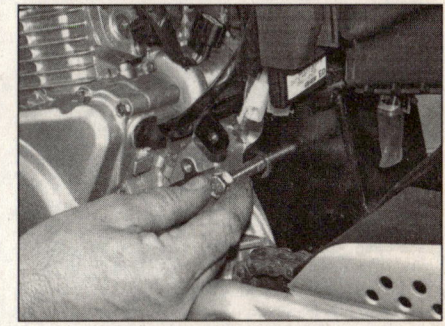

4.23a Withdraw the upper . . .

4.23b . . . and lower rear mounting bolts

4.23c Manoeuvre the engine out towards the right-hand side

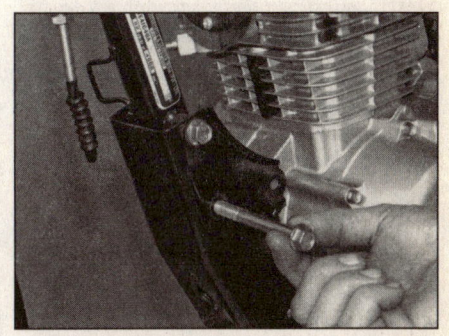

4.27 Install the front mounting bolts from the left-hand side

2•8 Engine, clutch and transmission

tighten the rear and then the front nuts and bolts to the torque settings specified at the beginning of this Chapter. **Note:** *Counter-hold the mounting bolts when tightening the nuts.*

29 The remainder of the installation procedure is the reverse of removal, noting the following:
- Make sure all wires, cables and hoses are correctly routed and connected, and secured by the relevant clips or ties.
- Tighten all bolts to the specified torque settings where given.
- Adjust the throttle and clutch cable freeplay (see Chapter 1).
- Adjust the drive chain (see Chapter 1).
- Refill the engine with oil to the correct level (see Chapter 1 and Pre-ride checks).

5 Engine overhaul – general information

1 Before disassembling the engine, the external surfaces of the unit should be thoroughly cleaned and degreased. This will prevent contamination of the engine internals, and will also make working a lot easier and cleaner. A high flash-point solvent, such as paraffin (kerosene) can be used, or better still, a proprietary engine cleaner such as Gunk. Use a paraffin brush or old paintbrush to work the solvent into the recesses of the engine casings. Take care to exclude solvent or water from the electrical components and intake and exhaust ports.

⚠️ **Warning: The use of petrol (gasoline) as a cleaning agent should be avoided because of the risk of fire.**

2 When the engine is clean and dry, clear a suitable area for working – a workbench is desirable for all operations once a component has been removed from the machine. Gather a selection of small containers and plastic bags so that parts can be grouped together in an easily identifiable manner. Some paper and a pen should be at hand so that notes can be made and labels attached where necessary. A supply of clean rag is also required. If the engine has been removed from the bike (see Section 4), have an assistant help you lift it onto the workbench.

3 Before commencing work, read through the appropriate section so that some idea of the necessary procedure can be gained. When removing components it should be noted that great force is seldom required. In many cases, a component's reluctance to be removed is indicative of an incorrect approach or removal method – if in any doubt, re-check with the text. In cases where fasteners have corroded, apply penetrating oil before disassembly.

4 When disassembling the engine, keep 'mated' parts together (e.g. valve assemblies, clutch plates etc. that have been in contact with each other during engine operation). These 'mated' parts must be reused or renewed as assemblies.

5 A complete engine/transmission disassembly should be done in the following general order with reference to the appropriate Sections.

Remove the valve cover
Remove the cam chain tensioner
Remove the camshaft and rocker arms
Remove the cylinder head
Remove the cylinder and piston
Remove the starter motor (see Chapter 8)
Remove the oil pump
Remove the clutch
Remove the primary drive gear
Remove the gearchange mechanism
Remove the starter clutch and gears
Remove the cam chain and blades
Separate the crankcase halves
Remove the crankshaft and connecting rod
Remove the selector drum and forks
Remove the transmission shafts

6 Reassembly is accomplished by reversing the general disassembly sequence.

6 Valve cover

Note: *The valve cover can be removed with the engine in the frame. If the engine has been removed, ignore the steps which don't apply.*

Removal

1 Remove the side panels and the fairing (see Chapter 7).

2 Unscrew the valve cover bolts, noting the location of the seals **(see illustrations)**. Discard the seals if they are damaged or deteriorated.

3 Lift the cover off **(see illustration)**. If it is stuck, tap gently around the sides with a rubber hammer or block of wood to dislodge it – do not lever it off with a screwdriver as this will damage the sealing surface.

4 The cover gasket is normally glued into the groove in the cover, and is best left there if it is reusable. If there are signs of oil leakage, or the gasket is in any way damaged, deformed or deteriorated, peel it off and remove any traces of sealant with a suitable solvent **(see illustrations)**.

5 Note the O-ring on the dowel that links the oil passage between the valve cover and camshaft holder and discard it as a new one

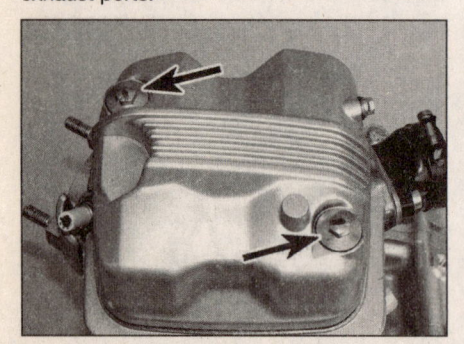

6.2a Undo the cover bolts . . .

6.2b . . . noting the location of the seals (arrowed)

6.3 Lift off the valve cover

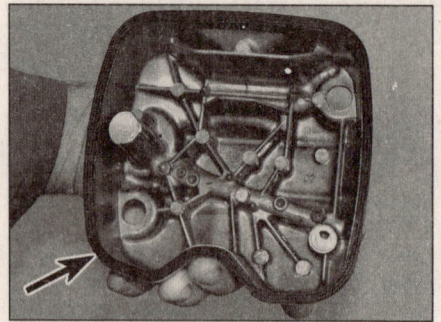

6.4a Cover gasket (arrowed) is glued in position

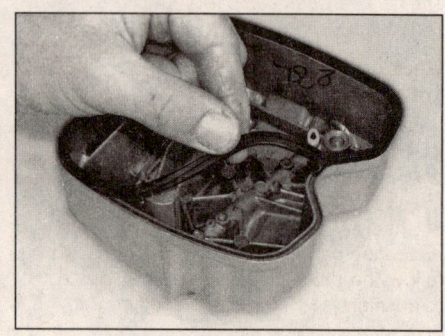

6.4b Only remove the gasket if it is damaged

Engine, clutch and transmission 2•9

6.5a Renew the O-ring (arrowed)

6.5b Ensure the dowel is secure

must be fitted **(see illustrations)**. *Note: Prior to installation, blow through the oil passage in the cover with compressed air to ensure it is clear.*

Installation

6 If a new cover gasket is being fitted, apply sealant in a few places around the groove in the cover to hold the gasket in position while the cover is being installed, then lay the gasket in place **(see illustrations 6.4b and a)**.
7 Fit a new O-ring onto the oil passage dowel and lubricate it with a smear of engine oil **(see illustration 6.5a)**.
8 Position the valve cover on the cylinder head, making sure the gasket stays in place.
9 Install the seals with the UP marks uppermost **(see illustration)**. Install the cover bolts and tighten them to the torque setting specified at the beginning of this Chapter.
10 Install the remaining components in the reverse order of removal. *Note: If required, check the engine oil circulation (see Section 3).*

7 Cam chain tensioner

Note: The cam chain tensioner can be removed with the engine in the frame. If the engine has been removed, ignore the steps which don't apply.

Removal

1 The cam chain tensioner is located on the rear, left-hand side of the cylinder **(see illustration 7.4a)**.
2 Remove the valve cover (see Section 6) and the spark plug (see Chapter 1).
3 Unscrew the timing inspection cap and the centre cap from the alternator cover, then follow the procedure in Chapter 1, Section 6 to position the piston at top dead centre (TDC) on its compression stroke.
4 Undo the tensioner cap screw and remove the O-ring **(see illustrations)**.

5 If the Honda service tool (Part No. 070MG-0010100) is available, insert it into the tensioner, turn it clockwise and then push it in to lock the tensioner plunger in the retracted position. Undo the mounting bolts, withdraw the tensioner and discard the gasket as a new one must be fitted. Remove the service tool.
6 Alternatively, insert a small flat-bladed screwdriver into the tensioner and turn it clockwise to retract the tensioner plunger. Hold the screwdriver in this position, then undo the mounting bolts and withdraw the tensioner **(see illustrations)**. Release the screwdriver – the plunger will spring back out, but can be easily reset on installation.

6.9 UP marks must be uppermost

7.4a Tensioner cap screw (A). Note mounting bolts (B)

7.4b Remove the O-ring

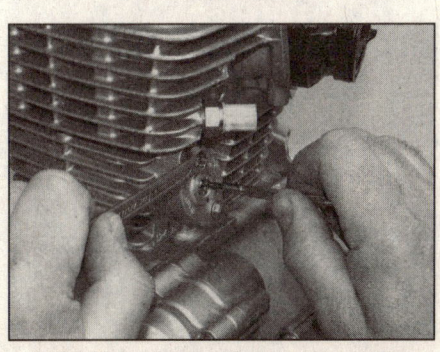

7.6a Use a screwdriver to retract the plunger . . .

7.6b . . . then remove the tensioner

2•10 Engine, clutch and transmission

7.7a Check the operation of the plunger (arrowed)

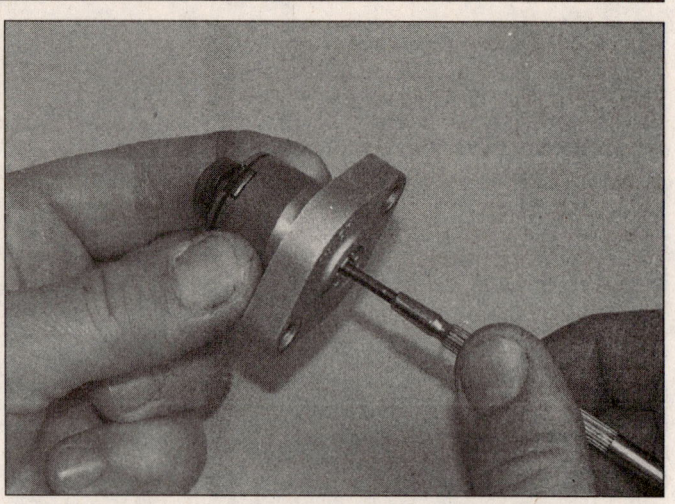

7.7b Use a screwdriver to retract the plunger

Check

7 Check that the plunger cannot be pushed back into the tensioner body **(see illustration)**. Insert a small flat-bladed screwdriver into the tensioner and turn it clockwise to retract the tensioner plunger **(see illustration)**. Now release the screwdriver – the plunger should spring back out freely. If the tensioner fails either of these checks replace it with a new one.

Installation

8 Clean the mating surfaces of the tensioner body and cylinder.
9 Ensure that the piston at TDC on its compression stroke (see Step 3).

10 Fit a new gasket onto the tensioner body.
11 If the Honda service tool is available, use it to lock the tensioner plunger in the retracted position (see Step 5). Install the tensioner and tighten the mounting bolts to the specified torque setting, then remove the service tool. Alternatively, retract the plunger using a small, flat-bladed screwdriver **(see illustration 7.7b)**. Secure the tensioner with its mounting bolts, then remove the screwdriver.
12 Lubricate a new O-ring with engine oil and install it in its groove, then tighten the cap screw securely **(see illustration 7.4b)**.
13 Install the remaining components in the reverse order of removal.

8 Camshaft and rocker arms

Note: *The camshaft and rocker arms can be removed with the engine in the frame. If the engine has been removed, ignore the steps which don't apply.*

Removal

1 Remove the valve cover (see Section 6) and the cam chain tensioner (see Section 7).
2 To remove the camshaft, first use the socket on the alternator nut to prevent the crankshaft turning and undo the bolts securing the camshaft sprocket **(see illustrations)**. Lift the sprocket off the camshaft and disengage it from the camchain **(see illustration)**. Secure the chain with a piece of wire to prevent it falling into the cam chain tunnel.
3 Note how the raised section on the left-hand end of the camshaft is facing upwards, then undo the bolt securing the camshaft retainer and lift it off, noting how it fits **(see illustration)**.
4 Press the rocker arms down against the tops of the valve stems and withdraw the camshaft together with its bearings **(see illustration)**.
5 Undo the sleeve nuts securing the camshaft holder evenly in a criss-cross pattern, noting

8.2a Hold the crankshaft . . .

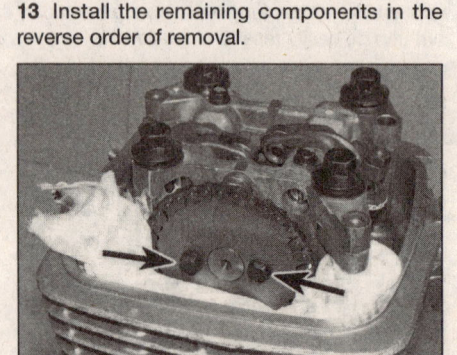

8.2b . . . undo the camshaft sprocket bolts (arrowed) . . .

8.2c . . . and lift off the sprocket

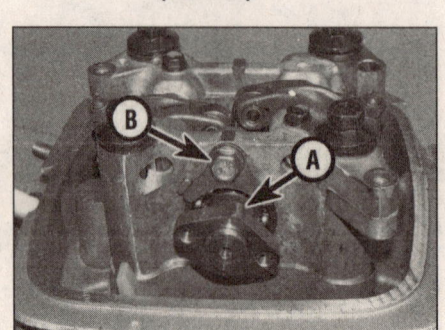

8.3 Raised section on camshaft (A). Camshaft retainer bolt (B)

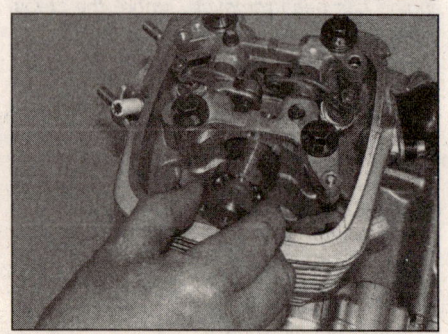

8.4 Withdraw the camshaft and bearings

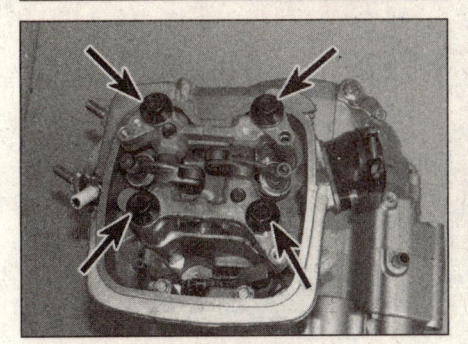

8.5a Undo the sleeve nuts . . .

8.5b . . . noting the washers (arrowed)

8.5c Note the dowels (arrowed) on the camshaft holder

the location of the washers **(see illustrations)**. Lift off the camshaft holder, noting the location of the dowels **(see illustration)**.

6 With the camshaft removed, avoid turning the crankshaft – the cam chain may drop down and bind between the crankshaft and case. Place a clean rag over the cylinder head to prevent anything falling inside.

7 Before removing the rocker arms, mark the arms and the shafts so that they can be installed in their original locations if required.

8 Working on one rocker arm at a time, undo the retaining bolt, withdraw the rocker shaft and lift out the arm **(see illustration)**. Keep related components together – slide each rocker arm back onto its shaft to aid inspection and installation.

Inspection

9 Clean the components with a suitable solvent and dry them thoroughly, using compressed air if available. Blow through the oil passage in the camshaft holder to ensure it is clear.

10 The camshaft bearings should be an interference fit on the shaft – if they are loose a new camshaft and bearing assembly will have to be fitted **(see illustration)**. Also check that the bearings turn smoothly and freely, and that there is no freeplay between the inner and outer races. Check that the bearing housings in the holder are not worn or damaged.

11 Inspect the camshaft lobes for heat discoloration (blue appearance), score marks, chipped areas, flat spots and pitting. Measure the height of each lobe with a micrometer **(see illustration)** and compare the results to the specifications listed at the beginning this Chapter. If damage is noted or the lobes are worn, the camshaft must be replaced with a new one.

12 Inspect the rocker arms for heat discoloration, score marks and flat spots or pitting on the surface of the valve clearance adjusters where they contact the valve stems **(see illustration)**. Check that the rollers turn freely. If damage is noted or wear is excessive, the rocker arms, adjusters and valves must be renewed as required. Ensure the oil holes in the arms are clear.

13 Check for freeplay between each rocker arm and its shaft. Measure the internal diameter of the arm bore and the corresponding diameter of the shaft and compare the results with the specifications **(see illustrations)**. Renew any component that is worn beyond its service limit.

14 Check the sprocket for wear and replace it with a new one if necessary. **Note:** *If the sprocket is worn, it is likely that the cam chain will also be worn, and so too the sprocket on the crankshaft (see Section 23).*

8.8 Withdraw the rocker shaft and lift out the arm

8.10 Camshaft and bearings (arrowed) are supplied as an assembly

8.11 Measuring the cam lobes with a micrometer

8.12 Inspect the adjuster tips (arrowed) for wear and pitting

8.13a Measuring the diameter of the arm bore . . .

8.13b . . . and the corresponding diameter of the shaft

2•12 Engine, clutch and transmission

8.16 Align the rocker shaft before installing the bolt

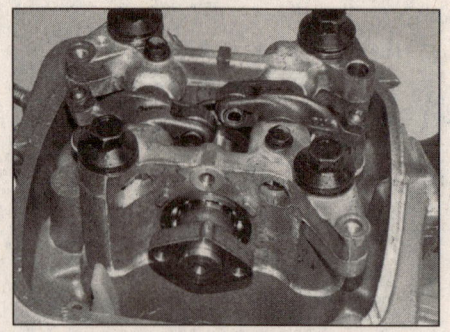

8.22 Installed position of the camshaft

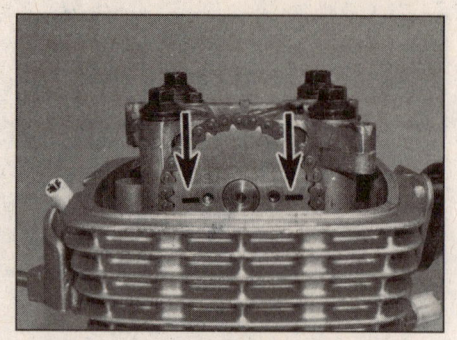

8.23 Align the camshaft sprocket as shown

Installation

15 Lubricate each rocker shaft and arm with engine oil.
16 Position the first rocker arm in the holder with the adjuster on the outside, then slide the shaft all the way through and secure it with the retaining bolt (see illustration 8.8). If required, the hole in the shaft can be aligned with the bolt using a flat-bladed screwdriver in the slot in the end of the shaft (see illustration). Tighten the bolt to the torque setting specified at the beginning of this Chapter.
17 Follow the same procedure to install the second rocker arm.
18 Ensure the dowels are in position in the camshaft holder, then fit the holder onto the cylinder head (see illustration 8.5c).
19 Ensure the threads of the camshaft holder nuts are clean. Lubricate the threads and the underside of the nuts with engine oil. Install the washers and tighten the nuts finger-tight (see illustration 8.5b).
20 Tighten the camshaft holder nuts evenly, in a criss-cross pattern, to the specified torque setting.
21 Check that the piston is still at TDC – the line next to the T mark on the alternator rotor aligns with the notch in the timing inspection hole (see Chapter 1, Section 6).
22 Lubricate the camshaft lobes and bearings with engine oil. Press the rocker arms down against the tops of the valve stems and slide the camshaft and bearings into the holder with the raised section on the left-hand end uppermost (see illustration). Install the camshaft retainer and tighten the bolt securely.

23 Free the cam chain, lift the front run of the chain to remove all slack and fit the camshaft sprocket into the chain – the index lines on the sprocket should be parallel with the mating surface of the head (see illustration). Fit the sprocket onto the end of the camshaft and align the bolt holes. Stuff some clean rag into the cam chain tunnel to avoid dropping the bolts into the crankcase.
24 Install the sprocket bolts, then use the socket on the alternator nut to prevent the crankshaft turning and tighten the sprocket bolts to the specified torque.
25 Install the cam chain tensioner (see Section 7). Check that the index lines on the sprocket are still correctly aligned with the cylinder head. If not, remove the tensioner, undo the sprocket bolts and correct the position of the sprocket before going any further.
Caution: If the marks are not aligned exactly as described, the valve timing will be incorrect and the valves may strike the piston, causing extensive damage to the engine.
26 Check the valve clearances (see Chapter 1).
27 Install the remaining components in the reverse order of removal.

9 Cylinder head removal and installation

Note: *The cylinder head can be removed with the engine in the frame. If the engine has been removed, ignore the steps which don't apply.*

Removal

1 Remove the exhaust system (see Chapter 4).
2 Remove the throttle body assembly (see Chapter 4). Plug the engine intake manifold with clean rag.
3 Disconnect the engine oil temperature sensor and oxygen sensor wiring connectors (see illustrations 4.17a and b).
4 Remove the valve cover (see Section 6) and the cam chain tensioner (see Section 7).
5 Remove the camshaft (see Section 8) but do not remove the camshaft holder at this stage.
6 Undo the two cylinder head bolts on the left-hand side next to the cam chain tunnel (see illustration). Undo the sleeve nuts securing the camshaft holder and remove the camshaft holder (see Section 8).
7 Pull the cylinder head up off the cylinder (see illustration). Note that the cylinder is held against the crankcase by the cylinder head fixings – if the cylinder lifts with the head the cylinder base gasket seal will be broken and the cylinder will have to be removed and a new base gasket fitted (see Section 11). If the head is stuck, tap around the joint with a soft-faced mallet to free it. Do not attempt to free the head by levering it off – you'll damage the sealing surfaces. As the head is lifted off, release the cam chain, but ensure it doesn't fall down the cam chain tunnel.
8 Remove the cylinder head gasket (see illustration). Ensure the cam chain is held securely and stuff a clean rag into the cam chain tunnel to prevent any debris falling in.

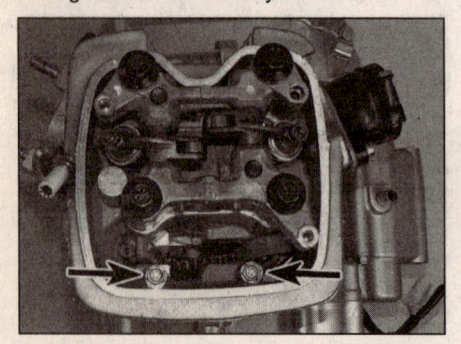

9.6 Location of the cylinder head bolts

9.7 Lift off the cylinder head

9.8 Remove the head gasket

Engine, clutch and transmission 2•13

9.9 Note the location of the dowels (arrowed)

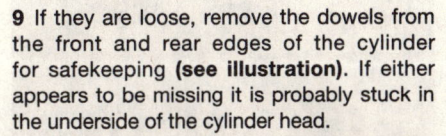

9.15 Install the head bolts finger-tight

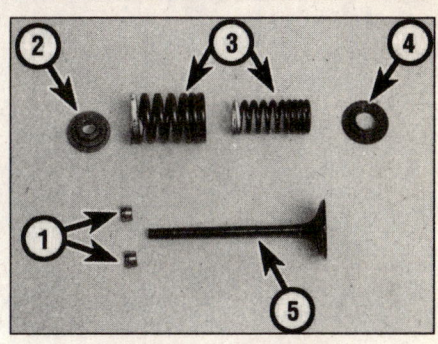

10.5 Valve components
1 Collets
2 Spring retainer
3 Springs
4 Spring seat
5 Valve

9 If they are loose, remove the dowels from the front and rear edges of the cylinder for safekeeping **(see illustration)**. If either appears to be missing it is probably stuck in the underside of the cylinder head.

10 Inspect the cylinder head gasket and the mating surfaces on the head and cylinder for signs of leakage, which could indicate that the head is distorted. If necessary, check the cylinder head with a straight-edge (see Section 10). Discard the old head gasket as a new one must be fitted on reassembly.

11 Clean any traces of old gasket material from the head and cylinder. If a scraper is used, take care not to scratch or gouge the soft aluminium. Be careful not to let any of the gasket material fall into the cylinder bore or cam chain tunnel.

Installation

12 If removed, fit the dowels into the cylinder **(see illustration 9.9)**.

13 Remove any rag from the cam chain tunnel. Ensure the cam chain is held securely. Install the cam chain guide blade if it has been removed **(see illustration 11.2)**.

14 Ensure the cylinder head and cylinder mating surfaces are clean. Lay the *new* head gasket over the studs and onto the cylinder, locating it over the dowels. Never re-use the old gasket.

15 Carefully fit the cylinder head over the studs and the cam chain and lower it onto the cylinder, making sure it locates correctly onto the dowels **(see illustration 9.7)**. Install the cylinder head bolts finger-tight **(see illustration)**.

16 Install the camshaft holder and tighten the nuts evenly, in a criss-cross pattern, to the specified torque setting (see Section 8). Tighten the cylinder head bolts the specified torque setting.

17 Install the camshaft, the cam chain tensioner and the valve cover.

18 Connect the engine oil temperature sensor and oxygen sensor wiring connectors **(see illustrations 4.17a and b)**.

19 Install the remaining components in the reverse order of removal.

10 Cylinder head and valve overhaul

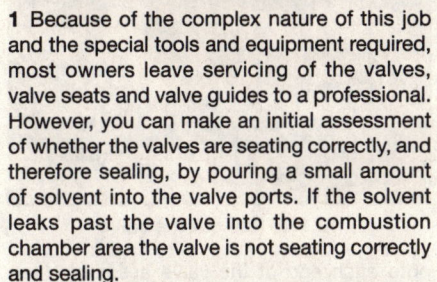

1 Because of the complex nature of this job and the special tools and equipment required, most owners leave servicing of the valves, valve seats and valve guides to a professional. However, you can make an initial assessment of whether the valves are seating correctly, and therefore sealing, by pouring a small amount of solvent into the valve ports. If the solvent leaks past the valve into the combustion chamber area the valve is not seating correctly and sealing.

2 With the correct tools (a valve spring compressor is essential – make sure it is suitable for motorcycle work), you can also remove the valves and associated components from the cylinder head, clean them and check them for wear to assess the extent of the work needed.

Unless seat cutting or guide replacement is required, the head can then be reassembled.

3 A dealer service department or specialist engineer can renew the guides and re-cut the valve seats.

4 After the valve service has been performed, be sure to clean the head very thoroughly before installation on the engine to remove any metal particles or abrasive grit that may still be present from the valve service operations. Use compressed air, if available, to blow out all the holes and passages.

Disassembly

Special tool: *A valve spring compressor suitable for motorcycle work is essential for this procedure (see Step 8).*

5 Before proceeding, arrange to label and store the valves along with their related components in such a way that they can be returned to their original locations without getting mixed up **(see illustration)**. Two small containers are ideal – alternatively, labelled plastic bags will do just as well.

6 If required, remove the engine oil temperature sensor and oxygen sensor **(see illustrations)**. If work is being undertaken on the cylinder head and there is a danger the sensors may be damaged, remove them for safekeeping. **Note:** *The sensors are part of the engine management system – see Chapter 4 for test details.*

7 If required, undo the bolts securing the intake manifold and remove the manifold,

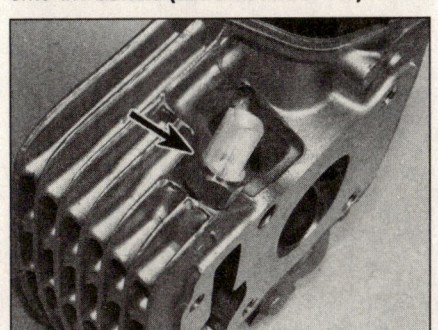

10.6a Location of the oil temperature sensor (arrowed)

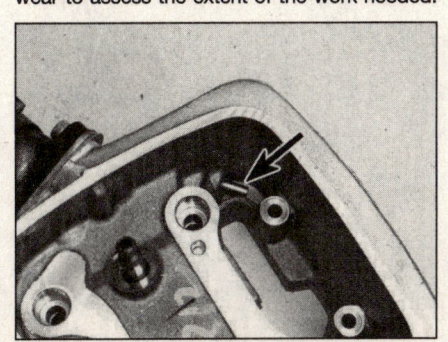

10.6b Oil temperature sensor probe inside head (arrowed)

10.6c Location of the oxygen sensor (arrowed)

2•14 Engine, clutch and transmission

10.7 Note location of the intake manifold

10.8a Install the valve spring compressor

10.8b Ensure the compressor locates on the valve . . .

10.8c . . . and the spring retainer

10.9 Removing the collets with a small screwdriver

10.10a Remove the spring retainer . . .

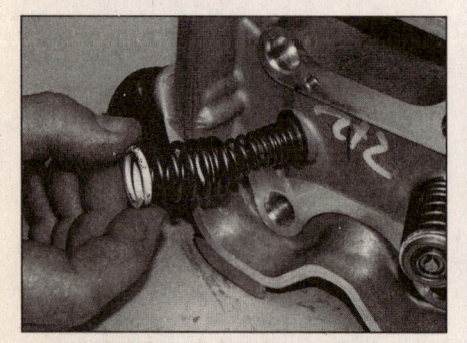

10.10b . . . and valve springs

10.11a Pull out the valve

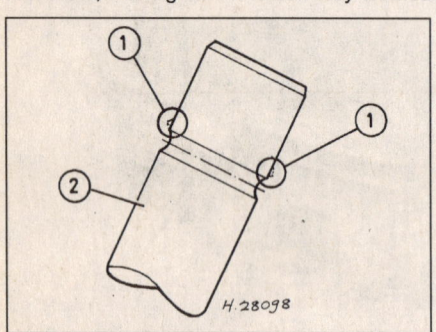

10.11b If necessary, deburr the valve stem (2) above the collet groove (1)

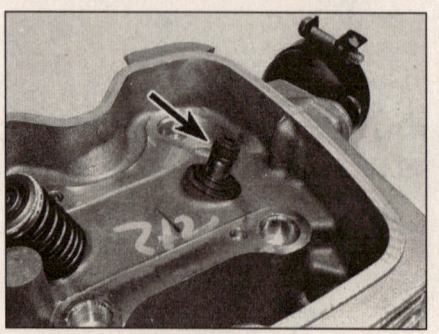

10.12a Pull the stem seal (arrowed) off with pliers . . .

10.12b . . . and remove the spring seat

noting how it fits **(see illustration)**. Note the location of the gasket and O-ring and discard them as new ones must be fitted. If the manifold is cracked or hardened, a new one must be fitted on reassembly.

8 Install the valve spring compressor on the first valve, making sure it is correctly located onto each end of the valve assembly **(see illustration)**. On the underside of the head, make sure the compressor only contacts the valve and not the soft aluminium of the head – if necessary, fit a spacer between them. On the top of the valve the compressor needs to be about the same size as the spring retainer – if it is too small it will be difficult to remove and install the collets **(see illustrations)**.

9 Compress the spring just enough to free the collets, then remove them using a magnet or a screwdriver with a dab of grease on it **(see illustration)**.

10 Carefully release the valve spring compressor and remove the spring retainer and spring(s), noting which way up each component fits **(see illustrations)**. **Note:** *CBF125M9 and MA models are fitted with one spring per valve. CBF125MB models onward (as used to illustrate this procedure) are fitted with two springs per valve.*

11 Pull the valve out from the underside of the head **(see illustration)**. If the valve binds in the guide and won't pull through, push it back into the head and deburr the area around the collet groove with a very fine file **(see illustration)**.

12 Pull the valve stem seal off the top of the valve guide with pliers and discard it **(see illustration)** – never re-use the old seals. Lift out the spring seat **(see illustration)**.

Engine, clutch and transmission 2•15

10.18 Check the head gasket mating surface for warpage

10.19 Measure the valve seat width

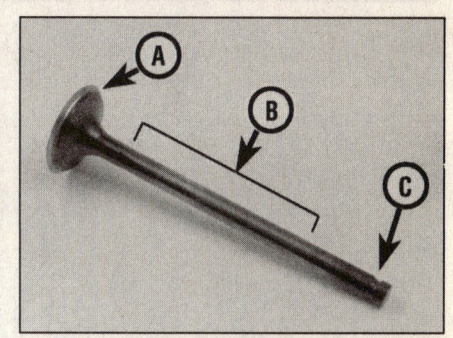

10.20 Examine the valve head (A), stem (B) and collet groove (C)

13 Repeat the procedure for the other valve. Remember to keep the parts for each valve separate so they can be reinstalled in the correct location.
14 Clean the cylinder head with solvent and dry it thoroughly. Compressed air will speed the drying process and ensure that all holes and recessed areas are clean. **Note:** *Do not use a wire brush mounted in a drill motor to clean the combustion chamber as the head material is soft and may be scratched or eroded away by the wire brush.*
15 Clean the valve spring(s), collets, retainers and spring seats with solvent and dry them thoroughly. Do the parts from one valve at a time so that no mixing of parts between valves occurs.
16 Remove any carbon deposits that may have formed on the valve heads using a scraper or a motorised wire brush. Again, make sure the valves do not get mixed-up.

Inspection

17 Check very carefully for cracks and other damage, especially around the valve seats and spark plug hole. If cracks are found, a new head will be required.
18 Using a precision straight-edge and a feeler gauge, check the head gasket mating surface for warpage **(see illustration)**. Refer to *Tools and Workshop Tips* in the Reference section for details of how to use the straight-edge. If the head is warped beyond the limit specified at the beginning of this Chapter, consult a Honda dealer or take it to a specialist repair shop for rectification.
19 Examine the valve seats in the combustion chamber. If they are pitted, cracked or burned, the head will require work beyond the scope of the home mechanic. Measure the valve seat width and compare it to this Chapter's *Specifications* **(see illustration)**. If it exceeds the service limit, or if it varies around its circumference, overhaul is required.
20 Examine the head of each valve for cracks, pits and burned spots, then check the valve stem and the collet groove area for wear and damage **(see illustration)**. Rotate the valve and check for any obvious indication that it is bent. Check the end of the stem for pitting and excessive wear. Renew the valve if necessary.
21 Clean the valve guides to remove any carbon build-up. Working on one valve and guide at a time, measure the valve stem diameter and note the results – take measurements in three different places to check for uneven wear **(see illustration)**. Now measure the inside diameter of the guide (at both ends and in the centre of the guide) with a small hole gauge (see *Tools and Workshop Tips* in the *Reference* section). Subtract the stem diameter from the guide diameter to obtain the stem-to-guide clearance. If the clearance is greater than the service limit listed in this Chapter's *Specifications*, renew whichever component is worn beyond its service limit. If the valve guide is within specifications, but is worn unevenly, it should be renewed.
22 Check the end of each valve spring for wear and pitting. Measure the spring free length and compare the result to the specifications **(see illustration)**. If any spring is shorter than specified it has sagged and must be replaced with a new one.

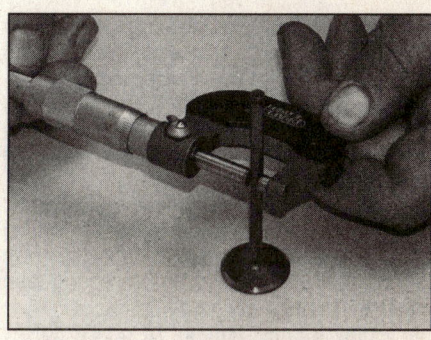

10.21 Measuring the valve stem diameter with a micrometer

23 Stand each spring upright on a flat surface and check it for bend with a set square **(see illustration)**. If the bend in any spring is excessive, it must be replaced with a new one.
24 Check the spring seats, retainers and collets for obvious wear and cracks. Any questionable parts should not be re-used, as extensive damage will occur in the event of failure during engine operation.
25 If the inspection indicates that no overhaul work is required, the valve components can be reinstalled in the head.

Reassembly

26 Ensure the cylinder head is clean and blow through all passages with compressed air.
27 Working on one valve at a time, lay the spring seat in place with its shouldered side facing up **(see illustration 10.12b)**. Lubricate the *new* valve stem seal with engine oil and fit it onto the top of the valve guide **(see illustration)**.

10.22 Measuring valve spring free length

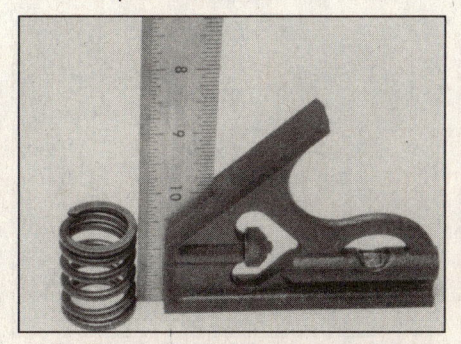

10.23 Check that the springs are not bent

10.27a Lubricate the new seal with engine oil . . .

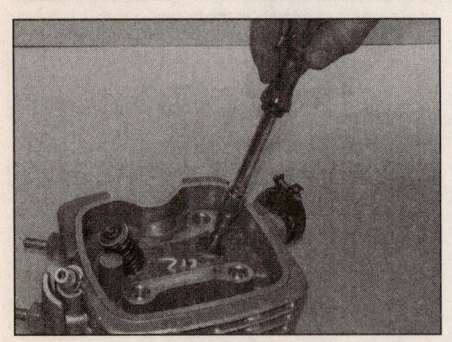

2•16 Engine, clutch and transmission

10.27b ... and press it on with a suitably-sized socket

10.32 Tap each valve stem lightly to seat the collets

Use an appropriate size deep socket to push the seal squarely over the end of the guide until it is felt to clip into place **(see illustration)**.

28 Lubricate the valve stem with engine oil, then install the valve in its guide, rotating it slowly to avoid damaging the seal **(see illustration 10.11a)**.

29 Install the spring(s), with the closer-wound coils facing down, followed by the spring retainer, with its shouldered side facing down so that it fits into the top of the spring **(see illustrations 10.10b and a)**.

30 Apply a small amount of grease to the collets to help hold them in place. Compress the spring with the valve spring compressor and install the collets **(see illustrations 10.8a and 9)**. When compressing the spring, depress it only as far as is absolutely necessary to slip the collets into place. Make certain that the collets are securely located in the collet groove and release the spring compressor.

31 Repeat the procedure for the other valve.
32 Support the cylinder head on blocks so the valves can't contact the work surface, then tap the end of each valve stem lightly with a hammer and punch to seat the collets in their grooves **(see illustration)**.
33 If removed, install the intake manifold using a new gasket and O-ring. Tighten the manifold bolts to the torque setting specified at the beginning of this Chapter **(see illustration 10.7)**.
34 If removed, install the engine oil temperature sensor with a new sealing washer. Tighten the sensor to the torque setting specified at the beginning of this Chapter.
35 If removed, install the oxygen sensor. Ensure the sensor threads are clean, then screw it in as far as possible by hand. Once the sensor is finger-tight, tighten it to the specified torque with a spark plug socket or dedicated oxygen sensor wrench.

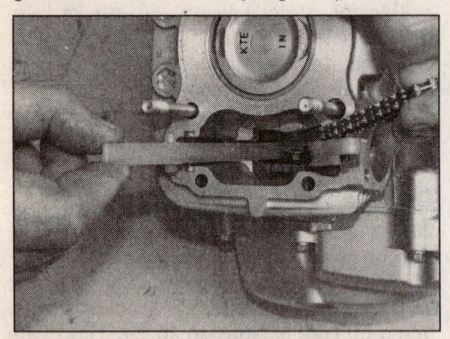

11.2 Lift out the cam chain guide blade

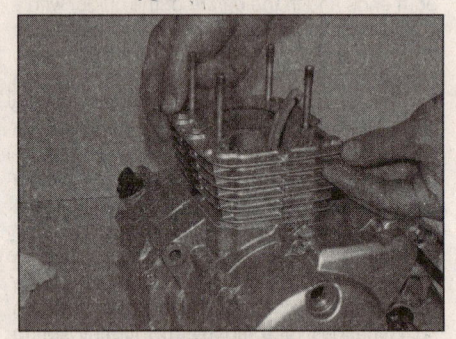

11.3 Ease the cylinder up off the crankcase

11 Cylinder

Note: *The cylinder can be removed with the engine in the frame. If the engine has been removed, ignore the steps which don't apply.*

Removal

1 Remove the cylinder head (see Section 9).
2 Lift out the cam chain guide blade, noting how it fits **(see illustration)**.
3 Ensure the cam chain is held securely, then ease the cylinder up off the crankcase **(see illustration)**. If the cylinder is stuck, tap around the joint with a soft-faced mallet to free it. Do not attempt to free the cylinder by levering it off – you'll damage the sealing surfaces.
4 Support the piston as the cylinder is lifted off to prevent the connecting rod or piston skirt hitting the crankcase **(see illustration)**. Note the location of the sound deadening inserts pressed between the cylinder fins **(see illustration)**.
5 Remove the cylinder base gasket and discard it as a new one must be used **(see illustration)**. If they are loose, remove the dowels from the crankcase for safekeeping – if either appears to be missing it is probably stuck in the underside of the cylinder.
6 Stuff clean rag into the cam chain tunnel and around the connecting rod to protect and support it and the piston and to prevent anything falling into the crankcase.
7 Clean any traces of old gasket material from the cylinder and crankcase. If a scraper is used, take care not to scratch or gouge the soft aluminium. Be careful not to let any of the gasket material fall into the engine.

Inspection

8 Use a precision straight-edge and a feeler gauge to check the top surface of the cylinder for warpage **(see illustration 10.18)**. Refer to *Tools and Workshop Tips* in the Reference section for details of how to use the straight-edge. If the cylinder is warped beyond the limit specified at the beginning of this Chapter, consult your Honda dealer or take it to a specialist repair shop for rectification.

11.4a Support the piston as the cylinder is lifted

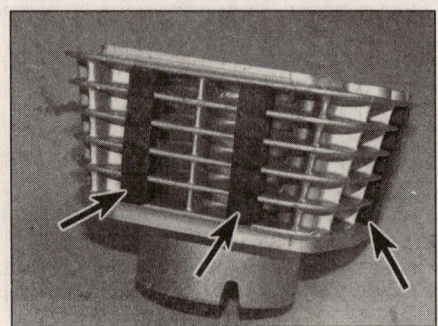

11.4b Note the location of the inserts (arrowed)

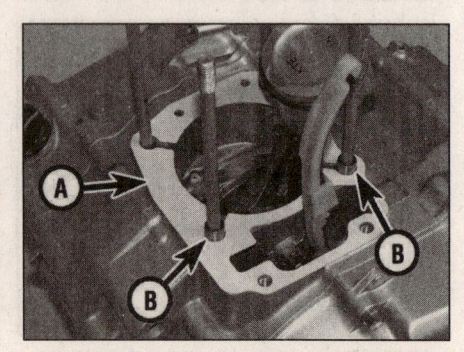

11.5 Remove the base gasket (A). Note location of the dowels (B)

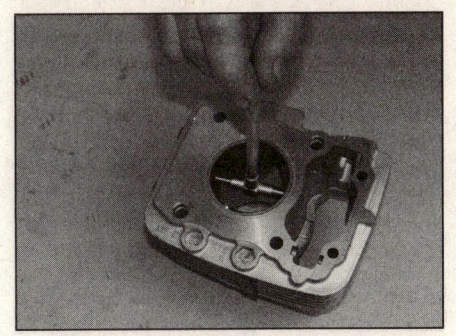

Engine, clutch and transmission 2•17

11.10a Measure the cylinder bore with a telescoping gauge . . .

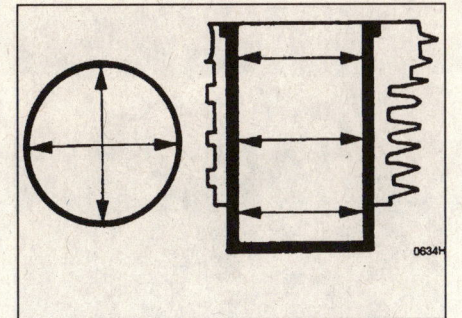

11.10b . . . in the directions shown

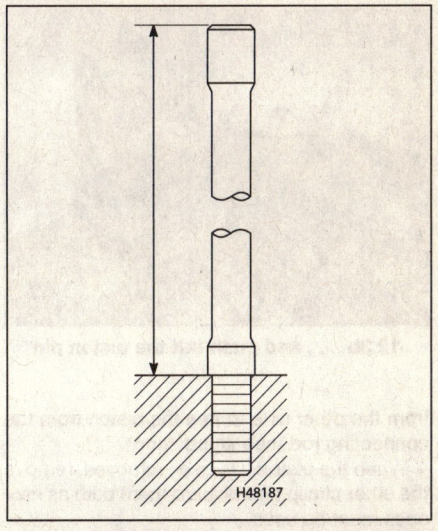

11.13 Installed length of the cylinder studs 113.4 to 115.4 mm

9 Inspect the cylinder wall carefully for scratches and score marks.

10 Using a telescoping bore gauge and a micrometer, check the dimensions of the cylinder bore to assess the amount of wear, taper and ovality. Measure near the top (but below the level of the top piston ring at TDC), centre and bottom (but above the level of the oil ring at BDC) of the bore, both parallel to and across the crankshaft axis **(see illustrations)**. Compare the results to the specifications at the beginning of this Chapter. If the bore is worn, oval or tapered beyond the service limit it can be re-bored and an oversize piston and ring set fitted. Four sizes of oversize piston (+0.25, +0.50, +0.75 and +1.0 mm) are available. Note that the engineer carrying out the re-bore must be aware of the required piston-to-bore clearance (see *Specifications*).

11 If the precision measuring tools are not available, take the piston and cylinder to a Honda dealer or specialist repair shop for assessment and advice.

12 Check that all the cylinder studs are tight in the crankcase. If any are loose, remove them and clean the threads before installation. If any studs are damaged they should be renewed.

13 Before installing a stud, ensure that the threads on the stud and in the crankcase are clean. When fitting the studs always screw the end with the longest thread into the crankcase. To avoid marking the studs when they are fitted, lock two nuts together on the upper thread, then tighten the stud using a spanner on the upper nut. Check the installed length of the studs by measuring the distance between the top and the crankcase surface **(see illustration)**.

Installation

14 If removed, fit the dowels over the studs and press them down firmly **(see illustration 11.5)**.

15 Remove the rags from around the piston and the cam chain tunnel, taking care not to let the connecting rod fall against the rim of the crankcase.

16 Ensure the cylinder and crankcase mating surfaces are clean. Lay the *new* base gasket over the studs and onto the crankcase, locating it over the dowels **(see illustration 11.5)**. Never re-use the old gasket.

17 Ensure the piston ring end gaps are correctly staggered **(see illustration 13.10)** then lubricate the piston, rings and cylinder bore with engine oil.

18 Rotate the crankshaft so that the piston is at its highest point – if possible have an assistant support the piston. Fit the cylinder over the studs and the cam chain and lower it onto the top of the piston.

19 Carefully compress and feed the top ring into the bore as the cylinder is pressed down – use your finger-tips and a small screwdriver to do this **(see illustration)**. Don't press the cylinder down too hard as this will only cause the ring to snag and take care not to score the surface of the piston skirt with the screwdriver.

20 Gradually lower the cylinder over the piston and feed the second ring and oil ring in using the same method.

21 Once all the rings are safely inside the bore, lower the cylinder onto the base gasket and press it down firmly **(see illustration)**.

22 Install the cam chain guide blade **(see illustration 11.2)**.

23 Install the remaining components in the reverse order of removal.

12 Piston

Note: *The piston can be removed with the engine in the frame.*

Removal

1 Remove the cylinder (see Section 11). Ensure that the crankcase and the cam chain tunnel are completely blocked with clean rag to prevent anything falling inside.

2 Note that the piston is marked IN – this mark faces the intake (rear) side of the engine. The mark may not be clearly visible until the piston is cleaned.

3 Carefully prise out the circlip on one side of the piston using needle-nose pliers or a small flat-bladed screwdriver inserted into the notch **(see illustration)**. Push the piston pin out

11.19 Feed the top ring into the cylinder bore

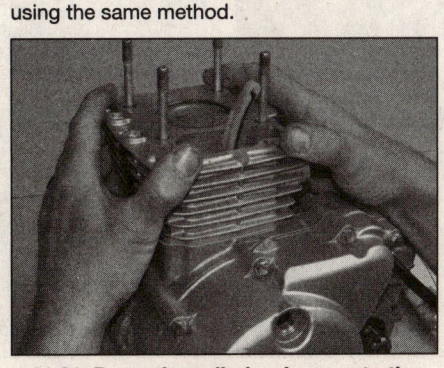

11.21 Press the cylinder down onto the base gasket

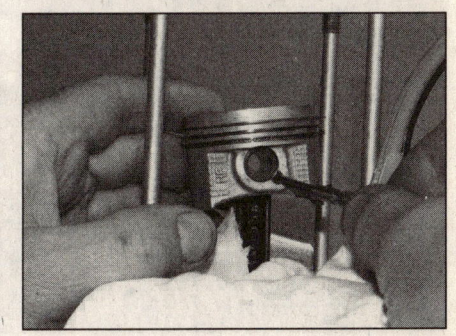

12.3a Prise out the circlip . . .

2•18 Engine, clutch and transmission

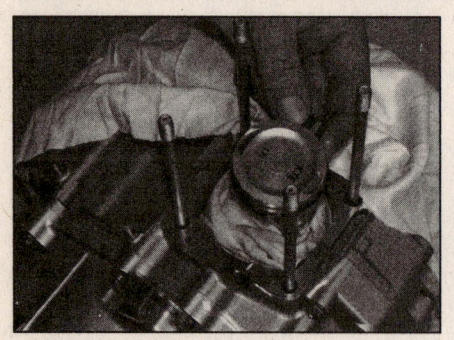

12.3b ... and push out the piston pin

12.5a Ease off the rings using thumbs ...

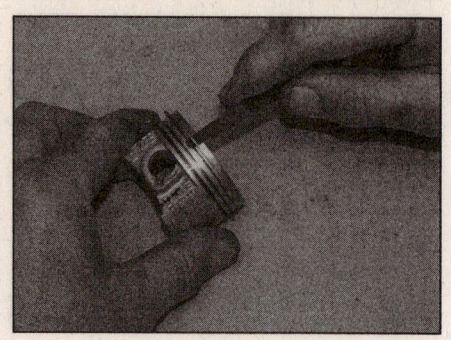

12.5b ... or a thin blade

from the other side to free the piston from the connecting rod **(see illustration)**.

4 When the piston has been removed, remove the other circlip and discard them both as new ones must be used.

> **HAYNES HiNT** If the piston pin is a tight fit, heat the piston gently with a hot air gun – this will expand the alloy piston sufficiently to release its grip on the pin. If the piston pin is particularly stubborn, extract it using a drawbolt tool, but be careful to protect the piston's working surfaces – see Tools and Workshop Tips in the Reference section.

5 Using your thumbs or a thin blade, carefully remove the rings from the piston **(see illustrations)**. Do not nick or gouge the piston in the process. Note which way up each ring fits and in which groove as they must be installed in their original positions if being re-used (see Section 13). The oil control ring (lowest on the piston) is composed of three separate components – the expander and the upper and lower side rails.

Note: *It is good practice to fit new piston rings when an engine is being overhauled.*

6 Clean all traces of carbon from the top of the piston. A hand-held wire brush or a piece of fine emery cloth can be used once most of the deposits have been scraped away. Do not, under any circumstances, use a wire brush mounted in a drill motor; the piston material is soft and will be eroded away by the brush.

7 Use a piston ring groove cleaning tool to remove any carbon deposits from the ring grooves. If a tool is not available, a piece broken off an old ring will do the job. Be very careful to remove only the carbon deposits. Do not remove any metal and do not nick or gouge the sides of the ring grooves.

8 Once the carbon has been removed, clean the piston with a suitable solvent and dry it thoroughly. Make sure the oil return holes at the back of the oil ring groove are clear.

Inspection

9 Carefully inspect the piston for cracks around the skirt, at the pin bosses and at the ring lands (between the ring grooves). Also check that the circlip grooves are not damaged. Normal piston wear appears as even, vertical wear on the thrust surfaces of the piston. If the skirt is scored or scuffed, the engine may have been suffering from overheating and/or abnormal combustion, which causes excessively high operating temperatures. The oil pump should be checked thoroughly.

10 In extreme cases, a hole in the top of the piston or burned areas around the edge of the piston crown indicate that pre-ignition or knocking under load have occurred, although the ECM should detect over-heating problems long before serious damage takes place. Check the symptoms of poor running in *Fault Finding* in the *Reference* section.

11 Check the piston-to-bore clearance by measuring the cylinder bore (see Section 11) and the piston diameter. Measure the piston 5 mm up from the bottom of the skirt and at 90° to the piston pin axis **(see illustration)**. Subtract the piston diameter from the bore diameter to obtain the clearance. If it is greater than the figure specified at the beginning of this Chapter, check whether it is the bore or piston, or both, that is worn beyond the service limit. If just the piston is worn, a new piston and ring set should be fitted. If the bore is worn the cylinder will have to be re-bored and an oversize piston fitted (see Section 11).

12 Measure the piston ring-to-groove clearance by fitting each ring in its groove and slipping a feeler gauge in beside it **(see illustration)**. Make sure you have the correct ring for the groove (see Step 5). Check the clearance at three or four locations around the groove. If the clearance is greater than specified, replace the piston and rings as a

12.11 Measuring the piston diameter

12.12 Measuring the ring-to-groove clearance

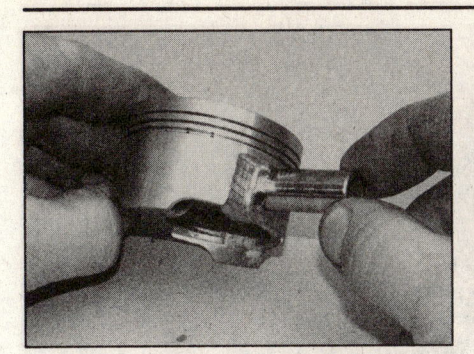

Engine, clutch and transmission 2•19

12.13a Checking the piston pin for freeplay in the piston

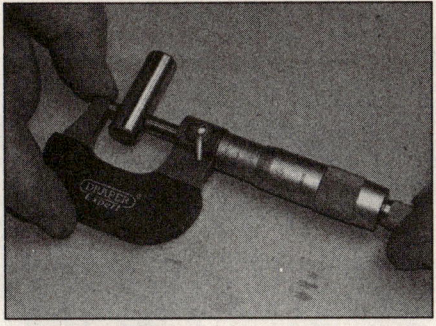

12.13b Measure the external diameter of the pin at both ends . . .

12.13c . . . and the internal diameter of the pin bore

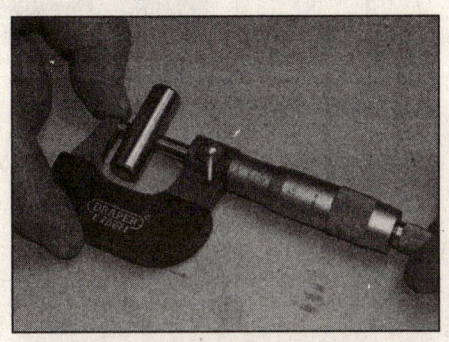

12.14a Measure the external diameter of the pin at the centre . . .

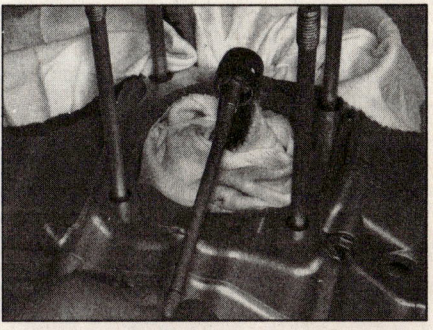

12.14b . . . and the internal diameter of the small-end

set. If new rings are being used, measure the clearance using the new rings. If the clearance is greater than that specified, the piston is worn and must be replaced with a new one.

13 Apply clean engine oil to the piston pin, insert it into the piston and check for any freeplay between the two **(see illustration)**. Measure the pin external diameter at each end **(see illustration)**, and the pin bores in the piston **(see illustration)**. Calculate the difference to obtain the piston-to-piston pin clearance and compare the result to the specifications at the beginning of this Chapter. If the clearance is greater than specified, replace the components that are worn beyond their specified limits.

14 Repeat the check and measurements between the middle of the pin and the connecting rod small-end **(see illustrations)**. If the small-end has worn beyond its service limit, a new crankshaft assembly will have to be fitted (see Section 23).

Installation

15 Inspect and install the piston rings (see Section 13).

16 Install a *new* circlip into one side of the piston – never re-use old circlips. When installing the circlips, compress them only just enough to fit them in the piston, and make sure they are properly seated in their grooves with the open end away from the removal notch **(see illustration 12.3a)**.

17 Lubricate the piston pin, the piston pin bore and the connecting rod small-end bore with engine oil, then install the piston on the connecting rod 3). Ensure the piston is fitted the correct way round (see Step 2).

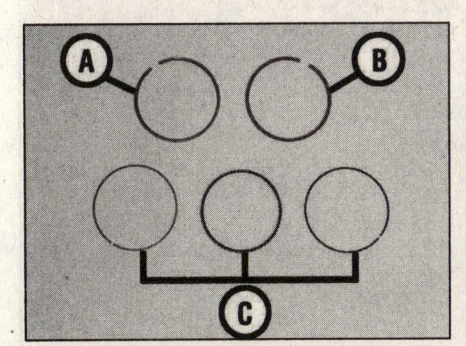

18 Insert the piston pin from the side without the circlip and push it all the way in. Secure the pin with the other *new* circlip.

19 Remove the rag from the crankcase openings and install the cylinder (see Section 11).

13 Piston rings

Inspection

1 It is good practice to fit new piston rings when an engine is being overhauled. Before

13.2 Piston ring set – top ring (A), second ring (B) and oil control ring (C)

13.3 Measuring piston ring installed end gap

installing the new rings, measure their end gaps as follows.

2 Lay out the piston rings so they can be identified for the measurement procedure **(see illustration)**. The upper surface of the top and second rings should have a manufacturer's mark at one end – the top ring is marked 'TOP 1' and the second ring is marked 'TOP 2'. Also note that the rings can be identified by their different cross-sections **(see illustration 13.10)**.

3 The end gaps are measured with the rings fitted inside the cylinder bore – insert a ring into the bottom of the bore and square it up with the cylinder walls by pushing it down with the top of the piston. The ring should be approximately 15 mm below the edge of the cylinder. Slip a feeler gauge between the ends of the ring to measure the gap and compare the result to *Specifications* at the beginning of this Chapter **(see illustration)**. Note that the gaps for each ring are different.

4 If the gap is larger or smaller than specified, check that you have the correct rings before proceeding. Excess end gap is not critical unless it exceeds the service limit.

Installation

5 The oil control ring (lowest on the piston) is installed first. It is composed of three separate components – the expander and the upper and lower side rails. Slip the expander into the groove, positioning its ends

2•20 Engine, clutch and transmission

13.5 Installing the oil ring expander

13.6 Installing the lower side rail

so that they touch but do not overlap **(see illustration)**.

6 Install the lower side rail. Do not use a piston ring installation tool on the oil ring side rails as they may be damaged. Instead, place one end of the side rail into the groove between the expander and the ring land **(see illustration)**. Hold it firmly in place and slide a finger or thin blade around the piston while pushing the rail into the groove. Next, install the upper side rail in the same manner.

7 After the oil control ring has been installed, check that both its upper and lower side rails can be turned smoothly in the ring groove.

8 Fit the second ring into the middle groove in the piston with its mark facing up (see Step 2). Do not expand the ring any more than is necessary to slide it into place. If required, use a piston ring installation tool to avoid breaking the ring.

9 Follow the same procedure to install the top ring into the top groove in the piston

10 Once the rings are correctly installed, check they move freely without snagging and stagger their end gaps as shown **(see illustration)**.

14 Oil pump

Note: *The oil pump can be removed with the engine in the frame. If the engine has been removed, ignore the steps which don't apply.*

Removal

1 Drain the engine oil (see Chapter 1).
2 Disconnect the lower end of the clutch cable and position it clear of the engine cover (see Section 16). On CBF125MD models onward remove the belly fairing (see Chapter 7).
3 Position a suitable container underneath the right-hand engine cover to catch any residual oil when the cover is removed. Undo the cover bolts evenly, noting the location of the clutch cable bracket, and draw the cover off **(see illustrations)**.
4 Remove the cover gasket and discard it;

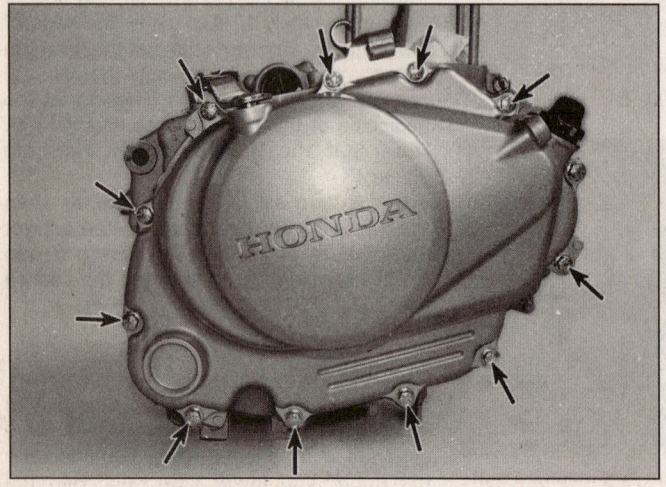

13.10 Stagger the ring end gaps as shown

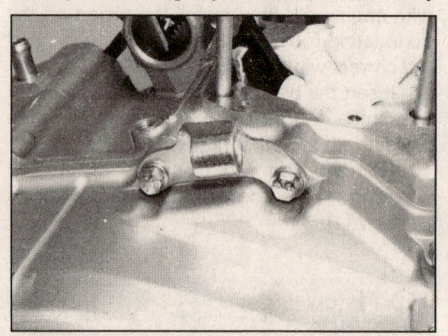

14.3a Note location of the clutch cable bracket

14.3b Undo the engine cover bolts . . .

14.3c . . . and draw the cover off

Engine, clutch and transmission 2•21

14.4 Location of the cover dowels

14.5 Remove the oil pump driven gear (arrowed)

note the location of the cover dowels and remove them for safe-keeping if they are loose **(see illustration)**.

5 Draw off the oil pump driven gear **(see illustration)**. If the gear teeth are worn or damaged, replace it with a new one.

6 Undo the pump mounting bolts and remove the pump **(see illustrations)**.

7 Undo the screw and lift off the back of the pump, noting how it fits **(see illustrations)**.

8 Remove the dowels **(see illustration)**.

9 Draw out the pump shaft and inner rotor and separate the rotor from the shaft – note the register mark on the face of the rotor **(see illustrations)**. Lift out the outer rotor, noting the register mark **(see illustration)**. **Note:** *The*

14.6a Undo the pump mounting bolts (arrowed) . . .

14.6b . . . and lift out the pump

14.7a Undo the screw (arrowed) . . .

14.7b . . . and remove the back of the pump

14.8 Remove the dowels

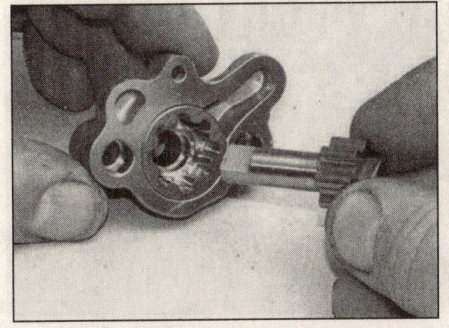

14.9a Draw out the pump shaft . . .

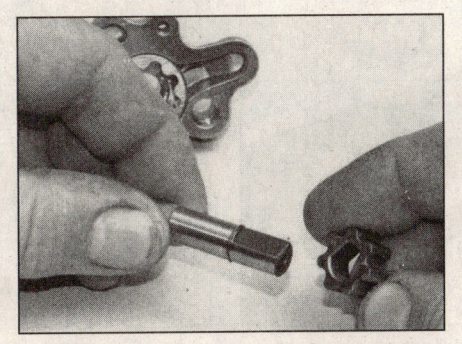

14.9b . . . and remove the inner rotor

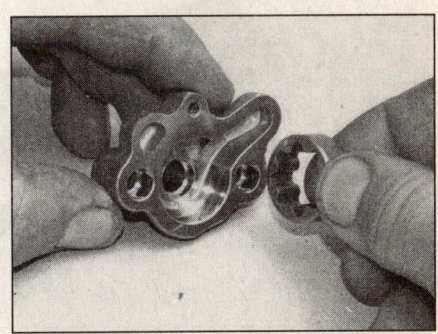

14.9c Lift out the outer rotor

2•22 Engine, clutch and transmission

14.13 Measuring inner rotor tip-to-outer rotor clearance

14.14a Measuring outer rotor-to-body clearance

register marks may face inwards or outwards – always ensure they are reassembled as noted on disassembly. Note the location of the circlip on the pump shaft.

Inspection

10 Clean all the components in a suitable solvent.
11 Inspect the pump body and rotors for scoring and wear. If any damage is evident, replace the components with new ones.
12 Fit the inner and outer rotors into the pump body as noted on removal.
13 Measure the clearance between the inner rotor tip and the outer rotor with a feeler gauge and compare it to the specification listed at the beginning of this Chapter **(see illustration)**. If the clearance is greater than the service limit, renew the rotors.
14 Measure the clearance between the outer rotor and the pump body and compare it to the specification listed at the beginning of this Chapter **(see illustration)**. Lay a straight-edge across the rotors and the pump body and, using a feeler gauge, measure the rotor end-float (the gap between the rotors and the straight-edge **(see illustration)**. If either

measurement is greater than the service limit, fit a new oil pump.

Installation

Note: *Prior to installation, lubricate the rotors with plenty of clean engine oil.*
15 Install the outer rotor in the pump body, ensuring it is the correct way round **(see illustration 14.9c)**. Fit the inner rotor onto the shaft and install the shaft **(see illustrations 14.9b and a)**.
16 Fit the dowels and the back of the pump and secure it with the screw **(see illustrations 14.8 and 7b and a)**. Check that the pump shaft turns freely.
17 Ensure the mating surfaces of the pump and crankcase are clean, then install the pump and tighten the mounting bolts to the specified torque setting. Install the oil pump driven gear **(see illustration 14.5)**.
18 Remove all traces of old gasket from the crankcase and cover surfaces.
19 If removed, install the cover dowels, then fit the new cover gasket making sure it locates correctly onto the dowels **(see illustration 14.4)**.
20 Install the engine cover.
21 Install the cover bolts finger-tight, not

forgetting the clutch cable bracket, then tighten the bolts evenly in a criss-cross pattern **(see illustration 14.3a and b)**.
22 Install the clutch cable (see Section 16) and adjust the freeplay (see Chapter 1)
23 Refill the engine with the recommended grade and type of oil (see Chapter 1). Refit the belly fairing (where fitted).

15 Clutch

Note 1: *The clutch can be removed with the engine in the frame. If the engine has been removed, ignore the steps which don't apply.*
Note 2: *The clutch centre nut and oil filter rotor nut must be discarded and new ones used on installation – it is best to obtain the new nuts in advance.*
Special tools: *A gear locking tool (see Step 3), a peg spanner (see Step 4) and a clutch centre holding tool (see Step 7) are required for this procedure.*

Removal

1 Drain the engine oil (see Chapter 1). Disconnect the lower end of the clutch cable and position it clear of the engine cover (see Section 16), then follow the procedure in Section 14 to remove the right-hand engine cover. Draw off the oil pump driven gear **(see illustration 14.5)**.
2 Remove the oil filter rotor cover and gasket (see Chapter 1, Section 18).
3 To loosen the filter rotor nut, the crankshaft drive gear and clutch driven gear must be locked. Honda produces a service tool to do this (Part No. 07724-0010200). Alternatively, use a piece of soft aluminium between the gear teeth as shown **(see illustration 15.4b)**.
4 With the crankshaft held securely, use a peg spanner to undo the nut **(see illustration)**.

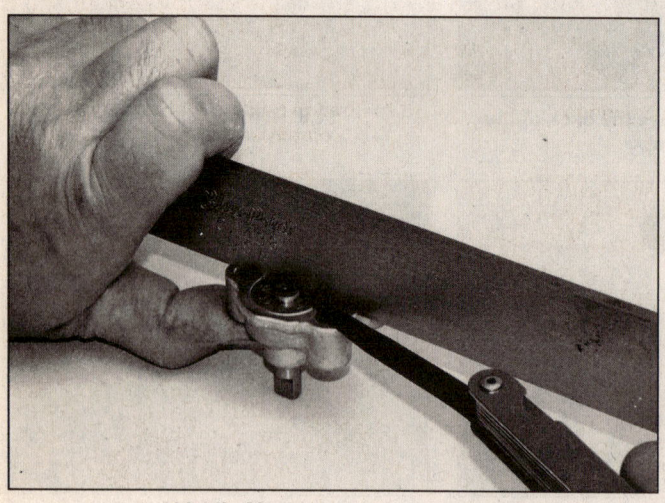

14.14b Measuring rotor end-float

15.4a Undo the nut using a peg spanner

Engine, clutch and transmission 2•23

15.4b Note the strip of aluminium (arrowed) used to lock the gears

15.5a Remove the nut . . .

15.5b . . . washer . . .

Honda produces a service tool to do this (Part No. 07716-0020100). Alternatively, use a commercially available tool as shown **(see illustration)**.

5 Remove the nut, washer and oil filter rotor **(see illustrations)**.

6 Lock the crankshaft drive gear and clutch driven gear to prevent the clutch from turning, then undo the clutch spring bolts a little at a time in a criss-cross pattern **(see illustration)**. Remove the bolts, lifter plate and springs **(see illustrations)**.

7 To loosen the clutch centre nut the clutch must be held to prevent it turning. Honda produces a service tool to do this (Part No. 07GMB-KT70101). Alternatively, a suitable tool can be made as shown **(see illustrations)**. Ensure the clutch centre is held securely when undoing the nut. **Note:** *Do not use the threaded projections for the spring bolts in the clutch pressure plate to hold the clutch - they are not strong enough.*

8 Remove the nut and washer **(see illustration)**.

9 Note the location of the outer friction plate tabs, then withdraw the clutch plates from the clutch housing as an assembly **(see illustration)**.

10 Remove the pressure plate from the back of the assembly – note the alignment of the

15.5c . . . and oil filter rotor

15.6a Undo the clutch spring bolts – note the position of the aluminium strip (arrowed)

15.6b Remove the spring bolts and lifter plate . . .

15.6c . . . and springs

15.7a Ensure holding tool locates against clutch centre webs . . .

15.7b . . . then undo the centre locknut

15.8 Remove the nut and washer (arrowed)

15.9 Withdraw the clutch plates as an assembly

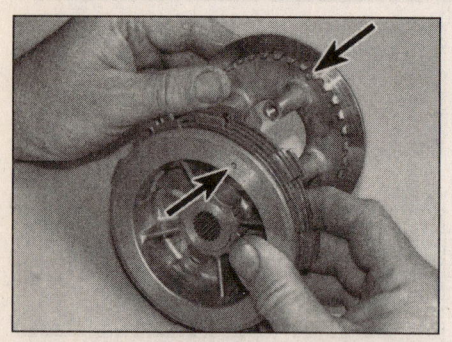

2•24 Engine, clutch and transmission

15.10 Remove the pressure plate, noting the register marks (arrowed)

15.11a Keep the plates in order

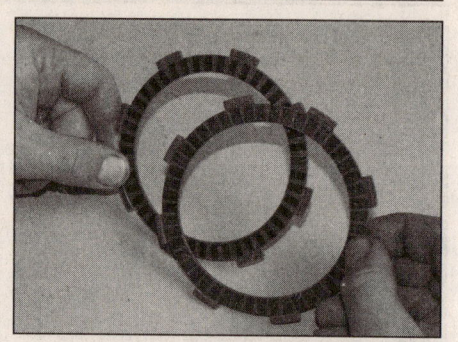

15.11b Note the width of the friction linings

register marks on the pressure plate and clutch centre **(see illustration).**
11 Keep the plates in their original order, even if they are being replaced with new ones. There are five friction plates and four plain plates. Note that the outer and innermost friction plates have wider friction linings than the others **(see illustrations).**
12 Remove the thrust washer and draw the clutch housing off the gearbox input shaft **(see illustrations).**
13 Slide the input shaft sleeve off the shaft **(see illustration).**

Inspection

14 After an extended period of service the clutch friction plates will wear and promote clutch slip. Measure the thickness of each friction plate using a Vernier caliper **(see illustration).** If any plate has worn to or beyond the service limits given in the *Specifications* at the beginning of this Chapter, or if any of the plates smell burnt or are glazed, the friction plates must be replaced with a new set.
15 The plain plates should not show any signs of excess heating (bluing). Check for warpage using a flat surface and feeler gauges **(see illustration).** If any plate exceeds the maximum permissible warpage, or shows signs of bluing, all plain plates must be replaced with a new set.
16 Inspect the clutch assembly for burrs and indentations in the slots in the housing and on the corresponding tabs on the friction plates **(see illustration).** Similarly check for wear between the slots in the clutch centre and the inner tongues of the plain plates **(see illustration).** Wear of this nature will cause clutch drag and slow disengagement during gear changes, since the plates will snag when the pressure plate is lifted. With care, a small amount of wear can be corrected by dressing with a fine file, but if this is excessive the worn components should be renewed.
17 Ensure the threads for the spring bolts

15.12a Remove the thrust washer . . .

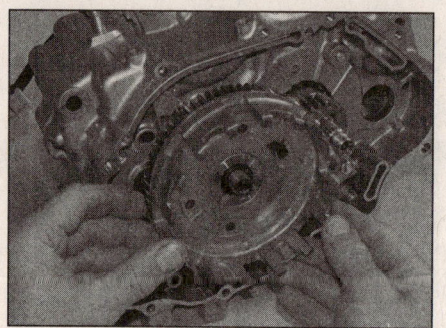

15.12b . . . and the clutch housing

15.13 Slide off the input shaft sleeve

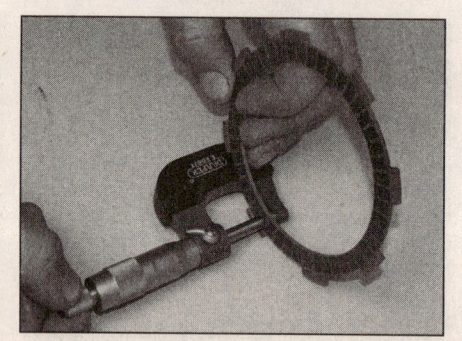

15.14 Measuring friction plate thickness with a Vernier caliper

15.15 Checking a plain plate for warpage

15.16a Inspect the clutch housing and friction plate tabs

15.16b Inspect the clutch centre and plain plate tongues

Engine, clutch and transmission 2•25

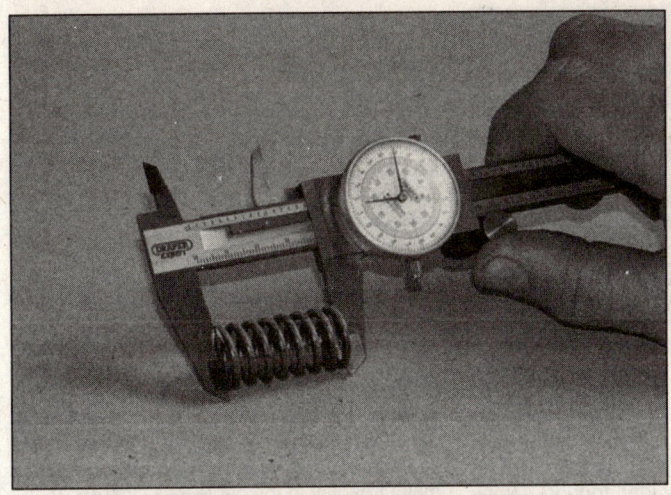

15.18 Measuring clutch spring free length

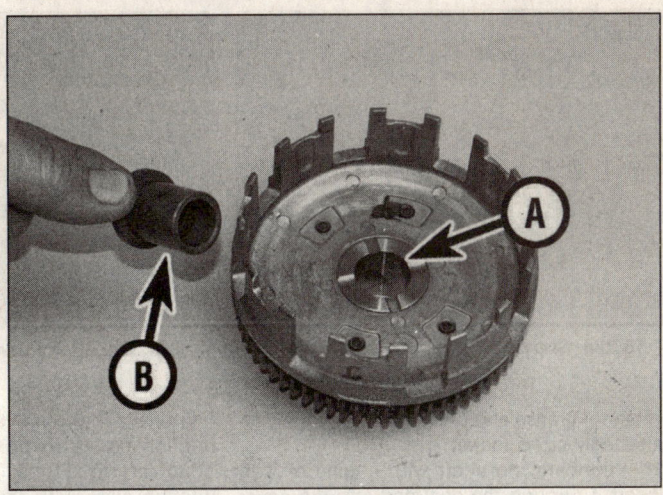

15.19 Inspect the bearing surfaces of the clutch housing (A) and input shaft sleeve (B)

in the clutch pressure plate are in good condition.
18 Measure the free length of each clutch spring using a Vernier caliper **(see illustration)**. Stand each spring upright on a flat surface and check it for bend by placing a set square against it. If any spring is shorter than specified, or if the bend in any spring is excessive, replace all the springs as a set.
19 Inspect the bearing surfaces of the clutch housing and the input shaft sleeve for wear **(see illustration)**. Measure the internal diameter of the housing and the external diameter of the sleeve and compare the results with the Specifications at the beginning of this Chapter. Measure the internal diameter of the sleeve and the external diameter of the input shaft. If there are any signs of wear, pitting or other damage the affected parts must be replaced with new ones. Refer to Section 26 for details of transmission disassembly.
20 Check the teeth of the primary driven gear on the outside of the clutch housing **(see illustration)** and the corresponding teeth of the primary drive gear on the crankshaft. Renew the clutch housing and the primary drive gear if the teeth are worn or chipped – refer to Section 18 for the primary drive gear.
21 The clutch housing incorporates a cush-drive mechanism – check that the springs are not loose or broken and that there is no

15.20 Primary driven gear (A) and cush drive spring (B)

backlash between the housing and the primary driven gear, otherwise replace the housing with a new one **(see illustration 15.20)**.
22 Check the bearing in the clutch lifter plate turns smoothly and that the bearing is secure in the lifter plate **(see illustration)**. If required, support the lifter plate on wooden blocks and press the bearing out from the inside. Turn the lifter plate over and install the new bearing from the outside. Refer to *Tools and Workshop Tips* in the *Reference* section for full details of bearing removal and installation.
23 Inspect the clutch lifter and the lower end of the clutch actuating shaft where it engages for wear **(see illustration)**. If the shaft is worn

15.22 Inspect the clutch lifter plate bearing

and needs renewing, of there is evidence of oil leakage from the seal at the top of the shaft, remove the shaft as follows. Note the location of the return spring **(see illustration)**. Note the protrusion on the shaft retaining pin and how the upper end of the spring locates around the pin, then drive the pin into the shaft with a suitable punch **(see illustration)**. Pull the shaft out of the cover and remove the return spring. Check the spring for fatigue or damage and renew it if necessary.
24 If required, carefully lever out the seal with a flat-bladed screwdriver, noting how it fits. Ensure the seal housing is clean and free from corrosion, then lubricate the new seal with a

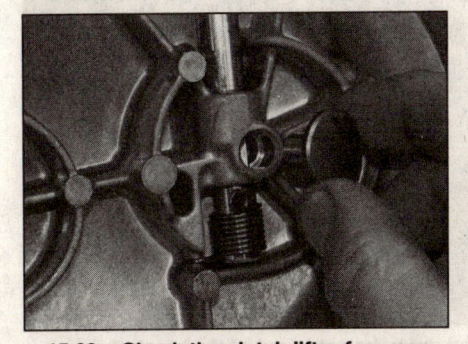

15.23a Check the clutch lifter for wear

15.23b Location of the shaft return spring

15.23c Shaft retaining pin (arrowed)

2•26 Engine, clutch and transmission

15.29a Start with the outermost friction plate . . .

15.29b . . . followed by a plain plate

smear of grease and press it into position with a suitably-sized socket.

25 Lubricate the shaft with engine oil and insert it through the seal and into the cover carefully to avoid damaging the seal. Don't forget to fit the return spring onto the lower end of the shaft **(see illustration 15.23b)**. Rotate the shaft and drive the retaining pin back out the noted amount, ensuring the upper end of the spring locates around the spring **(see illustration 15.23c)**.

Installation

26 Remove all traces of old gasket from the crankcase and cover surfaces.
27 Lubricate the input shaft sleeve with molybdenum oil (a 50/50 mix of engine oil and molybdenum grease), then slide it onto the input shaft **(see illustration 15.13)**.
28 Lubricate the primary driven gear with engine oil, slide the clutch housing onto the input shaft sleeve and install the thrust washer **(see illustration 15.12b and a)**. Ensure the primary driven gear engages correctly with the primary drive gear.
29 Coat each clutch plate with engine oil, then build up the plates on the clutch centre, starting with the outermost friction plate with the wider friction linings **(see illustration)**. Next, fit a plain plate followed by a friction plate and continue to alternate plain and friction plates to build up the clutch **(see illustration)**. Finally install the innermost friction plate with the wider friction linings **(see illustration 15.11a)**.
30 Install the pressure plate, ensuring the register marks align **(see illustration 15.10)**.
31 Install the assembled clutch in the clutch housing, ensuring the outer friction plate tabs locate in the shallow slots in the housing **(see illustration 15.9)**.
32 Install the washer. Lubricate the threads and seating surface of the new clutch centre nut with engine oil and install it finger-tight **(see illustration 15.8)**. Using the method employed on removal to hold the clutch (see Step 7), tighten the nut to the torque setting specified at the beginning of this Chapter.
33 Install the clutch springs, lifter plate and spring bolts, then lock the crankshaft drive gear and clutch driven gear and tighten the bolts evenly in a criss-cross pattern to the specified torque setting.
34 Ensure the inside of the oil filter rotor is clean, then install the rotor, washer and new nut **(see illustrations 15.5c, b and a)**. Using the method employed on removal to hold the crankshaft (see Step 3), tighten the nut to the torque setting specified at the beginning of this Chapter.
35 Install the rotor cover and gasket (see Chapter 1) and the oil pump driven gear **(see illustration 14.5)**.
36 Follow the procedure in Section 14 to install the right-hand engine cover. Check the operation of the clutch and adjust the cable freeplay as necessary (see Chapter 1).
37 Refill the engine with the recommended grade and type of oil (see Chapter 1).

16 Clutch cable

1 Start at the lower end of the cable. Counter-hold the adjuster nut and loosen the adjuster locknut, then turn the adjuster nut to make freeplay in the cable (see Chapter 1).
2 Free the cable end from the clutch actuating arm then draw the cable forward out of the bracket **(see illustrations)**.
3 At the handlebar end of the cable, refer to Chapter 5, Section 5, and displace the dust cover from the lever. Pull the outer cable end from the socket in the lever bracket and release the inner cable from the lever.
4 Remove the cable from the machine, noting its routing.

> **HAYNES HINT** *Before removing the cable from the bike, tape the lower end of the new cable to the upper end of the old cable. Slowly pull the lower end of the old cable out, guiding the new cable down into position. Using this method will ensure the cable is routed correctly.*

5 Installation is the reverse of removal. Apply silicone grease to the cable ends. Make sure the cable is correctly routed. Adjust the clutch lever freeplay (see Chapter 1).

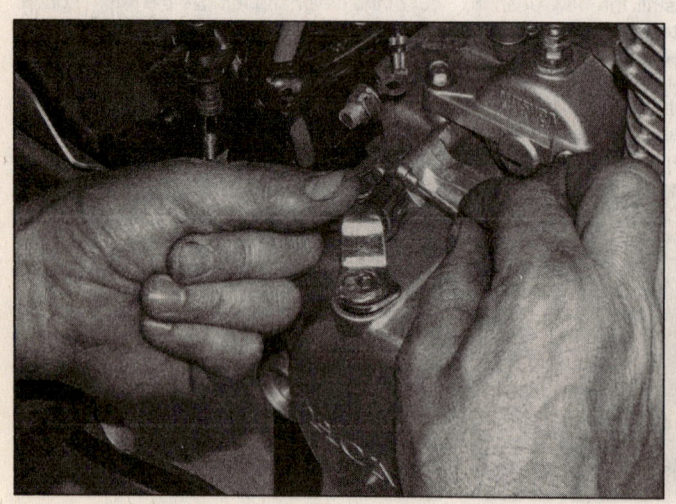

16.2a Free the cable end from the actuating arm . . .

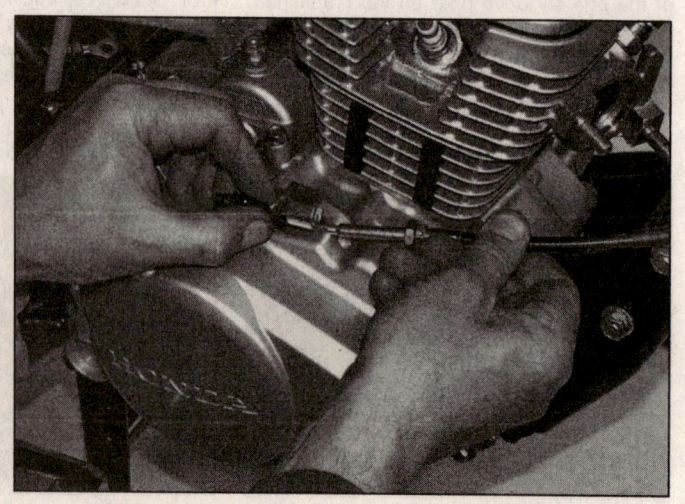

16.2b . . . then draw the cable out of the bracket

Engine, clutch and transmission 2•27

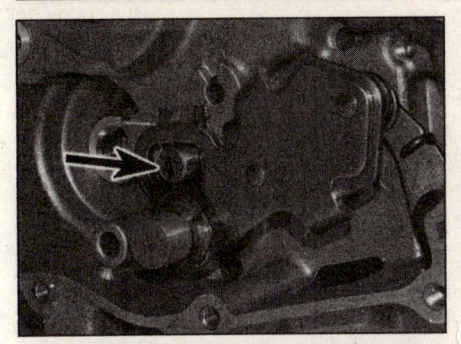

17.4a Note how the return spring fits each side of the locating pin (arrowed)

17.4b Note how the pawls (arrowed) locate onto the pins on the selector cam

17.4c Draw the gearchange shaft assembly out

17 Gearchange mechanism

Note: *The gearchange mechanism can be removed with the engine in the frame.*

Removal

1 Make sure the transmission is in neutral. Remove the front sprocket cover and chain guide (see Chapter 6). Undo the pinch bolt securing the gearchange arm and draw the arm off the shaft, noting the alignment of the arm to the shaft (see Chapter 5, Section 3).
2 Clean the exposed length of the gearchange shaft thoroughly – this will rule out the possibility of dirt entering the engine unit when the shaft is withdrawn. Clean off any corrosion with wire wool.
3 Remove the clutch (see Section 15).
4 Note how the ends of the gearchange shaft return spring fit on each side of the locating pin in the casing, and how the pawls on the selector arm locate onto the pins on the end of the selector cam, then draw the shaft assembly out **(see illustrations)**. Note the location of the thrust washer on the shaft.
5 Note how the ends of the stopper arm spring locate and how the roller on the arm locates in the neutral detent on the selector cam **(see illustration)**. Unscrew the stopper arm pivot bolt and remove the arm, washer and spring, noting how they fit **(see illustration)**.
6 Unscrew the bolt securing the gearchange cam and lift the cam off, noting how it locates onto the pins in the end of the selector drum **(see illustrations)**. Remove the pins for safekeeping **(see illustration)**.

Inspection

7 Check the selector arm for cracks, distortion and wear of its pawls **(see illustration)**. Check for any corresponding wear on the pins on the selector cam **(see illustration 17.9b)**. Check that the gearchange shaft is straight and that the splines on the end of the shaft are undamaged. If necessary, fit a new gearchange shaft and selector arm assembly.
8 Inspect the shaft return spring for fatigue, wear or damage **(see illustration 17.7)**. To remove the spring, first slide the thrust washer off the shaft, then slide off the circlip and discard it as a new one must be fitted. Note how the ends of the spring locate either side

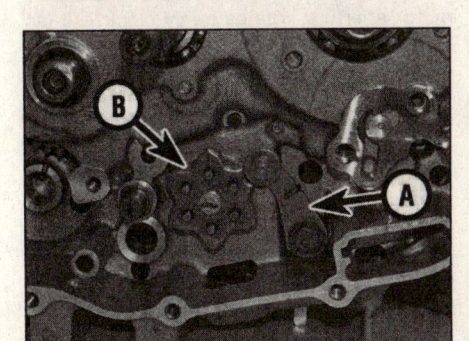

17.5a Location of the stopper arm (A) and gearchange cam (B)

17.5b Unscrew the pivot bolt and remove the assembly

17.6a Unscrew the bolt (arrowed) . . .

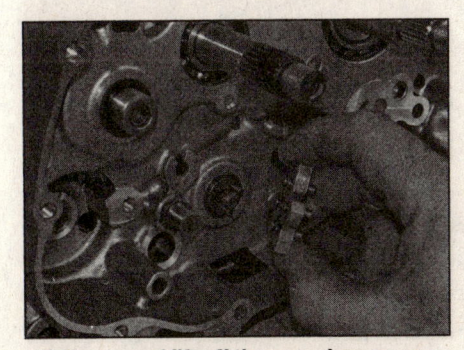

17.6b . . . and lift off the gearchange cam, noting the locating pins

17.6c Remove the pins for safekeeping

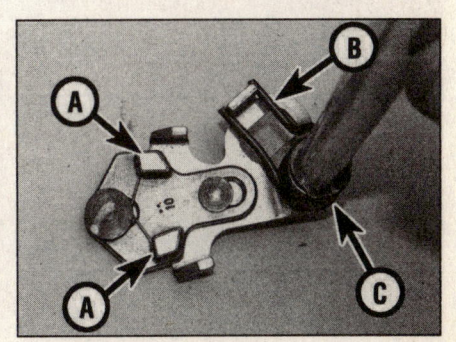

17.7 Selector arm pawls (A), return spring (B) and circlip (C)

2•28 Engine, clutch and transmission

17.9a Inspect the stopper arm components

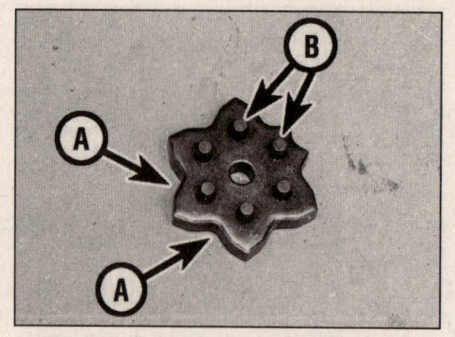

17.9b Selector drum cam detents (A) and pins (B)

of the tab on the selector arm, then ease the spring off. Install the new spring and secure it with a new circlip – open the circlip only enough to slide it along the shaft and ensure it is correctly located in its groove. Fit the thrust washer.

9 Check the stopper arm return spring for fatigue and wear and ensure that the stopper arm roller turns freely **(see illustration)**. Renew any components that are worn or damaged. Also check the detents in the selector drum cam for wear **(see illustration)**.

10 Check the condition of the shaft oil seal in the left-hand side of the crankcase. If it is damaged, deteriorated or shows signs of leakage it must be replaced with a new one. Lever out the old seal with a flat-bladed screwdriver **(see illustration 22.2b)**. Lubricate the new seal with a smear of engine oil and press it squarely into place using your thumbs or suitable socket.

11 If required, follow the procedure in Chapter 5 to remove and inspect the gearchange lever assembly.

Installation

12 Make sure the transmission is still in neutral. Clean the threads of the gearchange cam bolt and apply a suitable non-permanent thread-locking compound. Install the pins in the end of the selector drum, install the cam and secure it with the bolt **(see illustrations 17.6c, b and a)**. Tighten the bolt to the torque setting specified at the beginning of this Chapter.

13 Assemble the stopper arm, washer and spring on the stopper arm bolt and install the assembly **(see illustration 17.5b)**. Ensure the straight end of the spring is against the casing, the hooked end is around the arm, and the roller is located in the neutral detent on the cam **(see illustration 17.5a)**. Tighten the pivot bolt to the specified torque setting. Check that the arm moves freely.

14 Ensure the thrust washer is in place on the gearchange shaft, then install the shaft carefully to avoid damaging the seal on the left-hand side **(see illustration 17.4c)**. Fit the ends of the return spring on each side of the locating pin in the casing and align the pawls on the selector arm with the pins on the end of the selector cam **(see illustration 17.4b and a)**.

15 Install the remaining components in the reverse order of removal.

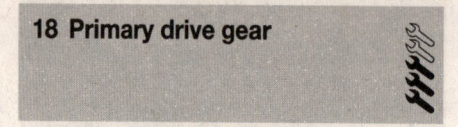

18 Primary drive gear

1 The primary drive gear is located on the right-hand side of the crankshaft behind the centrifugal oil filter. Follow the procedure in Section 15 to remove the oil filter rotor and clutch.

2 Draw off the drive gear, noting how it fits **(see illustration)**.

3 Draw off the crankshaft spacer, noting how it fits **(see illustration)**.

4 Remove the key from the crankshaft **(see illustration 18.2)**.

5 Installation is the reverse of removal, noting the following:

• Press the key firmly into the slot in the crankshaft **(see illustration)**.
• Ensure the spacer and drive gear are installed the correct way round **(see illustrations 18.3 and 2)**.

19 Starter clutch and gears

Note 1: *The starter clutch can be removed with the engine in the frame.*

Note 2: *The alternator rotor centre locknut must be discarded and a new one used on installation – it is best to obtain the new nut in advance.*

Special tools: *A strap wrench will be required to loosen the starter clutch retaining bolts and alternator rotor centre locknut (see Steps 10 and 11). A puller will be required to draw the alternator rotor off the crankshaft (see Step 12).*

Check

1 The operation of the starter clutch can be checked while it is in situ. First remove the starter motor (see Chapter 8). Check that the reduction gear, located inside the starter motor aperture, rotates freely clockwise (as you look at it from the right-hand side), but locks when rotated anti-clockwise. If not, the starter clutch or one of the intermediate gears is faulty and should be removed for inspection.

Removal

2 Remove the left-hand side panel (see Chapter 7). On CBF125MD models onward remove the belly fairing (see Chapter 7).

3 Remove the front sprocket cover and chain guide (see Chapter 6).

4 Trace the alternator and crankshaft position (CKP) sensor wiring from the back of the

18.2 Remove the primary drive gear . . .

18.3 . . . and the crankshaft spacer

18.5 Installed position of the crankshaft key (arrowed)

Engine, clutch and transmission 2•29

19.4 Alternator and CKP sensor wiring (arrowed)

19.5 Free the neutral switch and sidestand switch wiring

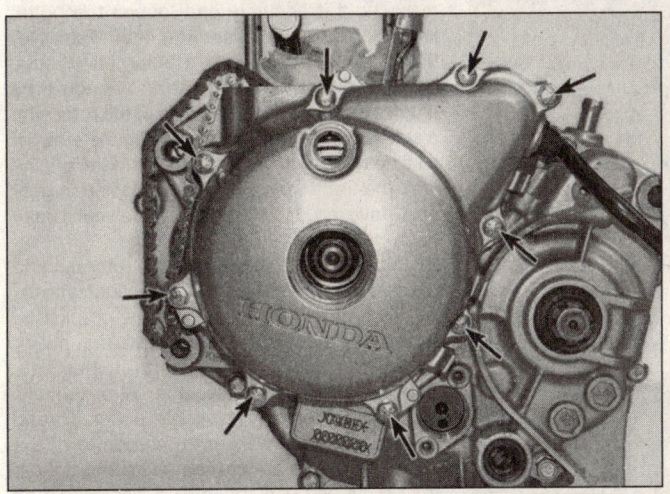

19.6a Undo the bolts (arrowed) . . .

19.6b . . . and remove the cover

alternator cover and disconnect it at the connectors **(see illustration)**.

5 Release the neutral switch and sidestand switch wiring from the guides on the cover **(see illustration)**.

6 Position a suitable container underneath the cover to catch any residual oil when it is removed. Undo the cover bolts evenly and draw the cover off, noting that it will be restrained by the force of the alternator rotor magnets **(see illustrations)**.

7 Remove the cover gasket and discard it; note the location of the cover dowels and remove them for safe-keeping if they are loose **(see illustration)**.

8 Note how the larger pinion on the reduction gear engages with the starter motor gear and the smaller pinion engages with the starter clutch driven gear. Remove the spacer, then withdraw the reduction gear shaft and remove the gear **(see illustrations)**.

9 Check the operation of the starter clutch – the driven gear on the starter clutch should rotate freely clockwise as you look at it, but should lock when rotated anti-clockwise **(see illustration 19.27)**. If not, the starter clutch is faulty and should be removed for inspection.

19.7 Location of the cover dowels (arrowed)

19.8a Remove the spacer . . .

19.8b . . . withdraw the shaft and remove the reduction gear

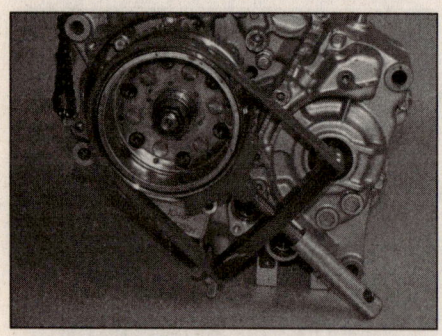

2•30 Engine, clutch and transmission

19.10 Holding the rotor using a strap wrench

19.11 Remove the nut and washer (arrowed)

19.12a Thread the puller onto the alternator rotor . . .

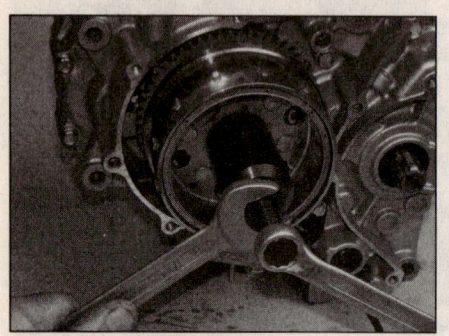

19.12b . . . then tighten the centre bolt . . .

19.12c . . . to displace the rotor

10 The starter clutch is secured to the back of the alternator rotor by six bolts (see illustration 19.15a). Before removing the rotor, hold it securely and loosen the bolts. Honda produces a service tool (Part No. 07725-0040001) to do this. Alternatively, use a commercially available strap wrench (see illustration). Clean the outside of the rotor with a suitable solvent before installing the strap. If a strap wrench is not available, and the engine is in the frame, place the transmission in gear and have an assistant apply the rear brake hard.

11 Now hold the rotor, undo the rotor nut and remove the nut and washer (see illustration).

12 To remove the rotor from the crankshaft taper it is necessary to use a rotor puller. Honda produces a service tool (Part No. 07933-KM10001) to do this. Alternatively, use a commercially available puller. Thread the puller all the way onto the centre of the rotor, then counter-hold the puller and tighten the centre bolt until the rotor is displaced (see illustrations).

13 Remove the rotor and the key from the crankshaft (see illustrations).

14 Slide the starter driven gear and the needle bearing off the crankshaft (see illustrations). If the starter driven gear has remained on the back of the alternator rotor, rotate it anti-clockwise and pull it off the rotor (see illustration).

19.13a Remove the rotor . . .

19.13b . . . and the crankshaft key

19.14a Slide off the starter driven gear . . .

19.14b . . . and the needle bearing

19.14c Free the gear by turning it anti-clockwise

Engine, clutch and transmission 2•31

19.15a Undo the bolts . . .

19.15b . . . and lift off the alternator rotor

19.16a Remove the cover

15 Undo the bolts securing the starter clutch assembly and separate it from the alternator rotor **(see illustrations)**.

Inspection

16 Remove the starter clutch cover **(see illustration)**. Clean all the components in a suitable solvent, then examine the rollers and springs inside the clutch housing **(see illustrations)**. Ensure the rollers turn freely against the pressure of the springs. If any components are worn, damaged or broken, renew the complete assembly.

17 Examine the outer surface of the driven gear hub for wear **(see illustration)**. Measure the outside diameter of the hub, then compare the result to the specification at the beginning of this Chapter. If the hub is worn the driven gear must be renewed.

18 Refer to *Tools and Workshop Tips* in the *Reference* section and inspect the needle bearing and the bearing surfaces of the crankshaft and the driven gear hub.

19 Inspect the teeth of the driven gear and reduction gear **(see illustration)**. Renew the gears as a set if worn or chipped teeth are discovered. Check the teeth on the starter motor shaft (see Chapter 8). Also check the reduction gear shaft for wear and ensure that the gear is not a loose fit on it.

Installation

20 Remove all traces of old gasket and sealant from the crankcase and cover surfaces.

21 Lubricate the clutch rollers with engine oil then fit the cover **(see illustrations 19.16b and a)**.

22 Fit the alternator rotor onto the clutch assembly and align the fixing bolt holes **(see illustration 19.15b)**.

23 Clean the threads of the starter clutch bolts, apply a suitable non-permanent thread-locking compound, then install the bolts finger-tight.

24 Hold the rotor with a strap wrench and tighten the bolts to the torque setting specified at the beginning of this Chapter **(see illustration)**.

25 Slide the needle bearing onto the

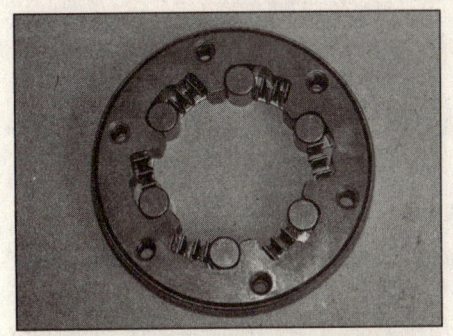

19.16b Note location of rollers and springs . . .

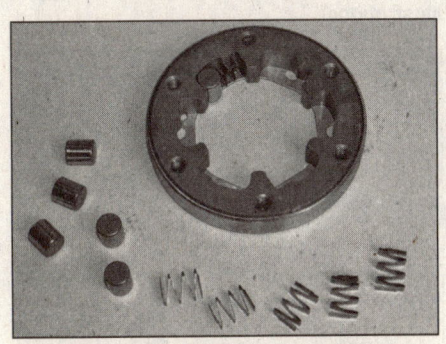

19.16c . . . and examine them for wear

19.17 Examine the driven gear hub (arrowed) for wear

19.19 Check the reduction gear teeth and the gear shaft

19.24 Tighten the bolts to the specified torque setting

19.26 Installed position of the crankshaft key (arrowed)

2•32 Engine, clutch and transmission

19.27 Rotate the starter driven gear to aid installation

crankshaft and lubricate it with molybdenum oil (a 50/50 mix of engine oil and molybdenum grease). Clean all traces of oil off the taper on the crankshaft. Fit the starter driven gear onto the bearing (see illustration 19.14a).

26 Press the key firmly into the slot in the crankshaft (see illustration).

27 Align the slot in the centre of the alternator rotor with the key and press the rotor all the way on – rotate the starter driven gear clockwise to help locate it in the starter clutch (see illustration).

28 Install the washer. Lubricate the threads and seating surface of the new alternator rotor centre nut with engine oil and install it finger-tight (see illustration 19.11). Using the method employed on removal to hold the alternator rotor (see Step 10), tighten the nut to the torque setting specified at the beginning of this Chapter.

29 Lubricate the reduction gear shaft with engine oil and install the gear, spacer and shaft (see illustrations 19.8b and a). Note: The larger pinion on the reduction gear should be outermost.

30 If removed, fit the dowels into the crankcase, then locate a new gasket onto the dowels (see illustration 19.7).

31 Install the alternator cover, ensuring it locates onto the dowels, then install the cover bolts and tighten them evenly in a criss-cross pattern.

32 Secure the wiring as noted on removal and reconnect the wiring connectors (see Steps 5 and 4).

33 Install the remaining components in the reverse order of removal.

34 Check the engine oil level and top-up as necessary (see Pre-ride checks).

20 Cam chain, tensioner blade and guide blade

Note: The cam chain and blades can be removed with the engine in the frame.

Removal

1 Remove the cylinder head (see Section 9), then lift out the cam chain guide blade (see illustration 11.2).

2 Remove the starter reduction gear and alternator rotor (see Section 19).

3 Undo the bolts securing the lower cam chain guide and remove the guide (see illustrations).

4 Remove the tensioner blade, noting how it fits (see illustrations).

5 Note how the cam chain locates on the crankshaft sprocket and mark the outer face of the chain with a dab of paint so that is can be assembled the same way round if it is to be reused. Slip the chain off the crankshaft sprocket and draw it out of the engine (see illustration).

Inspection

6 Except in cases of oil starvation, the cam chain should wear very little. If the chain has stretched excessively, and can no longer be correctly tensioned by the cam chain tensioner, it is likely that the guide and tensioner blades will be worn and in need of renewal as well.

7 Check all round the chain – if there is any discernible slack between the links, or if it is stiff or the links are binding or kinking, replace it with a new one (see illustration).

8 Also check the condition of the camshaft sprocket (see Section 8) and crankshaft sprocket. If the crankshaft sprocket is worn or damaged a new crankshaft will have to be fitted – the sprocket is an integral part of the crankshaft assembly (see Section 23). Note: Check the operation of the cam chain tensioner if the chain is slack but appears to be in good condition.

9 Examine the sliding surfaces of the guide and tensioner blades for signs of wear or damage. Check them carefully for cracks in the surface and along the edges. Install new components as necessary.

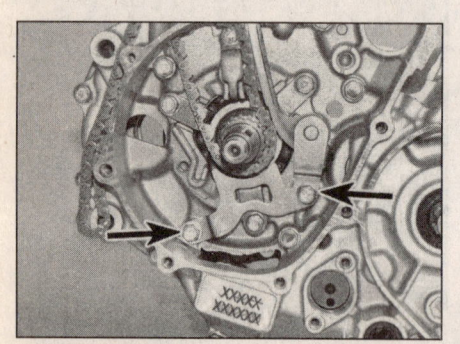

20.3a Undo the bolts (arrowed) . . .

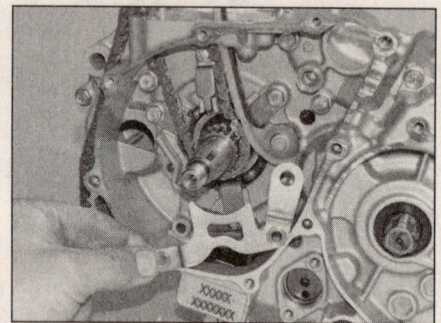

20.3b . . . and remove the lower guide

20.4a Note location of the lower end (arrowed) . . .

20.4b . . . of the tensioner blade

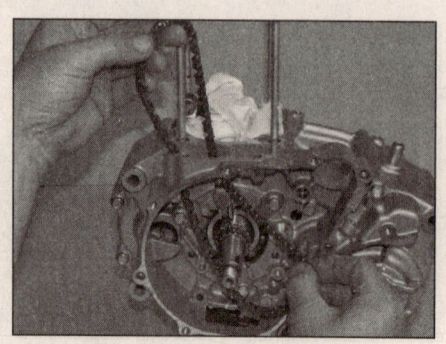

20.5 Removing the cam chain

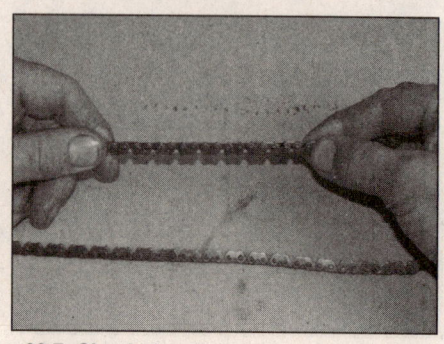

20.7 Check the chain for wear and slack

Engine, clutch and transmission 2•33

21.4a Undo the bolt . . .

21.4b . . . remove the plate . . .

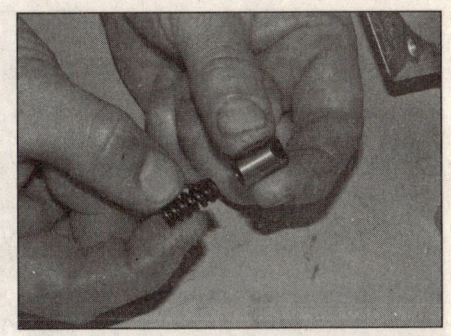

21.4c . . . and draw out the spring and retainer

21.4d Undo the bolts (arrowed) . . .

21.4e . . . remove the bearing retainers

21.5a Remove the circlip . . .

Installation

10 Installation is the reverse of removal, noting the following:
- If the original chain is being used, fit it as noted on removal (see Step 5).
- Tighten the lower cam chain guide mounting bolts securely.
- Lubricate the chain with engine oil.

21 Crankcase separation and reassembly

Note: *To separate the crankcase halves, the engine must be removed from the frame.*

Separation

1 To access the crankshaft and connecting rod assembly, transmission shafts, selector drum and forks, and their associated bearings, the crankcase halves must be separated.

2 Before the crankcases can be separated the following components must be removed:

Camshaft and rockers (Section 8)
Cylinder head (Section 9)
Cylinder (Section 11)
Piston (Section 12)
Starter motor (Chapter 8)
Oil pump (Section 14)
Clutch (Section 15)
Gearchange mechanism (Section 17)
Primary drive gear (Section 18)
Starter clutch and gears (Section 19)
Cam chain and blades (Section 20)

3 Make a cardboard template punched with holes to match all the crankcase bolts – as each bolt is removed, store it in its relative position in the template **(see illustration 21.6b)**. This will ensure all bolts are installed in the correct location on reassembly.

4 Starting on the left-hand side of the crankcase, undo the bolt securing the sprung retainer, remove the plate and draw out the retainer and spring **(see illustrations)**. Undo the bolts securing the main bearing retainers and remove the retainers **(see illustrations)**.

5 On the right-hand side of the crankcase, remove the circlip and thrust washer on the end of the transmission output shaft **(see illustrations)**. On M9 and MA models, remove the spacer and second thrust washer. Undo the upper front crankcase bolt **(see illustration)**.

21.5b . . . and thrust washer

21.5c Location of the right-hand upper front crankcase bolt (arrowed)

2•34 Engine, clutch and transmission

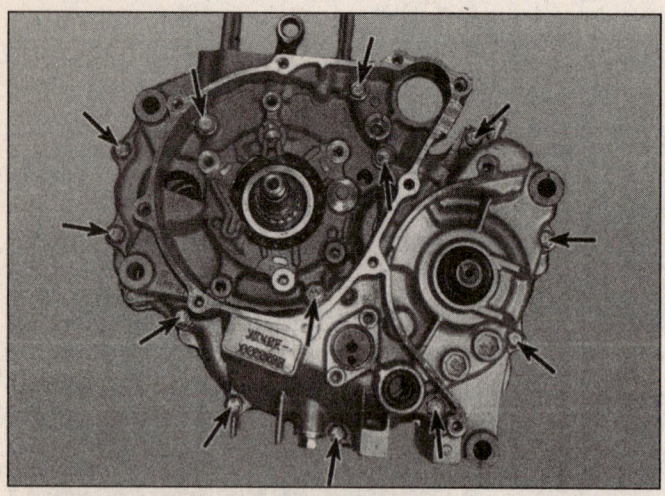

21.6a Undo the crankcase bolts . . .

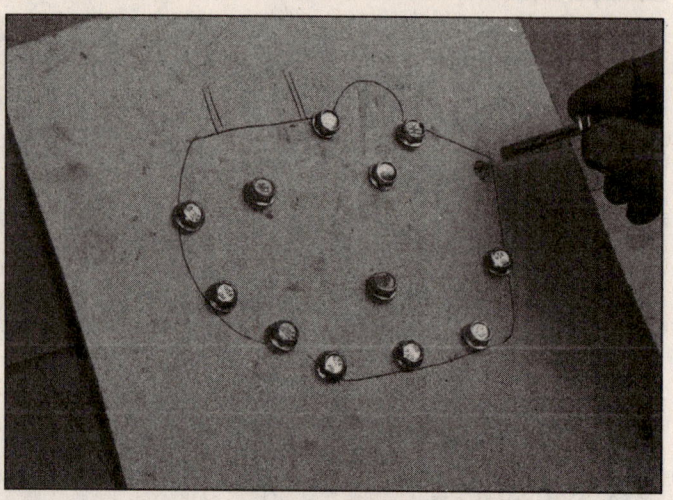

21.6b . . . and store them in the template

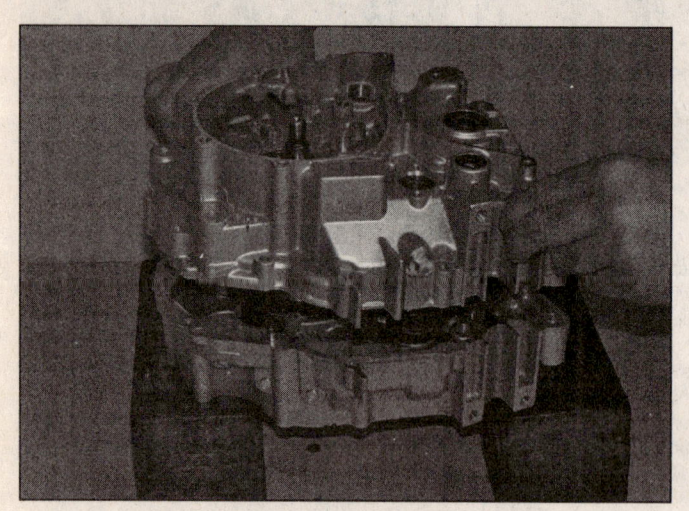

21.7 Lift off the left-hand crankcase half

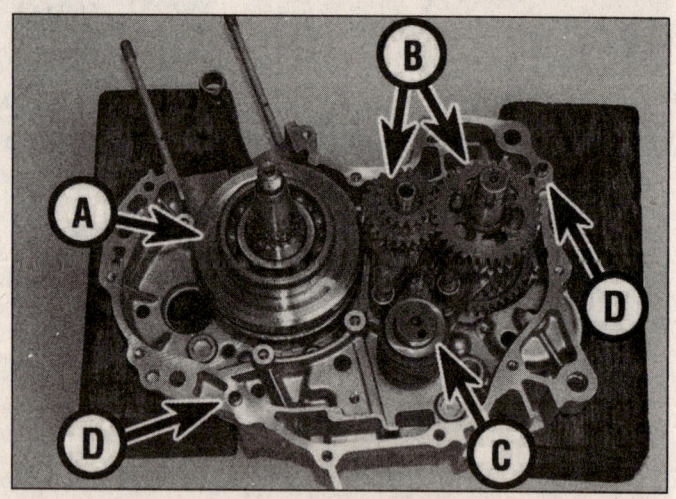

21.8 Crankshaft (A), transmission shafts (B), selector drum and forks (C) and dowels (D)

6 Support the crankcases on wooden blocks, left-hand side uppermost. Loosen the crankcase bolts evenly in a criss-cross pattern until they are finger-tight, then remove them and store them in the template **(see illustrations)**.

7 Carefully lift the left crankcase half off, using a soft-faced hammer to tap around the joint to initially separate the halves if necessary **(see illustration)**. Note: *If the halves do not separate easily, make sure all fasteners have been removed. Do not try and separate the halves by levering between the crankcase mating surfaces as they are easily damaged and will leak on reassembly. If necessary, use a hot air gun to heat the left-hand main bearing housing to aid disassembly.*

8 The left-hand crankcase half will come away leaving the crankshaft assembly, transmission shafts and selector drum and forks in the right-hand half **(see illustration)**. Note the location of the crankcase dowels and remove them for safekeeping if they are loose. The left-hand main bearing should remain on the crankshaft.

9 Refer to Section 22 for inspection of the crankcases and main bearings, and Sections 23 to 25 for removal and installation of the crankshaft assembly, selector drum and forks and transmission shafts. **Note:** *Always renew the transmission output shaft and gearchange shaft oil seals when the crankcases have been separated (see Section 22). Lubricate the seals with a smear of grease prior to reassembly.*

Reassembly

10 Remove all traces of old sealant from the crankcase mating surfaces with a suitable solvent, taking care not to nick or gouge the soft aluminium if a scraper is used. Use compressed air to blow through the oil galleries in the cases. Clean the threads of all the crankcase bolts.

11 Support the right-hand crankcase half securely on the work surface and ensure all the components are in place – if removed, fit the locating dowels **(see illustration 21.8)**.

12 Wipe the mating surfaces of both crankcase halves with a rag soaked in high flash-point solvent to remove all traces of oil. Apply a thin coating of suitable sealant to the mating surface of the left-hand half **(see illustration)**.

Caution: Apply the sealant only where indicated. Do not apply an excessive

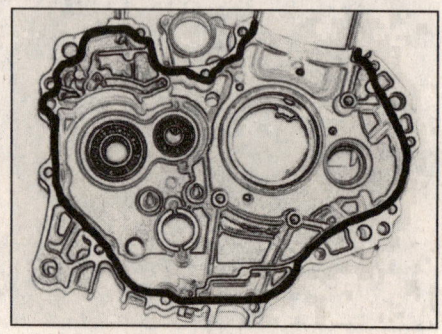

21.12 Apply a suitable sealant to the mating surface as shown

Engine, clutch and transmission 2•35

21.13 Ensure the crankcase halves are correctly aligned

21.17 Note location of chamfer (arrowed) on inner end of retainer

amount of sealant as it will ooze out when the case halves are assembled and may obstruct oil passages.

13 Carefully lower the left-hand crankcase half down onto the right-hand half, making sure the shafts and dowels all locate correctly. When you are sure everything is correctly aligned, press the halves together firmly **(see illustration)**.

Caution: *The crankcase halves should fit together without being forced. If the casings are not correctly seated, remove the left-hand half and investigate the problem. Do not attempt to pull them together using the crankcase bolts as the casing will crack and be ruined.*

14 Install the crankcase bolts and tighten them finger-tight **(see illustration 21.6a)**. Now tighten the bolts evenly and a little at a time in a criss-cross pattern to the torque setting specified at the beginning of this Chapter.

15 Support the connecting rod and stand the crankcases upright. Install the thrust washer, spacer and washer, or thrust washer only, as appropriate, on the right-hand end of the transmission output shaft and secure them with a new circlip **(see illustrations 21.5b and a)**. Install the upper front crankcase bolt and tighten it to the specified torque **(see illustration 21.5c)**.

16 Install the right-hand bearing retainers and tighten the retainer bolts to the specified torque.

17 Install the sprung retainer with the chamfered edge pressed against the outer race of the main bearing **(see illustration)**.

Install the spring, then fit the plate and tighten the bolt to the specified torque **(see illustrations 21.4b and a)**.

18 Support the connecting rod and check that the crankshaft and transmission shafts rotate smoothly and easily – in neutral, the transmission shafts should rotate freely and independently. If there are any signs of undue stiffness, tight or rough spots, or of any other problem, the fault must be rectified before proceeding further.

19 Install the remaining components in the reverse order of removal.

22 Crankcases and main bearings

1 After the crankcase halves have been separated (see Section 21), follow the procedures in Sections 23 to 25 for the removal of the crankshaft assembly, selector drum and forks and transmission shafts.

2 Note the position of the transmission output shaft and gearchange shaft oil seals in the left-hand crankcase half – lever the seals out carefully using a flat-bladed screwdriver or seal hook **(see illustrations)**. Discard the old seals as new ones must be fitted on reassembly.

Main bearings

3 The right-hand main bearing is in the right-hand crankcase half – the inner race can be lifted out to inspect the bearing rollers **(see illustrations)**. The left-hand main bearing is on the crankshaft **(see illustration)**.

4 If the main bearings have failed, excessive rumbling and vibration will be felt when the engine is running. Check the condition of the bearings – they should spin freely and smoothly without any rough spots (see *Tools and Workshop Tips* in the *Reference* section). If there is any doubt about their condition they must be renewed.

5 To remove and install the right-hand bearing requires the use of an hydraulic press – for this reason the job should be undertaken by a Honda dealer or specialist engineer. Note that prior to reassembly, the bearing inner race should be installed from the inside.

6 The left-hand main bearing is not available as a separate item – if the bearing is worn a new crankshaft assembly will have to be fitted.

22.2a Lever out the output shaft seal . . .

22.2b . . . and gearchange shaft oil seal

22.3a Lift out the bearing inner race . . .

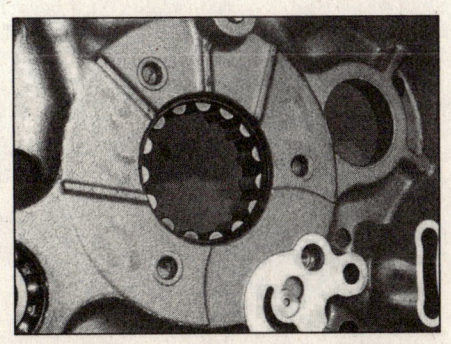

22.3b . . . to inspect the rollers

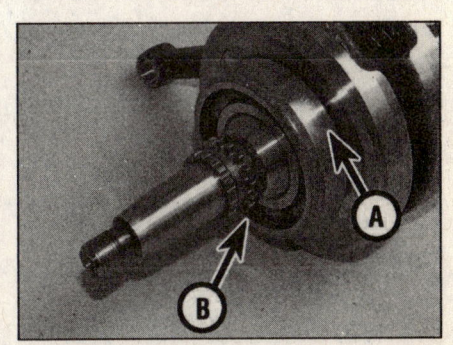

22.3c Location of the left-hand main bearing (A). Note camshaft sprocket (B)

22.11a Install the new oil seals . . .

22.11b . . . to the specified depth

23.2 Lift out the crankshaft assembly

Crankcases

7 Check both crankcase halves very carefully for cracks and damaged threads. Small cracks or holes in aluminium castings may be repaired with an epoxy resin adhesive as a temporary measure, or with one of the low temperature welding kits. Permanent repairs can only be effected by welding, and only a specialist in this process is in a position to advise on the economy or practical aspect of such a repair. If any damage is found that can't be repaired, renew both crankcase halves as a set.

8 Damaged threads can be reclaimed by using a thread insert of the Heli-Coil type, which is fitted after drilling and re-tapping the affected thread (see *Tools and Workshop Tips* in the *Reference* section). Most motorcycle dealers and small engineering firms offer a service of this kind. Sheared screws and studs can usually be removed with screw extractors which consist of a tapered, left thread screw of very hard steel. These are inserted into a pre-drilled hole in the broken fixing, and usually succeed in dislodging the most stubborn stud or screw (see *Tools and Workshop Tips* in the *Reference* section). If you are in any doubt about removing a sheared screw, consult a Honda dealer or automotive engineer.

9 Always wash the crankcases thoroughly after any repair work to ensure no dirt or metal swarf is trapped inside when the engine is rebuilt.

10 If any of the cylinder studs are loose or damaged, refer to the procedure in Section 11 to install them.

Reassembly

11 Locate the new transmission output shaft oil seal in position in the left-hand crankcase half, ensuring that it is the correct way round **(see illustration)**. Lubricate the seal with a smear of grease and use a suitably-sized socket to press it in. Check that the seal is the specified depth below the outer edge of its housing **(see illustration)**.

12 Following the same procedure, install the new gearchange shaft oil seal.

13 Install the transmission shafts, selector drum and forks and crankshaft assembly in the right-hand crankcase half, then reassemble the crankcase halves (see Section 21).

23 Crankshaft and connecting rod

Note: *To remove the crankshaft assembly the engine must be removed from the frame and the crankcases separated (see Section 21). The connecting rod and big-end bearing are an integral part of the crankshaft assembly – individual components are not available.*

Removal

1 When the crankcase halves are separated the crankshaft assembly remains in the right-hand crankcase half **(see illustration 21.8)**.

2 Lift out the crankshaft assembly **(see illustration)**. Note that the inner race of the right-hand main bearing is a sliding fit in the bearing **(see illustration 22.3a)**. The left-hand main bearing will remain on the crankshaft **(see illustration 22.3c)**.

Inspection

3 If the connecting rod (big-end) bearing has failed, there will be a pronounced knocking noise when the engine is running, particularly under load and increasing with engine speed.

4 Hold the crankshaft still and check for any radial (up and down) play in the big-end bearing by pushing and pulling the rod against the crank **(see illustration)**. There should be no discernable freeplay. If a dial gauge is available, measure the amount of radial clearance and compare the result with the service limit specified at the beginning of this Chapter.

5 Measure the connecting rod side clearance (the gap between the connecting rod big-end and the crankshaft web) with a feeler gauge and compare the result with the service limit **(see illustration)**.

6 If either clearance is greater than the service limit the big-end bearing has failed – replace the crankshaft assembly with a new one.

7 Place the crankshaft on V-blocks and check the runout using a dial gauge **(see illustration)**. Compare the reading to the maximum specified and renew the crankshaft if the runout exceeds the limit.

8 Refer to Section 12 and check the connecting rod small-end and piston pin for wear.

9 Check the cam chain sprocket for wear and damage **(see illustration 22.3c)**. Refer to

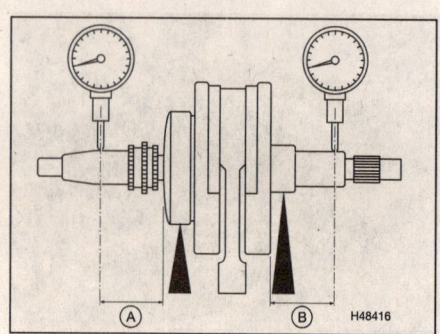

23.4 Checking for up and down play in the big-end bearing

23.5 Measuring the connecting rod side clearance

23.7 Check runout at the distances indicated – (A) 47.5 mm , (B) 43.0 mm

# Engine, clutch and transmission 2•37

Section 20 to check the condition of the cam chain.

10 Inspect the splines for the centrifugal oil filter and the slot for the primary drive gear Woodruff key. Inspect the crankshaft taper and slot for the alternator rotor Woodruff key. If there is any wear or damage a new crankshaft will have to be fitted.

Installation

Note: *During this procedure, take care not to knock the connecting rod against the edge of the crankcase opening.*

11 Support the right-hand crankcase half on wooden blocks. If removed, install the transmission shafts and selector drum and forks (see Sections 25 and 24).

12 If not already done, install the inner race of the right-hand main bearing **(see illustration 22.3a)**.

13 Align the connecting rod with the crankcase opening and lower the crankshaft into position **(see illustration 23.2)**. Ensure the crankshaft is fitted all the way into the main bearing, then support the connecting rod and check that the crankshaft rotates freely.

14 Reassemble the crankcase halves (see Section 21).

24 Selector drum and forks

Note: *To remove the selector drum and forks the engine must be removed from the frame and the crankcases separated (see Section 21).*

Removal

1 When the crankcase halves are separated the selector drum and forks remain in the right-hand crankcase half **(see illustration 21.8)**. Note how the guide pins on the forks locate in the grooves in the selector drum and note which grooves the pins locate in as an aid for installation. The selector drum should be in the neutral position.

2 Carefully lift out the shaft retaining the selector forks on the transmission output shaft so as not to disturb the position of the forks **(see illustration)**.

3 Note the position of the selector forks on the output shaft **(see illustration)**. Slide the upper fork out from the groove in the 5th gear pinion **(see illustration)**. Slide the lower fork out from the groove in the 4th gear pinion **(see illustration)**. Slide the forks back onto their shaft in the correct order and the right way round – the forks are marked R/L on the sides facing up **(see illustration)**.

4 Carefully lift out the shaft retaining the selector fork on the transmission input shaft **(see illustration)**.

5 Note the position of the selector fork, then slide it out from the groove in the 3rd gear pinion on the input shaft **(see illustration)**. Slide the fork back onto its shaft – the fork is marked C on the side facing up **(see illustration 24.3d)**.

6 Note the position of the selector drum and lift it out **(see illustration)**.

Inspection

7 Inspect the selector forks for any signs of wear or damage, especially around the fork

24.2 Lift out the output shaft selector forks' shaft

24.3a Note the position of the selector forks . . .

24.3b . . . then slide out the upper . . .

24.3c . . . and lower forks

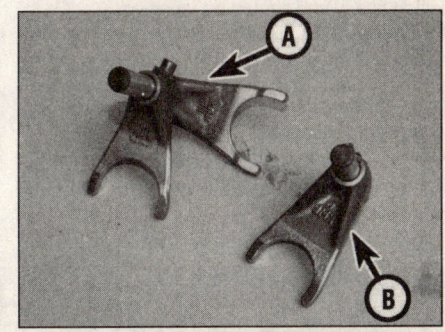

24.3d Output shaft forks (A) marked R/L. Input shaft fork (B) marked C

24.4 Lift out the input shaft selector fork shaft

24.5 Slide out the selector fork

24.6 Lift out the selector drum

2•38 Engine, clutch and transmission

24.7 Measure the fork end thickness

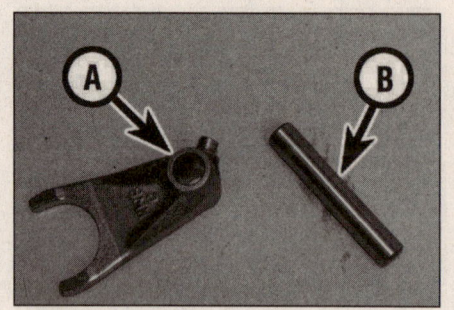

24.8 Measure the internal diameter of the fork bores (A) and the outside diameter of the shafts (B)

24.10 Examine the guide pins and selector drum grooves

ends where they engage with the grooves in the pinions. Using a micrometer, measure the ends of the forks and compare the results with the specifications at the beginning of this Chapter **(see illustration)**. Check that each fork fits correctly in its pinion groove. Check closely to see if the forks are bent. If the forks are worn or damaged in any way they must be replaced with new ones.

8 Check that the forks fit correctly on their shafts – they should be a sliding fit with no appreciable freeplay. Measure the internal diameter of the fork bores and the outside diameter of the shafts **(see illustration)**. Replace the forks and/or shafts with new ones if they are worn beyond their service limits.

9 Check that the selector fork shaft s are straight by rolling them on a flat surface such as a sheet of glass. A bent shaft will cause difficulty in selecting gears and make the gearchange action heavy and should be renewed.

10 Inspect the selector drum grooves and selector fork guide pins for signs of wear or damage **(see illustration)**. If any component shows signs of wear or damage the fork(s) and drum must be renewed.

11 Measure the outside diameter (OD) of the left and right-hand selector drum bearing journals and compare the results with the specifications – if either is worn beyond the service limit, renew the selector drum.

12 Measure the internal diameter (ID) of the left and right-hand selector drum bearings in the crankcase halves and compare the results with the specifications – if either is worn beyond the service limit have the cases inspected by a Honda dealer or specialist repair shop.

Installation

13 Lubricate the selector forks and selector drum with engine oil. Install the selector drum **(see illustration 24.6)**.

14 Install the input shaft selector fork marked C on the side facing up into the groove in the 3rd gear pinion **(see illustration 24.5)**. Align the guide pin with its groove in the selector drum and secure the fork with its shaft **(see illustration 24.4)**.

15 Install the output shaft selector forks marked R/L on the sides facing up into the grooves in the 4th and 5th gear pinions **(see illustrations 24.3c and b)**. Align the guide pins with their grooves in the selector drum and secure the forks with their shaft **(see illustrations 24.3a and 2)**.

16 Check that the forks, guide pins and selector drum are correctly aligned.

17 Reassemble the crankcase halves (see Section 21).

25 Transmission shafts and bearings

Note: *To remove the transmission shafts the engine must be removed from the frame and the crankcases separated (see Section 21).*

Removal

1 When the crankcase halves are separated the transmission shafts remain in the right-hand crankcase half **(see illustration 21.8)**. Before removing the shafts, lift out the crankshaft assembly (see Section 23) then follow the procedure in Section 24 to remove the selector drum and forks.

2 Don't try to pull the shafts out individually. Note the relative positions of the input and output shafts and how they fit together, then lift them out as an assembly – hold the bottom pinions on the shafts to prevent them dropping off **(see illustration 25.16a)**.

3 Note the thrust washer on the lower (right-hand) end of the output shaft which may stick to the bearing in the crankcase or fall off as the shaft is removed – retrieve the washer and fit it back onto the shaft with a dab of grease **(see illustration)**.

4 Lay the transmission shafts on a clean work surface **(see illustration)**.

25.3 Note location of the output shaft thrust washer

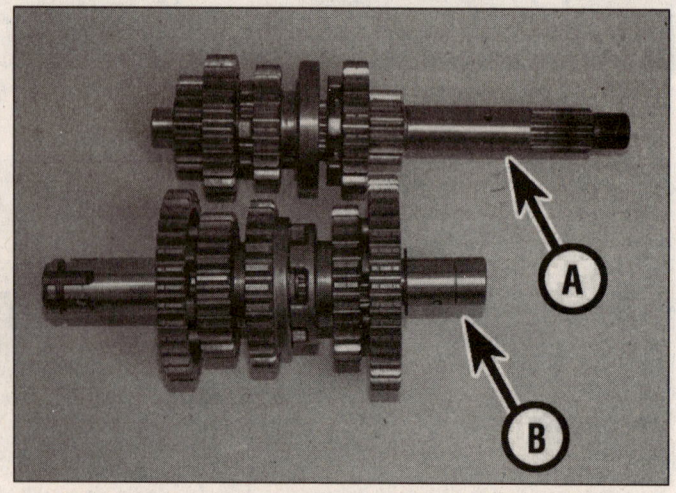

25.4 Note the relative positions of the gear pinions on the transmission input (A) and output (B) shafts

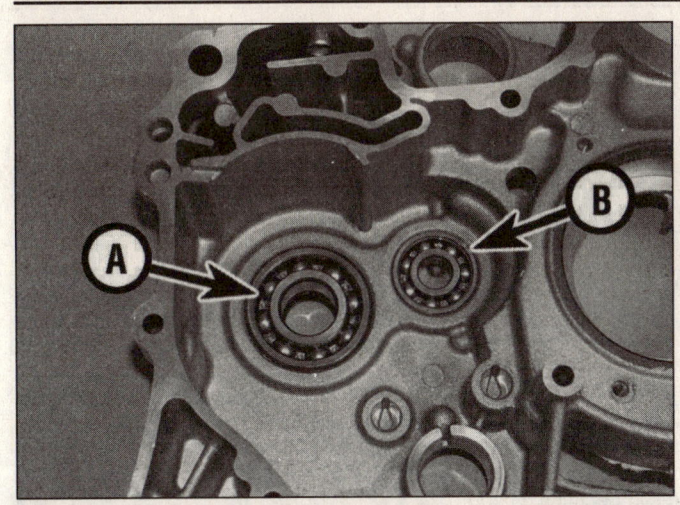

Engine, clutch and transmission 2•39

25.7a Left-hand crankcase transmission output (A) and input (B) shaft bearings

25.7b Right-hand crankcase transmission output (A) and input (B) shaft bearings

5 If necessary, the shafts can be disassembled and the components inspected for wear or damage (see Section 26).

6 Remove the transmission output shaft oil seal from the left-hand crankcase half **(see illustration 22.2a)**.

7 Check the condition of the transmission shaft bearings in both crankcase halves **(see illustrations)**. If required, flush the bearings with a suitable solvent then dry them thoroughly – use low pressure compressed air if it is available. Lubricate the bearings lightly with clean engine oil, then check them as described (see *Tools and Workshop Tips* in the *Reference* section).

8 Only remove the bearings if they need renewing. If the bearing on one end of a shaft needs renewing, it is good practice to renew the bearing on the other end at the same time. Before removing a bearing, note any markings indicating which way round it is fitted.

9 The input shaft bearing in the right-hand case is retained by two plates on the inside of the case – undo the bolts and remove the plates **(see illustration 25.7b)**. Heat the bearing housing with a hot air gun, then tap the bearing out from the outside using a bearing driver or a suitable socket. Prior to installation, smear the outside of the new bearing with clean oil. Heat the housing again and drive the bearing in squarely until it seats using a driver or socket that bears only on the bearing's outer race. Clean the bolt threads and apply a suitable non-permanent thread-locking compound. Install the retaining plates and tighten the bolts to the torque setting specified at the beginning of this Chapter.

10 To remove and install the output shaft bearing in the left-hand case, follow the procedure in Step 9, heating the bearing housing and driving the bearing out from the outside **(see illustration)**. On installation, ensure the driver bears only on the bearing's outer race.

11 To remove the input shaft bearing from the left-hand case and the output shaft bearing from the right-hand case, an expanding knife-edge bearing puller with slide-hammer attachment is required (see *Tools and Workshop Tips* in the *Reference* section). Follow the procedure in Step 9 to install the bearings.

> **HAYNES HiNT** *If any of the bearings are loose in their housings, or have seized and damaged their housings, have the condition of the casing assessed by a Honda dealer. A loose bearing can often be secured using a suitable bearing lock compound.*

Installation

12 If not already done, fit a new transmission output shaft oil seal (see Section 22). Lubricate the inside of the seal with engine oil.

13 Support the right-hand crankcase half on wooden blocks **(see illustration)**. Lubricate the transmission shaft bearings in both crankcase halves with engine oil.

14 Ensure the thrust washer is installed on

25.10 Drive the bearing (arrowed) out from the outside

25.13 Support the right-hand crankcase half on wooden blocks

2•40 Engine, clutch and transmission

25.16a Align the shafts with their bearings . . .

25.16b . . . and install the transmission assembly

the right-hand end of the output shaft and secure it in place with a dab of grease **(see illustration 26.24a)**.

15 Place the shafts side-by-side on the work surface and align the gear pinions **(see illustration 25.4)**.

16 Grasp the shafts assembly, align the right-hand ends of the shafts with the bearings in the right-hand casing and install the shafts **(see illustrations)**. Check that the gear pinions rotate freely.

17 Follow the procedures in Sections 24 and 23 to install the selector drum and forks and crankshaft assembly.

18 Reassemble the crankcase halves (see Section 21).

26 Transmission shaft overhaul

1 Remove the transmission shafts (see Section 25). Always disassemble the transmission shafts separately to avoid mixing up the components.

HAYNES HiNT *When disassembling the transmission shafts, place the parts on a long rod or thread a wire through them to keep them in order and facing the proper direction.*

⚠️ *Warning: The gear pinions are secured by circlips – fit new circlips on reassembly, never re-use the old circlips.*

Input shaft

Disassembly

2 Remove the thrust washer from the left-hand end of the shaft, then slide off the 2nd gear pinion **(see illustrations)**.

3 Slide off the 5th gear pinion, noting which way round it fits **(see illustration)**.

4 Slide off the thrust washer **(see illustration)**.

5 Slide off the 3rd gear pinion, noting which way round it fits **(see illustration)**.

6 Remove the circlip and splined washer securing the 4th gear pinion, then slide the pinion off, noting which way round it fits **(see illustrations)**.

26.2a Remove the thrust washer . . .

26.2b . . . and slide off the 2nd gear pinion

26.3 Slide off the 5th gear pinion

26.4 Slide off the thrust washer

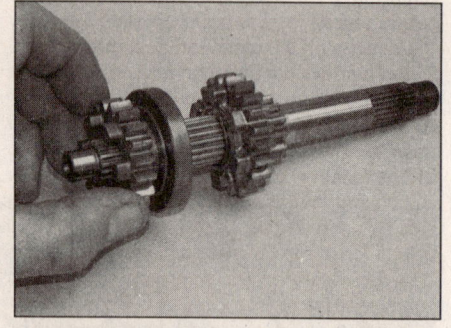

26.5 Slide off the 3rd gear pinion

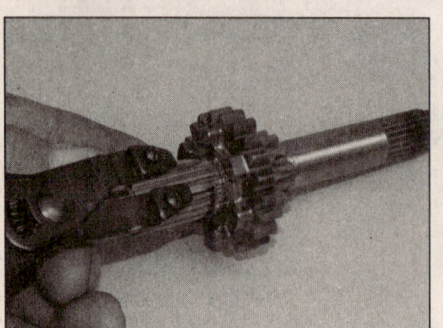

26.6a Remove the circlip . . .

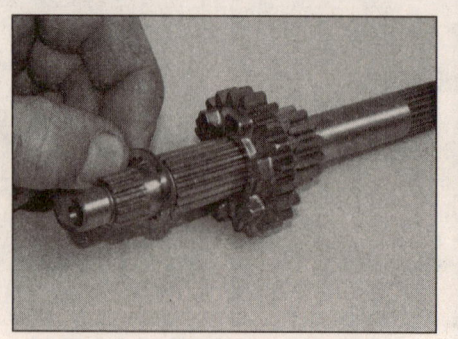

26.6b . . . and the splined washer

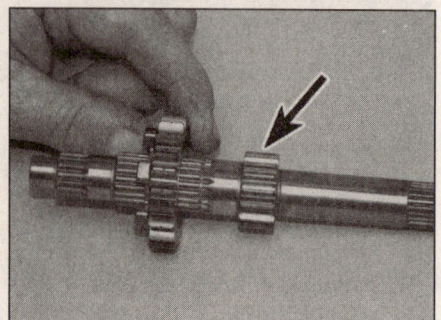

26.6c Slide off the 4th gear pinion. Note 1st gear pinion (arrowed)

Engine, clutch and transmission 2•41

26.10 Examine the dogs (arrowed) for wear and damage

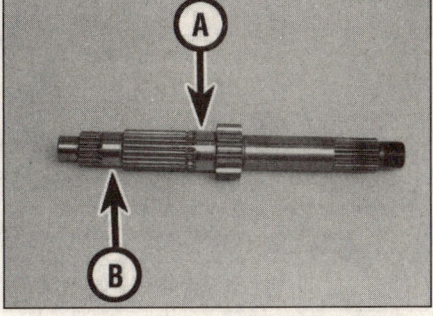

26.12 Position of the 4th (A) and 5th (B) gear pinions

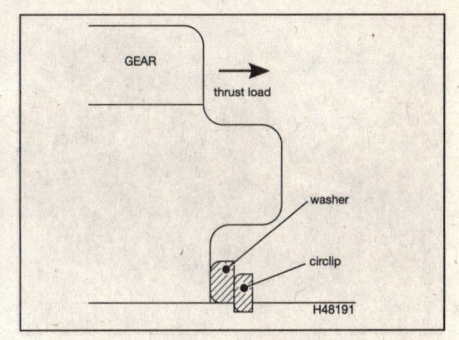

26.17 Correct fitting of stamped circlips and washers

7 The 1st gear pinion is integral with the shaft (see illustration 26.6c).

Inspection

8 Wash all of the components in suitable solvent and dry them off.
9 Check the gear teeth for cracking, chipping, pitting and other obvious wear or damage. Any pinion that is damaged must be renewed. Note: *If a pinion on the input shaft is damaged, check the corresponding pinion on the output shaft. Transmission pinions should be renewed in matched pairs.*
10 Inspect the dogs on the gears for cracks, chips, and excessive wear especially in the form of rounded edges (see illustration). Make sure mating gears engage properly. Replace the paired gears as a set if necessary.
11 Check for signs of scoring or bluing on the pinions and shaft. This could be caused by overheating due to inadequate lubrication. Check that all the oil holes and passages are clear. Replace any damaged components.
12 Measure the diameter of the shaft at the position of the 4th gear pinion and compare the result with the specification at the beginning of this Chapter (see illustration). Measure the inside diameter of the 4th gear pinion and compare the result with the specification.
13 Similarly, measure the diameter of the shaft at the position of the 5th gear pinion (see illustration 26.12) and measure the inside diameter of the 5th gear pinion. Compare the results with the specifications at the beginning of this Chapter.
14 If any components are worn beyond the service limit they should be renewed.
15 The shaft is unlikely to sustain damage unless the engine has seized, placing an unusually high loading on the transmission, or the machine has covered a very high mileage. Check the surface of the shaft and the shaft splines, and renew the shaft if it has scored or picked up, or if there are any cracks. If available, check the shaft runout using V-blocks and a dial gauge and replace the shaft with a new one if it is bent.

Reassembly

16 During reassembly, apply molybdenum disulphide oil (a 50/50 mixture of molybdenum disulphide grease and engine oil) to the bearing surfaces of the pinions and the selector fork groove in the 3rd gear pinion.
17 When installing the *new* circlip, do not expand the ends any further than is necessary to slide it along the shaft. Install the stamped circlip so that the chamfered side faces the pinion it secures (see illustration).
18 Slide the 4th gear pinion onto the shaft with its dogs facing away from the integral 1st gear (see illustration 26.6c). Slide the splined washer onto the shaft, then fit the circlip (see illustration 26.6b and a). Make sure the circlip locates correctly in the groove in the shaft (see illustration).
19 Slide on the 3rd gear pinion with the selector fork groove facing the 4th gear pinion (see illustration 26.5).

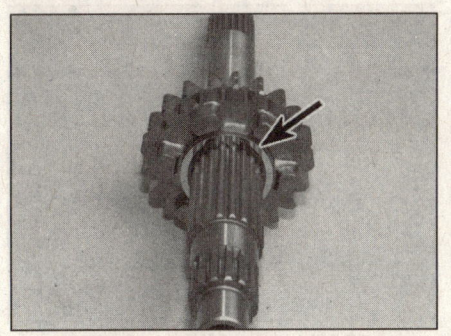

26.18 Installed position of the circlip (arrowed)

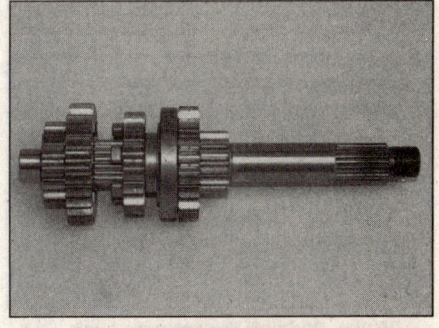

20 Slide on the thrust washer (see illustration 26.4).
21 Install the 5th gear pinion with the dog holes facing the 3rd gear pinion (see illustration 26.3).
22 Fit the 2nd gear pinion and thrust washer onto the end of the shaft (see illustrations 26.2b and a).
23 Check that all the components have been correctly installed (see illustration).

Output shaft

Disassembly

24 Remove the thrust washer from the left-hand end of the shaft, then slide off the 2nd gear pinion (see illustrations).

26.23 The assembled input shaft should look like this

26.24a Remove the thrust washer ...

26.24b ... and slide off the 2nd gear pinion

2•42 Engine, clutch and transmission

26.25a Slide off the 2nd gear bush . . .

26.25b . . . and thrust washer

26.26 Slide off the 5th gear pinion

26.27a Remove the thrust washer . . .

26.27b . . . then slide off the 1st gear pinion

25 Slide off the 2nd gear bush and the thrust washer **(see illustrations)**.
26 Slide off the 5th gear pinion, noting which way round it fits **(see illustration)**.
27 Remove the thrust washer from the right-hand end of the shaft, then slide off the 1st gear pinion **(see illustrations)**.
28 Slide off the 1st gear bush and the thrust washer **(see illustrations)**.
29 Slide off the 4th gear pinion, noting which way round it fits **(see illustration)**.
30 Remove the circlip and splined washer securing the 3rd gear pinion, then slide the pinion off, noting which way round it fits **(see illustrations)**.
31 Slide off the 3rd gear bush and thrust washer **(see illustrations)**.

26.28a Slide off the 1st gear bush . . .

26.28b . . . and thrust washer

26.29 Slide off the 4th gear pinion

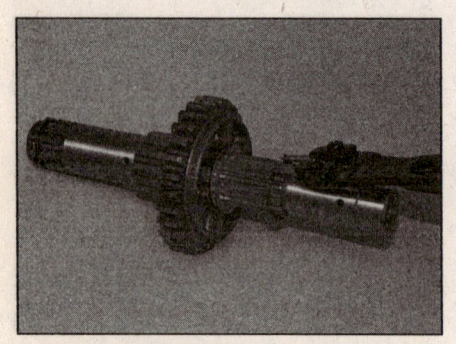

26.30a Remove the circlip . . .

26.30b . . . and splined washer

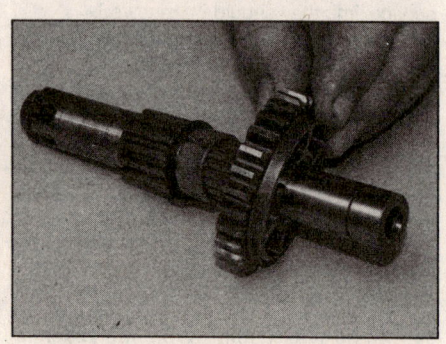

26.30c Slide off the 3rd gear pinion

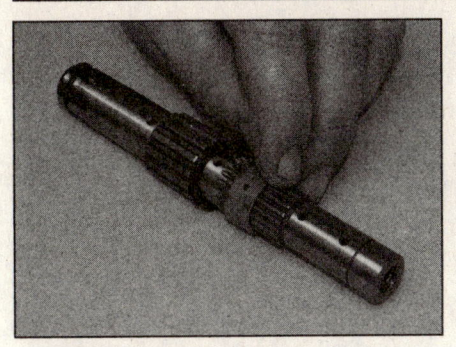

Engine, clutch and transmission 2•43

26.31a Slide off the 3rd gear bush . . .

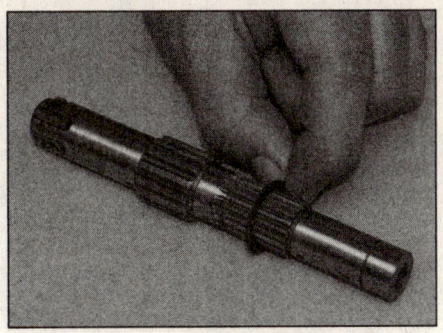

26.31b . . . and thrust washer

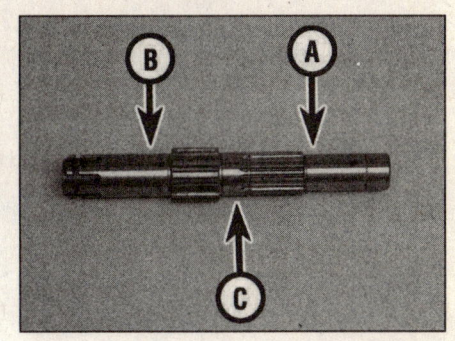

26.33a Position of the 1st (A), 2nd (B) and 3rd (C) gear bushes

Inspection

32 Refer to Steps 8 to 11 above. As well as checking the gear pinion dogs for wear and damage (see illustration 26.10), inspect the dog holes in the 1st and 2nd gear pinions (see illustrations 26.27b and 24b).

33 Measure the diameter of the shaft at the position of the 1st gear bush and compare the result with the specification at the beginning of this Chapter (see illustration). Measure the inside and outside diameters of the bush, and the inside diameter of the 1st gear pinion and compare the results with the specifications (see illustrations). If any components are worn beyond the service limit they should be renewed.

34 Similarly, measure the diameter of the shaft at the position of the 2nd and 3rd gear bushes, the inside and outside diameters of the 2nd and 3rd gear bushes and the inside diameters 2nd and 3rd gear pinions. Renew any component that is worn beyond the service limit.

35 Refer to Step 15 and check the shaft for wear and damage.

Reassembly

36 During reassembly, lubricate the bearing surfaces of the pinions, bushes and the selector fork grooves in the 4th and 5th gear pinions with molybdenum disulphide oil (a 50/50 mixture of molybdenum disulphide grease and engine oil). Refer to Step 17 when installing the *new* circlips.

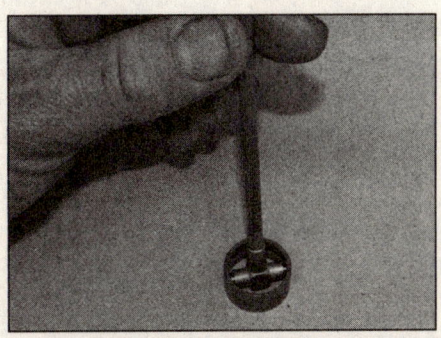

26.33b Measure the inside . . .

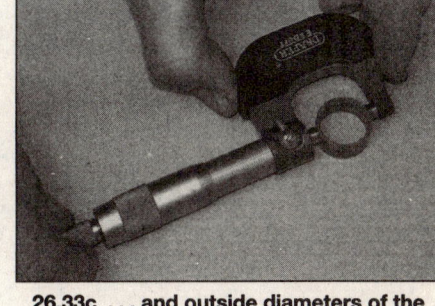

26.33c . . . and outside diameters of the bush

37 Slide the thrust washer and 3rd gear bush onto the shaft from the right-hand end (see illustrations 26.31b and a).

38 Install the 3rd gear pinion on its bush with the dog holes facing the right-hand end of the shaft (see illustration 26.30c).

39 Slide the splined washer onto the shaft, then fit the circlip (see illustration 26.30b and a). Make sure the circlip locates correctly in the groove in the shaft (see illustration).

40 Slide on the 4th gear pinion with the selector fork groove facing the 3rd gear pinion (see illustration 26.29).

41 Slide on the thrust washer and 1st gear bush (see illustrations 26.28b and a).

42 Install the 1st gear pinion on its bush with the concave side facing the 4th gear pinion (see illustration 26.27b).

43 Install the thrust washer and secure it with a dab of grease (see illustration 26.27a).

44 Slide the 5th gear pinion onto the shaft from the left-hand end with the selector fork groove facing the 3rd gear pinion (see illustration 26.26).

45 Slide on the thrust washer and 2nd gear bush (see illustrations 26.25b and a).

46 Install the 2nd gear pinion on its bush with the concave side facing the 5th gear pinion (see illustration 26.24b). Install the thrust washer (see illustration 26.24a).

47 Check that all the components have been correctly installed (see illustration).

26.33d Measure the inside diameter of the gear pinion

26.39 Installed position of the circlip

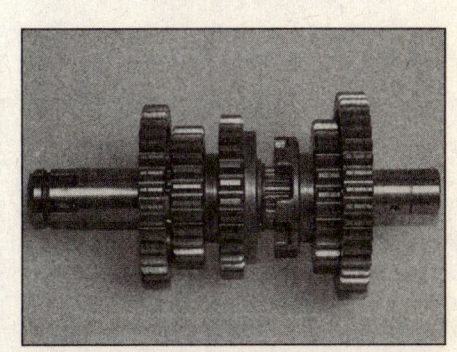

26.47 The assembled output shaft should look like this

27 Running-in procedure

1 Make sure the engine oil level is correct (see *Pre-ride checks*). Make sure there is fuel in the tank.
2 Turn the ignition ON and check that the gearbox into neutral.
3 With the throttle completely closed, start the engine and allow it to run at a moderately fast idle until it reaches operating temperature.
4 Check carefully that there are no oil or fuel leaks and make sure the transmission and controls, especially the brakes, function properly before road testing the machine.
5 Treat the machine gently for the first few miles to make sure oil has circulated throughout the engine and any new parts installed have started to seat.
6 Even greater care is necessary if the cylinder has been rebored and a new piston has been fitted, or if new bearings have been fitted in the crankcase – the bike will have to be run in as when new. This means greater use of the transmission and a restraining hand on the throttle until at least 300 miles (500 km) have been covered. There's no point in keeping to any set speed limit – but don't labour the engine and gradually increase performance up to the 300 miles (500 km) mark. Experience is the best guide, since it's easy to tell when an engine is running freely.
7 Upon completion of the road test, and after the engine has cooled down completely, check the engine oil level and top-up if necessary (see *Pre-ride checks*).
8 After 600 miles (1000 km) check the valve clearances (see Chapter 1).

Chapter 3
Ignition system

Contents

	Section number		Section number
Clutch switch	see Chapter 8	Ignition system check	2
General information	1	Ignition timing	5
Engine control module	see Chapter 4	Neutral switch	see Chapter 8
Ignition HT coil	3	Sidestand switch	see Chapter 8
Crankshaft position sensor	4	Spark plug	see Chapter 1
Ignition switch	see Chapter 8		

Degrees of difficulty

Easy, suitable for novice with little experience	Fairly easy, suitable for beginner with some experience	Fairly difficult, suitable for competent DIY mechanic	Difficult, suitable for experienced DIY mechanic	Very difficult, suitable for expert DIY or professional

Specifications

General information
Spark plug .... see Chapter 1

Crankshaft position sensor
Minimum peak voltage .... 0.7 volts

Ignition HT coil
Input voltage .... Battery voltage
Minimum primary peak voltage .... 100 volts

Torque wrench settings
Crankshaft position sensor bolts .... 12 Nm
Timing inspection cap .... 10 Nm

3•2 Ignition system

1 General information

All models are fitted with a fully transistorised electronic ignition system. The system consists of the crankshaft position (CKP) sensor, engine control module (ECM), ignition HT coil and spark plug.

The triggers on the alternator rotor, which is fitted to the left-hand end of the crankshaft, activate signals in the CKP sensor as the crankshaft rotates. The sensor sends those signals to the ECM which calculates the ignition timing and supplies the ignition HT coil with the power necessary to produce a spark at the plug. The ECM incorporates an electronic advance system. Although the ignition timing can be checked, there is no provision for adjusting the timing.

The system incorporates a safety interlock circuit which will cut the ignition if the sidestand is extended whilst the engine is running and in gear, or if a gear is selected whilst the engine is running and the sidestand is extended. It also prevents the engine from being started if the transmission is in gear unless the clutch lever is pulled in. See Chapter 8 for test details of the safety circuit components. A tip-over sensor will cut the ignition if the bike falls over whilst the engine is running. The TO sensor is part of the engine management system – see Chapter 4 for details.

Because of their nature, the individual ignition system components can be checked but not repaired. If ignition system troubles occur, and the faulty component can be isolated, the only cure for the problem is to replace the part with a new one. Keep in mind that most electrical parts, once purchased, cannot be returned. To avoid unnecessary expense, make very sure the faulty component has been positively identified before buying a replacement part.

2 Ignition system check

Warning: The energy levels in electronic systems can be very high. On no account should the ignition be switched on whilst the plug or plug cap is being held. Shocks from the HT circuit can be most unpleasant.

1 As no means of adjustment is available, any failure of the system can be traced to failure of a system component or a simple wiring fault. Of the two possibilities, the latter is by far the most likely. In the event of failure, check the system in a logical fashion, as described below.

2 Pull the cap off the spark plug (see Chapter 1). Fit a spare spark plug into the cap and lay the plug against the cylinder head with the threads contacting it. If necessary, hold the spark plug with an insulated tool.

Warning: Do not remove the spark plug from the engine to perform this check – atomised fuel being pumped out of the open spark plug hole could ignite, causing severe injury! Make sure the plug is securely held against the engine.

3 Check that the transmission is in neutral, then turn the ignition switch ON and turn the engine over on the starter motor. If the system is in good condition a regular, fat blue spark should be evident at the plug electrodes. If the spark appears thin or yellowish, or is non-existent, further investigation will be necessary.

4 The ignition system must be able to produce a spark which is capable of jumping a particular size gap – Honda do not give a specification, but a healthy system should produce a spark capable of jumping at least 6 mm. Simple ignition spark gap testing tools are commercially available – follow the manufacturer's instructions and check the spark **(see illustration)**.

5 If the test results are good the entire ignition system can be considered good. If the spark appears thin or yellowish, or is non-existent, further investigation is necessary.

6 Ignition faults can be divided into two categories, namely those where the ignition system has failed completely, and those which are due to a partial failure. The likely faults are listed below, starting with the most probable source of failure. Work through the list systematically, referring to the subsequent sections for full details of the necessary checks and tests, and to the Wiring Diagram at the end of Chapter 8. Before checking the following items ensure that the battery is fully charged and that all fuses are in good condition.

- Loose, corroded or damaged wiring connections, broken or shorted wiring between any of the component parts of the ignition system (see Chapter 8).
- Faulty HT lead or spark plug cap, faulty spark plug, dirty, worn or corroded plug electrodes, or incorrect gap between electrodes.
- Faulty ignition switch (see Chapter 8).
- Faulty neutral, clutch or sidestand switch, or safety circuit diode (see Chapter 8).
- Faulty ignition HT coil.
- Faulty crankshaft position (CKP) sensor.
- Faulty tip-over sensor.
- Faulty ECM.

7 If the above checks don't reveal the cause of the problem, have the ignition system tested by a Honda dealer.

3 Ignition HT coil

Caution: Ensure the ignition is switched OFF before disconnecting/reconnecting any ignition system wiring connectors. If a connector is disconnected/reconnected with the ignition switched ON the engine control module (ECM) could be damaged.
Special tools: A multimeter and peak voltage adapter are required for this procedure (see Step 3).

1 The ignition coil is located on the right-hand side of the frame underneath the fuel tank **(see illustration)**. Remove the fuel tank (see Chapter 4) for access.

2 Ensure that the spark plug and spark plug cap are in good condition (see Chapter 1).

Check

3 To test the ignition coil a multimeter with a minimum input resistance of 10 M-ohms is required in conjunction with a peak voltage adapter. Honda produces a peak voltage adapter (Part No. 07HGJ-0020100) for this purpose. If the appropriate equipment is not available the checks should be undertaken by a Honda dealer.

4 Support the machine on its centrestand and retract the sidestand. Check that the transmission is in neutral.

5 Pull the cap off the spark plug, connect a known good plug to the cap and earth (ground) the plug against the cylinder head.

6 To test the coil input voltage, back probe the black/blue wire terminal on the coil with the multimeter positive (+) probe and connect the negative (-) probe to earth (ground). Turn the ignition ON and note the voltage – see Specifications at the beginning of this Chapter.

7 If there is no input voltage, turn the ignition OFF and check for continuity in the wiring

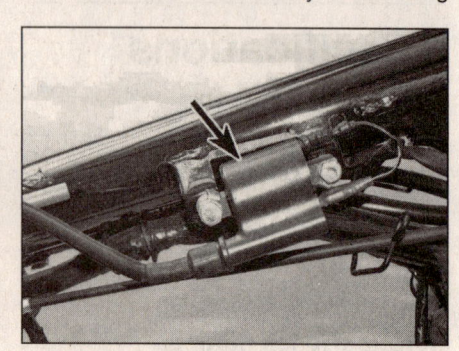

2.4 A typical spark gap testing tool

3.1 Location of the ignition HT coil (arrowed)

Ignition system 3•3

3.14 Note the location of the wiring connectors (arrowed)

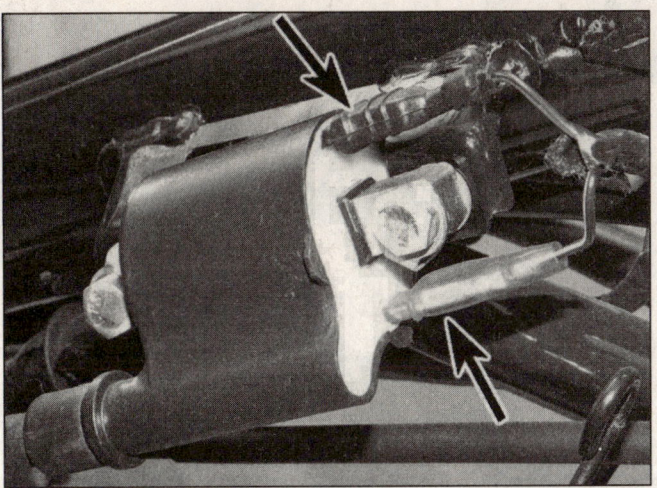

4.3a Location of the ECM (arrowed)

between the coil, the fusebox and the ignition switch (see *Wiring Diagram* at the end of Chapter 8).

8 If the input voltage is good, test the coil peak voltage as follows. Back probe the black/white wire terminal on the coil with the peak voltage adapter positive (+) probe and connect the negative (-) probe to earth (ground). Turn the ignition ON, crank the engine on the starter motor and note the peak voltage. Turn the ignition OFF. **Note:** *The machine's battery must be fully charged to perform this test successfully.* Compare the result with the specification at the beginning of this Chapter.

9 If the peak voltage is lower than specified it is likely that either the ignition HT coil or the ECM is faulty – have them checked by a Honda dealer.

10 If no peak voltage is recorded it is likely that either the CKP sensor or the ECM is faulty. Follow the procedure in Section 4 to test the CKP sensor. Have the ECM checked by a Honda dealer.

11 If both the input voltage and peak voltage are as specified but there is no spark across the plug electrodes, it is likely the ignition HT coil is faulty.

Removal and installation

12 If not already done, remove the fuel tank (see Chapter 4).
13 Disconnect the cap from the spark plug (see Chapter 1).
14 Disconnect the coil wiring connectors, noting how they fit **(see illustration)**.
15 Undo the bolts securing the coil and lift it off, noting the routing of the HT lead.
16 Installation is the reverse of removal.

4 Crankshaft position sensor

Caution: Ensure the ignition is switched OFF before disconnecting/reconnecting any ignition system wiring connectors. If a connector is disconnected/reconnected with the ignition switched ON the engine control module (ECM) could be damaged.
Special tools: *A multimeter and peak voltage adapter are required for this procedure (see Step 1).*

Check

1 To test the crankshaft position (CKP) sensor a multimeter with a minimum input resistance of 10 M-ohms is required in conjunction with a peak voltage adapter. Honda produces a peak voltage adapter (Part No. 07HGJ-0020100) for this purpose. If the appropriate equipment is not available the checks should be undertaken by a Honda dealer.

2 Support the machine on its centrestand and retract the sidestand. Check that the transmission is in neutral.

3 Remove the seats and the left-hand side panel (see Chapter 7) to access the ECM **(see illustration)**. Ease the ECM off its mounting bracket and disconnect the multi-pin wiring connector **(see illustrations)**.

4.3b Displace the ECM . . .

4.3c . . . and disconnect the multi-pin connector

3•4 Ignition system

4.7a Trace the wiring from the back of the cover . . .

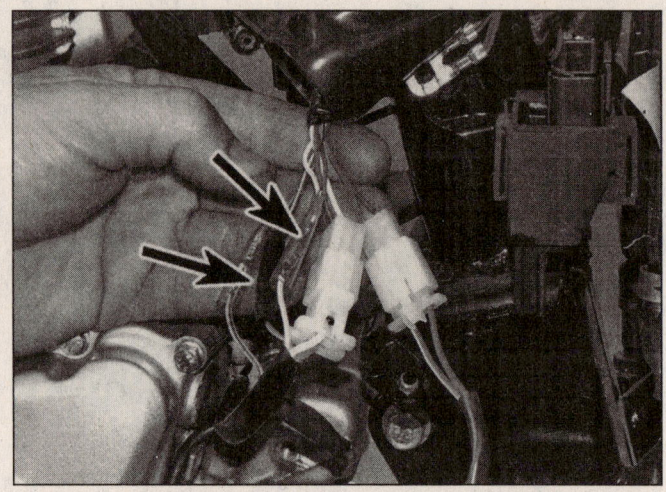

4.7b . . . and disconnect the CKP sensor connectors (arrowed)

4 Connect the peak voltage adapter probes to the white/yellow and blue/yellow wire terminals on the loom side of the multi-pin connector.

5 Turn the ignition ON, crank the engine on the starter motor and note the CKP sensor peak voltage. Turn the ignition OFF. **Note:** *The machine's battery must be fully charged to perform this test successfully.*

6 Compare the result with the specification at the beginning of this Chapter. If the result is below the specified minimum, repeat the test at the CKP sensor wiring connector as follows.

7 The CKP sensor is located inside the alternator cover on the left-hand side of the engine unit. Trace the wiring from the back of the alternator cover to the wiring boot **(see illustration)**. Draw the wiring out of the boot, then refer to the *Wiring Diagram* at the end of Chapter 8 and disconnect the two CKP sensor connectors **(see illustration)**.

8 Connect the peak voltage adapter probes to the wire terminals on the sensor side of the connectors and repeat the procedure in Step 5.

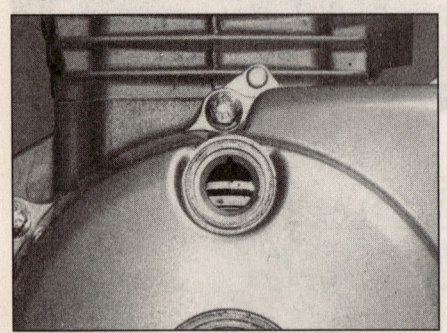

5.4 Unscrew the timing inspection cap and check position of the timing mark

9 If the result in the second test is as specified, inspect the wiring and connections between the wiring connector and the ECM for damage. If the result is again below the specified minimum, either the test equipment is not suitable for the task or the CKP sensor is faulty – have it checked by a Honda dealer.

Removal and installation

10 The CKP sensor is an integral part of the alternator stator assembly. If the sensor is faulty a new stator assembly will have to be fitted. Refer to Chapter 8 to remove and install the alternator stator assembly.

5 Ignition timing

General information

1 Since no provision exists for adjusting the ignition timing and since no component is subject to mechanical wear, there is no need for regular checks: only if investigating a fault such as a loss of power or a misfire, should the ignition timing be checked.

2 The ignition timing is checked dynamically (engine running) using a stroboscopic lamp. The inexpensive neon lamps should be adequate in theory, but in practice may produce a pulse of such low intensity that the timing mark remains indistinct. If possible, one of the more precise xenon tube lamps should be used, powered by an external source of the appropriate voltage. **Note:** *Do not use the machine's own battery, as an incorrect reading may result from stray impulses within the machine's electrical system.*

Check

3 Warm the engine up to normal operating temperature, then turn the ignition OFF.

4 Unscrew the timing inspection cap from the top of the alternator cover on the left-hand side of the engine **(see illustration)**.

5 The timing mark which indicates the firing point at idle speed is the line next to the 'F' mark on the alternator rotor.

> **HAYNES HiNT** *The timing marks can be highlighted with white paint to make them more visible under the stroboscope light.*

6 Connect the timing light to the HT lead as described in the manufacturer's instructions.

7 Start the engine and aim the strobe lamp at the inspection hole.

8 With the machine idling at the specified speed, the line next to the 'F' mark on the alternator rotor should align with the notch in the inspection hole (the static timing mark).

9 Slowly increase the engine speed whilst observing the 'F' mark. The mark should appear to move anti-clockwise, increasing in relation to the engine speed until it reaches full advance (no identification mark).

10 As already stated, there is no means of adjustment of the ignition timing on these machines. If the ignition timing is incorrect, or suspected of being incorrect, one of the ignition system components is at fault and the system must be tested as described in the preceding Sections of this Chapter.

11 On completion, install the timing inspection cap using a new O-ring if required. Lubricate the O-ring with a smear of engine oil. Tighten the cap to the torque setting specified at the beginning of the Chapter.

Chapter 4
Engine management system

Contents

	Section number
Air filter	see Chapter 1
Air filter housing	5
Catalytic converter	14
Crankshaft position sensor	see Chapter 3
Engine management system operation	7
Engine management system fault diagnosis	8
Engine management system components	9
Exhaust system	13
Fuel gauge	see Chapter 8
Fuel injector	11
Fuel pressure and delivery check	3
Fuel pump	4
Fuel level sensor	6
Fuel system check	see Chapter 1
Fuel tank	2
General information and precautions	1
Ignition HT coil	see Chapter 3
Spark plug	see Chapter 1
Throttle cable check and adjustment	see Chapter 1
Throttle body	10
Throttle cable	12

Degrees of difficulty

Easy, suitable for novice with little experience	**Fairly easy,** suitable for beginner with some experience	**Fairly difficult,** suitable for competent DIY mechanic	**Difficult,** suitable for experienced DIY mechanic	**Very difficult,** suitable for expert DIY or professional

Specifications

Fuel
Grade .... Unleaded. Minimum 91 RON (Research Octane Number)
Fuel tank capacity .... 13 litres

Fuel level sensor
Resistance
  Tank full .... 6 to 10 ohms
  Tank empty .... 90 to 96 ohms

Fuel pump
Fuel pressure, engine idling .... 43 psi (3.0 Bar)
Minimum fuel flow rate .... 27.7 ml every 10 seconds

Throttle body
ID number GQM6A

Engine management system

Throttle body sensor unit
   Input voltage .... 4.75 to 5.25 V
Manifold absolute pressure (MAP) sensor
   Output voltage
      Inspection 1 .... 2.6 to 3.2 V
      Inspection 2 (FI system back-up mode signal) .... 3.8 to 5.25 V
Engine oil temperature (EOT) sensor
   Input voltage .... 4.75 to 5.25 V
   Resistance at 20°C (68°F) .... 2.4 to 2.9 K-ohms
   Output voltage .... 2.7 to 3.1 V
Throttle position (TP) sensor
   Output voltage
      Throttle fully closed .... 0.29 to 0.71 V
      Throttle fully open .... 4.13 to 4.76 V
Intake air temperature (IAT) sensor
   Output voltage .... 2.7 to 3.1 V
   Input voltage .... 4.75 to 5.25 V
   Resistance .... 1.0 to 4.0 K-ohms at 20°C (68°F)
Fuel injector
   Input voltage .... Battery voltage
   Resistance .... 9.0 to 12.0 ohms at 20°C (68°F)
Idle air control valve (IACV)
   Resistance .... 117 to 143 ohms at 25°C (77°F)
Tip-over (TO) sensor
   Input voltage .... 4.75 to 5.25 V
   Output voltage
      Sensor horizontal .... 3.6 to 4.4 V
      Sensor tilted (see text) .... 0.7 to 1.3 V

Torque settings

Crankshaft position (CKP) sensor bolts .... 12 Nm
Engine oil temperature (EOT) sensor .... 14 Nm
Fuel hose union bolts .... 5 Nm
Fuel level sensor mounting nuts .... 9 Nm
Oxygen sensor .... 25 Nm
Exhaust header pipe flange nuts .... 11 Nm
Silencer mounting bolt .... 34 Nm

1 General information and precautions

General information

The engine management system combines the operations of the fuel and ignition systems. Together they are controlled by the engine control module (ECM) which ensures that the engine is running at optimum efficiency under all riding conditions.

Details of the ignition system and its components can be found in Chapter 3.

Fuel system

The fuel system consists of the fuel tank, fuel level sensor, a combined fuel pump (with pressure regulator and filter), the fuel hose, injector, throttle body assembly and control cable.

Fuel flows by gravity from the tank to the pump and is then pumped under pressure to the fuel injector. The fuel pump is switched on and off by the ignition switch. Operating pressure is maintained by the pressure regulator.

When it opens, the injector sprays fuel into the throttle body where it mixes with air and vaporises, before entering the cylinder where it is compressed and ignited. Fuel supply varies according to the engine's needs for starting, warming-up, idling, cruising and acceleration. The timing and duration of fuel delivery is determined by the ECM using the information obtained from the various sensors it monitors (see Section 7).

The exhaust system is a one-piece design comprising the header pipe and silencer. A catalytic converter is located inside the rear end of the header pipe.

Several of the fuel system service procedures are considered routine maintenance items and for that reason are covered in Chapter 1.

Note: *Individual engine management system components can be checked but not repaired. If system troubles occur, and the faulty component can be isolated, the only cure for the problem in most cases is to replace the part with a new one. Keep in mind that most electronic parts, once purchased, cannot be returned. To avoid unnecessary expense, make very sure the faulty component has been positively identified before buying a new part.*

Precautions

⚠️ **Warning:** *Petrol (gasoline) is extremely flammable, so take extra precautions when you work on any part of the fuel system. Always remove the battery (see Chapter 8). Don't smoke or allow open flames or bare light bulbs near the work area, and don't work in a garage where a natural gas-type appliance is present. If you spill any fuel on your skin, rinse it off immediately with soap and water. When you perform any kind of work on the fuel system, wear safety glasses and have a fire extinguisher suitable for a class B type fire (flammable liquids) on hand.*

Ensure the ignition is switched OFF before disconnecting or reconnecting any fuel injection system wiring connector. If a connector is disconnected or reconnected with the ignition switched ON, the engine control module (ECM) may be damaged.

Always perform service procedures in a well-ventilated area to prevent a build-up of fumes.

Never work in a building containing a gas appliance with a pilot light, or any other form

Engine management system

of naked flame. Ensure that there are no naked light bulbs or any sources of flame or sparks nearby.

Do not smoke (or allow anyone else to smoke) while in the vicinity of petrol (gasoline) or of components containing it. Remember the possible presence of vapour from these sources and move well clear before smoking.

Check all electrical equipment belonging to the house, garage or workshop where work is being undertaken (see the *Safety first!* section of this manual). Remember that certain electrical appliances such as drills, cutters etc, create sparks in the normal course of operation and must not be used near petrol (gasoline) or any component containing it. Again, remember the possible presence of fumes before using electrical equipment.

Always mop up any spilt fuel and safely dispose of the rag used.

Any stored fuel that is drained off during servicing work must be kept in sealed containers that are suitable for holding petrol (gasoline), and clearly marked as such; the containers themselves should be kept in a safe place. Note that this last point applies equally to the fuel tank if it is removed from the machine; also remember to keep its filler cap closed at all times.

Read the *Safety first!* section of this manual carefully before starting work.

2 Fuel tank

Warning: *Refer to the precautions given in Section 1 before starting work.*

Note: *If the fuel tank is removed from the bike, it should not be placed in an area where sparks or open flames could ignite the fumes coming out of the tank. Be especially careful inside garages where a natural gas-type appliance is located, because the pilot light could cause an explosion.*

Removal

1 Ensure the ignition is switched OFF.
2 Remove the seats, the side panels and the fairing (see Chapter 7).
3 No fuel tap is fitted to the tank; if it is more than half full it is advisable to siphon some fuel out into a suitable container before removing the tank. Alternatively, fit a suitable clamp to the fuel supply hose, release the clip securing the hose to the union on the fuel pump and disconnect the hose **(see illustration)**. Have a piece of rag ready to catch any residual fuel. Release the clamp and drain the fuel from the tank into a suitable container **(see illustration)**.
4 Disconnect the fuel level sensor wiring connector **(see illustration)**.
5 Fit clamps to the fuel supply and vapour return hoses, then release the clips securing the hoses to the unions on the fuel pump and disconnect the hoses **(see illustration)**.

2.3a Disconnecting the hose from the pump union

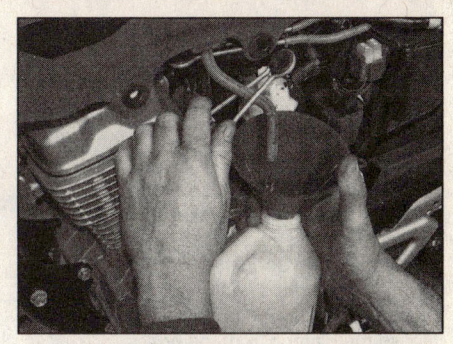

2.3b Drain the fuel into a suitable container

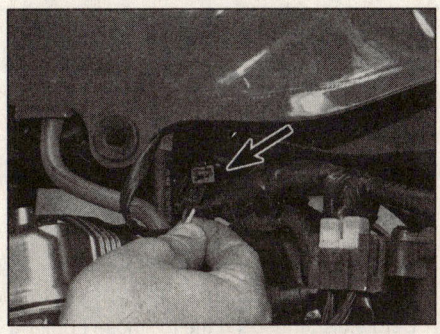

2.4 Fuel level sensor wiring connector (arrowed)

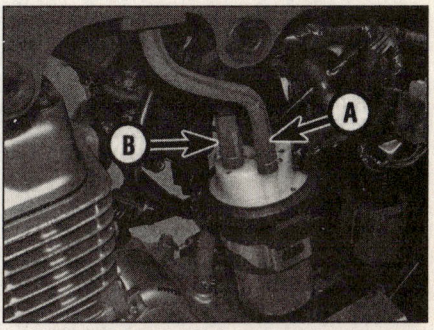

2.5 Fuel supply (A) and vapour return (B) hoses

6 Make sure the fuel cap is secure.
7 Undo the bolt securing the rear of the tank and remove the collar **(see illustration)**.
8 Lift the rear of the tank and disconnect the breather hoses, noting how they fit **(see illustration)**.

9 Pull the tank back off the front mounting bushes and lift it off **(see illustration)**.
10 Inspect the tank mounting bushes for signs of damage or deterioration and replace them with new ones if necessary **(see illustration)**.

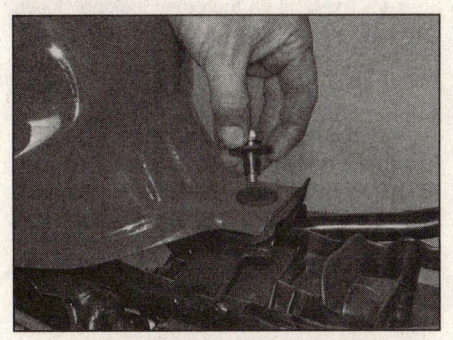

2.7 Remove the bolt and collar

2.8 Disconnect the breather hoses from the tank unions (arrowed)

2.9 Pull the tank back and lift it off

2.10 Inspect the mounting bushes on both sides

4•4 Engine management system

Installation

11 Push the tank forwards and ensure it is located securely on the mounting bushes. Install the breather hoses on their unions on the underside of the tank (see illustration 2.8).
12 Lower the rear of the tank and install the mounting bolt and collar (see illustration 2.7). Tighten the bolt securely
13 Install the vapour return hose and fuel supply hose onto their unions on the pump and secure them with the clips. If fitted, release the clamps from the hoses.
14 Connect the fuel level sensor wiring connector (see illustration 2.4).
15 With fuel in the tank, check fuel flow as follows – turn the ignition ON and check that the fuel pump operates for approximately 2 seconds then switches off. Turn the ignition OFF. Check the hose unions for fuel leaks.
16 Install the remaining components in the reverse order of removal.

Repair

17 All repairs to the fuel tank should be carried out by a professional who has experience in this critical and potentially dangerous work. Even after cleaning and flushing of the fuel system, explosive fumes can remain and ignite during repair of the tank.

3 Fuel pressure and delivery check

⚠️ **Warning:** *Refer to the precautions given in Section 1 before starting work.*
Special Tools: *A fuel pressure gauge, hose and adapter are required for the pressure check (see Step 3). A suitable calibrated container and length of fuel hose are required for the fuel delivery check (see Step 10).*

1 The fuel pump is located on the left-hand side below the fuel tank (see illustration). Remove the seats and the left-hand side panel for access (see Chapter 7).
2 When the ignition is switched ON, it should be possible to hear the pump run for approximately 2 seconds until the system is up to pressure. If you can't hear anything, check

3.1 Location of the fuel pump

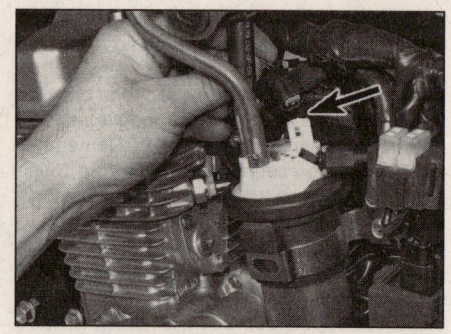

the pump electrical circuit and associated components (see Section 4). If the pump appears to be good, check the fuel pressure and delivery as follows.

Fuel pressure check

3 To check the fuel pressure, a suitable gauge, gauge adapter, hoses and hose union are needed. Honda provides service tools (Part Nos. 07406-0040004, 07ZAJ-S5A0111, 07ZAJ-S5A0130, 07ZAJ-S5A0120 and 07ZAJ-S5A0150) for this purpose.
4 Before disconnecting the fuel hose from the fuel pump, relieve the fuel pressure as follows. Disconnect the fuel pump wiring connector (see illustration). Start the engine and allow it to idle until it stalls through lack of fuel. Turn the ignition OFF.
5 Note the location of the rubber security cap on the end of the hose connector then pull the cap out of the connector (see illustration). Squeeze the tabs on the green locking sleeve together to release the hose connector from the pump union (see illustration). **Note:** *Honda recommends that a new locking sleeve is fitted whenever the fuel hose is disconnected. See Section 10 for further details.*
6 Use the service tools to connect the gauge between the pump union and the supply hose to the injector.
7 Reconnect the pump wiring connector, then turn the ignition ON and start the engine. Note the fuel pressure at idle and compare the result with the specification at the beginning of this Chapter. Turn the ignition OFF, disconnect the fuel pump wiring connector, then follow

3.4 Fuel pump wiring connector (arrowed)

the procedure in Step 4 relieve any pressure in the fuel hoses and service equipment before removing the equipment.
8 If the pressure is too high, either the pump or pressure regulator is faulty. Individual components are not available – a new pump assembly will have to be fitted (see Section 4).
9 If the pressure is too low, first check for a leak between the fuel hose and the injector. If there is no leakage, ensure the tank breather hoses and unions are clear. Check the fuel delivery (see Steps 10 to 12). Finally check the pump (see Section 4).

Fuel delivery check

10 Follow the procedure in Steps 4 and 5 to disconnect the fuel hose from the fuel pump union. Connect a length of suitable hose to the pump union and place the open end of the hose in a calibrated container capable for holding approximately 500 cc of fuel. **Note:** *The fuel pressure check hose Part No. 07ZAJ-S5A0130 is ideal for this purpose.*
11 Turn the ignition ON – the pump should operate for 2 seconds. Repeat the procedure five times (total delivery time 10 seconds).
12 Measure the amount of fuel that has flowed into the container and compare it to the amount specified at the beginning of this Chapter.
13 If the flow rate is below the minimum, first check the battery condition (see Chapter 8). If the battery is good, ensure that the tank breather hoses and unions are clear. If no fault can be found, either the fuel filter is blocked or the pump motor is defective; no individual components are available, a new fuel pump must be fitted (see Section 4).

4 Fuel pump

⚠️ **Warning:** *Refer to the precautions given in Section 1 before starting work.*

Voltage check

1 The fuel pump is located on the left-hand side below the fuel tank (see illustration 3.1). Remove the seats and the left-hand side panel for access (see Chapter 7).

3.5a Location of the rubber security cap (arrowed)

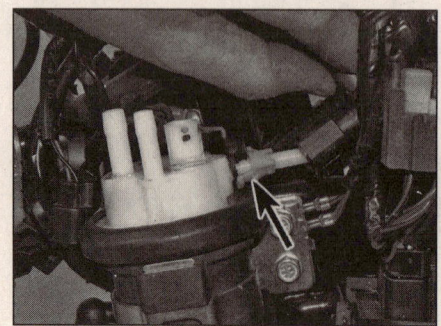

3.5b Disconnect the fuel hose. Note locking sleeve (arrowed)

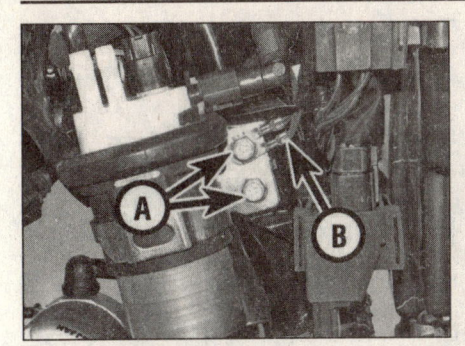

Engine management system 4•5

4.10 Pump mounting bolts (A). Note earth wires (B)

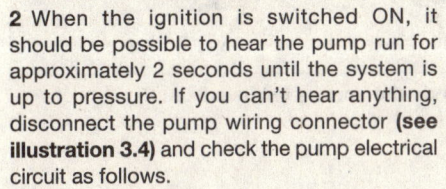

4.11 Remove the pump and mounting bracket

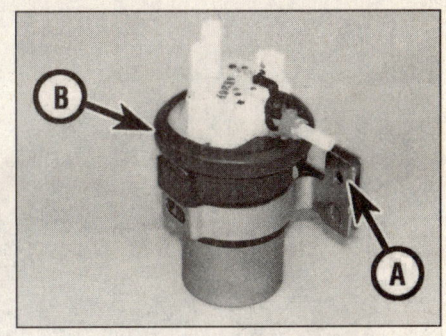

4.12 Remove the mounting bracket (A) and rubber sleeve (B)

2 When the ignition is switched ON, it should be possible to hear the pump run for approximately 2 seconds until the system is up to pressure. If you can't hear anything, disconnect the pump wiring connector **(see illustration 3.4)** and check the pump electrical circuit as follows.

3 Using a multimeter set to the volts scale, connect the meter positive (+) probe to the black/blue wire terminal and the negative (-) probe to the brown wire terminal on the loom side of the connector. Turn the ignition ON – there should be battery voltage for approximately 2 seconds.

4 If there is battery voltage it is likely the pump is faulty – have it checked by a Honda dealer.

5 If there is no voltage, first check the main fuse and circuit fuse B (see Chapter 8). Check the ignition switch and then inspect the wiring between the pump, the fusebox and the switch for damage (see Wiring Diagram at the end of Chapter 8).

6 If all the components are good it is likely the ECM is faulty – have it checked by a Honda dealer.

Removal and installation

Note: *The fuel pump cannot be disassembled.*

7 The fuel pump is located on the left-hand side below the fuel tank **(see illustration 3.1)**. Remove the seats and the left-hand side panel for access (see Chapter 7).

8 Follow the procedure in Section 3 to relieve the fuel pressure and disconnect the hose from the fuel pump union.

9 Follow the procedure in Section 2 to disconnect the fuel supply and vapour return hoses from the pump.

10 Undo the pump mounting bolts, noting the location of the earth (ground) wires **(see illustration)**.

11 If not already done, disconnect the pump wiring connector, then lift the pump off **(see illustration)**.

12 Remove the mounting bracket and rubber sleeve from the pump **(see illustration)**.

13 Installation is the reverse of removal. **Note:** *Honda recommends that a new locking sleeve is fitted whenever the fuel pressure hose is disconnected.*

5 Air filter housing

1 Remove the seats and the left and right-hand side panels (see Chapter 7).

2 Follow the procedure in Chapter 1 to remove the air filter cover and element.

3 Undo the screw securing the wiring clip to the left-hand side of the filter housing **(see illustration)**.

4 Undo the front and rear mounting bolts on the left-hand side **(see illustrations)**.

5 Undo the mounting bolt on the right-hand side **(see illustration)**.

6 Loosen the clamp securing the intake duct to the throttle body and detach the duct **(see illustration)**.

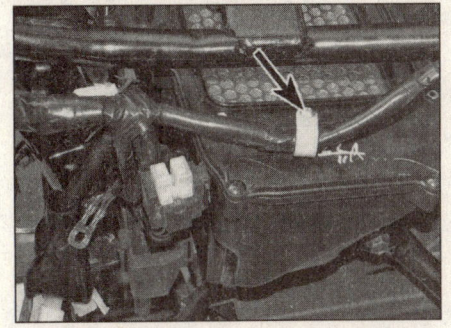

5.3 Release the wiring clip (arrowed)

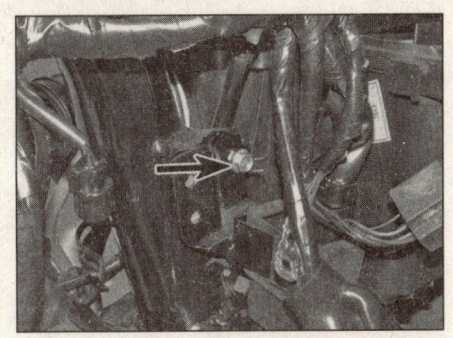

5.4a Undo the left-hand front . . .

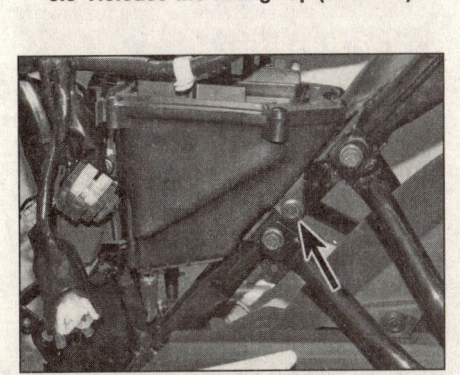

5.4b . . . and rear mounting bolts (arrowed)

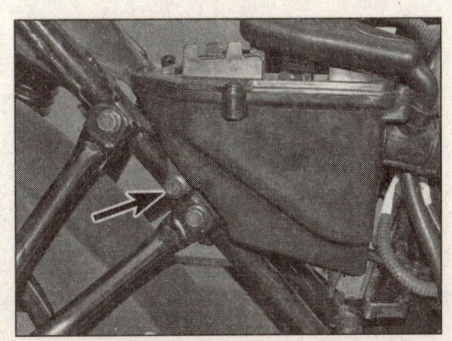

5.5 Undo the right-hand mounting bolt (arrowed)

5.6 Loosen the clamp (arrowed) securing the intake duct

4•6 Engine management system

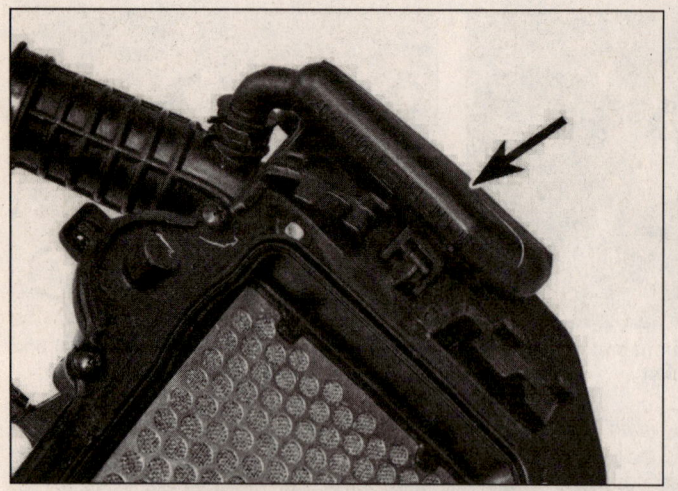

5.8 Location of the resonator (arrowed)

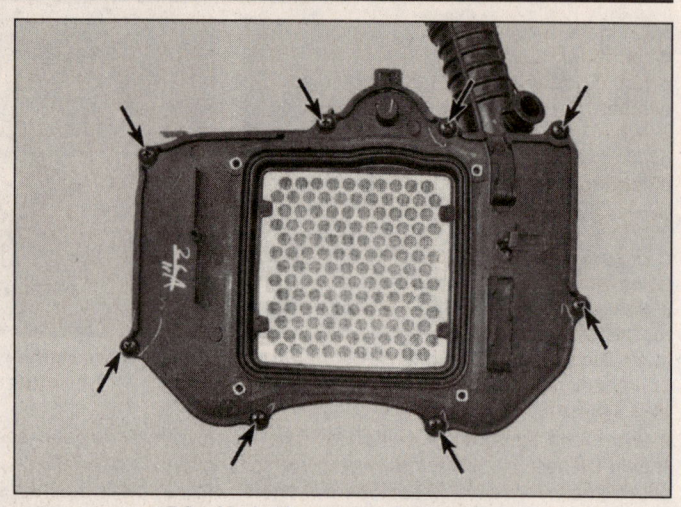

5.9a Undo the screws (arrowed) . . .

5.9b . . . and remove the sub filter

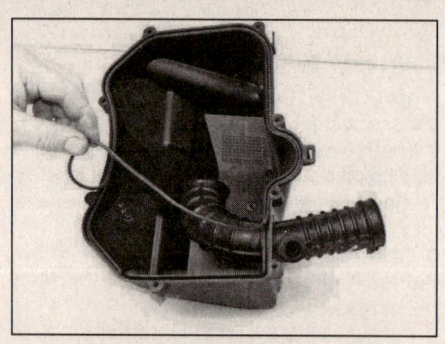

5.9c Note location of the seal

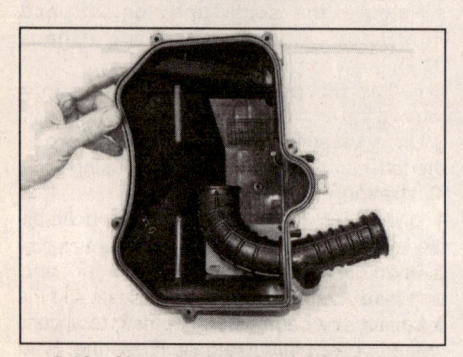

5.10a Note the location of the intake duct . . .

5.10b . . . then draw it out of the housing

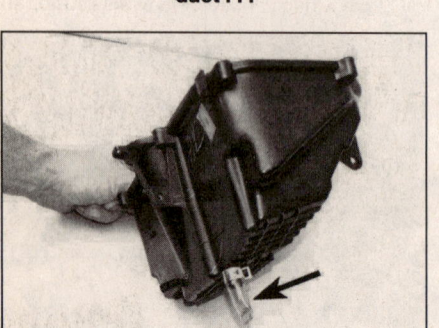

5.11 Remove the housing drain (arrowed)

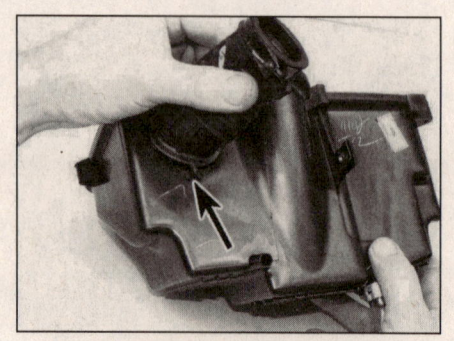

5.12 Align the duct with the housing (arrowed)

7 Manoeuvre the air filter housing out on the right-hand side.
8 Note the location of the resonator **(see illustration)**. If required, release the clip securing the resonator and lift it off.
9 Undo the screws securing the sub filter and lift it off, noting the location of the seal **(see illustrations)**.
10 Note the location of the intake duct then draw it out of the housing **(see illustrations)**.
11 Release the clip securing the drain to the underside of the housing and remove it **(see illustration)**.
12 Installation is the reverse of removal, noting the following:
● Renew the housing seal if it is deteriorated.
● Align the tab on the intake duct with the notch on the outside of the housing **(see illustration)**.
● Ensure the intake duct is pushed firmly onto the throttle body and tighten the clamp securely **(see illustration 5.6)**.

6 Fuel level sensor

1 The fuel level sensor is located inside the fuel tank. If the sensor is thought to be faulty, remove and check it as follows.

Removal

2 Remove the fuel tank (see Section 2) and drain any residual fuel into a suitable container. Support the tank upside down on some clean rag to prevent damage to the paintwork.

Engine management system 4•7

3 Undo the sensor mounting nuts evenly **(see illustration)**.
4 Lift out the sensor, taking care not to damage the float arm **(see illustration)**.
5 Note the location of the O-ring seal and discard it as a new one must be fitted **(see illustration)**.

Check

6 Ensure that the float arm moves up and down freely.
7 Using a multimeter set to the ohms scale, measure the resistance between the terminals in the sensor wiring connector with the float up (tank full) and the float down (tank empty) **(see illustration)**.
8 Compare the results with the specifications at the beginning of this Chapter. If the results are not as specified the sensor is faulty and a new one must be fitted.

Installation

9 Installation is the reverse of removal, noting the following:
- Lubricate the new O-ring seal with a smear of engine oil.
- Tighten the mounting nuts evenly to the specified torque setting.

7 Engine management system operation

1 The engine management system consists of the fuel system and the ignition circuit, controlled and co-ordinated by the engine control module (ECM). An overview of the engine management system can be found in Section 1.
2 To ensure optimum engine efficiency, the ECM monitors signals from the following components:
- Manifold absolute pressure (MAP) sensor
- Engine oil temperature (EOT) sensor
- Throttle position (TP) sensor
- Intake air temperature (IAT) sensor
- Oxygen sensor
- Idle air control valve (IACV)
- Tip-over (TO) sensor
- Crankshaft position (CKP) sensor (see Chapter 3)

3 The FI warning light in the instrument cluster should come on briefly when the ignition is switched ON, then go out – this serves as a check that the engine management system circuit is working correctly. If the warning light does not come on, or comes on and stays on, carry out the checks below.
4 In the event of an abnormality in any of the components or sensor signals, the FI warning light comes on and the ECM determines whether the engine can still be run safely. If it can, a back-up mode substitutes the sensor signal with a fixed signal, restricting performance but allowing the bike to be ridden home or to a dealer. If the fault is serious, the fuel and ignition systems will be shut down and the engine will not run.
5 Once a fault has been indicated by the FI warning light, the fault code should be accessed from the system and appropriate checks undertaken (see Sections 8 and 9).
6 The system incorporates two safety circuits. The sidestand switch, clutch switch and neutral switch circuit which prevent or stop the engine running if the transmission is in gear whilst the sidestand is down, and prevents the engine from starting if the transmission is in gear unless the sidestand is up and the clutch lever is pulled in (see Chapter 8 for component test details). The tip-over sensor circuit, which automatically switches off the fuel pump and cuts power to the ignition and injection circuits if the motorcycle falls over (see Section 9).

FI warning light check

7 If the light does not come on, first check the warning light bulb in the instrument cluster (see Chapter 8).
8 If the bulb is good, remove the seats and the left-hand side panel (see Chapter 7) to access the ECM **(see illustration)**. Ease the ECM off its mounting bracket and disconnect the multi-pin wiring connector **(see illustrations)**.

6.3 Undo the sensor mounting nuts (arrowed)

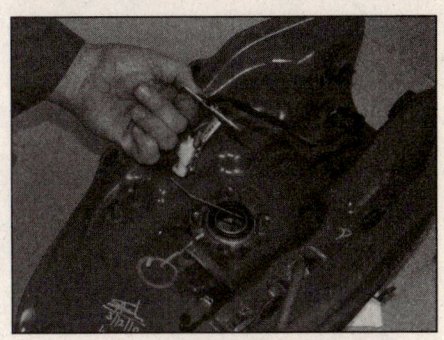

6.4 Remove the sensor carefully

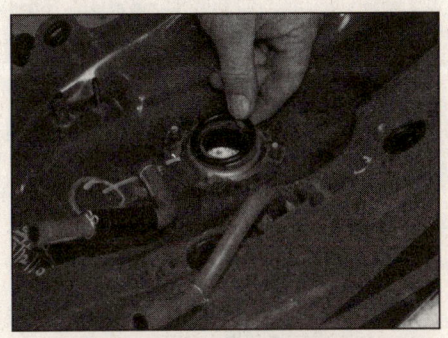

6.5 Location of the O-ring seal

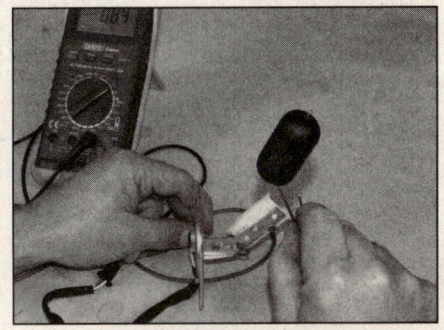

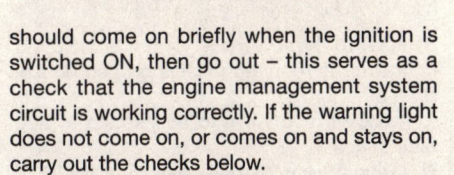

6.7 Checking the fuel level sensor resistance

7.8a Location of the ECM (arrowed)

7.8b Displace the ECM . . .

7.8c . . . and disconnect the multi-pin connector

4•8 Engine management system

7.12a Location of the DLC

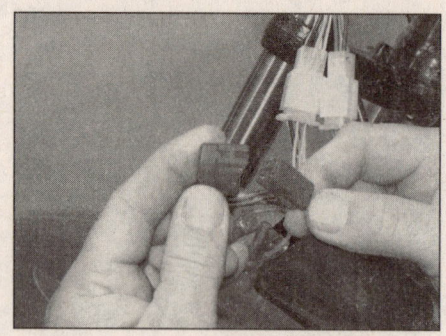

7.12b Remove the DLC cap

9 Using an insulated jumper wire, connect the white/blue wire terminal on the loom side of the ECM connector to earth (ground) and turn the ignition ON.

10 If the FI warning light comes on it is likely the ECM is faulty – have it checked by a Honda dealer. If the light does not come on, check for continuity between the white/blue wire terminal and the instrument cluster. If there is continuity it is likely the instrument cluster is faulty – have it checked by a Honda dealer.

11 If, when the ignition is switched ON, the FI warning light comes on and stays on, ensure the ignition is switched OFF, then follow the procedure in Step 8 to disconnect the ECM multi-pin connector. Turn the ignition ON – the warning light should turn off.

12 If the warning light turns off, ensure the ignition is switched OFF, then check for a short circuit in the blue wire between the ECM connector and the data link connector (DLC). The DLC is located inside the boot for the headlight assembly wiring connectors on the left-hand side inside the fairing **(see illustration)** – remove the fairing for access (see Chapter 7). Unclip the DLC cap to access the blue wire terminal **(see illustration)**. If the wiring is good it is likely the ECM is faulty – have it checked by a Honda dealer.

13 If the warning light comes on, check for a short circuit in the white/blue wire between the ECM connector and the instrument cluster. If the wiring is good it is likely the ECM is faulty – have it checked by a Honda dealer.

14 If the engine will not start and the warning light does not come on, check the ECM wiring (see Section 9).

8 Engine management system fault diagnosis

Special tools: *A Service Check Short (SCS) connector is required for this procedure (see Step 3).*

1 There are two ways to access the system fault codes:
- Using the Honda Diagnostic System (HDS) pocket tester – fault codes are displayed as a hyphenated number. The digits in front of the hyphen indicate the faulty component, those behind the hyphen indicate a specific failure symptom.
- Using the Service Check Short (SCS) connector – fault codes are displayed by the FI warning light as a series of flashes.

2 Both units connect to the data link connector (DLC) at the front of the bike **(see illustrations 7.12a and b)**.

3 For the purpose of this manual the SCS connector (Part No. 070PZ-ZY30100) has been used to access the fault codes.

4 Follow the procedure in Section 7 to access the DLC. Ensure the ignition is switched OFF, then unclip the DLC cap and install the SCS connector – the connector links the blue and green/black wire terminals inside the DLC.

5 Turn the ignition ON and the FI light should start to flash, denoting the fault code(s) as follows.

6 The FI light emits short (0.5 second) and long (1.3 second) flashes – the short flashes represent the units and the long flashes represent the tens. For example, fault code 7 is represented as seven short flashes; fault code 21 is represented as two long flashes and one short flash.

7 If there is more than one fault code, the codes are displayed in numerical order, lowest to highest.

8 Note the fault codes and keep the SCS connector connected until you have finished reading the fault code(s). Turn the ignition OFF and disconnect the SCS connector.

9 Compare the codes with the fault code table to identify the faulty components, then refer to Section 9 for checking procedures.

10 To delete the fault code from the system memory once the fault has been corrected, install the SCS connector (see Step 4) and turn the ignition ON. Disconnect the SCS link wire, then as soon as the FI light comes on, reconnect the link wire. The FI light should go off and then start flashing to denote the code has been erased. Turn the ignition OFF.

Code	Faulty component – ECM response	Possible causes
1	Manifold absolute pressure (MAP) sensor – engine will run in fail-safe mode	Faulty wiring or wiring connector Faulty, damaged or improperly installed sensor
7	Engine oil temperature (ECT) sensor – engine hard to start when cold, temperature signal fixed at 75°C	Faulty wiring or wiring connector Faulty, damaged or improperly installed sensor
8	Throttle position (TP) sensor – engine will run in fail-safe mode, poor acceleration	Faulty wiring or wiring connector Faulty, damaged or improperly installed sensor
9	Intake air temperature (IAT) sensor – engine will run, temperature signal fixed at 35°C	Faulty wiring or wiring connector Faulty, damaged or improperly installed sensor
12	Fuel injector – engine will not run, fuel and ignition systems turned OFF	Faulty wiring or wiring connector Faulty or damaged fuel injector
21	Oxygen sensor – engine will run	Faulty wiring or wiring connector Faulty, damaged or improperly installed sensor
29	Idle air control valve (IACV) – engine will run, hard to start, rough idling	Faulty wiring or wiring connector Faulty, damaged or improperly installed valve
33	ECM fault code memory malfunction – engine will run	Faulty ECM – will not retain self diagnosis information
54	Tip-over sensor – engine will run, safety circuit not functioning	Faulty wiring or wiring connector Faulty sensor

Engine management system 4•9

9 Engine management system components

Caution: *Ensure the ignition is switched OFF before disconnecting/reconnecting any engine management system wiring connectors. If a connector is disconnected/reconnected with the ignition switched ON the engine control module (ECM) could be damaged.*

1 If a fault is indicated on any of the system components, first check the wiring and connectors between the appropriate component and the engine control module (ECM) – see *Wiring Diagram* at the end of Chapter 8. A continuity test (see Chapter 8, Section 2) of all wires will locate a break or short in any circuit. Inspect the terminals inside the wiring connectors and ensure that they are not loose or corroded. Spray the inside of the connectors with a proprietary electrical terminal cleaner before reconnection. Where appropriate, remove the sensor and check the sensor head and clean it if it is dirty – an accumulation of dirt could affect the signal it transmits. Recheck the FI warning light to see if the fault has been cleared before proceeding.

2 It is possible to undertake some checks on system components using a multimeter (see Chapter 8, Section 2) and comparing the results with the specifications at the beginning of this Chapter. **Note:** *Different meters may give slightly different results to those specified even though the component being tested is not faulty – do not consign a component to the bin before having it double-checked.* If the appropriate equipment is not available, the checks should be undertaken by a Honda dealer.

3 Honda produces a test harness and pin box (Part No. 070MZ-MCA0100) for checking circuits to-and-from the ECM. If this is not available, you will need needle probes for your multimeter to enable you to back-probe the ECM connector terminals with the connector connected. For the purpose of this manual checks are described by back-probing the connector terminals – if the service equipment is available, connect the meter probes to the designated terminals on the pin box.

4 If, after a thorough check, the source of a fault has not been identified, it is possible that the ECM itself is faulty. A Honda dealer will be able to check the ECM using a Honda Diagnostic System tester, but it is worthwhile checking the ECM wiring beforehand (see Steps 63 to 65).

Throttle body sensor unit

5 The MAP, TP and IAT sensors are located in the sensor unit on the left-hand side of the throttle body assembly **(see illustration 10.15)**. Before undertaking tests on the individual sensors, test the unit power input circuit as follows.

6 Remove the seats and left and right-hand side panels for access (see Chapter 7).

7 To check the unit input voltage, displace the ECM **(see illustration 7.8b)** to access the loom side of the wiring connector. Do not disconnect the connector. With the ignition OFF, back-probe the yellow/red wire terminal 6 with the meter positive (+) probe and the green/orange wire terminal 4 with the meter negative (-) probe. Turn the ignition ON and check the input voltage. Turn the ignition OFF. If the result is not within the range specified at the beginning of this Chapter it is likely the ECM is faulty – have it checked by a Honda dealer.

8 If the result is good, disconnect the sensor unit wiring connector **(see illustration)**. Connect the meter positive (+) probe to the yellow/red wire terminal and the negative (-) probe to the green/orange wire terminal on the loom side of the connector. Turn the ignition ON and check the input voltage again, then turn the ignition OFF. The result should be as specified.

9 If the result is not as specified, check for continuity between the yellow/red wire terminal and earth (ground). Continuity indicates a short circuit in the yellow/red wire. Next, check for continuity in the yellow/red and green/orange wires between the ECM connector and the sensor unit connector. Continuity indicates an intermittent fault in the wiring – check carefully for damage. No continuity indicates a broken wire.

Manifold absolute pressure (MAP) sensor

Check

10 The MAP sensor is located in the sensor unit on the left-hand side of the throttle body assembly. If the initial sensor unit checks (see Steps 5 to 9) have failed to identify a fault, re-connect both wiring connectors. Back-probe the ECM light green/yellow terminal 27 with the meter positive (+) probe and the green/orange wire terminal 4 with the meter negative (-) probe. Turn the ignition ON and check the MAP sensor output voltage. Turn the ignition OFF. A result within the range for Inspection 1 indicates an intermittent fault or poor contacts in the wiring connectors.

11 If the result is not as specified, disconnect the sensor unit wiring connector **(see illustration 9.8)**. Connect the meter positive (+) probe to the light green/yellow wire terminal on the loom side of the connector and the negative (-) probe to the green/orange wire terminal. Turn the ignition ON, note the voltage, then turn the ignition OFF. A result within the specified range for Inspection 2 indicates a faulty MAP sensor.

12 If the result is not as specified, check for continuity between the light green/yellow wire terminal and earth (ground). Continuity indicates a short circuit in the light green/yellow wire. Next, back-probe the ECM light green/yellow wire terminal 27 and check for continuity in the wire between the ECM and the sensor unit connector. No continuity indicates a broken wire. If the wiring is good it is likely the ECM is faulty – have it checked by a Honda dealer.

Removal and installation

13 The MAP sensor is an integral part of the throttle body sensor unit (see Section 10).

Engine oil temperature (EOT) sensor

Check

14 The EOT sensor is located in the rear of the cylinder head **(see illustration)**. Remove the seats and left-hand side panel (see Chapter 7), then displace the fuel pump (see Section 4) to access the sensor wiring connector.

15 To check the sensor input voltage, disconnect the wiring connector. Connect the meter positive (+) probe to the yellow/blue wire terminal on the loom side of the connector and the negative (-) probe to earth (ground). Turn the ignition ON, note the voltage, then turn the ignition OFF.

16 If the result is not within the range specified at the beginning of this Chapter, check for continuity between the yellow/blue wire terminal and earth (ground). Continuity indicates a short circuit in the yellow/blue wire.

17 If the input voltage is within the specified range, check the resistance between the sensor terminals and compare the result with the specification. If the resistance is outside the specified range the EOT sensor is faulty and a new one must be fitted (see Chapter 2, Section 10).

9.8 Throttle body sensor wiring connector (arrowed)

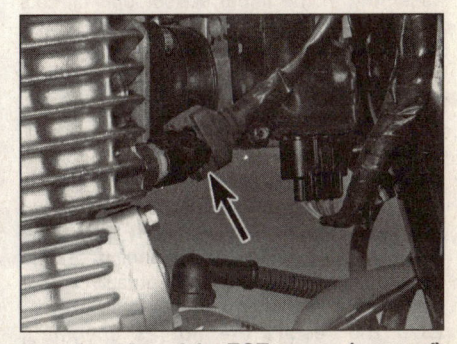

9.14 Location of the EOT sensor (arrowed)

9.33 Location of the fuel injector (arrowed)

9.38a Location of the oxygen sensor (arrowed)

9.38b Check the sensor connector (arrowed)

18 If the resistance is good, check for continuity in the yellow/blue wire between the ECM terminal 24 and the corresponding terminal in the EOT sensor connector, and in the green/orange wire between the ECM terminal 4 and the corresponding terminal in the EOT sensor connector. No continuity indicates a broken wire.

19 If the wiring is good, ensure the ECM and EOT sensor connectors are securely connected. Back-probe the ECM yellow/blue wire terminal 24 with the meter positive (+) probe and the green/orange wire terminal 4 with the meter negative (-) probe. Turn the ignition ON and check the output voltage. Turn the ignition OFF. A result within the range specified at the beginning of this Chapter indicates an intermittent fault or poor connector contacts.

20 If the result is not as specified it is likely the ECM is faulty – have it checked by a Honda dealer.

Removal and installation

21 Follow the procedure in Chapter 2, Section 10. Note that it is not necessary to remove the cylinder head – if necessary, displace the fuel pump (see Section 4) for access. Have a rag ready to catch any residual oil when the sensor is removed. Fit a new sealing washer on installation.

Throttle position (TP) sensor

Check

22 The TP sensor is located in the sensor unit on the left-hand side of the throttle body assembly. If the initial sensor unit checks (see Steps 5 to 9) have failed to identify a fault, re-connect both wiring connectors. Back-probe the ECM yellow wire terminal 5 with the meter positive (+) probe and the green/orange wire terminal 4 with the meter negative (-) probe. Turn the ignition ON and check the output voltage with the throttle fully closed and with the throttle fully open. Turn the ignition OFF. A result within the ranges specified at the beginning of this Chapter indicates an intermittent fault or poor connector contacts.

23 If the results are not as specified, disconnect the ECM and sensor unit wiring connectors. Check for continuity between the yellow wire terminal in the sensor connector and earth (ground). Continuity indicates a short circuit in the yellow wire.

24 Check for continuity in the yellow wire between the ECM terminal 5 and the corresponding terminal in the sensor connector. No continuity indicates a broken wire.

25 If the wiring is good, either the TP sensor or the ECM is faulty – have the components checked by a Honda dealer.

Removal and installation

26 The TP sensor is an integral part of the throttle body sensor unit (see Section 10).

Intake air temperature (IAT) sensor

Check

27 The IAT sensor is located in the sensor unit on the left-hand side of the throttle body assembly. If the initial sensor unit checks (see Steps 5 to 9) have failed to identify a fault, re-connect both wiring connectors. Back-probe the ECM grey/blue wire terminal 14 with the meter positive (+) probe and the green/orange wire terminal 4 with the meter negative (-) probe. Turn the ignition ON and check the output voltage. Turn the ignition OFF. A result within the range specified at the beginning of this Chapter indicates an intermittent fault or poor connector contacts.

28 If the result is not as specified, disconnect the sensor unit wiring connector (see illustration 9.8). Connect the meter positive (+) probe to the grey/blue wire terminal and the negative (-) probe to the green/orange wire terminal on the loom side of the connector. Turn the ignition ON and check the input voltage, then turn the ignition OFF.

29 If the input voltage is within the specified range, check the sensor resistance as follows. Connect the sensor unit wiring connector. Back-probe the ECM grey/blue wire terminal 14 and the green/orange wire terminal 4 and note the reading. A result within the range specified at the beginning of this Chapter indicates a faulty ECM – have it checked by a Honda dealer. If the result is outside the specified range the IAT sensor is faulty.

30 If the result is not as specified, check for continuity between the grey/blue wire terminal in the sensor connector and earth (ground). Continuity indicates a short circuit in the grey/blue wire.

31 Check for continuity in the grey/blue wire between the ECM terminal 14 and the corresponding terminal in the sensor connector. No continuity indicates a broken wire.

Removal and installation

32 The IAT sensor is an integral part of the throttle body sensor unit (see Section 10).

Fuel injector

33 The fuel injector is located on the top of the throttle body assembly (see illustration). Access to the injector wiring connector is extremely restricted – if required, follow the procedure in Section 10 to temporarily displace the throttle body assembly (see illustration 10.8).

34 To check the injector input voltage, first disconnect the wiring connector (see illustration 10.9). Connect the meter (+) probe to the black/blue wire terminal on the loom side of the connector and the negative (-) probe to earth (ground). Turn the ignition ON and check for battery voltage. Turn the ignition OFF. No voltage indicates a fault in the black/blue wire.

35 If the input voltage is good, check for continuity between the pink/green wire terminal on the loom side of the injector connector and earth (ground). Continuity indicates a short circuit in the pink/green wire.

36 Check for continuity in the pink/green wire between the ECM terminal 16 and the corresponding terminal in the injector connector. No continuity indicates a broken wire.

37 If the wiring is good, check the resistance between the injector terminals and compare the result with the specification at the beginning of this Chapter. If the resistance is outside the specified range the injector is faulty and a new one must be fitted (see Section 11). If the result is good it is likely the ECM is faulty – have it checked by a Honda dealer.

Oxygen sensor

38 The oxygen sensor is located above the exhaust manifold at the front of the engine unit (see illustration). Remove the fairing (see Chapter 7) and check that the sensor cap and sub-loom wiring connector are secure (see illustration).

39 Start the engine and warm it up to normal operating temperature, then check the FI warning light after a short test-ride. If the warning light has turned off, poor connector contacts were at fault.

40 If the warning light is still indicating an oxygen sensor fault, disconnect the sub-loom wiring connector and check for continuity between the black/orange wire terminal on the main loom side of the connector and earth (ground). Continuity indicates a short circuit in the black/orange wire.

41 Check for continuity in the black/orange wire between the ECM terminal 3 and the corresponding terminal in the connector. No continuity indicates a broken wire.

42 If the wiring is good, substitute a known good oxygen sensor and sub-loom for the existing ones (see Chapter 2, Section 10). Warm-up the engine and test ride the machine, then check the warning light again – if it has turned off, the original oxygen sensor and sub-loom were faulty. If the warning light is still indicating an oxygen sensor fault it is likely the ECM is faulty – have it checked by a Honda dealer.

Idle air control valve (IACV)

Check

43 The IACV is located on the right-hand side of the throttle body assembly (see illustration). Remove the right-hand side panel for access (see Chapter 7).

44 Back-probe the following pairs of ECM connector wire terminals and check the IACV resistance – brown/black wire terminal 20 and black/yellow wire terminal 21; brown/yellow wire terminal 31 and brown/white wire terminal 32. If the results are not within the range specified at the beginning of this Chapter the IACV is faulty.

45 If the results are within the specified range, disconnect the IACV wiring connector and check for continuity between each of the wire terminals on the loom side of the connector and earth (ground). Continuity indicates a short circuit in the wire tested.

46 Check for continuity in the individual wires between the ECM and the IACV connector – brown/black wire terminal 20, black/yellow wire terminal 21, brown/yellow wire terminal 31 and brown/white wire terminal 32. No continuity indicates a broken wire. If the wiring

9.43 Location of the IACV

is good it is likely the ECM is faulty – have it checked by a Honda dealer.

Removal and installation

47 Follow the procedure in Section 10. **Note:** *It is not necessary to remove the throttle body before removing the IACV.*

Tip over (TO) sensor

48 The TO sensor is located on the front, left-hand side below the fuel tank (see illustration). Remove the fairing (see Chapter 7) for access.

49 To check the input voltage, disconnect the sensor wiring connector, then connect the meter (+) probe to the yellow/red wire terminal on the loom side of the connector and the negative (-) probe to the green/orange wire terminal. Turn the ignition ON and check the input voltage. Turn the ignition OFF.

50 If the result is not within the range specified at the beginning of this Chapter, check for continuity between the yellow/red wire terminal in the sensor connector and earth (ground). Continuity indicates a short circuit in the yellow/red wire.

51 Back-probe the ECM yellow/red wire terminal 6 and check for continuity on the yellow/red wire between the ECM and the appropriate terminal in the sensor connector. Back-probe the ECM green/orange wire terminal 4 and check for continuity on the green/orange wire between the ECM and the appropriate terminal in the sensor connector. No continuity indicates a broken wire.

52 If the wiring is good it is likely the ECM is faulty – have it checked by a Honda dealer.

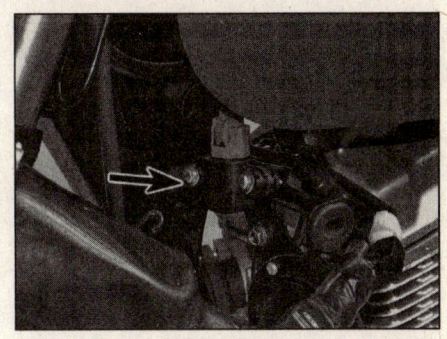

9.48 Location of the TO sensor (arrowed)

53 If the input voltage is as specified, check for continuity between the red/blue wire terminal on the loom side of the sensor connector and earth (ground). Continuity indicates a short circuit in the red/blue wire.

54 Back-probe the ECM red/blue wire terminal 26 and check for continuity on the red/blue wire between the ECM and the appropriate terminal in the sensor connector. No continuity indicates a broken wire.

55 If the wiring is good, reconnect the sensor wiring connector and test the operation of the sensor as follows. Back-probe the ECM red/blue wire terminal 26 with the meter positive (+) probe and the green/orange wire terminal 4 with the meter negative (-) probe. Undo the screws securing the sensor to its bracket (see illustration). Turn the ignition ON and check the output voltage, first with the senor held horizontally and then with it tilted at an angle between 50° and 60° (see illustrations).

56 Turn the ignition OFF. If the results are not within the ranges specified at the beginning of this Chapter the TO sensor is faulty and a new one must be fitted.

Removal and installation

57 Remove the fairing (see Chapter 7).

58 Disconnect the sensor wiring connector.

59 Undo the screws securing the sensor to its bracket, noting the location of the washers and spacers (see illustration 9.55a).

60 On installation, ensure the sensor is secured to its bracket with the UP mark facing up. Ensure the spacers and washers are correctly assembled and tighten the mounting screws securely.

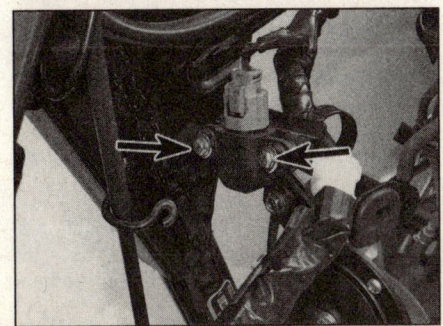

9.55a TO sensor mounting screws (arrowed)

9.55b Hold the sensor horizontally . . .

9.55c . . . and then tilted as described

4•12 Engine management system

ECM

61 The ECM is located behind the left-hand side panel **(see illustration 7.8a)**. Remove the seats and side panel (see Chapter 7) for access.

62 Failure of the ECM can only be determined conclusively by using a Honda Diagnostic System tester or by substituting it for a known good unit. If the problem is then rectified, the original unit is confirmed faulty. However, it is worthwhile checking the ECM wiring beforehand as follows.

63 Displace the ECM and disconnect the multi-pin wiring connector **(see illustrations 7.8b and c)**. Connect the meter positive (+) probe to the black/blue wire terminal 1 on the loom side of the connector and the negative (-) probe to earth (ground). Turn the ignition ON and check for battery voltage. Turn the ignition OFF.

64 If there is no voltage, first check the fuses, then check for a short circuit or break in the black/blue wire (see Chapter 8). If the fuses and wiring are good, check the operation of the ignition switch (see Chapter 8).

65 If battery voltage is shown, check for continuity between the green wire terminal 9 on the loom side of the connector and earth (ground). Similarly, check for continuity between the green wire terminal 10 and the green/black wire terminal 2 on the loom side of the connector and earth (ground). If all three checks indicate continuity it is likely the ECM is faulty – have it checked by a Honda dealer. No continuity indicates a broken wire.

Removal and installation

66 To remove the ECM follow the procedure in Section 7 **(see illustrations 7.8a, b and c)**.
67 Inspect the terminals on the ECM and inside the wiring connector for damage and corrosion.
68 Check the ECM holder for damage and deterioration and renew it if necessary.
69 On installation, align the wiring connector carefully, then press it into place ensuring it is secure.

10 Throttle body

> **Warning:** Refer to the precautions given in Section 1 before starting work.

Removal

1 Remove the seats and the side panels (see Chapter 7).
2 Follow the procedure in Section 3 to relieve the fuel pressure in the hose between the pump and the throttle body assembly, then disconnect the hose from the pump.
3 Disconnect the throttle cable from the pulley and the bracket on the throttle body assembly (see Section 12).
4 Disconnect the throttle body sensor unit wiring connector **(see illustration 9.8)**.
5 Disconnect the IACV wiring connector **(see illustration)**.
6 Loosen the clamp screw securing the throttle body assembly to the intake manifold **(see illustration)**. Note how the throttle body aligns with the manifold.
7 Loosen the clamp securing the intake duct to the throttle body and detach the duct **(see illustration)**.
8 Ease the throttle body assembly out from the intake manifold **(see illustration)**.
9 Pull back the boot and disconnect the fuel injector wiring connector **(see illustration)**.

Caution: Stuff clean rag into the cylinder head intake manifold after removing the throttle body assembly to prevent anything from falling inside.

10 To disconnect the fuel hose from the injector union, note the location of the rubber security cap on the end of the connector then pull the cap out of the connector **(see illustration)**. Squeeze the tabs on the green locking sleeve together to release the connector from the union **(see illustration)**.

10.5 Disconnect the IACV wiring connector

10.6 Loosen the manifold clamp screw (arrowed)

10.7 Loosen the intake duct clamp screw (arrowed)

10.8 Ease the throttle body assembly off

10.9 Disconnect the fuel injector wiring connector

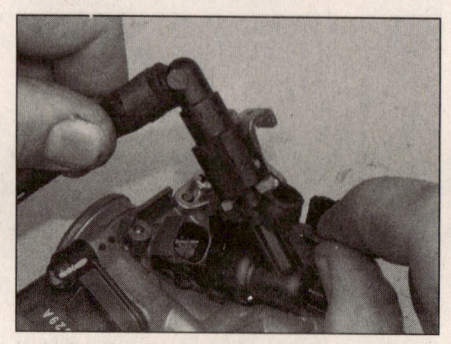

10.10a Pull the cap out of the connector

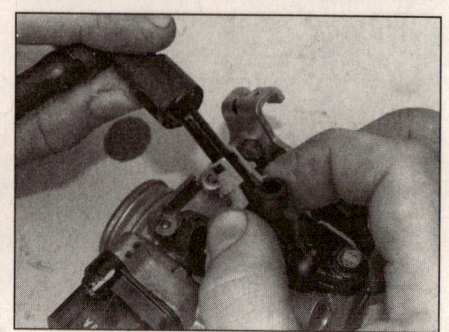

10.10b Release the connector from the union

Engine management system 4•13

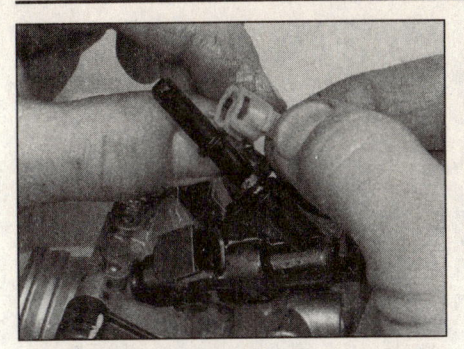

10.10c Remove the locking sleeve from the union

10.10d Draw off the security cap

10.13 Check the operation of the throttle pulley (arrowed)

Remove the locking sleeve, noting how it fits on the union **(see illustration)**. **Note:** *Honda recommends that a new locking sleeve is fitted whenever the fuel hose is disconnected.* Draw off the security cap, noting how it fits **(see illustration)**.

Inspection

Caution: The throttle body assembly must be treated as a complete unit. Do not loosen any nuts/bolts/screws other than as directed here or in Section 12 as they are pre-set at the factory to ensure correct operation. The only components on the assembly which may be removed are the sensor unit, IACV and fuel injector.

11 Clean the assembly with suitable solvent using a nylon-bristled brush to remove stubborn deposits.

Caution: Use only a dedicated carburettor cleaner or petroleum-based solvent for carburettor cleaning, following the manufacturer's instructions. DO NOT use caustic cleaners.

12 Inspect the throttle body for cracks or any other damage which may result in air leaks.

13 Check that the throttle pulley moves smoothly and freely in the body **(see illustration)**. Inspect the pulley shaft and throttle body for wear. Check the condition of the pulley shaft spring.

14 If required, remove the fuel injector (see Section 11).

15 If required, undo the screws securing the throttle body sensor unit using a suitable tamper-proof Torx bit **(see illustration)**. **Note:** *If the sensor unit is removed the TP sensor will have to be reset after the throttle body has been installed on the bike (see Steps 29 to 32).* Lift the sensor unit off carefully, noting how the throttle position sensor shaft locates over the end of the throttle shaft. Remove the sensor gasket and discard it as a new one must be fitted. Blow compressed air into the holes and air passages in the throttle body to ensure they are clear.

16 Prior to installation, install a new sensor unit gasket. Align the probe of the IAT sensor with its hole in the throttle body and ensure the throttle position sensor shaft is aligned with the end of the throttle shaft. Tighten the Torx screws securely.

17 If required, remove the IACV as follows. **Note:** *The IACV can be removed without removing the throttle body assembly – if not already done, disconnect the IACV wiring connector.* Undo the screws securing the IACV using a suitable Torx bit **(see illustration)**. Note the location of the set plate and remove it, then carefully draw the valve slide out from the throttle body noting how the slot in the slide fits on the pin in the housing **(see illustrations)**. Note how the slot in the set plate aligns with the tab on the back of the valve body **(see illustration)**.

18 To check the operation of the IACV, temporarily connect the wiring connector, then turn the ignition ON. The valve slide should rotate into the valve body and then out again. Turn the ignition OFF and disconnect the wiring connector.

19 Prior to installation, turn the valve slide clockwise until it seats on the body **(see**

10.15 Sensor unit is secured by Torx screws (arrowed)

10.17a IACV is secured by Torx screws (arrowed)

10.17b Remove the set plate

10.17c Note how the slide slot locates on the pin (arrowed)

10.17d Note how the set plate slot (arrowed) locates on the tab

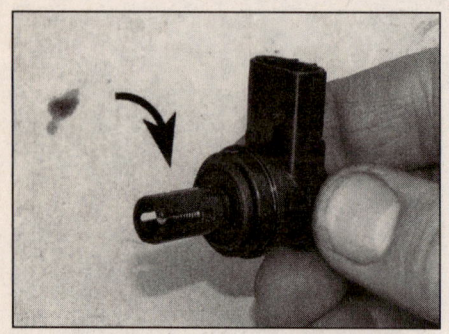

4•14 Engine management system

10.19 Turn the valve slide clockwise

10.22 Install the security cap

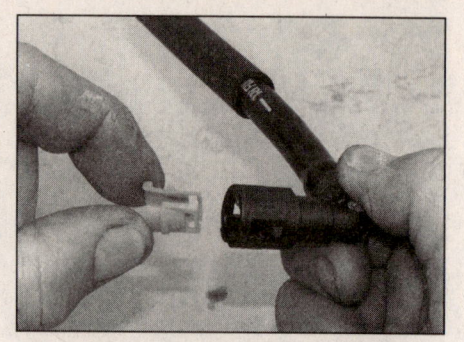

10.23a Fit a new locking sleeve

10.23b Ensure security cap is aligned with the locking sleeve . . .

10.23c . . . then press the connector on until the sleeve clicks

10.25a Press the throttle body into the manifold firmly

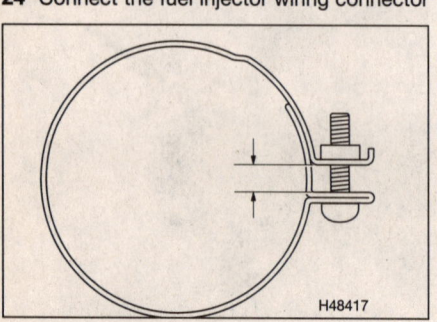

10.25b End clearance 7 to 9 mm when fully tightened

11.3a Undo the bolts (arrowed) . . .

illustration). Align the slot in the slide with the pin in the housing and install the IACV. Fit the set plate as noted on removal, then tighten the Torx screws securely.

20 Inspect the clamp on the intake manifold (see illustration 10.6) – if it is corroded or damaged it must be renewed. If the manifold is hardened or split new one should be fitted (see Chapter 2, Section 10).

Installation

21 If removed, install the fuel injector (see Section 11).

22 Ensure the rubber security cap is installed on the fuel hose union (see illustration).

23 Fit a new locking sleeve into the fuel hose connector (see illustration). Slide the connector onto the union, ensure the security cap is aligned with the locking sleeve, then press the connector on until the locking sleeve clicks into position (see illustrations).

24 Connect the fuel injector wiring connector and install the boot (see illustration 10.9).

25 Make sure the intake duct and manifold clamps are positioned correctly. Fit the intake duct over the end of the throttle body, then align the throttle body with the manifold and press it in firmly to ensure it is fully engaged – a squirt of WD-40 or a smear of oil will ease entry (see illustration). Tighten the clamp screws securely. Ensure that the clearance between the ends of the manifold clamp are as specified (see illustration).

26 Connect the throttle body sensor unit wiring connector and the IACV wiring connector (see Steps 4 and 5).

27 Install the throttle cable (see Section 12). Check the operation of the cable and adjust it as necessary (see Chapter 1).

28 Installation the remaining components in the reverse order of removal.

29 To reset the TP sensor, first follow the procedure in Section 8 to delete any fault codes using the SCS connector. On completion, turn the ignition OFF but leave the link wire connected.

30 Disconnect the EOT sensor wiring connector (see Section 9) and connect the terminals on the loom side of the connector using an insulated jumper wire. Turn the ignition ON, then immediately disconnect the jumper wire.

31 If the TP sensor has been reset the FI light will emit short (0.3 second) flashes. If the FI light remains on continuously the sensor has not been reset – repeat the procedure.

32 Once the sensor has been reset, turn the ignition OFF. Reconnect the EOT sensor connector, disconnect the SCS connector and install the DLC cap.

11 Fuel injector

Warning: Refer to the precautions given in Section 1 before starting work.

1 The fuel injector is located on the top of the throttle body assembly. A fault with the injector should be indicated by the FI warning light (see Section 8). Follow the procedure in Section 9 to test the injector.

Removal

2 Remove the throttle body assembly and disconnect the fuel hose from the injector union (see Section 10).

3 Undo the bolts securing the injector fuel union (see illustration). Carefully lift the fuel

Engine management system 4•15

11.3b ... and lift off the fuel union

11.4 Remove the lower seal

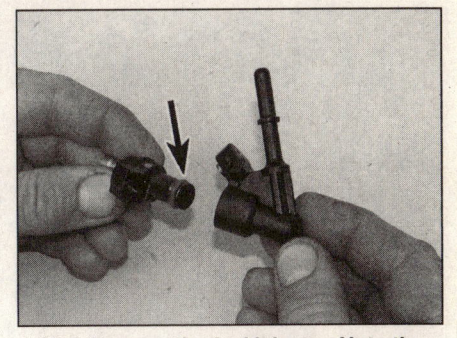

11.5 Remove the fuel injector. Note the O-ring (arrowed)

union off the throttle body – the fuel injector will come away with the union **(see illustration)**.
4 Note the location of the lower injector seal and remove it carefully **(see illustration)**.
5 Ease the injector out from the fuel union noting how it fits **(see illustration)**.
6 Remove the upper injector O-ring – discard the seal and O-ring as new ones must be fitted.
7 Inspect the end of the fuel injector for accumulations of carbon and signs of damage. Check that the terminals in the wiring connector are clean.
8 Modern fuels contain detergents which should keep the injector clean and free of gum or varnish from fuel residue. If the injector is suspected of being blocked, clean it through with injector cleaner. If the injector is clean but its performance is suspect, take it to a Honda dealer for assessment.

Installation

Note: Apply a smear of engine oil to the new seal and O-ring before reassembly.
9 Installation is the reverse of removal, noting the following:

- Install the new O-ring onto the injector carefully.
- Ensure the injector is correctly aligned with the fuel union before installation. Pres the injector in firmly taking care not to twist it **(see illustration 11.5)**.
- Install the new seal in the throttle body.
- Ensure the injector and fuel union are correctly aligned with the throttle body before installation **(see illustration 11.3b)**.
- Tighten the fuel union bolts evenly to the specified torque.
- Install the remaining components in the reverse order of removal.

12 Throttle cable

⚠ *Warning: Refer to the precautions given in Section 1 before proceeding.*

Removal

1 Remove the seats, the side panels and the fairing (see Chapter 7), then follow the procedure in Section 2 to remove the fuel tank.
2 Note the location of the throttle cable on the throttle pulley **(see illustration)**.
3 Loosen the upper locknut on the cable adjuster and free the adjuster from the bracket, noting how it locates **(see illustration)**. Disconnect the inner cable end from the pulley **(see illustration)**.

12.2 Note how the cable fits on the pulley (arrowed)

12.3a Free the cable adjuster (arrowed) from the bracket

12.3b Disconnect the cable end from the pulley

4•16 Engine management system

12.4 Upper cable adjuster (arrowed)

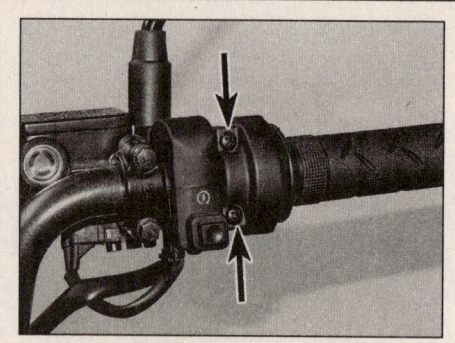

12.5a Undo the screws (arrowed) . . .

12.5b . . . and separate the halves of the housing

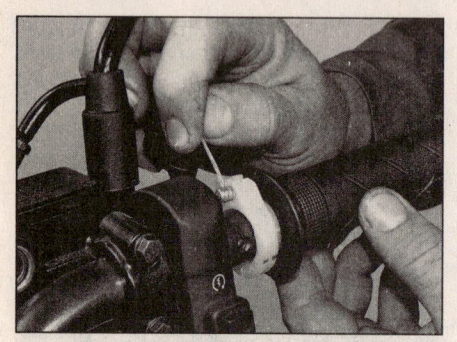

12.6a Detach the inner cable end from the twistgrip . . .

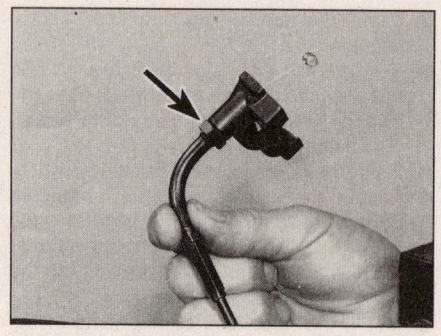

12.6b . . . then undo the cable elbow nut (arrowed)

12.7 Note routing of the throttle cable through guide (arrowed)

4 Pull back the boot to expose the adjuster at the upper end of the cable (see illustration). Loosen the adjuster locknut and turn the adjuster all the way in.

5 Undo the throttle twistgrip housing screws and separate the halves of the housing, noting how they align with the handlebar (see illustrations).

6 Detach the inner cable end from the twistgrip, then undo the cable elbow nut and separate the cable from the housing (see illustrations).

7 Note the routing of the cable around the steering head and through the guide on the frame, then take the cable off (see illustration).

Installation

8 Route the cable through the guides, then fit the upper end into the front half of the twistgrip housing and tighten the elbow nut finger-tight (see illustration 12.6b). Lubricate both ends of the inner cable with multi-purpose grease.

9 Fit the inner cable end onto the twistgrip (see illustration 12.6a). Assemble the twistgrip housing on the handlebar as noted on removal and tighten the housing screws securely (see illustrations 12.5b and a).

10 Turn the upper cable adjuster all the way in, then turn it out one turn.

11 At the lower end of the cable, fit the inner cable end onto the throttle pulley, then locate the adjuster on the bracket with the locknuts either side of the bracket (see illustrations 12.3b and a). Adjust the locknuts so the cable freeplay is as specified in Chapter 1 and tighten the locknuts.

12 Operate the throttle twistgrip to check that it opens and closes freely.

13 Turn the handlebars back-and-forth to make sure the cable doesn't cause the steering to bind.

14 Tighten the locknut on the upper cable adjuster, then slide the boot over the adjuster.

15 Install the remaining components in the reverse order of removal.

16 Start the engine and check that the idle speed does not rise as the handlebars are turned. If it does, the cable is routed incorrectly. Correct the problem before riding the motorcycle.

13 Exhaust system

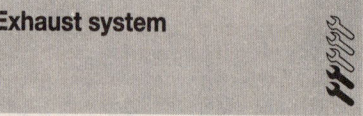

⚠️ *Warning: If the engine has been running the exhaust system will be very hot. Allow the system to cool before carrying out any work.*

Removal

1 On CBF125MD models onward remove the belly fairing (see Chapter 7).

2 Undo the nuts securing the header pipe flange and pull the flange off the exhaust studs (see illustrations). Undo the bolt securing the silencer to its mounting bracket,

13.2a Undo the nuts (arrowed) . . .

13.2b . . . and pull the flange off the exhaust studs

Engine management system 4•17

13.2c Undo the nut (arrowed)

13.3a Withdraw the bolt (arrowed) . . .

13.3b . . . and remove the exhaust system

13.4 Prise out the exhaust seal

13.5a Withdraw the spacer . . .

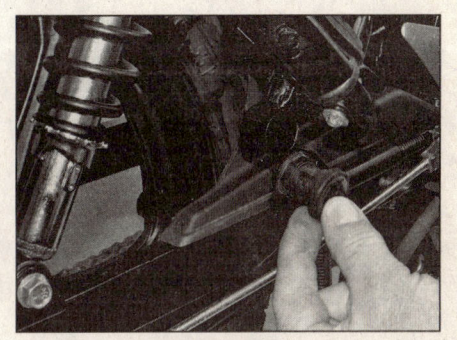

13.5b . . . and check the condition of the grommet

noting the location of the washer **(see illustration)**.

3 Support the exhaust system and withdraw the bolt, then lift the exhaust system off **(see illustrations)**.

4 Prise the exhaust seal out from the port and discard it as a new one must be fitted **(see illustration)**.

5 If required, withdraw the spacer from the silencer mounting bracket and check the condition of the grommet **(see illustrations)**. Replace the grommet with a new one if it is damaged or deteriorated.

Installation

6 Installation is the reverse of removal, noting the following:
- Apply a dab of grease to the exhaust seal to hold it in place **(see illustration 13.4)**.
- Apply a smear of copper grease to all nuts and studs to prevent them from seizing.
- Align the header pipe with the port, install the flange and nuts finger-tight, then fit the silencer mounting bolt.
- Ensure the system is correctly aligned before tightening any of the fixings.
- Tighten the header pipe flange nuts first, then the silencer mounting nut.

- Tighten the fixings to the torque settings specified at the beginning of this Chapter.
- Run the engine and check the system for leaks.

14 Catalytic converter

General information

1 A catalytic converter is incorporated in the exhaust system midway between the header pipe and the silencer to minimise the level of exhaust pollutants released into the atmosphere.

2 The catalytic converter consists of a heat tube impregnated with a catalyst material, over which the hot exhaust gases pass. Through chemical reactions it converts carbon monoxide, nitrous oxide and unburned hydrocarbons into carbon dioxide, nitrogen and water vapour

Precautions

3 The catalytic converter is a reliable and simple device which needs no maintenance in itself, but there are some facts of which an owner should be aware if the converter is to function properly for its full service life.

- DO NOT use leaded or lead replacement petrol (gasoline) – the additives will coat the precious metals, reducing their converting efficiency and will eventually destroy the catalytic converter.
- Always keep the ignition and fuel systems well-maintained in accordance with the manufacturer's schedule – if the fuel/air mixture is suspected of being incorrect have it checked on an exhaust gas analyser.
- If the engine develops a misfire, do not ride the bike at all (or at least as little as possible) until the fault is cured.
- DO NOT use fuel or engine oil additives – these may contain substances harmful to the catalytic converter.
- DO NOT continue to use the bike if the engine burns oil to the extent of leaving a visible trail of blue smoke.
- Remember that the catalytic converter is FRAGILE – do not strike or drop the exhaust system during servicing.

Notes

Chapter 5
Frame and suspension

Contents

	Section number
Footrests, brake pedal and gearchange lever	3
Fork oil change	7
Fork overhaul	8
Fork removal and installation	6
Frame inspection and repair	2
General information	1
Handlebars and levers	5
Handlebar switches	see Chapter 8
Rear shock absorbers	11

	Section number
Stands	4
Stand lubrication	see Chapter 1
Sidestand switch	see Chapter 8
Steering head bearing check and adjustment	see Chapter 1
Steering head bearings	10
Steering stem	9
Suspension check and adjustment	see Chapter 1
Swingarm	12

Degrees of difficulty

Easy, suitable for novice with little experience	Fairly easy, suitable for beginner with some experience	Fairly difficult, suitable for competent DIY mechanic	Difficult, suitable for experienced DIY mechanic	Very difficult, suitable for expert DIY or professional

Specifications

Front forks

Fork oil type	10 W fork oil
Fork oil capacity	146 ± 2.5 cc
Fork oil level*	167 mm
Fork spring free length	372.7 mm
Fork tube runout limit	0.2 mm

*Oil level is measured from the top of the tube with the fork spring removed and the leg fully compressed.

Torque settings

Footrest bracket bolts	39 Nm
Fork damper bolts	20 Nm
Fork top bolts	44 Nm
Fork top caps	22 Nm
Fork clamp bolts	32 Nm
Front brake master cylinder clamp bolts	9 Nm
Handlebar clamp bolts	12 Nm
Handlebar bracket nuts	39 Nm
Shock absorber top nut	34 Nm
Shock absorber bottom bolt	34 Nm
Sidestand pivot bolt	10 Nm
Sidestand pivot bolt nut	29 Nm
Steering head bearing adjuster	
Initial setting	25 Nm
Final setting	1.5 Nm
Steering stem nut	74 Nm
Swingarm pivot bolt nut	54 Nm

5•2 Frame and suspension

1 General information

All models have an open loop steel frame with a box-section steel swingarm.
Front suspension is by a pair of conventional, non-adjustable, oil-damped telescopic forks.
The rear swingarm is supported by twin shock absorbers which are adjustable for spring preload.

2 Frame inspection and repair

1 The frame should not require attention unless accident damage has occurred. In most cases, fitting a new frame is the only satisfactory remedy for such damage. Frame specialists have the jigs and other equipment necessary for straightening a frame to the required standard of accuracy, but even then there is no simple way of assessing to what extent it may have been over-stressed.
2 After a high mileage, the frame should be examined closely for signs of cracking or splitting at the welded joints. Loose engine mounting bolts can cause ovaling or fracturing of the mounting points. Minor damage can often be repaired by specialised welding, depending on the extent and nature of the damage.
3 Remember that a frame that is out of alignment will cause handling problems. If, as the result of an accident, misalignment is suspected, it will be necessary to strip the machine completely so the frame can be thoroughly checked.

3 Footrests, brake pedal and gearchange lever

Footrests

1 To remove a rider's footrest, first straighten and remove the split pin on the bottom of the footrest pivot pin and remove the washer (see illustration). Discard the split pin as a new one must be used.
2 Withdraw the pivot pin and lift off the footrest, noting the location of the spacer.
3 If required undo the bolt on the underside and remove the bottom plate, then separate the rubber from the peg. All components are available individually.
4 To remove the footrest brackets, follow the procedure in Steps 8 to 12 (right-hand side) and 16 to 22 (left-hand side).
5 To remove a passenger's footrest, follow the procedure in Steps 1 to 3 (see illustration).
6 The passenger's footrest brackets are bolted to the rear sub-frame (see illustration). Before removing the right-hand bracket, follow the procedure in Chapter 4 to remove the exhaust system.
7 Installation is the reverse of removal. Apply a small amount of multi-purpose grease to the pivot pin. Use new split pins on the pivot pins, and bend the ends as shown (see illustration 3.1).

Brake pedal assembly

8 The brake pedal assembly is mounted on the right-hand footrest bracket (see illustration 3.12a). Remove the exhaust system (see Chapter 4) for access.
9 Unhook the rear brake light switch spring from the brake arm behind the footrest bracket (see illustration).
10 Disconnect the brake rod from the brake arm on the rear brake backplate (see Chapter 6). Unhook the brake pedal return spring (see illustrations).
11 Undo the lower bracket mounting bolt (see illustration).

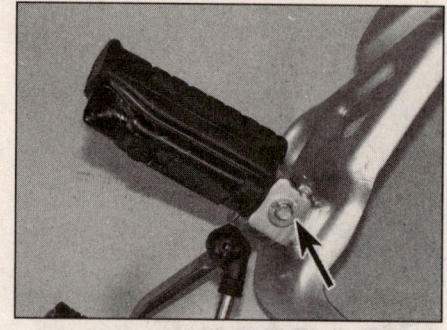

3.1 Remove the split pin and washer (arrowed)

3.5 Split pin and washer (arrowed) – passenger's footrest

3.6 Footrest bracket mounting bolts (arrowed)

3.9 Unhook the brake light switch spring (arrowed)

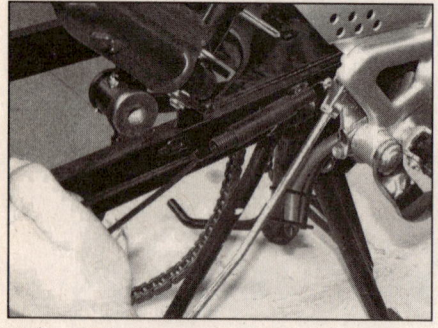

3.10a Unhook the pedal return spring . . .

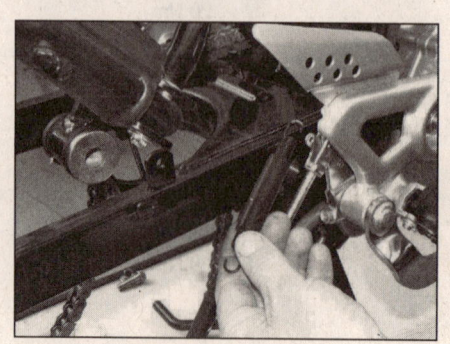

3.10b . . . and remove it

3.11 Location of the lower mounting bolt (arrowed)

Frame and suspension 5•3

12 Undo the nut on the swingarm pivot bolt and lift the bracket and brake pedal assembly off **(see illustrations)**.

13 To separate the brake rod from the brake arm, straighten and remove the split pin, then pull out the pivot pin **(see illustration)**. Discard the split pin as a new one must be used.

14 To remove the brake pedal and brake arm, first note the alignment marks on the arm and pedal shaft – if no marks are visible, make your own **(see illustration)**. Undo the pinch bolt and ease the arm off the shaft.

15 Installation is the reverse of removal, noting the following:
- Apply a small amount of multi-purpose grease to the brake pedal shaft and brake rod pivot pin.
- Align the brake arm with pedal shaft **(see illustration 3.14)** then tighten the pinch bolt securely.
- Use a new split pin on the brake rod pivot pin and bend the ends as shown **(see illustration 3.13)**.
- Tighten the bracket mounting bolt and swingarm pivot bolt nut to the torque settings specified at the beginning of this Chapter.
- Don't forget to reconnect the brake pedal return spring and rear brake light switch spring.
- Check the operation of the rear brake (see Chapter 1).

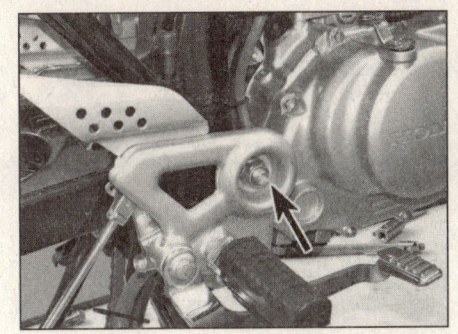

3.12a Undo the pivot bolt nut (arrowed) . . .

3.12b . . . and lift the assembly off

Gearchange lever assembly

16 Remove the front sprocket cover (see Chapter 6).

17 Note the position of the gearchange lever, rod and gearchange arm **(see illustration)**. Mark the alignment of the gearchange arm on the gearchange shaft **(see illustration)**. Undo the pinch bolt securing the gearchange

3.13 Brake rod pivot pin (arrowed)

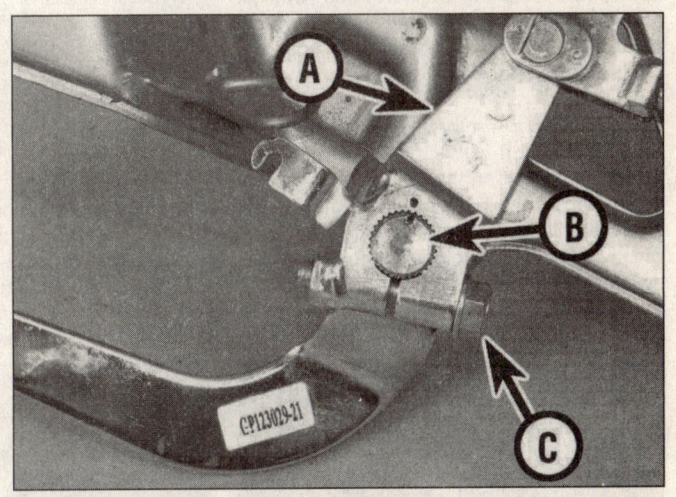

3.14 Alignment marks between brake arm (A) and pedal shaft (B). Note pinch bolt (C)

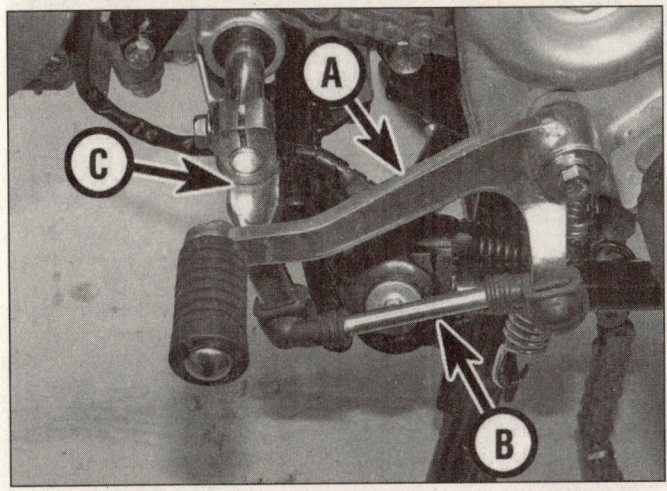

3.17a Note position of gearchange lever (A), rod (B) and gearchange arm (C)

3.17b Mark alignment between the gearchange arm and shaft

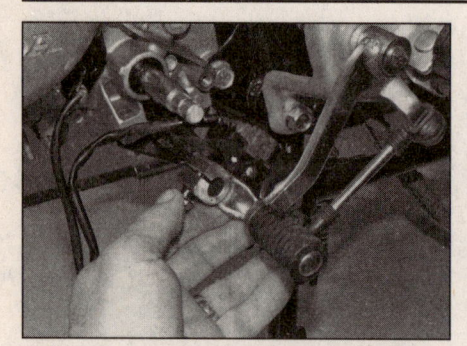

5•4 Frame and suspension

3.17c Draw the arm off the shaft

3.21 Location of the lower mounting bolt (arrowed)

4.1 Location of the sidestand springs (arrowed)

arm and draw the arm off the shaft **(see illustration)**.

18 Remove the bolt and washer securing the gearchange lever and lift the assembly off.

19 If required, displace the boots at both ends of the rod and remove the split pins and washers securing the rod to the gearchange lever and arm. Use new split pins on reassembly.

20 Before removing the left-hand footrest bracket it is necessary to remove the swingarm pivot bolt. If the rear wheel is in position, ensure it is supported before beginning the procedure.

21 Undo the lower bracket mounting bolt **(see illustration)**.

22 Undo the nut on the swingarm pivot bolt, then support the bracket and withdraw the bolt **(see illustrations 12.6a, b and c)**. Slide the pivot bolt back into position to support the swingarm.

23 Installation is the reverse of removal, noting the following:

- Tighten the bracket mounting bolt and swingarm pivot bolt nut to the torque settings specified at the beginning of this Chapter.
- Apply a small amount of multi-purpose grease to the gearchange lever pivot.
- Align the gearchange arm with the gearchange shaft **(see illustration 3.17b)** then tighten the pinch bolt securely.

4 Stands

Sidestand

1 The sidestand pivots on a bracket bolted to the underside of the crankcase. Springs between the bracket and the stand ensure that it is held in the retracted or extended position **(see illustration)**.

2 To remove the sidestand, support the bike using the centrestand or an auxiliary stand. Remove the seats and the left-hand side panel (see Chapter 7). Remove the front sprocket cover and chain guide (see Chapter 6, Section 16). Trace the wiring from the sidestand switch and disconnect the wiring connector inside the wiring boot **(see illustration)**. Release the wiring from any clips or ties and feed it back to the switch.

3 If required, remove the stand springs at this stage. Ensure the bike is supported securely, then unhook the lower end of the springs from the lug on the stand.

4 Undo the bolts securing the sidestand bracket and lift it off **(see illustrations)**.

5 Note how the peg on the sidestand locates on the switch, then undo the switch mounting bolt and washer and lift off the switch **(see illustrations)**.

6 Undo the pivot bolt locknut, then undo the pivot bolt and separate the stand from its bracket **(see illustration)**.

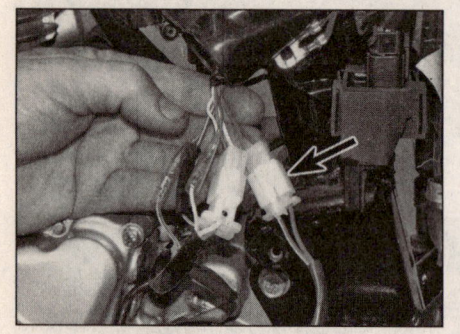

4.2 Disconnect the sidestand switch connector (arrowed)

4.4a Undo the mounting bolts . . .

4.4b . . . and remove the sidestand assembly

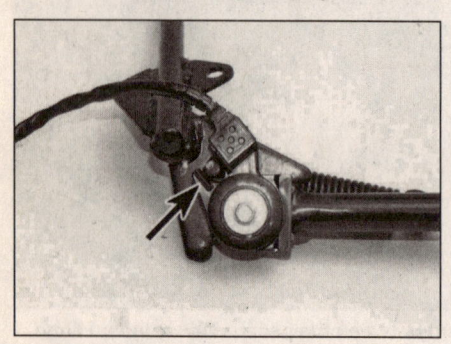

4.5a Note location of peg (arrowed) . . .

4.5b . . . then remove the switch

4.6 Location of pivot bolt locknut (arrowed)

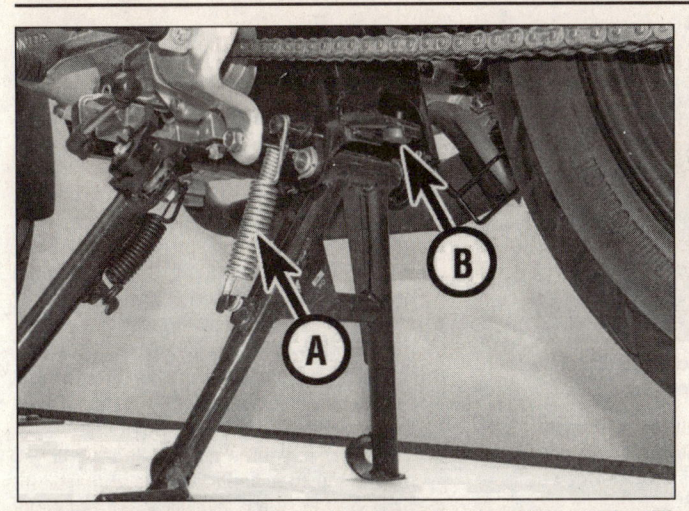

Frame and suspension 5•5

4.14 Location of the centrestand springs (A) and rubber cushion (B)

4.17 Remove the split pin and washer (arrowed)

7 Inspect the stand carefully for wear and damage. Clean the stand bracket and pivot bolt and inspect them for wear – fit a new bolt if necessary.

8 Prior to installation, lubricate the bracket and pivot bolt with multi-purpose grease. Fit the stand onto the bracket, tighten the pivot bolt to the torque setting specified at the beginning of this Chapter, then tighten the locknut to the specified torque. Check that the stand pivots freely around the bolt.

9 Install the sidestand switch ensuring it is correctly located around the peg on the stand. Tighten the switch bolt securely.

10 Install the sidestand bracket and tighten the mounting bolts securely.

11 If removed, hook the upper ends of the springs over the lug on the stand bracket, then pull the springs down carefully and hook them over the lug on the stand. It is essential that the springs are in good condition and capable of holding the stand up when not in use – an accident is almost certain to occur if the stand extends while the machine is in motion.

12 Reconnect the sidestand switch wiring connector and secure the wiring as noted on removal. Check the operation of the switch (see Chapter 1).

13 Install the remaining components in the reverse order of removal.

Centrestand

14 The centrestand pivots on a tube held between two brackets on the underside of the frame. Springs between the frame and the stand ensure that it is held in the retracted or extended position **(see illustration)**. When the stand is retracted the springs should hold it firmly against a rubber cushion on the underside of the frame.

15 To remove the centrestand, first remove the exhaust system (see Chapter 4).

16 Support the bike using an auxiliary stand. Ease the lower end of the springs off the lug on the stand, then remove the springs, noting how they fit.

17 Straighten and remove the split pin and washer securing the pivot tube – discard the split pin as a new one must be used **(see illustration)**.

18 Withdraw the pivot tube from the right-hand side and remove the stand.

19 Inspect the stand carefully for wear and damage. Clean off all old grease and corrosion. Inspect the pivot tube for wear and ensure the rubber cushion on the frame is in good condition. Renew any components as necessary.

20 Prior to installation, lubricate the pivot tube with multi-purpose grease. Fit the stand between the mounting brackets, slide in the pivot tube and secure it with the washer and a new split pin. Check that the stand pivots freely.

21 Install the springs. It is essential that the springs are in good condition and are capable of holding the stand up when not in use. A broken or weak spring is an obvious safety hazard.

5 Handlebars and levers

Handlebars

Note: *If required, the handlebars can be displaced without removing the switch housings, clutch lever or the front brake master cylinder.*

1 Support the machine securely in an upright position. If required, remove the fuel tank to avoid damaging its paintwork (see Chapter 4).

2 Remove the mirrors (see Chapter 7).

3 Undo the screws retaining the left and right-hand bar end-weights and remove the weights **(see illustration)**.

4 Disconnect the wiring connectors for the front brake light switch, then undo the front brake master cylinder clamp bolts and remove the back of the clamp **(see illustrations)**.

5.3 Remove the bar end-weights (arrowed)

5.4a Disconnect the brake light switch connectors

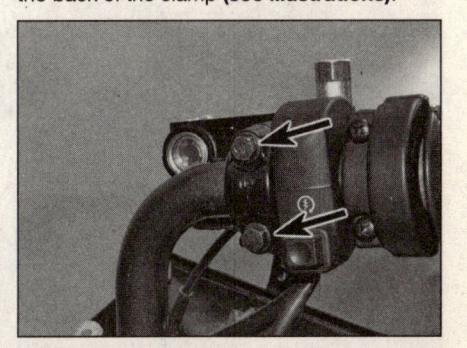

5.4b Front brake master cylinder clamp bolts (arrowed)

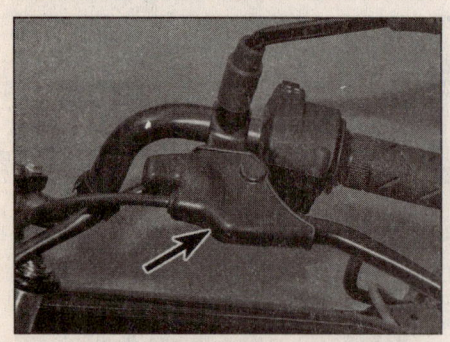

5•6 Frame and suspension

5.9a Displace the cover . . .

5.9b . . . and disconnect the clutch switch wiring connectors

5 Secure the master cylinder assembly clear of the handlebar and ensure no strain is placed on the brake hose. Keep the fluid reservoir upright to prevent air entering the system.

6 Follow the procedure in Chapter 4 to detach the throttle cable from the twistgrip. Slide the twistgrip off the handlebar.

7 Release any ties securing the wiring to the handlebars

8 Follow the procedure in Chapter 8 to separate the two halves of the right-hand switch housing and position them away from the handlebar.

9 Displace the cover from the clutch lever bracket and disconnect the wiring connectors for the clutch switch **(see illustrations)**.

10 Follow the procedure in Chapter 8 to separate the two halves of the left-hand switch housing and position them away from the handlebar.

11 Pull the left-hand grip off the handlebar. **Note:** *The grip will probably be stuck in place – it may be necessary to slit the grip with a sharp knife in order to remove it.*

12 Loosen the clutch lever bracket clamp bolt and slide the bracket off the handlebar.

13 If the handlebar brackets are to be removed, loosen the retaining nuts on the underside of the top yoke **(see illustration 9.11c)**.

14 Loosen the handlebar clamp bolts, then support the handlebars and remove the clamp **(see illustration)**. Lift the handlebars off. If required, remove the handlebar brackets **(see illustration)**.

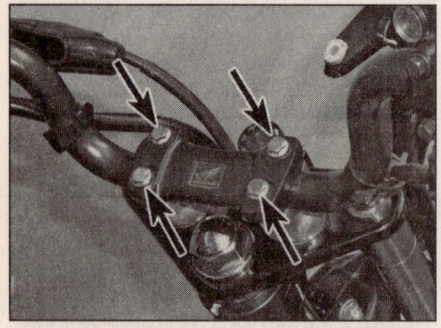

15 Installation is the reverse of removal, noting the following:

- If removed, install the handlebar brackets and tighten the retaining nuts finger-tight.
- Align the punch mark on the handlebars with the mating surface of the right-hand bracket **(see illustration 5.15a)**.
- Install the handlebar clamp with the punch marks at the front **(see illustration 5.14a)**.
- Tighten the clamp bolts to the torque setting specified at the beginning of this Chapter – tighten the front bolts first.
- If applicable, tighten the handlebar bracket nuts to the specified torque setting.
- Slide on the clutch lever bracket and align it with the punch mark on the underside of the handlebar. Tighten the bracket bolt securely.
- Follow the procedure in Chapter 8 to install the left-hand switch housing.
- Connect the clutch switch wiring connectors.
- If a new left-hand grip is being fitted, secure it with a suitable adhesive.
- Follow the procedure in Chapter 8 to install the right-hand switch housing.
- Install the twistgrip and throttle cable (see Chapter 4).
- Align the front brake master cylinder clamp joint with the punch mark on the top of the handlebar **(see illustration 5.15b)**. Install the back of the master cylinder clamp with the UP mark facing up. Tighten the clamp bolts to the specified torque setting – tighten the upper bolt first.
- Connect the front brake light switch wiring connectors.
- Secure the wiring to the handlebars as noted on removal.
- Check the operation of the front brake light switch and clutch switch before riding the motorcycle.

5.14a Handlebar clamp bolts (arrowed)

5.14b Location of handlebar brackets (arrowed)

5.15a Align punch mark (arrowed) with mating surface of bracket

5.15b Align clamp joint with the punch mark (arrowed)

Frame and suspension 5•7

Levers

16 To remove the front brake lever, first undo the pivot bolt locknut, then unscrew the bolt and remove the lever **(see illustrations)**.

17 To remove the clutch lever, first follow the procedure in Chapter 2 to disconnect the cable from the lever.

18 Undo the locknut on the underside of the lever **(see illustration)**, then unscrew the pivot bolt and remove the lever.

19 Installation is the reverse of removal, noting the following.
- Apply silicone grease to the contact area between the front brake master cylinder pushrod tip and the brake lever.
- Apply multi-purpose grease to the pivot bolts and the contact areas between the levers and their brackets.
- Tighten the pivot bolts securely first, then tighten the locknuts. Check the operation of the levers.
- Adjust clutch cable freeplay (see Chapter 1).

6 Fork removal and installation

Removal

1 Remove the fairing (see Chapter 7).
2 Displace the handlebars (see Section 5).
3 Remove the front wheel and secure the brake caliper to the machine so that it is clear of the front forks (see Chapter 6).
4 Remove the front mudguard (see Chapter 7).
5 Note the routing of the cables, hose and wiring around the fork legs.
6 Working on one fork leg at a time, remove the fork top bolt and washer, then loosen the fork clamp bolt in the bottom yoke **(see illustrations)**.
7 If the fork is to be disassembled, or if the fork oil is being changed, pull the leg down through the bottom yoke a short way and temporarily tighten the clamp bolt to hold the leg. Loosen the fork top cap **(see illustration)**. Now loosen the clamp bolt again.
8 Remove the fork leg by twisting it and pulling it down **(see illustration)**.

HAYNES HiNT *If the fork legs are seized in the yokes, spray the area with penetrating oil and allow time for it to soak in before trying again.*

Installation

9 Remove all traces of corrosion from the fork inner tube and the yokes. Make sure you install the fork legs the correct way round – the right-hand fork outer tube has the lugs to carry the brake caliper.
10 Slide the fork leg up through the bottom yoke and into the top yoke, making sure all cables, hoses and wiring are routed on the correct side of the tube. If the fork top cap has not been fully tightened, temporarily clamp the leg in the bottom yoke and tighten the cap to the torque setting specified at the beginning of this Chapter.
11 Slide the fork leg all the way up until

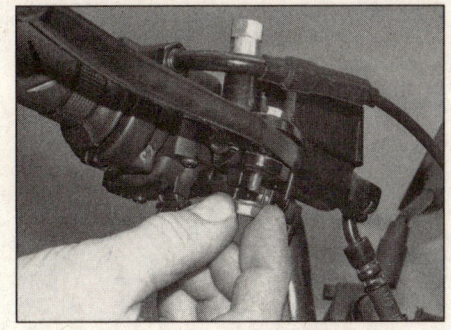

5.16a Undo the pivot bolt locknut . . .

5.16b . . . then unscrew the bolt . . .

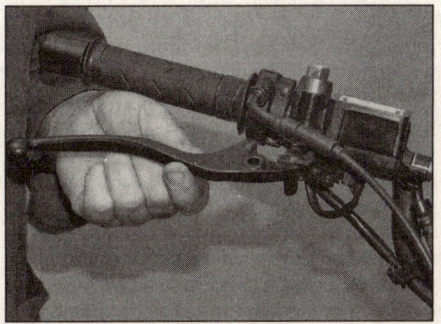

5.16c . . . and remove the lever

5.18 Unscrew the clutch lever pivot locknut (arrowed)

6.6a Remove the fork top bolt and washer

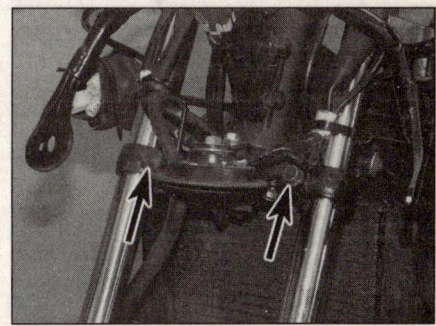

6.6b Bottom yoke fork clamp bolts (arrowed)

6.7 Loosen the fork top cap

6.8 Removing the fork leg

6.11 Push fork top cap (arrowed) fully into the yoke

7.3 Unscrew the fork top cap

the top cap is located in the top yoke **(see illustration)**. Install the top bolt and washer and tighten the bolt to the specified torque.
12 Tighten the fork clamp bolts to the specified torque.
13 Install the remaining components in the reverse order of removal.
14 Check the operation of the front forks and brake before riding the motorcycle.

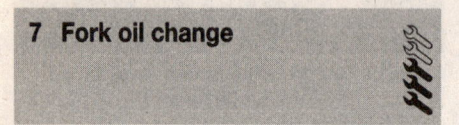

7 Fork oil change

1 After a high mileage the fork oil will deteriorate and its damping and lubrication qualities will be impaired. Always change the oil in both fork legs.
2 Follow the procedure in Section 6 to remove the fork legs, ensuring the top caps are loosened as described.
3 Working on one fork leg at a time, support the leg in an upright position and unscrew the cap **(see illustration)**. Note: *The cap is under pressure from the fork spring so use a ratchet tool that does not need to be removed from the cap as you unscrew it. Maintain some downward pressure on the cap, particularly as you come to the end of the threads.*
4 Note the location of the O-ring on the cap and discard it as a new one must be fitted **(see illustration)**.
5 Compress the fork inner tube down into the outer tube and remove the spacer, the spring seat and spring **(see illustrations)**. Note which way up the spring is fitted. Wipe any excess oil off the spring.

6 Invert the fork leg over a suitable container and pump the fork to expel as much oil as possible. Support the fork upside down in the container and allow it to drain for a few minutes. If the oil contains metal particles inspect the internal components for wear (see Section 8).
7 Hold the fork leg upright and slowly pour in the specified quantity of the correct grade of fork oil (see Specifications at the beginning of this Chapter) **(see illustration)**. Pump the fork up-and-down several times to expel any trapped air, then compress the inner tube fully and measure the oil level to the top of the tube **(see illustration)**. Add or subtract oil until it is at the specified level.
8 Pull the inner tube up and install the spring with its closer-wound coils at the bottom **(see illustration 7.5c)**.
9 Install the spring seat and the spacer **(see illustration 7.5b and a)**.
10 Fit a new O-ring into the groove in the top cap and lubricate it with a smear of fork oil, then thread the cap into the fork tube, compressing the spring as you do. Keep downward pressure on the spring and ensure the cap is not cross-threaded **(see illustration 7.3)**. The cap can be tightened fully to the specified torque setting once the leg has been installed and is securely held in the bottom yoke.
11 Install the fork legs (see Section 6).

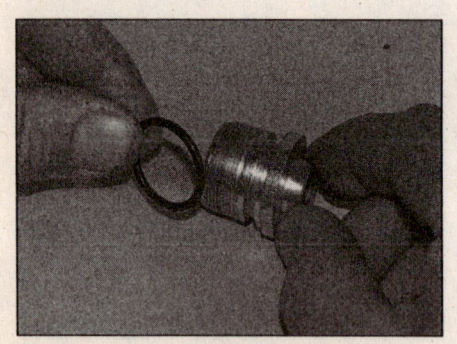

7.4 Note location of the O-ring

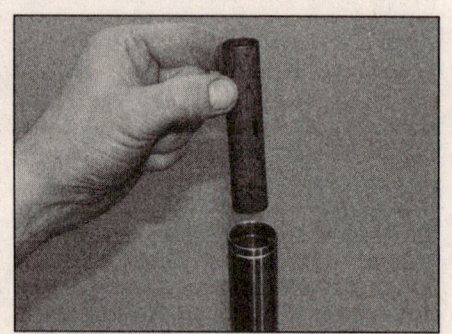

7.5a Remove the spacer . . .

7.5b . . . the spring seat . . .

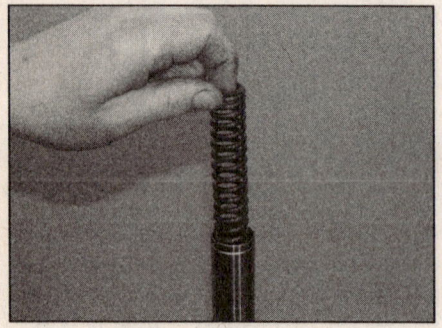

7.5c . . . and spring

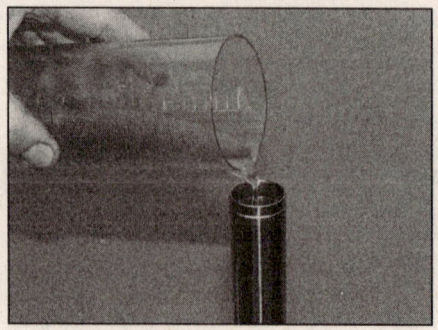

7.7a Pour the oil into the tube . . .

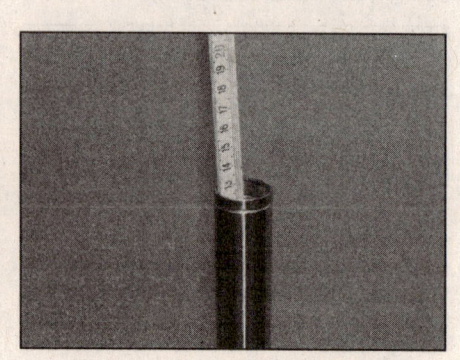

7.7b . . . then measure the level

Frame and suspension 5•9

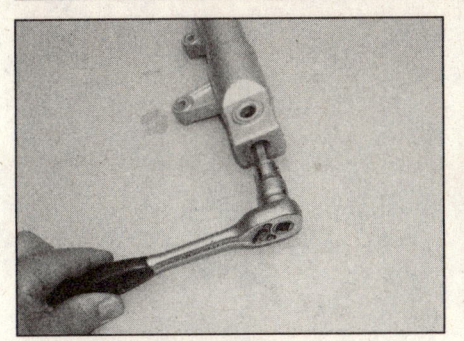

8.3 Loosen the damper bolt

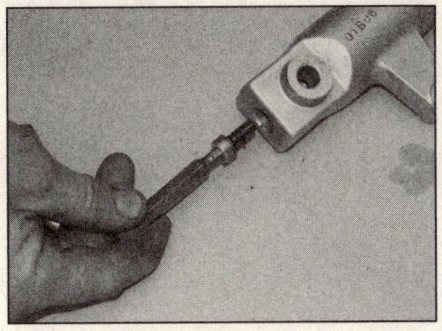

8.5 Remove the damper bolt and sealing washer

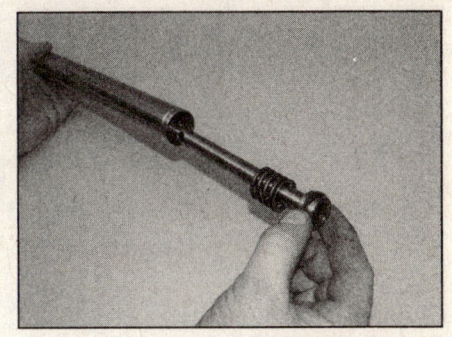

8.6 Tip out the damper and rebound spring

8 Fork overhaul

Disassembly

1 Follow the procedure in Section 6 to remove the fork legs, ensuring the top caps are loosened as described.
2 Always dismantle the fork legs separately to avoid interchanging parts. Store all components in separate, clearly marked containers.
3 Start by loosening the damper bolt in the underside of the outer tube **(see illustration)**. To prevent the damper from turning inside the leg, hold the fork leg upside-down and compress it so that the spring exerts maximum pressure on the damper. If the bolt will not loosen, or the damper turns inside the leg, try again once the spring has been removed (see Step 5). Alternatively, use an air-wrench if available.
4 Follow the procedure in Section 7 to unscrew the top cap and remove the spacer, the spring seat and spring, then drain the oil out of the fork leg.
5 Remove the previously loosed damper bolt and its sealing washer **(see illustration)**. Discard the sealing washer as a new one must be used. If the damper bolt was not loosened earlier, insert a length of wood doweling, tapered on the end to engage the head of the damper, into the fork leg. Press the leg down onto the doweling and undo the bolt.
6 Tip the damper and rebound spring out of the fork leg **(see illustration)**.
7 Carefully prise out the dust seal from the top of the outer tube **(see illustration)**. Discard the seal as a new one must be used.
8 Withdraw the inner tube from the outer tube, then tip out the damper seat noting which way up it fits **(see illustrations)**.
9 Remove the oil seal retaining clip, taking care not to scratch the surface of the inner tube **(see illustration)**.
10 Prise out the oil seal from the outer tube using either a seal hook or an internal puller with slide-hammer attachment **(see illustrations)**. Take care not to damage the seal housing. Discard the seal as a new one must be used.

Inspection

11 Clean all parts in solvent and blow them dry with compressed air, if available. Examine the inner tube for score marks, scratches, flaking of the chrome finish and excessive or abnormal wear. Look for dents in the tube and

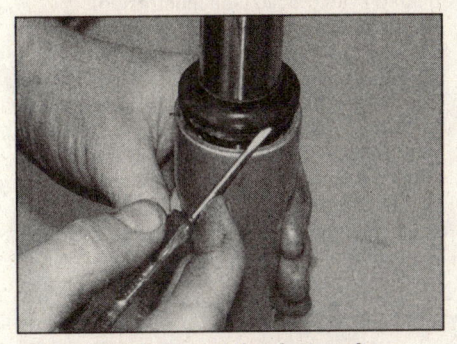

8.7 Prise out the dust seal

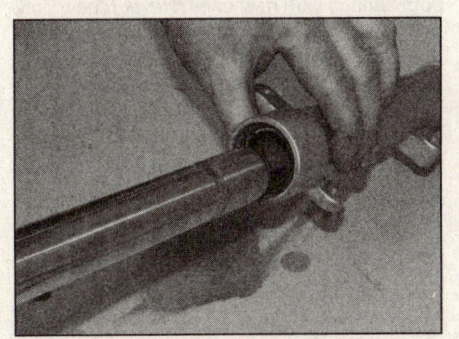

8.8a Separate the fork tubes . . .

8.8b . . . then tip out the damper seat

8.9 Remove the oil seal retaining clip

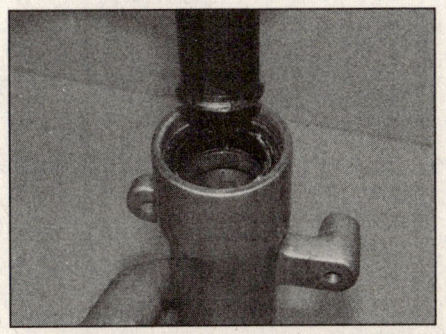

8.10a Locate the puller under the oil seal then expand the puller . . .

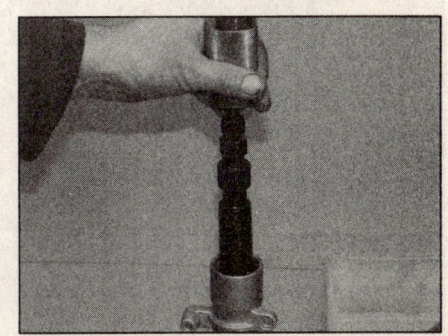

8.10b . . . and jar the seal out using the slide-hammer attachment

5•10 Frame and suspension

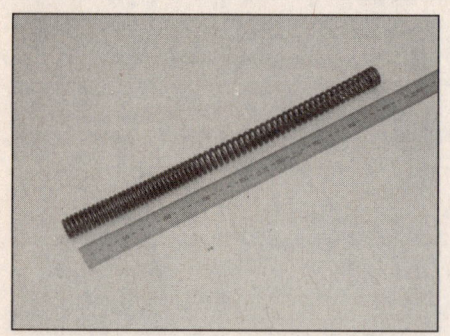

8.14 Measure the free length of the spring

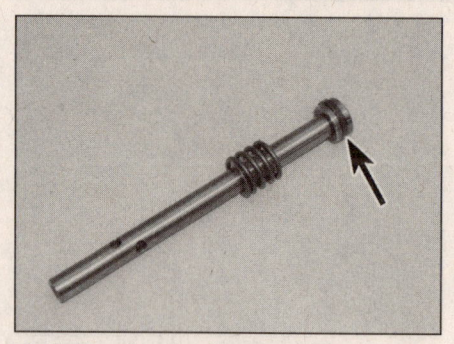

8.15 Examine the damper and piston ring (arrowed)

8.16a Fit the oil seal . . .

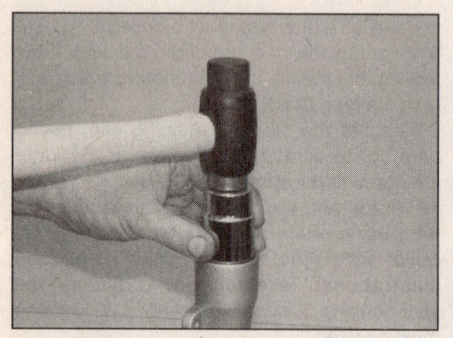

8.16b . . . and drive it into place

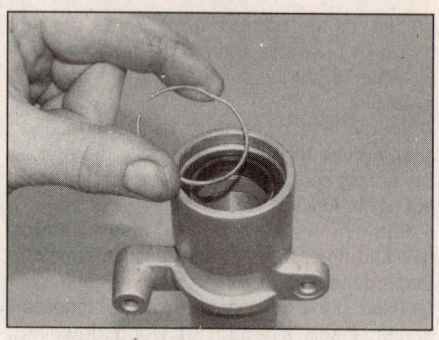

8.17 Fit the seal retaining clip

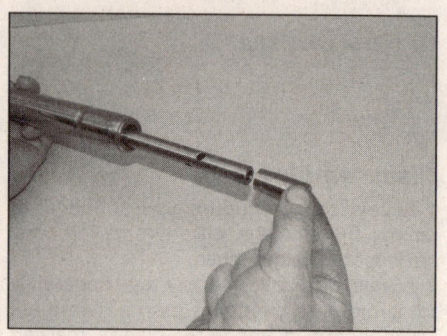

8.18a Fit the seat on the bottom of the damper . . .

replace the tube in both forks if any are found.
12 Check the inner tube runout using V-blocks and a dial gauge, or have it done by a Honda dealer. If the amount of runout exceeds the service limit specified, the tube should be renewed.

⚠ **Warning:** *If the tube is bent or exceeds the runout limit, it should not be straightened; replace it with a new one.*

13 Examine the internal surface of the outer tube for score marks, scratches and excessive or abnormal wear and renew the outer tube if necessary. Examine the fork seal housing in the top of the outer tube for nicks, gouges and scratches. If damage is evident, leaks will occur.

14 Check the fork spring for cracks and other damage. Measure the spring free length and compare the result to the specification at the beginning of this Chapter **(see illustration)**. If the spring is defective or has sagged, replace both springs with new ones. Never renew only one spring. Also check the rebound spring.
15 Check the damper and its piston ring for damage and wear, and renew them if necessary **(see illustration)**. Do not remove the ring from the piston unless it requires renewal.

Reassembly

16 Lubricate the new oil seal with a smear of fork oil, then press it squarely into its housing in the top of the outer tube – the markings on the seal should face upwards. Use a driver or suitable socket to drive the seal in until it seats and the retaining clip groove is visible above it **(see illustrations)**.
17 Fit the retaining clip ensuring it is correctly located in its groove **(see illustration)**.
18 If removed, install the new piston ring into the groove in the damper, then slide the rebound spring onto the damper **(see illustration 8.15)**. Insert the damper into the top of the inner tube and slide it down so that it projects fully from the bottom of the tube, then install the damper seat **(see illustrations)**.
19 Lubricate the inner tube with fork oil, then insert the assembly into the outer tube **(see illustration)**.
20 Clean the threads of the damper bolt and

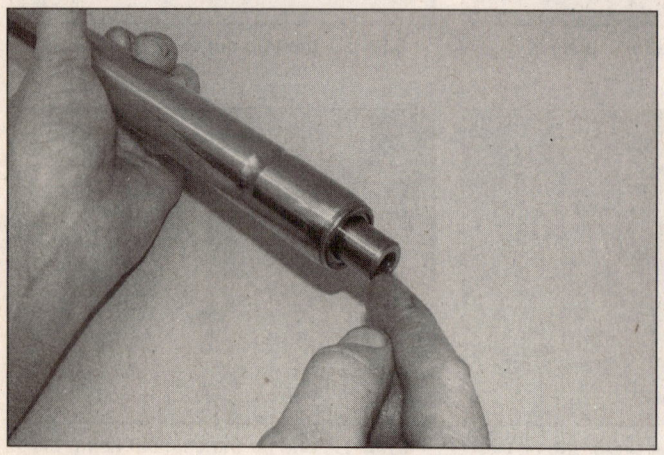

8.18b . . . then push it into the bottom of the inner tube

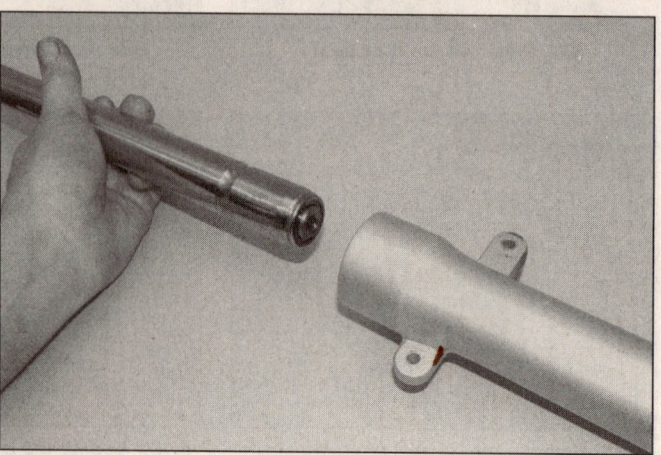

8.19 Assemble the fork tubes

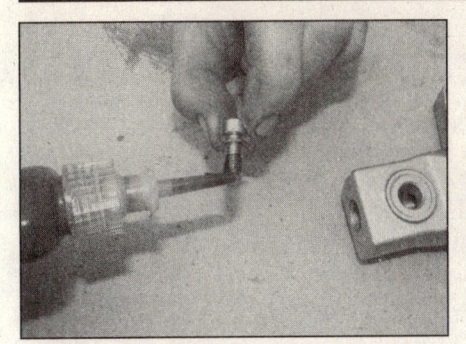

Frame and suspension 5•11

8.20a Fit the bolt using threadlock and a new sealing washer ...

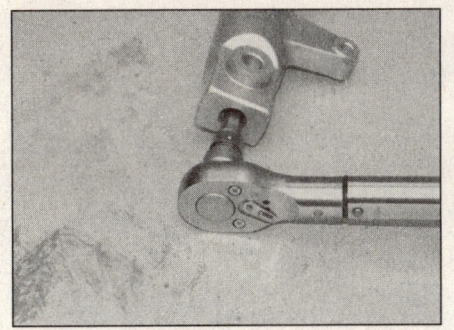

8.20b ... and tighten it to the specified torque

8.21 Install the new dust seal

apply a few drops of a suitable non-permanent thread-locking compound. Fit a new sealing washer to the damper bolt, then install the bolt into the bottom of the outer tube and tighten it to the torque setting specified at the beginning of this Chapter **(see illustrations)**. If the damper rotates inside the tube, hold it with spring pressure or a wooden dowel as on disassembly (see Steps 3 and 5).

21 Compress the fork leg fully, then lubricate the inside of the new dust seal with fork oil, slide it down the inner tube and press it into position **(see illustration)**.

22 Follow the procedure in Section 7 to fill the fork with the specified quantity of oil, then install the spring, spring seat, spacer and top cap.

23 Follow the procedure in Section 6 to install the fork legs.

9 Steering stem

Removal

Note: *Uncaged ball bearings are fitted. When the steering stem is removed, hold a suitable contained below the steering head to catch the ball bearings if they fall out.*

Special tool: *A peg spanner will be required to tighten the bearing adjuster nut to the specified torque setting (see Step 18).*

1 Remove the fairing (see Chapter 7).
2 Displace the handlebars (see Section 5).
3 Remove the front wheel and secure the brake caliper to the machine so that it is clear of the front forks (see Chapter 6).
4 Undo the bolt securing the front brake hose guide to the bottom yoke **(see illustration)**.
5 Remove the front mudguard (see Chapter 7).
6 Trace the wiring from the ignition switch on the underside of the top yoke and disconnect it at the connector **(see illustration)**. Free the wiring from any clips or ties and feed it back to the switch.
7 Undo the screws securing the switch cover **(see illustration 9.6)** and remove the cover **(see illustration)**.
8 Undo the bolts securing the cable guide and remove the guide **(see illustration)**.
9 Loosen the steering stem nut **(see illustration)**.

9.4 Bolt (arrowed) secures front brake hose guide

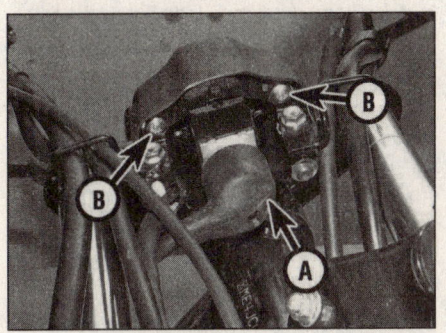

9.6 Ignition switch wiring (A), cover screws (B)

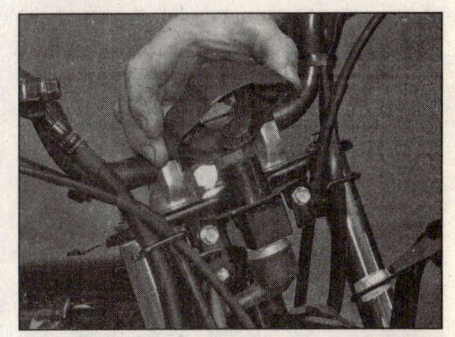

9.7 Remove the ignition switch cover

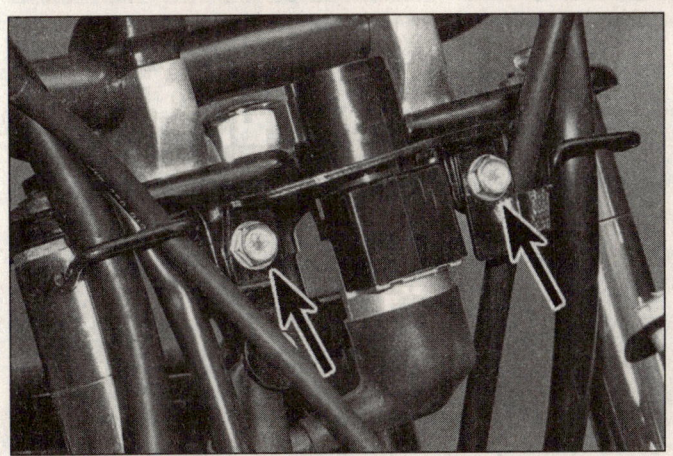

9.8 Bolts (arrowed) secure cable guide

9.9 Loosen the steering stem nut (arrowed)

5•12 Frame and suspension

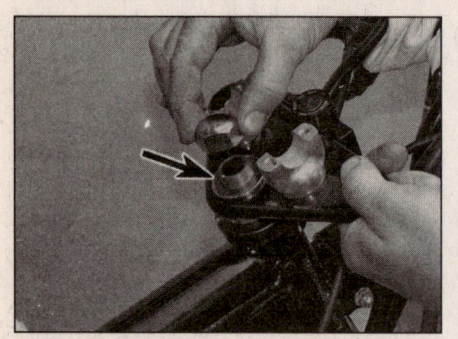

9.11a Remove the steering stem nut and washer (arrowed)

9.11b Lift off the top yoke

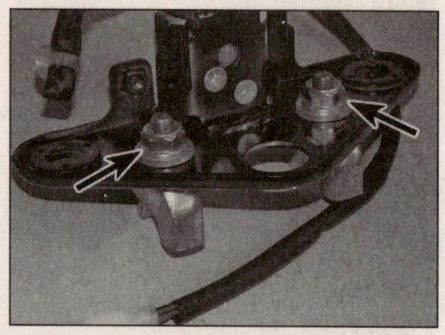

9.11c Nuts (arrowed) secure the handlebar brackets

10 Follow the procedure in Section 6 to remove the front fork legs.

11 Unscrew the steering stem nut and remove the washer **(see illustrations)**. Lift the top yoke up off the steering stem **(see illustration)**. Note the location of the nuts securing the handlebar brackets **(see illustration)**.

12 Support the bottom yoke and unscrew the bearing adjuster using a C-spanner if required **(see illustration)**. Note the location of the cover on the adjuster.

13 Lift off the upper bearing inner race **(see illustration)**. Note the location of the ball bearings in the upper outer race. **Note:** *There are 18 ball bearings in both steering head races. If the grease has been washed out of the bearings they may fall out when the steering stem is removed. Use a magnetic tool to retrieve the ball bearings.*

14 Carefully lower the steering stem out of the steering head – be prepared to catch any loose ball bearings **(see illustration)**.

15 Remove all traces of old grease from the bearings and races using a suitable solvent, then check them for wear or damage as described in Section 10.

Installation

16 Apply a liberal quantity of grease to the bearing races in the frame and on the steering stem. Stick the lower bearing balls into the grease on the steering stem inner race and the upper bearing balls into the grease on the steering head outer race **(see illustrations)**.

17 Lift the steering stem up through the steering head and install the upper bearing inner race **(see illustration 9.13)**. Press the race down firmly, then thread the combined adjuster and cover onto the stem and tighten it finger-tight **(see illustration)**.

18 If the Honda service tool (Part No. 07702-0020001) or a suitable peg spanner and a torque wrench are available, tighten the adjuster to the initial torque setting specified at the beginning of this Chapter. Turn the steering stem through its full lock several times to settle the bearings, then slacken the adjuster completely. Tighten the adjuster to the final torque setting.

19 If the special tools are not available, a peg spanner can be made by cutting castellations

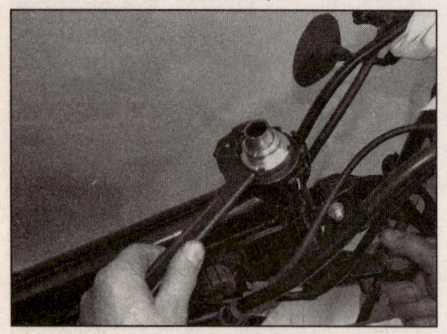

9.12 Unscrewing the bearing adjuster using a C-spanner

9.13 Remove the upper bearing inner race

9.14 Lower the steering stem out – note the ball bearings (arrowed)

9.16a Assemble the lower ball bearings on the stem . . .

9.16b . . . and the upper ball bearings in the steering head

9.17 Install the adjuster finger-tight

Frame and suspension 5•13

into an old socket **(see illustration)**. Alternatively, tighten the adjuster using a C-spanner so that bearing play is eliminated but the steering is able to move freely from lock-to-lock, then slacken the nut so that it is loose. Now tighten it lightly – the nut must be literally on the point of being loose.

Caution: Take great care not to apply excessive pressure because this will cause premature failure of the bearings.

20 Fit the top yoke onto the steering stem, then fit the steering stem nut with its washer and tighten it finger-tight **(see illustrations 9.11b and a)**. Temporarily install the fork legs to align the top and bottom yokes, but do not tighten the bottom yoke clamp bolts. Now tighten the steering stem nut to the torque setting specified at the beginning of this Chapter.

21 Install the remaining components in the reverse of the removal.

22 Recheck the steering head bearing adjustment as described in Chapter 1.

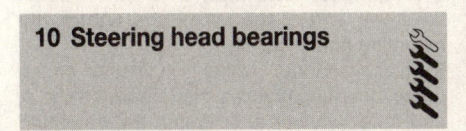

10 Steering head bearings

Note: *Do not attempt to remove the outer races from the steering head or the lower inner race from the steering stem unless they are to be renewed.*

Inspection

1 Remove the steering stem (see Section 9).
2 Remove all traces of old grease from the ball bearings and races using a suitable solvent, then inspect them for wear or damage.
3 The inner and outer races should be polished and free from indentations **(see illustrations)**. The bearing balls should be polished and free from signs of wear, pitting or discoloration (see *Bearing fault finding* in the *Reference* section).
4 If there are any signs of wear on any of the bearing components, both upper and lower bearing assemblies must be renewed as a set. **Note:** *Once the outer races in the steering head and the lower bearing inner race have been removed they should be discarded – do not reuse them.*

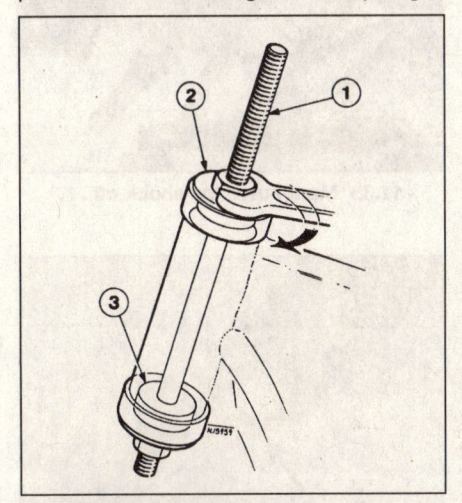

Renewal

5 The outer races are an interference fit in the steering head – tap them from position using a suitable drift located on the exposed inner lip of the race **(see illustration)**. Tap firmly and evenly around each race to ensure that it is driven out squarely. Curve the end of the drift slightly to improve access if necessary. Alternatively, remove the outer races using a bearing puller with slide-hammer attachment (see *Tools and Workshop Tips* in the *Reference* section).

6 Install the new outer races using a drawbolt arrangement **(see illustration)**. Ensure the drawbolt washer rests only on the outer edge of the race and does not contact the bearing surface. Ensure both races are drawn all the way into their seats.

> **HAYNES HiNT** *Installation of new bearing outer races is made much easier if the races are left overnight in the freezer. This causes them to contract slightly making them a looser fit. Alternatively, use a freeze spray.*

7 To remove the lower inner race from the steering stem, use two screwdrivers placed on opposite sides to work it free, using blocks of wood to improve leverage and protect the yoke, or tap under it using a cold chisel **(see illustrations)**. If you use a cold chisel, fit the

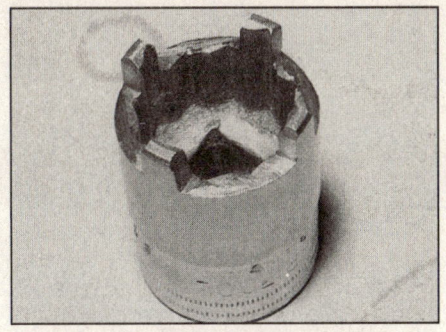

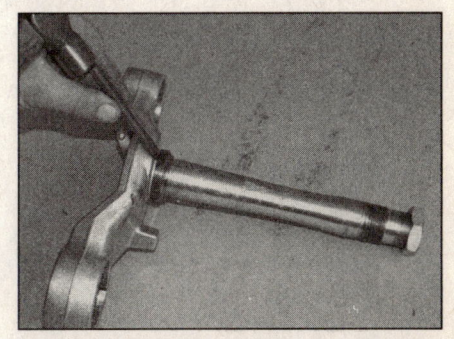

9.19 A peg spanner can be made by cutting castellations into an old socket

10.3a Inspect the inner . . .

10.3b . . . and outer bearing races

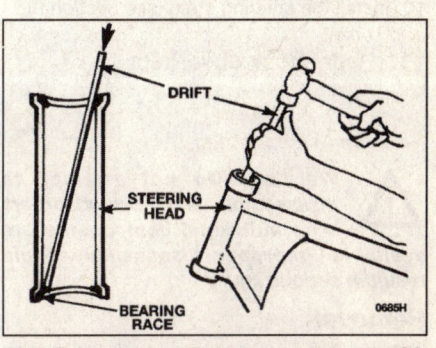

10.5 Drive the bearing outer races out with a brass drift as shown

10.6 Drawbolt arrangement for fitting steering head bearing outer races

1 Long bolt or threaded bar
2 Thick washer
3 Guide for lower outer race

10.7a Removing the lower inner race using screwdrivers

10.7b Removing the lower inner race with a cold chisel

5•14 Frame and suspension

steering stem nut to protect the threads on the end of the stem. If the race is firmly in place it will be necessary to use a puller **(see illustration)**, or split the race using an angle grinder – be very careful not to gouge the steering stem

8 Remove the dust seal from the bottom of the stem and replace it with a new one.

9 Fit the new lower inner race onto the steering stem. Tap the new race into position using a length of tubing with an internal diameter slightly larger than the steering stem **(see illustration)**. Ensure that the drift rests only on the inner edge of the race and does not contact the bearing surface.

10 Install the steering stem (see Section 9).

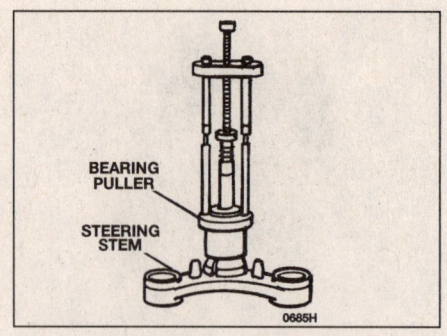

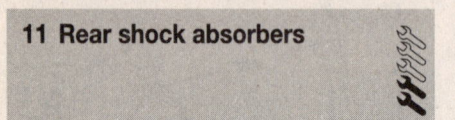

11 Rear shock absorbers

Warning: Do not attempt to disassemble the shock absorbers – no individual components are available. Improper disassembly could result in serious injury.

Removal

1 Support the machine securely in an upright position. Position a support under the rear wheel so that it does not drop when the shock absorbers are removed, but also making sure that the weight of the machine is off the rear suspension so that the shocks are not compressed.

2 Working on one side at a time, unscrew the lower shock absorber mounting bolt **(see illustration)**.

3 Undo the upper shock absorber mounting nut and washer **(see illustration)**. Pull the shock towards the rear of the bike so that it is free of the lower mounting bracket, and then pull it off the upper mounting bracket **(see illustration)**. Note the location of the inner washer on the upper mounting bracket **(see illustration)**.

Inspection

4 Inspect the shock absorbers for obvious physical damage and oil leakage. Check the springs for looseness, cracks or signs of fatigue **(see illustration)**. If either shock absorber is in any way faulty, renew both shocks as a pair.

5 Ensure that the spring pre-load adjusters are clean and free from corrosion **(see illustration)**. Using the C-spanner from the bike's toolkit, check that the adjusters move freely.

6 Inspect the bushes in the upper and lower shock absorber mounts for wear or damage and renew them if necessary.

Installation

7 Working on one side at a time, install the lower end of the shock and tighten the mounting bolt finger-tight.

8 Ensure the inner washer is in position on the upper mounting bracket, then install the shock and outer washer and tighten the mounting nut finger-tight.

9 Support the machine upright on its wheels so that the weight is taken on the shock absorbers and swingarm pivot bushes, then tighten the mounting nuts and bolts to the torque setting specified at the beginning of this Chapter.

10 Follow the procedure in Chapter 1 to

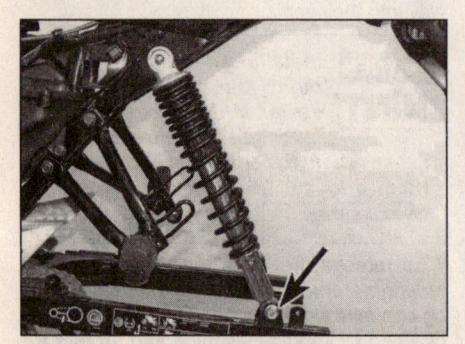

10.7c Set-up for removing the lower race with a puller

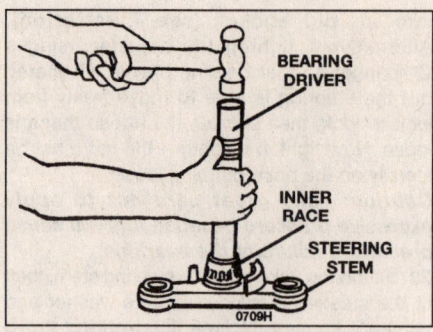

10.9 Set-up for installing the lower inner race

11.2 Unscrew the lower shock mounting bolt (arrowed)

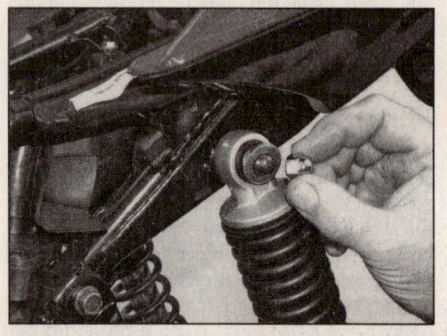

11.3a Unscrew the upper shock mounting bolt and washer

11.3b Manoeuvre the shock off . . .

11.3c . . . and note location of inner washer

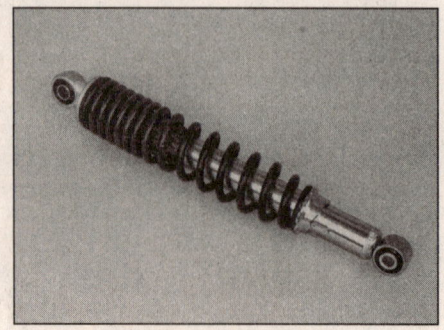

11.4 Examine the shocks for damage, oil leaks and corrosion

11.5 Check the spring pre-load adjusters (arrowed)

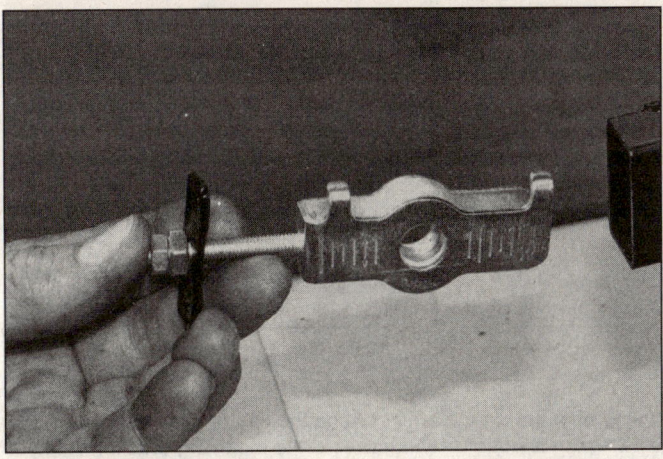

Frame and suspension 5•15

12.1 Withdraw the chain adjusters from the swingarm

12.2a Position of the locating tabs on swingarm

12.2b Undo the left . . .

12.2c . . . and right-hand mounting screws (arrowed)

12.6a Undo the nut . . .

adjust the spring pre-load. **Note:** *Always ensure both shock absorber pre-load adjusters are adjusted equally.*

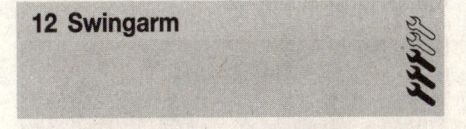

12 Swingarm

Removal

1 Remove the rear wheel (see Chapter 6). Note the location of the chain adjusters and remove them for safekeeping, noting how they fit **(see illustration)**.
2 Note how the chainguard/hugger assembly locates in the tabs on the swingarm **(see illustration)**. Undo the screws securing the assembly and lift it off **(see illustrations)**.
3 Unhook the brake pedal return spring from the lug on the swingarm **(see illustrations 3.10a and b)**.
4 Remove the shock absorbers (see Section 11).
5 At this point, if required, check the swingarm bushes as described in Chapter 1.
6 Undo the nut on the right-hand end of the swingarm pivot bolt, then drive the pivot bolt part-way out using a suitable punch taking care not to damage the threads on the end of the bolt **(see illustrations)**. Support the swingarm, withdraw the bolt fully and lift the swingarm out **(see illustration)**.

Inspection

7 Thoroughly clean the swingarm, removing all traces of dirt, corrosion and grease. Clean the pivot bolt and remove any corrosion using wire wool).

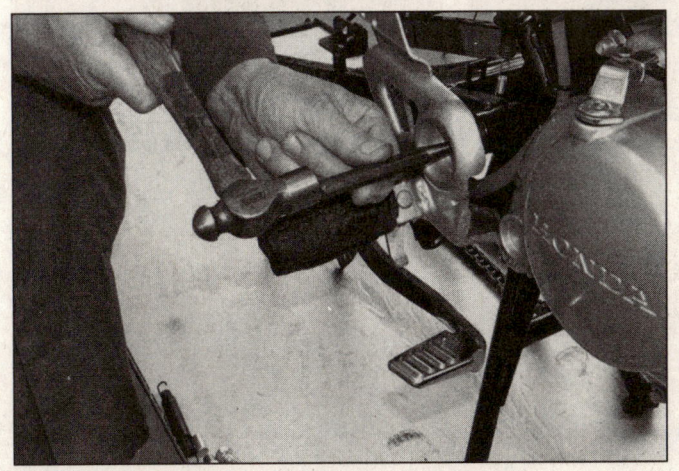

12.6b . . . and displace the pivot bolt

12.6c Support the swingarm and withdraw the pivot bolt

5•16 Frame and suspension

12.8a Location of the drive chain slider (arrowed)

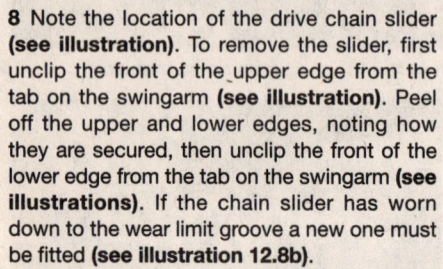

12.8b Unclip the front upper edge. Note wear limit groove (arrowed)

12.8c Peel the chain slider off . . .

8 Note the location of the drive chain slider **(see illustration)**. To remove the slider, first unclip the front of the upper edge from the tab on the swingarm **(see illustration)**. Peel off the upper and lower edges, noting how they are secured, then unclip the front of the lower edge from the tab on the swingarm **(see illustrations)**. If the chain slider has worn down to the wear limit groove a new one must be fitted **(see illustration 12.8b)**.

9 If required, straighten and remove the split pin, then undo the nut on the shouldered bolt securing the rear brake torque arm to the underside of the swingarm **(see illustration)**. Remove the plain washer and the spring washer, then withdraw the bolt and remove the torque arm, noting how it locates between the two halves of its mounting bracket. Discard the split pin as a new one must be used.

10 Temporarily install the swingarm pivot bolt, the chain adjusters and the rear axle. Lay the swingarm on the work surface and support it so that the pivot bolt is level (check this with a spirit level), then check the level of the axle. If the axle is not level, the swingarm is out of true and must be renewed.

11 Check the pivot bolt for straightness by rolling it on a flat surface such as a piece of plate glass (if the equipment is available, place the bolt in V-blocks and measure the runout using a dial gauge). If the bolt is bent or the runout excessive, or if it shows signs of wear, it must be renewed.

12 Examine the swingarm bushes for wear and deterioration **(see illustration)**. If the checks detailed in Chapter 1 show the bushes to be worn, consult your Honda dealer – Honda do not list swingarm bushes separately and a new swingarm may have to be fitted.

13 Examine the chain adjusters for wear and damage – they should be a sliding fit inside the ends of the swingarm **(see illustration 12.1)**. Ensure the threads, adjuster nuts and locknuts are in good condition

Installation

14 If removed, install the rear brake torque arm, locating the end of the arm between the two halves of its mounting bracket. Apply a smear of grease to the shouldered bolt, then fit the bolt from the inside of the bracket. Fit the spring washer, plain washer and nut on the outside of the bracket and tighten the nut securely. Secure the nut with a new split pin **(see illustration 12.9)**.

15 If removed, install the chain slider **(see illustrations 12.8d, c, b and a)**.

16 Apply a smear of grease to the pivot bolt. Position the swingarm in the frame between the pivot bolt lugs and install the pivot bolt from the left-hand side – if the drive chain is in place on the front sprocket, don't forget to position the swingarm between the top and bottom runs of the chain as it is manoeuvred into the frame **(see illustration 12.6c)**.

17 Counter-hold the pivot bolt and tighten the pivot bolt nut to the torque setting specified at the beginning of this Chapter.

18 Install the remaining components in the reverse order of removal.

12.8d . . . then unclip the front lower edge

12.9 Split pin (arrowed) secures torque arm bolt

12.12 Examine the bushes (arrowed) for wear

Chapter 6
Brakes, wheels and final drive

Contents

	Section number
Brake light switches	see Chapter 8
Brake wear check	see Chapter 1
Brake system check	see Chapter 1
Drive chain	15
Drive chain maintenance	see Chapter 1
Front brake bleeding and fluid change	7
Front brake caliper	3
Front brake disc	4
Front brake fluid level	see Pre-ride checks
Front brake hose and fittings	6
Front brake master cylinder	5
Front brake pads	2
Front wheel	11

	Section number
General information	1
Rear drum brake	8
Rear sprocket coupling dampers	17
Rear wheel	12
Sprockets	16
Tyre maintenance	see Pre-ride checks
Tyres	14
Wheel alignment	10
Wheel bearing check	see Chapter 1
Wheel bearings	13
Wheel check	see Chapter 1
Wheel inspection and repair	9

Degrees of difficulty

Easy, suitable for novice with little experience	**Fairly easy,** suitable for beginner with some experience	**Fairly difficult,** suitable for competent DIY mechanic	**Difficult,** suitable for experienced DIY mechanic	**Very difficult,** suitable for expert DIY or professional

Specifications

Front brake
Brake fluid type .... DOT 4
Caliper bore ID
   Service limit .... 25.460 mm
Caliper piston OD
   Service limit .... 25.310 mm
Disc thickness
   Service limit .... 3.5 mm
Disc maximum runout .... 0.10 mm
Master cylinder bore ID
   Service limit .... 12.755 mm
Master cylinder piston OD
   Service limit .... 12.645 mm

6•2 Brakes, wheels and final drive

Rear brake
Brake drum ID
   Service limit .... 131.00 mm
Brake pedal freeplay .... see Chapter 1

Wheels
Maximum wheel runout (front and rear)
   Axial (side-to-side) .... 1.0 mm
   Radial (out-of-round) .... 1.0 mm
Maximum axle runout (front and rear) .... 0.20 mm

Tyres
Tyre pressures .... see Pre-ride checks
Tyre sizes
   Front .... 80/100-17 MC (46P)
   Rear .... 100/90-17 MC (55P)

Final drive
Sprocket sizes
   Front (engine) sprocket 16T
   Rear (wheel) sprocket
      France 43T
      Rest of Europe 42T
Drive chain slack and lubricant .... SAE 80 or 90 gear oil or aerosol chain lubricant suitable for O-ring chains
Drive chain
   Type RK428 KRO-118LE
   Length .... 118 links
   Soft link
      Pin projection from side plate .... 1.10 mm
      Diameter of staked pin .... 4.75 to 4.95 mm

Torque settings
Front brake caliper bleed valve .... 5.4 Nm
Front brake caliper mounting bolts .... 30 Nm
Front brake disc bolts .... 42 Nm
Front brake hose banjo bolts .... 34 Nm
Front brake master cylinder clamp bolts .... 9 Nm
Front brake pad retaining pin .... 17 Nm
Front axle nut .... 54 Nm
Front sprocket retainer plate bolts .... 12 Nm
Rear axle nut .... 54 Nm
Rear brake arm pinch bolt .... 10 Nm
Rear brake torque arm nuts .... 22 Nm
Rear sprocket nuts .... 32 Nm

1 General information

The front brake is a single, hydraulically operated disc brake. The sliding-type caliper contains two pistons.

The rear brake is a single leading shoe drum brake connected to the brake pedal by a rod.

All models are fitted with six-spoke cast alloy wheels designed for tubeless tyres only.

The drive to the rear wheel is by chain and sprockets.

Caution: Disc brake components rarely require disassembly. Do not disassemble components unless absolutely necessary. If an hydraulic brake hose is loosened or disconnected, the union sealing washers must be renewed and the system bled upon reassembly. Do not use solvents on internal brake components. Solvents will cause the seals to swell and distort. Use only clean brake fluid of the correct type for cleaning. Use care when working with brake fluid as it can injure your eyes and it will damage painted surfaces and plastic parts.

2 Front brake pads

Warning: The dust created by the brake system is harmful to your health. Never blow it out with compressed air and don't inhale any of it. An approved filtering mask should be worn when working on the brakes.

Removal

1 Unscrew the pad retaining pin (see illustration).

2.1 Unscrew the pad retaining pin (arrowed)

Brakes, wheels and final drive 6•3

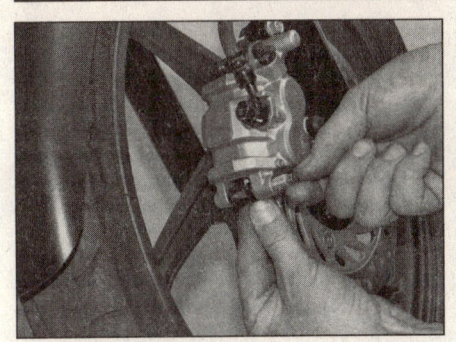

2.2a Partially withdraw the pin . . .

2.2b . . . and remove the inner pad . . .

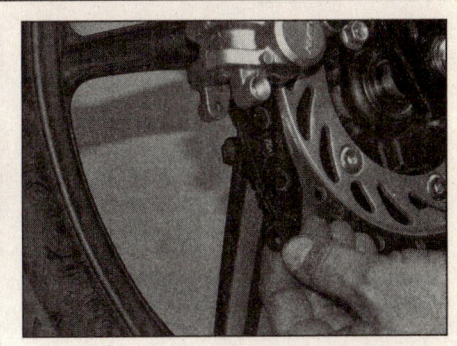

2.2c . . . then remove the outer pad

2 Partially withdraw the pin and remove the inner pad, then withdraw the pin completely and remove the outer pad **(see illustrations)**. Note how the pads fit each side of the brake disc. **Note:** *Do not operate the brake lever while the pads are out of the caliper.*

3 Inspect the surface of each pad for contamination and check that the friction material has not worn beyond its service limit (see Chapter 1) – if necessary, measure the thickness of the friction material. If either pad is worn down to, or beyond, the service limit, is fouled with oil or grease, or heavily scored or damaged, fit a set of new pads. **Note:** *It is not possible to degrease the friction material; if the pads are contaminated in any way they must be replaced with new ones.*

4 Check that each pad has worn evenly at each end, and that each has the same amount of wear as the other. If uneven wear is noticed, one of the pistons is probably sticking in the caliper, or the caliper is seized on its slider pins – in either case the caliper must be overhauled (see Section 3).

5 If the pads are in good condition clean them carefully, using a fine wire brush which is completely free of oil and grease to remove all traces of road dirt and corrosion. Using a pointed instrument, dig out any embedded particles of foreign matter. If required, spray with a dedicated brake cleaner to remove any dust.

6 Check the condition of the brake disc (see Section 4).

7 Remove all traces of corrosion from the pad pin and check it for wear and damage. Renew the pin if necessary.

8 If new pads are being fitted, temporarily install the old pads, then press the caliper against its mounting bracket to push the pistons into the caliper to create room for the new pads. If the pistons appear to be stuck, displace the caliper (see Section 3) and clean the inside with a dedicated brake system cleaner. Note the location of the pad spring inside the caliper **(see illustration)**. Ease the pistons back using a piece of wood and a pair of grips, or use a commercially available piston-pushing tool **(see illustrations)**. **Note:** *Due to the increased friction material thickness of new pads, it may be necessary to remove the master cylinder reservoir cover and siphon out some fluid (see Section 7).*

9 If either piston appears seized, the caliper will have to be overhauled (see Section 3).

Installation

10 If removed, install the brake caliper (see Section 3).

11 Smear the backs of the pads with copper-based grease, making sure that none gets on the front or sides of the pads.

12 Fit the outer pad into the caliper **(see illustration 2.2c)**. Ensure the upper end of the pad locates correctly against the pad retainer and secure the pad with the pad pin **(see illustrations)**. **Note:** *Ensure the brake pads locate correctly on each side of the disc with the friction material facing the disc.*

13 Fit the inner pad **(see illustration 2.2b)**, locating its curved end over the post on the

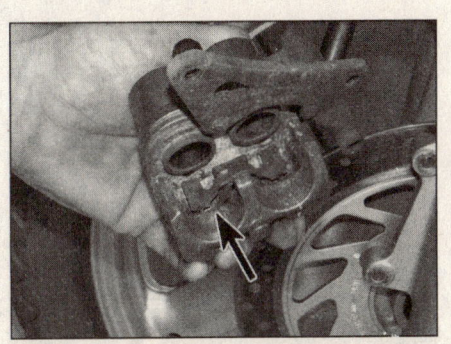

2.8a Location of the pad spring (arrowed)

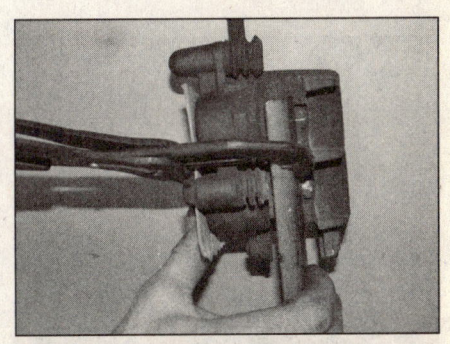

2.8b Push the pistons back using some grips and a piece of wood . . .

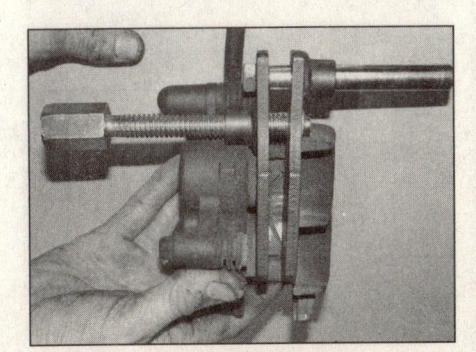

2.8c . . . or a piston-pushing tool

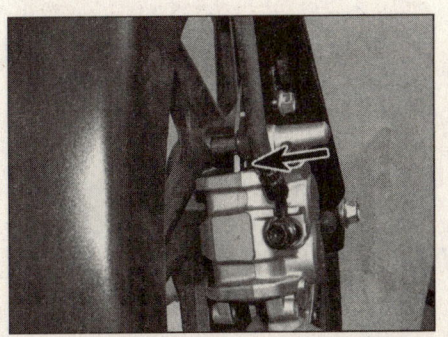

2.12a Locate outer pad against pad retainer (arrowed) . . .

2.12b . . . and secure it with the pad pin

6•4 Brakes, wheels and final drive

caliper bracket **(see illustration)**. Press the pad against the pad spring and secure it with the pin **(see illustration 2.2a)**. Tighten the pad pin to the torque setting specified at the beginning of this Chapter.

14 Operate the brake lever several times to bring the pads into contact with the disc.

15 Check the fluid level in the master cylinder reservoir and top-up if necessary (see *Pre-ride checks*).

16 Check the operation of the brake before riding the motorcycle.

3 Front brake caliper

⚠️ **Warning:** *If a caliper is in need of an overhaul all old brake fluid should be flushed from the system. Also, the dust created by the brake system may contain asbestos, which is harmful to your health. Never blow it out with compressed air and do not inhale any of it. An approved filtering mask should be worn when working on the brakes. Overhaul of the brake caliper must be done in a spotlessly clean work area to avoid contamination and possible failure of the brake hydraulic system components. Do not, under any circumstances, use petroleum-based solvents to clean brake parts. Use clean DOT 4 brake fluid, dedicated brake cleaner or denatured alcohol only. To prevent damage from spilled brake fluid, always cover paintwork when working on the braking system.*

2.13 Locate inner pad over the post (arrowed)

Removal

Special tool: *A source of compressed air is required to ease the pistons out from the brake caliper (see Step 11).*

Note: *If the caliper is being overhauled (usually due to sticking pistons or fluid leaks) read through the entire procedure first and make sure that you have obtained all the new parts required, including some new DOT 4 brake fluid.*

1 If required, undo the right-hand mudguard mounting bolt and free the brake hose guide **(see illustration)**.

2 If the caliper assembly is just being displaced from the front forks, unscrew the mounting bolts and slide it off the disc **(see illustrations)**. Secure the caliper to the bike with a cable-tie to avoid straining the brake hose. **Note:** *Do not operate the brake lever while the caliper is off the disc.*

3 If the caliper is being completely removed or overhauled, first loosen the pad pin **(see illustration 2.1)**, then follow the procedure in Section 7 and drain the brake fluid.

4 Unscrew the brake hose banjo bolt and detach the banjo union, noting its alignment with the caliper **(see illustration)**. Wrap a small plastic bag around the banjo union and secure the hose in an upright position to minimise fluid loss. Discard the sealing washers, as new ones must be fitted on reassembly.

5 Undo the caliper mounting bolts and slide the caliper off the disc **(see illustrations 3.2a and b)**.

6 Unscrew the pad pin and remove the pads (see Section 2).

Overhaul

7 Slide the caliper off the bracket **(see illustration)**.

8 Remove the pad spring, noting how it fits **(see illustration)** then clean the exterior of the caliper and bracket with denatured alcohol or brake system cleaner. Have some clean rag ready to catch any spilled brake fluid.

9 Clean off all traces of corrosion and hardened grease from the slider pins on the bracket and make sure the lower slider pin is tight.

10 Examine the boots in the caliper and

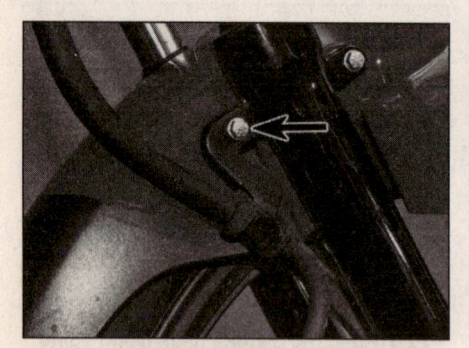

3.1 Bolt (arrowed) secures the brake hose guide

3.2a Unscrew the mounting bolts (arrowed) . . .

3.2b . . . and slide the caliper off the disc

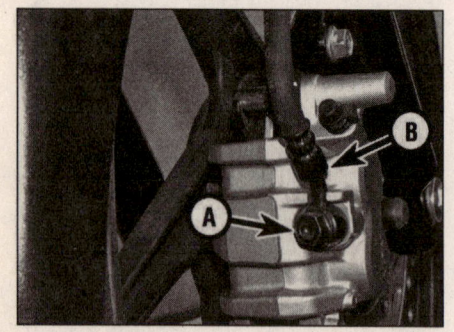

3.4 Banjo bolt (A) and brake hose banjo union (B)

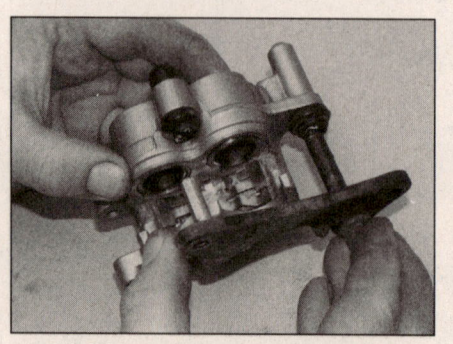

3.7 Slide the caliper off the bracket

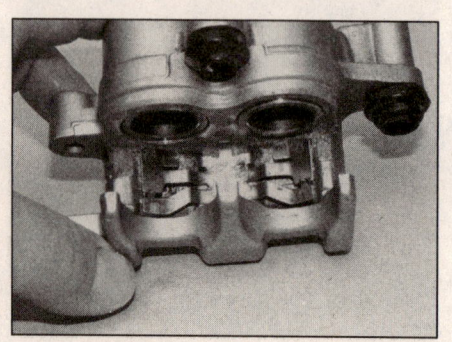

3.8 Remove the pad spring

Brakes, wheels and final drive 6•5

renew them if they are damaged, deformed or deteriorated **(see illustration)**.

11 Hold the caliper piston-side down on the workbench on a cushion of clean rag, then apply low pressure compressed air into the fluid inlet to ease the pistons out **(see illustration)**. Make sure both pistons are displaced at the same time. Mark each piston head and caliper bore with a felt marker to ensure that the pistons can be matched to their original bores on reassembly.

12 If one piston sticks in its bore, block the free piston with a piece of wood, then try to ease the other piston out as before **(see illustration)**. Do not try to remove a piston by levering it out or by using pliers or other grips. If the piston has completely seized you will have to replace the caliper with a new one.

13 Remove the (outer) dust seal and the (inner) piston seal from each piston bore using a soft wooden or plastic tool to avoid scratching the bore **(see illustration)**. Discard the seals as new ones must be fitted.

14 Clean the pistons and bores with fresh brake fluid and blow compressed air through the fluid galleries in the caliper to ensure they are clear (make sure the air is filtered and unlubricated).

Caution: Do not, under any circumstances, use a petroleum-based solvent to clean brake parts.

15 Inspect each caliper bore and piston for signs of corrosion, nicks and burrs and loss of plating. If surface defects are present, the pistons and/or the caliper assembly must be replaced with new ones. If the necessary measuring equipment is available, compare the dimensions of the caliper bores and pistons to those specified at the beginning of this Chapter, and obtain new pistons or a new caliper if necessary.

16 Lubricate the new piston seals with fresh brake fluid and install them in the inner grooves in the caliper bores **(see illustrations)**.

17 Lubricate the new dust seals with silicone grease and install them in the outer grooves in the caliper bores.

18 Lubricate the pistons with clean brake fluid and install them closed-end first into the caliper bores. Using your thumbs, push the pistons all the way in, making sure they enter the bores squarely and taking care not to displace the seals **(see illustration)**.

19 Install the pad spring, then apply a smear of silicone-based grease to the slider pins and side the caliper onto the bracket **(see illustrations 3.8 and 7)**.

Installation

20 If the caliper has not been overhauled, ease the brake pads apart so that they will fit either side of the disc, then install the caliper assembly and tighten the mounting bolts to the torque setting specified at the beginning of this Chapter **(see illustrations 3.2b and a)**.

21 If the caliper has been overhauled, install the caliper assembly on the right-hand fork outer tube and tighten the mounting bolts to the specified torque setting **(see illustration)**.

22 Install the brake pads (see Section 2).

23 Connect the brake hose to the caliper – locate the banjo union between the lugs on the caliper and use new sealing washers on

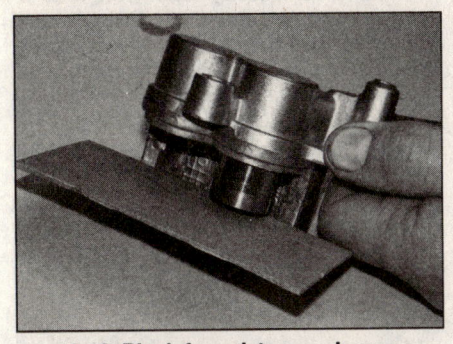

3.10 Examine slider pin boots (arrowed)

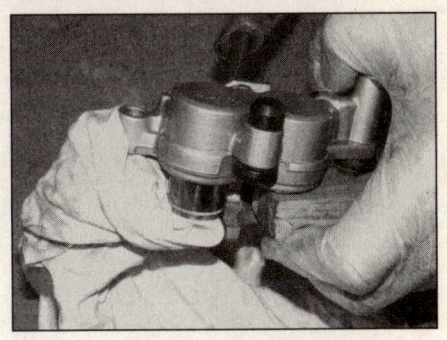

3.11 Ease the pistons out with compressed air

3.12 Block free piston as shown

3.13 Remove the seals and discard them

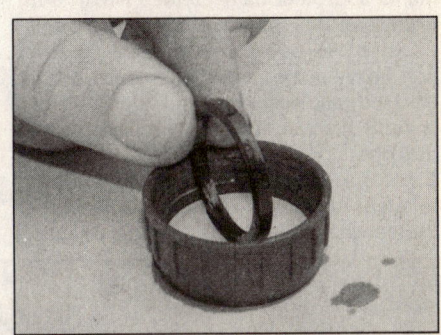

3.16a Lubricate the new piston seals with brake fluid . . .

3.16b . . . and install them in their grooves

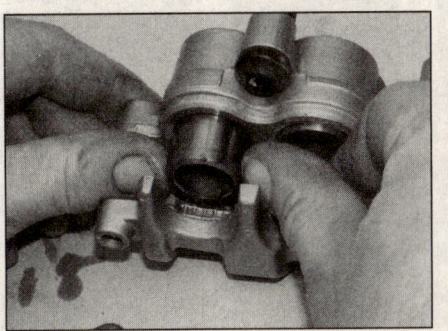

3.18 Push the pistons all the way in

3.21 Slide the caliper onto the bracket

6•6 Brakes, wheels and final drive

3.23 Use new sealing washers on both sides of the union

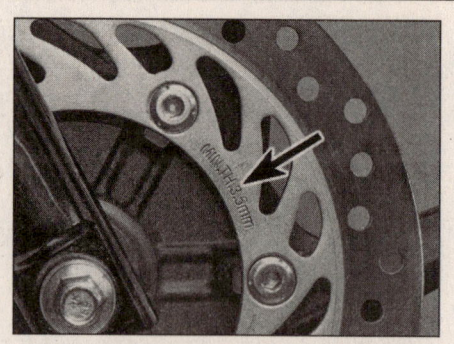

4.1 Inspect the surface of the disc. Note minimum thickness mark (arrowed)

both sides of the union **(see illustration)**. Tighten the banjo bolt to the specified torque setting.

24 If removed, secure the brake hose guide **(see illustration 3.1)**.

25 Fill the master cylinder reservoir with new DOT 4 brake fluid and follow the *Fluid change* procedure in Section 7 to refill the system. Check that there are no fluid leaks.

26 Check the operation of the brake before riding the motorcycle.

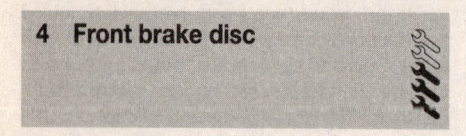

4 Front brake disc

Inspection

1 Inspect the surface of the disc for score marks and other damage **(see illustration)**. Light scratches are normal after use and won't affect brake operation, but deep grooves and heavy score marks will reduce braking efficiency and accelerate pad wear. If the disc is badly grooved it must be replaced with a new one.

2 The disc must not be machined or allowed to wear down to a thickness less than the service limit as listed in this Chapter's *Specifications*. The minimum thickness is also stamped on the disc **(see illustration 4.1)**. Measure the thickness of the disc with a micrometer and replace it with a new one if necessary.

3 To check if the disc is warped, position the bike on an auxiliary stand with the front wheel raised off the ground. Mount a dial gauge to the fork leg, with the gauge plunger touching the surface of the disc about 10 mm from the outer edge **(see illustration)**. Rotate the wheel and watch the gauge needle, comparing the reading with the limit listed in *Specifications* at the beginning of this Chapter. If the runout is greater than the service limit, check the wheel bearings for play (see Chapter 1). If the bearings are worn, install new ones (see Section 13) and repeat this check. If the disc runout is still excessive, a new disc will have to be fitted.

Removal

4 Remove the wheel (see Section 11).

5 If you are not replacing the disc with a new one, mark the relationship of the disc to the wheel, so it can be installed in the same position. Unscrew the disc retaining bolts, loosening them evenly and a little at a time in a criss-cross pattern to avoid distorting the disc, then remove the disc **(see illustration)**.

Installation

6 Before installing the disc, make sure there is no dirt or corrosion where it seats on the hub. If the disc does not sit flat when it is bolted down, it will appear to be warped when checked or when the front brake is applied.

7 Install the disc on the wheel with its marked side facing out, aligning the previously applied matchmarks (if you're reinstalling the original disc).

8 Clean the threads of the disc mounting bolts, then apply a suitable non-permanent thread locking compound. Install the bolts and tighten them evenly and a little at a time in a criss-cross pattern to the torque setting specified at the beginning of this Chapter. Clean the disc using acetone or brake system cleaner. If a new disc has been installed remove any protective coating from its working surfaces. **Note:** *Always fit new brake pads when installing a new disc.*

9 Install the front wheel (see Section 11).

10 Operate the brake lever several times to bring the pads into contact with the disc.

11 Check the operation of the brake before riding the motorcycle.

5 Front brake master cylinder

⚠️ *Warning: If the brake master cylinder is in need of an overhaul all old brake fluid should be flushed from the system. Overhaul must be done in a spotlessly clean work area to avoid contamination and possible failure of the brake hydraulic system components. Do not, under any circumstances, use petroleum-based solvents to clean brake parts; use clean DOT 4 brake fluid, dedicated brake cleaner or denatured alcohol only. To prevent damage from spilled brake fluid, always cover paintwork when working on the braking system.*

4.3 Checking disc runout

4.5 Front brake disc retaining bolts (arrowed)

Brakes, wheels and final drive 6•7

5.5 Disconnect the switch wiring connectors

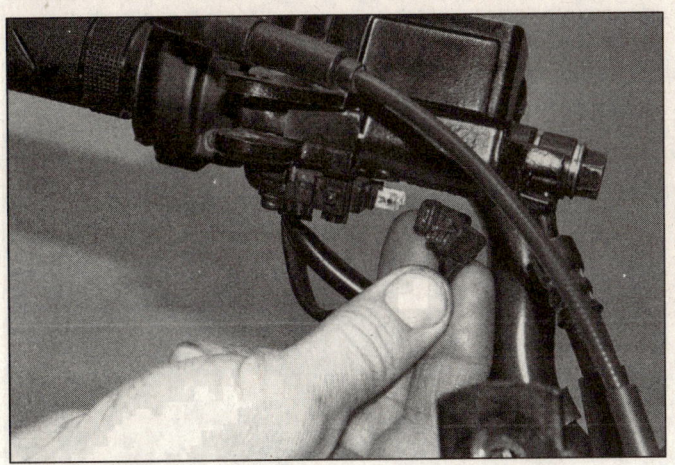

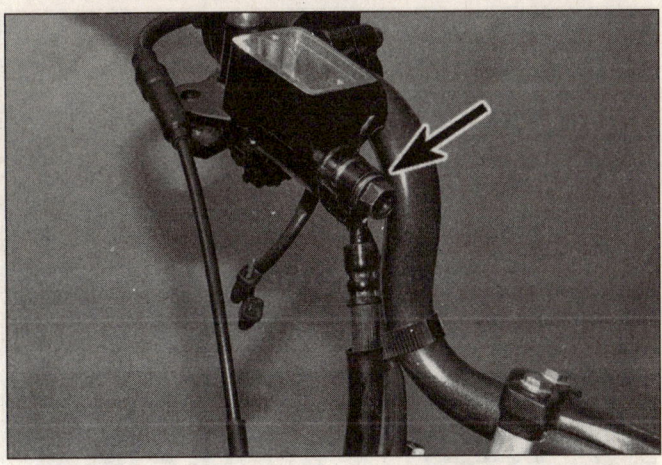

5.6 Note alignment of banjo union (arrowed) with caliper

Removal

Note: *If the master cylinder is being overhauled (usually due to sticking or poor action, or fluid leaks) read through the entire procedure first and make sure that you have obtained all the new parts required, including some new DOT 4 brake fluid.*

1 If the master cylinder is just being displaced from the handlebars, remove the right-hand mirror (see Chapter 7), then follow the procedure in Chapter 5, Section 5.

2 If the master cylinder is being completely removed or overhauled, follow the procedure in Section 7 and siphon out the brake fluid. Temporarily install the diaphragm, diaphragm plate and cover.

3 Remove the right-hand mirror (see Chapter 7).

4 Follow the procedure in Chapter 5, Section 5, and remove the front brake lever.

5 Disconnect the front brake light switch wiring connectors **see illustration**).

6 Unscrew the brake hose banjo bolt and detach the banjo union, noting its alignment with the master cylinder **(see illustration)**. Wrap a small plastic bag around the banjo union and secure the hose in an upright position to minimise fluid loss. Discard the sealing washers, as new ones must be fitted on reassembly.

7 Undo the master cylinder clamp bolts and remove the back of the clamp **(see illustration)**. Lift the master cylinder off the handlebar.

8 Remove the reservoir cover, diaphragm plate and diaphragm and wipe any remaining brake fluid out of the reservoir with a clean rag.

9 If required, undo the screw securing the brake light switch to the bottom of the master cylinder and remove the switch **(see illustration)**.

Overhaul

10 Remove the rubber boot from the master cylinder **(see illustration)**.

11 Note the location of the circlip securing the master cylinder piston **(see illustration)**. Depress the piston and use circlip pliers to remove the circlip.

12 Draw out the piston assembly and the spring, noting how they fit **(see illustration)**. If the piston is difficult to remove, apply low pressure compressed air to the brake fluid outlet. Lay the parts out in the proper order to aid reassembly.

13 Clean the inside of the master cylinder and reservoir with fresh brake fluid. If compressed air is available, blow it through the fluid galleries to ensure they are clear (make sure the air is filtered and unlubricated).

Caution: *Do not, under any circumstances, use a petroleum-based solvent to clean brake parts.*

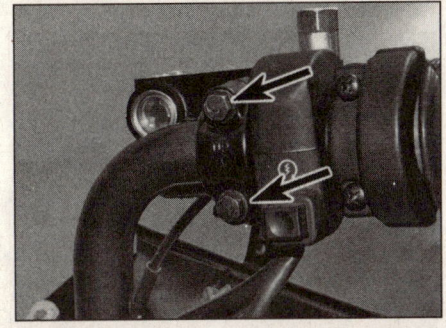

5.7 Master cylinder clamp bolts (arrowed)

5.9 Screw (arrowed) secures brake light switch

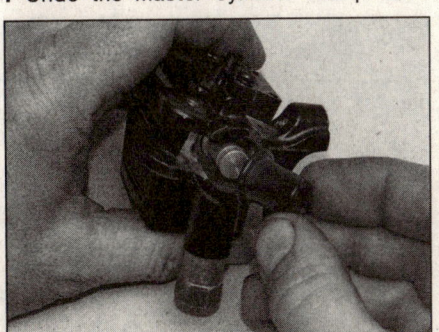

5.10 Remove the rubber boot

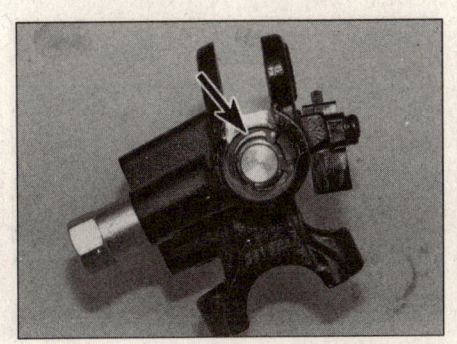

5.11 Note location of the circlip

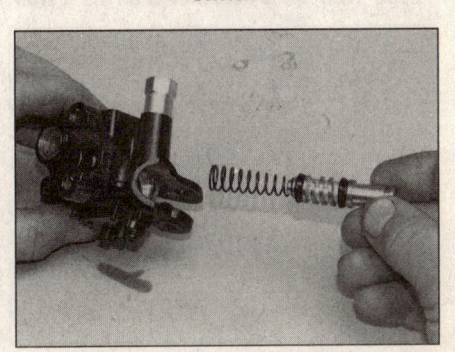

5.12 Draw out the piston assembly and spring

6•8 Brakes, wheels and final drive

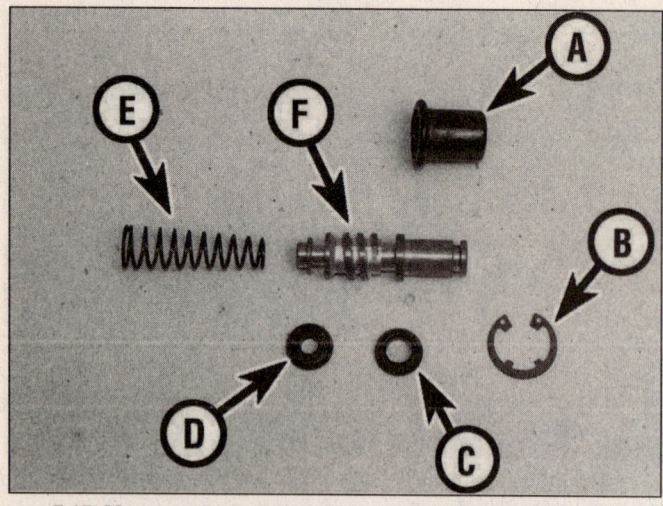

5.15 Master cylinder rebuild kit – dust boot (A), circlip (B), secondary seal (C), primary seal (D), spring (E) and piston (F)

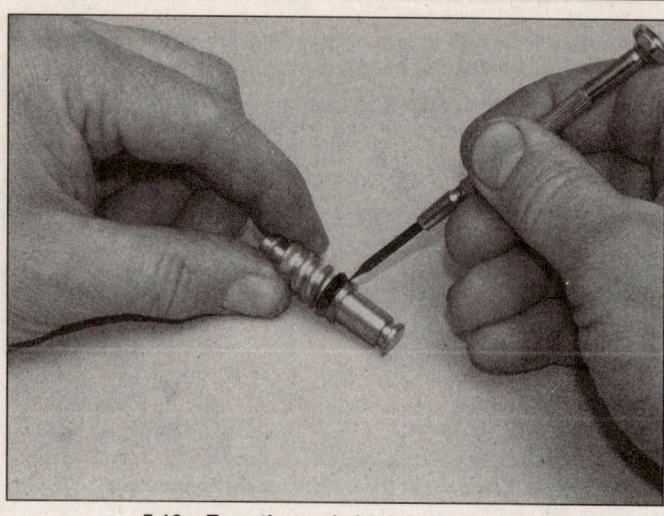

5.16a Ease the seals into their grooves

14 Check the master cylinder bore for corrosion, scratches, nicks and score marks. If the necessary measuring equipment is available, compare the dimensions of the piston and bore to those given in the Specifications at the beginning of this Chapter. If damage or wear is evident, the master cylinder must be replaced with a new one. If the master cylinder is in poor condition, then the caliper should be checked as well.

15 The dust boot, circlip, piston, seals and the spring are all included in the master cylinder rebuild kit **(see illustration)**. Use all of the new parts, regardless of the apparent condition of the old ones.

16 If the seals are not fitted to the piston, first lubricate them with fresh brake fluid. Ease the thinner secondary seal into its groove in the middle of the piston, then ease the thicker primary seal into its groove in the inner end of the piston **(see illustrations)**. Note: *When the piston is inserted into the master cylinder, the wider ends of the seals should go in first.*

17 Lubricate the master cylinder bore and the piston assembly with brake fluid, then fit the narrow end of the spring onto the piston **(see illustration)**. Carefully slide the assembly into the master cylinder **(see illustration 5.12)**.

18 Push the piston all the way in, compressing the spring, then secure it with the new circlip, making sure it locates properly in its groove **(see illustration 5.11)**.

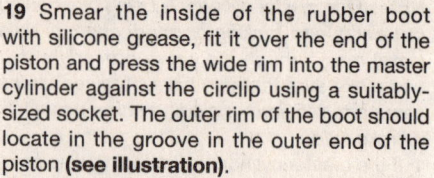

19 Smear the inside of the rubber boot with silicone grease, fit it over the end of the piston and press the wide rim into the master cylinder against the circlip using a suitably-sized socket. The outer rim of the boot should locate in the groove in the outer end of the piston **(see illustration)**.

20 Inspect the fluid reservoir diaphragm and fit a new one if it is damaged or deteriorated.

Installation

21 If the master cylinder has just been displaced from the handlebars, follow the procedure in Steps 23 and 25.

22 If the master cylinder has been completely removed or overhauled, install the brake light switch and tighten the screw securely. **(see illustration 5.9)**.

23 Align the master cylinder clamp joint with the punch mark on the top of the handlebar **(see illustration)**. Fit the back of the clamp with its UP mark facing up **(see illustration 5.7)**. Tighten the upper clamp bolt to the torque setting specified at the beginning of this Chapter, followed by the lower bolt so that any gap is at the bottom of the clamp joint.

24 Connect the brake hose to the master cylinder, using new sealing washers on both sides of the banjo union **(see illustration)**. Align the hose as noted on removal, then

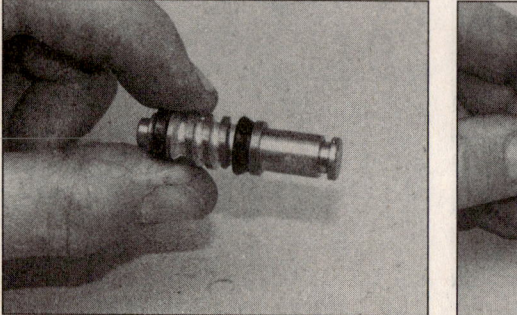

5.16b New seals assembled on the piston

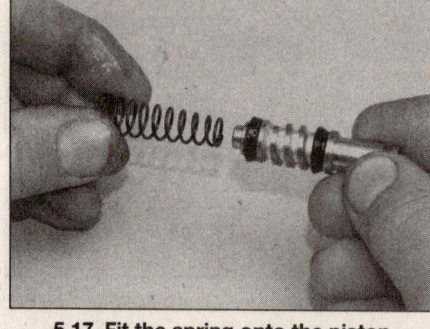

5.17 Fit the spring onto the piston

5.19 Ensure rim of the boot (arrowed) locates in groove in piston

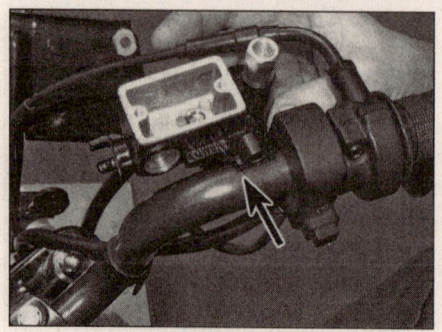

5.23 Align the clamp joint with the punch mark

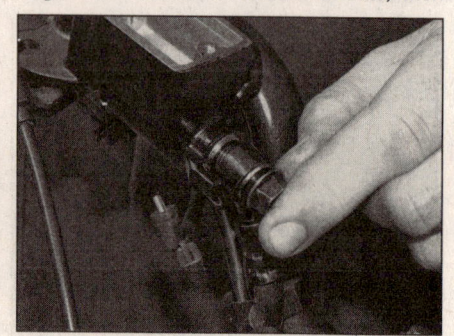

5.24 Use new sealing washers on both sides of the union

tighten the banjo bolt to the specified torque setting.
25 Connect the brake light switch wiring connectors **(see illustration 5.5)**.
26 Install the brake lever (see Chapter 5).
27 Fill the fluid reservoir with new DOT 4 brake fluid and follow the *Fluid change* procedure in Section 7 to refill the system. Check that there are no fluid leaks.
28 Install the right-hand mirror.
29 Check the operation of the brake before riding the motorcycle.

6 Front brake hose and fittings

Inspection

1 Brake hose condition should be checked regularly and the hose replaced with a new one if it shows signs of hardening, cracking or abrasion.
2 Twist and flex the hose while looking for cracks, bulges and seeping hydraulic fluid. Check extra carefully around the area where the hose connects with the banjo unions, as these are common areas for hose failure.
3 Inspect the banjo unions connected to the brake hose. If the unions are rusted, scratched or cracked, fit a new hose.

Removal and installation

4 The brake hose has banjo unions on both ends. Cover the surrounding area with plenty of rags and unscrew the banjo bolt at both ends of the hose, noting the alignment of the union with the master cylinder or brake caliper **(see illustrations 5.6 and 3.4)**. Free the hose from any clips or guides and remove it, noting its routing. Discard the sealing washers. **Note:** *Do not operate the brake lever while a brake hose is disconnected.*
5 Position the new hose, making sure it isn't twisted or otherwise strained, and ensure that it is correctly routed through any clips or guides and is clear of all moving components.
6 Check that the unions align correctly, then install the banjo bolts, using new sealing washers on both sides of the unions **(see illustrations 5.24 and 3.23)**. Tighten the banjo

7.2 Set-up for bleeding the front brake

bolts to the torque setting specified at the beginning of this Chapter.
7 Flush the old brake fluid from the system, refill with new DOT 4 brake fluid and bleed the air from the system (see Section 7).
8 Check the operation of the brake before riding the motorcycle.

7 Front brake bleeding and fluid change

Bleeding

1 Bleeding the brake is simply the process of removing air from the brake fluid reservoir, master cylinder, the hose and the brake caliper. Bleeding is necessary whenever a brake system connection is loosened, after a component or hose is replaced with a new one, or when the master cylinder or caliper is overhauled. Leaks in the system may also allow air to enter, but leaking brake fluid will reveal their presence and warn you of the need for repair.
2 To bleed the brake, you will need some new DOT 4 brake fluid, a length of clear flexible hose, a small container partially filled with clean brake fluid, some rags, a spanner to fit the brake caliper bleed valve, and help from an assistant **(see illustration)**. Bleeding kits that include the hose, a one-way valve and a container are available and greatly simplify the task.
3 Cover painted components to prevent damage in the event that brake fluid is spilled.
4 Refer to *Pre-ride checks* and remove the reservoir cover, diaphragm plate and diaphragm and slowly pump the brake lever a few times, until no air bubbles can be seen floating up from the holes in the bottom of the reservoir **(see illustration)**. This bleeds the air from the master cylinder end of the line. Temporarily refit the reservoir cover.
5 Pull the dust cap off the bleed valve **(see illustration)**. If using a ring spanner fit it onto the valve **(see illustrations 7.2)**. Attach one end of the hose to the bleed valve and, unless you're using a one-man kit, submerge the other end in the clean brake fluid in the container.

> **HAYNES HINT** To avoid damaging the bleed valve during the procedure, loosen it and then tighten it temporarily with a ring spanner before attaching the hose. With the hose attached, the valve can then be opened and closed either with an open-ended spanner, or by leaving the ring spanner located on the valve and fitting the hose above it.

6 Check the fluid level in the reservoir. Do not allow the fluid level to drop below the lower mark during the procedure **(see illustration)**.
7 Slowly pump the brake lever three or four times and hold it in while opening the bleed valve. When the valve is opened, brake fluid will flow out of the caliper into the clear tubing, and the lever will move toward the handlebar. If there is air in the system there will be air bubbles in the brake fluid coming out of the caliper.
8 Tighten the bleed valve, then release the brake lever gradually. Repeat the process until no air bubbles are visible in the brake fluid leaving the caliper, and the lever is firm when applied, topping the reservoir up when necessary. On completion, disconnect the hose, then tighten the bleed valve to the torque setting specified at the beginning of this Chapter and install the dust cap.

> **HAYNES HINT** If it is not possible to produce a firm feel to the lever the fluid may be aerated. Let the brake fluid in the system stabilise for a few hours and then repeat the procedure when the tiny bubbles in the system have settled out.

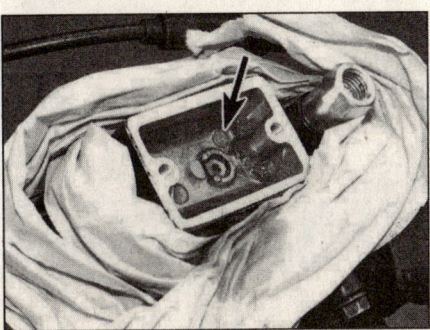

7.4 Air bubbles (arrowed) indicate air in the upper end of the system

7.5 Pull the dust cap off the bleed valve (arrowed)

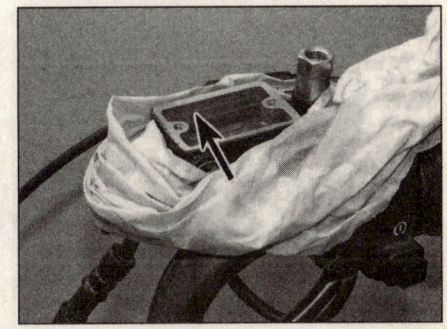

7.6 Fluid level lower mark (arrowed) cast inside reservoir

6•10 Brakes, wheels and final drive

9 Top-up the reservoir, then install the diaphragm, diaphragm plate, and cover. Wipe up any spilled brake fluid. Check the entire system for fluid leaks.
10 Check the operation of the brake before riding the motorcycle.

Fluid change

11 Changing the brake fluid is a similar process to bleeding the brakes and requires the same materials (see Step 2) plus a suitable syringe for siphoning the fluid out of the master cylinder reservoir. Also ensure that the container is large enough to take all the old fluid when it is flushed out of the system.
12 Follow Steps 3 and 5, then remove the reservoir cover, diaphragm plate and diaphragm and siphon the old fluid out of the reservoir.
13 Wipe the reservoir clean, then fill it with new brake fluid.
14 Slowly pump the brake lever three or four times and hold it in while opening the caliper bleed valve. When the valve is opened, brake fluid will flow out of the caliper into the clear tubing, and the lever will move toward the handlebar.
15 Tighten the bleed valve, then release the brake lever gradually. Keep the reservoir topped-up with new fluid to above the LOWER level at all times or air may enter the system and greatly increase the length of the task. Repeat the process until new fluid can be seen emerging from the caliper bleed valve.

> **HAYNES HINT** *Old brake fluid is invariably much darker in colour than new fluid, making it easy to see when all old fluid has been expelled from the system.*

16 Disconnect the hose, then tighten the bleed valve to the torque setting specified at the beginning of this Chapter and install the dust cap.
17 Top-up the reservoir, then install the diaphragm, diaphragm plate, and cover. Wipe up any spilled brake fluid. Check the entire system for fluid leaks.

8.3 Installed position of the rear brake shoes – note brake cam (arrowed)

18 Check the operation of the brake before riding the motorcycle.

Draining the system for overhaul

19 Follow the procedure in Steps 11 and 12, then connect the syringe to the caliper bleed valve using a length of hose. Open the bleed valve and draw the fluid out from the brake hose and caliper. **Note:** *After draining, a small amount of brake fluid will remain in the system. Take care when disconnecting the brake hose to avoid spilling fluid onto painted surfaces.*

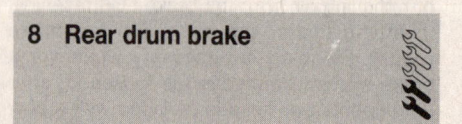

8 Rear drum brake

Removal

1 Before you start, check the position of the rear brake wear indicator (see Chapter 1).
2 Remove the rear wheel (see Section 12).
3 Lift off the brake plate. Mark the brake shoes to aid reassembly – if they are not going to be renewed they must be installed in their original positions (see illustration). Note the position of the brake springs and mark the end of the brake cam to aid reassembly. Ensure the springs hold the shoes together firmly otherwise they should be renewed (see Step 9).
4 Fold the shoes toward each other to release

8.4 Remove the shoes and springs as an assembly

the spring tension and lift the shoes and springs off as an assembly **(see illustration)**.

Inspection

5 Check the brake linings for wear, damage and signs of contamination **(see illustration)**. Note that it is not possible to degrease the friction material – if the linings are contaminated in any way, new brake shoes must be fitted.
6 If the wear indicator shows that the linings are worn down to the service limit (see Step 1), renew the shoes as a pair.
7 Check the ends of the shoes where they contact the brake cam and pivot post **(see illustration)**. Renew the shoes if there's visible wear.
8 If the linings are in good condition, clean them carefully using a fine wire brush which is completely free of oil and grease, to remove all traces of dirt and corrosion. Using a pointed instrument, dig out any embedded particles of foreign matter.
9 Examine the springs – if they are sprained and do not hold the shoes together tightly when in place, discard them and fit a new pair.
10 Clean all old grease from the brake cam and pivot post and check them for wear and damage **(see illustration)**. If the pivot post is worn or loose, a new backplate will have to be fitted.
11 To renew the brake cam, first note the alignment between the marks on the brake arm and the outer end of the cam shaft, then

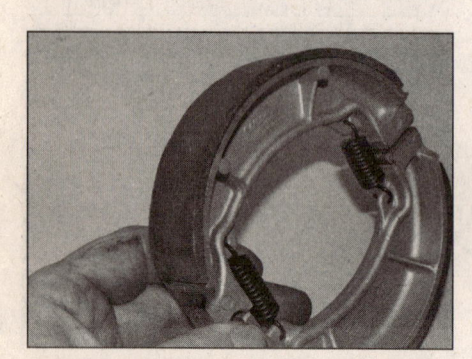

8.5 Examine the linings for wear and damage

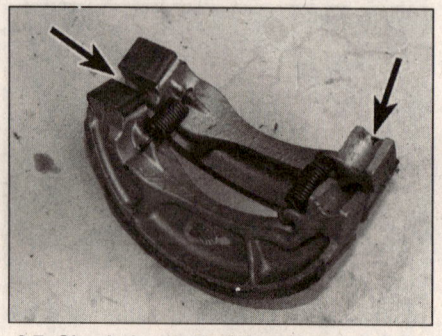

8.7 Check the ends of the shoes for wear (arrowed)

8.10 Brake cam (A) and pivot post (B)

Brakes, wheels and final drive 6•11

8.11 Brake arm and cam shaft alignment marks (arrowed)

8.14a Inspect the inside of the brake drum

8.14b Measure the inside diameter of the drum

remove the brake arm pinch bolt and pull the arm off the shaft **(see illustration)**.
12 Note how the wear indicator locates on the shaft, them pull the cam shaft out of the backplate. Note the location of the seal.
13 Lubricate the brake cam shaft with lithium-based grease and install it in the backplate, then fit the seal, the wear indicator and brake arm. Check the alignment of the components **(see illustration 8.11)**. Tighten the pinch bolt to the torque setting specified at the beginning of this Chapter.
14 Inspect the inside of the brake drum for wear or damage and measure the inside diameter of the drum at several points with a vernier caliper **(see illustrations)**. If the measurements are uneven (indicating that the drum is out-of-round) or if there deep scratches in the surface, have the drum skimmed by a brake specialist. If the wear or damage cannot be corrected within the service limit specified at the beginning of this Chapter, the wheel must be renewed.

Installation
15 Apply a smear of lithium-based grease to the pivot post and the faces of the brake cam.
Caution: Do not apply too much grease otherwise there is a risk of it contaminating the brake drum and linings.
16 Assemble the brake shoes and springs, position the shoes in a V on the brake plate, then fold the them down into position **(see illustration 8.4)**. Make sure the ends of the shoes fit correctly on the pivot post and cam **(see illustration 8.3)**.
17 Check the operation of the brake arm.
18 Install the brake plate, then install the rear wheel (see Section 12).
19 Check and adjust the brake pedal freeplay (see Chapter 1).

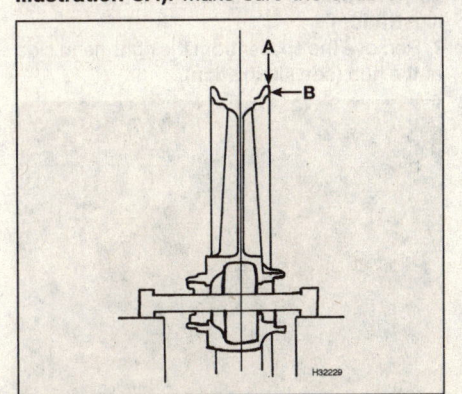

9 Wheel inspection and repair

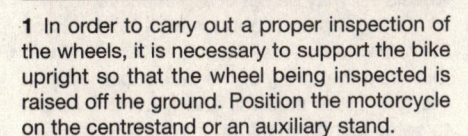

1 In order to carry out a proper inspection of the wheels, it is necessary to support the bike upright so that the wheel being inspected is raised off the ground. Position the motorcycle on the centrestand or an auxiliary stand.
2 Clean the wheels thoroughly to remove mud and dirt that may interfere with the inspection procedure or mask defects. Make a general check of the wheels (see Chapter 1) and tyres (see *Pre-ride checks*).
3 Attach a dial gauge to the fork or the swingarm and position its tip against the side of the wheel rim. Spin the wheel slowly and check the axial (side-to-side) runout of the rim **(see illustration)**.
4 In order to accurately check radial (out of round) runout with the dial gauge, remove the wheel from the machine, and the tyre from the wheel. With the axle clamped in a vice and the dial gauge positioned on the top of the rim, the wheel can be rotated to check the runout **(see illustration 9.3)**.
5 An easier, though slightly less accurate, method is to attach a stiff wire pointer to the fork or the swingarm and position the end a fraction of an inch from the wheel rim where the wheel and tyre join. If the wheel is true, the distance from the pointer to the rim will be constant as the wheel is rotated. **Note:** *If wheel runout is excessive, check the wheel bearings very carefully before renewing the wheel.*

10 Wheel alignment

1 Misalignment of the wheels due to a bent frame or forks can cause strange and possibly serious handling problems. If the frame or forks are at fault, repair by a frame specialist or renewal are the only options.
2 To check wheel alignment you will need an assistant, a length of string or a perfectly straight piece of wood and a ruler. A plumb bob or spirit level for checking that the wheels are vertical will also be required.
3 In order to make a proper check of the wheels it is necessary to support the bike in an upright position, using the centrestand or an auxiliary stand.
4 First ensure that the chain adjuster markings coincide on each side of the swingarm (see Chapter 1, Section 1). Next, measure the width of both tyres at their widest points. Subtract the smaller measurement from the larger measurement, then divide the difference by two. The result is the amount of offset that should exist between the front and rear tyres on both sides of the machine.
5 If a string is used, have your assistant hold one end of it about halfway between the floor and the rear axle, with the string touching the back edge of the rear tyre sidewall.
6 Run the other end of the string forward and pull it tight so that it is roughly parallel to the floor **(see illustration)**. Slowly bring the string into contact with the front edge of the rear tyre sidewall, then turn the front wheel until it is parallel with the string. Measure the distance from the front tyre sidewall to the string.

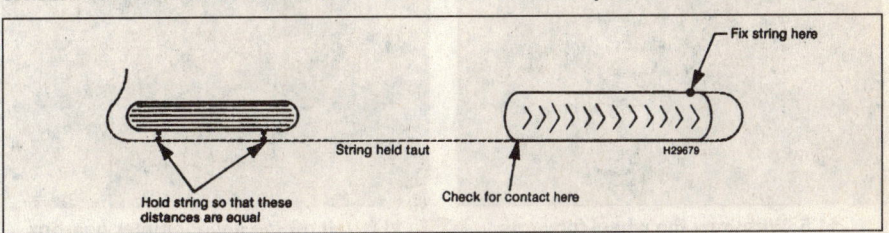

9.3 Check the wheel for radial (out-of-round) runout (A) and axial (side-to-side) runout (B)

10.6 Wheel alignment check using string

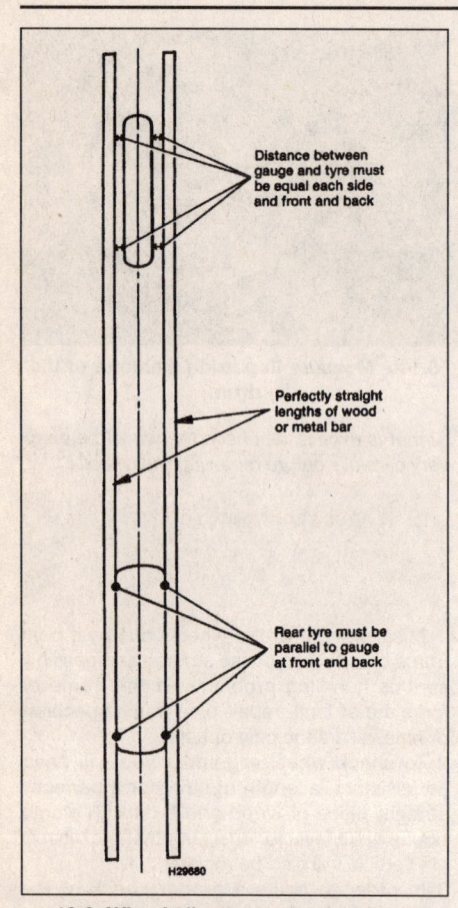

6•12 Brakes, wheels and final drive

10.8 Wheel alignment check using a straight-edge

11.3a Release the tab ...

11.3b ... and disconnect the speedometer cable

7 Repeat the procedure on the other side of the motorcycle. The distance from the front tyre sidewall to the string should be equal on both sides.

8 As previously mentioned, a perfectly straight length of wood or metal bar may be substituted for the string **(see illustration)**.

9 If the distance between the string and tyre is greater on one side, or if the rear wheel appears to be out of alignment, have your machine checked by a Honda dealer or frame specialist.

10 If the front-to-back alignment is correct, the wheels still may be out of alignment vertically.

11 Using a plumb bob or spirit level, check the rear wheel to make sure it is vertical. To do this, hold the string of the plumb bob against the tyre upper sidewall and allow the weight to settle just off the floor. If the string touches both the upper and lower tyre sidewalls and is perfectly straight, the wheel is vertical. If it is not, adjust the stand until it is.

12 Once the rear wheel is vertical, check the front wheel in the same manner. If both wheels are not perfectly vertical, the frame and/or major suspension components are bent.

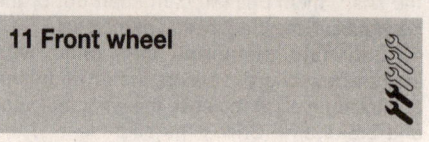

11 Front wheel

Removal

1 Support the motorcycle on an auxiliary stand so that the front wheel is off the ground. Always make sure the motorcycle is securely supported.

2 Displace the front brake caliper (see Section 3). Secure the caliper to the machine with a cable-tie so that no strain is placed on the brake hose. There is no need to disconnect the hose from the caliper. **Note:** *Do not operate the front brake lever while the caliper is off the disc.*

3 Release the tab securing the speedometer cable and disconnect the cable from the speedometer gearbox **(see illustrations)**. Note the location of the O-ring on the lower end of the cable.

4 Unscrew the axle nut, then support the wheel and withdraw the axle from the right-hand side **(see illustrations)**.

5 Lower the wheel and draw it forwards **(see illustration)**.

6 Lift off the speedometer gearbox noting how it locates on the drive tabs in the hub **(see illustration)**.

7 Remove the spacer from the right-hand side of the hub **(see illustration)**.

11.4a Unscrew the axle nut (arrowed) ...

11.4b ... and withdraw the axle from the right-hand side

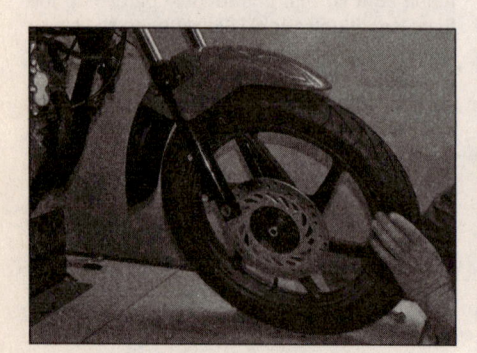

11.5 Withdraw the wheel forwards

11.6 Lift off the speedometer gearbox noting how it fits

11.7 Remove the right-hand axle spacer

Brakes, wheels and final drive 6•13

11.13 Ensure the ridges on the speedometer gearbox are correctly aligned (arrowed)

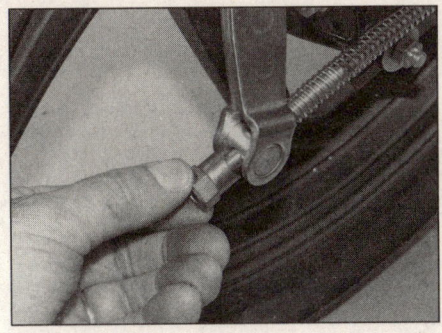

12.2a Unscrew the rear brake adjuster nut

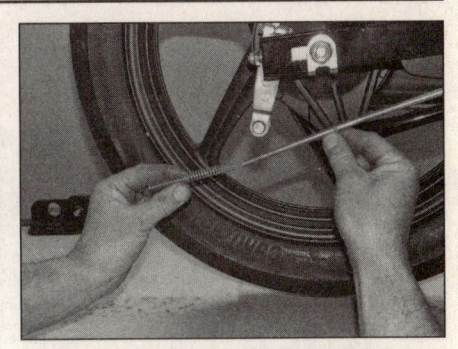

12.2b Note location of the brake rod spring . . .

Caution: *Don't lay the wheel down and allow it to rest on the disc – it could become warped. Set the wheel on wood blocks so the disc doesn't support the weight of the wheel.*

8 Clean all old grease off the axle, spacer, bearing seals and the speedometer gearbox.
9 Check the axle is straight by rolling it on a flat surface such as a piece of plate glass (first remove any corrosion using wire wool). If the equipment is available, place the axle in V-blocks and measure the runout using a dial gauge. If the axle is bent or the runout exceeds the limit specified, replace it with a new one.
10 Check the condition of the wheel bearings and seals (see Section 13).

Installation

11 Apply a smear of grease to the inside of the bearing seals then install the spacer on the right-hand side and the speedometer gearbox on the left **(see illustrations 11.7 and 6)**.
12 Manoeuvre the wheel into position between the forks, making sure the brake disc is on the right-hand side.
13 Lubricate the axle with a smear of grease, then lift the wheel into position and slide the axle through from the right-hand side **(see illustration 11.4b)**. Ensure the ridges on the speedometer gearbox are aligned with the tab on the inside of the left-hand fork outer tube **(see illustration)**.
14 Counter-hold the axle and tighten the axle nut to the torque setting specified at the beginning of this Chapter.
15 Lubricate the speedometer cable O-ring

12.2c . . . and brake arm trunnion

with a smear of grease, then connect the cable (see Step 3).
16 Install the brake caliper (see Section 3). Operate the brake lever to bring the pads into contact with the disc.
17 Check the operation of the brake before riding the motorcycle.

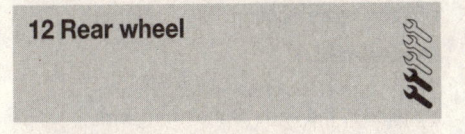

12 Rear wheel

Removal

1 Position the motorcycle on the centrestand so that the rear wheel is off the ground. Always make sure the motorcycle is securely supported.
2 Unscrew the rear brake adjuster nut **(see illustration)** and disconnect the brake rod

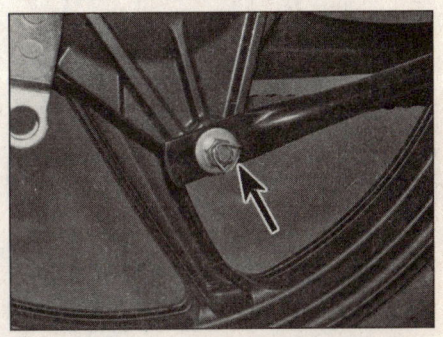

12.3a Remove the split pin and nut (arrowed) . . .

from the brake arm. Note the location of the brake rod spring and brake arm trunnion and remove them for safekeeping **(see illustrations)**. Alternatively, slide the spring and trunnion onto the rod and secure them with the adjuster nut.
3 Straighten and remove the split pin, then undo the nut securing the rear brake torque arm to the brake plate **(see illustration)**. Discard the split pin as a new one must be used. Remove the plain washer and the rubber washer **(see illustration)** then disconnect the torque arm from the brake plate
4 Loosen the rear axle nut, then loosen the locknut on the left and right-hand chain adjusters and turn both adjuster nuts to create some slack in the chain (see Chapter 1).
5 Unscrew the axle nut and remove the right-hand axle plate, noting how it fits **(see illustrations)**.

12.3b . . . and remove the plain washer and rubber washer

12.5a Unscrew the axle nut . . .

12.5b . . . and remove the axle plate

6•14 Brakes, wheels and final drive

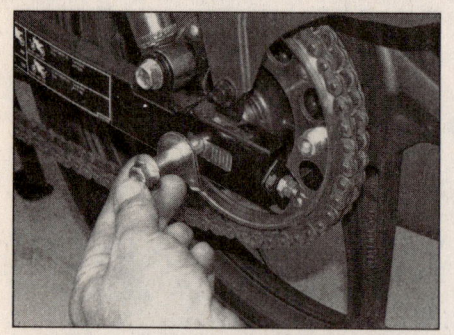

12.6a Partially withdraw the axle ...

12.6b ... and remove the right-hand spacer

12.7a Lift the chain off the sprocket

12.7b Remove the left-hand axle spacer

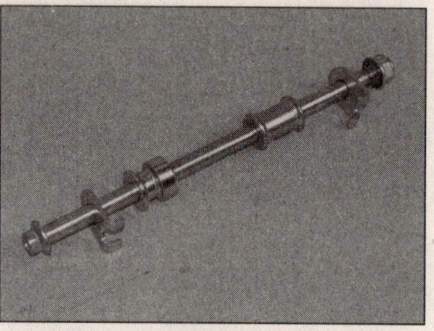

12.8 Keep the axle plates and spacers in the correct order

6 Support the wheel and partially withdraw the axle from the left-hand side so that the right-hand spacer can be removed **(see illustrations)**.
7 Withdraw the axle, lower the wheel to the ground and lift the chain off the sprocket **(see illustration)**. Draw the wheel rearwards and remove the left-hand spacer, noting how it fits **(see illustration)**. Keep the wheel upright – if you need to lay it down, first lift the brake plate off the brake drum.

Caution: Don't lay the wheel down and allow it to rest on the sprocket – it could become warped. Set the wheel on wood blocks so the sprocket doesn't support the weight of the wheel.

8 If required, slide the axle plates and spacers onto the axle in the proper order to aid reassembly **(see illustration)**.
9 Clean all old grease off the axle, spacers and bearing seals. If required, remove the sprocket coupling (see Section 17).
10 Check the axle is straight by rolling it on a flat surface such as a piece of plate glass (first remove any corrosion using wire wool). If the equipment is available, place the axle in V-blocks and measure the runout using a dial gauge. If the axle is bent or the runout exceeds the limit specified, replace it with a new one.
11 Check the condition of the wheel bearings and seals (see Section 13).

Installation

12 Ensure both chain adjusters are correctly installed in the ends of the swingarm.
13 If removed, install the sprocket coupling and apply a smear of grease to the inside of the coupling bearing seal. Ensure the brake plate is correctly installed on the brake drum.
14 Install the left-hand spacer, then manoeuvre the wheel into position between the ends of the swingarm with the sprocket on the left-hand side and fit the drive chain onto the sprocket **(see illustrations 12.7b and a)**.
15 Lubricate the axle with a smear of grease and fit the left-hand axle plate, then lift the wheel into position and insert the axle from the left-hand side **(see illustration 12.6a)**. Install the right-hand spacer between the brake plate and the swingarm **(see illustration 12.6b)** then push the axle all the way through.
16 Check that everything is correctly aligned, then fit the right-hand axle plate and tighten the axle nut finger-tight **(see illustrations 12.5b and a)**.
17 Fit the torque arm onto the shouldered bolt on the brake plate, then install the rubber washer and plain washer and tighten the nut to the torque setting specified at the beginning of this Chapter **(see illustrations 12.3b)**. Secure the nut with a new split pin and bend the ends as shown **(see illustration 12.3a)**.
18 Install the brake rod spring and brake arm trunnion, then connect the rod to the brake arm and thread on the adjuster nut **(see illustrations 12.2b, c and a)**.
19 Check and adjust the drive chain slack (see Chapter 1).
20 Check and adjust the brake pedal freeplay (see Chapter 1).

13 Wheel bearings

Note: *Always renew the wheel bearings in pairs, never individually. Never reuse bearings once they have been removed.*

Front wheel bearings

Caution: Don't lay the wheel down and allow it to rest on the disc – it could become warped. Set the wheel on wood blocks so the wheel rim supports the weight of the wheel, or keep the wheel upright. Don't operate the brake lever with the wheel removed.

1 Remove the wheel (see Section 11).
2 Lever out the bearing seal from each side of the hub using a flat-bladed screwdriver or a seal hook **(see illustration)**. Take care not to damage the hub. Discard the seals as new ones must be fitted on reassembly.
3 Remove the speedometer drive plate from the left-hand side **(see illustration)**.

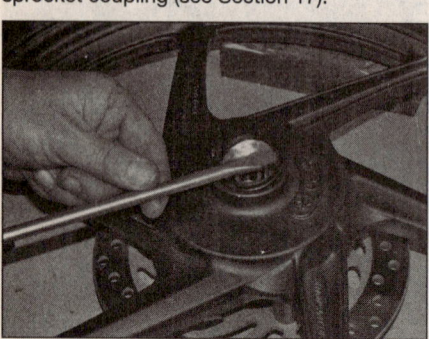

13.2 Lever out the bearing seal

13.3 Remove the speedometer drive plate

Brakes, wheels and final drive 6•15

13.4 Inspect the wheel bearings (arrowed)

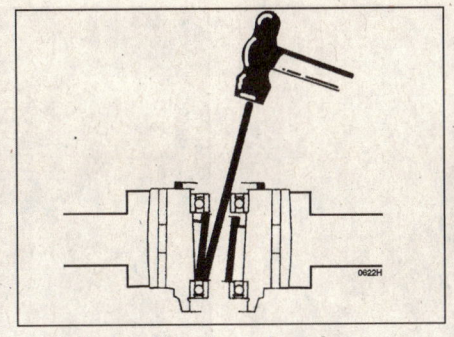

13.5a Position the rod as shown . . .

13.5b . . . to drive out the wheel bearings

4 Inspect the bearings – check that the inner race turns smoothly, quietly and freely and that the outer race is a tight fit in the hub **(see illustration)**.

5 If the bearings are worn, remove them using a metal rod (preferably a brass punch) inserted through the centre of the opposite bearing and locating it on the inner race, pushing the bearing spacer aside to expose it **(see illustration)**. Curve the end of the rod to obtain better purchase if necessary. Strike the rod with a hammer, working evenly around the bearing, to drive it from the hub **(see illustration)**. Remove the spacer which fits between the bearings.

6 Turn the wheel over and remove the other bearing using the same procedure.

7 Thoroughly clean the hub area of the wheel with a suitable solvent and inspect the bearing seats for scoring and wear. If the seats are damaged, consult a Honda dealer before reassembling the wheel.

8 The new bearings can be installed in the hub using a drawbolt arrangement (see *Tools and Workshop Tips* in the *Reference* section) or by using a bearing driver or suitable socket. Ensure that the drawbolt washer or driver (as applicable) bears only on the bearing's outer race and does not contact the bearing housing. Prior to installation, pack the inner, open side of the bearings with multi-purpose grease.

9 Install the right-hand bearing first, with the sealed side facing outwards. Ensure the bearing is fitted squarely and all the way into its seat.

10 Turn the wheel over. Lubricate the bearing spacer with a smear of grease, then install the spacer. Install the left-hand bearing, sealed side facing outwards, driving it in until it is fully seated **(see illustration)**.

11 Lubricate the right-hand bearing seal with a smear of grease and press it into the hub – level the seal with the rim of the hub with a small block of wood **(see illustration)**.

12 Turn the wheel over.

13 Install the speedometer drive plate, ensuring the tabs are facing upwards and are correctly located **(see illustration)**.

14 Lubricate the left-hand bearing seal with a smear of grease and press it into the hub – level the seal with the rim of the hub with a small block of wood.

15 Clean the brake disc using acetone or brake system cleaner, then install the front wheel (see Section 11).

Rear wheel bearings

16 Remove the wheel (see Section 12) and lift the sprocket coupling out of the hub (see Section 17).

17 Inspect the bearings in both sides of the hub – check that the inner race turns smoothly, quietly and freely and that the outer race is a tight fit in the hub **(see illustrations)**.

18 If the bearings are worn, follow the procedure in Steps 5 and 6 to drive them both out and remove the spacer.

19 Thoroughly clean the hub area of the wheel with a suitable solvent and inspect the bearing seats for scoring and wear. If the seats are damaged, consult a Honda dealer before reassembling the wheel.

20 The new bearings can be installed in the hub using a drawbolt arrangement or by using a bearing driver or suitable socket (see

13.10 Drive the bearings in until fully seated

13.11 Installed position of the bearing seal

13.13 Drive plate tabs (arrowed) face upwards

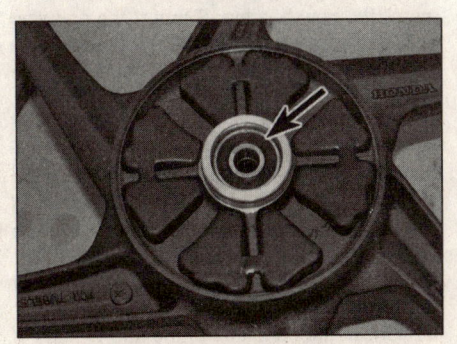

13.17a Inspect the left . . .

13.17b . . . and right-hand rear wheel bearings

13.24 Remove the coupling bearing spacer

13.26 Drive out the bearing from the inside

13.29 Installed position of the bearing seal

13.31 Fit a new hub O-ring if required

Step 8). Don't forget to lubricate the bearings with multi-purpose grease prior to installation.
21 Install the left-hand bearing first, with the sealed side facing outwards. Ensure the bearing is fitted squarely and all the way into its seat.
22 Turn the wheel over. Lubricate the bearing spacer with a smear of grease, then install the spacer. Install the right-hand bearing, sealed side facing outwards, driving it in until it is fully seated.

Sprocket coupling bearing

23 Lever out the bearing seal on the outside of the coupling using a flat-bladed screwdriver or a seal hook **(see illustration 13.2)**. Take care not to damage the seal housing. Discard the seal as a new one should be fitted on reassembly.
24 Remove the spacer from inside the coupling bearing **(see illustration)**.
25 Inspect the bearing – check that the inner races turn smoothly, quietly and freely, and that the outer race is a tight fit in the coupling.

26 If the bearing is worn, support the coupling sprocket side down and drive it out using a suitably-sized socket **(see illustration)**.
27 Thoroughly clean the bearing seat with a suitable solvent and inspect it for scoring and wear. If the seat is damaged, consult a Honda dealer before reassembling the wheel.
28 Use a bearing driver or suitable socket to install the new bearing. Support the coupling sprocket side up and install the bearing with the marked side uppermost. Ensure that the driver bears only on the bearing's outer race. Ensure the bearing is fitted squarely and all the way onto its seat.
29 Lubricate the new seal with a smear of grease, then press it into the coupling. Level the seal with the rim of the coupling with a small block of wood **(see illustration)**.
30 Check the sprocket coupling/rubber dampers (see Section 17).
31 Check the condition of the hub O-ring – if it is damaged or flattened, remove it and fit a new one **(see illustration)**. Ensure the O-ring is correctly located in its groove and lubricate it with a smear of grease.
32 Install the sprocket coupling (see Section 17) then install the rear wheel (see Section 12).

14 Tyres

General information

1 The wheels fitted to the machines covered in this manual are designed to take tubeless tyres only.
2 Tyre sizes are given in *Bike spec* at the beginning of this manual. They are also listed in the Owner's Handbook and on the tyre information label on the swingarm.
3 Refer to the *Pre-ride checks* listed at the beginning of this manual for tyre maintenance.

Brakes, wheels and final drive 6•17

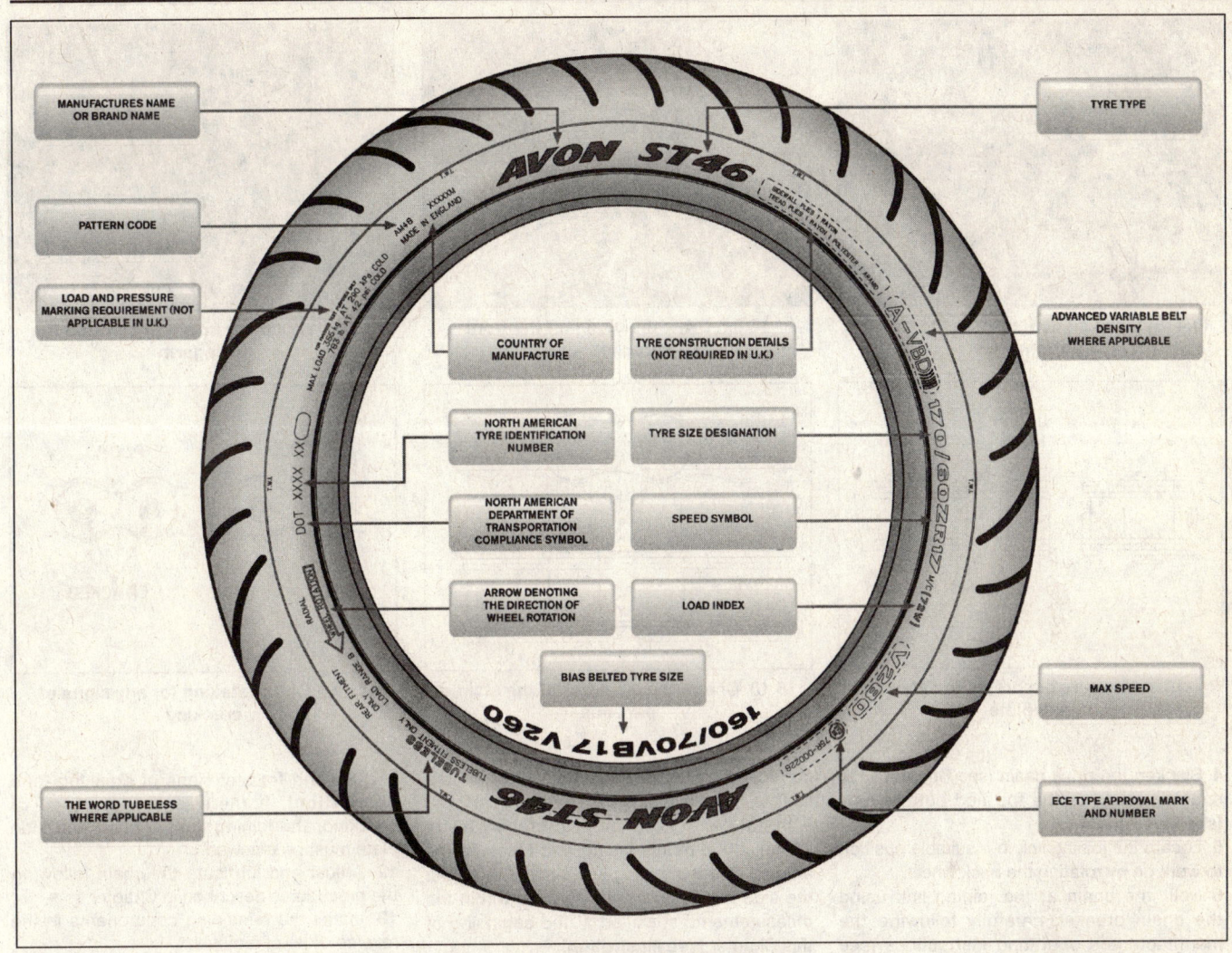

14.4 Common tyre sidewall markings

Labels around the tyre diagram:
- MANUFACTURES NAME OR BRAND NAME
- PATTERN CODE
- LOAD AND PRESSURE MARKING REQUIREMENT (NOT APPLICABLE IN U.K.)
- COUNTRY OF MANUFACTURE
- NORTH AMERICAN TYRE IDENTIFICATION NUMBER
- NORTH AMERICAN DEPARTMENT OF TRANSPORTATION COMPLIANCE SYMBOL
- ARROW DENOTING THE DIRECTION OF WHEEL ROTATION
- BIAS BELTED TYRE SIZE
- THE WORD TUBELESS WHERE APPLICABLE
- TYRE TYPE
- TYRE CONSTRUCTION DETAILS (NOT REQUIRED IN U.K.)
- ADVANCED VARIABLE BELT DENSITY WHERE APPLICABLE
- TYRE SIZE DESIGNATION
- SPEED SYMBOL
- LOAD INDEX
- MAX SPEED
- ECE TYPE APPROVAL MARK AND NUMBER

Fitting new tyres

4 When selecting new tyres, refer to the tyre information in the Owner's Handbook. Ensure that front and rear tyre types are compatible, the correct size and correct speed rating **(see illustration)**. If necessary seek advice from a Honda dealer or tyre fitting specialist.

5 It is recommended that tyres are fitted by a motorcycle tyre specialist rather than attempted in the home workshop. This is particularly relevant in the case of tubeless tyres because the force required to break the seal between the wheel rim and tyre bead is substantial, and is usually beyond the capabilities of an individual working with normal tyre levers. Additionally, the specialist will be able to balance the wheels after tyre fitting and renew the tyre valve.

6 Note that punctured tubeless tyres can in some cases be repaired. Repairs must be carried out by a motorcycle tyre fitting specialist. Honda advise that a repaired tyre should not be used at speeds above 50 mph (80 kmh) for the first 24 hours, and not above 75 mph (120 kmh) thereafter.

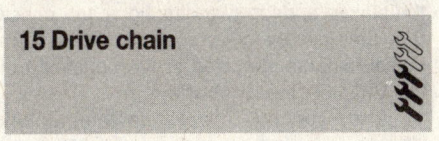

15 Drive chain

Cleaning

1 Refer to Chapter 1 for details of routine cleaning with the chain installed on the sprockets.

2 If the chain is extremely dirty remove it from the motorcycle and soak it in paraffin (kerosene) for approximately five or six minutes, then clean it using a soft brush.

Caution: Don't use gasoline (petrol), solvent or other cleaning fluids which might damage its internal sealing properties. Don't use high-pressure water. Remove the chain, wipe it off, then blow dry it with compressed air immediately. The entire process shouldn't take longer than ten minutes – if it does, the O-rings in the chain rollers could be damaged.

Removal and installation

Special tool: *The original equipment chain has a staked-type joining link which can be disassembled using either Honda service tool, Part No. 07HMH-MR10103, or one of several commercially-available drive chain cutting/staking tools. Such chains can be identified by the joining link side plate's identification marks (and usually its different colour), as well as by the staked ends of the link's two pins which look as if they have been deeply centre-punched, instead of peened over as with all the other pins.*

Note: *If the chain is to be reused, clean it as described and wipe all old grease and dirt off the sprockets, swingarm chain slider and front sprocket cover. If the chain is to be renewed, fit new front and rear sprockets as described in Section 16.*

3 To remove the chain, first remove the front sprocket cover and chain guide (see Section 16).

6•18 Brakes, wheels and final drive

15.4 Slacken chain for access to top and bottom runs

15.6a Draw the chain off the front sprocket . . .

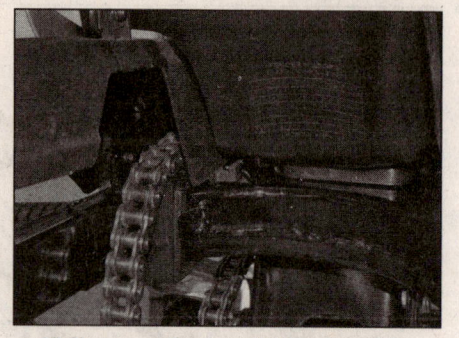

15.6b . . . noting how it fits around the swingarm

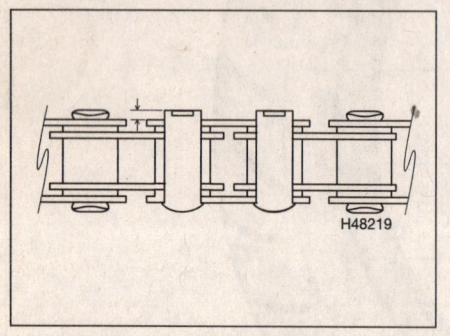

15.9 Measure pin projection above sideplate

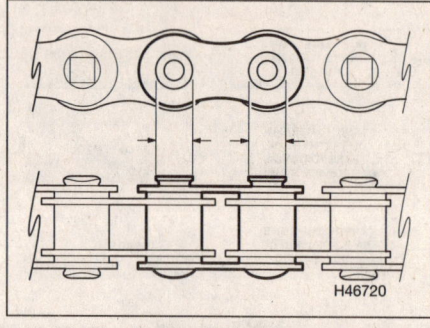

15.10 Check the diameter of the staked pin ends

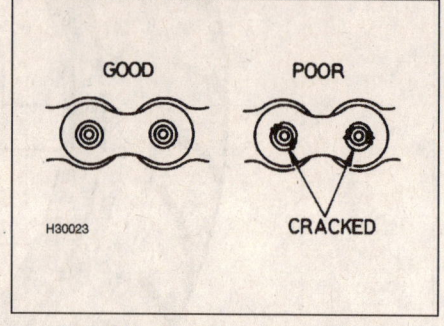

15.11 Check staking for any signs of cracking

4 Slacken the drive chain (see Chapter 1) to enable access to the top and bottom runs **(see illustration)**.
5 Locate the joining link in a suitable position to work on by rotating the back wheel.
6 Split the chain at the joining link using the chain breaker, carefully following the manufacturer's operating instructions (see also Section 8 in *Tools and Workshop Tips* in the *Reference* section). Draw the chain off the front sprocket, noting how it fits around the swingarm, and lift it off **(see illustrations)**.
7 On installation, fit the chain around the front and rear sprockets, leaving the two ends in a convenient position to work on.
8 Refer to Section 8 in *Tools and Workshop Tips* in the *Reference* section. Install the new joining link from the inside with the four O-rings correctly located between the link plates. DO NOT re-use old joining link components.
9 Install the new side plate with its identification marks facing out. Measure the amount that the joining link pins project from the side plate and check they are within the measurements specified at the beginning of this Chapter **(see illustration)**.
10 Stake the new link using the drive chain cutting/staking tool, carefully following the instructions of both the chain manufacturer and the tool manufacturer. Ensure the chain is staked correctly by measuring the diameter of the staked ends in two directions and check that they are evenly staked and within the measurements specified at the beginning of this Chapter **(see illustration)**.
11 After staking, check the joining link and staking for any signs of cracking **(see illustration)**. If there is any evidence of cracking, the joining link, O-rings and side plate must be renewed.
12 Adjust and lubricate the chain following the procedures described in Chapter 1.
13 Install the remaining components in the reverse order of removal.

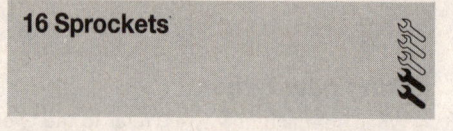

16 Sprockets

Check

1 Undo the bolts securing the front sprocket cover and remove it **(see illustrations)**. Lift off the chain guide **(see illustration)**.

16.1a Undo the bolts (arrowed) . . .

16.1b . . . and remove the front sprocket cover

16.1c Remove the chain guide

Brakes, wheels and final drive 6•19

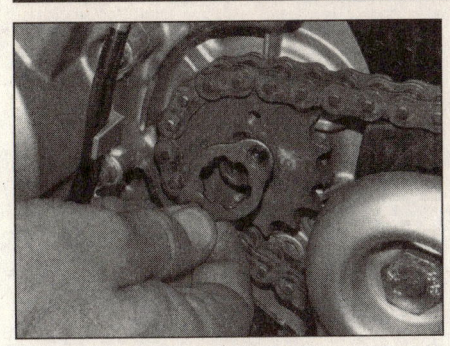

16.5 Remove the retainer plate ...

16.6 ... and draw the front sprocket off

16.9 Sprocket mounting nuts (arrowed)

2 Check the wear pattern on both sprockets (see Chapter 1, Section 1). If the sprocket teeth are worn excessively, replace the chain and both sprockets as a set – worn sprockets can ruin a new drive chain and vice versa.

Removal and installation

Front sprocket

3 Remove the front sprocket cover and chain guide (see Step 1).
4 If only the front sprocket is being removed, slacken the drive chain (see Chapter 1) – the sprocket can then be pulled off the transmission output shaft with the chain *in situ*.
5 Unscrew the sprocket retainer plate bolts, turn the plate to unlock it from the splines on the output shaft, then slide it off the shaft **(see illustration)**.
6 Lift the chain off the sprocket and slide the sprocket off the shaft **(see illustration)**. Note which way round the sprocket is fitted.
7 Installation is the reverse of removal, noting the following:
- Ensure the marked side of the sprocket faces out.
- Ensure the retainer plate is correctly installed.
- Tighten the retainer plate bolts to the torque setting specified at the beginning of this Chapter.

Rear sprocket

8 Remove the rear wheel (see Section 12). Support the wheel on wooden blocks with the sprocket uppermost.
9 Unscrew the nuts securing the sprocket to the sprocket coupling, then lift off the sprocket, noting which way round it fits **(see illustration)**.
10 Check the condition of the sprocket studs and replace them all with new ones if any are damaged. Prior to installation, clean the stud threads and apply a suitable non-permanent thread-locking compound. Follow the procedure in *Tools and Workshop Tips* to lock 2 nuts together on the stud to aid installation. Make sure the studs are tight.
11 Before installing the sprocket, make sure there is no dirt or corrosion where it seats on the hub. Fit the sprocket with the marked side facing out, then install the nuts and tighten them evenly and in a criss-cross sequence to the torque setting specified at the beginning of this Chapter.
12 Install the rear wheel (see Section 12).

17 Rear sprocket coupling dampers

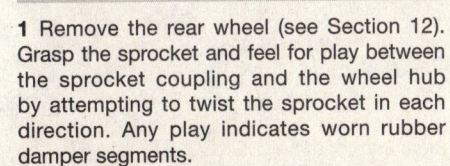

1 Remove the rear wheel (see Section 12). Grasp the sprocket and feel for play between the sprocket coupling and the wheel hub by attempting to twist the sprocket in each direction. Any play indicates worn rubber damper segments.
2 Lift the sprocket coupling out from the wheel hub leaving the rubber dampers in position. Note the spacer inside the coupling and remove it if it is loose **(see illustration 13.24)**.
3 Examine the vanes on the back of the coupling for cracks or any obvious signs of damage.
4 Lift the rubber damper segments from the wheel and check them for cracks, hardening and general deterioration **(see illustration)**. Renew them as a set if necessary.
5 Check the condition of the hub O-ring – if it is damaged or flattened, replace it with a new one **(see illustration 13.31)**.
6 Inspect the sprocket coupling bearing see Section 13.
7 Installation is the reverse of removal. Lubricate the hub O-ring with a smear of grease. Make sure the spacer is correctly installed in the coupling. Align the vanes with the dampers and press the coupling in firmly.

17.4 Examine the damper segments

Chapter 7
Bodywork

Contents

	Section number		Section number
Belly fairing	10	Rear mudguard	9
Fairing panels	6	Seat cowling	8
Front mudguard	7	Seats	2
General information	1	Side panels	3
Mirrors	4	Windshield	5

Degrees of difficulty

Easy, suitable for novice with little experience	Fairly easy, suitable for beginner with some experience	Fairly difficult, suitable for competent DIY mechanic	Difficult, suitable for experienced DIY mechanic	Very difficult, suitable for expert DIY or professional

1 General information

This Chapter covers the procedures necessary to remove and install the bodywork. Since many service and repair operations on these motorcycles require the removal of the body panels, the procedures are grouped here and referred to from other Chapters.

In the case of damage to the bodywork, it is usually necessary to remove the broken component and replace it with a new (or used) one. The material that the body panels are composed of doesn't lend itself to conventional repair techniques. Note that there are however some companies that specialize in 'plastic welding' and there are a number of DIY bodywork repair kits now available for motorcycles.

When attempting to remove any body panel, first study it closely, noting any fasteners and associated fittings, to be sure of returning everything to its correct place on installation. In some cases the aid of an assistant will be required when removing panels, to help avoid the risk of damage to paintwork. Once the evident fasteners have been removed, try to withdraw the panel as described but DO NOT FORCE IT – if it will not release, check that all fasteners have been removed and try again.

When installing a body panel, first study it closely, noting any fasteners and associated fittings removed with it, to be sure of returning everything to its correct place. Check that all fasteners are in good condition, including the rubber mounts; replace any faulty fasteners with new ones before the panel is reassembled. Check also that all mounting brackets are straight and repair them or replace them with new ones if necessary before attempting to install the panel.

Tighten the fasteners securely, but be careful not to overtighten any of them or the panel may break (not always immediately) due to the uneven stress.

Wellnuts

Wellnuts have a metal thread retained inside a rubber bush. The bush is a firm press fit in a body panel or windshield **(see illustration 5.2)**. Avoid overtightening the screw, otherwise the bush will twist in the panel and damage the locating hole.

Self-tapping screws

When a panel is removed, note the location of the screws. If they engage in plastic lugs on the back of an adjacent panel, check the condition of each lug and ensure it is not split or the thread stripped. If necessary, repair a damaged lug with a proprietary repair kit.

If the screws engage in U-clips, check that the clips are a firm fit on the mounting lug and that they are not sprained **(see illustration 6.16)**. If necessary, fit new U-clips.

7•2 Bodywork

2.1 Release the seat catch

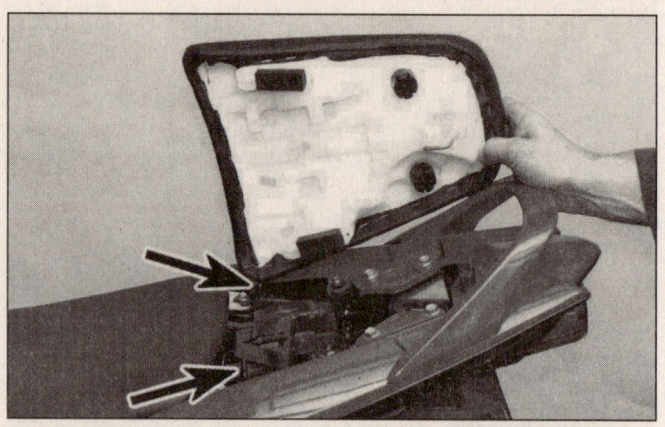

2.2 Draw the seat rearwards to free it from the frame brackets (arrowed)

2 Seats

Removal

1 Insert the ignition key into the seat lock located below the seat cowling on the left-hand side, release the seat catch and lift the rear of the passenger's seat **(see illustration)**.
2 Draw the seat rearwards to disengage the tabs on the underside from the brackets on the frame **(see illustration)**.
3 To remove the rider's seat, undo the bolts securing the rear of the seat, noting the location of the spacers **(see illustrations)**.
4 Draw the seat rearwards to disengage the tabs on the underside from the rear of the fuel tank **(see illustrations)**.
5 The seat catch mechanism is located on the rear of the frame – remove the seat cowling (see Section 8) and the rear mudguard (see Section 9) for access **(see illustration)**. If, for any reason, the lock or catch mechanism are renewed, always check the operation of the catch before installing the passenger's seat.

Installation

6 Make sure the tabs at the front of the rider's seat are fitted correctly under the rear of the fuel tank. Fit the spacers on the mounting bolts and tighten the bolts securely.
7 Slide the passenger's seat forwards to engage the tabs with the frame brackets, then push down on the back of the seat to engage the catch.

2.3a Undo the bolts (arrowed) . . .

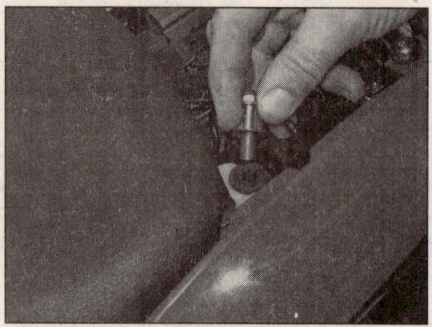

2.3b . . . noting location of the spacers

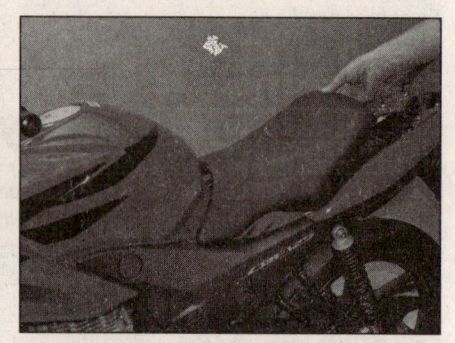

2.4a Draw the seat rearwards . . .

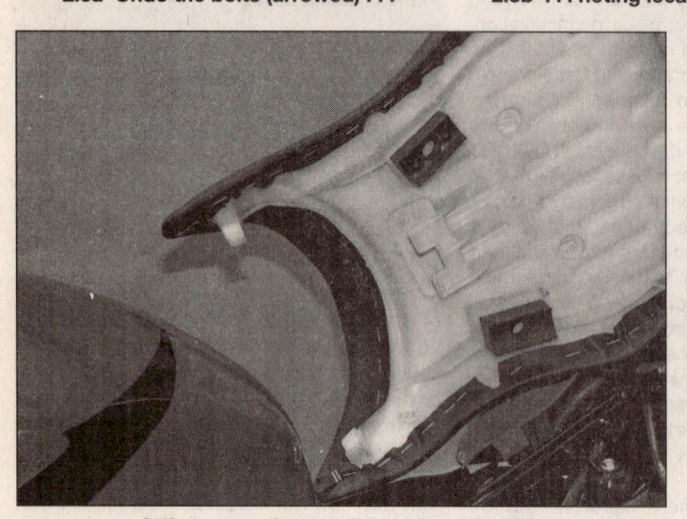

2.4b . . . to release tabs on the underside

2.5 Location of the seat catch mechanism

Bodywork 7•3

3.2 Undo the screws (arrowed)

3.3a Free the top edge of the panel (arrowed) . . .

3 Side panels

Removal

1 Remove the seats (see Section 2).
2 Undo the screws securing the forward edge of the side panel **(see illustration)**.
3 Ease the top edge away from the fuel tank to release the pegs on the back of the panel from the grommets, then unhook the rear edge of the panel from the tab on the front edge of the seat cowling **(see illustrations)**.

Installation

4 Prior to Installation, ensure the grommets are correctly located in the bottom edge of the fuel tank **(see illustration)**.
5 Secure the rear edge of the panel, then press the pegs firmly into the grommets. If required, lubricate the grommets with WD-40 or similar.
6 Tighten the fixing screws to secure the panel.

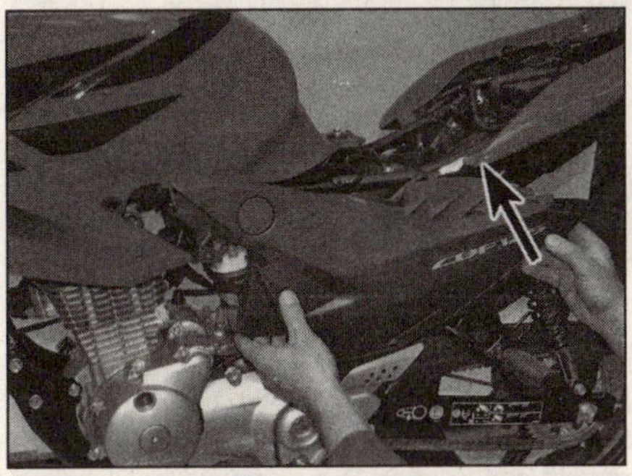

4 Mirrors

Removal

1 Lift the rubber boot off the mirror bracket **(see illustration)**.
2 Loosen the locknut on the mirror stem, then unscrew the mirror **(see illustrations)**. Both mirrors have right-hand threads – turn anti-clockwise to unscrew.
3 If required, unscrew the mirror adapter **(see illustration)**. Both adapters have left-hand threads – turn clockwise to unscrew.

Installation

4 If removed, turn the mirror adapters anti-clockwise and tighten them securely.

3.3b . . . and unhook the rear edge from the tab (arrowed)

3.4 Ensure the grommets (arrowed) are correctly located

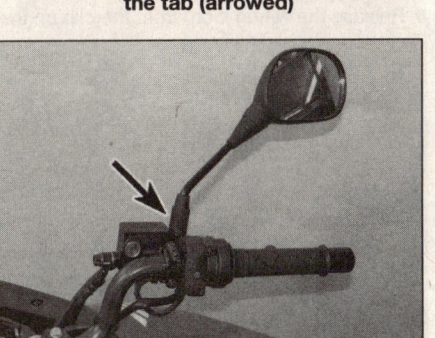

4.1 Lift the rubber boot (arrowed)

4.2a Loosen the locknut (arrowed) . . .

4.2b . . . and unscrew the mirror stem

4.3 Mirror adapter has a left-hand thread

7•4 Bodywork

5 Screw the mirror stem fully into the adapter and position it as required. Counter-hold the adapter and tighten the locknut.
6 Position the rubber boot over the locknut and adapter.

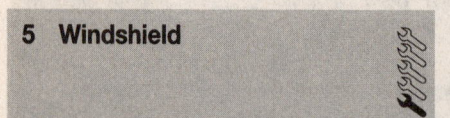

5 Windshield

1 Undo the screws securing the windshield, noting the location of the plastic washers, and lift it off **(see illustrations)**.
2 Inspect the wellnuts in the fairing **(see illustration)** – if they are loose, new ones must be fitted. Apply a smear of grease to the screw threads on installation.

6 Fairing panels

Inner fairing panels

1 Working on one panel at a time, undo the screw securing the panel **(see illustration)**.
2 Ease the rear upper edge of the panel out from underneath the edge of the fairing panel **(see illustration)**.
3 Release the top edge of the panel from the spring retainer on the back of the fairing panel and lift it out **(see illustration)**.
4 On installation, ensure the rear upper edge of the inner panel is correctly positioned before clipping it into place and securing it with the screw **(see illustration)**.

5.1a Undo the screws (arrowed) . . .

5.1b . . . noting the location of the washers . . .

5.1c . . . and lift the windshield off

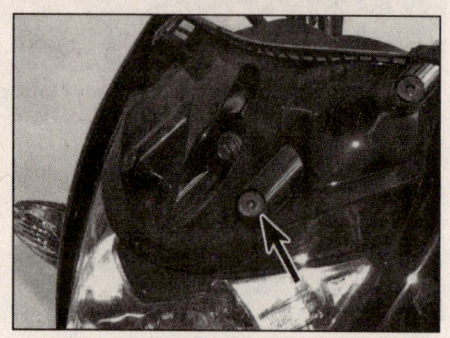

5.2 Check that the wellnuts (arrowed) are secure

Fairing

5 Remove the seats (see Section 2), side panels (see Section 3), windshield (see Section 5) and inner fairing panels (see above).
6 Release the wiring loom from the clip on the inner left-hand side of the fairing and displace the boot **(see illustration)**. Refer to the *Wiring Diagram* at the end of Chapter 8 and disconnect the connectors for the headlight assembly and turn signals **(see illustration)**.

6.1 Undo screw (arrowed) securing the panel

6.2 Ease the edge (arrowed) out from under the fairing panel

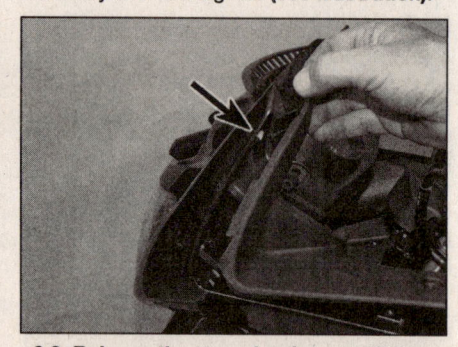

6.3 Release the top edge (arrowed) from the spring retainer

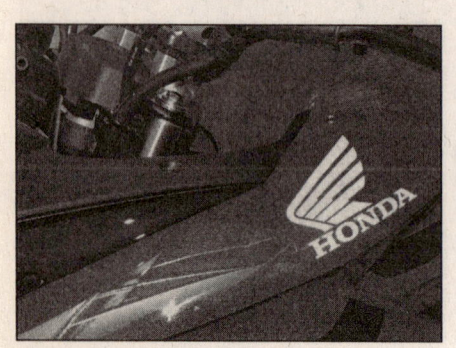

6.4 Ensure correct alignment of panels before securing

6.6a Displace the wiring boot (arrowed) . . .

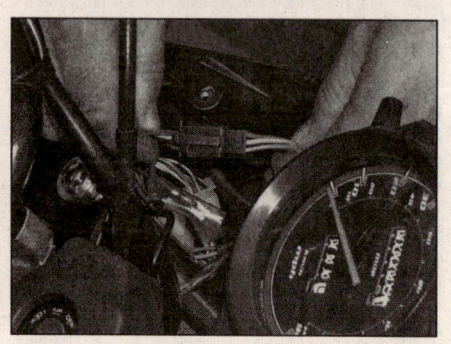

6.6b . . . and disconnect the connectors

Bodywork 7•5

6.8 Undo the screws (arrowed)

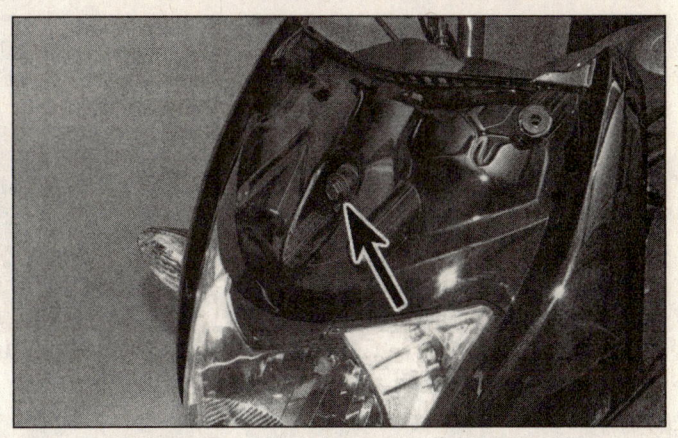

6.9 Location of central mounting bolt (arrowed)

7 Release the speedometer cable from the clip on the lower left-hand edge of the fairing **(see illustration 6.15)**.
8 Undo the screws on both sides securing the fairing to the fuel tank **(see illustration)**.
9 Undo the central mounting bolt, noting the location of the spacer **(see illustration)**.
10 Draw the fairing forwards and off the bike **(see illustration)**.

11 Note the location of the rubber covers on the fuel tank mounting tabs and remove them for safekeeping if they are loose **(see illustration)**.
12 Follow the procedures in Chapter 8 to remove the headlight unit and turn signals.
13 Note the location of the support stay on the inside of the fairing. The fairing is secured to the stay by self-tapping screws and the turn signal stems (see Chapter 8, Sections 7 and 12).
14 If required, undo the screws securing the right-hand fairing side panel **(see illustration)**. Note how the tab on the side panel locates in the slot in the headlight panel, then release the tab carefully and separate the panels **(see illustration)**.
15 Before removing the left-hand side panel,

6.10 Draw the fairing forwards

6.11 Note the location of the rubber covers

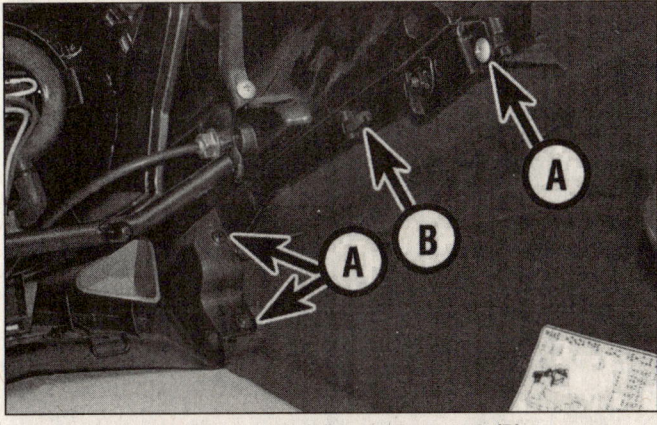

6.14a Undo screws (A) and release tab (B) . . .

6.14b . . . to release the right-hand panel

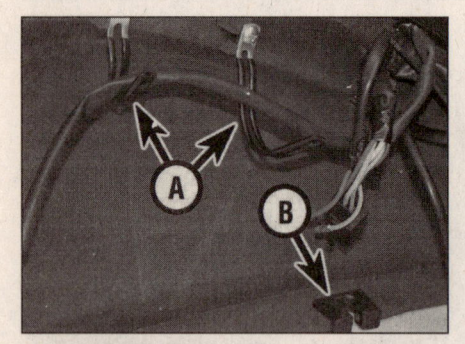

6.15 Wiring clips (A) and speedo cable clip (B)

6.16 Ensure the U-clips are secure

6.18 Inspect the grommets (arrowed) in the fairing bracket

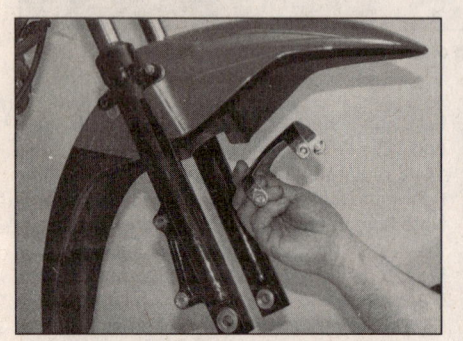

7.2 Remove the support bracket

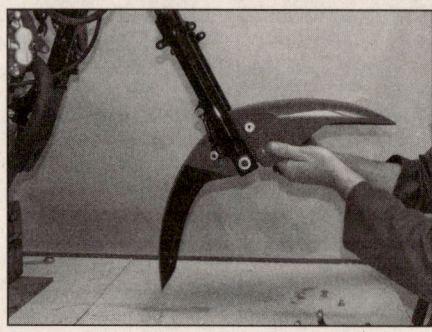

7.3 Lower the mudguard

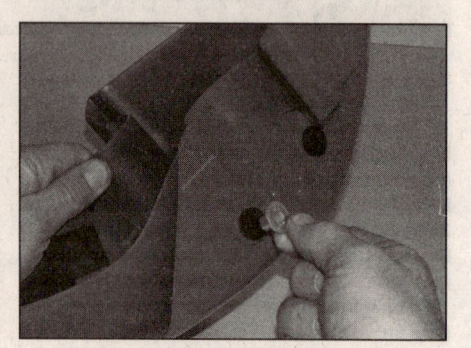

7.4 Note location of spacers and grommets

release the headlight and turn signal relay wiring from the clips and note the location of the clip for the speedometer cable **(see illustration)**. Unclip the turn signal relay from its bracket (see Chapter 8, Section 10). Follow the procedure in Step 14 to separate the side panel from the headlight panel.
16 Note the location of the U-clips on the inside of the side panels and ensure they are secure **(see illustration)**.
17 Note the location of the grommet for the fairing central mounting bolt and the windshield wellnuts in the headlight panel. Renew any components that are damaged or deteriorated.
18 Inspect the grommets in the fairing bracket and renew them if they are damaged or deteriorated **(see illustration)**. Check that the bracket mounting bolts are tightened securely.
19 Installation is the reverse of removal. Ensure all wiring connectors are secure and test the operation of the headlight and turn signals before riding the motorcycle.

7 Front mudguard

1 Undo the right-hand mudguard mounting bolt to free the brake hose guide, then remove the front wheel (see Chapter 6).
2 Undo the remaining mudguard mounting bolts and remove the bracket from inside the mudguard **(see illustration)**.
3 Lower the mudguard to remove it **(see illustration)**.
4 Note the location of the spacers and grommets in the sides of the mudguard **(see illustration)**. Remove the spacers for safekeeping if they are loose. Replace the grommets with new ones if they are damaged or deteriorated.
5 Installation is the reverse of removal.

8 Seat cowling

Removal
1 Remove the seats (see Section 2).
2 Undo the bolts securing the passenger handle and lift the handle off **(see illustrations)**.

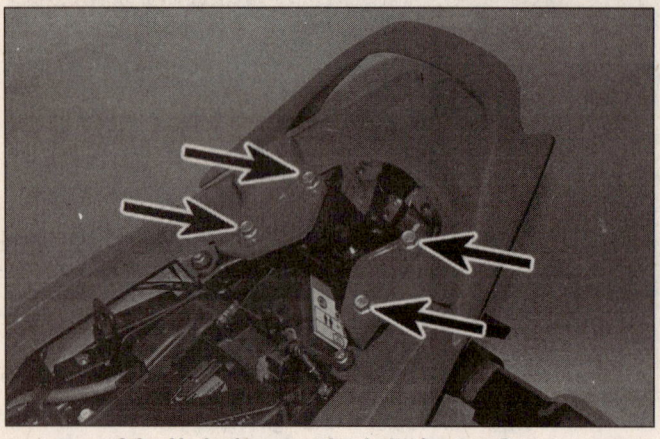

8.2a Undo the mounting bolts (arrowed) . . .

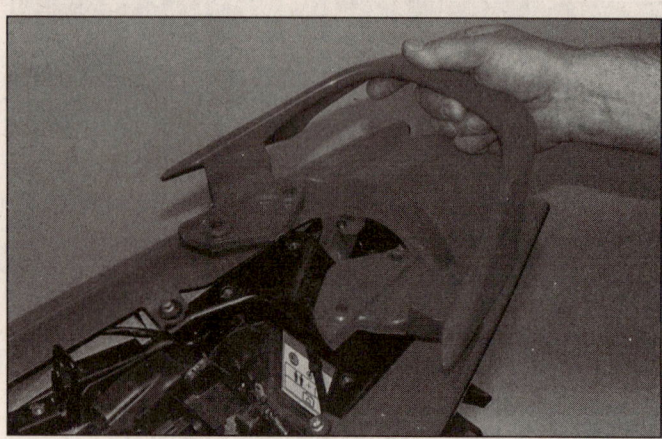

8.2b . . . and lift the handle off

Bodywork 7•7

8.3a Undo the bolts (arrowed) . . .

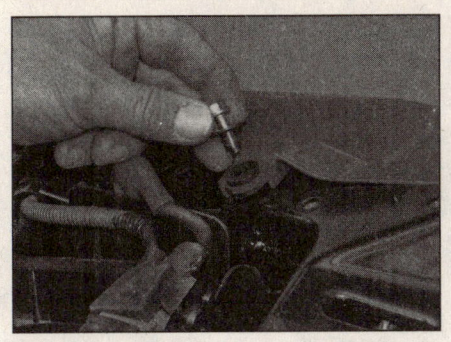

8.3b . . . noting location of the spacers

8.4 Disconnect the tail light wiring connector

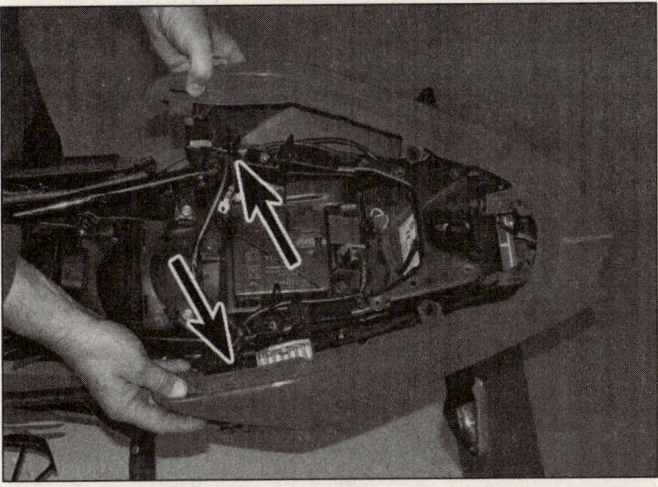

8.5 Release the pegs (arrowed) from the grommets on the frame

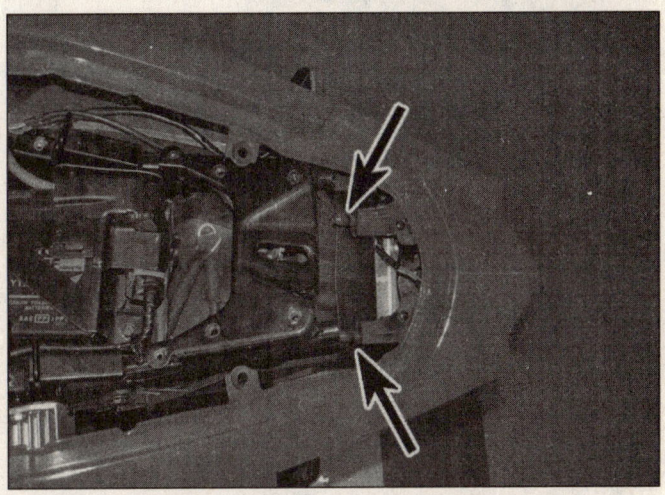

8.6a Release the pegs (arrowed) . . .

3 Undo the bolts securing the seat cowling, noting the location of the spacers **(see illustrations)**.
4 Locate the wiring connector for the tail light unit behind the cowling on the right-hand side and disconnect it **(see illustration)**.
5 Ease the forward edges of the cowling apart to release the pegs from the grommets on the frame **(see illustration)**.
6 Ease the cowling towards the rear to release the pegs from the grommets in the top of the rear mudguard and lift it off **(see illustrations)**.
7 Note the location of the grommets in the upper mountings and renew them if they are damaged or deteriorated **(see illustration)**.

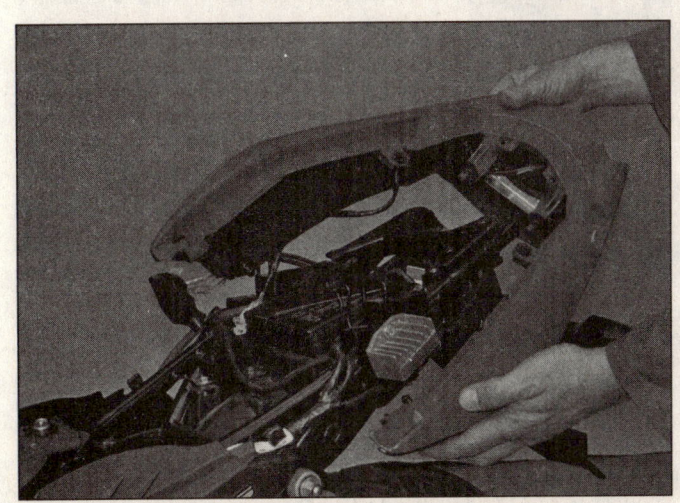

8.6b . . . and remove the seat cowling

8.7 Check the condition of the grommets (arrowed)

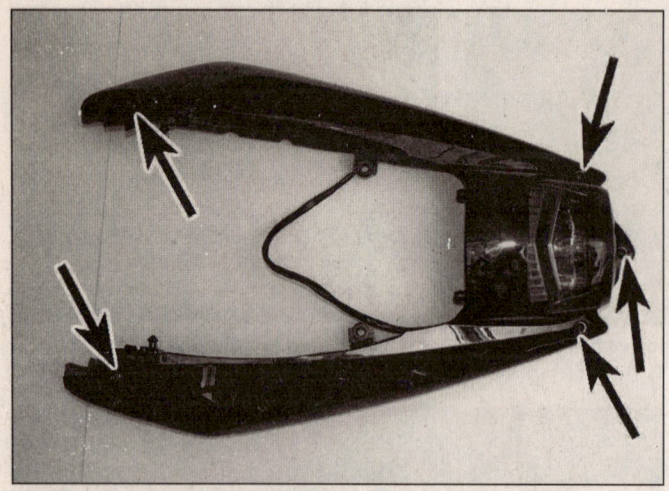

7•8 Bodywork

8.8a Undo the screws (arrowed)

8.8b Release the spring retainers from the brackets

8 If required, to separate the two halves of the cowling, undo the self-tapping screws **(see illustration)**. Ease the two halves apart to release the spring retainers on the underside of the top half from the brackets on the bottom half **(see illustration)**.

Installation

9 Installation is the reverse of removal. Ensure the wiring is correctly routed. Ensure the two halves of the cowling are aligned accurately before clipping them together. Test the operation of the tail light and brake light before riding the motorcycle.

9 Rear mudguard

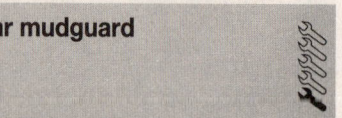

9.3 Note how the mudguard locates

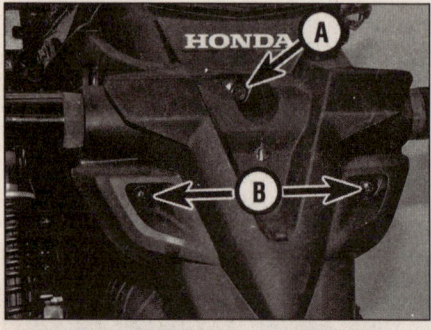

9.4a Undo the bolt (A) and screws (B) . . .

9.4b . . . and lift the mudguard off

1 Remove the seats (see Section 2) and the seat cowling (see Section 8).
2 If applicable, remove the licence plate.
3 Note how the top of the mudguard locates over the rear turn signals bracket and the seat lock, and how the forward edge hooks over the rear edge of the underseat panel **(see illustration)**.
4 Undo the bolt and screws securing the mudguard and lift it off **(see illustrations)**.
5 Installation is the reverse of removal.
6 The rear hugger and chain guard assembly are fixed to the swingarm – refer to Chapter 5 for details.

10 Belly fairing

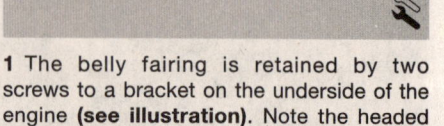

10.1a Belly fairing is retained by a screw on each side

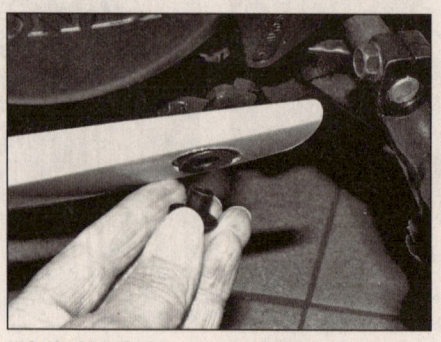

10.1b Headed spacer locates in grommet

1 The belly fairing is retained by two screws to a bracket on the underside of the engine **(see illustration)**. Note the headed spacer which fits inside the grommet **(see illustration)**.
2 Once removed, the right-hand half can be separated from the main section by removing the three screws from the inside. If removing the fairing as part of the engine removal procedure, also unbolt its mounting bracket from the underside.
3 When refitting, note the fairing tabs locate on the frame's engine mounting bracket.

Chapter 8
Electrical system

Contents

	Section number
Alternator	27
Battery	3
Brake light switches	13
Brake/tail light bulb	8
Brake/tail light unit	9
Charging system testing	26
Clutch switch	21
Electrical system fault finding	2
Fuses	4
General information	1
Handlebar switches	16
Headlight	7
Headlight and sidelight bulbs	6
Horn	17
Ignition safety interlock circuit	18

	Section number
Ignition switch	15
Ignition system components	see Chapter 3
Instrument cluster	14
Lighting system check	5
Neutral switch	19
Regulator/rectifier	28
Sidestand switch	20
Starter safety circuit diode	22
Starter motor overhaul	25
Starter motor removal and installation	24
Starter relay	23
Turn signal assemblies	12
Turn signal bulbs	11
Turn signal circuit check	10

Degrees of difficulty

| **Easy,** suitable for novice with little experience | **Fairly easy,** suitable for beginner with some experience | **Fairly difficult,** suitable for competent DIY mechanic | **Difficult,** suitable for experienced DIY mechanic | **Very difficult,** suitable for expert DIY or professional |

Specifications

Battery
Capacity	12 V, 6 Ah
Voltage	
Fully-charged	12.7 to 12.9 V
Needs charging	below 12.4 V
Charging rate	
Normal	0.6 A for 5 to 10 hrs
Quick	3.0 A for 1 hr (max)

Charging system
Alternator stator coil resistance	0.2 to 1.0 ohms
Alternator output	170 W @ 5000 rpm
Current leakage	0.1 mA (max)
Regulated voltage output	15.5 V @ 5000 rpm

Starter motor
Brush length	
Standard	10.0 to 10.05 mm

Fuses
Main fuse	15 A
Circuit fuses	10 A x 2

Bulbs
Headlight	35/35 W
Sidelight	5 W
Brake/tail light	21/5 W
Turn signal lights	21 W x 4 (amber)
Instrument lights	1.7 W x 2
Warning lights	
Turn signal	1.7 W
High beam	1.7 W
Neutral indicator	1.7 W
FI warning light	1.7 W

Torque settings
Alternator rotor nut	74 Nm
Alternator stator wiring clamp bolts	12 Nm
CKP sensor bolts	12 Nm
Neutral switch	12 Nm
Starter motor housing bolts	5 Nm

1 General information

All models covered in this manual have a 12 volt electrical system charged by a three-phase alternator with a separate regulator/rectifier.

The regulator maintains the charging system output within the specified range to prevent overcharging, and the rectifier converts the ac (alternating current) output of the alternator to dc (direct current) to power the lights and other components and to charge the battery. The alternator rotor is mounted on the left-hand end of the crankshaft.

The starter motor is mounted on top of the crankcase behind the cylinder. The starting system includes the motor, the battery, the relay and the various wires and switches. Some of the switches are part of a safety circuit which prevents the engine from being started initially if the sidestand is down or the engine is in gear. The system will also cut the engine should the sidestand extend while the bike is being ridden – see Chapter 1 for checks on the system.

Note: *Keep in mind that electrical parts, once purchased, often cannot be returned. To avoid unnecessary expense, make very sure the faulty component has been positively identified before buying a replacement part.*

2 Electrical system fault finding

1 A typical electrical circuit consists of an electrical component, the switches, relays, etc, related to that component and the wiring and connectors that link the component to the battery and the frame.

2 Before tackling any troublesome electrical circuit, first study the wiring diagram thoroughly to get a complete picture of what makes up that individual circuit. Trouble spots, for instance, can often be narrowed down by noting if other components related to that circuit are operating properly or not. If several components or circuits fail at one time, chances are the fault lies either in the fuse or in the common earth (ground) connection, as several circuits are often routed through the same fuse and earth (ground) connections.

3 Electrical problems often stem from simple causes, such as loose or corroded connections or a blown fuse. Prior to any electrical fault finding, always visually check the condition of the fuse, wires and connections in the problem circuit. Intermittent failures can be especially frustrating, since you can't always duplicate the failure when it's convenient to test. In such situations, a good practice is to clean all connections in the affected circuit, whether or not they appear to be good. All of the connections and wires should also be wiggled to check for looseness which can cause intermittent failure.

4 A multimeter will enable a full range of electrical tests to be made. If you don't have a multimeter it is highly advisable to obtain one – they are not expensive and will enable a full range of electrical tests to be made. Go for a modern digital one with LCD display as they are easier to use. A continuity tester and/or test light are useful for certain electrical checks as an alternative, though are limited in their usefulness compared to a multimeter **(see illustrations)**.

Continuity checks

5 The term continuity describes the uninterrupted flow of electricity through an electrical circuit. Continuity can be checked with a multimeter set either to its continuity function (a beep is emitted when continuity is found), or to the resistance (ohms / Ω) function, or with a dedicated continuity tester. Both instruments are powered by an internal battery, therefore the checks are made with the ignition OFF. As a safety precaution, always disconnect the battery negative (-ve) lead before making continuity checks, particularly if ignition switch checks are being made.

6 If using a multimeter, select the continuity

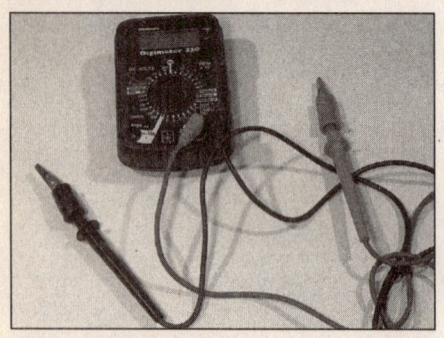

2.4a A digital multimeter can be used for all electrical tests

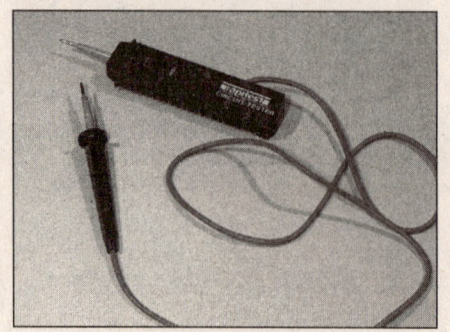

2.4b A battery powered continuity tester

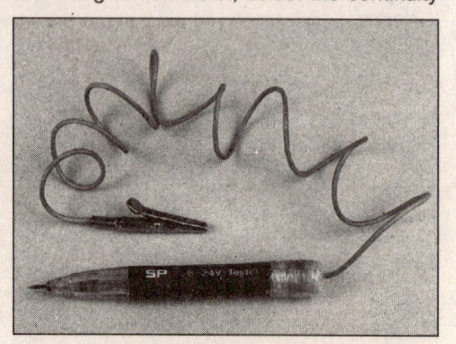

2.4c A simple test light can be used for voltage checks

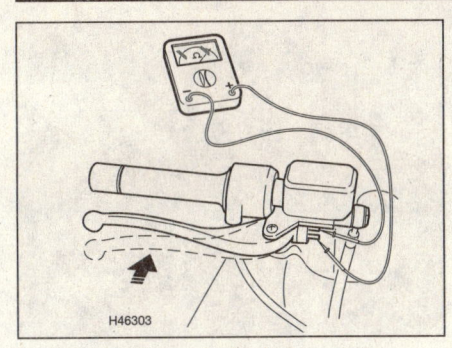

Electrical system 8•3

2.10 Testing a brake light switch for continuity

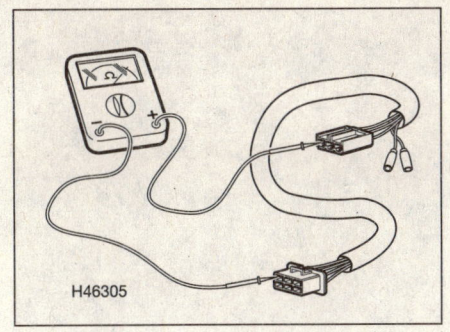

2.12 Testing for continuity in a wiring loom

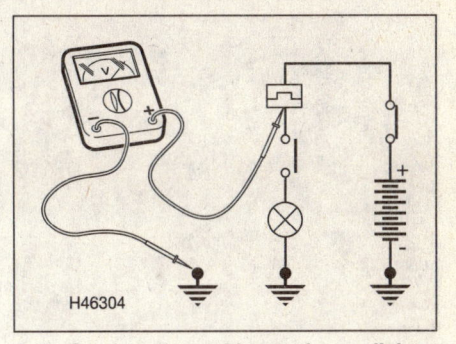

2.15 Connect the multimeter in parallel, or across the load, as shown

function if it has one, or the resistance (ohms) function. Touch the meter probes together and check that a beep is emitted or the meter reads zero, which indicates continuity. If there is no continuity there will be no beep or the meter will show infinite resistance. After using the meter, always switch it OFF to conserve its battery.

7 A continuity tester can be used in the same way – its light should come on or it should beep to indicate continuity in the switch ON position, but should be off or silent in the OFF position.

8 Note that the polarity of the test probes doesn't matter for continuity checks, although care should be taken to follow specific test procedures if a diode or solid-state component is being checked.

Switch continuity checks

9 If a switch is at fault, trace its wiring to the wiring connectors. Separate the connectors and inspect them for security and condition. A build-up of dirt or corrosion here will most likely be the cause of the problem – clean up and apply a water dispersant such as WD40, or alternatively use a dedicated contact cleaner and protection spray.

10 If using a multimeter, select the continuity function if it has one, or the resistance (ohms/Ω) function, and connect its probes to the terminals in the connector **(see illustration)**. Simple ON/OFF type switches, such as brake light switches, only have two wires whereas combination switches, like the handlebar switches, have many wires. Study the wiring diagram to ensure that you are connecting to the correct pair of wires. Continuity should be indicated with the switch ON and no continuity with it OFF.

Wiring continuity checks

11 Many electrical faults are caused by damaged wiring, often due to incorrect routing or chaffing on frame components. Loose, wet or corroded wire connectors can also be the cause of electrical problems.

12 A continuity check can be made on a single length of wire by disconnecting it at each end and connecting the meter or continuity tester probes to each end of the wire **(see illustration)**. Continuity (low or no resistance – zero ohms) should be indicated

if the wire is good. If no continuity (high resistance) is shown, suspect a broken wire.

13 To check for continuity to earth in any earth wire connect one probe of your meter or tester to the earth wire terminal in the connector and the other to the frame, engine, or battery earth (-) terminal. Continuity (low or no resistance – zero ohms) should be indicated if the wire is good. If no continuity (high resistance) is shown, suspect a broken wire or corroded or loose earth point (see below).

Voltage checks

14 A voltage check can determine whether power is reaching a component. Use a multimeter set to the dc voltage scale, or a test light. The test light is the cheaper component, but the meter has the advantage of being able to give a voltage reading.

15 Connect the meter or test light in parallel, i.e. across the load **(see illustration)**.

16 First identify the relevant wiring circuit by referring to the wiring diagram at the end of this manual. If other electrical components share the same power supply, take note whether they are working correctly – this is useful information in deciding where to start checking the circuit.

17 If using a meter, check first that the meter leads are plugged into the correct terminals on the meter (red to positive (+), black to negative (-). Set the meter to the dc volts function, where necessary at a range suitable for the battery voltage – 0 to 20 volts dc. Connect the meter red probe (+) to the power supply wire

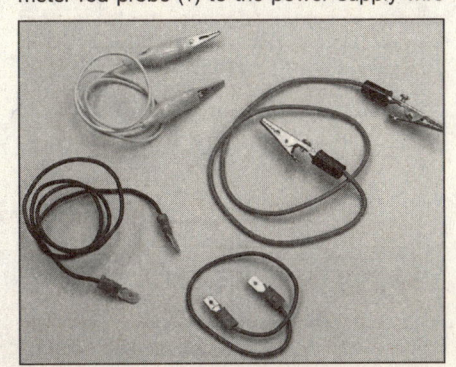

2.23 A selection of jumper wires for making earth (ground) checks

and the black probe to a good metal earth (ground) on the motorcycle's frame or directly to the battery negative terminal. Battery voltage should be shown on the meter with the ignition switch, and if necessary any other relevant switch, ON.

18 If using a test light, connect its positive (+) probe to the power supply terminal and its negative (-) probe to a good earth (ground) on the motorcycle's frame. With the switch, and if necessary any other relevant switch, ON, the test light should illuminate.

19 If no voltage is indicated, work back towards the switch continuing to check for voltage. When you reach a point where there is voltage, you know the problem lies between that point and your last check point.

Earth (ground) checks

20 Earth connections are made either directly to the engine (such as the starter motor which only has a positive feed) or to the engine or frame via the earth circuit of the appropriate wiring system (see the *Wiring Diagram* at the end of this Chapter).

21 Corrosion is a common cause of a poor earth connection, as is a loose earth terminal fastener.

22 If total or multiple component failure is experienced, check the security of the main earth lead from the negative (-) terminal of the battery, the earth leads bolted to the engine (at the front of the crankcase and the rear of the cylinder head), and the main earth point(s) on the frame. If corroded, dismantle the connection and clean all surfaces back to bare metal. Remake the connection and prevent further corrosion from forming by smearing battery terminal grease over the connection.

23 To check the earth of a component, use an insulated jumper wire to temporarily bypass its earth connection **(see illustration)** – connect one end of the jumper wire to the earth terminal or metal body of the component and the other end to the motorcycle's frame. If the circuit works with the jumper wire installed, the earth circuit is faulty.

24 To check an earth wire first check for corroded or loose connections, then check the wiring for continuity (Steps 12 and 13) between each connector in the circuit in turn, and then to its earth point, to locate the break.

8•4 Electrical system

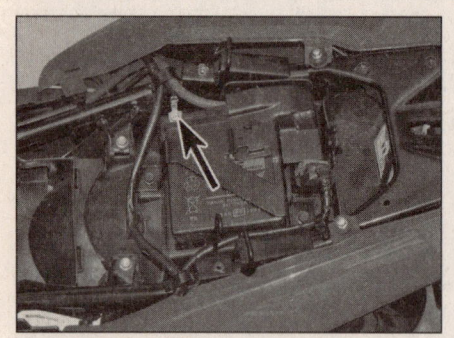

3.2 Unscrew the negative (-) terminal first

3.3a Undo the bolts (arrowed) . . .

3.3b . . . and remove the battery bracket

3 Battery

Caution: *Be extremely careful when handling or working around the battery. The electrolyte is very caustic and an explosive gas (hydrogen) is given off when the battery is charging. Always disconnect the battery negative (-ve) lead first, and reconnect it last.*

Removal and installation

1 Make sure the ignition is switched OFF. Remove the seats for access (see Chapter 7).
2 Unscrew the negative (-) terminal bolt and disconnect the lead from the battery **(see illustration)**.
3 Undo the bolts securing the battery bracket and remove the bracket **(see illustrations)**.
4 Lift off the red insulating cover to access the positive (+) terminal, then unscrew the bolt and disconnect the lead **(see illustration)**. Lift the battery out.
5 Prior to installation, ensure the battery terminals and lead ends are clean (see Step 9). Fit the battery into its holder and reconnect the leads, connecting the positive (+) terminal first.

> **HAYNES HINT**
> *Battery corrosion can be kept to a minimum by applying a layer of battery terminal grease or petroleum jelly (Vaseline) to the terminals after the leads have been connected. DO NOT use a mineral based grease.*

6 Secure the battery with its bracket, then install the seats.

Inspection

7 The battery fitted to all machines covered in this manual is of the maintenance-free (sealed) type – however, the following checks should still be performed.
8 Check the condition of the battery by measuring the voltage at the terminals. Connect the voltmeter positive (+) probe to the battery positive (+) terminal, and connect the negative (-) probe to the negative (-) terminal **(see illustration)**. When fully-charged there should be 12.7 to 12.9 volts present. If the voltage falls below 12.4 volts remove the battery and recharge it (see Steps 13 to 19).
9 Check the battery terminals and leads are tight and free of corrosion. If corrosion is evident, remove the battery and clean the terminals and lead ends with a wire brush, knife or wire wool.
10 Keep the battery case clean to prevent current leakage, which can discharge the battery over a period of time (especially when it sits unused). If necessary, wash the outside of the case with a solution of baking soda and water. Rinse the battery thoroughly, then dry it.
11 Look for cracks in the case and replace the battery with a new one if any are found. If acid has been spilled on the frame or battery holder, neutralise it with a baking soda and water solution, dry it thoroughly, then touch up any damaged paint.
12 If the motorcycle sits unused for long periods of time, disconnect the leads from the battery terminals, negative (-) terminal first. Check the battery condition regularly and charge the battery once every month.

Charging

13 Ensure the battery charger is suitable for charging a 12 volt battery.
14 Remove the battery (see Steps 1 to 4). Before switching the charger ON, connect it to the battery, making sure that the positive (+) lead on the charger is connected to the positive (+) terminal on the battery, and the negative (-) lead is connected to the negative (-) terminal.
15 Honda recommends that the battery is charged at a rate of 0.6 amps for 5 to 10 hours. Exceeding this figure can cause the battery to overheat, buckling the plates and rendering it useless. Few owners will have access to an expensive current controlled charger, so if a normal domestic charger is used, check that after a possible initial peak, the charge rate falls to a safe level **(see illustration)**. **Note:** *In emergencies the battery can be charged at a maximum rate of 3.0 amps for a period of 1 hour. However, this is not recommended and the low amp charge is by far the safer method of charging the battery.*
16 If the battery becomes hot during charging **STOP**. Further charging will cause damage
17 After charging, allow the battery to stand for 30 minutes, then measure its terminal voltage (see Step 8). If the voltage is below 12.7 volts, charge the battery again and repeat the voltage measuring process. If the voltage is still low, the battery is failing and should be replaced with a new one.

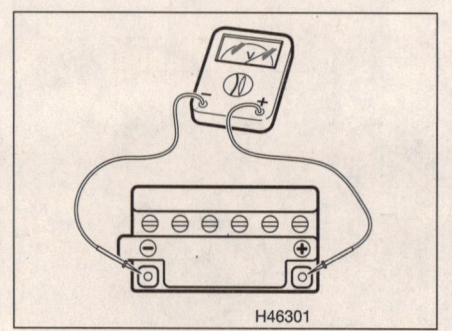

3.4 Disconnect the positive (+) terminal

3.8 Checking the battery voltage

3.15 Use of a dedicated motorcycle charger ensures a safe charge rate

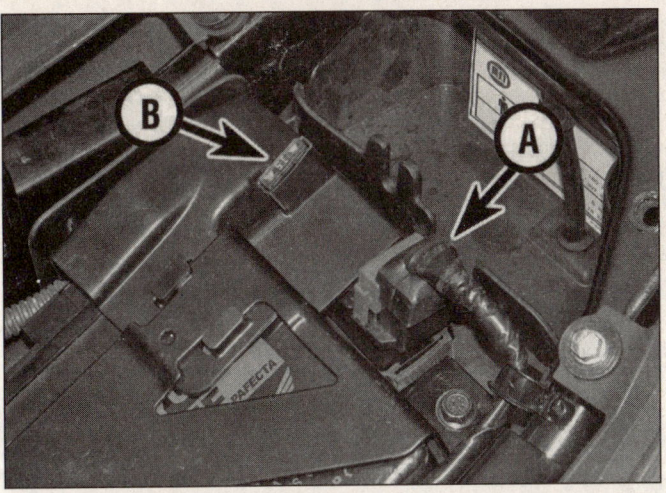

Electrical system 8•5

4.3 Location of the starter relay (A). Note spare fuse (B)

4.4 Unclip the relay wiring connector

18 Install the battery (see Steps 5 and 6).
19 If the recharged battery discharges rapidly when left disconnected, it is likely that an internal short caused by physical damage or sulphation has occurred. A new battery will be required. A good battery will tend to lose its charge at approximately 1% per day.

4 Fuses

1 The electrical systems are protected by fuses. If a fuse blows, be sure to check the appropriate wiring circuit very carefully for evidence of a short-circuit (see the *Wiring Diagram* at the end of this Chapter). Look for bare wires and chafed, melted or burned insulation, or a damaged switch. If the fuse is renewed before the cause is located, the new fuse will blow immediately.
2 Occasionally a fuse will blow or cause an open-circuit for no obvious reason. Corrosion of the fuse and fusebox terminals may occur and cause poor electrical contact. If this happens, remove the corrosion with a knife or wire wool, then spray the terminals with electrical contact cleaner.
3 The main fuse is integral with the starter relay located next to the battery – remove the passenger's seat (see Chapter 7) for access **(see illustration)**.
4 To check the main fuse, first disconnect the battery negative lead and remove the battery bracket (see Section 3). Unclip the relay wiring connector **(see illustration)**.
5 The circuit fuses are housed in the fusebox behind the left-hand side panel **(see illustration)** – remove the side panel for access (see Chapter 7).
6 To check either of the circuit fuses, unclip the fusebox lid **(see illustration)**.
7 The fuses should be removed and checked visually **(see illustration)**. If you can't pull the fuse out with your fingertips, use a pair of long-nose pliers. The fuses are identified as sub fuse A and B on the *Wiring Diagram* at the end of this Chapter.
8 A blown fuse is easily identified by a break in the element **(see illustration)**. Each fuse is clearly marked with its rating and must only be replaced by a fuse of the correct rating. A spare main fuse is located in a holder on the battery bracket **(see illustration 4.3)**. A spare circuit fuse is located in the fusebox **(see illustration 4.6)**.
9 If a spare fuse is used, always replace it with a new one so that a spare of each rating is carried on the bike at all times.

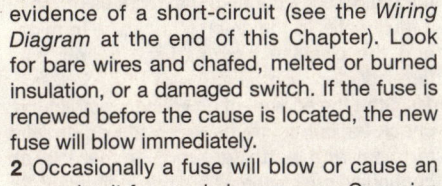

⚠ **Warning:** *Never put in a fuse of a higher rating or bridge the terminals with any other substitute, however temporary it may be. Serious damage may be done to the circuit, or a fire may start.*

4.5 Location of fusebox

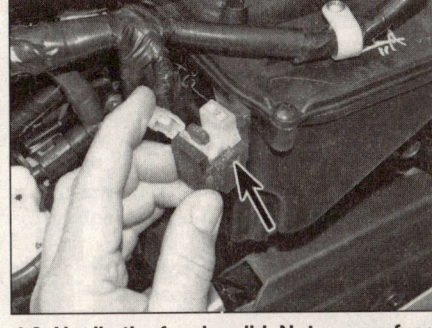

4.6 Unclip the fusebox lid. Note spare fuse (arrowed)

4.7 Pull out the fuse for a visual check

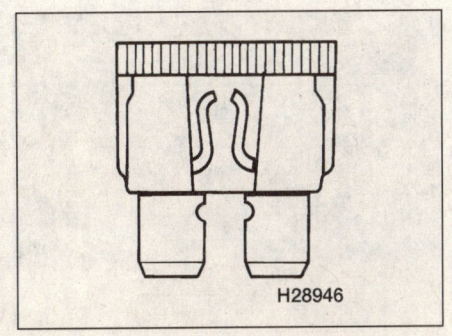

4.8 A blown fuse can be identified by a break in its element

5 Lighting system check

Note: *All lighting is controlled by the ignition switch. The brake light, turn signals and horn operate when the ignition is turned ON; the headlight, sidelight, tail light and instrument cluster lights operate when the engine is running.*

1 The battery provides power for operation of the turn signals and brake light. If none of these work, always check battery voltage before proceeding. Low battery voltage indicates either a faulty battery or a defective charging system. Refer to Section 3 for battery checks and Section 26 for charging system tests. Also, check the condition of the fuses (see Section 4) – if there is more than one problem at the same time, it is likely to be a fault relating to a multi-function component, such as one of the fuses governing more than one circuit, or the ignition switch.
2 When checking for a blown filament in a bulb, it is advisable to back up a visual check with a continuity test of the filament as it is not always apparent that a bulb has blown. When testing for continuity, remember that on single terminal bulbs it is the metal body of the bulb that is the earth (ground).

Headlight

3 If one headlight beam fails to work, first check the bulb (see Section 6). If both headlight beams fail to work, check the wiring, connectors and dimmer switch.
4 Disconnect the headlight bulb wiring connector (see Section 6) and check for battery voltage on the supply side of the connector. Connect the negative probe of a multimeter to the green wire (earth) terminal, and the positive probe to the blue wire terminal for the high beam or the white wire terminal for the low beam. Don't forget to select either high or low beam as appropriate at the dimmer switch.
5 Start the engine – if no voltage is indicated, check for continuity between the green wire terminal and earth (ground). If there is no continuity, check the earth (ground) circuit for an open or poor connection.
6 If the earth circuit is good, refer to the *Wiring Diagram* at the end of this Chapter and check the yellow wire between the components in the lighting circuit, and check the components themselves. **Note:** *Refer to Chapter 7, Section 6, and check the headlight assembly sub-loom connector. Check the sub-loom wiring for continuity – no continuity indicates a break in the wiring.*

Sidelight

7 If the sidelight fails to work, first check the bulb (see Section 6).
8 Next, refer to Chapter 7, Section 6, and disconnect the headlight assembly sub-loom connector. Check for battery voltage on the supply side of the connector – connect the negative probe of a multimeter to the green wire (earth) terminal, and the positive probe to the yellow wire terminal.
9 Start the engine – if no voltage is indicated, check for continuity between the green wire terminal and earth (ground). If there is no continuity, check the earth (ground) circuit for an open or poor connection.

10 If the earth circuit is good, refer to *Wiring Diagrams* at the end of this Chapter and check the wiring between the components in the lighting circuit, and check the components themselves.
11 If voltage is indicated, check for continuity between the terminals on the sidelight side of the wiring connector and the corresponding terminals in the bulbholder – no continuity indicates a break in the sub-loom circuit.

Tail light

12 If the tail light fails to work, first check the bulb (Section 8).
13 If they are good, refer to the *Wiring Diagram* at the end of this Chapter and check the wiring and connectors as follows.
14 Follow the procedure in Chapter 7, Section 8, to access the tail light wiring connector.
15 Disconnect the wiring connector and check for battery voltage on the supply side of the connector – connect the negative probe of a multimeter to the green (earth) wire terminal, and the positive probe to the yellow wire terminal.
16 Start the engine – if no voltage is indicated, check for continuity between the green wire terminal and earth (ground). If there is no continuity, check the earth (ground) circuit for an open or poor connection.
17 If the earth circuit is good, refer to the *Wiring Diagram* at the end of this Chapter and check the wiring between the components in the lighting circuit, and check the components themselves.
18 If voltage is indicated, remove the tail light bulb (see Section 8) and check for continuity between the wiring connector and the terminals in the bulbholder – no continuity indicates a break in the circuit.

Brake light

19 If the brake light fails to work, first check the bulb (Section 8), then sub fuse A (Section 4).
20 If they are good, follow the procedure in Chapter 7, Section 8, to access the tail light wiring connector.
21 Disconnect the wiring connector and check for battery voltage on the supply side of the connector – connect the negative probe of a multimeter to the green (earth) wire terminal, and the positive probe to the green/yellow wire terminal. Turn the ignition ON. Check first with the front brake lever pulled in, then with the rear brake pedal pressed down.
22 If no voltage is indicated in either test, check the appropriate brake light switch (see Section 13), then the wiring between the brake light connector and the switches.
23 Check for continuity to earth (ground) in the green wire on the loom side of the wiring connector. If there is no continuity, check the earth (ground) circuit for a broken or poor connection.
24 If voltage is indicated, remove the bulb and check for continuity between the terminals on the tail light side of the wiring connector and the corresponding terminals in the bulbholder – no continuity indicates a break in the circuit.

Turn signals

25 See Section 10.

6 Headlight and sidelight bulbs

Note: *The headlight bulb is of the quartz-halogen type. Do not touch the bulb glass as skin acids will shorten the bulb's service life. If the bulb is accidentally touched, it should be wiped carefully when cold with a rag soaked in methylated spirit and dried before fitting. Use a paper towel or dry cloth when handling new bulbs to prevent injury if the bulb should break and to increase bulb life.*

Headlight

1 Follow the procedure in Chapter 7, Section 6, to remove the inner fairing panels. Access to the headlight and sidelight bulbs is gained from the rear of the headlight unit.
2 Disconnect the wiring connector, then pull back the tab to remove the dust cover **(see illustrations)**.
3 Release the retaining clip, noting how it fits, then lift out the bulb, noting how it

6.2a Disconnect the wiring connector . . .

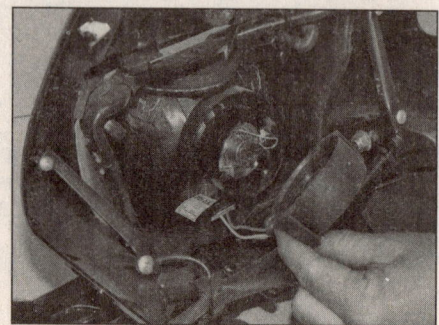

6.2b . . . and remove the dust cover

Electrical system 8•7

6.3a Release the retaining clip . . .

6.3b . . . and lift out the bulb

6.6 Pull out the sidelight bulbholder

locates in the back of the headlight unit **(see illustrations)**.

4 Installation is the reverse of removal, noting the following:
- Line up the tabs on the new bulb with the slots in the headlight unit.
- Ensure the retaining clip is secure and check that the dust cover is correctly installed.
- Check the operation of the headlight before riding the motorcycle.

Sidelight

5 Refer to Step 1 to access the rear of the headlight unit.
6 Pull the bulbholder out from the lower edge of the headlight unit **(see illustration)**.
7 The bulb is of the capless type – pull it out of the bulbholder carefully **(see illustration)**.
8 Installation is the reverse of removal. Check the operation of the sidelight.

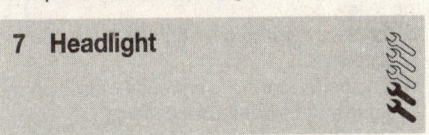

7 Headlight

Headlight aim

Note: *An improperly adjusted headlight may cause problems for oncoming traffic or provide poor, unsafe illumination of the road ahead. Before adjusting the headlight aim, be sure to consult with local traffic laws and regulations – for UK models refer to MOT Test Checks in the Reference section.*

1 Before making any adjustment, check that the tyre pressures are correct and the suspension is adjusted as required. Make any adjustments to the headlight aim with the machine on level ground, with the fuel tank half full and with an assistant sitting on the seat.
2 The headlight can be adjusted vertically by first loosening the bolt on the underside of the fairing **(see illustration)**.
3 Tip the headlight upwards or downwards to the desired position, then tighten the bolt securely.

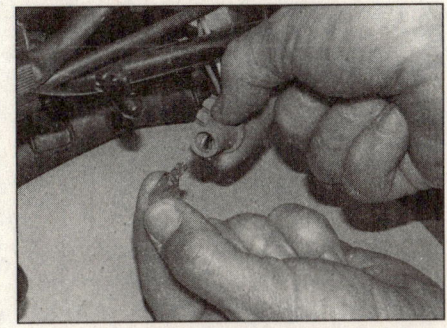

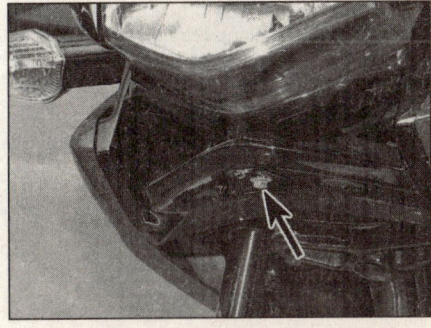

6.7 Remove the bulb carefully

7.2 Vertical adjuster bolt (arrowed)

Removal and installation

4 Follow the procedure in Chapter 7 to remove the fairing.
5 Remove the turn signal assemblies (see Section 12).
6 Undo the screws securing the support stay on the inside of the fairing **(see illustration)**. Release the wiring from any ties and remove the stay.
7 If required, disconnect the headlight wiring connector **(see illustration 6.2a)**. Alternatively, release the headlight assembly sub-loom from the clips on the inside of the fairing **see illustration)**.

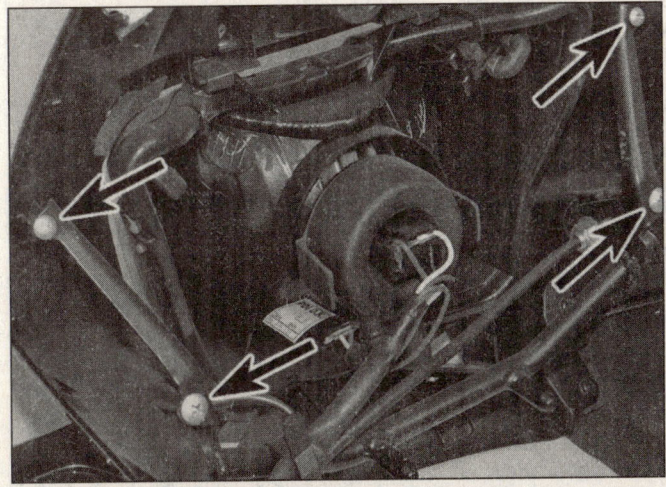

7.6 Location of support stay screws (arrowed)

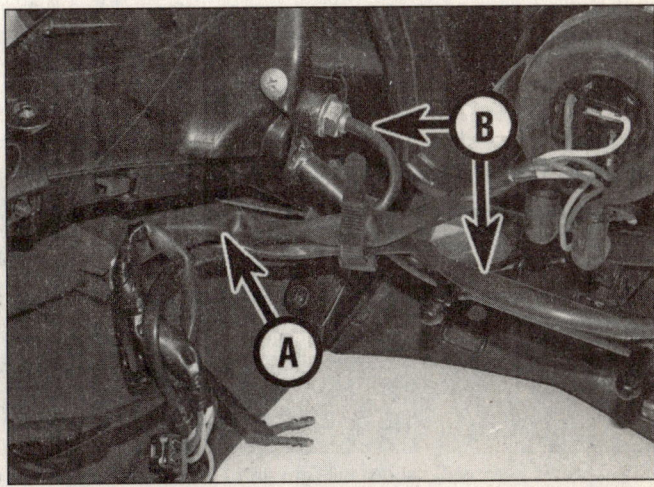

7.7 Headlight assembly sub-loom (A). Turn signal wiring (B)

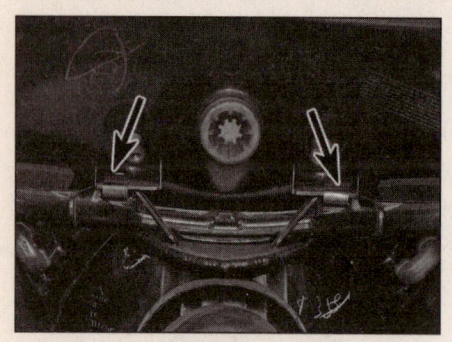

7.9 Spring clips (arrowed) secure top of the headlight unit

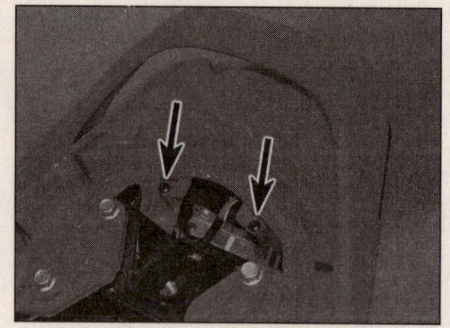

8.2a Undo the screws (arrowed) . . .

8.2b . . . and lift off the cover

8 Unscrew the headlight adjuster bolt on the underside of the fairing **(see illustration 7.2)**.
9 Ease out the spring clips securing the top of the headlight unit **(see illustration)** and remove the unit.
10 Installation is the reverse of removal, noting the following:
- Ensure the spring clips are securely fitted – fit new ones if they are sprained.
- Tighten the adjuster bolt finger-tight.
- Make sure all the wiring is correctly routed, connected and secured.
- Check the operation of the headlight and sidelight.
- Adjust the headlight aim.

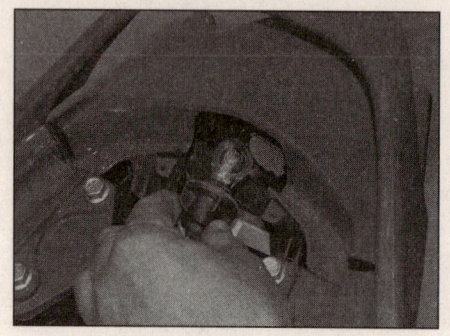

8.3 Turn the bulbholder anti-clockwise

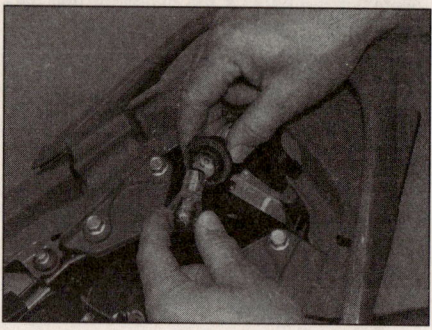

8.4 Push bulb in and turn it anti-clockwise

8 Brake/tail light bulb

Note: *It is a good idea to use a paper towel or dry cloth when handling the new bulb to prevent injury if it breaks, and to increase bulb life.*

1 Remove the passenger's seat (see Chapter 7).
2 Undo the screws securing the tail light cover and lift it off **(see illustrations)**.
3 Turn the bulbholder anti-clockwise and pull it out **(see illustration)**.
4 Push the bulb in and turn it anti-clockwise to release it from the holder **(see illustration)**.
5 Check the terminals for corrosion and clean them if necessary.

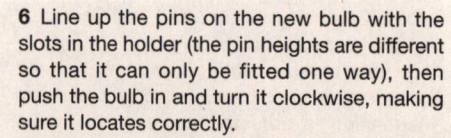

6 Line up the pins on the new bulb with the slots in the holder (the pin heights are different so that it can only be fitted one way), then push the bulb in and turn it clockwise, making sure it locates correctly.
7 Install the bulbholder and the tail light cover.
8 Check the operation of the brake/tail light.

9 Brake/tail light unit

Note: *A clear panel in the underside of the lens facilitates illumination of the licence plate.*
1 Remove the seat cowling and separate the two halves of the cowling (see Chapter 7).
2 Undo the screws securing the light unit,

noting the location of the washers **(see illustration)**.
3 Installation is the reverse of removal, noting the following:
- Take care not to over-tighten the mounting screws.
- Ensure the wiring is correctly routed on the right-hand side of the cowling.
- Check the operation of the tail and brake light before riding the motorcycle.

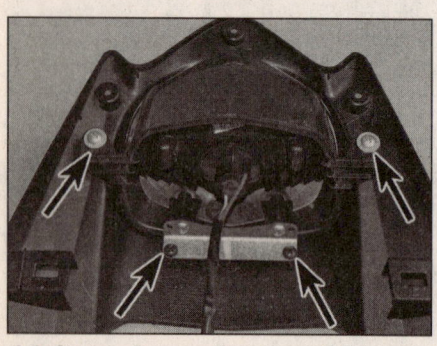

10 Turn signal circuit check

1 Most turn signal problems are the result of a burned out bulb or corroded socket. This is especially true when the turn signals function on one side (although possibly too quickly), but fail to work on the other side. If this is the case, first check the bulbs, the bulb sockets and the wiring connectors.
2 If all the turn signals fail to work, first check sub fuse A (see Section 4) and then the relay, relay wiring and connectors as follows (see *Wiring Diagram* at the end of this Chapter). Refer to Section 16 for switch testing procedures.

Relay

3 The turn signal relay is located inside the fairing on the left-hand side **(see illustration)** – remove the inner fairing panel for access (see Chapter 7).

9.2 Screws (arrowed) secure tail light unit

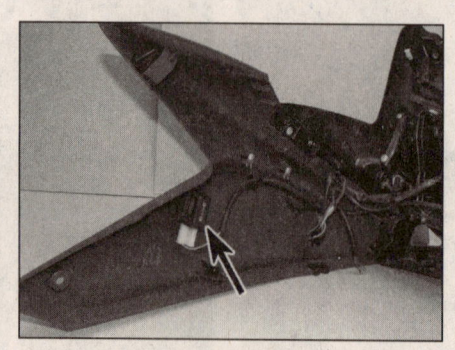

10.3 Location of the turn signal relay (arrowed)

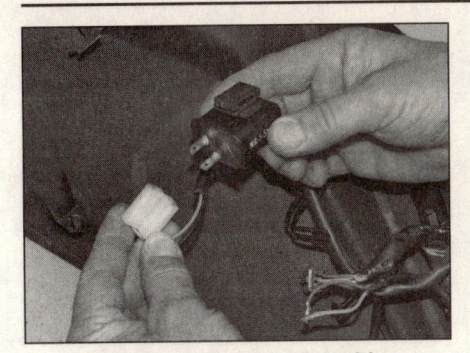

Electrical system 8•9

10.4 Disconnect the relay wiring connector

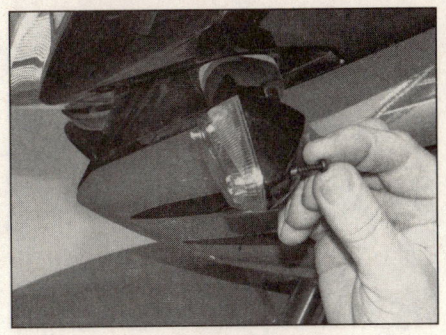

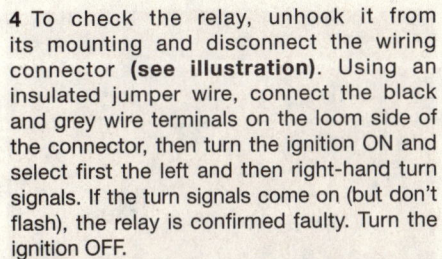

11.2a Undo the screws . . .

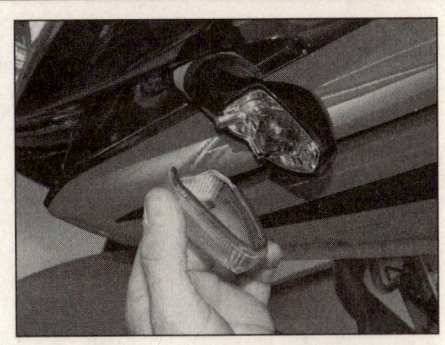

11.2b . . . and remove the lens

4 To check the relay, unhook it from its mounting and disconnect the wiring connector **(see illustration)**. Using an insulated jumper wire, connect the black and grey wire terminals on the loom side of the connector, then turn the ignition ON and select first the left and then right-hand turn signals. If the turn signals come on (but don't flash), the relay is confirmed faulty. Turn the ignition OFF.

5 If the turn signals on either side do not come on, check the wiring for continuity between the switch and the appropriate turn signals.

6 If none of the turn signals come on, check the grey wire for continuity between the relay connector and the switch, then check the black wire for continuity between the relay connector and the fusebox.

11 Turn signal bulbs

Note 1: *It is a good idea to use a paper towel or dry cloth when handling the new bulb to prevent injury if the bulb should break and to increase bulb life.*

Note 2: *Take care not to over-tighten the lens screws as it is easy to strip the threads or crack the lens.*

1 The procedure for changing the turn signal bulbs is the same for the front and rear assemblies.

11.2c Note location of the drain hole (arrowed)

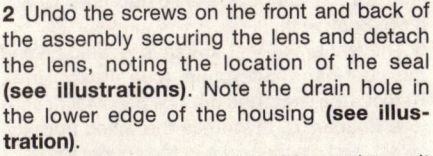

2 Undo the screws on the front and back of the assembly securing the lens and detach the lens, noting the location of the seal **(see illustrations)**. Note the drain hole in the lower edge of the housing **(see illustration)**.

3 Push the bulb into the holder and turn it anti-clockwise to remove it.

4 Check the socket terminal for corrosion and clean it if necessary.

5 Line up the pins of the new bulb with the slots in the socket – note that the pins are offset and will only fit in one position **(see illustration)**. Push the bulb in and turn it clockwise until it locks into place. Check the operation of the bulb.

6 Ensure the seal is in position, then fit the lens onto the housing and secure it with the screws **(see illustrations 11.2c, b and a)**.

11.5 Align the bulb with the socket

12 Turn signal assemblies

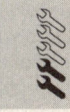

Front

1 Follow the procedure in Chapter 7 to remove the fairing.

2 Note the routing of the turn signal wiring inside the fairing and free it from any clips or ties **(see illustration 7.7)**.

3 To remove the complete signal assembly, undo the nut on the housing stem **(see illustration)**, then draw the stem out from the fairing.

4 To remove the signal housing only, undo the screw on the underside of the housing, then draw the housing off the stem **(see illustrations)**.

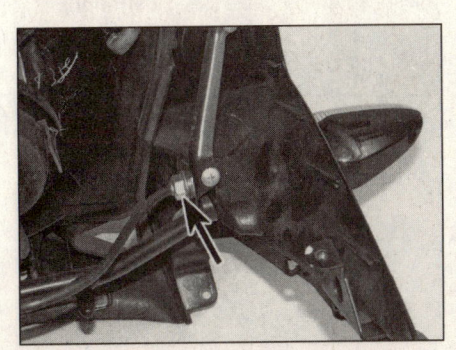

12.3 Nut (arrowed) secures turn signal housing stem

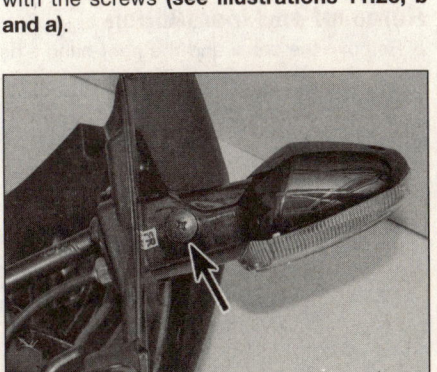

12.4a Undo the screw (arrowed) . . .

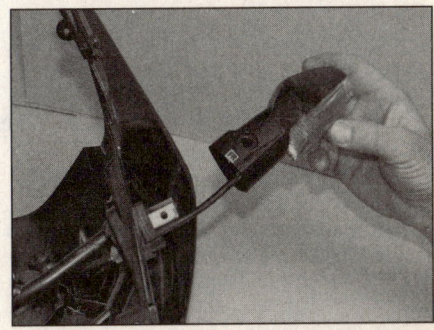

12.4b . . . and draw the housing off

12.7a Turn signal connectors (arrowed) on right-hand side

12.7b Feed the wiring back to the turn signals

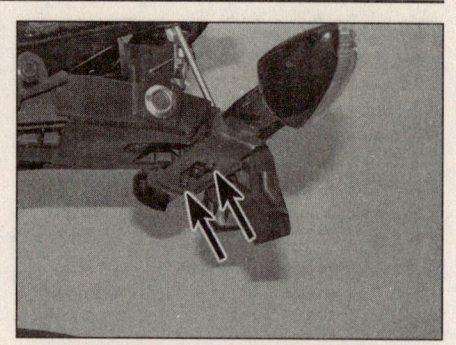

12.8a Undo the bolts (arrowed)...

5 Installation is the reverse of removal, noting the following:
• Ensure the wiring is correctly routed and secured.
• Check the operation of the turn signals before riding the motorcycle.

Rear

6 Follow the procedure in Chapter 7 to remove the seats, seat cowling and rear mudguard.
7 Trace the turn signal wiring along the right-hand side of the frame and disconnect it at the connectors **(see illustration)**. Release the wiring from any clips or ties and feed it back to the turn signals **(see illustration)**.
8 To remove the complete signal assembly and mounting bracket, undo the bolts on the underside of the bracket and lift the assembly off **(see illustrations)**.
9 To remove the left or right-hand signal assembly only, undo the nut on the housing stem **(see illustration)**, then draw the wiring out through the mounting bracket.
10 To remove the signal housing only, follow the procedure in Step 4.
11 Installation is the reverse of removal, noting the following:
• Ensure the wiring is correctly routed and secured.
• Check the operation of the turn signals before riding the motorcycle.

13 Brake light switches

Check

1 Before checking the switches, and if not already done, check the brake light circuit (see Section 5).
2 The front brake light switch is mounted on the underside of the brake master cylinder. Disconnect the wiring connectors from the switch (see Chapter 6, Section 5).
3 Using a continuity tester, connect the probes to the terminals of the switch. With the brake lever at rest, there should be no continuity. With the brake lever applied, there should be continuity.
4 If the switch does not behave as described, replace it with a new one – the front brake

12.8b ...and remove the turn signal assembly

light switch cannot be adjusted (see Chapter 6, Section 5).
5 The rear brake light switch is located behind the right-hand side panel **(see illustration)**. Remove the seats and the side panel for access (see Chapter 7), then trace the wiring from the switch and disconnect it at the connector.
6 Using a continuity tester, connect the probes to the terminals on the switch side of the connector. With the brake pedal at rest, there should be no continuity. With the brake pedal applied, there should be continuity. If the switch does not behave as described, check that it is adjusted correctly (see Chapter 1, Section 2). If the switch still does not work, replace it with a new one.
7 If the switches are good, refer to the *Wiring Diagram* at the end of this chapter and check the wiring for continuity.

Removal and installation

8 Remove the seats and the right-hand side

13.5 Location of rear brake light switch

12.9 Nut (arrowed) secures turn signal housing stem

panel (see Chapter 7). Disconnect the switch wiring connector, then feed the wiring down to the switch.
9 Unhook the brake light switch spring from the brake pedal. Unscrew the switch from its adjuster and remove it.
10 Installation is the reverse of removal. Check and adjust the switch (see Chapter 1, Section 2).

14 Instrument cluster

Removal and installation

1 Follow the procedure in Chapter 7 to remove the fairing.
2 Unscrew the knurled ring and disconnect the speedometer cable **(see illustration)**.

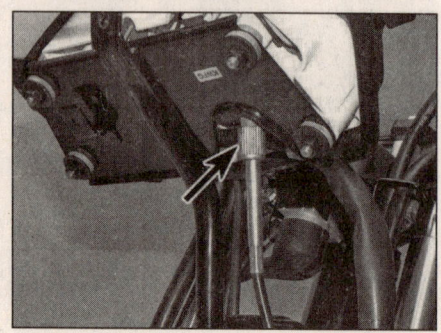

14.2 Unscrew the knurled ring (arrowed) and disconnect the speedo cable

Electrical system 8•11

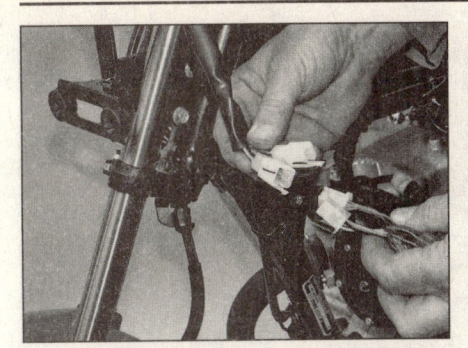

14.3 Instrument cluster wiring connectors

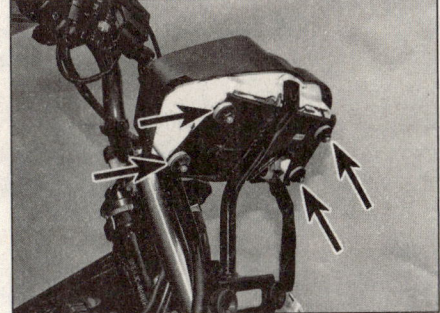

14.4a Undo the nuts (arrowed) . . .

14.4b . . . and lift the instrument cluster off

3 Trace the wiring from the instrument cluster and disconnect it at the connectors **(see illustration)**. Release the wiring from any clips or ties.
4 Undo the nuts securing the instrument cluster, noting the location of the washers **(see illustration)**. Lift the instrument cluster off its mounting bracket, noting the location of the grommets in the bracket **(see illustration)**. Renew the grommets if they are damaged or deteriorated.
5 To remove the top cover, first undo the screw securing the trip reset knob and pull the knob out **(see illustrations)**.
6 Undo the screws securing the cover and lift it off **(see illustrations)**.
7 The instruments are secured by screws on the underside of the case **(see illustration)**. CBF125M9 and MA models are equipped with a speedometer and fuel gauge; CBF125MB models onward are equipped with a speedometer and combined tachometer and fuel gauge. Prior to removal, note the location of the instrument illumination and warning light bulbholders, and the terminals for the instrument wiring connectors **(see illustration)**.
8 Installation is the reverse of removal, noting the following:
● Ensure the terminal screws are tightened securely.

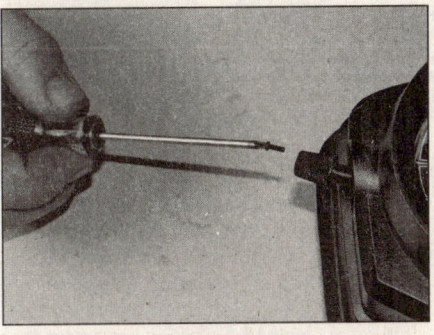

14.5a Undo the screw . . .

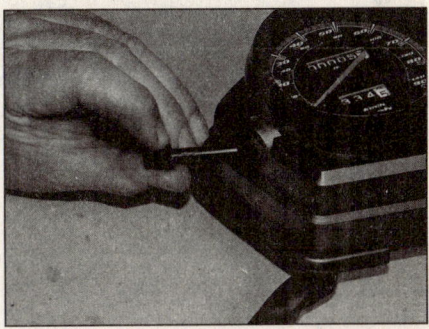

14.5b . . . and pull out the trip reset knob

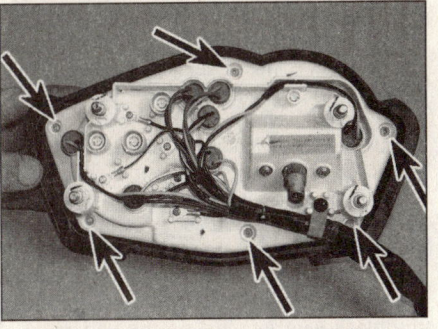

14.6a Undo the screws (arrowed) . . .

14.6b . . . and remove the cover

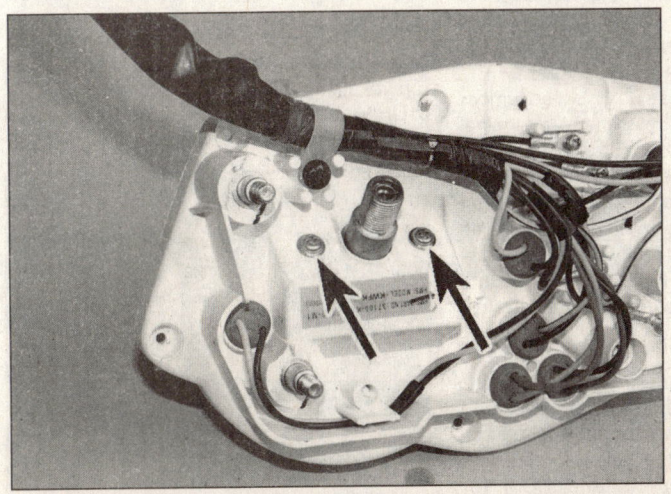

14.7a Screws (arrowed) secure instruments – speedometer shown

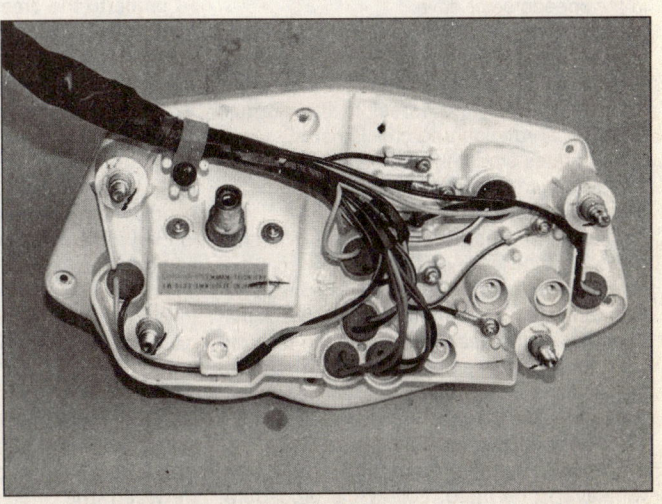

14.7b Note location of bulbholders and wiring terminals

8•12 Electrical system

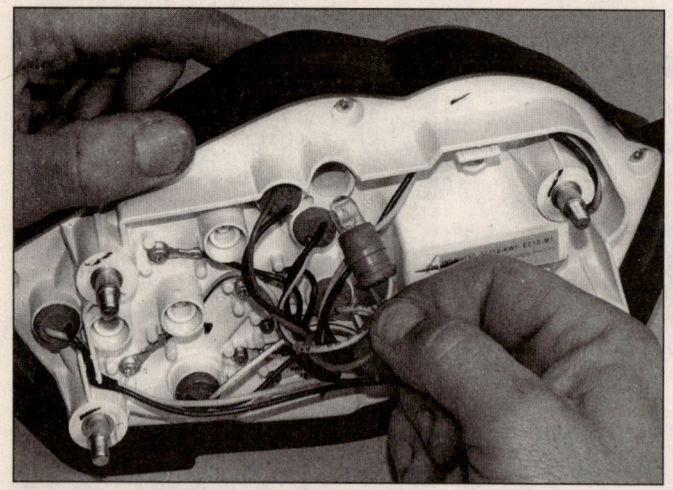

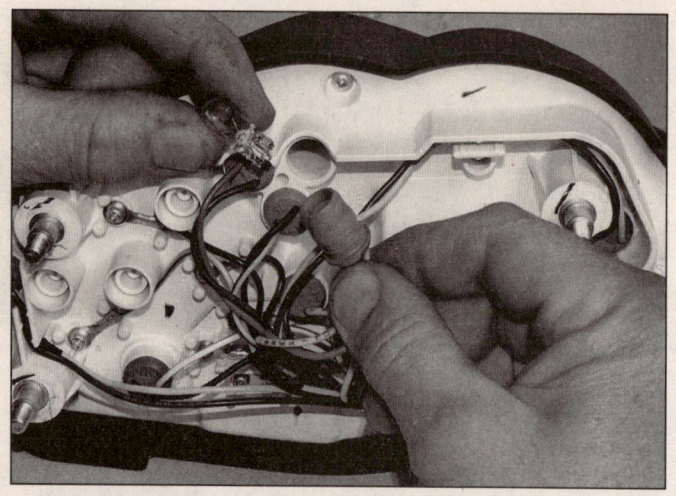

14.10 Pull out the bulbholder

14.11 Remove the bulb carefully

- Secure the sub-loom with its clip.
- Ensure the grommets are in place on the mounting bracket.
- Secure the wiring as noted on removal.

Instrument and warning light bulbs

9 To renew a light bulb, first follow the procedure in Steps 1 to 4 to remove the instrument cluster.
10 Prise out the appropriate bulbholder **(see illustration)**.
11 The bulb is of the capless type – pull it out of the bulbholder carefully **(see illustration)**.
12 Installation is the reverse of removal. Check the operation of the light.

Speedometer and cable

13 If the speedometer doesn't work, first remove the fairing (see Chapter 7) and check the cable and drive as follows.
14 Unscrew the knurled ring and disconnect the cable **(see illustration 14.2)**. The end of the inner cable should be squared to connect in the speedometer drive.
15 Support the machine on an auxiliary stand so that the front wheel is off the ground. Always make sure the motorcycle is securely supported. Turn the wheel in the normal direction of rotation and check that the inner cable rotates smoothly. If the cable does not rotate, either the cable or the speedometer gearbox is faulty.
16 Refer to Chapter 6, Section 11, and disconnect the lower end of the cable from the speedometer gearbox. If the cable appears to be good, remove the front wheel and check the operation of the gearbox. Inspect the tabs on the drive plate for damage – if required, remove the left-hand wheel bearing seal and renew the drive plate (see Chapter 6, Section 13).
17 If all the components are good it is likely the speedometer is faulty and a new one will have to be fitted. Follow the procedure in Steps 3 to 7 to remove and install the speedometer.

Fuel gauge

18 If the fuel gauge doesn't work, first check the operation of the fuel level sensor (see Chapter 4).
19 If the sensor is good, remove the fairing (see Chapter 7), then disconnect the instrument cluster 6-pin wiring connector **(see illustration 14.3)** and the fuel level sensor wiring connector (see Chapter 4, Section 2).
20 Check for continuity in the yellow/white wire between the terminals on the loom side of the two connectors. Check for continuity between the green wire terminal in the fuel level sensor wiring connector and earth (ground). No continuity indicates a break in the yellow/white or green wires.
21 If there is continuity, reconnect the fuel level sensor connector. Remove the instrument cluster (see Steps 2 to 4), then reconnect the instrument cluster wiring connectors. Using a multimeter, connect the positive (+) probe to the black wire terminal on the underside of the instrument cluster case and the negative (-) probe to the green wire terminal. Turn the ignition ON and check for battery voltage. No voltage indicates a break or short circuit in the black wire, or a break in the green wire.
22 If there is voltage, use an insulated jumper wire to connect the yellow/white wire terminal on the underside of the instrument cluster case to earth (ground). If the fuel gauge needle moves there is a break or short circuit in the yellow/white wire. If the needle remains static the fuel gauge is faulty and a new one will have to be fitted. Follow the procedure in Steps 5 to 7 to remove and install the fuel gauge.

Tachometer

23 CBF125MB models onward are equipped with a combined tachometer and fuel gauge. Apart from checking the yellow/green wire between the instruments and ECM for continuity, no information is available for testing the tachometer.

15 Ignition switch

Warning: To prevent the risk of short circuits, disconnect the battery negative (–) lead before making any ignition switch checks.

Check

1 The combined ignition switch and steering lock is located on the front of the fork top yoke.
2 To test the switch, first remove the fairing (see Chapter 7).
3 Trace the wiring from the underside of the switch and disconnect the connector (see the Wiring Diagram at the end of this Chapter).
4 Check for continuity between the red and red/black wire terminals on the switch side of the connector. There should be no continuity between the terminals with the switch in the OFF position and continuity with the switch ON.

Removal and installation

5 To remove the switch, first remove the fork top yoke (see Chapter 5, Section 9).
6 Undo the screws securing the switch assembly **(see illustration)**.

15.6 Screws (arrowed) secure ignition switch

Electrical system 8•13

16.8a Undo the screws (arrowed) . . .

16.8b . . . and split the housing – note register plate

16.9 Undo the screws on the underside of the housing

7 Prior to installation, clean the threads of the mounting screws and apply a suitable non-permanent thread-locking compound. Align the switch assembly with the plate on the underside of the yoke and tighten the screws securely.
8 Check the operation of the steering lock.
9 Make sure the wiring is correctly routed and securely connected.

16 Handlebar switches

Check

1 Generally speaking, the switches are reliable and trouble-free. Most problems, when they do occur, are caused by dirty or corroded contacts, but wear and breakage of internal parts is a possibility that should not be overlooked. If breakage does occur, the entire switch and related wiring harness will have to be replaced with a new one, as individual parts are not available.
2 The switches can be checked for continuity using a multimeter or a continuity test light. Always disconnect the battery negative (-) lead, which will prevent the possibility of a short circuit, before making the checks.
3 Remove the fairing (see Chapter 7). Trace the wiring from the switch to be tested and disconnect the wiring connector.
4 Check for continuity between the terminals of the switch connector with the switch in the various positions i.e. switch off – no continuity,

switch on – continuity (see the *Wiring Diagram* at the end of this Chapter). Continuity should exist between the terminals connected by a solid line on the diagram when the switch is in the indicated position.
5 If the check indicates a problem exists, displace the switch housing, clean out any old grease and spray the switch contacts with electrical contact cleaner. If they are accessible, the contacts can be scraped clean with a small knife. If switch components are damaged or broken, it will be obvious when the switch is disassembled.

Removal and installation

6 Follow the procedure in Step 3 to disconnect the appropriate wiring connector. Feed the wiring back to the switch, freeing it from any clips or ties and noting its routing.
7 If removing the right-hand switch, disconnect the wires from the front brake light switch (see Section 13). If removing the left-hand switch, disconnect the wires from the clutch switch **(see illustration 21.3)**.
8 To remove the left-hand switch, undo the screws on the underside of the housing and free the switch from the handlebar by separating the two halves – note the location of the register plate in the lower half of the housing **(see illustrations)**. Prior to installation, lubricate the switch mechanism and contacts with silicone grease. Locate the peg on the lower half of the housing in the hole in the underside of the handlebar and tighten the housing screws securely.
9 To remove the right-hand housing, undo

the screws on the underside of the housing and free the switch from the handlebar by separating the two halves **(see illustration)**. Note the location of the switch housing screws – if they are different lengths they must be returned to their correct positions. Follow the procedure in Step 8 to clean and lubricate the switch contacts. Make sure the peg in the housing locates in the hole in the handlebar.
10 Check the operation of the switches before riding the motorcycle.

17 Horn

Check

1 The horn is located at the front of the machine on the left-hand side **(see illustration)**.
2 Disconnect the wiring connectors from the back of the horn **(see illustration)**. Using two insulated jumper wires, apply voltage from a fully-charged 12V battery directly to the terminals on the horn. If the horn doesn't sound, replace it with a new one.
3 If the horn works check sub fuse A (Section 4), then refer to the *Wiring Diagram* at the end of this Chapter and check for battery voltage in the wire from the horn button to the horn with the ignition ON and the horn button pressed. If voltage is present, check the other wire to the horn for continuity to earth (ground).
4 If no voltage was present, check for continuity in the wire between the horn and the horn button, and the horn button and the fuse.
5 If all the wiring and connectors are good, check the button contacts in the switch housing (see Section 16).

Removal and installation

6 Disconnect the wiring connectors from the back of the horn, then undo the mounting bolt, noting the location of the rubber washers and spacer.
7 Installation is the reverse of removal. Ensure the horn bracket is correctly aligned with the mounting on the frame and tighten the mounting bolt securely. Ensure the wiring connectors are secure and check the operation of the horn before riding the motorcycle.

17.1 Location of the horn (arrowed)

17.2 Disconnect the wiring connectors

18 Ignition safety interlock circuit

1 The safety interlock circuit prevents the engine from starting if the sidestand is down, unless the transmission is in neutral. If the sidestand is up, the engine can be started with the clutch lever pulled in and the transmission in neutral or in gear. It also stops the engine running if the transmission is in gear and the sidestand is lowered.

2 If, after checking the components referred to in Chapter 3, an ignition fault cannot be traced, check the operation of the following components as described in this Chapter.
- Neutral switch
- Sidestand switch
- Clutch switch
- Starter safety circuit diode

19 Neutral switch

1 The neutral switch is part of the starter safety circuit (see Section 18).

Check

2 The neutral switch is located on the lower left-hand side of the crankcase forward of the gearchange shaft **(see illustration)**.
3 Remove the seats and the left-hand side panel (see Chapter 7).
4 Trace the wiring from the switch and disconnect the connector (see the *Wiring Diagram* at the end of this Chapter).
5 Ensure the transmission is in neutral. Check for continuity between the switch side of the connector and earth (ground). There should be continuity. Now repeat the test with the transmission in gear – there should be no continuity.
6 If the results are not as described the switch is faulty and a new one will have to be fitted. Follow the procedure in Steps 11 to 18
7 If the switch is good but the neutral warning light does not come on, first check sub fuse A (see Section 4) and the bulb (see Section 14).

19.2 Location of the neutral switch (arrowed)

8 Check the starter circuit diode (see Section 22).
9 Refer to the *Wiring Diagram* at the end of this Chapter and check for a break or short circuit in the wire between the ignition switch and the starter relay. Similarly, check the wiring between the neutral warning light and the ignition switch, and between the neutral warning light and the neutral switch.

Removal and installation

10 If not already done, remove the seats and the left-hand side panel (see Chapter 7).
11 Remove the front sprocket cover and chain guide (see Chapter 6, Section 16). Clean the area around the switch thoroughly before starting – this will make work much easier and rule out the possibility of dirt falling inside.
12 Trace the wiring from the switch and disconnect the connector. Note the route of the wiring, then feed it down to the switch.
13 Ensure the transmission is in neutral. Unscrew the mounting bolts and draw the switch out from the crankcase **(see illustration)**. Note the location of the O-ring and discard it as a new one must be fitted.
14 Note the location of the drive pin and withdraw the pin and spring **(see illustrations)**. Inspect the pin and spring for wear and damage and renew them if necessary.
15 Prior to installation, fit a new switch O-ring and lubricate it with a smear of engine oil **(see illustration)**.
16 Ensure the spring and drive pin are correctly installed, then align the electrical contact on the inside of the switch with the pin

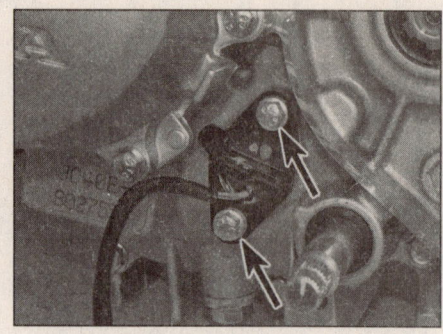

19.13 Neutral switch mounting bolts (arrowed)

and press the switch into its recess. Tighten the switch mounting bolts securely.
17 Route the wiring as noted on removal and reconnect the wiring connector. Check the operation of the switch.
18 Install the remaining components in the reverse order of removal.

20 Sidestand switch

1 The sidestand switch is part of the starter safety circuit (see Section 18).

Check

2 The switch is mounted on the stand pivot (see Chapter 5, Section 4). To check the operation of the switch, remove the seats and the left-hand side panel (see Chapter 7). Trace the wiring from the switch and disconnect the wiring connector as described in Chapter 5.
3 Check for continuity between the wire terminals on the switch side of the connector. There should be no continuity with the stand DOWN and continuity with the stand UP. If the switch does not perform as described it is faulty and must be renewed.

Removal and installation

4 If not already done, remove the seats and the left-hand side panel (see Chapter 7).
5 Remove the front sprocket cover and chain guide (see Chapter 6, Section 16).
6 Disconnect the switch wiring connector.

19.14a Note location of the drive pin (arrowed) ...

19.14b ... then withdraw the pin and spring

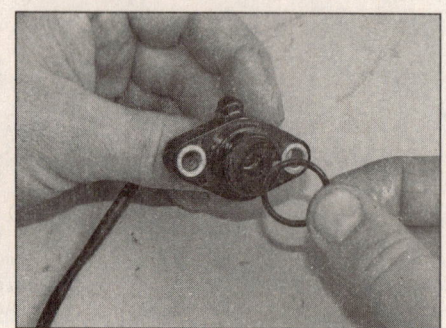

19.15 Fit a new O-ring to the switch

Electrical system 8•15

21.3 Disconnect the clutch switch connectors

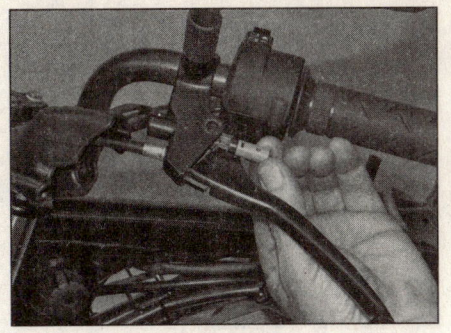

21.5 Withdraw the switch from inside the lever bracket

21.6 Push the switch all the way into the bracket

Note the route of the wiring, then feed it down to the switch.
7 Follow the procedure in Chapter 5 to remove the switch and wiring – it is not necessary to remove the stand bracket to do this.
8 Follow the procedure in Chapter 5 to install the switch. Check the operation of the switch (see Step 3).
9 Secure the wiring as noted on removal and ensure the connector is secure
10 Install the remaining components in the reverse order of removal.

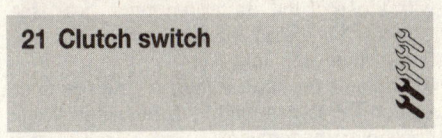

21 Clutch switch

1 The clutch switch is part of the starter safety circuit (see Section 18).

Check

2 The switch is located in the clutch lever bracket.
3 To check the switch, displace the dust cover and disconnect the wiring connectors **(see illustration)**. Check for continuity between the wire terminals on the switch. There should be no continuity with the lever out and continuity with it pulled in. If the switch does not perform as described it is faulty and must be renewed.

Removal and installation

4 If not already done, disconnect the switch wiring connectors.
5 The switch is secured by the handlebar lever. Follow the procedure in Chapter 5 to remove the pivot bolt and displace the lever, then withdraw the switch from inside the lever bracket **(see illustration)**.
6 Installation is the reverse of removal. Push the switch all the way into the bracket with a suitable small rod or punch **(see illustration)**. Secure the clutch lever with the pivot bolt and tighten the locknut on the underside securely.
7 Reconnect the wiring connectors and replace the dust cover.

22 Starter safety circuit diode

1 The diode for the starter safety circuit is located in the wiring loom secured inside the fairing – remove the fairing for access.
2 Unclip the diode from the wiring loom **(see illustration)**.
3 Using a multimeter, connect the positive (+) probe to the diode A terminal and the negative (-) probe to the diode B terminal **(see illustration)**. The diode should show continuity. Now reverse the probes. The diode should show no continuity.
4 Repeat the test between the C and B terminals. Connect the positive (+) probe to the C terminal and the negative (-) probe to the B terminal. The diode should show continuity. Now reverse the probes. The diode should show no continuity.
5 If the results are not as stated, the diode is faulty and a new one must be fitted.

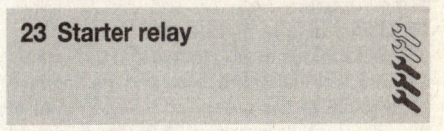

23 Starter relay

Relay check

1 If the starter circuit is faulty, first check the main fuse and sub fuse B (see Section 4).
2 The starter relay is located next to the battery – remove the passenger's seat (see Chapter 7) for access **(see illustration 4.3)**.
3 Remove the battery bracket (see Section 3). Do not disconnect the battery negative (-) lead for this test.
4 Pull back the relay terminal cover and unscrew the bolt securing the starter motor lead **(see illustration)**. Position the lead away from the relay terminal. Ensure the transmission is in neutral, then turn the ignition ON and press the starter button – the relay should be heard to click. Turn the ignition OFF.
5 If the relay doesn't click, remove and test it as follows.
6 Disconnect the battery negative (-) lead (see Section 3).

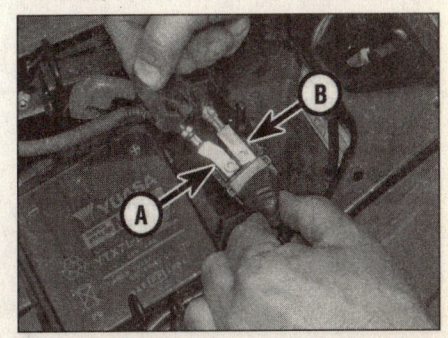

22.2 Starter safety circuit diode

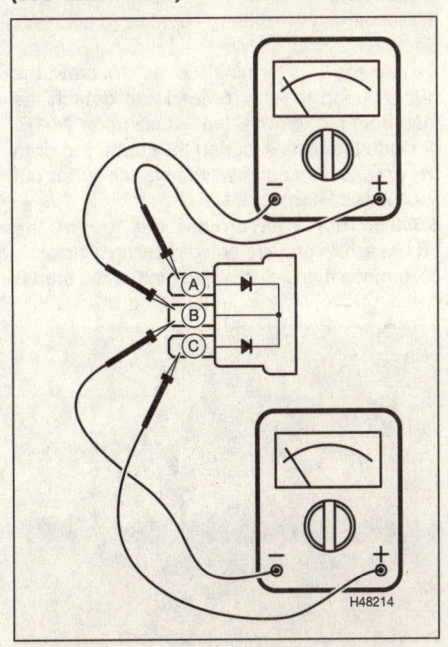

22.3 Diode check – connect the meter probes as described

23.4 Starter motor lead (A), battery lead (B)

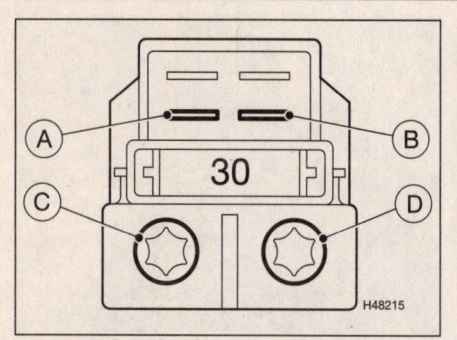

8•16 Electrical system

23.9 Starter relay terminal identification – green/red wire (A), yellow/red wire (B), starter motor lead (C), and battery lead (D)

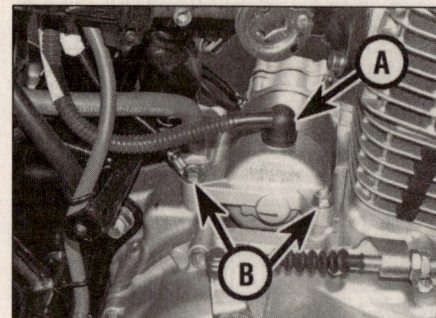

24.1 Location of the starter motor. Note terminal cover (A) and mounting bolts (B)

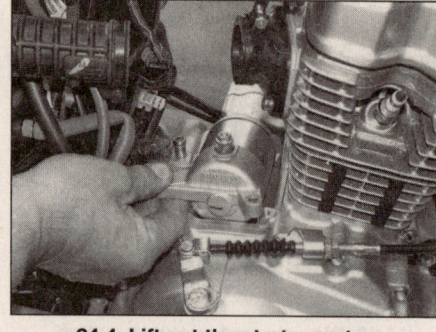

24.4 Lift out the starter motor

7 Disconnect the relay wiring connector **(see illustration 4.4)**.
8 Unscrew the bolt securing the battery positive (+) lead to the relay and detach the lead **(see illustration 23.4)**. Remove the relay from its holder.
9 Using a multimeter, check for continuity between the relay's starter motor and battery lead terminals **(see illustration)**. There should be no continuity.
10 Using a fully-charged 12 volt battery, connect the positive (+) terminal to the yellow/red wire terminal of the relay, and the negative (-) terminal to the green/red wire terminal of the relay **(see illustration 23.9)**. There should now be continuity between the starter motor and battery lead terminals.
11 If the results are not as stated, the relay is faulty and a new one must be fitted.
12 Installation is the reverse of removal. Ensure the terminal bolts are tightened securely. If a new relay is being fitted, don't forget to fit the main fuse. Connect the negative (-) lead last when reconnecting the battery.

Relay circuit check

13 Displace the wiring boot to access the rear of the relay wiring connector. Using a multimeter, backprobe the yellow/red wire terminal on the connector with the meter positive (+) probe and connect the meter negative (-) probe to earth (ground). Turn the ignition ON and press the starter button – there should be battery voltage. If there is no voltage, check the wiring between the relay wiring connector and the starter button (see *Wiring Diagrams* at the end of this Chapter).
14 Disconnect the relay wiring connector **(see illustration 4.4)**. Press the starter button and check for continuity between the green/red wire terminal on the loom side of the connector and earth (ground). Note that the components of the starter safety circuit must be in their correct positions (see Sections 19, 20 and 21). If there is no continuity, check the wiring and components of the starter safety circuit.

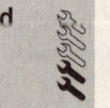

24 Starter motor removal and installation

Removal

1 The starter motor is mounted on top of the crankcase behind the cylinder **(see illustration)**.
2 Disconnect the battery negative (-) lead (see Section 3).
3 Displace the terminal cover, unscrew the nut securing the starter lead and detach the lead from the terminal **(see illustration 24.1)**.
4 Undo the bolts securing the starter motor to the crankcase and draw the starter motor out **(see illustration)**.
5 Clean the area around the top of the crankcase to prevent any dirt falling inside.
6 Remove the O-ring on the end of the starter motor and discard it as a new one must be used **(see illustration)**.

Installation

7 Ensure the mounting face of the crankcase is clean. Fit a new O-ring onto the end of the starter motor, making sure it is seated in its groove. Apply a smear of engine oil to the O-ring.
8 Manoeuvre the starter motor into position, ensuring the teeth on the shaft mesh correctly with those of the starter reduction gear (see Chapter 2). Install the mounting bolts and tighten them securely.
9 Connect the starter lead to the terminal, tighten the terminal nut securely, then fit the cover over the terminal.
10 Connect the battery negative (-) lead.

25 Starter motor overhaul

Disassembly

1 Remove the starter motor (see Section 24).
2 Note the alignment marks between the main housing and the front and rear covers, or make your own if they aren't clear **(see illustration)**.
3 Unscrew the two long bolts, noting the location of the O-rings **(see illustration)**. Discard the O-rings as new ones must be used.

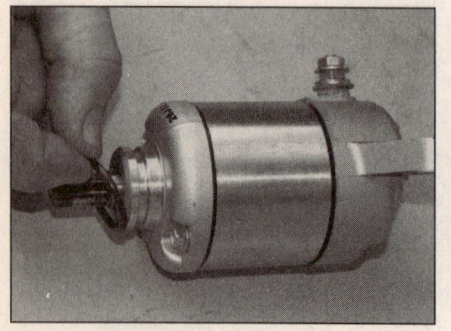

24.6 Remove the O-ring

25.2 Note alignment marks

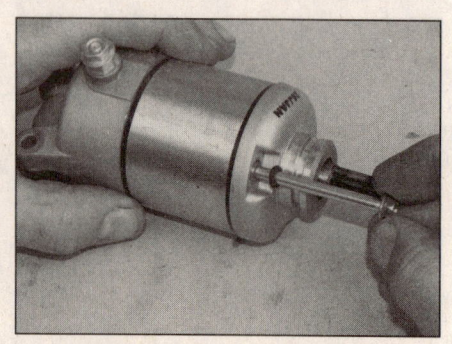

25.3 Unscrew the long bolts

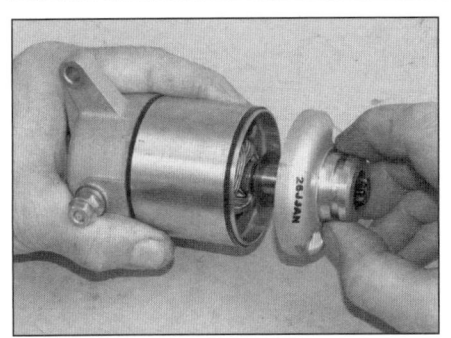

Electrical system 8•17

25.4a Remove front cover . . .

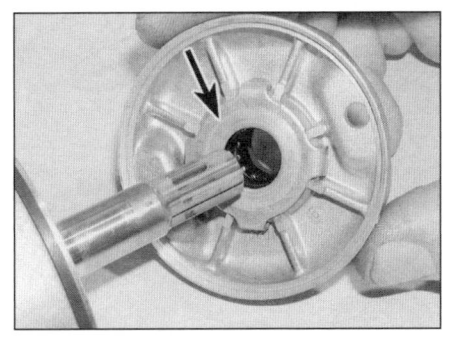

25.4b . . . note location of tabbed washer (arrowed)

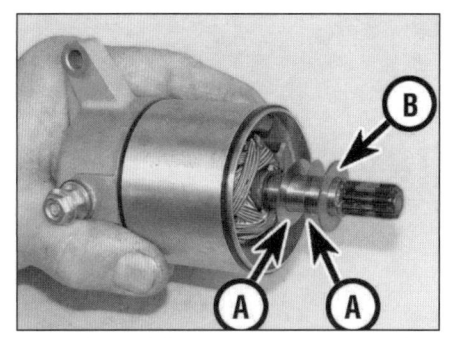

25.5 Shims (A) and insulating washer (B)

25.6a Remove the front cover O-ring . . .

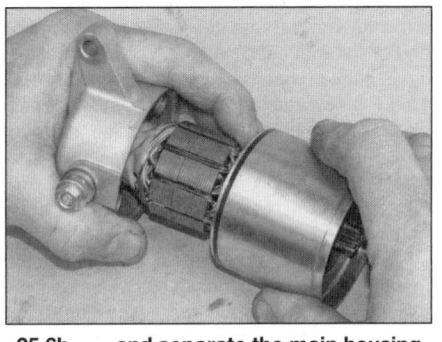

25.6b . . . and separate the main housing from the rear cover

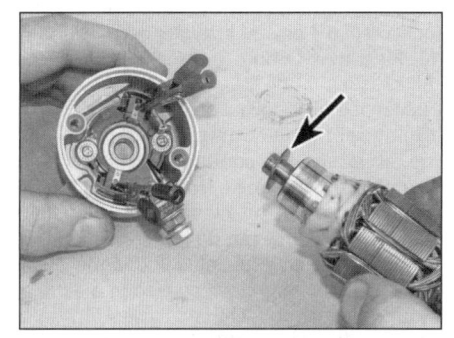

25.7 Remove the shims (arrowed) from the end of the shaft

4 Remove the front cover from the motor and remove the tabbed washer from inside the front cover **(see illustrations)**.

5 Remove the shims and insulating washer from the front end of the armature shaft, noting the order in which they are fitted **(see illustration)**.

6 Remove the front cover O-ring, then draw off the main housing and remove the rear cover O-ring **(see illustrations)**. Discard the O-rings as new ones must be fitted.

7 Remove the rear cover and brushplate assembly from the armature commutator, noting the shims on the end of the armature shaft **(see illustrations)**.

8 Ease the brushes and brush springs out from their holders, noting that positive (+) brush is attached to the terminal and the negative (-) brush is attached to the brushplate **(see illustration)**.

Inspection

9 Check the general condition of all the starter motor components. Some parts, such as the brushes, brush springs and O-rings are available separately, otherwise a new starter motor will have to be fitted. The parts that are most likely to require attention are the brushes. Measure the length of the brushes and compare the result with the specification at the beginning of this Chapter **(see illustration)**. If either of the brushes is worn excessively or otherwise damaged, renew them as a set.

10 Check for continuity between the positive (+) brush and the brush terminal; there should be continuity (zero resistance) **(see illustration)**. Check for continuity between

the terminal and the housing; there should be no continuity (infinite resistance). Check for continuity between the positive (+) and negative (-) brushes; there should be no continuity.

11 If required, undo the screw securing the

25.8 Location of the positive (A) and negative (B) brushes

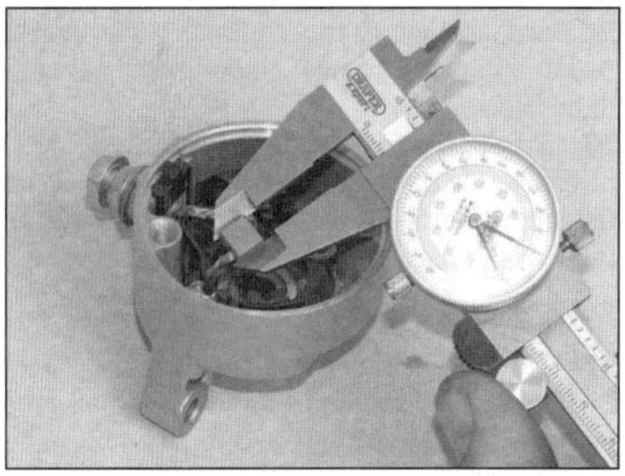

negative (-) brush and remove the brush **(see illustration)**. To remove the positive (+) brush, undo the nut on the terminal and remove the washer and insulating washers, noting the order in which they are fitted. Withdraw the

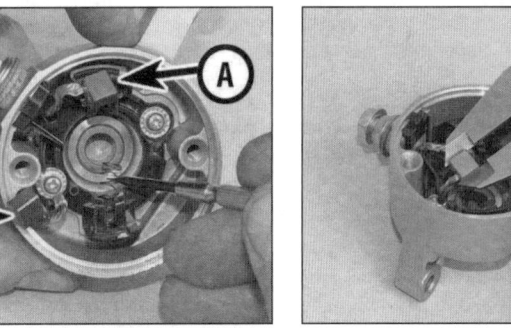

25.9 Measure brush length

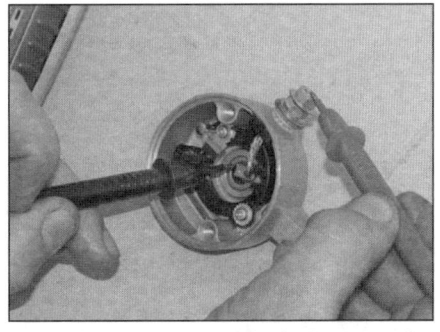

25.10 Checking for continuity between the positive brush and terminal

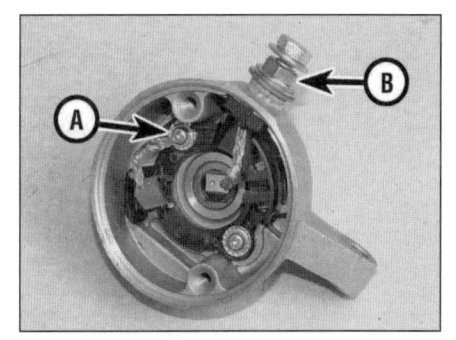

25.11 Screw (A) secures negative brush. Positive brush is connected to the terminal (B)

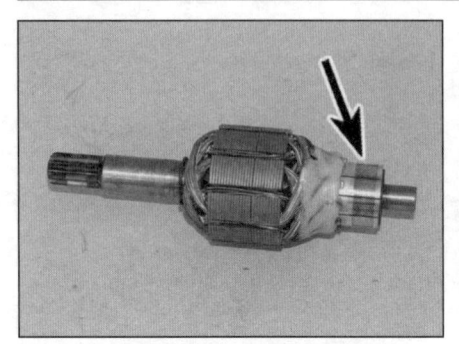

8•18 Electrical system

25.13 Inspect the commutator bars (arrowed) for damage

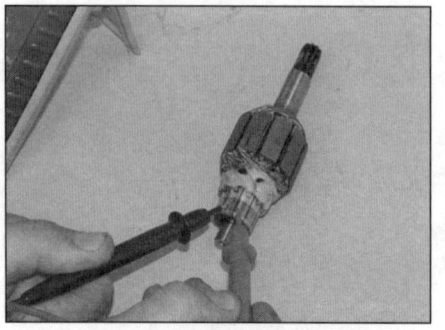

25.14a Checking for continuity between the commutator bars

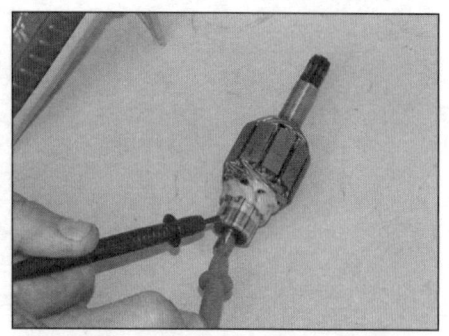

25.14b Checking for continuity between commutator bars and the armature shaft

terminal from inside the cover, noting the location of the square insulator and O-ring.

12 Fit a new O-ring to the terminal. Install the brushes in the reverse order of removal. Tighten the terminal nut securely.

13 Inspect the commutator bars on the armature for scoring, scratches and discoloration **(see illustration)**. The commutator can be cleaned and polished with crocus cloth – but do not use sandpaper or emery paper. After cleaning, wipe away any residue with a cloth soaked in electrical system cleaner or denatured alcohol.

14 Check for continuity between the commutator bars **(see illustration)**. Continuity (zero resistance) should exist between each bar and all of the others. Also, check for continuity between the commutator bars and the armature shaft **(see illustration)**. There should be no continuity (infinite resistance). If the checks indicate otherwise, the armature is defective.

15 Check the front end of the armature shaft for worn, cracked or broken teeth. If the shaft is damaged or worn, a new starter motor will have to be fitted.

16 Inspect the front and rear covers for signs of cracks or damage. Inspect the front cover oil seal and needle bearing **(see illustration)**. Inspect the plain bearing in the rear cover.

Reassembly

17 Slide the springs and brushes back into position in their holders – use some small clips to hold them in place to aid reassembly **(see illustration)**.

18 Slide the shims onto the rear end of the armature shaft **(see illustration 25.7)**. Lubricate the shaft with a smear of grease, then insert the shaft into the rear cover. Remove the clips and check that each brush is securely pressed against the commutator by its spring.

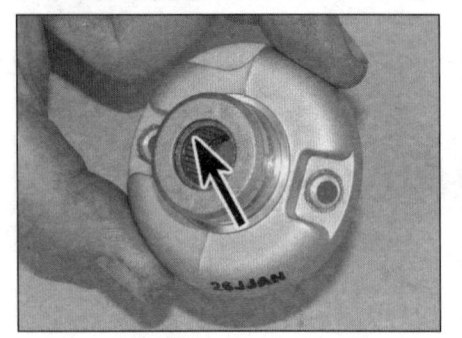

19 Fit a new rear cover O-ring onto the main housing, then fit the housing over the armature and onto the rear cover, aligning the marks made on removal **(see illustration 25.6b)**. Fit a new front cover O-ring onto the main housing **(see illustration 25.6a)**.

20 Slide the insulating washer and shims onto the front end of the armature shaft and lubricate the shaft with a smear of grease **(see illustration 25.5)**. Apply a smear of grease to the inside of the front cover oil seal and fit the tabbed washer into the cover, making sure the tabs locate correctly **(see illustration 25.4b)**. Install the cover on the main housing, aligning the marks made on removal **(see illustration 25.2)**.

21 Slide a new O-ring onto each of the long bolts. Check the marks made on removal are correctly aligned, then install the long bolts and tighten them to the torque setting specified at the beginning of this Chapter.

22 Install the starter motor (see Section 24).

26 Charging system testing

1 If the performance of the charging system is suspect, the system as a whole should be checked first, followed by testing of the individual components. **Note:** *Before beginning the checks, make sure the battery is fully charged and that all system connections are clean and tight.*

2 Checking the output of the charging system and the performance of the various components within the charging system requires the use of a multimeter. If a multimeter is not available, the job of checking the charging system should be left to a Honda dealer.

3 When making the checks, follow the procedures carefully to prevent incorrect connections or short circuits resulting in irreparable damage to electrical system components.

Leakage test

Caution: Always connect an ammeter in series, never in parallel with the battery, otherwise it will be damaged. Do not turn the ignition ON or operate the starter motor when the ammeter is connected – a sudden surge in current will blow the meter's fuse.

4 Ensure the ignition is OFF, then disconnect the battery negative (-) lead (see Section 3).

5 Set the multimeter to the Amps function and connect its negative (-) probe to the battery negative (-) terminal, and positive (+) probe to the disconnected negative (-) lead **(see illustration)**. Always set the meter to a high amps range initially and then bring it down to the mA (milli Amps) range; if there is a high current flow in the circuit it may blow the meter's fuse.

6 Battery current leakage should not exceed the maximum limit (see *Specifications* at the beginning of this Chapter). If a higher leakage rate is shown, disconnect the regulator/rectifier wiring connector (see Section 28) and test the leakage again. If the leakage rate is now within the specification the regulator/rectifier is probably faulty (see Section 28). If the leakage

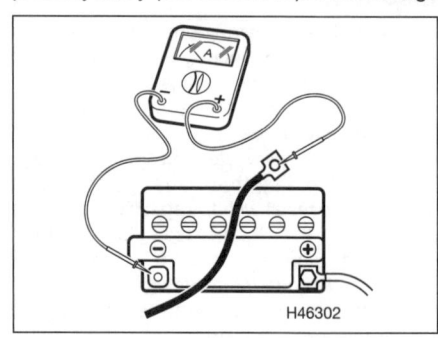

25.16 Check the oil seal and bearing (arrowed)

25.17 Using small clips to hold the brushes in position

26.5 Set-up for checking current leakage

Electrical system 8•19

rate is still too high, either there is a short circuit in the wiring or the ignition switch is faulty. Refer to the *Wiring Diagram* at the end of this Chapter to systematically disconnect individual electrical components and repeat the test until the source is identified. **Note:** *If an after-market immobiliser or alarm is fitted, its current draw should be taken into account.*

7 Once the tests have been completed, reconnect the battery negative (-) lead.

Regulated output test

8 Start the engine and warm it up to operating temperature. Turn the engine OFF. Remove the seats (see Chapter 7).
9 Connect a multimeter set to the 0-20 volts DC scale to the terminals of the battery; positive (+) meter probe to battery positive (+) terminal and the negative (-) meter probe to battery negative (-) terminal **(see illustration)**.
10 Start the engine, switch the headlight high beam ON, then slowly increase the engine speed to 5000 rpm and note the reading obtained.
11 Compare the result with the specification at the beginning of this Chapter. If the regulated voltage output is outside the specification, check the alternator and the regulator (see Sections 27 and 28).

> **HAYNES HiNT** Clues to a faulty regulator are constantly blowing bulbs, with brightness varying considerably with engine speed, and battery overheating.

27 Alternator

Special tool: *A rotor strap and rotor puller are necessary to remove the alternator rotor from the crankshaft (see Chapter 2).*

Check

1 Remove the seat and the left-hand side panel (see Chapter 7).
2 Refer to the *Wiring Diagram* at the end of this Chapter, then trace the wiring from the back of the alternator cover on the left-hand side of the engine to the wiring boot and disconnect the alternator connector (see Chapter 2, Section 19).

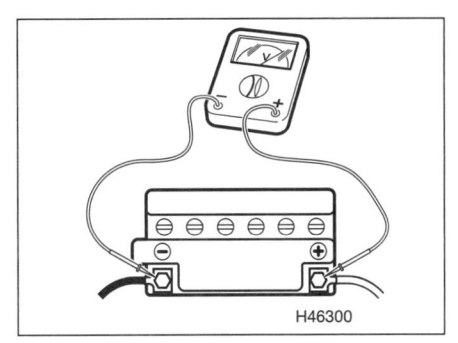

26.9 Set-up for regulated voltage output check

3 Using a multimeter set to the ohms scale, connect the meter probes to the white and green wire terminals on the alternator side of the connector and measure the resistance. If the result is outside the range shown in *Specifications* at the beginning of this Chapter, the alternator stator coil assembly is faulty and should be renewed. **Note:** *Before condemning the stator coils, check the fault is not due to damaged wiring between the connector and coils.*

Removal

4 Follow the procedure in Chapter 2, Section 19, to remove the alternator cover. The stator coil assembly is located inside the cover **(see illustration)**. **Note:** *The CKP sensor is an integral part of the alternator stator coil assembly.*
5 To remove the stator from the cover, first undo the bolts securing the CKP sensor and the wiring clamp **(see illustration)**. Ease the wiring grommet out of the cut-out in the cover. Undo the bolts securing the stator and lift it out together with the CKP sensor and wiring sub-loom.
6 If required, follow the procedure in Chapter 2, Section 19, to remove the alternator rotor.

Installation

7 Remove all traces of old gasket and sealant from the crankcase and cover surfaces.
8 Apply a suitable sealant to the wiring grommet, then fit the stator and CKP sensor into the cover, aligning the grommet with the cut-out **(see illustration 27.5)**.
9 Install the stator bolts and tighten them securely.
10 Install the wiring clamp. Clean the threads of the wiring clamp and CKP sensor bolts and apply a suitable non-permanent thread-locking compound, then tighten the mounting bolts to the torque setting specified at the beginning of this Chapter.
11 Follow the procedure in Chapter 2, Section 19, to install the alternator rotor and cover.
12 Don't forget to check the engine oil level and top-up as necessary (see *Pre-ride checks*).

28 Regulator/rectifier

Check

1 The regulator/rectifier is located inside the seat cowling on the left-hand side of the frame – remove the cowling for access (see Chapter 7).
2 If, after checking the charging system (see Section 26) and the alternator (see Section 27), the regulator/rectifier is thought to be faulty, check the wiring as follows.
3 Disconnect the regulator/rectifier wiring connector from the underside of the unit **(see illustration)**. Inspect the connector for loose or corroded terminals.
4 Using a multimeter, connect the meter positive (+) probe to the red wire terminal on the loom side of the connector and the negative (-) probe to earth (ground) and check for battery voltage. There should be battery voltage at all times.
5 Check for continuity between the green wire terminal on the loom side of the connector and earth (ground). There should be continuity.
6 Measure the resistance between the white wire terminal and earth (ground). The meter should register stator coil resistance.
7 If all the results are as specified it is likely the regulator/rectifier unit is faulty – have it checked by a Honda dealer.

Removal and installation

8 If not already done, remove the seat cowling (see Chapter 7).
9 Disconnect the wiring connector **(see illustration 28.3)**.
10 Undo the mounting bolt and remove the regulator/rectifier.
11 Installation is the reverse of removal. Tighten the mounting bolts securely. Ensure the wiring terminals are clean and free from corrosion.

27.4 Location of the stator coil assembly (arrowed)

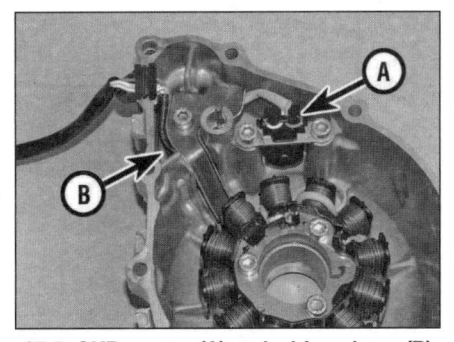

27.5 CKP sensor (A) and wiring clamp (B)

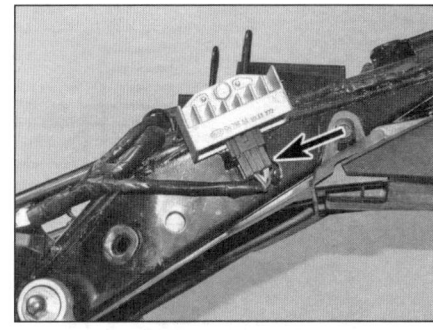

28.3 Regulator/rectifier wiring connector (arrowed)

8•20 Wiring diagram

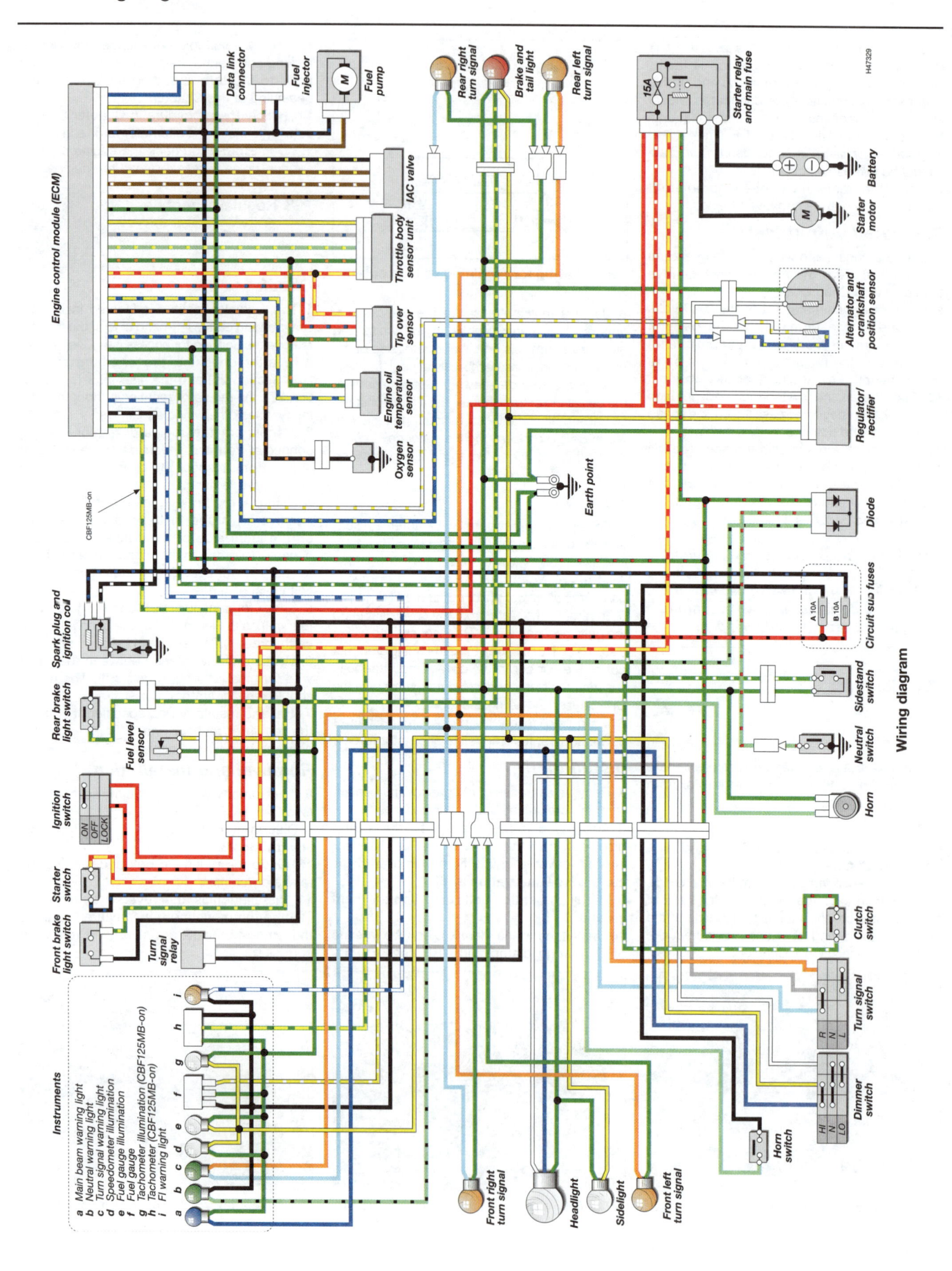

Reference

Tools and Workshop Tips — REF•2
- Building up a tool kit and equipping your workshop ● Using tools
- Understanding bearing, seal, fastener and chain sizes and markings
- Repair techniques

Security — REF•20
- Locks and chains
- U-locks ● Disc locks
- Alarms and immobilisers
- Security marking systems ● Tips on how to prevent bike theft

Lubricants and fluids — REF•23
- Engine oils
- Transmission (gear) oils
- Coolant/anti-freeze
- Fork oils and suspension fluids ● Brake/clutch fluids
- Spray lubes, degreasers and solvents

Conversion Factors — REF•26
- Formulae for conversion of the metric (SI) units used throughout the manual into Imperial measures

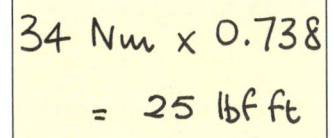

34 Nm × 0.738 = 25 lbf ft

MOT Test Checks — REF•27
- A guide to the UK MOT test ● Which items are tested ● How to prepare your motorcycle for the test and perform a pre-test check

Storage — REF•32
- How to prepare your motorcycle for going into storage and protect essential systems ● How to get the motorcycle back on the road

Fault Finding — REF•35
- Common faults and their likely causes ● Links to main chapters for testing and repair procedures

Technical Terms Explained — REF•44
- Component names, technical terms and common abbreviations explained

Index — REF•48

REF•2 Tools and Workshop Tips

Buying tools

A toolkit is a fundamental requirement for servicing and repairing a motorcycle. Although there will be an initial expense in building up enough tools for servicing, this will soon be offset by the savings made by doing the job yourself. As experience and confidence grow, additional tools can be added to enable the repair and overhaul of the motorcycle. Many of the specialist tools are expensive and not often used so it may be preferable to hire them, or for a group of friends or motorcycle club to join in the purchase.

As a rule, it is better to buy more expensive, good quality tools. Cheaper tools are likely to wear out faster and need to be renewed more often, nullifying the original saving.

> **Warning:** To avoid the risk of a poor quality tool breaking in use, causing injury or damage to the component being worked on, always aim to purchase tools which meet the relevant national safety standards.

The following lists of tools do not represent the manufacturer's service tools, but serve as a guide to help the owner decide which tools are needed for this level of work. In addition, items such as an electric drill, hacksaw, files, soldering iron and a workbench equipped with a vice, may be needed. Although not classed as tools, a selection of bolts, screws, nuts, washers and pieces of tubing always come in useful.

For more information about tools, refer to the Haynes *Motorcycle Workshop Practice Techbook* (Bk. No. 3470).

Manufacturer's service tools

Inevitably certain tasks require the use of a service tool. Where possible an alternative tool or method of approach is recommended, but sometimes there is no option if personal injury or damage to the component is to be avoided. Where required, service tools are referred to in the relevant procedure.

Service tools can usually only be purchased from a motorcycle dealer and are identified by a part number. Some of the commonly-used tools, such as rotor pullers, are available in aftermarket form from mail-order motorcycle tool and accessory suppliers.

Maintenance and minor repair tools

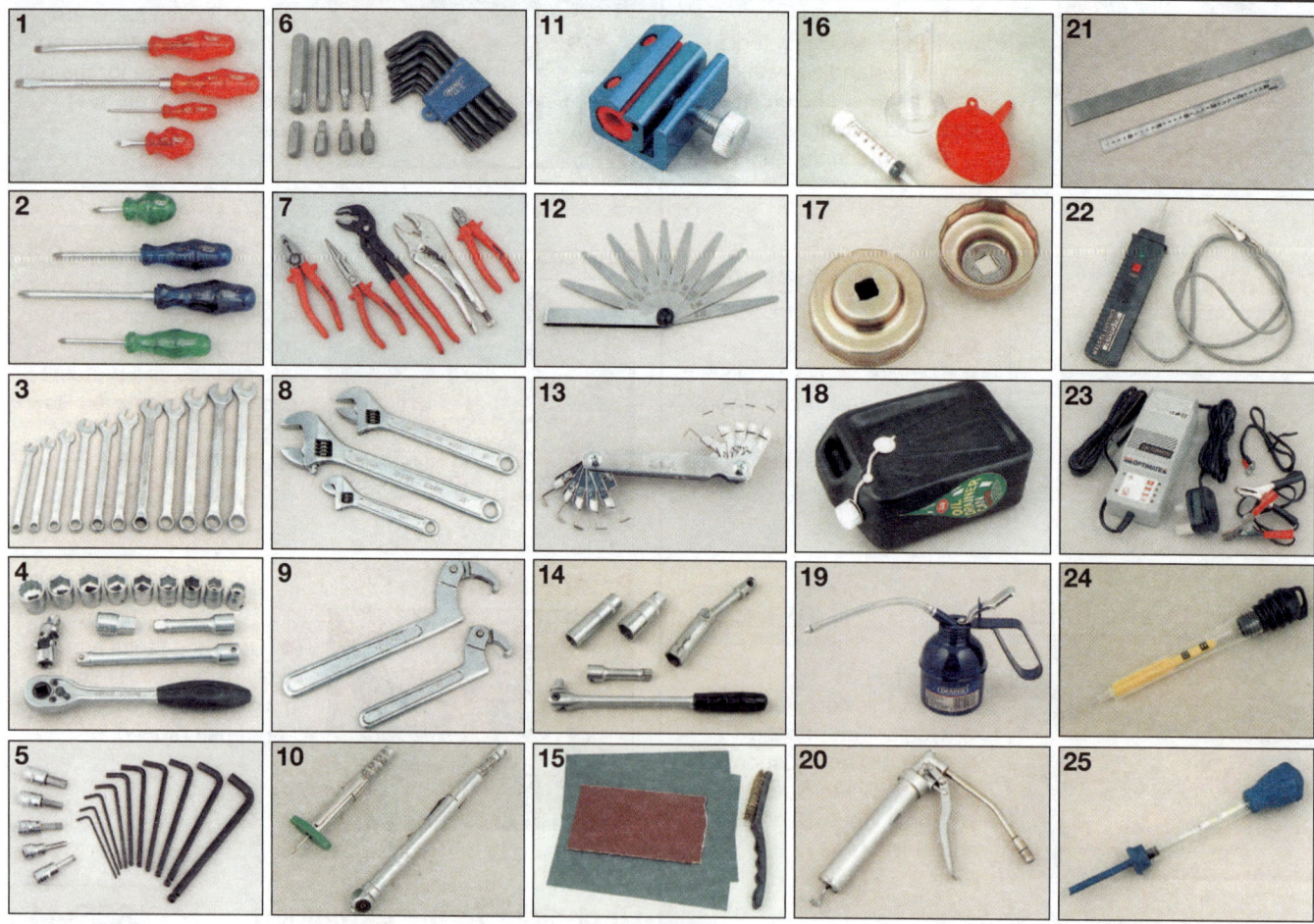

1 Set of flat-bladed screwdrivers
2 Set of Phillips head screwdrivers
3 Combination open-end and ring spanners
4 Socket set (3/8 inch or 1/2 inch drive)
5 Set of Allen keys or bits
6 Set of Torx keys or bits
7 Pliers, cutters and self-locking grips (Mole grips)
8 Adjustable spanners
9 C-spanners
10 Tread depth gauge and tyre pressure gauge
11 Cable oiler clamp
12 Feeler gauges
13 Spark plug gap measuring tool
14 Spark plug spanner or deep plug sockets
15 Wire brush and emery paper
16 Calibrated syringe, measuring vessel and funnel
17 Oil filter adapters
18 Oil drainer can or tray
19 Pump type oil can
20 Grease gun
21 Straight-edge and steel rule
22 Continuity tester
23 Battery charger
24 Hydrometer (for battery specific gravity check)
25 Anti-freeze tester (for liquid-cooled engines)

Tools and Workshop Tips REF•3

Repair and overhaul tools

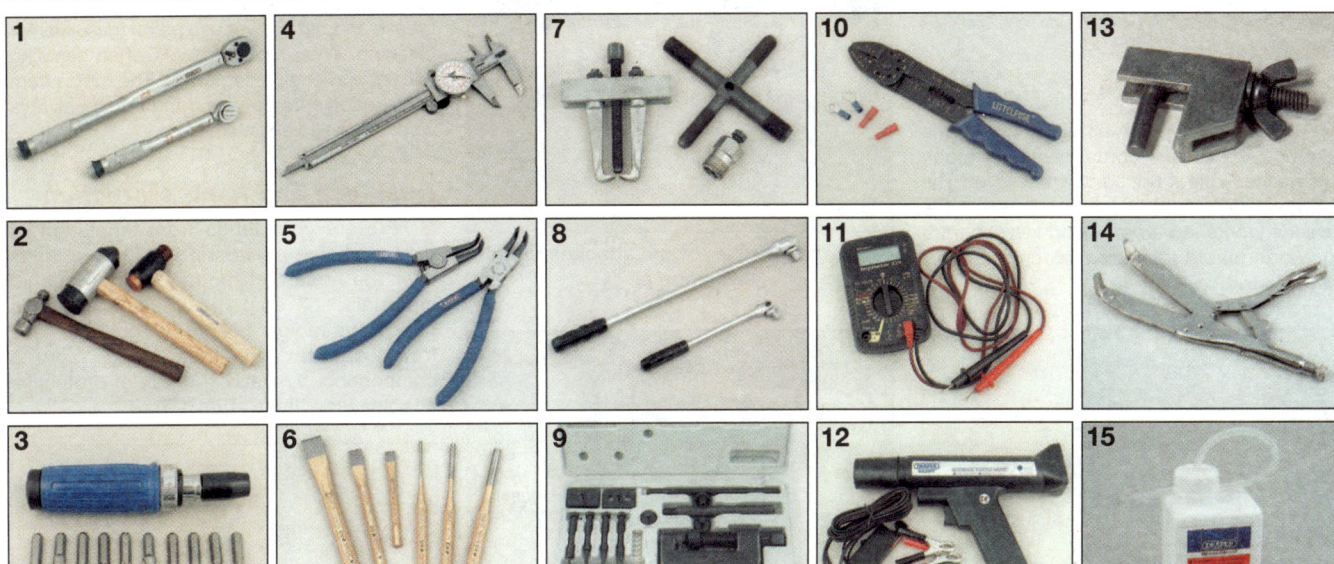

1 Torque wrench (small and mid-ranges)
2 Conventional, plastic or soft-faced hammers
3 Impact driver set
4 Vernier gauge
5 Circlip pliers (internal and external, or combination)
6 Set of cold chisels and punches
7 Selection of pullers
8 Breaker bars
9 Chain breaking/riveting tool set
10 Wire stripper and crimper tool
11 Multimeter (measures amps, volts and ohms)
12 Stroboscope (for dynamic timing checks)
13 Hose clamp (wingnut type shown)
14 Clutch holding tool
15 One-man brake/clutch bleeder kit

Specialist tools

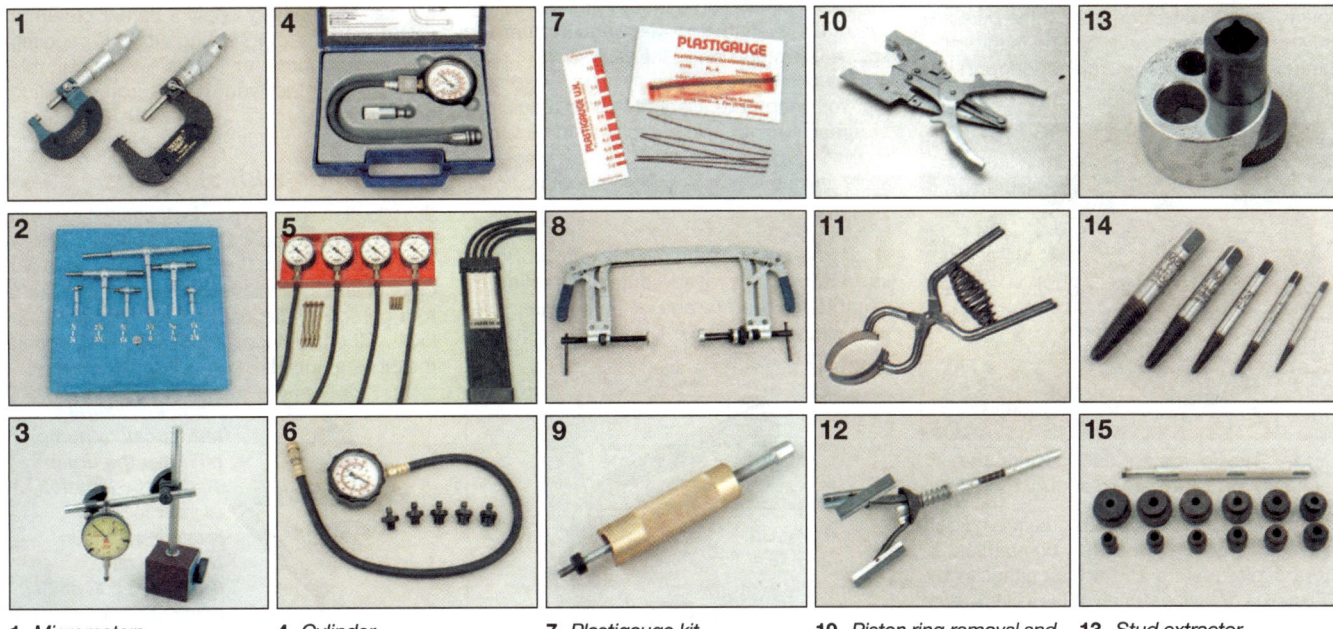

1 Micrometers (external type)
2 Telescoping gauges
3 Dial gauge
4 Cylinder compression gauge
5 Vacuum gauges (left) or manometer (right)
6 Oil pressure gauge
7 Plastigauge kit
8 Valve spring compressor (4-stroke engines)
9 Piston pin drawbolt tool
10 Piston ring removal and installation tool
11 Piston ring clamp
12 Cylinder bore hone (stone type shown)
13 Stud extractor
14 Screw extractor set
15 Bearing driver set

REF•4 Tools and Workshop Tips

1 Workshop equipment and facilities

The workbench

● Work is made much easier by raising the bike up on a ramp - components are much more accessible if raised to waist level. The hydraulic or pneumatic types seen in the dealer's workshop are a sound investment if you undertake a lot of repairs or overhauls **(see illustration 1.1)**.

1.1 Hydraulic motorcycle ramp

● If raised off ground level, the bike must be supported on the ramp to avoid it falling. Most ramps incorporate a front wheel locating clamp which can be adjusted to suit different diameter wheels. When tightening the clamp, take care not to mark the wheel rim or damage the tyre - use wood blocks on each side to prevent this.
● Secure the bike to the ramp using tie-downs **(see illustration 1.2)**. If the bike has only a sidestand, and hence leans at a dangerous angle when raised, support the bike on an auxiliary stand.

1.2 Tie-downs are used around the passenger footrests to secure the bike

● Auxiliary (paddock) stands are widely available from mail order companies or motorcycle dealers and attach either to the wheel axle or swingarm pivot **(see illustration 1.3)**. If the motorcycle has a centrestand, you can support it under the crankcase to prevent it toppling whilst either wheel is removed **(see illustration 1.4)**.

1.3 This auxiliary stand attaches to the swingarm pivot

1.4 Always use a block of wood between the engine and jack head when supporting the engine in this way

Fumes and fire

● Refer to the Safety first! page at the beginning of the manual for full details. Make sure your workshop is equipped with a fire extinguisher suitable for fuel-related fires (Class B fire - flammable liquids) - it is not sufficient to have a water-filled extinguisher.
● Always ensure adequate ventilation is available. Unless an exhaust gas extraction system is available for use, ensure that the engine is run outside of the workshop.
● If working on the fuel system, make sure the workshop is ventilated to avoid a build-up of fumes. This applies equally to fume build-up when charging a battery. Do not smoke or allow anyone else to smoke in the workshop.

Fluids

● If you need to drain fuel from the tank, store it in an approved container marked as suitable for the storage of petrol (gasoline) **(see illustration 1.5)**. Do not store fuel in glass jars or bottles.

1.5 Use an approved can only for storing petrol (gasoline)

● Use proprietary engine degreasers or solvents which have a high flash-point, such as paraffin (kerosene), for cleaning off oil, grease and dirt - never use petrol (gasoline) for cleaning. Wear rubber gloves when handling solvent and engine degreaser. The fumes from certain solvents can be dangerous - always work in a well-ventilated area.

Dust, eye and hand protection

● Protect your lungs from inhalation of dust particles by wearing a filtering mask over the nose and mouth. Many frictional materials still contain asbestos which is dangerous to your health. Protect your eyes from spouts of liquid and sprung components by wearing a pair of protective goggles **(see illustration 1.6)**.

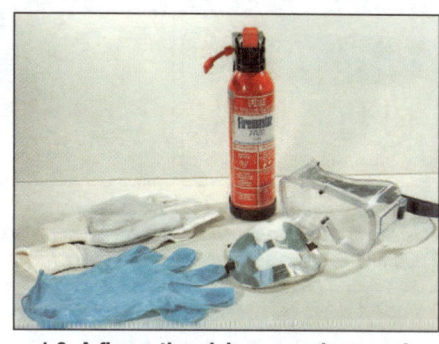

1.6 A fire extinguisher, goggles, mask and protective gloves should be at hand in the workshop

● Protect your hands from contact with solvents, fuel and oils by wearing rubber gloves. Alternatively apply a barrier cream to your hands before starting work. If handling hot components or fluids, wear suitable gloves to protect your hands from scalding and burns.

What to do with old fluids

● Old cleaning solvent, fuel, coolant and oils should not be poured down domestic drains or onto the ground. Package the fluid up in old oil containers, label it accordingly, and take it to a garage or disposal facility. Contact your local authority for location of such sites or ring the oil care hotline.

Note: It is illegal and anti-social to dump oil down the drain. To find the location of your local oil recycling bank in the UK, call 08708 506 506 or visit www.oilbankline.org.uk

In the USA, note that any oil supplier must accept used oil for recycling.

Tools and Workshop Tips

2 Fasteners -
screws, bolts and nuts

Fastener types and applications

Bolts and screws

● Fastener head types are either of hexagonal, Torx or splined design, with internal and external versions of each type **(see illustrations 2.1 and 2.2)**; splined head fasteners are not in common use on motorcycles. The conventional slotted or Phillips head design is used for certain screws. Bolt or screw length is always measured from the underside of the head to the end of the item **(see illustration 2.11)**.

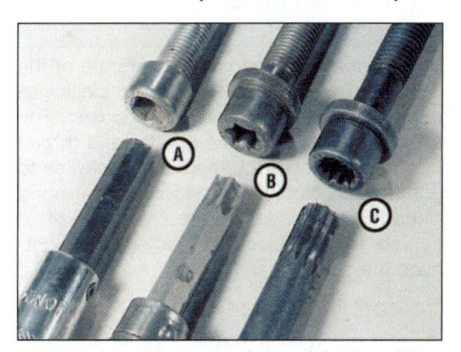

2.1 Internal hexagon/Allen (A), Torx (B) and splined (C) fasteners, with corresponding bits

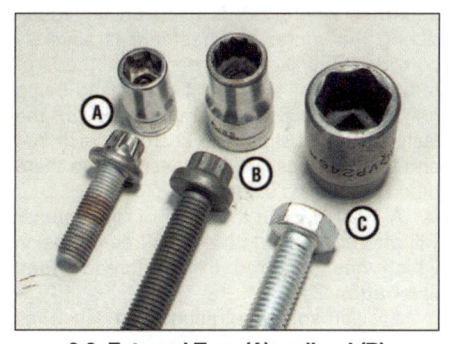

2.2 External Torx (A), splined (B) and hexagon (C) fasteners, with corresponding sockets

● Certain fasteners on the motorcycle have a tensile marking on their heads, the higher the marking the stronger the fastener. High tensile fasteners generally carry a 10 or higher marking. Never replace a high tensile fastener with one of a lower tensile strength.

Washers (see illustration 2.3)

● Plain washers are used between a fastener head and a component to prevent damage to the component or to spread the load when torque is applied. Plain washers can also be used as spacers or shims in certain assemblies. Copper or aluminium plain washers are often used as sealing washers on drain plugs.

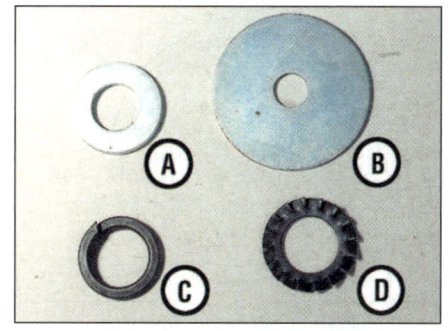

2.3 Plain washer (A), penny washer (B), spring washer (C) and serrated washer (D)

● The split-ring spring washer works by applying axial tension between the fastener head and component. If flattened, it is fatigued and must be renewed. If a plain (flat) washer is used on the fastener, position the spring washer between the fastener and the plain washer.

● Serrated star type washers dig into the fastener and component faces, preventing loosening. They are often used on electrical earth (ground) connections to the frame.

● Cone type washers (sometimes called Belleville) are conical and when tightened apply axial tension between the fastener head and component. They must be installed with the dished side against the component and often carry an OUTSIDE marking on their outer face. If flattened, they are fatigued and must be renewed.

● Tab washers are used to lock plain nuts or bolts on a shaft. A portion of the tab washer is bent up hard against one flat of the nut or bolt to prevent it loosening. Due to the tab washer being deformed in use, a new tab washer should be used every time it is disturbed.

● Wave washers are used to take up endfloat on a shaft. They provide light springing and prevent excessive side-to-side play of a component. Can be found on rocker arm shafts.

Nuts and split pins

● Conventional plain nuts are usually six-sided **(see illustration 2.4)**. They are sized by thread diameter and pitch. High tensile nuts carry a number on one end to denote their tensile strength.

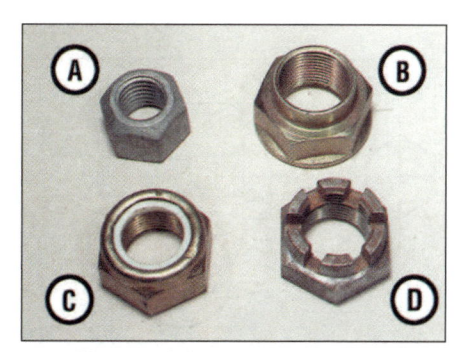

2.4 Plain nut (A), shouldered locknut (B), nylon insert nut (C) and castellated nut (D)

● Self-locking nuts either have a nylon insert, or two spring metal tabs, or a shoulder which is staked into a groove in the shaft - their advantage over conventional plain nuts is a resistance to loosening due to vibration. The nylon insert type can be used a number of times, but must be renewed when the friction of the nylon insert is reduced, ie when the nut spins freely on the shaft. The spring tab type can be reused unless the tabs are damaged. The shouldered type must be renewed every time it is disturbed.

● Split pins (cotter pins) are used to lock a castellated nut to a shaft or to prevent slackening of a plain nut. Common applications are wheel axles and brake torque arms. Because the split pin arms are deformed to lock around the nut a new split pin must always be used on installation - always fit the correct size split pin which will fit snugly in the shaft hole. Make sure the split pin arms are correctly located around the nut **(see illustrations 2.5 and 2.6)**.

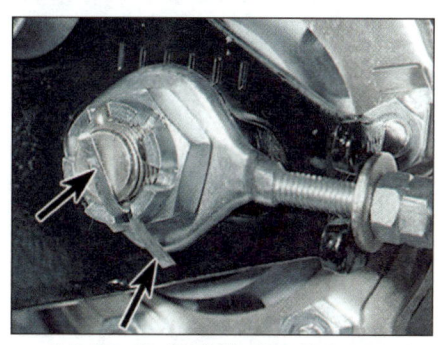

2.5 Bend split pin (cotter pin) arms as shown (arrows) to secure a castellated nut

2.6 Bend split pin (cotter pin) arms as shown to secure a plain nut

Caution: If the castellated nut slots do not align with the shaft hole after tightening to the torque setting, tighten the nut until the next slot aligns with the hole - never slacken the nut to align its slot.

● R-pins (shaped like the letter R), or slip pins as they are sometimes called, are sprung and can be reused if they are otherwise in good condition. Always install R-pins with their closed end facing forwards **(see illustration 2.7)**.

REF•6 Tools and Workshop Tips

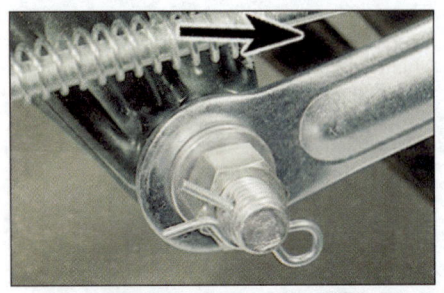

2.7 Correct fitting of R-pin. Arrow indicates forward direction

Circlips (see illustration 2.8)

● Circlips (sometimes called snap-rings) are used to retain components on a shaft or in a housing and have corresponding external or internal ears to permit removal. Parallel-sided (machined) circlips can be installed either way round in their groove, whereas stamped circlips (which have a chamfered edge on one face) must be installed with the chamfer facing away from the direction of thrust load **(see illustration 2.9)**.

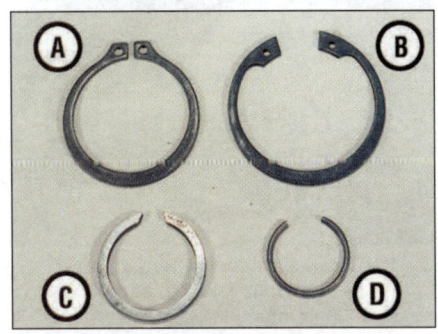

2.8 External stamped circlip (A), internal stamped circlip (B), machined circlip (C) and wire circlip (D)

● Always use circlip pliers to remove and install circlips; expand or compress them just enough to remove them. After installation, rotate the circlip in its groove to ensure it is securely seated. If installing a circlip on a splined shaft, always align its opening with a shaft channel to ensure the circlip ends are well supported and unlikely to catch **(see illustration 2.10)**.

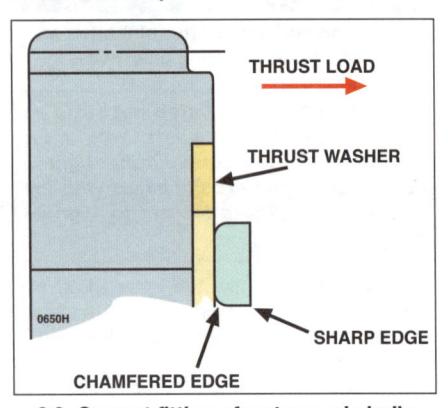

2.9 Correct fitting of a stamped circlip

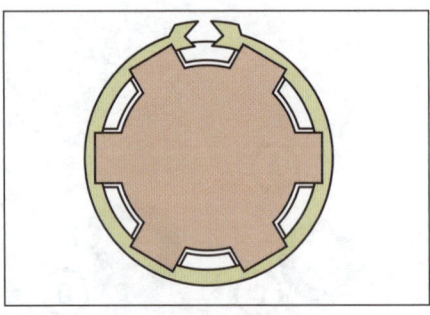

2.10 Align circlip opening with shaft channel

● Circlips can wear due to the thrust of components and become loose in their grooves, with the subsequent danger of becoming dislodged in operation. For this reason, renewal is advised every time a circlip is disturbed.

● Wire circlips are commonly used as piston pin retaining clips. If a removal tang is provided, long-nosed pliers can be used to dislodge them, otherwise careful use of a small flat-bladed screwdriver is necessary. Wire circlips should be renewed every time they are disturbed.

Thread diameter and pitch

● Diameter of a male thread (screw, bolt or stud) is the outside diameter of the threaded portion **(see illustration 2.11)**. Most motorcycle manufacturers use the ISO (International Standards Organisation) metric system expressed in millimetres, eg M6 refers to a 6 mm diameter thread. Sizing is the same for nuts, except that the thread diameter is measured across the valleys of the nut.

● Pitch is the distance between the peaks of the thread **(see illustration 2.11)**. It is expressed in millimetres, thus a common bolt size may be expressed as 6.0 x 1.0 mm (6 mm thread diameter and 1 mm pitch). Generally pitch increases in proportion to thread diameter, although there are always exceptions.

● Thread diameter and pitch are related for conventional fastener applications and the accompanying table can be used as a guide. Additionally, the AF (Across Flats), spanner or socket size dimension of the bolt or nut **(see illustration 2.11)** is linked to thread and pitch specification. Thread pitch can be measured with a thread gauge **(see illustration 2.12)**.

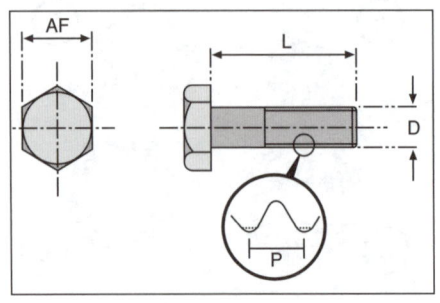

2.11 Fastener length (L), thread diameter (D), thread pitch (P) and head size (AF)

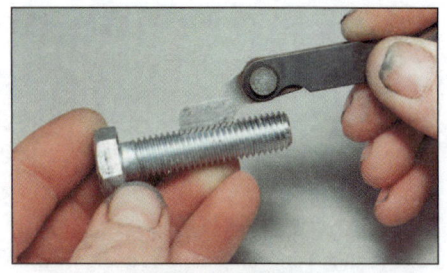

2.12 Using a thread gauge to measure pitch

AF size	Thread diameter x pitch (mm)
8 mm	M5 x 0.8
8 mm	M6 x 1.0
10 mm	M6 x 1.0
12 mm	M8 x 1.25
14 mm	M10 x 1.25
17 mm	M12 x 1.25

● The threads of most fasteners are of the right-hand type, ie they are turned clockwise to tighten and anti-clockwise to loosen. The reverse situation applies to left-hand thread fasteners, which are turned anti-clockwise to tighten and clockwise to loosen. Left-hand threads are used where rotation of a component might loosen a conventional right-hand thread fastener.

Seized fasteners

● Corrosion of external fasteners due to water or reaction between two dissimilar metals can occur over a period of time. It will build up sooner in wet conditions or in countries where salt is used on the roads during the winter. If a fastener is severely corroded it is likely that normal methods of removal will fail and result in its head being ruined. When you attempt removal, the fastener thread should be heard to crack free and unscrew easily - if it doesn't, stop there before damaging something.

● A smart tap on the head of the fastener will often succeed in breaking free corrosion which has occurred in the threads **(see illustration 2.13)**.

● An aerosol penetrating fluid (such as WD-40) applied the night beforehand may work its way down into the thread and ease removal. Depending on the location, you may be able to make up a Plasticine well around the fastener head and fill it with penetrating fluid.

2.13 A sharp tap on the head of a fastener will often break free a corroded thread

Tools and Workshop Tips REF•7

• If you are working on an engine internal component, corrosion will most likely not be a problem due to the well lubricated environment. However, components can be very tight and an impact driver is a useful tool in freeing them (see illustration 2.14).

2.14 Using an impact driver to free a fastener

• Where corrosion has occurred between dissimilar metals (eg steel and aluminium alloy), the application of heat to the fastener head will create a disproportionate expansion rate between the two metals and break the seizure caused by the corrosion. Whether heat can be applied depends on the location of the fastener - any surrounding components likely to be damaged must first be removed (see illustration 2.15). Heat can be applied using a paint stripper heat gun or clothes iron, or by immersing the component in boiling water - wear protective gloves to prevent scalding or burns to the hands.

2.15 Using heat to free a seized fastener

• As a last resort, it is possible to use a hammer and cold chisel to work the fastener head unscrewed (see illustration 2.16). This will damage the fastener, but more importantly extreme care must be taken not to damage the surrounding component.

Caution: Remember that the component being secured is generally of more value than the bolt, nut or screw - when the fastener is freed, do not unscrew it with force, instead work the fastener back and forth when resistance is felt to prevent thread damage.

2.16 Using a hammer and chisel to free a seized fastener

Broken fasteners and damaged heads

• If the shank of a broken bolt or screw is accessible you can grip it with self-locking grips. The knurled wheel type stud extractor tool or self-gripping stud puller tool is particularly useful for removing the long studs which screw into the cylinder mouth surface of the crankcase or bolts and screws from which the head has broken off (see illustration 2.17). Studs can also be removed by locking two nuts together on the threaded end of the stud and using a spanner on the lower nut (see illustration 2.18).

2.17 Using a stud extractor tool to remove a broken crankcase stud

2.18 Two nuts can be locked together to unscrew a stud from a component

• A bolt or screw which has broken off below or level with the casing must be extracted using a screw extractor set. Centre punch the fastener to centralise the drill bit, then drill a hole in the fastener (see illustration 2.19). Select a drill bit which is approximately half to three-quarters the

2.19 When using a screw extractor, first drill a hole in the fastener . . .

diameter of the fastener and drill to a depth which will accommodate the extractor. Use the largest size extractor possible, but avoid leaving too small a wall thickness otherwise the extractor will merely force the fastener walls outwards wedging it in the casing thread.

• If a spiral type extractor is used, thread it anti-clockwise into the fastener. As it is screwed in, it will grip the fastener and unscrew it from the casing (see illustration 2.20).

2.20 . . . then thread the extractor anti-clockwise into the fastener

• If a taper type extractor is used, tap it into the fastener so that it is firmly wedged in place. Unscrew the extractor (anti-clockwise) to draw the fastener out.

> ⚠ **Warning: Stud extractors are very hard and may break off in the fastener if care is not taken - ask an engineer about spark erosion if this happens.**

• Alternatively, the broken bolt/screw can be drilled out and the hole retapped for an oversize bolt/screw or a diamond-section thread insert. It is essential that the drilling is carried out squarely and to the correct depth, otherwise the casing may be ruined - if in doubt, entrust the work to an engineer.

• Bolts and nuts with rounded corners cause the correct size spanner or socket to slip when force is applied. Of the types of spanner/socket available always use a six-point type rather than an eight or twelve-point type - better grip

REF•8 Tools and Workshop Tips

2.21 Comparison of surface drive ring spanner (left) with 12-point type (right)

is obtained. Surface drive spanners grip the middle of the hex flats, rather than the corners, and are thus good in cases of damaged heads **(see illustration 2.21)**.

● Slotted-head or Phillips-head screws are often damaged by the use of the wrong size screwdriver. Allen-head and Torx-head screws are much less likely to sustain damage. If enough of the screw head is exposed you can use a hacksaw to cut a slot in its head and then use a conventional flat-bladed screwdriver to remove it. Alternatively use a hammer and cold chisel to tap the head of the fastener around to slacken it. Always replace damaged fasteners with new ones, preferably Torx or Allen-head type.

> **HAYNES HiNT**
>
> *A dab of valve grinding compound between the screw head and screwdriver tip will often give a good grip.*

Thread repair

● Threads (particularly those in aluminium alloy components) can be damaged by overtightening, being assembled with dirt in the threads, or from a component working loose and vibrating. Eventually the thread will fail completely, and it will be impossible to tighten the fastener.

● If a thread is damaged or clogged with old locking compound it can be renovated with a thread repair tool (thread chaser) **(see illustrations 2.22 and 2.23)**; special thread

2.22 A thread repair tool being used to correct an internal thread

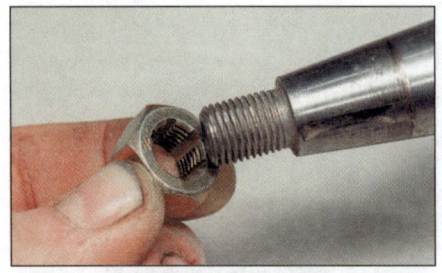

2.23 A thread repair tool being used to correct an external thread

chasers are available for spark plug hole threads. The tool will not cut a new thread, but clean and true the original thread. Make sure that you use the correct diameter and pitch tool. Similarly, external threads can be cleaned up with a die or a thread restorer file **(see illustration 2.24)**.

2.24 Using a thread restorer file

● It is possible to drill out the old thread and retap the component to the next thread size. This will work where there is enough surrounding material and a new bolt or screw can be obtained. Sometimes, however, this is not possible - such as where the bolt/screw passes through another component which must also be suitably modified, also in cases where a spark plug or oil drain plug cannot be obtained in a larger diameter thread size.

● The diamond-section thread insert (often known by its popular trade name of Heli-Coil) is a simple and effective method of renewing the thread and retaining the original size. A kit can be purchased which contains the tap, insert and installing tool **(see illustration 2.25)**. Drill out the damaged thread with the size drill specified **(see illustration 2.26)**. Carefully retap the thread **(see illustration 2.27)**. Install the

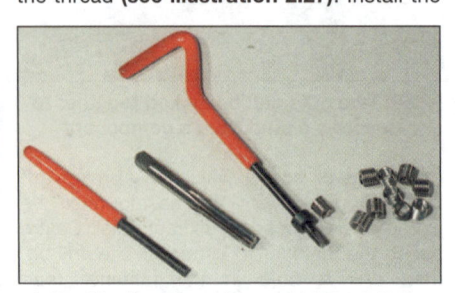

2.25 Obtain a thread insert kit to suit the thread diameter and pitch required

2.26 To install a thread insert, first drill out the original thread . . .

2.27 . . . tap a new thread . . .

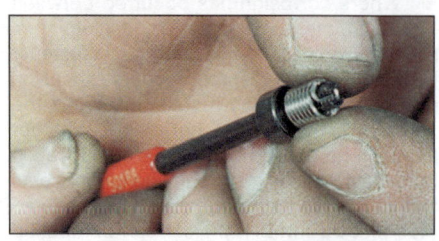

2.28 . . . fit insert on the installing tool . . .

2.29 . . . and thread into the component . . .

2.30 . . . break off the tang when complete

insert on the installing tool and thread it slowly into place using a light downward pressure **(see illustrations 2.28 and 2.29)**. When positioned between a 1/4 and 1/2 turn below the surface withdraw the installing tool and use the break-off tool to press down on the tang, breaking it off **(see illustration 2.30)**.

● There are epoxy thread repair kits on the market which can rebuild stripped internal threads, although this repair should not be used on high load-bearing components.

Tools and Workshop Tips

Thread locking and sealing compounds

● Locking compounds are used in locations where the fastener is prone to loosening due to vibration or on important safety-related items which might cause loss of control of the motorcycle if they fail. It is also used where important fasteners cannot be secured by other means such as lockwashers or split pins.

● Before applying locking compound, make sure that the threads (internal and external) are clean and dry with all old compound removed. Select a compound to suit the component being secured - a non-permanent general locking and sealing type is suitable for most applications, but a high strength type is needed for permanent fixing of studs in castings. Apply a drop or two of the compound to the first few threads of the fastener, then thread it into place and tighten to the specified torque. Do not apply excessive thread locking compound otherwise the thread may be damaged on subsequent removal.

● Certain fasteners are impregnated with a dry film type coating of locking compound on their threads. Always renew this type of fastener if disturbed.

● Anti-seize compounds, such as copper-based greases, can be applied to protect threads from seizure due to extreme heat and corrosion. A common instance is spark plug threads and exhaust system fasteners.

3 Measuring tools and gauges

Feeler gauges

● Feeler gauges (or blades) are used for measuring small gaps and clearances (see illustration 3.1). They can also be used to measure endfloat (sideplay) of a component on a shaft where access is not possible with a dial gauge.

● Feeler gauge sets should be treated with care and not bent or damaged. They are etched with their size on one face. Keep them clean and very lightly oiled to prevent corrosion build-up.

3.1 Feeler gauges are used for measuring small gaps and clearances - thickness is marked on one face of gauge

● When measuring a clearance, select a gauge which is a light sliding fit between the two components. You may need to use two gauges together to measure the clearance accurately.

Micrometers

● A micrometer is a precision tool capable of measuring to 0.01 or 0.001 of a millimetre. It should always be stored in its case and not in the general toolbox. It must be kept clean and never dropped, otherwise its frame or measuring anvils could be distorted resulting in inaccurate readings.

● External micrometers are used for measuring outside diameters of components and have many more applications than internal micrometers. Micrometers are available in different size ranges, eg 0 to 25 mm, 25 to 50 mm, and upwards in 25 mm steps; some large micrometers have interchangeable anvils to allow a range of measurements to be taken. Generally the largest precision measurement you are likely to take on a motorcycle is the piston diameter.

● Internal micrometers (or bore micrometers) are used for measuring inside diameters, such as valve guides and cylinder bores. Telescoping gauges and small hole gauges are used in conjunction with an external micrometer, whereas the more expensive internal micrometers have their own measuring device.

External micrometer

Note: *The conventional analogue type instrument is described. Although much easier to read, digital micrometers are considerably more expensive.*

● Always check the calibration of the micrometer before use. With the anvils closed (0 to 25 mm type) or set over a test gauge (for the larger types) the scale should read zero (see illustration 3.2); make sure that the anvils (and test piece) are clean first. Any discrepancy can be adjusted by referring to the instructions supplied with the tool. Remember that the micrometer is a precision measuring tool - don't force the anvils closed, use the ratchet (4) on the end of the micrometer to close it. In this way, a measured force is always applied.

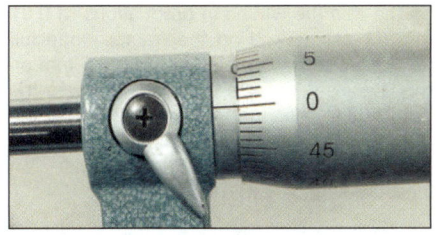

3.2 Check micrometer calibration before use

● To use, first make sure that the item being measured is clean. Place the anvil of the micrometer (1) against the item and use the thimble (2) to bring the spindle (3) lightly into contact with the other side of the item (see illustration 3.3). Don't tighten the thimble down because this will damage the micrometer - instead use the ratchet (4) on the end of the micrometer. The ratchet mechanism applies a measured force preventing damage to the instrument.

● The micrometer is read by referring to the linear scale on the sleeve and the annular scale on the thimble. Read off the sleeve first to obtain the base measurement, then add the fine measurement from the thimble to obtain the overall reading. The linear scale on the sleeve represents the measuring range of the micrometer (eg 0 to 25 mm). The annular scale

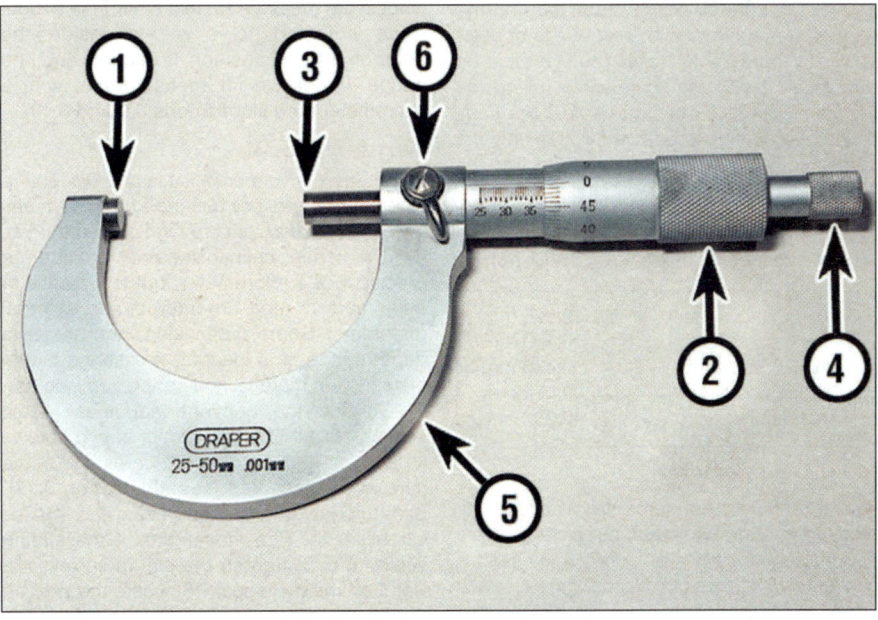

3.3 Micrometer component parts

1 Anvil
2 Thimble
3 Spindle
4 Ratchet
5 Frame
6 Locking lever

REF•10 Tools and Workshop Tips

on the thimble will be in graduations of 0.01 mm (or as marked on the frame) - one full revolution of the thimble will move 0.5 mm on the linear scale. Take the reading where the datum line on the sleeve intersects the thimble's scale. Always position the eye directly above the scale otherwise an inaccurate reading will result.

In the example shown the item measures 2.95 mm **(see illustration 3.4)**:

Linear scale	2.00 mm
Linear scale	0.50 mm
Annular scale	0.45 mm
Total figure	**2.95 mm**

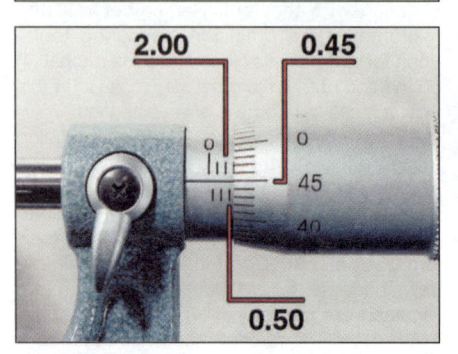

3.4 Micrometer reading of 2.95 mm

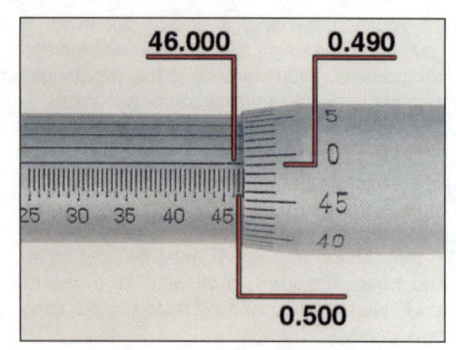

3.5 Micrometer reading of 46.99 mm on linear and annular scales . . .

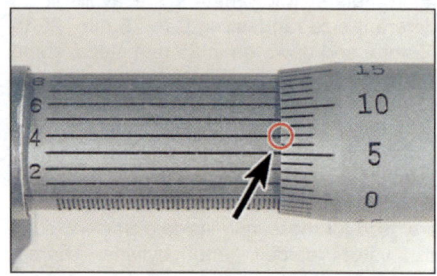

3.6 . . . and 0.004 mm on vernier scale

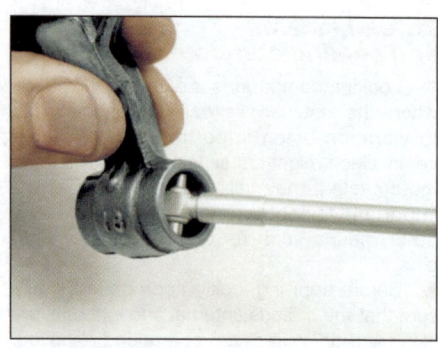

3.7 Expand the telescoping gauge in the bore, lock its position . . .

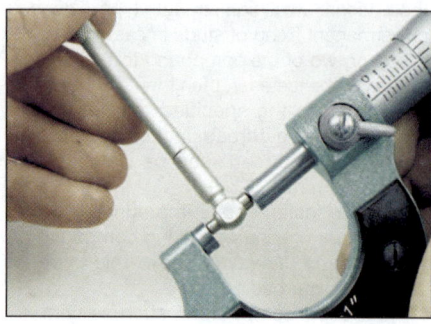

3.8 . . . then measure the gauge with a micrometer

Most micrometers have a locking lever (6) on the frame to hold the setting in place, allowing the item to be removed from the micrometer.
● Some micrometers have a vernier scale on their sleeve, providing an even finer measurement to be taken, in 0.001 increments of a millimetre. Take the sleeve and thimble measurement as described above, then check which graduation on the vernier scale aligns with that of the annular scale on the thimble **Note:** *The eye must be perpendicular to the scale when taking the vernier reading - if necessary rotate the body of the micrometer to ensure this.* Multiply the vernier scale figure by 0.001 and add it to the base and fine measurement figures.

In the example shown the item measures 46.994 mm **(see illustrations 3.5 and 3.6)**:

Linear scale (base)	46.000 mm
Linear scale (base)	00.500 mm
Annular scale (fine)	00.490 mm
Vernier scale	00.004 mm
Total figure	**46.994 mm**

Internal micrometer

● Internal micrometers are available for measuring bore diameters, but are expensive and unlikely to be available for home use. It is suggested that a set of telescoping gauges and small hole gauges, both of which must be used with an external micrometer, will suffice for taking internal measurements on a motorcycle.
● Telescoping gauges can be used to measure internal diameters of components. Select a gauge with the correct size range, make sure its ends are clean and insert it into the bore. Expand the gauge, then lock its position and withdraw it from the bore **(see illustration 3.7)**. Measure across the gauge ends with a micrometer **(see illustration 3.8)**.
● Very small diameter bores (such as valve guides) are measured with a small hole gauge. Once adjusted to a slip-fit inside the component, its position is locked and the gauge withdrawn for measurement with a micrometer **(see illustrations 3.9 and 3.10)**.

Vernier caliper

Note: *The conventional linear and dial gauge type instruments are described. Digital types are easier to read, but are far more expensive.*
● The vernier caliper does not provide the precision of a micrometer, but is versatile in being able to measure internal and external diameters. Some types also incorporate a depth gauge. It is ideal for measuring clutch plate friction material and spring free lengths.
● To use the conventional linear scale vernier, slacken off the vernier clamp screws (1) and set its jaws over (2), or inside (3), the item to be measured **(see illustration 3.11)**. Slide the jaw into contact, using the thumbwheel (4) for fine movement of the sliding scale (5) then tighten the clamp screws (1). Read off the main scale (6) where the zero on the sliding scale (5) intersects it, taking the whole number to the left of the zero; this provides the base measurement. View along the sliding scale and select the division which

3.9 Expand the small hole gauge in the bore, lock its position . . .

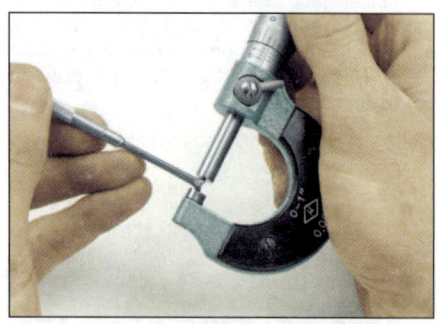

3.10 . . . then measure the gauge with a micrometer

lines up exactly with any of the divisions on the main scale, noting that the divisions usually represents 0.02 of a millimetre. Add this fine measurement to the base measurement to obtain the total reading.

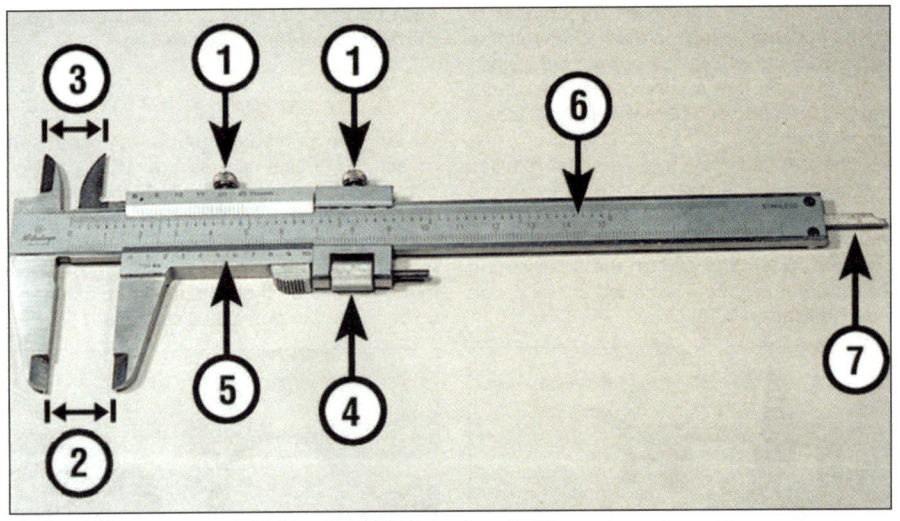

Tools and Workshop Tips   REF•11

Plastigauge

- Plastigauge is a plastic material which can be compressed between two surfaces to measure the oil clearance between them. The width of the compressed Plastigauge is measured against a calibrated scale to determine the clearance.
- Common uses of Plastigauge are for measuring the clearance between crankshaft journal and main bearing inserts, between crankshaft journal and big-end bearing inserts, and between camshaft and bearing surfaces. The following example describes big-end oil clearance measurement.
- Handle the Plastigauge material carefully to prevent distortion. Using a sharp knife, cut a length which corresponds with the width of the bearing being measured and place it carefully across the journal so that it is parallel with the shaft (see illustration 3.15). Carefully install both bearing shells and the connecting rod. Without rotating the rod on the journal tighten its bolts or nuts (as applicable) to the specified torque. The connecting rod and bearings are then disassembled and the crushed Plastigauge examined.

3.11 Vernier component parts (linear gauge)

1 Clamp screws
2 External jaws
3 Internal jaws
4 Thumbwheel
5 Sliding scale
6 Main scale
7 Depth gauge

In the example shown the item measures 55.92 mm (see illustration 3.12):

Base measurement	55.00 mm
Fine measurement	00.92 mm
Total figure	**55.92 mm**

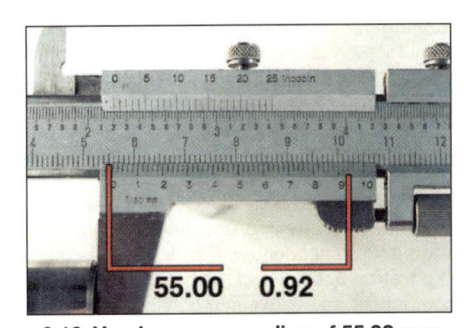

- Some vernier calipers are equipped with a dial gauge for fine measurement. Before use, check that the jaws are clean, then close them fully and check that the dial gauge reads zero. If necessary adjust the gauge ring accordingly. Slacken the vernier clamp screw (1) and set its jaws over (2), or inside (3), the item to be measured (see illustration 3.13). Slide the jaws into contact, using the thumbwheel (4) for fine movement. Read off the main scale (5) where the edge of the sliding scale (6) intersects it, taking the whole number to the left of the zero; this provides the base measurement. Read off the needle position on the dial gauge (7) scale to provide the fine measurement; each division represents 0.05 of a millimetre. Add this fine measurement to the base measurement to obtain the total reading.

In the example shown the item measures 55.95 mm (see illustration 3.14):

Base measurement	55.00 mm
Fine measurement	00.95 mm
Total figure	**55.95 mm**

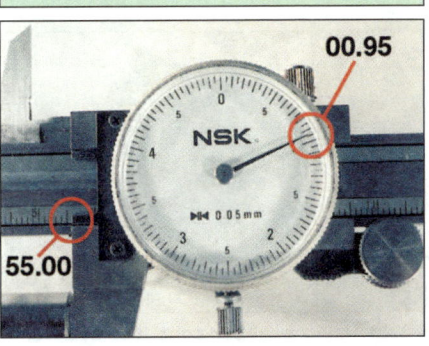

3.12 Vernier gauge reading of 55.92 mm

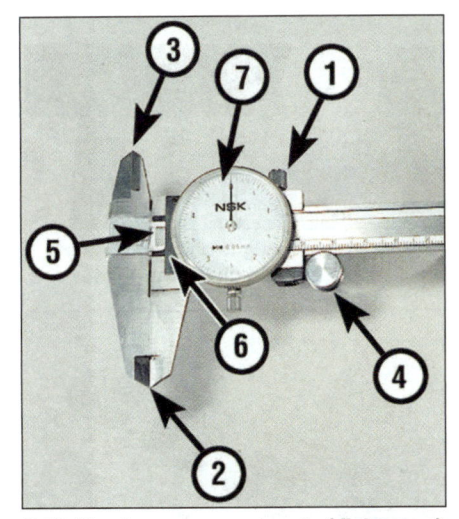

3.13 Vernier component parts (dial gauge)

1 Clamp screw
2 External jaws
3 Internal jaws
4 Thumbwheel
5 Main scale
6 Sliding scale
7 Dial gauge

3.14 Vernier gauge reading of 55.95 mm

3.15 Plastigauge placed across shaft journal

- Using the scale provided in the Plastigauge kit, measure the width of the material to determine the oil clearance (see illustration 3.16). Always remove all traces of Plastigauge after use using your fingernails.

Caution: Arriving at the correct clearance demands that the assembly is torqued correctly, according to the settings and sequence (where applicable) provided by the motorcycle manufacturer.

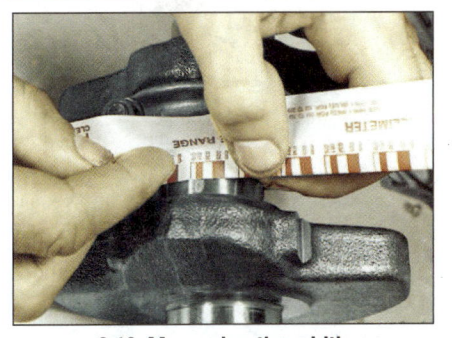

3.16 Measuring the width of the crushed Plastigauge

REF•12 Tools and Workshop Tips

Dial gauge or DTI (Dial Test Indicator)

● A dial gauge can be used to accurately measure small amounts of movement. Typical uses are measuring shaft runout or shaft endfloat (sideplay) and setting piston position for ignition timing on two-strokes. A dial gauge set usually comes with a range of different probes and adapters and mounting equipment.

● The gauge needle must point to zero when at rest. Rotate the ring around its periphery to zero the gauge.

● Check that the gauge is capable of reading the extent of movement in the work. Most gauges have a small dial set in the face which records whole millimetres of movement as well as the fine scale around the face periphery which is calibrated in 0.01 mm divisions. Read off the small dial first to obtain the base measurement, then add the measurement from the fine scale to obtain the total reading.

In the example shown the gauge reads 1.48 mm (see illustration 3.17):

Base measurement	1.00 mm
Fine measurement	0.48 mm
Total figure	**1.48 mm**

3.17 Dial gauge reading of 1.48 mm

● If measuring shaft runout, the shaft must be supported in vee-blocks and the gauge mounted on a stand perpendicular to the shaft. Rest the tip of the gauge against the centre of the shaft and rotate the shaft slowly whilst watching the gauge reading (see illustration 3.18). Take several measurements along the length of the shaft and record the maximum gauge reading as the amount of runout in the shaft. **Note:** *The reading obtained will be total runout at that point - some manufacturers specify that the runout figure is halved to compare with their specified runout limit.*

● Endfloat (sideplay) measurement requires that the gauge is mounted securely to the surrounding component with its probe touching the end of the shaft. Using hand pressure, push and pull on the shaft noting the maximum endfloat recorded on the gauge (see illustration 3.19).

3.19 Using a dial gauge to measure shaft endfloat

● A dial gauge with suitable adapters can be used to determine piston position BTDC on two-stroke engines for the purposes of ignition timing. The gauge, adapter and suitable length probe are installed in the place of the spark plug and the gauge zeroed at TDC. If the piston position is specified as 1.14 mm BTDC, rotate the engine back to 2.00 mm BTDC, then slowly forwards to 1.14 mm BTDC.

Cylinder compression gauges

● A compression gauge is used for measuring cylinder compression. Either the rubber-cone type or the threaded adapter type can be used. The latter is preferred to ensure a perfect seal against the cylinder head. A 0 to 300 psi (0 to 20 Bar) type gauge (for petrol/gasoline engines) will be suitable for motorcycles.

● The spark plug is removed and the gauge either held hard against the cylinder head (cone type) or the gauge adapter screwed into the cylinder head (threaded type) (see illustration 3.20). Cylinder compression is measured with the engine turning over, but not running - carry out the compression test as described in *Fault Finding Equipment*. The gauge will hold the reading until manually released.

Oil pressure gauge

● An oil pressure gauge is used for measuring engine oil pressure. Most gauges come with a set of adapters to fit the thread of the take-off point (see illustration 3.21). If the take-off point specified by the motorcycle manufacturer is an external oil pipe union, make sure that the specified replacement union is used to prevent oil starvation.

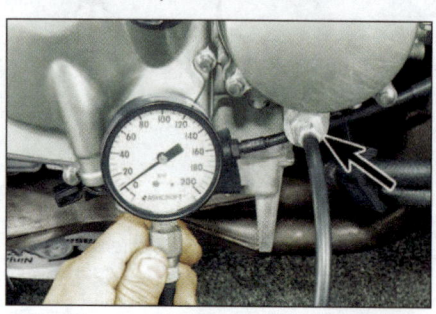

3.21 Oil pressure gauge and take-off point adapter (arrow)

● Oil pressure is measured with the engine running (at a specific rpm) and often the manufacturer will specify pressure limits for a cold and hot engine.

Straight-edge and surface plate

● If checking the gasket face of a component for warpage, place a steel rule or precision straight-edge across the gasket face and measure any gap between the straight-edge and component with feeler gauges (see illustration 3.22). Check diagonally across the component and between mounting holes (see illustration 3.23).

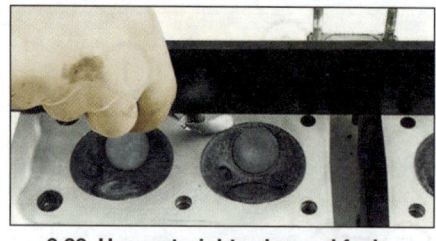

3.22 Use a straight-edge and feeler gauges to check for warpage

3.18 Using a dial gauge to measure shaft runout

3.20 Using a rubber-cone type cylinder compression gauge

3.23 Check for warpage in these directions

Tools and Workshop Tips REF•13

- Checking individual components for warpage, such as clutch plain (metal) plates, requires a perfectly flat plate or piece or plate glass and feeler gauges.

4 Torque and leverage

What is torque?

- Torque describes the twisting force about a shaft. The amount of torque applied is determined by the distance from the centre of the shaft to the end of the lever and the amount of force being applied to the end of the lever; distance multiplied by force equals torque.
- The manufacturer applies a measured torque to a bolt or nut to ensure that it will not slacken in use and to hold two components securely together without movement in the joint. The actual torque setting depends on the thread size, bolt or nut material and the composition of the components being held.
- Too little torque may cause the fastener to loosen due to vibration, whereas too much torque will distort the joint faces of the component or cause the fastener to shear off. Always stick to the specified torque setting.

Using a torque wrench

- Check the calibration of the torque wrench and make sure it has a suitable range for the job. Torque wrenches are available in Nm (Newton-metres), kgf m (kilograms-force metre), lbf ft (pounds-feet), lbf in (inch-pounds). Do not confuse lbf ft with lbf in.
- Adjust the tool to the desired torque on the scale (see illustration 4.1). If your torque wrench is not calibrated in the units specified, carefully convert the figure (see *Conversion Factors*). A manufacturer sometimes gives a torque setting as a range (8 to 10 Nm) rather than a single figure - in this case set the tool midway between the two settings. The same torque may be expressed as 9 Nm ± 1 Nm. Some torque wrenches have a method of locking the setting so that it isn't inadvertently altered during use.

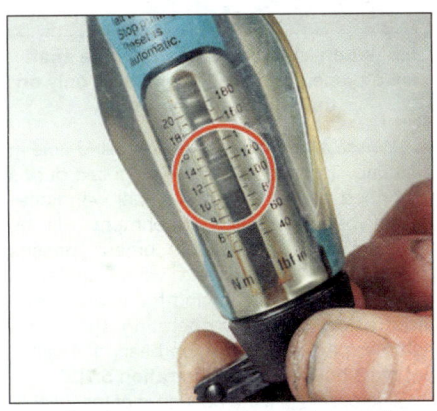

- Install the bolts/nuts in their correct location and secure them lightly. Their threads must be clean and free of any old locking compound. Unless specified the threads and flange should be dry - oiled threads are necessary in certain circumstances and the manufacturer will take this into account in the specified torque figure. Similarly, the manufacturer may also specify the application of thread-locking compound.
- Tighten the fasteners in the specified sequence until the torque wrench clicks, indicating that the torque setting has been reached. Apply the torque again to double-check the setting. Where different thread diameter fasteners secure the component, as a rule tighten the larger diameter ones first.
- When the torque wrench has been finished with, release the lock (where applicable) and fully back off its setting to zero - do not leave the torque wrench tensioned. Also, do not use a torque wrench for slackening a fastener.

Angle-tightening

- Manufacturers often specify a figure in degrees for final tightening of a fastener. This usually follows tightening to a specific torque setting.
- A degree disc can be set and attached to the socket (see illustration 4.2) or a protractor can be used to mark the angle of movement on the bolt/nut head and the surrounding casting (see illustration 4.3).

4.2 Angle tightening can be accomplished with a torque-angle gauge ...

4.1 Set the torque wrench index mark to the setting required, in this case 12 Nm

4.3 ... or by marking the angle on the surrounding component

Loosening sequences

- Where more than one bolt/nut secures a component, loosen each fastener evenly a little at a time. In this way, not all the stress of the joint is held by one fastener and the components are not likely to distort.
- If a tightening sequence is provided, work in the REVERSE of this, but if not, work from the outside in, in a criss-cross sequence (see illustration 4.4).

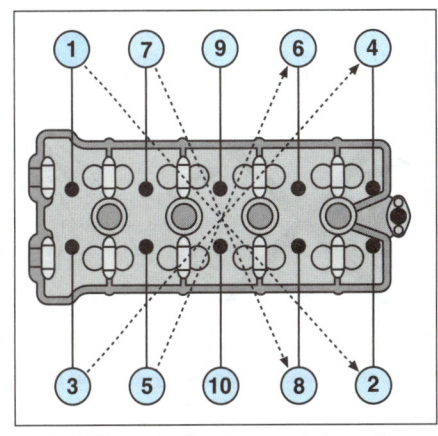

4.4 When slackening, work from the outside inwards

Tightening sequences

- If a component is held by more than one fastener it is important that the retaining bolts/nuts are tightened evenly to prevent uneven stress build-up and distortion of sealing faces. This is especially important on high-compression joints such as the cylinder head.
- A sequence is usually provided by the manufacturer, either in a diagram or actually marked in the casting. If not, always start in the centre and work outwards in a criss-cross pattern (see illustration 4.5). Start off by securing all bolts/nuts finger-tight, then set the torque wrench and tighten each fastener by a small amount in sequence until the final torque is reached. By following this practice,

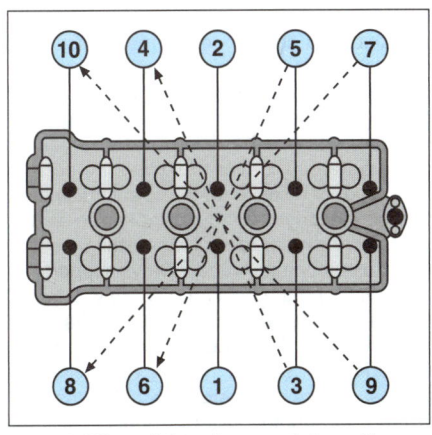

4.5 When tightening, work from the inside outwards

REF•14 Tools and Workshop Tips

the joint will be held evenly and will not be distorted. Important joints, such as the cylinder head and big-end fasteners often have two- or three-stage torque settings.

Applying leverage

● Use tools at the correct angle. Position a socket wrench or spanner on the bolt/nut so that you pull it towards you when loosening. If this can't be done, push the spanner without curling your fingers around it **(see illustration 4.6)** - the spanner may slip or the fastener loosen suddenly, resulting in your fingers being crushed against a component.

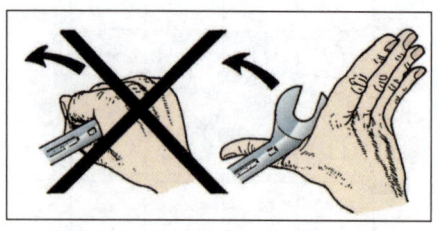

4.6 If you can't pull on the spanner to loosen a fastener, push with your hand open

● Additional leverage is gained by extending the length of the lever. The best way to do this is to use a breaker bar instead of the regular length tool, or to slip a length of tubing over the end of the spanner or socket wrench.
● If additional leverage will not work, the fastener head is either damaged or firmly corroded in place (see *Fasteners*).

5 Bearings

Bearing removal and installation

Drivers and sockets

● Before removing a bearing, always inspect the casing to see which way it must be driven out - some casings will have retaining plates or a cast step. Also check for any identifying markings on the bearing and if installed to a certain depth, measure this at this stage. Some roller bearings are sealed on one side - take note of the original fitted position.
● Bearings can be driven out of a casing using a bearing driver tool (with the correct size head) or a socket of the correct diameter. Select the driver head or socket so that it contacts the outer race of the bearing, not the balls/rollers or inner race. Always support the casing around the bearing housing with wood blocks, otherwise there is a risk of fracture. The bearing is driven out with a few blows on the driver or socket from a heavy mallet. Unless access is severely restricted (as with wheel bearings), a pin-punch is not recommended unless it is moved around the bearing to keep it square in its housing.

● The same equipment can be used to install bearings. Make sure the bearing housing is supported on wood blocks and line up the bearing in its housing. Fit the bearing as noted on removal - generally they are installed with their marked side facing outwards. Tap the bearing squarely into its housing using a driver or socket which bears only on the bearing's outer race - contact with the bearing balls/rollers or inner race will destroy it **(see illustrations 5.1 and 5.2)**.
● Check that the bearing inner race and balls/rollers rotate freely.

5.1 Using a bearing driver against the bearing's outer race

5.2 Using a large socket against the bearing's outer race

Pullers and slide-hammers

● Where a bearing is pressed on a shaft a puller will be required to extract it **(see illustration 5.3)**. Make sure that the puller clamp or legs fit securely behind the bearing and are unlikely to slip out. If pulling a bearing

5.3 This bearing puller clamps behind the bearing and pressure is applied to the shaft end to draw the bearing off

off a gear shaft for example, you may have to locate the puller behind a gear pinion if there is no access to the race and draw the gear pinion off the shaft as well **(see illustration 5.4)**.

Caution: Ensure that the puller's centre bolt locates securely against the end of the shaft and will not slip when pressure is applied. Also ensure that puller does not damage the shaft end.

5.4 Where no access is available to the rear of the bearing, it is sometimes possible to draw off the adjacent component

● Operate the puller so that its centre bolt exerts pressure on the shaft end and draws the bearing off the shaft.
● When installing the bearing on the shaft, tap only on the bearing's inner race - contact with the balls/rollers or outer race with destroy the bearing. Use a socket or length of tubing as a drift which fits over the shaft end **(see illustration 5.5)**.

5.5 When installing a bearing on a shaft use a piece of tubing which bears only on the bearing's inner race

● Where a bearing locates in a blind hole in a casing, it cannot be driven or pulled out as described above. A slide-hammer with knife-edged bearing puller attachment will be required. The puller attachment passes through the bearing and when tightened expands to fit firmly behind the bearing **(see illustration 5.6)**. By operating the slide-hammer part of the tool the bearing is jarred out of its housing **(see illustration 5.7)**.
● It is possible, if the bearing is of reasonable weight, for it to drop out of its housing if the casing is heated as described opposite. If this

Tools and Workshop Tips REF•15

5.6 Expand the bearing puller so that it locks behind the bearing . . .

5.7 . . . attach the slide hammer to the bearing puller

method is attempted, first prepare a work surface which will enable the casing to be tapped face down to help dislodge the bearing - a wood surface is ideal since it will not damage the casing's gasket surface. Wearing protective gloves, tap the heated casing several times against the work surface to dislodge the bearing under its own weight **(see illustration 5.8)**.

5.8 Tapping a casing face down on wood blocks can often dislodge a bearing

● Bearings can be installed in blind holes using the driver or socket method described above.

Drawbolts

● Where a bearing or bush is set in the eye of a component, such as a suspension linkage arm or connecting rod small-end, removal by drift may damage the component. Furthermore, a rubber bushing in a shock absorber eye cannot successfully be driven out of position. If access is available to a engineering press, the task is straightforward. If not, a drawbolt can be fabricated to extract the bearing or bush.

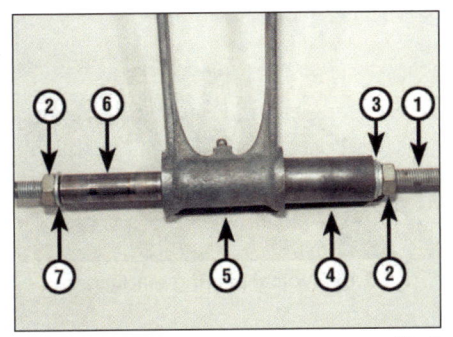

5.9 Drawbolt component parts assembled on a suspension arm

1 Bolt or length of threaded bar
2 Nuts
3 Washer (external diameter greater than tubing internal diameter)
4 Tubing (internal diameter sufficient to accommodate bearing)
5 Suspension arm with bearing
6 Tubing (external diameter slightly smaller than bearing)
7 Washer (external diameter slightly smaller than bearing)

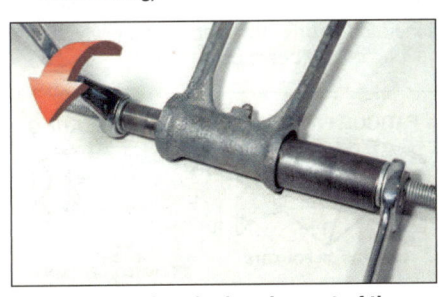

5.10 Drawing the bearing out of the suspension arm

● To extract the bearing/bush you will need a long bolt with nut (or piece of threaded bar with two nuts), a piece of tubing which has an internal diameter larger than the bearing/bush, another piece of tubing which has an external diameter slightly smaller than the bearing/bush, and a selection of washers **(see illustrations 5.9 and 5.10)**. Note that the pieces of tubing must be of the same length, or longer, than the bearing/bush.
● The same kit (without the pieces of tubing) can be used to draw the new bearing/bush back into place **(see illustration 5.11)**.

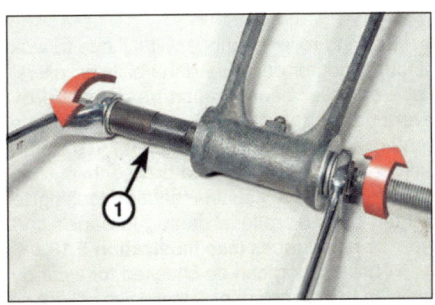

5.11 Installing a new bearing (1) in the suspension arm

Temperature change

● If the bearing's outer race is a tight fit in the casing, the aluminium casing can be heated to release its grip on the bearing. Aluminium will expand at a greater rate than the steel bearing outer race. There are several ways to do this, but avoid any localised extreme heat (such as a blow torch) - aluminium alloy has a low melting point.

● Approved methods of heating a casing are using a domestic oven (heated to 100°C) or immersing the casing in boiling water **(see illustration 5.12)**. Low temperature range localised heat sources such as a paint stripper heat gun or clothes iron can also be used **(see illustration 5.13)**. Alternatively, soak a rag in boiling water, wring it out and wrap it around the bearing housing.

> **Warning:** *All of these methods require care in use to prevent scalding and burns to the hands. Wear protective gloves when handling hot components.*

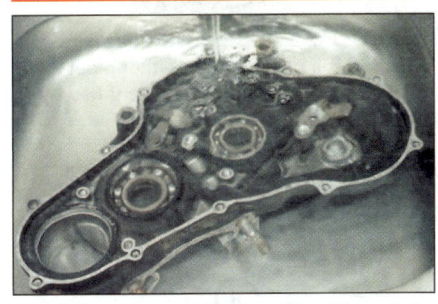

5.12 A casing can be immersed in a sink of boiling water to aid bearing removal

5.13 Using a localised heat source to aid bearing removal

● If heating the whole casing note that plastic components, such as the neutral switch, may suffer - remove them beforehand.

● After heating, remove the bearing as described above. You may find that the expansion is sufficient for the bearing to fall out of the casing under its own weight or with a light tap on the driver or socket.

● If necessary, the casing can be heated to aid bearing installation, and this is sometimes the recommended procedure if the motorcycle manufacturer has designed the housing and bearing fit with this intention.

Tools and Workshop Tips

- Installation of bearings can be eased by placing them in a freezer the night before installation. The steel bearing will contract slightly, allowing easy insertion in its housing. This is often useful when installing steering head outer races in the frame.

Bearing types and markings

- Plain shell bearings, ball bearings, needle roller bearings and tapered roller bearings will all be found on motorcycles (see illustrations 5.14 and 5.15). The ball and roller types are usually caged between an inner and outer race, but uncaged variations may be found.

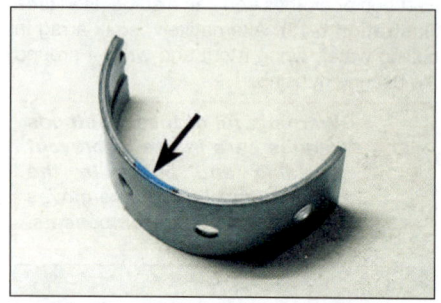

5.14 Shell bearings are either plain or grooved. They are usually identified by colour code (arrow)

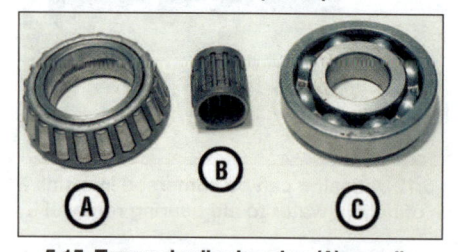

5.15 Tapered roller bearing (A), needle roller bearing (B) and ball journal bearing (C)

- Shell bearings (often called inserts) are usually found at the crankshaft main and connecting rod big-end where they are good at coping with high loads. They are made of a phosphor-bronze material and are impregnated with self-lubricating properties.
- Ball bearings and needle roller bearings consist of a steel inner and outer race with the balls or rollers between the races. They require constant lubrication by oil or grease and are good at coping with axial loads. Taper roller bearings consist of rollers set in a tapered cage set on the inner race; the outer race is separate. They are good at coping with axial loads and prevent movement along the shaft - a typical application is in the steering head.
- Bearing manufacturers produce bearings to ISO size standards and stamp one face of the bearing to indicate its internal and external diameter, load capacity and type (see illustration 5.16).
- Metal bushes are usually of phosphor-bronze material. Rubber bushes are used in suspension mounting eyes. Fibre bushes have also been used in suspension pivots.

5.16 Typical bearing marking

Bearing fault finding

- If a bearing outer race has spun in its housing, the housing material will be damaged. You can use a bearing locking compound to bond the outer race in place if damage is not too severe.
- Shell bearings will fail due to damage of their working surface, as a result of lack of lubrication, corrosion or abrasive particles in the oil (see illustration 5.17). Small particles of dirt in the oil may embed in the bearing material whereas larger particles will score the bearing and shaft journal. If a number of short journeys are made, insufficient heat will be generated to drive off condensation which has built up on the bearings.

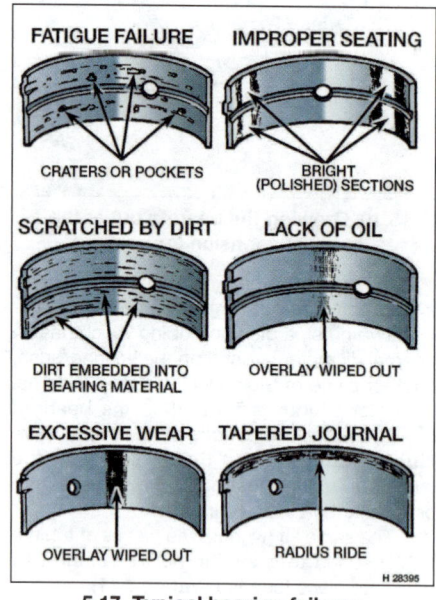

5.17 Typical bearing failures

- Ball and roller bearings will fail due to lack of lubrication or damage to the balls or rollers. Tapered-roller bearings can be damaged by overloading them. Unless the bearing is sealed on both sides, wash it in paraffin (kerosene) to remove all old grease then allow it to dry. Make a visual inspection looking to dented balls or rollers, damaged cages and worn or pitted races (see illustration 5.18).
- A ball bearing can be checked for wear by listening to it when spun. Apply a film of light oil to the bearing and hold it close to the ear - hold the outer race with one hand and spin the inner

5.18 Example of ball journal bearing with damaged balls and cages

5.19 Hold outer race and listen to inner race when spun

race with the other hand (see illustration 5.19). The bearing should be almost silent when spun; if it grates or rattles it is worn.

6 Oil seals

Oil seal removal and installation

- Oil seals should be renewed every time a component is dismantled. This is because the seal lips will become set to the sealing surface and will not necessarily reseal.
- Oil seals can be prised out of position using a large flat-bladed screwdriver (see illustration 6.1). In the case of crankcase seals, check first that the seal is not lipped on the inside, preventing its removal with the crankcases joined.

6.1 Prise out oil seals with a large flat-bladed screwdriver

- New seals are usually installed with their marked face (containing the seal reference code) outwards and the spring side towards the fluid being retained. In certain cases, such as a two-stroke engine crankshaft seal, a double lipped seal may be used due to there being fluid or gas on each side of the joint.

Tools and Workshop Tips

- Use a bearing driver or socket which bears only on the outer hard edge of the seal to install it in the casing - tapping on the inner edge will damage the sealing lip.

Oil seal types and markings

- Oil seals are usually of the single-lipped type. Double-lipped seals are found where a liquid or gas is on both sides of the joint.
- Oil seals can harden and lose their sealing ability if the motorcycle has been in storage for a long period - renewal is the only solution.
- Oil seal manufacturers also conform to the ISO markings for seal size - these are moulded into the outer face of the seal (see illustration 6.2).

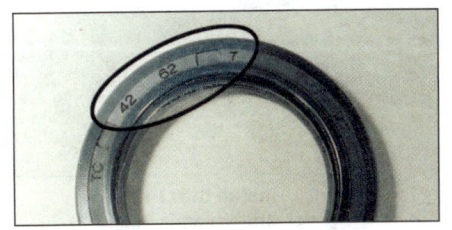

6.2 These oil seal markings indicate inside diameter, outside diameter and seal thickness

7 Gaskets and sealants

Types of gasket and sealant

- Gaskets are used to seal the mating surfaces between components and keep lubricants, fluids, vacuum or pressure contained within the assembly. Aluminium gaskets are sometimes found at the cylinder joints, but most gaskets are paper-based. If the mating surfaces of the components being joined are undamaged the gasket can be installed dry, although a dab of sealant or grease will be useful to hold it in place during assembly.
- RTV (Room Temperature Vulcanising) silicone rubber sealants cure when exposed to moisture in the atmosphere. These sealants are good at filling pits or irregular gasket faces, but will tend to be forced out of the joint under very high torque. They can be used to replace a paper gasket, but first make sure that the width of the paper gasket is not essential to the shimming of internal components. RTV sealants should not be used on components containing petrol (gasoline).
- Non-hardening, semi-hardening and hard setting liquid gasket compounds can be used with a gasket or between a metal-to-metal joint. Select the sealant to suit the application: universal non-hardening sealant can be used on virtually all joints; semi-hardening on joint faces which are rough or damaged; hard setting sealant on joints which require a permanent bond and are subjected to high temperature and pressure. **Note:** *Check first if the paper gasket has a bead of sealant impregnated in its surface before applying additional sealant.*
- When choosing a sealant, make sure it is suitable for the application, particularly if being applied in a high-temperature area or in the vicinity of fuel. Certain manufacturers produce sealants in either clear, silver or black colours to match the finish of the engine. This has a particular application on motorcycles where much of the engine is exposed.
- Do not over-apply sealant. That which is squeezed out on the outside of the joint can be wiped off, whereas an excess of sealant on the inside can break off and clog oilways.

Breaking a sealed joint

- Age, heat, pressure and the use of hard setting sealant can cause two components to stick together so tightly that they are difficult to separate using finger pressure alone. Do not resort to using levers unless there is a pry point provided for this purpose (see illustration 7.1) or else the gasket surfaces will be damaged.
- Use a soft-faced hammer (see illustration 7.2) or a wood block and conventional hammer to strike the component near the mating surface. Avoid hammering against cast extremities since they may break off. If this method fails, try using a wood wedge between the two components.

Caution: *If the joint will not separate, double-check that you have removed all the fasteners.*

7.1 If a pry point is provided, apply gently pressure with a flat-bladed screwdriver

7.2 Tap around the joint with a soft-faced mallet if necessary - don't strike cooling fins

Removal of old gasket and sealant

- Paper gaskets will most likely come away complete, leaving only a few traces stuck on

> **HAYNES HiNT**
>
> *Most components have one or two hollow locating dowels between the two gasket faces. If a dowel cannot be removed, do not resort to gripping it with pliers - it will almost certainly be distorted. Install a close-fitting socket or Phillips screwdriver into the dowel and then grip the outer edge of the dowel to free it.*

the sealing faces of the components. It is imperative that all traces are removed to ensure correct sealing of the new gasket.
- Very carefully scrape all traces of gasket away making sure that the sealing surfaces are not gouged or scored by the scraper (see illustrations 7.3, 7.4 and 7.5). Stubborn deposits can be removed by spraying with an aerosol gasket remover. Final preparation of

7.3 Paper gaskets can be scraped off with a gasket scraper tool . . .

7.4 . . . a knife blade . . .

7.5 . . . or a household scraper

REF•18 Tools and Workshop Tips

7.6 Fine abrasive paper is wrapped around a flat file to clean up the gasket face

7.7 A kitchen scourer can be used on stubborn deposits

8.1 Tighten the chain breaker to push the pin out of the link . . .

8.2 . . . withdraw the pin, remove the tool . . .

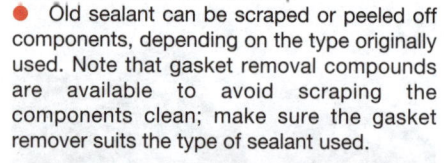

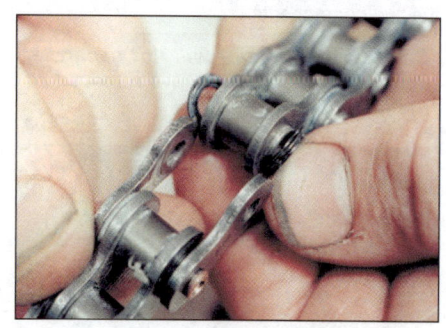

8.3 . . . and separate the chain link

8.4 Insert the new soft link, with O-rings, through the chain ends . . .

8.5 . . . install the O-rings over the pin ends . . .

8.6 . . . followed by the sideplate

8.7 Push the sideplate into position using a clamp

the gasket surface can be made with very fine abrasive paper or a plastic kitchen scourer **(see illustrations 7.6 and 7.7)**.

• Old sealant can be scraped or peeled off components, depending on the type originally used. Note that gasket removal compounds are available to avoid scraping the components clean; make sure the gasket remover suits the type of sealant used.

8 Chains

Breaking and joining final drive chains

• Drive chains for all but small bikes are continuous and do not have a clip-type connecting link. The chain must be broken using a chain breaker tool and the new chain securely riveted together using a new soft rivet-type link. Never use a clip-type connecting link instead of a rivet-type link, except in an emergency. Various chain breaking and riveting tools are available, either as separate tools or combined as illustrated in the accompanying photographs - read the instructions supplied with the tool carefully.

⚠ **Warning: The need to rivet the new link pins correctly cannot be overstressed - loss of control of the motorcycle is very likely to result if the chain breaks in use.**

• Rotate the chain and look for the soft link. The soft link pins look like they have been deeply centre-punched instead of peened over like all the other pins **(see illustration 8.9)** and its sideplate may be a different colour. Position the soft link midway between the sprockets and assemble the chain breaker tool over one of the soft link pins **(see illustration 8.1)**. Operate the tool to push the pin out through the chain **(see illustration 8.2)**. On an O-ring chain, remove the O-rings **(see illustration 8.3)**. Carry out the same procedure on the other soft link pin.

Caution: Certain soft link pins (particularly on the larger chains) may require their ends to be filed or ground off before they can be pressed out using the tool.

• Check that you have the correct size and strength (standard or heavy duty) new soft link - do not reuse the old link. Look for the size marking on the chain sideplates **(see illustration 8.10)**.

• Position the chain ends so that they are engaged over the rear sprocket. On an O-ring chain, install a new O-ring over each pin of the link and insert the link through the two chain ends **(see illustration 8.4)**. Install a new O-ring over the end of each pin, followed by the sideplate (with the chain manufacturer's marking facing outwards) **(see illustrations 8.5 and 8.6)**. On an unsealed chain, insert the link through the two chain ends, then install the sideplate with the chain manufacturer's marking facing outwards.

• Note that it may not be possible to install the sideplate using finger pressure alone. If using a joining tool, assemble it so that the plates of the tool clamp the link and press the sideplate over the pins **(see illustration 8.7)**. Otherwise, use two small sockets placed over

Tools and Workshop Tips REF•19

8.8 Assemble the chain riveting tool over one pin at a time and tighten it fully

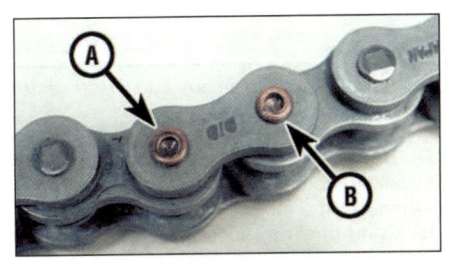

8.9 Pin end correctly riveted (A), pin end unriveted (B)

the rivet ends and two pieces of the wood between a G-clamp. Operate the clamp to press the sideplate over the pins.
- Assemble the joining tool over one pin (following the maker's instructions) and tighten the tool down to spread the pin end securely **(see illustrations 8.8 and 8.9)**. Do the same on the other pin.

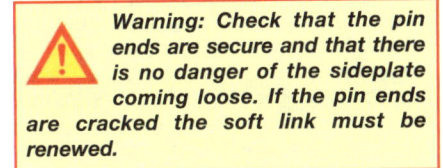

> ⚠ **Warning: Check that the pin ends are secure and that there is no danger of the sideplate coming loose. If the pin ends are cracked the soft link must be renewed.**

Final drive chain sizing

- Chains are sized using a three digit number, followed by a suffix to denote the chain type **(see illustration 8.10)**. Chain type is either standard or heavy duty (thicker sideplates), and also unsealed or O-ring/X-ring type.
- The first digit of the number relates to the pitch of the chain, ie the distance from the centre of one pin to the centre of the next pin **(see illustration 8.11)**. Pitch is expressed in eighths of an inch, as follows:

8.10 Typical chain size and type marking

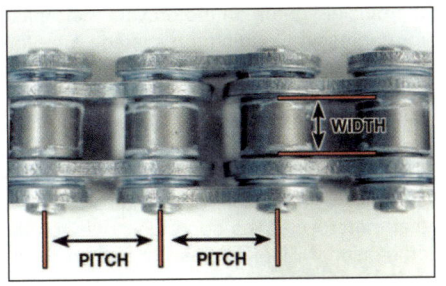

8.11 Chain dimensions

| Sizes commencing with a 4 (eg 428) have a pitch of 1/2 inch (12.7 mm) |
| Sizes commencing with a 5 (eg 520) have a pitch of 5/8 inch (15.9 mm) |
| Sizes commencing with a 6 (eg 630) have a pitch of 3/4 inch (19.1 mm) |

- The second and third digits of the chain size relate to the width of the rollers, again in imperial units, eg the 525 shown has 5/16 inch (7.94 mm) rollers **(see illustration 8.11)**.

9 Hoses

Clamping to prevent flow

- Small-bore flexible hoses can be clamped to prevent fluid flow whilst a component is worked on. Whichever method is used, ensure that the hose material is not permanently distorted or damaged by the clamp.
  a) A brake hose clamp available from auto accessory shops **(see illustration 9.1)**.
  b) A wingnut type hose clamp **(see illustration 9.2)**.
  c) Two sockets placed each side of the hose and held with straight-jawed self-locking grips **(see illustration 9.3)**.
  d) Thick card each side of the hose held between straight-jawed self-locking grips **(see illustration 9.4)**.

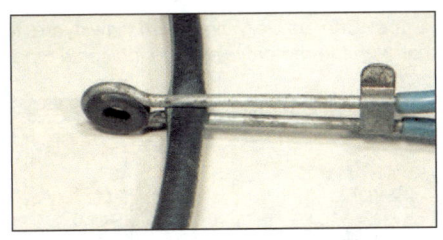

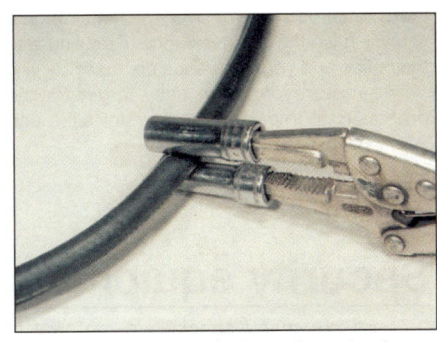

9.1 Hoses can be clamped with an automotive brake hose clamp ...

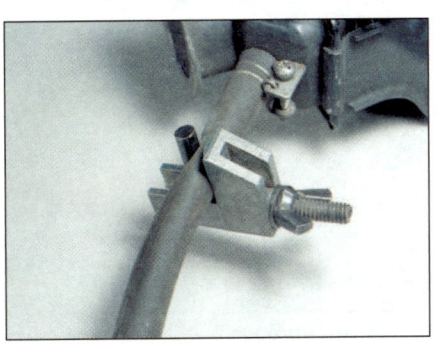

9.2 ... a wingnut type hose clamp ...

9.3 ... two sockets and a pair of self-locking grips ...

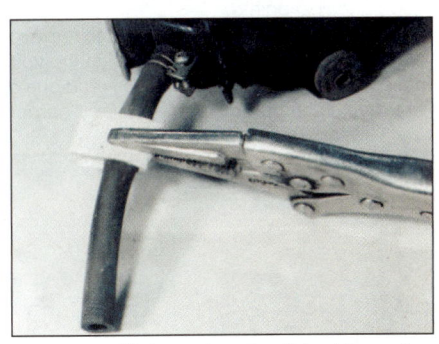

9.4 ... or thick card and self-locking grips

Freeing and fitting hoses

- Always make sure the hose clamp is moved well clear of the hose end. Grip the hose with your hand and rotate it whilst pulling it off the union. If the hose has hardened due to age and will not move, slit it with a sharp knife and peel its ends off the union **(see illustration 9.5)**.
- Resist the temptation to use grease or soap on the unions to aid installation; although it helps the hose slip over the union it will equally aid the escape of fluid from the joint. It is preferable to soften the hose ends in hot water and wet the inside surface of the hose with water or a fluid which will evaporate.

9.5 Cutting a coolant hose free with a sharp knife

Security

Introduction

In less time than it takes to read this introduction, a thief could steal your motorcycle. Returning only to find your bike has gone is one of the worst feelings in the world. Even if the motorcycle is insured against theft, once you've got over the initial shock, you will have the inconvenience of dealing with the police and your insurance company.

The motorcycle is an easy target for the professional thief and the joyrider alike and the official figures on motorcycle theft make for depressing reading; on average a motorcycle is stolen every 16 minutes in the UK!

Motorcycle thefts fall into two categories, those stolen 'to order' and those taken by opportunists. The thief stealing to order will be on the look out for a specific make and model and will go to extraordinary lengths to obtain that motorcycle. The opportunist thief on the other hand will look for easy targets which can be stolen with the minimum of effort and risk.

Whilst it is never going to be possible to make your machine 100% secure, it is estimated that around half of all stolen motorcycles are taken by opportunist thieves. Remember that the opportunist thief is always on the look out for the easy option: if there are two similar motorcycles parked side-by-side, they will target the one with the lowest level of security. By taking a few precautions, you can reduce the chances of your motorcycle being stolen.

Security equipment

There are many specialised motorcycle security devices available and the following text summarises their applications and their good and bad points.

Once you have decided on the type of security equipment which best suits your needs, we recommended that you read one of the many equipment tests regularly carried out by the motorcycle press. These tests compare the products from all the major manufacturers and give impartial ratings on their effectiveness, value-for-money and ease of use.

No one item of security equipment can provide complete protection. It is highly recommended that two or more of the items described below are combined to increase the security of your motorcycle (a lock and chain plus an alarm system is just about ideal). The more security measures fitted to the bike, the less likely it is to be stolen.

Lock and chain

Pros: *Very flexible to use; can be used to secure the motorcycle to almost any immovable object. On some locks and chains, the lock can be used on its own as a disc lock (see below).*

Cons: *Can be very heavy and awkward to carry on the motorcycle, although some types will be supplied with a carry bag which can be strapped to the pillion seat.*

● Heavy-duty chains and locks are an excellent security measure **(see illustration 1)**. Whenever the motorcycle is parked, use the lock and chain to secure the machine to a solid, immovable object such as a post or railings. This will prevent the machine from being ridden away or being lifted into the back of a van.

● When fitting the chain, always ensure the chain is routed around the motorcycle frame or swingarm **(see illustrations 2 and 3)**. Never merely pass the chain around one of the wheel rims; a thief may unbolt the wheel and lift the rest of the machine into a van, leaving you with just the wheel! Try to avoid having excess chain free, thus making it difficult to use cutting tools, and keep the chain and lock off the ground to prevent thieves attacking it with a cold chisel. Position the lock so that its lock barrel is facing downwards; this will make it harder for the thief to attack the lock mechanism.

1 Ensure the lock and chain you buy is of good quality and long enough to shackle your bike to a solid object

2 Pass the chain through the bike's frame, rather than just through a wheel . . .

3 . . . and loop it around a solid object

Security

U-locks

Pros: *Highly effective deterrent which can be used to secure the bike to a post or railings. Most U-locks come with a carrier which allows the lock to be easily carried on the bike.*

Cons: *Not as flexible to use as a lock and chain.*

● These are solid locks which are similar in use to a lock and chain. U-locks are lighter than a lock and chain but not so flexible to use. The length and shape of the lock shackle limit the objects to which the bike can be secured **(see illustration 4)**.

Disc locks

Pros: *Small, light and very easy to carry; most can be stored underneath the seat.*

Cons: *Does not prevent the motorcycle being lifted into a van. Can be very embarrassing if you forget to remove the lock before attempting to ride off!*

● Disc locks are designed to be attached to the front brake disc. The lock passes through one of the holes in the disc and prevents the wheel rotating by jamming against the fork/brake caliper **(see illustration 5)**. Some are equipped with an alarm siren which sounds if the disc lock is moved; this not only acts as a theft deterrent but also as a handy reminder if you try to move the bike with the lock still fitted.

● Combining the disc lock with a length of cable which can be looped around a post or railings provides an additional measure of security **(see illustration 6)**.

Alarms and immobilisers

Pros: *Once installed it is completely hassle-free to use. If the system is 'Thatcham' or 'Sold Secure-approved', insurance companies may give you a discount.*

Cons: *Can be expensive to buy and complex to install. No system will prevent the motorcycle from being lifted into a van and taken away.*

● Electronic alarms and immobilisers are available to suit a variety of budgets. There are three different types of system available: pure alarms, pure immobilisers, and the more expensive systems which are combined alarm/immobilisers **(see illustration 7)**.

● An alarm system is designed to emit an audible warning if the motorcycle is being tampered with.

● An immobiliser prevents the motorcycle being started and ridden away by disabling its electrical systems.

● When purchasing an alarm/immobiliser system, check the cost of installing the system unless you are able to do it yourself. If the motorcycle is not used regularly, another consideration is the current drain of the system. All alarm/immobiliser systems are powered by the motorcycle's battery; purchasing a system with a very low current drain could prevent the battery losing its charge whilst the motorcycle is not being used.

U-locks can be used to secure the bike to a solid object – ensure you purchase one which is long enough

A typical disc lock attached through one of the holes in the disc

A disc lock combined with a security cable provides additional protection

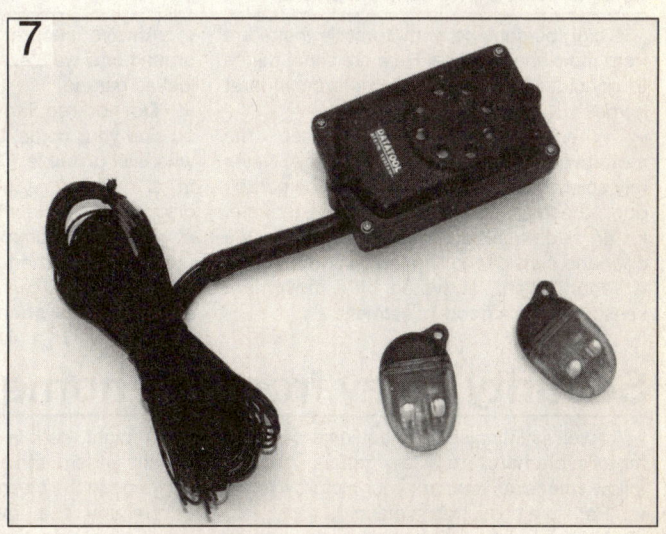

A typical alarm/immobiliser system

REF•22 Security

Indelible markings can be applied to most areas of the bike – always apply the manufacturer's sticker to warn off thieves

Chemically-etched code numbers can be applied to main body panels . . .

. . . again, always ensure that the kit manufacturer's sticker is applied in a prominent position

Security marking kits

Pros: *Very cheap and effective deterrent. Many insurance companies will give you a discount on your insurance premium if a recognised security marking kit is used on your motorcycle.*

Cons: *Does not prevent the motorcycle being stolen by joyriders.*

● There are many different types of security marking kits available. The idea is to mark as many parts of the motorcycle as possible with a unique security number **(see illustrations 8, 9 and 10)**. A form will be included with the kit to register your personal details and those of the motorcycle with the kit manufacturer. This register is made available to the police to help them trace the rightful owner of any motorcycle or components which they recover should all other forms of identification have been removed. Always apply the warning stickers provided with the kit to deter thieves.

Ground anchors, wheel clamps and security posts

Pros: *An excellent form of security which will deter all but the most determined of thieves.*

Cons: *Awkward to install and can be expensive.*

● Whilst the motorcycle is at home, it is a good idea to attach it securely to the floor or a solid wall, even if it is kept in a securely locked garage. Various types of ground anchors, security posts and wheel clamps are available for this purpose **(see illustration 11)**. These security devices are either bolted to a solid concrete or brick structure or can be cemented into the ground.

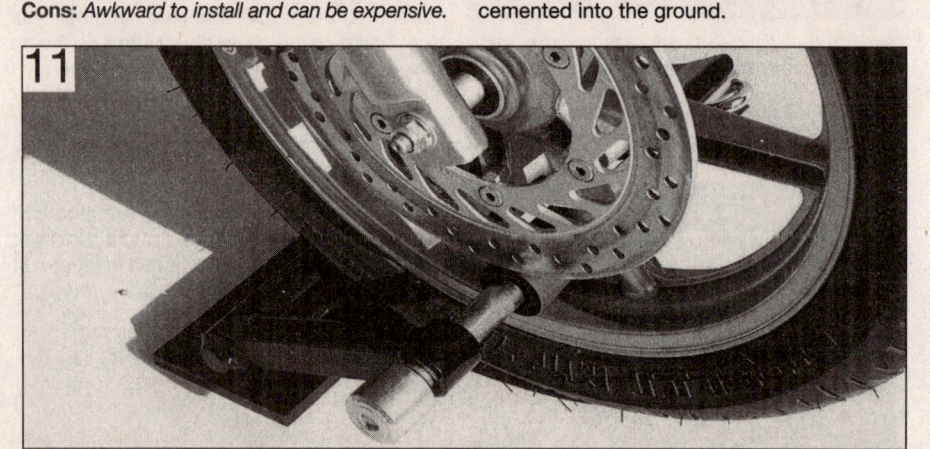

Permanent ground anchors provide an excellent level of security when the bike is at home

Security at home

A high percentage of motorcycle thefts are from the owner's home. Here are some things to consider whenever your motorcycle is at home:

✔ Where possible, always keep the motorcycle in a securely locked garage. Never rely solely on the standard lock on the garage door, these are usual hopelessly inadequate. Fit an additional locking mechanism to the door and consider having the garage alarmed. A security light, activated by a movement sensor, is also a good investment.

✔ Always secure the motorcycle to the ground or a wall, even if it is inside a securely locked garage.

✔ Do not regularly leave the motorcycle outside your home, try to keep it out of sight wherever possible. If a garage is not available, fit a motorcycle cover over the bike to disguise its true identity.

✔ It is not uncommon for thieves to follow a motorcyclist home to find out where the bike is kept. They will then return at a later date. Be aware of this whenever you are returning home on your motorcycle. If you suspect you are being followed, do not return home, instead ride to a garage or shop and stop as a precaution.

✔ When selling a motorcycle, do not provide your home address or the location where the bike is normally kept. Arrange to meet the buyer at a location away from your home. Thieves have been known to pose as potential buyers to find out where motorcycles are kept and then return later to steal them.

Security away from the home

As well as fitting security equipment to your motorcycle here are a few general rules to follow whenever you park your motorcycle.

✔ Park in a busy, public place.

✔ Use car parks which incorporate security features, such as CCTV.

✔ At night, park in a well-lit area, preferably directly underneath a street light.

✔ Engage the steering lock.

✔ Secure the motorcycle to a solid, immovable object such as a post or railings with an additional lock. If this is not possible, secure the bike to a friend's motorcycle. Some public parking places provide security loops for motorcycles.

✔ Never leave your helmet or luggage attached to the motorcycle. Take them with you at all times.

Lubricants and fluids

A wide range of lubricants, fluids and cleaning agents is available for motor-cycles. This is a guide as to what is available, its applications and properties.

Four-stroke engine oil

● Engine oil is without doubt the most important component of any four-stroke engine. Modern motorcycle engines place a lot of demands on their oil and choosing the right type is essential. Using an unsuitable oil will lead to an increased rate of engine wear and could result in serious engine damage. Before purchasing oil, always check the recommended oil specification given by the manufacturer. The manufacturer will state a recommended 'type or classification' and also a specific 'viscosity' range for engine oil.

● The oil 'type or classification' is identified by its API (American Petroleum Institute) rating. The API rating will be in the form of two letters, e.g. SG. The S identifies the oil as being suitable for use in a petrol (gasoline) engine (S stands for spark ignition) and the second letter, ranging from A to J, identifies the oil's performance rating. The later this letter, the higher the specification of the oil; for example API SG oil exceeds the requirements of API SF oil. **Note:** *On some oils there may also be a second rating consisting of another two letters, the first letter being C, e.g. API SF/CD. This rating indicates the oil is also suitable for use in a diesel engines (the C stands for compression ignition) and is thus of no relevance for motorcycle use.*

● The 'viscosity' of the oil is identified by its SAE (Society of Automotive Engineers) rating. All modern engines require multigrade oils and the SAE rating will consist of two numbers, the first followed by a W, e.g. 10W/40. The first number indicates the viscosity rating of the oil at low temperatures (W stands for winter – tested at –20°C) and the second number represents the viscosity of the oil at high temperatures (tested at 100°C). The lower the number, the thinner the oil. For example an oil with an SAE 10W/40 rating will give better cold starting and running than an SAE 15W/40 oil.

● As well as ensuring the 'type' and 'viscosity' of the oil match the recommendations, another consideration to make when buying engine oil is whether to purchase a standard mineral-based oil, a semi-synthetic oil (also known as a synthetic blend or synthetic-based oil) or a fully-synthetic oil. Although all oils will have a similar rating and viscosity, their cost will vary considerably; mineral-based oils are the cheapest, the fully-synthetic oils the most expensive with the semi-synthetic oils falling somewhere in-between. This decision is very much up to the owner, but it should be noted that modern synthetic oils have far better lubricating and cleaning qualities than traditional mineral-based oils and tend to retain these properties for far longer. Bearing in mind the operating conditions inside a modern, high-revving motorcycle engine it is highly recommended that a fully synthetic oil is used. The extra expense at each service could save you money in the long term by preventing premature engine wear.

● As a final note always ensure that the oil is specifically designed for use in motorcycle engines. Engine oils designed primarily for use in car engines sometimes contain additives or friction modifiers which could cause clutch slip on a motorcycle fitted with a wet-clutch.

Two-stroke engine oil

● Modern two-stroke engines, with their high power outputs, place high demands on their oil. If engine seizure is to be avoided it is essential that a high-quality oil is used. Two-stroke oils differ hugely from four-stroke oils. The oil lubricates only the crankshaft and piston(s) (the transmission has its own lubricating oil) and is used on a total-loss basis where it is burnt completely during the combustion process.

● The Japanese have recently introduced a classification system for two-stroke oils, the JASO rating. This rating is in the form of two letters, either FA, FB or FC – FA is the lowest classification and FC the highest. Ensure the oil being used meets or exceeds the recommended rating specified by the manufacturer.

● As well as ensuring the oil rating matches the recommendation, another consideration to make when buying engine oil is whether to purchase a standard mineral-based oil, a semi-synthetic oil (also known as a synthetic blend or synthetic-based oil) or a fully-synthetic oil. The cost of each type of oil varies considerably; mineral-based oils are the cheapest, the fully-synthetic oils the most expensive with the semi-synthetic oils falling somewhere in-between. This decision is very much up to the owner, but it should be noted that modern synthetic oils have far better lubricating properties and burn cleaner than traditional mineral-based oils. It is therefore recommended that a fully synthetic oil is used. The extra expense could save you money in the long term by preventing premature engine wear, engine performance will be improved, carbon deposits and exhaust smoke will be reduced.

Lubricants and fluids

● Always ensure that the oil is specifically designed for use in an injector system. Many high quality two-stroke oils are designed for competition use and need to be pre-mixed with fuel. These oils are of a much higher viscosity and are not designed to flow through the injector pumps used on road-going two-stroke motorcycles.

Transmission (gear) oil

● On a two-stroke engine, the transmission and clutch are lubricated by their own separate oil bath which must be changed in accordance with the Maintenance Schedule.
● Although the engine and transmission units of most four-strokes use a common lubrication supply, there are some exceptions where the engine and gearbox have separate oil reservoirs and a dry clutch is used.
● Motorcycle manufacturers will either recommend a monograde transmission oil or a four-stroke multigrade engine oil to lubricate the transmission.
● Transmission oils, or gear oils as they are often called, are designed specifically for use in transmission systems. The viscosity of these oils is represented by an SAE number, but the scale of measurement applied is different to that used to grade engine oils. As a rough guide a SAE90 gear oil will be of the same viscosity as an SAE50 engine oil.

Shaft drive oil

● On models equipped with shaft final drive, the shaft drive gears are will have their own oil supply. The manufacturer will state a recommended 'type or classification' and also a specific 'viscosity' range in the same manner as for four-stroke engine oil.
● Gear oil classification is given by the number which follows the API GL (GL standing for gear lubricant) rating, the higher the number, the higher the specification of the oil, e.g. API GL5 oil is a higher specification than API GL4 oil. Ensure the oil meets or exceeds the classification specified and is of the correct viscosity. The viscosity of gear oils is also represented by an SAE number but the scale of measurement used is different to that used to grade engine oils. As a rough guide an SAE90 gear oil will be of the same viscosity as an SAE50 engine oil.
● If the use of an EP (Extreme Pressure) gear oil is specified, ensure the oil purchased is suitable.

Fork oil and suspension fluid

● Conventional telescopic front forks are hydraulic and require fork oil to work. To ensure the forks function correctly, the fork oil must be changed in accordance with the Maintenance Schedule.
● Fork oil is available in a variety of viscosities, identified by their SAE rating; fork oil ratings vary from light (SAE 5) to heavy (SAE 30). When purchasing fork oil, ensure the viscosity rating matches that specified by the manufacturer.
● Some lubricant manufacturers also produce a range of high-quality suspension fluids which are very similar to fork oil but are designed mainly for competition use. These fluids may have a different viscosity rating system which is not to be confused with the SAE rating of normal fork oil. Refer to the manufacturer's instructions if in any doubt.

Brake and clutch fluid

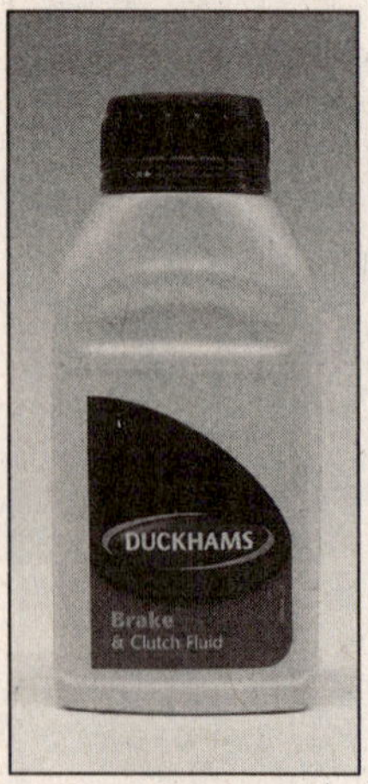

● All disc brake systems and some clutch systems are hydraulically operated. To ensure correct operation, the hydraulic fluid must be changed in accordance with the Maintenance Schedule.
● Brake and clutch fluid is classified by its DOT rating with most motorcycle manufacturers specifying DOT 3 or 4 fluid. Both fluid types are glycol-based and can be mixed together without adverse effect; DOT 4 fluid exceeds the requirements of DOT 3 fluid. Although it is safe to use DOT 4 fluid in a system designed for use with DOT 3 fluid, never use DOT 3 fluid in a system which specifies the use of DOT 4 as this will adversely affect the system's performance. The type required for the system will be marked on the fluid reservoir cap.
● Some manufacturers also produce a DOT 5 hydraulic fluid. DOT 5 hydraulic fluid is silicone-based and is not compatible with the glycol-based DOT 3 and 4 fluids. Never mix DOT 5 fluid with DOT 3 or 4 fluid as this will seriously affect the performance of the hydraulic system.

Coolant/antifreeze

● When purchasing coolant/antifreeze, always ensure it is suitable for use in an aluminium engine and contains corrosion inhibitors to prevent possible blockages of the internal coolant passages of the system. As a general rule, most coolants are designed to be used neat and should not be diluted whereas antifreeze can be mixed with distilled water to provide a coolant solution of the required strength. Refer to the manufacturer's instructions on the bottle.
● Ensure the coolant is changed in accordance with the Maintenance Schedule.

Chain lube

● Chain lube is an aerosol-type spray lubricant specifically designed for use on motorcycle final drive chains. Chain lube has two functions, to minimise friction between the final drive chain and sprockets and to prevent corrosion of the chain. Regular use of a good-quality chain lube will extend the life of the drive chain and sprockets and thus maximise the power being transmitted from the transmission to the rear wheel.
● When using chain lube, always allow some time for the solvents in the lube to evaporate before riding the motorcycle. This will minimise the amount of lube which will

Lubricants and fluids

'fling' off from the chain when the motorcycle is used. If the motorcycle is equipped with an 'O-ring' chain, ensure the chain lube is labelled as being suitable for use on 'O-ring' chains.

Degreasers and solvents

- There are many different types of solvents and degreasers available to remove the grime and grease which accumulate around the motorcycle during normal use. Degreasers and solvents are usually available as an aerosol-type spray or as a liquid which you apply with a brush. Always closely follow the manufacturer's instructions and wear eye protection during use. Be aware that many solvents are flammable and may give off noxious fumes; take adequate precautions when using them (see *Safety First!*).
- For general cleaning, use one of the many solvents or degreasers available from most motorcycle accessory shops. These solvents are usually applied then left for a certain time before being washed off with water.

Brake cleaner is a solvent specifically designed to remove all traces of oil, grease and dust from braking system components. Brake cleaner is designed to evaporate quickly and leaves behind no residue.

Carburettor cleaner is an aerosol-type solvent specifically designed to clear carburettor blockages and break down the hard deposits and gum often found inside carburettors during overhaul.

Contact cleaner is an aerosol-type solvent designed for cleaning electrical components. The cleaner will remove all traces of oil and dirt from components such as switch contacts or fouled spark plugs and then dry, leaving behind no residue.

Gasket remover is an aerosol-type solvent designed for removing stubborn gaskets from engine components during overhaul. Gasket remover will minimise the amount of scraping required to remove the gasket and therefore reduce the risk of damage to the mating surface.

Spray lubricants

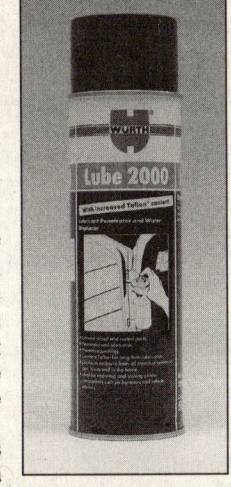

- Aerosol-based spray lubricants are widely available and are excellent for lubricating lever pivots and exposed cables and switches. Try to use a lubricant which is of the dry-film type as the fluid evaporates, leaving behind a dry-film of lubricant. Lubricants which leave behind an oily residue will attract dust and dirt which will increase the rate of wear of the cable/lever.
- Most lubricants also act as a moisture dispersant and a penetrating fluid. This means they can also be used to 'dry out' electrical components such as wiring connectors or switches as well as helping to free seized fasteners.

Greases

- Grease is used to lubricate many of the pivot-points. A good-quality multi-purpose grease is suitable for most applications but some manufacturers will specify the use of specialist greases for use on components such as swingarm and suspension linkage bushes. These specialist greases can be purchased from most motorcycle (or car) accessory shops; commonly specified types include molybdenum disulphide grease, lithium-based grease, graphite-based grease, silicone-based grease and high-temperature copper-based grease.

Gasket sealing compounds

- Gasket sealing compounds can be used in conjunction with gaskets, to improve their sealing capabilities, or on their own to seal metal-to-metal joints. Depending on their type, sealing compounds either set hard or stay relatively soft and pliable. 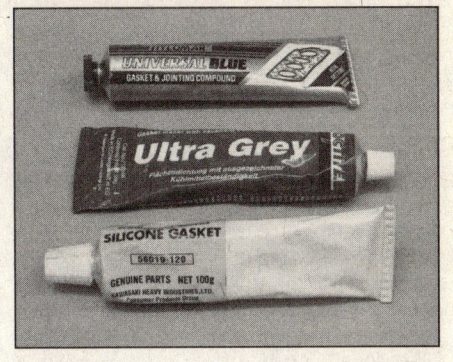
- When purchasing a gasket sealing compound, ensure that it is designed specifically for use on an internal combustion engine. General multi-purpose sealants available from DIY stores may appear visibly similar but they are not designed to withstand the extreme heat or contact with fuel and oil encountered when used on an engine (see 'Tools and Workshop Tips' for further information).

Thread locking compound

- Thread locking compounds are used to secure certain threaded fasteners in position to prevent them from loosening due to vibration. Thread locking compounds can be purchased from most motorcycle (and car) accessory shops. Ensure the threads of the both components are completely clean and dry before sparingly applying the locking compound (see 'Tools and Workshop Tips' for further information).

Fuel additives

- Fuel additives which protect and clean the fuel system components are widely available. These additives are designed to remove all traces of deposits that build up on the carburettors/injectors and prevent wear, helping the fuel system to operate more efficiently. If a fuel additive is being used, check that it is suitable for use with your motorcycle, especially if your motorcycle is equipped with a catalytic converter.
- Octane boosters are also available. These additives are designed to improve the performance of highly-tuned engines being run on normal pump-fuel and are of no real use on standard motorcycles.

Conversion factors

Length (distance)
Inches (in)	x 25.4	= Millimetres (mm)	x 0.0394	=	Inches (in)
Feet (ft)	x 0.305	= Metres (m)	x 3.281	=	Feet (ft)
Miles	x 1.609	= Kilometres (km)	x 0.621	=	Miles

Volume (capacity)
Cubic inches (cu in; in^3)	x 16.387	= Cubic centimetres (cc; cm^3)	x 0.061	=	Cubic inches (cu in; in^3)
Imperial pints (Imp pt)	x 0.568	= Litres (l)	x 1.76	=	Imperial pints (Imp pt)
Imperial quarts (Imp qt)	x 1.137	= Litres (l)	x 0.88	=	Imperial quarts (Imp qt)
Imperial quarts (Imp qt)	x 1.201	= US quarts (US qt)	x 0.833	=	Imperial quarts (Imp qt)
US quarts (US qt)	x 0.946	= Litres (l)	x 1.057	=	US quarts (US qt)
Imperial gallons (Imp gal)	x 4.546	= Litres (l)	x 0.22	=	Imperial gallons (Imp gal)
Imperial gallons (Imp gal)	x 1.201	= US gallons (US gal)	x 0.833	=	Imperial gallons (Imp gal)
US gallons (US gal)	x 3.785	= Litres (l)	x 0.264	=	US gallons (US gal)

Mass (weight)
Ounces (oz)	x 28.35	= Grams (g)	x 0.035	=	Ounces (oz)
Pounds (lb)	x 0.454	= Kilograms (kg)	x 2.205	=	Pounds (lb)

Force
Ounces-force (ozf; oz)	x 0.278	= Newtons (N)	x 3.6	=	Ounces-force (ozf; oz)
Pounds-force (lbf; lb)	x 4.448	= Newtons (N)	x 0.225	=	Pounds-force (lbf; lb)
Newtons (N)	x 0.1	= Kilograms-force (kgf; kg)	x 9.81	=	Newtons (N)

Pressure
Pounds-force per square inch (psi; lbf/in^2; lb/in^2)	x 0.070	= Kilograms-force per square centimetre (kgf/cm^2; kg/cm^2)	x 14.223	=	Pounds-force per square inch (psi; lbf/in^2; lb/in^2)
Pounds-force per square inch (psi; lbf/in^2; lb/in^2)	x 0.068	= Atmospheres (atm)	x 14.696	=	Pounds-force per square inch (psi; lbf/in^2; lb/in^2)
Pounds-force per square inch (psi; lbf/in^2; lb/in^2)	x 0.069	= Bars	x 14.5	=	Pounds-force per square inch (psi; lbf/in^2; lb/in^2)
Pounds-force per square inch (psi; lbf/in^2; lb/in^2)	x 6.895	= Kilopascals (kPa)	x 0.145	=	Pounds-force per square inch (psi; lbf/in^2; lb/in^2)
Kilopascals (kPa)	x 0.01	= Kilograms-force per square centimetre (kgf/cm^2; kg/cm^2)	x 98.1	=	Kilopascals (kPa)
Millibar (mbar)	x 100	= Pascals (Pa)	x 0.01	=	Millibar (mbar)
Millibar (mbar)	x 0.0145	= Pounds-force per square inch (psi; lbf/in^2; lb/in^2)	x 68.947	=	Millibar (mbar)
Millibar (mbar)	x 0.75	= Millimetres of mercury (mmHg)	x 1.333	=	Millibar (mbar)
Millibar (mbar)	x 0.401	= Inches of water (inH$_2$O)	x 2.491	=	Millibar (mbar)
Millimetres of mercury (mmHg)	x 0.535	= Inches of water (inH$_2$O)	x 1.868	=	Millimetres of mercury (mmHg)
Inches of water (inH$_2$O)	x 0.036	= Pounds-force per square inch (psi; lbf/in^2; lb/in^2)	x 27.68	=	Inches of water (inH$_2$O)

Torque (moment of force)
Pounds-force inches (lbf in; lb in)	x 1.152	= Kilograms-force centimetre (kgf cm; kg cm)	x 0.868	=	Pounds-force inches (lbf in; lb in)
Pounds-force inches (lbf in; lb in)	x 0.113	= Newton metres (Nm)	x 8.85	=	Pounds-force inches (lbf in; lb in)
Pounds-force inches (lbf in; lb in)	x 0.083	= Pounds-force feet (lbf ft; lb ft)	x 12	=	Pounds-force inches (lbf in; lb in)
Pounds-force feet (lbf ft; lb ft)	x 0.138	= Kilograms-force metres (kgf m; kg m)	x 7.233	=	Pounds-force feet (lbf ft; lb ft)
Pounds-force feet (lbf ft; lb ft)	x 1.356	= Newton metres (Nm)	x 0.738	=	Pounds-force feet (lbf ft; lb ft)
Newton metres (Nm)	x 0.102	= Kilograms-force metres (kgf m; kg m)	x 9.804	=	Newton metres (Nm)

Power
Horsepower (hp)	x 745.7	= Watts (W)	x 0.0013	=	Horsepower (hp)

Velocity (speed)
Miles per hour (miles/hr; mph)	x 1.609	= Kilometres per hour (km/hr; kph)	x 0.621	=	Miles per hour (miles/hr; mph)

Fuel consumption*
Miles per gallon (mpg)	x 0.354	= Kilometres per litre (km/l)	x 2.825	=	Miles per gallon (mpg)

Temperature

Degrees Fahrenheit = (°C x 1.8) + 32   Degrees Celsius (Degrees Centigrade; °C) = (°F - 32) x 0.56

It is common practice to convert from miles per gallon (mpg) to litres/100 kilometres (l/100km), where mpg x l/100 km = 282

MOT Test Checks REF•27

About the MOT Test

In the UK, all vehicles more than three years old are subject to an annual test to ensure that they meet minimum safety requirements. A current test certificate must be issued before a machine can be used on public roads, and is required before a road fund licence can be issued. Riding without a current test certificate will also invalidate your insurance.

For most owners, the MOT test is an annual cause for anxiety, and this is largely due to owners not being sure what needs to be checked prior to submitting the motorcycle for testing. The simple answer is that a fully roadworthy motorcycle will have no difficulty in passing the test.

This is a guide to getting your motorcycle through the MOT test. Obviously it will not be possible to examine the motorcycle to the same standard as the professional MOT tester, particularly in view of the equipment required for some of the checks. However, working through the following procedures will enable you to identify any problem areas before submitting the motorcycle for the test.

It has only been possible to summarise the test requirements here, based on the regulations in force at the time of printing. Test standards are becoming increasingly stringent, although there are some exemptions for older vehicles. More information about the MOT test can be obtained from the TSO publications, *How Safe is your Motorcycle* and *The MOT Inspection Manual for Motorcycle Testing*.

Many of the checks require that one of the wheels is raised off the ground. If the motorcycle doesn't have a centre stand, note that an auxiliary stand will be required. Additionally, the help of an assistant may prove useful.

Certain exceptions apply to machines under 50 cc, machines without a lighting system, and Classic bikes - if in doubt about any of the requirements listed below seek confirmation from an MOT tester prior to submitting the motorcycle for the test.

Check that the frame number is clearly visible.

Electrical System

Lights, turn signals, horn and reflector

✔ With the ignition on, check the operation of the following electrical components. **Note:** The electrical components on certain small-capacity machines are powered by the generator, requiring that the engine is run for this check.

a) *Headlight and tail light*. Check that both illuminate in the low and high beam switch positions.
b) *Position lights*. Check that the front position (or sidelight) and tail light illuminate in this switch position.
c) *Turn signals*. Check that all flash at the correct rate, and that the warning light(s) function correctly. Check that the turn signal switch works correctly.
d) *Hazard warning system (where fitted)*. Check that all four turn signals flash in this switch position.
e) *Brake stop light*. Check that the light comes on when the front and rear brakes are independently applied. Models first used on or after 1st April 1986 must have a brake light switch on each brake.
f) *Horn*. Check that the sound is continuous and of reasonable volume.

✔ Check that there is a red reflector on the rear of the machine, either mounted separately or as part of the tail light lens.

✔ Check the condition of the headlight, tail light and turn signal lenses.

Headlight beam height

✔ The MOT tester will perform a headlight beam height check using specialised beam setting equipment **(see illustration 1)**. This equipment will not be available to the home mechanic, but if you suspect that the headlight is incorrectly set or may have been maladjusted in the past, you can perform a rough test as follows.

✔ Position the bike in a straight line facing a brick wall. The bike must be off its stand, upright and with a rider seated. Measure the height from the ground to the centre of the headlight and mark a horizontal line on the wall at this height. Position the motorcycle 3.8 metres from the wall and draw a vertical line up the wall central to the centreline of the motorcycle. Switch to dipped beam and check that the beam pattern falls slightly lower than the horizontal line and to the left of the vertical line **(see illustration 2)**.

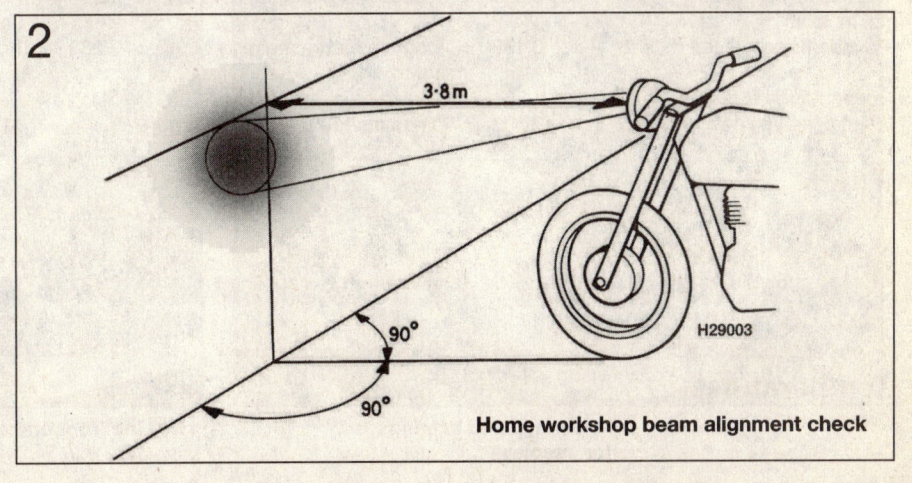

Headlight beam height checking equipment

Home workshop beam alignment check

MOT Test Checks

Exhaust System and Final Drive

Exhaust

✔ Check that the exhaust mountings are secure and that the system does not foul any of the rear suspension components.
✔ Start the motorcycle. When the revs are increased, check that the exhaust is neither holed nor leaking from any of its joints. On a linked system, check that the collector box is not leaking due to corrosion.
✔ Note that the exhaust decibel level ("loudness" of the exhaust) is assessed at the discretion of the tester. If the motorcycle was first used on or after 1st January 1985 the silencer must carry the BSAU 193 stamp, or a marking relating to its make and model, or be of OE (original equipment) manufacture. If the silencer is marked NOT FOR ROAD USE, RACING USE ONLY or similar, it will fail the MOT.

Final drive

✔ On chain or belt drive machines, check that the chain/belt is in good condition and does not have excessive slack. Also check that the sprocket is securely mounted on the rear wheel hub. Check that the chain/belt guard is in place.
✔ On shaft drive bikes, check for oil leaking from the drive unit and fouling the rear tyre.

Steering and Suspension

Steering

✔ With the front wheel raised off the ground, rotate the steering from lock to lock. The handlebar or switches must not contact the fuel tank or be close enough to trap the rider's hand. Problems can be caused by damaged lock stops on the lower yoke and frame, or by the fitting of non-standard handlebars.
✔ When performing the lock to lock check, also ensure that the steering moves freely without drag or notchiness. Steering movement can be impaired by poorly routed cables, or by overtight head bearings or worn bearings. The tester will perform a check of the steering head bearing lower race by mounting the front wheel on a surface plate, then performing a lock to lock check with the weight of the machine on the lower bearing (see illustration 3).
✔ Grasp the fork sliders (lower legs) and attempt to push and pull on the forks (see illustration 4). Any play in the steering head bearings will be felt. Note that in extreme cases, wear of the front fork bushes can be misinterpreted for head bearing play.
✔ Check that the handlebars are securely mounted.
✔ Check that the handlebar grip rubbers are secure. They should by bonded to the bar left end and to the throttle cable pulley on the right end.

Front wheel mounted on a surface plate for steering head bearing lower race check

Front suspension

✔ With the motorcycle off the stand, hold the front brake on and pump the front forks up and down (see illustration 5). Check that they are adequately damped.

Checking the steering head bearings for freeplay

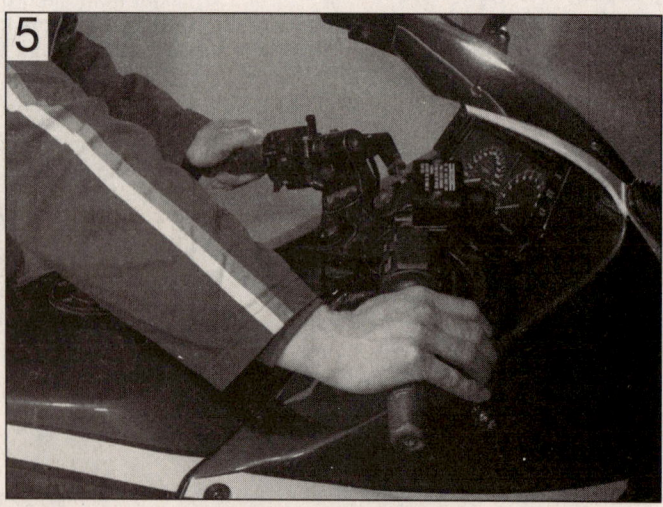

Hold the front brake on and pump the front forks up and down to check operation

MOT Test Checks REF•29

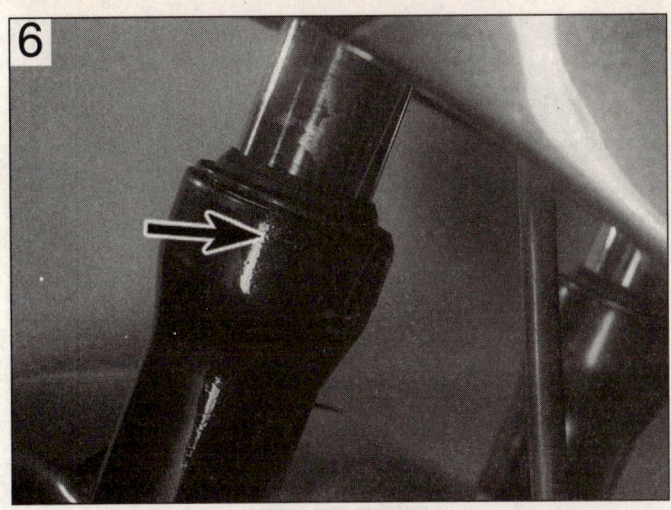

6

Inspect the area around the fork dust seal for oil leakage (arrow)

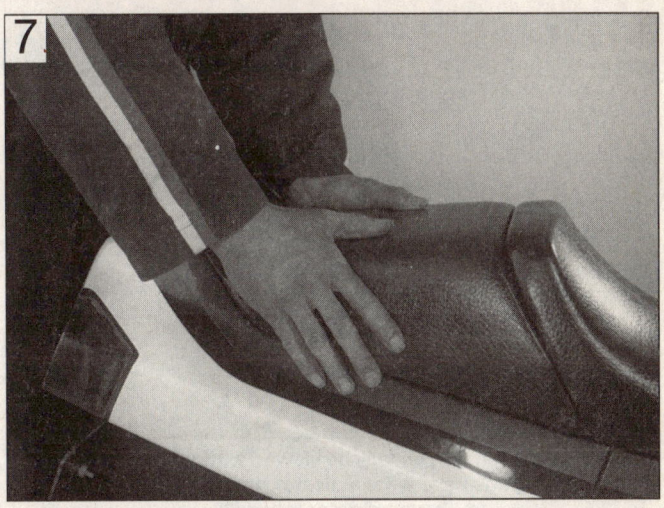

7

Bounce the rear of the motorcycle to check rear suspension operation

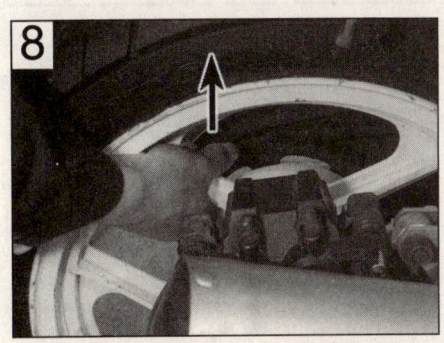

8

Checking for rear suspension linkage play

✔ Inspect the area above and around the front fork oil seals **(see illustration 6)**. There should be no sign of oil on the fork tube (stanchion) nor leaking down the slider (lower leg). On models so equipped, check that there is no oil leaking from the anti-dive units.

✔ On models with swingarm front suspension, check that there is no freeplay in the linkage when moved from side to side.

Rear suspension

✔ With the motorcycle off the stand and an assistant supporting the motorcycle by its handlebars, bounce the rear suspension **(see illustration 7)**. Check that the suspension components do not foul on any of the cycle parts and check that the shock absorber(s) provide adequate damping.

✔ Visually inspect the shock absorber(s) and check that there is no sign of oil leakage from its damper. This is somewhat restricted on certain single shock models due to the location of the shock absorber.

✔ With the rear wheel raised off the ground, grasp the wheel at the highest point and attempt to pull it up **(see illustration 8)**. Any play in the swingarm pivot or suspension linkage bearings will be felt as movement.

Note: *Do not confuse play with actual suspension movement.* Failure to lubricate suspension linkage bearings can lead to bearing failure **(see illustration 9)**.

✔ With the rear wheel raised off the ground, grasp the swingarm ends and attempt to move the swingarm from side to side and forwards and backwards - any play indicates wear of the swingarm pivot bearings **(see illustration 10)**.

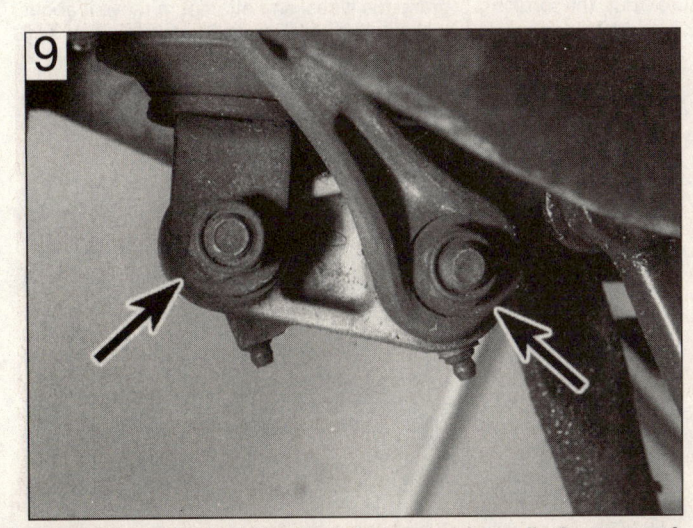

9

Worn suspension linkage pivots (arrows) are usually the cause of play in the rear suspension

10

Grasp the swingarm at the ends to check for play in its pivot bearings

REF•30 MOT Test Checks

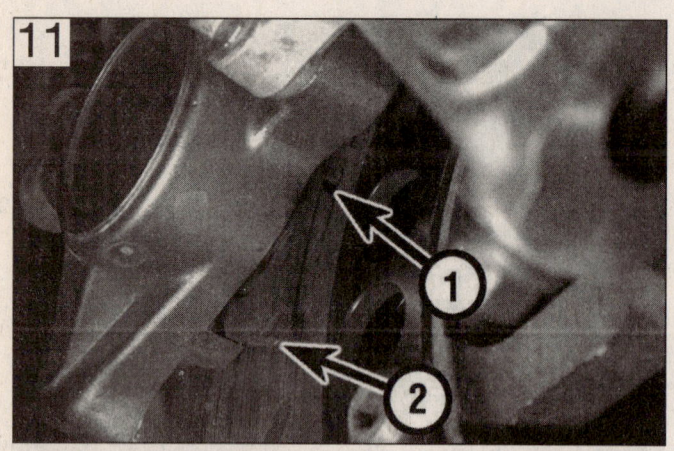

Brake pad wear can usually be viewed without removing the caliper. Most pads have wear indicator grooves (1) and some also have indicator tangs (2)

On drum brakes, check the angle of the operating lever with the brake fully applied. Most drum brakes have a wear indicator pointer and scale.

Brakes, Wheels and Tyres

Brakes

✔ With the wheel raised off the ground, apply the brake then free it off, and check that the wheel is about to revolve freely without brake drag.
✔ On disc brakes, examine the disc itself. Check that it is securely mounted and not cracked.
✔ On disc brakes, view the pad material through the caliper mouth and check that the pads are not worn down beyond the limit **(see illustration 11)**.
✔ On drum brakes, check that when the brake is applied the angle between the operating lever and cable or rod is not too great **(see illustration 12)**. Check also that the operating lever doesn't foul any other components.
✔ On disc brakes, examine the flexible hoses from top to bottom. Have an assistant hold the brake on so that the fluid in the hose is under pressure, and check that there is no sign of fluid leakage, bulges or cracking. If there are any metal brake pipes or unions, check that these are free from corrosion and damage. Where a brake-linked anti-dive system is fitted, check the hoses to the anti-dive in a similar manner.
✔ Check that the rear brake torque arm is secure and that its fasteners are secured by self-locking nuts or castellated nuts with split-pins or R-pins **(see illustration 13)**.
✔ On models with ABS, check that the self-check warning light in the instrument panel works.
✔ The MOT tester will perform a test of the motorcycle's braking efficiency based on a calculation of rider and motorcycle weight. Although this cannot be carried out at home, you can at least ensure that the braking systems are properly maintained. For hydraulic disc brakes, check the fluid level, lever/pedal feel (bleed of air if its spongy) and pad material. For drum brakes, check adjustment, cable or rod operation and shoe lining thickness.

Wheels and tyres

✔ Check the wheel condition. Cast wheels should be free from cracks and if of the built-up design, all fasteners should be secure. Spoked wheels should be checked for broken, corroded, loose or bent spokes.
✔ With the wheel raised off the ground, spin the wheel and visually check that the tyre and wheel run true. Check that the tyre does not foul the suspension or mudguards.
✔ With the wheel raised off the ground, grasp the wheel and attempt to move it about the axle (spindle) **(see illustration 14)**. Any play felt here indicates wheel bearing failure.

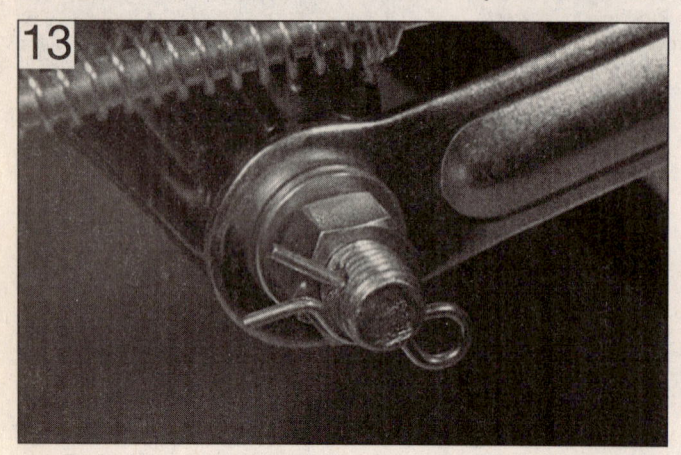

Brake torque arm must be properly secured at both ends

Check for wheel bearing play by trying to move the wheel about the axle (spindle)

MOT Test Checks REF•31

Checking the tyre tread depth

Tyre direction of rotation arrow can be found on tyre sidewall

Castellated type wheel axle (spindle) nut must be secured by a split pin or R-pin

Two straightedges are used to check wheel alignment

✓ Check the tyre tread depth, tread condition and sidewall condition **(see illustration 15)**.
✓ Check the tyre type. Front and rear tyre types must be compatible and be suitable for road use. Tyres marked NOT FOR ROAD USE, COMPETITION USE ONLY or similar, will fail the MOT.

✓ If the tyre sidewall carries a direction of rotation arrow, this must be pointing in the direction of normal wheel rotation **(see illustration 16)**.
✓ Check that the wheel axle (spindle) nuts (where applicable) are properly secured. A self-locking nut or castellated nut with a split-pin or R-pin can be used **(see illustration 17)**.
✓ Wheel alignment is checked with the motorcycle off the stand and a rider seated. With the front wheel pointing straight ahead, two perfectly straight lengths of metal or wood and placed against the sidewalls of both tyres **(see illustration 18)**. The gap each side of the front tyre must be equidistant on both sides. Incorrect wheel alignment may be due to a cocked rear wheel (often as the result of poor chain adjustment) or in extreme cases, a bent frame.

General checks and condition

✓ Check the security of all major fasteners, bodypanels, seat, fairings (where fitted) and mudguards.

✓ Check that the rider and pillion footrests, handlebar levers and brake pedal are securely mounted.

✓ Check for corrosion on the frame or any load-bearing components. If severe, this may affect the structure, particularly under stress.

Sidecars

A motorcycle fitted with a sidecar requires additional checks relating to the stability of the machine and security of attachment and swivel joints, plus specific wheel alignment (toe-in) requirements. Additionally, tyre and lighting requirements differ from conventional motorcycle use. Owners are advised to check MOT test requirements with an official test centre.

REF•32 Storage

Preparing for storage

Before you start

If repairs or an overhaul is needed, see that this is carried out now rather than left until you want to ride the bike again.

Give the bike a good wash and scrub all dirt from its underside. Make sure the bike dries completely before preparing for storage.

Engine

- Remove the spark plug(s) and lubricate the cylinder bores with approximately a teaspoon of motor oil using a spout-type oil can **(see illustration 1)**. Reinstall the spark plug(s). Crank the engine over a couple of times to coat the piston rings and bores with oil. If the bike has a kickstart, use this to turn the engine over. If not, flick the kill switch to the OFF position and crank the engine over on the starter **(see illustration 2)**. If the nature on the ignition system prevents the starter operating with the kill switch in the OFF position, remove the spark plugs and fit them back in their caps; ensure that the plugs are earthed (grounded) against the cylinder head when the starter is operated **(see illustration 3)**.

Warning: It is important that the plugs are earthed (grounded) away from the spark plug holes otherwise there is a risk of atomised fuel from the cylinders igniting.

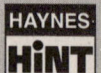

HAYNES HiNT *On a single cylinder four-stroke engine, you can seal the combustion chamber completely by positioning the piston at TDC on the compression stroke.*

- Drain the carburettor(s) otherwise there is a risk of jets becoming blocked by gum deposits from the fuel **(see illustration 4)**.

- If the bike is going into long-term storage, consider adding a fuel stabiliser to the fuel in the tank. If the tank is drained completely, corrosion of its internal surfaces may occur if left unprotected for a long period. The tank can be treated with a rust preventative especially for this purpose. Alternatively, remove the tank and pour half a litre of motor oil into it, install the filler cap and shake the tank to coat its internals with oil before draining off the excess. The same effect can also be achieved by spraying WD40 or a similar water-dispersant around the inside of the tank via its flexible nozzle.

- Make sure the cooling system contains the correct mix of antifreeze. Antifreeze also contains important corrosion inhibitors.

- The air intakes and exhaust can be sealed off by covering or plugging the openings. Ensure that you do not seal in any condensation; run the engine until it is hot,

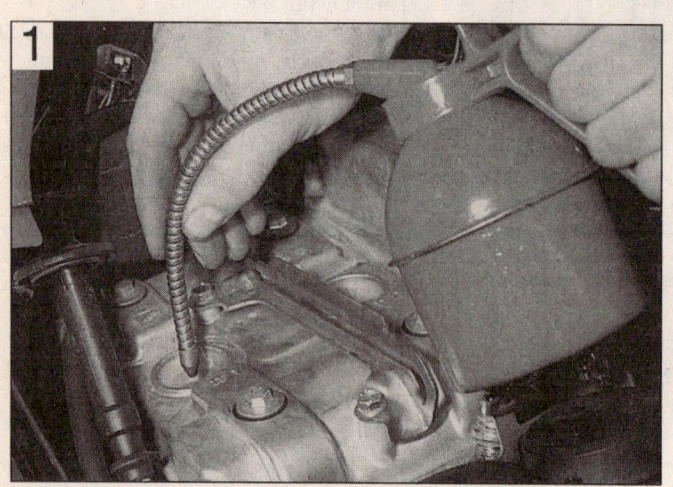

1 Squirt a drop of motor oil into each cylinder

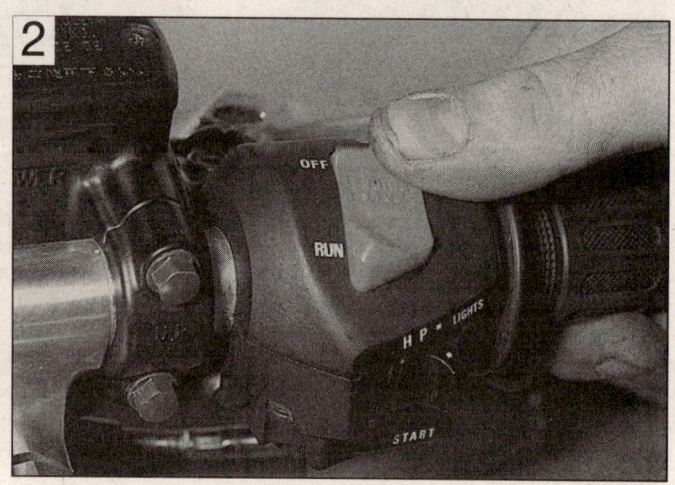

2 Flick the kill switch to OFF . . .

3 . . . and ensure that the metal bodies of the plugs (arrows) are earthed against the cylinder head

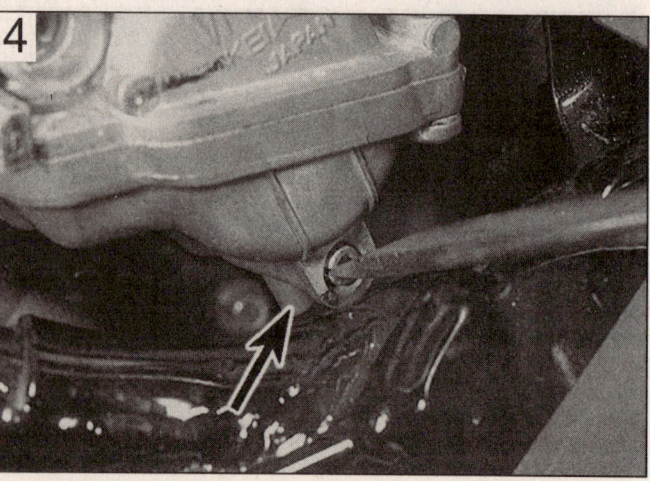

4 Connect a hose to the carburettor float chamber drain stub (arrow) and unscrew the drain screw

Storage

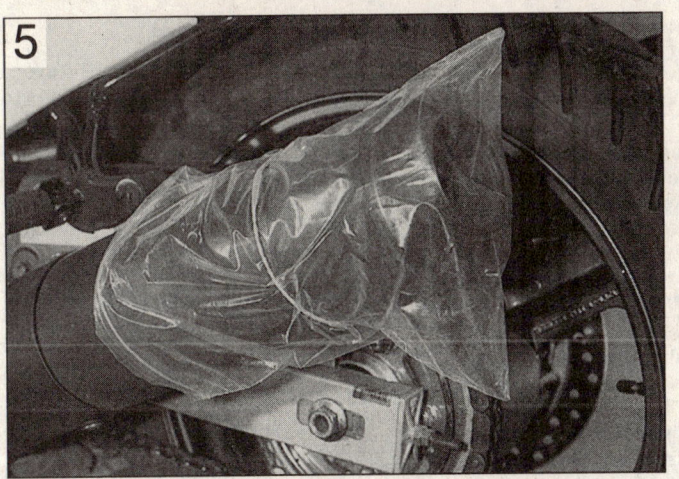

Exhausts can be sealed off with a plastic bag

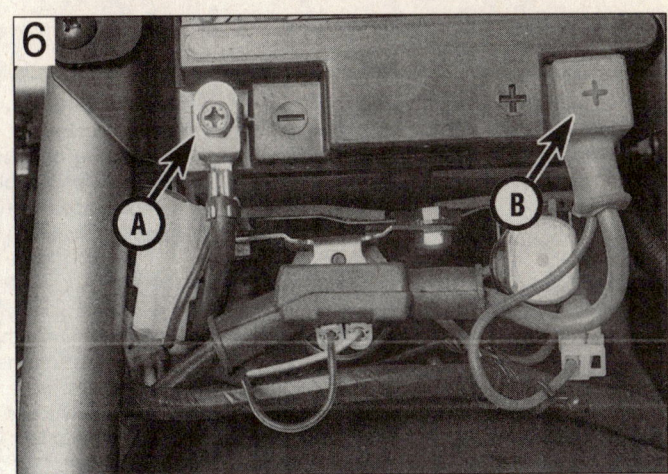

Disconnect the negative lead (A) first, followed by the positive lead (B)

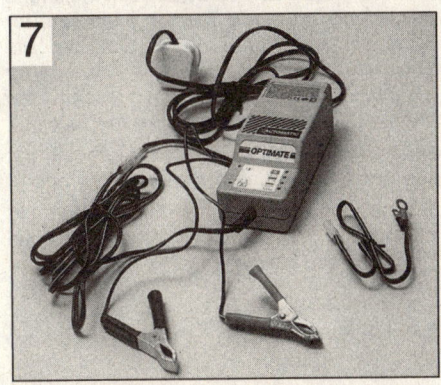

Use a suitable battery charger - this kit also assess battery condition

then switch off and allow to cool. Tape a piece of thick plastic over the silencer end(s) **(see illustration 5)**. Note that some advocate pouring a tablespoon of motor oil into the silencer(s) before sealing them off.

Battery

● Remove it from the bike - in extreme cases of cold the battery may freeze and crack its case **(see illustration 6)**.

● Check the electrolyte level and top up if necessary (conventional refillable batteries). Clean the terminals.
● Store the battery off the motorcycle and away from any sources of fire. Position a wooden block under the battery if it is to sit on the ground.
● Give the battery a trickle charge for a few hours every month **(see illustration 7)**.

Tyres

● Place the bike on its centrestand or an auxiliary stand which will support the motorcycle in an upright position. Position wood blocks under the tyres to keep them off the ground and to provide insulation from damp. If the bike is being put into long-term storage, ideally both tyres should be off the ground; not only will this protect the tyres, but will also ensure that no load is placed on the steering head or wheel bearings.
● Deflate each tyre by 5 to 10 psi, no more or the beads may unseat from the rim, making subsequent inflation difficult on tubeless tyres.

Pivots and controls

● Lubricate all lever, pedal, stand and footrest pivot points. If grease nipples are fitted to the rear suspension components, apply lubricant to the pivots.
● Lubricate all control cables.

Cycle components

● Apply a wax protectant to all painted and plastic components. Wipe off any excess, but don't polish to a shine. Where fitted, clean the screen with soap and water.
● Coat metal parts with Vaseline (petroleum jelly). When applying this to the fork tubes, do not compress the forks otherwise the seals will rot from contact with the Vaseline.
● Apply a vinyl cleaner to the seat.

Storage conditions

● Aim to store the bike in a shed or garage which does not leak and is free from damp.
● Drape an old blanket or bedspread over the bike to protect it from dust and direct contact with sunlight (which will fade paint). This also hides the bike from prying eyes. Beware of tight-fitting plastic covers which may allow condensation to form and settle on the bike.

Getting back on the road

Engine and transmission

● Change the oil and replace the oil filter. If this was done prior to storage, check that the oil hasn't emulsified - a thick whitish substance which occurs through condensation.
● Remove the spark plugs. Using a spout-type oil can, squirt a few drops of oil into the cylinder(s). This will provide initial lubrication as the piston rings and bores comes back into contact. Service the spark plugs, or fit new ones, and install them in the engine.

● Check that the clutch isn't stuck on. The plates can stick together if left standing for some time, preventing clutch operation. Engage a gear and try rocking the bike back and forth with the clutch lever held against the handlebar. If this doesn't work on cable-operated clutches, hold the clutch lever back against the handlebar with a strong elastic band or cable tie for a couple of hours **(see illustration 8)**.
● If the air intakes or silencer end(s) were blocked off, remove the bung or cover used.
● If the fuel tank was coated with a rust

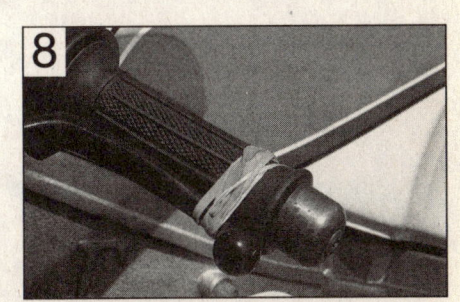

Hold clutch lever back against the handlebar with elastic bands or a cable tie

Storage

preventative, oil or a stabiliser added to the fuel, drain and flush the tank and dispose of the fuel sensibly. If no action was taken with the fuel tank prior to storage, it is advised that the old fuel is disposed of since it will go off over a period of time. Refill the fuel tank with fresh fuel.

Frame and running gear

- Oil all pivot points and cables.
- Check the tyre pressures. They will definitely need inflating if pressures were reduced for storage.
- Lubricate the final drive chain (where applicable).
- Remove any protective coating applied to the fork tubes (stanchions) since this may well destroy the fork seals. If the fork tubes weren't protected and have picked up rust spots, remove them with very fine abrasive paper and refinish with metal polish.
- Check that both brakes operate correctly. Apply each brake hard and check that it's not possible to move the motorcycle forwards, then check that the brake frees off again once released. Brake caliper pistons can stick due to corrosion around the piston head, or on the sliding caliper types, due to corrosion of the slider pins. If the brake doesn't free after repeated operation, take the caliper off for examination. Similarly drum brakes can stick due to a seized operating cam, cable or rod linkage.
- If the motorcycle has been in long-term storage, renew the brake fluid and clutch fluid (where applicable).
- Depending on where the bike has been stored, the wiring, cables and hoses may have been nibbled by rodents. Make a visual check and investigate disturbed wiring loom tape.

Battery

- If the battery has been previously removal and given top up charges it can simply be reconnected. Remember to connect the positive cable first and the negative cable last.
- On conventional refillable batteries, if the battery has not received any attention, remove it from the motorcycle and check its electrolyte level. Top up if necessary then charge the battery. If the battery fails to hold a charge and a visual checks show heavy white sulphation of the plates, the battery is probably defective and must be renewed. This is particularly likely if the battery is old. Confirm battery condition with a specific gravity check.
- On sealed (MF) batteries, if the battery has not received any attention, remove it from the motorcycle and charge it according to the information on the battery case - if the battery fails to hold a charge it must be renewed.

Starting procedure

- If a kickstart is fitted, turn the engine over a couple of times with the ignition OFF to distribute oil around the engine. If no kickstart is fitted, flick the engine kill switch OFF and the ignition ON and crank the engine over a couple of times to work oil around the upper cylinder components. If the nature of the ignition system is such that the starter won't work with the kill switch OFF, remove the spark plugs, fit them back into their caps and earth (ground) their bodies on the cylinder head. Reinstall the spark plugs afterwards.
- Switch the kill switch to RUN, operate the choke and start the engine. If the engine won't start don't continue cranking the engine - not only will this flatten the battery, but the starter motor will overheat. Switch the ignition off and try again later. If the engine refuses to start, go through the fault finding procedures in this manual. **Note:** *If the bike has been in storage for a long time, old fuel or a carburettor blockage may be the problem. Gum deposits in carburettors can block jets - if a carburettor cleaner doesn't prove successful the carburettors must be dismantled for cleaning.*
- Once the engine has started, check that the lights, turn signals and horn work properly.
- Treat the bike gently for the first ride and check all fluid levels on completion. Settle the bike back into the maintenance schedule.

Fault Finding REF•35

This Section provides an easy reference-guide to the more common faults that are likely to afflict your machine. Obviously, the opportunities are almost limitless for faults to occur as a result of obscure failures, and to try and cover all eventualities would require a book. Indeed, a number have been written on the subject.

Successful troubleshooting is not a mysterious 'black art' but the application of a bit of knowledge combined with a systematic and logical approach to the problem. Approach any troubleshooting by first accurately identifying the symptom and then checking through the list of possible causes, starting with the simplest or most obvious and progressing in stages to the most complex.

Take nothing for granted, but above all apply liberal quantities of common sense.

The main symptom of a fault is given in the text as a major heading below which are listed the various systems or areas which may contain the fault. Details of each possible cause for a fault and the remedial action to be taken are given, in brief, in the paragraphs below each heading. Further information should be sought in the relevant Chapter.

1 Engine doesn't start or is difficult to start
- [ ] Starter motor doesn't rotate
- [ ] Starter motor rotates but engine does not turn over
- [ ] No fuel flow
- [ ] Engine flooded
- [ ] No spark or weak spark
- [ ] Compression low
- [ ] Stalls after starting
- [ ] Rough idle

2 Poor running at low speed
- [ ] Spark weak
- [ ] Fuel/air mixture incorrect
- [ ] Compression low
- [ ] Poor acceleration

3 Poor running or no power at high speed
- [ ] Firing incorrect
- [ ] Fuel/air mixture incorrect
- [ ] Compression low
- [ ] Knocking or pinking
- [ ] Miscellaneous causes

4 Overheating
- [ ] Firing incorrect
- [ ] Fuel/air mixture incorrect
- [ ] Compression too high
- [ ] Engine load excessive
- [ ] Lubrication inadequate
- [ ] Miscellaneous causes

5 Clutch problems
- [ ] Clutch slipping
- [ ] Clutch not disengaging completely

6 Gearchange problems
- [ ] Doesn't go into gear, or lever doesn't return
- [ ] Jumps out of gear
- [ ] Overselects

7 Abnormal engine noise
- [ ] Knocking or pinking
- [ ] Piston slap or rattling
- [ ] Valve noise
- [ ] Other noise

8 Abnormal driveline noise
- [ ] Clutch noise
- [ ] Transmission noise
- [ ] Final drive noise

9 Abnormal frame and suspension noise
- [ ] Front end noise
- [ ] Shock absorber noise
- [ ] Brake noise

10 Excessive exhaust smoke
- [ ] White smoke
- [ ] Black smoke
- [ ] Brown smoke

11 Poor handling or stability
- [ ] Handlebar hard to turn
- [ ] Handlebar shakes or vibrates excessively
- [ ] Handlebar pulls to one side
- [ ] Poor shock absorbing qualities

12 Braking problems
- [ ] Brakes are spongy or don't hold
- [ ] Brake lever or pedal pulsates
- [ ] Brakes drag

13 Electrical problems
- [ ] Battery dead or weak
- [ ] Battery overcharged

Fault Finding

1 Engine doesn't start or is difficult to start

Starter motor doesn't rotate

- ☐ Fuse blown. Check main fuse and sub fuse B (Chapter 8).
- ☐ Battery voltage low. Check and recharge battery (Chapter 8).
- ☐ Starter motor defective. Make sure the wiring to the starter is secure. Make sure the starter relay clicks when the start button is pushed. If the relay clicks, then the fault is probably in the wiring or motor.
- ☐ Starter relay faulty. Check it according to the procedure in Chapter 8.
- ☐ Starter button not contacting. The contacts could be wet, corroded or dirty. Disassemble and clean the switch (Chapter 8).
- ☐ Wiring open or shorted. Check all wiring connections and harnesses to make sure that they are dry, tight and not corroded. Also check for broken or frayed wires that can cause a short to earth (see *Wiring Diagram*, Chapter 8).
- ☐ Ignition switch defective. Check the switch according to the procedure in Chapter 8. Replace the switch with a new one if it is defective.
- ☐ Faulty neutral/sidestand/clutch switch or diode. Check the wiring to each switch and the switch itself, and check the diode, according to the procedures in Chapter 8.
- ☐ Fuel injection system shutdown due to system fault (Chapter 4).

Starter motor rotates but engine does not turn over

- ☐ Starter clutch defective. Inspect and repair or replace (Chapter 2).
- ☐ Damaged idle/reduction or starter gears. Inspect and replace the damaged parts (Chapter 2).

No fuel flow

- ☐ No fuel in tank.
- ☐ Breather hose obstructed. Usually caused by dirt or a trapped hose.
- ☐ Fuel pump failure or filter clogged. Check fuel flow (Chapter 4).
- ☐ Fuel injection system fault (Chapter 4).
- ☐ Fuel hose clogged. Detach the fuel hose and carefully blow through it.

Engine flooded

- ☐ Injector needle valve worn or stuck open. A piece of dirt, rust or other debris can cause the needle to seat improperly, causing excess fuel to be admitted to the throttle body. In this case, the injector should be cleaned (Chapter 4). If the injector is damaged it must be renewed.
- ☐ Starting technique incorrect. Under normal circumstances (i.e. if all the components of the fuel injection system are good) the machine should start with the throttle closed.

No spark or weak spark

- ☐ Ignition switch OFF.
- ☐ Battery voltage low. Check and recharge battery as necessary (Chapter 8).
- ☐ Spark plug dirty, defective or worn out. Locate reason for fouled plug using spark plug condition chart and follow the plug maintenance procedures in Chapter 1.
- ☐ Spark plug cap or lead faulty. Check condition. Replace either or both components if cracks or deterioration are evident.
- ☐ Spark plug cap not making good contact. Make sure that the plug cap fits snugly over the plug end.
- ☐ Ignition system fault (Chapter 3).
- ☐ Ignition HT coil defective (Chapter 3).
- ☐ Ignition switch shorted. This is usually caused by water, corrosion, damage or excessive wear. If cleaning with electrical contact cleaner does not help, renew the switch (Chapter 8).
- ☐ Wiring shorted or broken. Make sure that all wiring connections are clean, dry and tight. Look for chafed and broken wires.

Compression low

- ☐ Spark plug loose. Remove the plug and inspect the threads. Reinstall and tighten to the specified torque (Chapter 1).
- ☐ Cylinder head not sufficiently tightened down. If a cylinder head is suspected of being loose, then there's a chance that the gasket or head is damaged if the problem has persisted for any length of time. The cylinder head fixings should be tightened to the correct torque in the correct sequence (Chapter 2).
- ☐ Improper valve clearance. This means that the valve is not closing completely and compression pressure is leaking past the valve. Check and adjust the valve clearances (Chapter 1).
- ☐ Cylinder and/or piston worn. Excessive wear will cause compression pressure to leak past the rings. This is usually accompanied by worn rings as well. A top-end overhaul is necessary (Chapter 2).
- ☐ Piston rings worn, weak, broken, or sticking. Broken or sticking piston rings usually indicate a lubrication or carburetion problem that causes excess carbon deposits or seizures to form on the piston and rings. Top-end overhaul is necessary (Chapter 2).
- ☐ Cylinder head gasket damaged. If the head is allowed to become loose, or if excessive carbon build-up on the piston crown and combustion chamber causes extremely high compression, the head gasket may leak. Retorquing the head is not always sufficient to restore the seal, so gasket replacement is necessary (Chapter 2).
- ☐ Cylinder head warped. This is caused by overheating or improperly tightened head fixings. Machine shop resurfacing or head replacement is necessary (Chapter 2).
- ☐ Valve spring broken or weak. Caused by component failure or wear; the valve springs must be replaced as a set (Chapter 2).
- ☐ Valve not seating properly. This is caused by a bent valve (from over-revving or improper valve adjustment), burned valve or seat or an accumulation of carbon deposits on the seat. The valves must be cleaned and/or replaced and the seats serviced if possible (Chapter 2).

Stalls after starting

- ☐ Ignition malfunction (Chapter 3).
- ☐ Faulty idle air control valve. Check the operation of the IACV (Chapter 4).
- ☐ Fuel injection system malfunction (Chapter 4).
- ☐ Fuel contaminated. The fuel can be contaminated with either dirt or water, or can change chemically if the machine is allowed to sit for several months or more. Drain the tank and fuel system (Chapter 4).
- ☐ Intake air leak. Check the throttle body connection with the cylinder head (Chapter 4).
- ☐ Engine idle speed incorrect. Check possible causes (Chapter 1).

Rough idle

- ☐ Ignition malfunction (Chapter 3).
- ☐ Idle speed incorrect. Check possible causes (Chapter 1).
- ☐ Fuel injection system fault (Chapter 4).
- ☐ Fuel contaminated. The fuel can be contaminated with either dirt or water, or can change chemically if the machine is allowed to sit for several months or more. Drain the tank and fuel system (Chapter 4).
- ☐ Intake air leak. Check the throttle body connection with the cylinder head (Chapter 4).
- ☐ Air filter clogged. Renew the air filter element (Chapter 1).
- ☐ Fuel injection system fault (Chapter 4).

Fault Finding REF•37

2 Poor running at low speed

Spark weak

- [ ] Battery voltage low. Check and recharge battery (Chapter 8).
- [ ] Spark plug fouled, defective or worn out. Refer to Chapter 1 for spark plug maintenance.
- [ ] Spark plug cap or lead defective. Refer to Chapter 3 for details on the ignition system.
- [ ] Spark plug cap not making contact.
- [ ] Incorrect spark plug. Wrong type, heat range or cap configuration. Check and install correct plug listed in Chapter 1.
- [ ] Ignition system defective (Chapter 3).
- [ ] Ignition HT coil defective (Chapter 3).

Compression low

- [ ] Spark plug loose. Remove the plug and inspect the threads. Reinstall and tighten to the specified torque (Chapter 1).
- [ ] Cylinder head not sufficiently tightened down. If a cylinder head is suspected of being loose, then there's a chance that the gasket and head are damaged if the problem has persisted for any length of time. The cylinder head fixings should be tightened to the correct torque in the correct sequence (Chapter 2).
- [ ] Improper valve clearance. This means that the valve is not closing completely and compression pressure is leaking past the valve. Check and adjust the valve clearances (Chapter 1).
- [ ] Cylinder and/or piston worn. Excessive wear will cause compression pressure to leak past the rings. This is usually accompanied by worn rings as well. A top-end overhaul is necessary (Chapter 2).
- [ ] Piston rings worn, weak, broken, or sticking. Broken or sticking piston rings usually indicate a lubrication or carburetion problem that causes excess carbon deposits or seizures to form on the piston and rings. Top-end overhaul is necessary (Chapter 2).
- [ ] Cylinder head gasket damaged. If the head is allowed to become loose, or if excessive carbon build-up on the piston crown and combustion chamber causes extremely high compression, the head gasket may leak. Retorquing the head is not always sufficient to restore the seal, so gasket replacement is necessary (Chapter 2).
- [ ] Cylinder head warped. This is caused by overheating or improperly tightened head fixings. Machine shop resurfacing or head replacement is necessary (Chapter 2).
- [ ] Valve spring broken or weak. Caused by component failure or wear; the springs should be renewed as a set (Chapter 2).
- [ ] Valve not seating properly. This is caused by a bent valve (from over-revving or improper valve adjustment), burned valve or seat or an accumulation of carbon deposits on the seat. The valves must be cleaned and/or replaced and the seats serviced if possible (Chapter 2).

Poor acceleration

- [ ] Throttle body leaking or dirty (Chapter 4).
- [ ] Fuel flow restricted. Check the fuel pressure and fuel flow, and all the hoses from the tank (Chapter 4). If the breather hose is blocked a vacuum can form in the tank which will restrict flow.
- [ ] Timing not advancing. The crankshaft position sensor or the ECM may be defective. If so, they must be replaced with new ones, as they can't be repaired.
- [ ] Engine oil viscosity too high. Using a heavier oil than that recommended can damage the oil pump or lubrication system and cause drag on the engine.
- [ ] Brakes dragging. Usually caused by debris which has entered the brake piston seals (disc brake), sticking brake operating mechanism or badly adjusted brake (drum brake), or from a warped disc or bent axle. Repair as necessary (Chapter 6).

Fault Finding

3 Poor running or no power at high speed

Firing incorrect
- [ ] Air filter restricted. Renew filter element (Chapter 1).
- [ ] Spark plug fouled, defective or worn out. See Chapter 1 for spark plug maintenance.
- [ ] Spark plug cap or lead wiring defective. See Chapter 3 for details of the ignition system.
- [ ] Spark plug cap not in good contact.
- [ ] Incorrect spark plug. Wrong type, heat range or cap configuration. Check and install correct plug listed in Chapter 1.
- [ ] Ignition system defective (Chapter 3).
- [ ] Ignition HT coil defective (Chapter 3).
- [ ] Fuel injection system fault (Chapter 4).

Fuel/air mixture incorrect
- [ ] Air filter clogged, poorly sealed, or missing (Chapter 1).
- [ ] Air filter housing poorly sealed. Look for cracks, holes or loose clamps, and replace or repair defective parts.
- [ ] Fuel pump faulty, or its filter is blocked (Chapter 4).
- [ ] Fuel injector clogged. Either a very bad batch of fuel with an unusual additive has been used, or some other foreign material has entered the tank. Check the fuel pressure and delivery. In some cases, if a machine has been unused for several months, the fuel turns to a varnish-like liquid which can cause the injector needle to stick to its seat. Drain the tank and fuel system (Chapter 4).
- [ ] Fuel tank breather hose blocked.
- [ ] Intake manifold loose. Check for cracks, breaks, tears or loose clamps.
- [ ] Fuel hose clogged. Detach the fuel hose and carefully blow through it.

Compression low
- [ ] Spark plug loose. Remove the plug and inspect the threads. Reinstall and tighten to the specified torque (Chapter 1).
- [ ] Cylinder head not sufficiently tightened down. If a cylinder head is suspected of being loose, then there's a chance that the gasket and head are damaged if the problem has persisted for any length of time. The cylinder head fixings should be tightened to the proper torque in the correct sequence (Chapter 2).
- [ ] Improper valve clearance. This means that the valve is not closing completely and compression pressure is leaking past the valve. Check and adjust the valve clearances (Chapter 1).
- [ ] Cylinder and/or piston worn. Excessive wear will cause compression pressure to leak past the rings. This is usually accompanied by worn rings as well. A top-end overhaul is necessary (Chapter 2).
- [ ] Piston rings worn, weak, broken, or sticking. Broken or sticking piston rings usually indicate a lubrication or carburetion problem that causes excess carbon deposits or seizures to form on the piston and rings. Top-end overhaul is necessary (Chapter 2).
- [ ] Cylinder head gasket damaged. If the head is allowed to become loose, or if excessive carbon build-up on the piston crown and combustion chamber causes extremely high compression, the head gasket may leak. Retorquing the head is not always sufficient to restore the seal, so gasket replacement is necessary (Chapter 2).
- [ ] Cylinder head warped. This is caused by overheating or improperly tightened head fixings. Machine shop resurfacing or head replacement is necessary (Chapter 2).
- [ ] Valve spring broken or weak. Caused by component failure or wear; renew the springs as a set (Chapter 2).
- [ ] Valve not seating properly. This is caused by a bent valve (from over-revving or improper valve adjustment), burned valve or seat or an accumulation of carbon deposits on the seat. The valves must be cleaned and/or replaced and the seats serviced if possible (Chapter 2).

Knocking or pinking
- [ ] Carbon build-up on the piston and in the combustion chamber. Remove the cylinder head and clean the piston and combustion chamber (Chapter 2).
- [ ] Incorrect or poor quality fuel. Old or improper grades of fuel can cause detonation. This causes the piston to rattle, thus the knocking or pinking sound. Drain old fuel and always use the recommended fuel grade.
- [ ] Spark plug heat range incorrect. Uncontrolled detonation indicates the plug heat range is too hot. The plug in effect becomes a glow plug, raising cylinder temperatures. Install the proper heat range plug (Chapter 1).
- [ ] Fuel injection system fault (Chapter 4).

Miscellaneous causes
- [ ] Throttle valve doesn't open fully. Adjust the cable freeplay (Chapter 1).
- [ ] Clutch slipping. May be caused by loose or worn clutch components. Refer to Chapter 2 for clutch overhaul procedures.
- [ ] Engine oil viscosity too high. Using a heavier oil than the one recommended can damage the oil pump or lubrication system and cause drag on the engine.
- [ ] Brakes dragging. Usually caused by debris which has entered the brake piston seals (disc brake), sticking brake operating mechanism or badly adjusted brake (drum brake), or from a warped disc or bent axle. Repair as necessary.

Fault Finding REF•39

4 Overheating

Engine overheats
- [ ] Oil level low. Check and top-up oil (see *Pre-ride checks*).
- [ ] Oil pump defective. Remove the pump and check the components (Chapter 2).
- [ ] Clogged cylinder head or cylinder fins. Remove any obstructions and clean the fins by washing thoroughly and blowing through with compressed air.

Firing incorrect
- [ ] Spark plug fouled, defective or worn out. See Chapter 1 for spark plug maintenance.
- [ ] Incorrect spark plug.
- [ ] Faulty ignition HT coil (Chapter 3).

Fuel/air mixture incorrect
- [ ] Air filter clogged, poorly sealed or missing (Chapter 1).
- [ ] Air filter housing poorly sealed. Look for cracks, holes or loose clamps and replace or repair.
- [ ] Fuel pump faulty, or its filter is blocked (see Chapter 4).
- [ ] Fuel injector clogged. Either a very bad batch of fuel with an unusual additive has been used, or some other foreign material has entered the tank. Check the fuel pressure and delivery. In some cases, if a machine has been unused for several months, the fuel turns to a varnish-like liquid which can cause an injector needle to stick to its seat. Drain the tank and fuel system (Chapter 4).
- [ ] Fuel tank breather hose blocked.
- [ ] Intake manifold loose. Check for cracks, breaks, tears or loose clamps.
- [ ] Fuel hose clogged. Detach the fuel hose and carefully blow through it.

Compression too high
- [ ] Carbon build-up on the piston and in the combustion chamber. Remove the cylinder head and clean the piston and combustion chamber (Chapter 2).
- [ ] Improperly machined head surface.

Engine load excessive
- [ ] Clutch slipping. Can be caused by damaged, loose or worn clutch components. Refer to Chapter 2 for overhaul procedures.
- [ ] Engine oil level too high. The addition of too much oil will cause pressurisation of the crankcase and inefficient engine operation. Check the level (*Pre-ride checks*).
- [ ] Engine oil viscosity too high. Using a heavier oil than the one recommended in can damage the oil pump or lubrication system as well as cause drag on the engine.
- [ ] Brakes dragging. Usually caused by debris which has entered the brake piston seals (disc brake), sticking brake operating mechanism or badly adjusted brake (drum brake), or from a warped disc or bent axle. Repair as necessary.

Lubrication inadequate
- [ ] Engine oil level too low. Friction caused by intermittent lack of lubrication or from oil that is overworked can cause overheating. The oil provides a definite cooling function in the engine. Check the oil level (*Pre-ride checks*).
- [ ] Poor quality engine oil or incorrect viscosity or type. Oil is rated not only according to viscosity but also according to type. Check the Specifications section and change to the correct oil (*Pre-ride checks*).
- [ ] Faulty oil pump causing reduced pressure in system. Check the pump for wear (see Chapter 2).

5 Clutch problems

Clutch slipping
- [ ] Cable freeplay insufficient. Check and adjust cable (Chapter 1).
- [ ] Friction plates worn or warped. Overhaul the clutch assembly (Chapter 2).
- [ ] Plain plates worn or warped (Chapter 2).
- [ ] Clutch spring(s) broken or weak. Old or heat-damaged (from slipping clutch) springs should be replaced with new ones (Chapter 2).
- [ ] Clutch release mechanism defective. Replace any defective parts (Chapter 2).
- [ ] Clutch centre or housing unevenly worn. This causes improper engagement of the plates. Replace the damaged or worn parts (Chapter 2).

Clutch not disengaging completely
- [ ] Cable freeplay excessive. Check and adjust cable (Chapter 1).
- [ ] Clutch plates warped or damaged. This will cause clutch drag, which in turn will cause the machine to creep. Overhaul the clutch assembly (Chapter 2).
- [ ] Clutch spring tension uneven. Usually caused by a sagged or broken spring. Check and replace the springs as a set (Chapter 2).
- [ ] Engine oil deteriorated. Old, thin, worn out oil will not provide proper lubrication for the plates, causing the clutch to drag. Change the oil and clean the filter and strainer (Chapter 1).
- [ ] Engine oil viscosity too high. Using a heavier oil than recommended can cause the plates to stick together, putting a drag on the engine. Change to the correct weight oil (*Pre-ride checks*).
- [ ] Clutch housing seized on input shaft. Lack of lubrication, severe wear or damage can cause the housing to seize on the shaft. Overhaul of the clutch, and perhaps transmission, may be necessary to repair the damage (Chapter 2).
- [ ] Clutch release mechanism defective. Worn or damaged release mechanism parts can stick and fail to apply force to the pressure plate. Overhaul the clutch cover components (Chapter 2).
- [ ] Loose clutch centre nut. Causes drum and centre misalignment putting a drag on the engine. Engagement adjustment continually varies. Overhaul the clutch assembly (Chapter 2).

REF•40 Fault Finding

6 Gearchange problems

Doesn't go into gear or lever doesn't return
- [ ] Clutch not disengaging.
- [ ] Selector fork(s) bent or seized due to lack of lubrication. Overhaul the transmission (Chapter 2).
- [ ] Gear(s) stuck on shaft. Most often caused by a lack of lubrication or excessive wear in transmission bearings and bushes. Overhaul the transmission (Chapter 2).
- [ ] Selector drum binding. Caused by lubrication failure or excessive wear. Replace the drum and bearings (Chapter 2).
- [ ] Gearchange lever return spring weak or broken (Chapter 2).
- [ ] Gearchange lever broken. Splines stripped out of lever or shaft, caused by allowing the lever to get loose or from dropping the machine. Replace necessary parts (Chapter 2).
- [ ] Gearchange mechanism stopper arm broken or worn. Full engagement and rotary movement of selector drum results. Replace the arm (Chapter 2).
- [ ] Stopper arm spring broken. Allows arm to float, causing sporadic selector operation. Replace spring (Chapter 2).

Jumps out of gear
- [ ] Selector fork(s) worn. Overhaul the transmission (Chapter 2).
- [ ] Gear groove(s) worn in selector drum. Overhaul the transmission (Chapter 2).
- [ ] Gear dogs or dog slots worn or damaged. The gears should be inspected and replaced. No attempt should be made to service the worn parts.

Overselects
- [ ] Stopper arm spring weak or broken (Chapter 2).
- [ ] Gearchange shaft return spring post broken or distorted (Chapter 2).

7 Abnormal engine noise

Knocking or pinking
- [ ] Carbon build-up on the piston and in the combustion the chamber. Remove the cylinder head and clean the piston and combustion chamber (Chapter 2).
- [ ] Incorrect or poor quality fuel. Old or improper fuel can cause detonation. This causes the piston to rattle, thus the knocking or pinking sound. Drain the old fuel and always use the recommended grade fuel (Chapter 4).
- [ ] Spark plug heat range incorrect. Uncontrolled detonation indicates that the plug heat range is too hot. The plug in effect becomes a glow plug, raising cylinder temperatures. Install the proper heat range plug (Chapter 1).
- [ ] Fuel injection system fault (Chapter 4).

Piston slap or rattling
- [ ] Cylinder-to-piston clearance excessive. Inspect and overhaul top-end parts (Chapter 2).
- [ ] Connecting rod bent. Caused by over-revving, piston seizure or broken valve. Replace the damaged parts (Chapter 2).
- [ ] Piston pin or piston pin bore worn or seized from wear or lack of lubrication. Replace damaged parts (Chapter 2).
- [ ] Piston ring(s) worn, broken or sticking. Overhaul the top-end (Chapter 2).
- [ ] Piston seizure damage. Usually from lack of lubrication or overheating. Replace the piston and rebore the cylinder, as necessary (Chapter 2).
- [ ] Connecting rod small or big-end clearance excessive. Caused by excessive wear or lack of lubrication. Replace worn parts.

Valve noise
- [ ] Incorrect valve clearances. Adjust the clearances by referring to Chapter 1.
- [ ] Valve spring broken or weak. Renew the valve springs as a set (Chapter 2).
- [ ] Camshaft, camshaft bearings or cylinder head worn or damaged. Lack of lubrication at high rpm is usually the cause of damage. Insufficient oil or failure to change the oil at the recommended intervals are the chief causes (Chapter 2).

Other noise
- [ ] Cylinder head gasket leaking.
- [ ] Exhaust pipe leaking at cylinder head connection. Caused by improper fit of pipe or loose exhaust flange. Renew the seal and ensure all exhaust fasteners are tightened evenly. Failure to do this will lead to a leak (Chapter 4).
- [ ] Crankshaft runout excessive. Caused by a bent crankshaft (from over-revving) or damage from an upper cylinder component failure.
- [ ] Engine mounting bolts loose. Tighten all engine mount bolts to the specified torque (Chapter 2).
- [ ] Crankshaft bearings worn (Chapter 2).
- [ ] Cam chain tensioner defective. Replace according to the procedure in Chapter 2.
- [ ] Cam chain, sprockets or guides worn (Chapter 2).

Fault Finding REF•41

8 Abnormal driveline noise

Clutch noise
- ☐ Clutch housing/friction plate clearance excessive (Chapter 2).
- ☐ Loose or damaged clutch pressure plate and/or bolts (Chapter 2).

Transmission noise
- ☐ Bearings worn. Also includes the possibility that the shafts are worn. Overhaul the transmission (Chapter 2).
- ☐ Gears worn or chipped (Chapter 2).
- ☐ Metal chips jammed in gear teeth. Probably pieces from a broken clutch, gear or selector mechanism that were picked up by the gears. This will cause early bearing failure (Chapter 2).
- ☐ Engine oil level too low. Causes a howl from transmission. Also affects engine power and clutch operation (*Pre-ride checks*).

Final drive noise
- ☐ Chain not adjusted properly (Chapter 1).
- ☐ Front or rear sprocket loose. Tighten fasteners (Chapter 6).
- ☐ Sprocket(s) worn. Renew sprockets and chain as a set (Chapter 6).
- ☐ Rear sprocket warped. Replace (Chapter 6).
- ☐ Sprocket coupling worn. Check coupling, dampers and bearing (Chapter 6).

9 Abnormal frame and suspension noise

Front end noise
- ☐ Low oil level or improper viscosity oil in forks. This can sound like spurting and is usually accompanied by irregular fork action (Chapter 5).
- ☐ Fork spring weak or broken. Makes a clicking or scraping sound. Fork oil, when drained, will have a lot of metal particles in it (Chapter 5).
- ☐ Steering head bearings loose or damaged. Clicks when braking. Check and adjust or replace as necessary (Chapters 1 and 5).
- ☐ Fork clamp bolts loose. Make sure all fork clamp bolts are tightened to the specified torque (Chapter 5).
- ☐ Fork tube bent. Good possibility if machine has been in an accident. Have both tubes checked for runout. Replace defective tube(s) with a new one (Chapter 5).
- ☐ Front axle loose. Tighten to the specified torque (Chapter 6).

Shock absorber noise
- ☐ Fluid level incorrect caused by defective seal. Rear shock will be covered with oil. Replace both shocks (Chapter 5).
- ☐ Defective shock absorber with internal damage. This is in the body of the shock and can't be remedied – renew the shocks as a pair (Chapter 5).
- ☐ Bent or damaged shock body. Replace the shocks (Chapter 5).

Brake noise (front)
- ☐ Worn brake pads – if there is no friction material left there will be a metal-on-metal grinding sound, and the disc will be damaged (Chapter 1).
- ☐ Squeal caused by dust on brake pads. Usually found in combination with glazed pads. Clean using brake cleaning solvent (Chapter 6).
- ☐ Contamination of brake pads. Oil or brake fluid causing brake to chatter or squeal. Fit a new set of pads (Chapter 6).
- ☐ Pads glazed. Caused by excessive heat from prolonged use or from contamination. A very fine flat file can be used to roughen the pad surfaces, but pad replacement is recommended as a cure (Chapter 6).
- ☐ Disc warped. Can cause a chattering, clicking or intermittent squeal. Usually accompanied by a pulsating lever and uneven braking. Replace the disc (Chapter 6).
- ☐ Loose or worn wheel bearings. Check and replace as needed (Chapter 6).

Brake noise (rear)
- ☐ Accumulation of dust inside brake drum. Braking efficiency may also be affected. Remove rear wheel and clean drum.
- ☐ Worn brake shoes – if there is no friction material left there will be a metal-on-metal grinding sound, and the brake drum will be damaged (Chapter 1).
- ☐ Loose or worn wheel bearings. Check and replace as needed (Chapter 6).

10 Excessive exhaust smoke

White smoke
- [ ] Piston oil control ring worn. The ring(s) may be broken or damaged, causing oil from the crankcase to be pulled past the piston into the combustion chamber. Replace the piston rings as a set (Chapter 2).
- [ ] Cylinder worn or scored. Caused by overheating or oil starvation. The cylinder will have to be rebored and a new piston and rings installed.
- [ ] Valve oil seal damaged or worn. Replace oil seals with new ones (Chapter 2).
- [ ] Valve guide worn. Perform a complete valve job (Chapter 2).
- [ ] Engine oil level too high, which causes the oil to be forced past the rings. Drain oil to the proper level (Chapter 1 and *Pre-ride checks*).
- [ ] Head gasket broken between oil return and cylinder. Causes oil to be pulled into the combustion chamber. Replace the head gasket and check the head for warpage (Chapter 2).
- [ ] Abnormal crankcase pressurisation, which forces oil past the rings. Clogged breather or hose usually the cause (Chapter 2).

Black smoke
- [ ] Air filter clogged. Renew the element (Chapter 1).
- [ ] Fuel injection system malfunction (Chapter 4).

Brown smoke
- [ ] Air filter poorly sealed or not installed (Chapter 1).
- [ ] Fuel flow insufficient. Fuel pump faulty or its filter is blocked (see Chapter 4). Fuel injector clogged. Either a very bad batch of fuel with an unusual additive has been used, or some other foreign material has entered the tank. Check the fuel pressure and delivery (Chapter 4).
- [ ] Intake manifold loose (Chapter 4).
- [ ] Fuel injection system malfunction (Chapter 4).

11 Poor handling or stability

Handlebar hard to turn
- [ ] Steering stem nut too tight (Chapter 5).
- [ ] Bearings damaged. Roughness can be felt as the bars are turned from side-to-side (Chapter 1). Replace bearings and races (Chapter 5).
- [ ] Races dented or worn. Denting results from wear in only one position (e.g. straight-ahead), from a collision or hitting a pothole or from crashing the machine. Replace races and bearings (Chapter 5).
- [ ] Steering stem lubrication inadequate. Causes are grease getting hard from age or being washed out by high pressure washers. Disassemble steering head and grease the bearings (Chapter 5).
- [ ] Steering stem bent. Caused by a collision, hitting a pothole or by crashing the machine. Replace damaged part. Don't try to straighten the steering stem (Chapter 5).
- [ ] Front tyre air pressure too low (*Pre-ride checks*).

Handlebar shakes or vibrates excessively
- [ ] Tyres worn or out of balance (*Pre-ride checks*).
- [ ] Swingarm bushes worn (Chapter 5).
- [ ] Wheel rim(s) warped or damaged. Inspect wheels for runout (Chapter 6).
- [ ] Wheel bearings worn. Worn front or rear wheel bearings can cause poor tracking. Worn front bearings will cause wobble (Chapters 1 and 6).
- [ ] Handlebar clamp bolts loose (Chapter 5).
- [ ] Steering stem nut or fork clamp bolts loose. Tighten them to the specified torque (Chapter 5).
- [ ] Engine mounting bolts loose. Will cause excessive vibration with increased engine rpm (Chapter 2).

Handlebar pulls to one side
- [ ] Frame bent. Definitely suspect this if the machine has been crashed. May or may not be accompanied by cracking near the bend. Replace the frame (Chapter 5).
- [ ] Wheel out of alignment. Caused by improper location of axle spacers (Chapter 6) or from bent steering stem or frame (Chapter 5). Check wheel alignment (Chapter 6).
- [ ] Swingarm bent or twisted. Caused by age (metal fatigue) or impact damage. Replace the swingarm (Chapter 5).
- [ ] Steering stem bent. Caused by a collision, hitting a pothole or by crashing the machine. Replace damaged part. Don't try to straighten the steering stem (Chapter 5).
- [ ] Fork leg bent. Disassemble the forks and replace the damaged parts (Chapter 5).
- [ ] Fork oil level uneven. Caused by leaking oil seals. Renew seals and fill forks to the correct level (Chapter 5).

Poor shock absorbing qualities
- [ ] Too hard:
    a) Fork oil level too high (Chapter 5).
    b) Fork oil viscosity too thick. Use a lighter oil (see the Specifications in Chapter 5).
    c) Fork tube bent. Causes a harsh, sticking feeling (Chapter 5).
    d) Fork internal damage (Chapter 5).
    e) Rear shock shaft or body bent or damaged (Chapter 5).
    f) Rear shock internal damage.
    g) Tyre pressure too high (*Pre-ride checks*).
- [ ] Too soft:
    a) Fork or shock oil insufficient and/or leaking (Chapter 5).
    b) Fork oil level too low (Chapter 5).
    c) Fork oil viscosity too thin (Chapter 5).
    d) Fork springs weak or broken (Chapter 5).
    e) Rear shock internal damage or leakage (Chapter 5).
    f) Rear shock spring weak or broken (Chapter 5).

Fault Finding REF•43

12 Braking problems

Brakes are spongy or don't hold (disc brake)
- [ ] Air in brake line or brake fluid leak. Caused by inattention to master cylinder fluid level or by leakage. Locate problem and bleed brake (Chapter 6).
- [ ] Pads or disc worn (Chapters 1 and 6).
- [ ] Contaminated pads. Caused by contamination with oil, grease, brake fluid, etc. Replace pads. Clean disc thoroughly with brake cleaner (Chapter 6).
- [ ] Brake fluid deteriorated. Fluid is old or contaminated. Drain system, replenish with new fluid and bleed the system (Chapter 6).
- [ ] Master cylinder internal parts worn or damaged causing fluid to bypass (Chapter 6).
- [ ] Master cylinder bore scratched by foreign material or broken spring. Repair or replace master cylinder (Chapter 6).
- [ ] Disc warped. Replace disc (Chapter 6).

Brake doesn't hold (drum brake)
- [ ] Brake incorrectly adjusted (Chapter 1).
- [ ] Brake shoes worn. Renew shoes (Chapter 6).

Brake lever pulsates (disc brake)
- [ ] Disc warped. Replace disc (Chapter 6).
- [ ] Wheel axle bent. Replace axle (Chapter 6).
- [ ] Brake caliper bolts loose (Chapter 6).
- [ ] Wheel warped or otherwise damaged (Chapter 6).
- [ ] Wheel bearings damaged or worn (Chapter 6).

Brake pedal pulsates (drum brake)
- [ ] Brake drum out of round. Renew rear wheel or seek advice on having the drum skimmed (Chapter 6).
- [ ] Wheel bearings damaged or worn (Chapter 6).

Brakes drag (disc brake)
- [ ] Master cylinder piston seized. Caused by wear or damage to piston or cylinder bore (Chapter 6).
- [ ] Lever/pedal balky or stuck. Check pivot and lubricate (Chapter 5).
- [ ] Brake caliper piston seized in bore. Caused by wear or ingestion of dirt past deteriorated seal (Chapter 6).
- [ ] Brake caliper slider pins damaged or sticking, causing caliper to bind. Lube the slider pins (Chapter 6).
- [ ] Brake pad damaged. Pad material separated from backing plate. Usually caused by faulty manufacturing process or from contact with chemicals. Replace pads (Chapter 6).
- [ ] Pads improperly installed (Chapter 6).

Brakes drag (drum brake)
- [ ] Brake pedal freeplay insufficient (Chapter 1).
- [ ] Brake shoe springs weak or broken (Chapter 6).
- [ ] Brake shoe operating cam sticking due to lack of lubrication (Chapter 6).

13 Electrical problems

Battery dead or weak
- [ ] Battery faulty or worn out. Check the terminal voltage and renew battery if recharging doesn't work (Chapter 8).
- [ ] Battery leads making poor contact. Clean and reconnect (Chapter 8).
- [ ] Load excessive. Caused by addition of high wattage lights or other electrical accessories.
- [ ] Ignition switch defective. Switch either earths internally or fails to shut off system. Replace the switch (Chapter 8).
- [ ] Regulator/rectifier defective (Chapter 8).
- [ ] Alternator stator coil open or shorted (Chapter 8).
- [ ] Wiring faulty. Wiring earthed or connections loose in ignition, charging or lighting circuits (Chapter 8).

Battery overcharged
- [ ] Regulator/rectifier defective. Overcharging is noticed when battery gets excessively warm (Chapter 8).
- [ ] Battery defective. Replace battery with a new one (Chapter 8).
- [ ] Battery amperage too low, wrong type or size. Install manufacturer's specified amp-hour battery to handle charging load (Chapter 8).

Technical Terms Explained

A

ABS (Anti-lock braking system) A system, usually electronically controlled, that senses incipient wheel lockup during braking and relieves hydraulic pressure at wheel which is about to skid.
Aftermarket Components suitable for the motorcycle, but not produced by the motorcycle manufacturer.
Allen key A hexagonal wrench which fits into a recessed hexagonal hole.
Alternating current (ac) Current produced by an alternator. Requires converting to direct current by a rectifier for charging purposes.
Alternator Converts mechanical energy from the engine into electrical energy to charge the battery and power the electrical system.
Ampere (amp) A unit of measurement for the flow of electrical current. Current = Volts ÷ Ohms.
Ampere-hour (Ah) Measure of battery capacity.
Angle-tightening A torque expressed in degrees. Often follows a conventional tightening torque for cylinder head or main bearing fasteners **(see illustration)**.

Angle-tightening cylinder head bolts

Antifreeze A substance (usually ethylene glycol) mixed with water, and added to the cooling system, to prevent freezing of the coolant in winter. Antifreeze also contains chemicals to inhibit corrosion and the formation of rust and other deposits that would tend to clog the radiator and coolant passages and reduce cooling efficiency.
Anti-dive System attached to the fork lower leg (slider) to prevent fork dive when braking hard.
Anti-seize compound A coating that reduces the risk of seizing on fasteners that are subjected to high temperatures, such as exhaust clamp bolts and nuts.
API American Petroleum Institute. A quality standard for 4-stroke motor oils.
Asbestos A natural fibrous mineral with great heat resistance, commonly used in the composition of brake friction materials. Asbestos is a health hazard and the dust created by brake systems should never be inhaled or ingested.
ATF Automatic Transmission Fluid. Often used in front forks.
ATU Automatic Timing Unit. Mechanical device for advancing the ignition timing on early engines.
ATV All Terrain Vehicle. Often called a Quad.
Axial play Side-to-side movement.
Axle A shaft on which a wheel revolves. Also known as a spindle.

B

Backlash The amount of movement between meshed components when one component is held still. Usually applies to gear teeth.
Ball bearing A bearing consisting of a hardened inner and outer race with hardened steel balls between the two races.
Bearings Used between two working surfaces to prevent wear of the components and a build-up of heat. Four types of bearing are commonly used on motorcycles: plain shell bearings, ball bearings, tapered roller bearings and needle roller bearings.
Bevel gears Used to turn the drive through 90°. Typical applications are shaft final drive and camshaft drive **(see illustration)**.

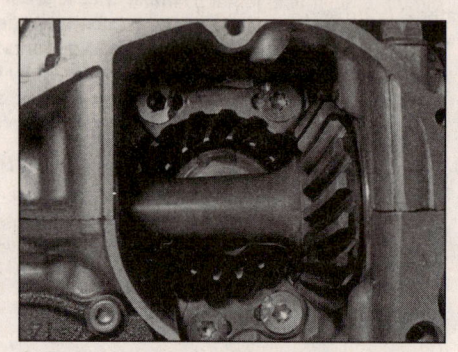

Bevel gears are used to turn the drive through 90°

BHP Brake Horsepower. The British measurement for engine power output. Power output is now usually expressed in kilowatts (kW).
Bias-belted tyre Similar construction to radial tyre, but with outer belt running at an angle to the wheel rim.
Big-end bearing The bearing in the end of the connecting rod that's attached to the crankshaft.
Bleeding The process of removing air from an hydraulic system via a bleed nipple or bleed screw.
Bottom-end A description of an engine's crankcase components and all components contained there-in.
BTDC Before Top Dead Centre in terms of piston position. Ignition timing is often expressed in terms of degrees or millimetres BTDC.
Bush A cylindrical metal or rubber component used between two moving parts.
Burr Rough edge left on a component after machining or as a result of excessive wear.

C

Cam chain The chain which takes drive from the crankshaft to the camshaft(s).
Canister The main component in an evaporative emission control system (California market only); contains activated charcoal granules to trap vapours from the fuel system rather than allowing them to vent to the atmosphere.
Castellated Resembling the parapets along the top of a castle wall. For example, a castellated wheel axle or spindle nut.
Catalytic converter A device in the exhaust system of some machines which converts certain pollutants in the exhaust gases into less harmful substances.
Charging system Description of the components which charge the battery, ie the alternator, rectifer and regulator.
Circlip A ring-shaped clip used to prevent endwise movement of cylindrical parts and shafts. An internal circlip is installed in a groove in a housing; an external circlip fits into a groove on the outside of a cylindrical piece such as a shaft. Also known as a snap-ring.
Clearance The amount of space between two parts. For example, between a piston and a cylinder, between a bearing and a journal, etc.
Coil spring A spiral of elastic steel found in various sizes throughout a vehicle, for example as a springing medium in the suspension and in the valve train.
Compression Reduction in volume, and increase in pressure and temperature, of a gas, caused by squeezing it into a smaller space.
Compression damping Controls the speed the suspension compresses when hitting a bump.
Compression ratio The relationship between cylinder volume when the piston is at top dead centre and cylinder volume when the piston is at bottom dead centre.
Continuity The uninterrupted path in the flow of electricity. Little or no measurable resistance.
Continuity tester Self-powered bleeper or test light which indicates continuity.
Cp Candlepower. Bulb rating commonly found on US motorcycles.
Crossply tyre Tyre plies arranged in a criss-cross pattern. Usually four or six plies used, hence 4PR or 6PR in tyre size codes.
Cush drive Rubber damper segments fitted between the rear wheel and final drive sprocket to absorb transmission shocks **(see illustration)**.

Cush drive rubbers dampen out transmission shocks

D

Degree disc Calibrated disc for measuring piston position. Expressed in degrees.
Dial gauge Clock-type gauge with adapters for measuring runout and piston position. Expressed in mm or inches.
Diaphragm The rubber membrane in a master cylinder or carburettor which seals the upper chamber.
Diaphragm spring A single sprung plate often used in clutches.
Direct current (dc) Current produced by a dc generator.

Technical Terms Explained REF•45

Decarbonisation The process of removing carbon deposits - typically from the combustion chamber, valves and exhaust port/system.
Detonation Destructive and damaging explosion of fuel/air mixture in combustion chamber instead of controlled burning.
Diode An electrical valve which only allows current to flow in one direction. Commonly used in rectifiers and starter interlock systems.
Disc valve (or rotary valve) A induction system used on some two-stroke engines.
Double-overhead camshaft (DOHC) An engine that uses two overhead camshafts, one for the intake valves and one for the exhaust valves.
Drivebelt A toothed belt used to transmit drive to the rear wheel on some motorcycles. A drivebelt has also been used to drive the camshafts. Drivebelts are usually made of Kevlar.
Driveshaft Any shaft used to transmit motion. Commonly used when referring to the final driveshaft on shaft drive motorcycles.

E

Earth return The return path of an electrical circuit, utilising the motorcycle's frame.
ECU (Electronic Control Unit) A computer which controls (for instance) an ignition system, or an anti-lock braking system.
EGO Exhaust Gas Oxygen sensor. Sometimes called a Lambda sensor.
Electrolyte The fluid in a lead-acid battery.
EMS (Engine Management System) A computer controlled system which manages the fuel injection and the ignition systems in an integrated fashion.
Endfloat The amount of lengthways movement between two parts. As applied to a crankshaft, the distance that the crankshaft can move side-to-side in the crankcase.
Endless chain A chain having no joining link. Common use for cam chains and final drive chains.
EP (Extreme Pressure) Oil type used in locations where high loads are applied, such as between gear teeth.
Evaporative emission control system Describes a charcoal filled canister which stores fuel vapours from the tank rather than allowing them to vent to the atmosphere. Usually only fitted to California models and referred to as an EVAP system.
Expansion chamber Section of two-stroke engine exhaust system so designed to improve engine efficiency and boost power.

F

Feeler blade or gauge A thin strip or blade of hardened steel, ground to an exact thickness, used to check or measure clearances between parts.
Final drive Description of the drive from the transmission to the rear wheel. Usually by chain or shaft, but sometimes by belt.
Firing order The order in which the engine cylinders fire, or deliver their power strokes, beginning with the number one cylinder.
Flooding Term used to describe a high fuel level in the carburettor float chambers, leading to fuel overflow. Also refers to excess fuel in the combustion chamber due to incorrect starting technique.
Free length The no-load state of a component when measured. Clutch, valve and fork spring lengths are measured at rest, without any preload.
Freeplay The amount of travel before any action takes place. The looseness in a linkage, or an assembly of parts, between the initial application of force and actual movement. For example, the distance the rear brake pedal moves before the rear brake is actuated.
Fuel injection The fuel/air mixture is metered electronically and directed into the engine intake ports (indirect injection) or into the cylinders (direct injection). Sensors supply information on engine speed and conditions.
Fuel/air mixture The charge of fuel and air going into the engine. See **Stoichiometric ratio**.
Fuse An electrical device which protects a circuit against accidental overload. The typical fuse contains a soft piece of metal which is calibrated to melt at a predetermined current flow (expressed as amps) and break the circuit.

G

Gap The distance the spark must travel in jumping from the centre electrode to the side electrode in a spark plug. Also refers to the distance between the ignition rotor and the pickup coil in an electronic ignition system.
Gasket Any thin, soft material - usually cork, cardboard, asbestos or soft metal - installed between two metal surfaces to ensure a good seal. For instance, the cylinder head gasket seals the joint between the block and the cylinder head.
Gauge An instrument panel display used to monitor engine conditions. A gauge with a movable pointer on a dial or a fixed scale is an analogue gauge. A gauge with a numerical readout is called a digital gauge.
Gear ratios The drive ratio of a pair of gears in a gearbox, calculated on their number of teeth.
Glaze-busting see **Honing**
Grinding Process for renovating the valve face and valve seat contact area in the cylinder head.
Gudgeon pin The shaft which connects the connecting rod small-end with the piston. Often called a piston pin or wrist pin.

H

Helical gears Gear teeth are slightly curved and produce less gear noise that straight-cut gears. Often used for primary drives.

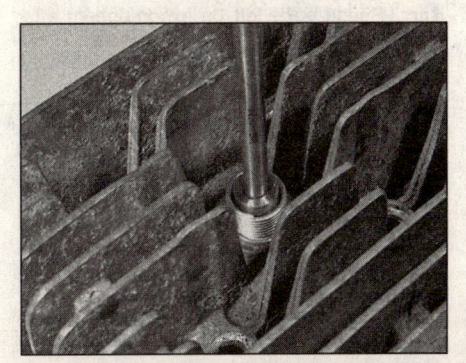

Installing a Helicoil thread insert in a cylinder head

Helicoil A thread insert repair system. Commonly used as a repair for stripped spark plug threads **(see illustration)**.
Honing A process used to break down the glaze on a cylinder bore (also called glaze-busting). Can also be carried out to roughen a rebored cylinder to aid ring bedding-in.
HT (High Tension) Description of the electrical circuit from the secondary winding of the ignition coil to the spark plug.
Hydraulic A liquid filled system used to transmit pressure from one component to another. Common uses on motorcycles are brakes and clutches.
Hydrometer An instrument for measuring the specific gravity of a lead-acid battery.
Hygroscopic Water absorbing. In motorcycle applications, braking efficiency will be reduced if DOT 3 or 4 hydraulic fluid absorbs water from the air - care must be taken to keep new brake fluid in tightly sealed containers.

I

lbf ft Pounds-force feet. An imperial unit of torque. Sometimes written as ft-lbs.
lbf in Pound-force inch. An imperial unit of torque, applied to components where a very low torque is required. Sometimes written as in-lbs.
IC Abbreviation for Integrated Circuit.
Ignition advance Means of increasing the timing of the spark at higher engine speeds. Done by mechanical means (ATU) on early engines or electronically by the ignition control unit on later engines.
Ignition timing The moment at which the spark plug fires, expressed in the number of crankshaft degrees before the piston reaches the top of its stroke, or in the number of millimetres before the piston reaches the top of its stroke.
Infinity (∞) Description of an open-circuit electrical state, where no continuity exists.
Inverted forks (upside down forks) The sliders or lower legs are held in the yokes and the fork tubes or stanchions are connected to the wheel axle (spindle). Less unsprung weight and stiffer construction than conventional forks.

J

JASO Quality standard for 2-stroke oils.
Joule The unit of electrical energy.
Journal The bearing surface of a shaft.

K

Kickstart Mechanical means of turning the engine over for starting purposes. Only usually fitted to mopeds, small capacity motorcycles and off-road motorcycles.
Kill switch Handebar-mounted switch for emergency ignition cut-out. Cuts the ignition circuit on all models, and additionally prevent starter motor operation on others.
km Symbol for kilometre.
kmh Abbreviation for kilometres per hour.

L

Lambda (λ) sensor A sensor fitted in the exhaust system to measure the exhaust gas oxygen content (excess air factor).

Technical Terms Explained

Lapping see **Grinding**.
LCD Abbreviation for Liquid Crystal Display.
LED Abbreviation for Light Emitting Diode.
Liner A steel cylinder liner inserted in a aluminium alloy cylinder block.
Locknut A nut used to lock an adjustment nut, or other threaded component, in place.
Lockstops The lugs on the lower triple clamp (yoke) which abut those on the frame, preventing handlebar-to-fuel tank contact.
Lockwasher A form of washer designed to prevent an attaching nut from working loose.
LT Low Tension Description of the electrical circuit from the power supply to the primary winding of the ignition coil.

M

Main bearings The bearings between the crankshaft and crankcase.
Maintenance-free (MF) battery A sealed battery which cannot be topped up.
Manometer Mercury-filled calibrated tubes used to measure intake tract vacuum. Used to synchronise carburettors on multi-cylinder engines.
Micrometer A precision measuring instrument that measures component outside diameters **(see illustration)**.

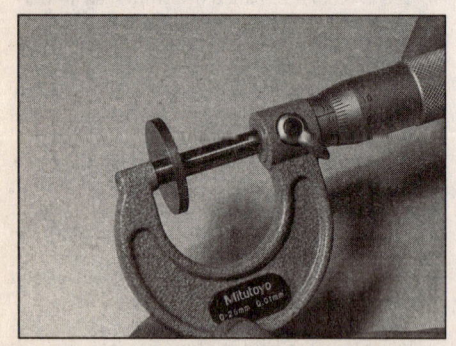

Tappet shims are measured with a micrometer

MON (Motor Octane Number) A measure of a fuel's resistance to knock.
Monograde oil An oil with a single viscosity, eg SAE80W.
Monoshock A single suspension unit linking the swingarm or suspension linkage to the frame.
mph Abbreviation for miles per hour.
Multigrade oil Having a wide viscosity range (eg 10W40). The W stands for Winter, thus the viscosity ranges from SAE10 when cold to SAE40 when hot.
Multimeter An electrical test instrument with the capability to measure voltage, current and resistance. Some meters also incorporate a continuity tester and buzzer.

N

Needle roller bearing Inner race of caged needle rollers and hardened outer race. Examples of uncaged needle rollers can be found on some engines. Commonly used in rear suspension applications and in two-stroke engines.
Nm Newton metres.
NOx Oxides of Nitrogen. A common toxic pollutant emitted by petrol engines at higher temperatures.

O

Octane The measure of a fuel's resistance to knock.
OE (Original Equipment) Relates to components fitted to a motorcycle as standard or replacement parts supplied by the motorcycle manufacturer.
Ohm The unit of electrical resistance. Ohms = Volts ÷ Current.
Ohmmeter An instrument for measuring electrical resistance.
Oil cooler System for diverting engine oil outside of the engine to a radiator for cooling purposes.
Oil injection A system of two-stroke engine lubrication where oil is pump-fed to the engine in accordance with throttle position.
Open-circuit An electrical condition where there is a break in the flow of electricity - no continuity (high resistance).
O-ring A type of sealing ring made of a special rubber-like material; in use, the O-ring is compressed into a groove to provide the sealing action.
Oversize (OS) Term used for piston and ring size options fitted to a rebored cylinder.
Overhead cam (sohc) engine An engine with single camshaft located on top of the cylinder head.
Overhead valve (ohv) engine An engine with the valves located in the cylinder head, but with the camshaft located in the engine block or crankcase.
Oxygen sensor A device installed in the exhaust system which senses the oxygen content in the exhaust and converts this information into an electric current. Also called a Lambda sensor.

P

Plastigauge A thin strip of plastic thread, available in different sizes, used for measuring clearances. For example, a strip of Plastigauge is laid across a bearing journal. The parts are assembled and dismantled; the width of the crushed strip indicates the clearance between journal and bearing.
Polarity Either negative or positive earth (ground), determined by which battery lead is connected to the frame (earth return). Modern motorcycles are usually negative earth.
Pre-ignition A situation where the fuel/air mixture ignites before the spark plug fires. Often due to a hot spot in the combustion chamber caused by carbon build-up. Engine has a tendency to 'run-on'.
Pre-load (suspension) The amount a spring is compressed when in the unloaded state. Preload can be applied by gas, spacer or mechanical adjuster.
Premix The method of engine lubrication on older two-stroke engines. Engine oil is mixed with the petrol in the fuel tank in a specific ratio. The fuel/oil mix is sometimes referred to as "petroil".
Primary drive Description of the drive from the crankshaft to the clutch. Usually by gear or chain.
PS Pfedestärke - a German interpretation of BHP.
PSI Pounds-force per square inch. Imperial measurement of tyre pressure and cylinder pressure measurement.
PTFE Polytetrafluroethylene. A low friction substance.
Pulse secondary air injection system A process of promoting the burning of excess fuel present in the exhaust gases by routing fresh air into the exhaust ports.

Q

Quartz halogen bulb Tungsten filament surrounded by a halogen gas. Typically used for the headlight **(see illustration)**.

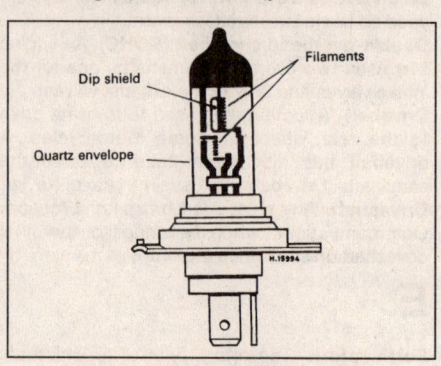

Quartz halogen headlight bulb construction

R

Rack-and-pinion A pinion gear on the end of a shaft that mates with a rack (think of a geared wheel opened up and laid flat). Sometimes used in clutch operating systems.
Radial play Up and down movement about a shaft.
Radial ply tyres Tyre plies run across the tyre (from bead to bead) and around the circumference of the tyre. Less resistant to tread distortion than other tyre types.
Radiator A liquid-to-air heat transfer device designed to reduce the temperature of the coolant in a liquid cooled engine.
Rake A feature of steering geometry - the angle of the steering head in relation to the vertical **(see illustration)**.

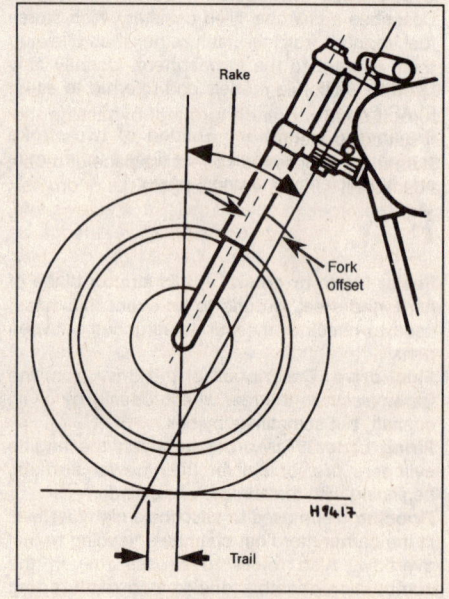

Steering geometry

Technical Terms Explained REF•47

Rebore Providing a new working surface to the cylinder bore by boring out the old surface. Necessitates the use of oversize piston and rings.
Rebound damping A means of controlling the oscillation of a suspension unit spring after it has been compressed. Resists the spring's natural tendency to bounce back after being compressed.
Rectifier Device for converting the ac output of an alternator into dc for battery charging.
Reed valve An induction system commonly used on two-stroke engines.
Regulator Device for maintaining the charging voltage from the generator or alternator within a specified range.
Relay A electrical device used to switch heavy current on and off by using a low current auxiliary circuit.
Resistance Measured in ohms. An electrical component's ability to pass electrical current.
RON (Research Octane Number) A measure of a fuel's resistance to knock.
rpm revolutions per minute.
Runout The amount of wobble (in-and-out movement) of a wheel or shaft as it's rotated. The amount a shaft rotates 'out-of-true'. The out-of-round condition of a rotating part.

S

SAE (Society of Automotive Engineers) A standard for the viscosity of a fluid.
Sealant A liquid or paste used to prevent leakage at a joint. Sometimes used in conjunction with a gasket.
Service limit Term for the point where a component is no longer useable and must be renewed.
Shaft drive A method of transmitting drive from the transmission to the rear wheel.
Shell bearings Plain bearings consisting of two shell halves. Most often used as big-end and main bearings in a four-stroke engine. Often called bearing inserts.
Shim Thin spacer, commonly used to adjust the clearance or relative positions between two parts. For example, shims inserted into or under tappets or followers to control valve clearances. Clearance is adjusted by changing the thickness of the shim.
Short-circuit An electrical condition where current shorts to earth (ground) bypassing the circuit components.
Skimming Process to correct warpage or repair a damaged surface, eg on brake discs or drums.
Slide-hammer A special puller that screws into or hooks onto a component such as a shaft or bearing; a heavy sliding handle on the shaft bottoms against the end of the shaft to knock the component free.
Small-end bearing The bearing in the upper end of the connecting rod at its joint with the gudgeon pin.
Spalling Damage to camshaft lobes or bearing journals shown as pitting of the working surface.
Specific gravity (SG) The state of charge of the electrolyte in a lead-acid battery. A measure of the electrolyte's density compared with water.
Straight-cut gears Common type gear used on gearbox shafts and for oil pump and water pump drives.
Stanchion The inner sliding part of the front forks, held by the yokes. Often called a fork tube.
Stoichiometric ratio The optimum chemical air/fuel ratio for a petrol engine, said to be 14.7 parts of air to 1 part of fuel.
Sulphuric acid The liquid (electrolyte) used in a lead-acid battery. Poisonous and extremely corrosive.
Surface grinding (lapping) Process to correct a warped gasket face, commonly used on cylinder heads.

T

Tapered-roller bearing Tapered inner race of caged needle rollers and separate tapered outer race. Examples of taper roller bearings can be found on steering heads.
Tappet A cylindrical component which transmits motion from the cam to the valve stem, either directly or via a pushrod and rocker arm. Also called a cam follower.
TCS Traction Control System. An electronically-controlled system which senses wheel spin and reduces engine speed accordingly.
TDC Top Dead Centre denotes that the piston is at its highest point in the cylinder.
Thread-locking compound Solution applied to fastener threads to prevent slackening. Select type to suit application.
Thrust washer A washer positioned between two moving components on a shaft. For example, between gear pinions on gearshaft.
Timing chain See **Cam Chain**.
Timing light Stroboscopic lamp for carrying out ignition timing checks with the engine running.
Top-end A description of an engine's cylinder block, head and valve gear components.
Torque Turning or twisting force about a shaft.
Torque setting A prescribed tightness specified by the motorcycle manufacturer to ensure that the bolt or nut is secured correctly. Undertightening can result in the bolt or nut coming loose or a surface not being sealed. Overtightening can result in stripped threads, distortion or damage to the component being retained.
Torx key A six-point wrench.
Tracer A stripe of a second colour applied to a wire insulator to distinguish that wire from another one with the same colour insulator. For example, Br/W is often used to denote a brown insulator with a white tracer.
Trail A feature of steering geometry. Distance from the steering head axis to the tyre's central contact point.
Triple clamps The cast components which extend from the steering head and support the fork stanchions or tubes. Often called fork yokes.
Turbocharger A centrifugal device, driven by exhaust gases, that pressurises the intake air. Normally used to increase the power output from a given engine displacement.
TWI Abbreviation for Tyre Wear Indicator. Indicates the location of the tread depth indicator bars on tyres.

U

Universal joint or U-joint (UJ) A double-pivoted connection for transmitting power from a driving to a driven shaft through an angle. Typically found in shaft drive assemblies.
Unsprung weight Anything not supported by the bike's suspension (ie the wheel, tyres, brakes, final drive and bottom (moving) part of the suspension).

V

Vacuum gauges Clock-type gauges for measuring intake tract vacuum. Used for carburettor synchronisation on multi-cylinder engines.
Valve A device through which the flow of liquid, gas or vacuum may be stopped, started or regulated by a moveable part that opens, shuts or partially obstructs one or more ports or passageways. The intake and exhaust valves in the cylinder head are of the poppet type.
Valve clearance The clearance between the valve tip (the end of the valve stem) and the rocker arm or tappet/follower. The valve clearance is measured when the valve is closed. The correct clearance is important - if too small the valve won't close fully and will burn out, whereas if too large noisy operation will result.
Valve lift The amount a valve is lifted off its seat by the camshaft lobe.
Valve timing The exact setting for the opening and closing of the valves in relation to piston position.
Vernier caliper A precision measuring instrument that measures inside and outside dimensions. Not quite as accurate as a micrometer, but more convenient.
VIN Vehicle Identification Number. Term for the bike's engine and frame numbers.
Viscosity The thickness of a liquid or its resistance to flow.
Volt A unit for expressing electrical "pressure" in a circuit. Volts = current x ohms.

W

Water pump A mechanically-driven device for moving coolant around the engine.
Watt A unit for expressing electrical power. Watts = volts x current.
Wear limit see **Service limit**
Wet liner A liquid-cooled engine design where the pistons run in liners which are directly surrounded by coolant **(see illustration)**.

Wet liner arrangement

Wheelbase Distance from the centre of the front wheel to the centre of the rear wheel.
Wiring harness or loom Describes the electrical wires running the length of the motorcycle and enclosed in tape or plastic sheathing. Wiring coming off the main harness is usually referred to as a sub harness.
Woodruff key A key of semi-circular or square section used to locate a gear to a shaft. Often used to locate the alternator rotor on the crankshaft.
Wrist pin Another name for gudgeon or piston pin.

Index

Note: References throughout this index are in the form - "Chapter number" • "Page number"

A

Acknowledgements – 0•8
Air filter – 1•17
  housing – 4•5
Air temperature sensor – 4•10
Alternator – 8•19

B

Battery – 8•4
Bearing seal lips lubricant – 1•2
Belly fairing – 7•8
Bike spec – 0•9
Bleeding brakes and fluid change – 6•9
Bodywork – 7•1 *et seq*
  fairing – 7•4
  general information – 7•1
  mirrors – 7•3
  mudguards – 7•6, 7•8
  seat cowling – 7•6
  seats – 7•2
  self-tapping screws – 7•1
  side panels – 7•3
  wellnuts – 7•1
  windshield – 7•4
Bolts – 1•16
Brake fluid – 1•2
  change – 1•8, 6•9
  level – 0•14
Brake lever pivot and piston tip lubricant – 1•2
Brake light – 8•6
  switches – 8•10
Brake pedal assembly – 5•2
  freeplay check and adjustment – 1.7
  lubricant – 1•2
Brake/tail light – 8•8
Brakes, wheels and final drive – 6•1 *et seq*
  bleeding brakes and fluid change – 6•9
  brake hose and fittings – 6•9
  brake system – 1•7
  caliper – 6•4
  chain – 6•17
  disc – 6•6
  draining the system for overhaul – 6•10
  drive chain – 6•17
  drum brake – 6•10
  general information – 6•2
  master cylinder – 6•6
  pads – 6•2
  sprockets – 6•16, 6•18, 6•19
  tyres – 6•16
  wheel bearings – 6•14
  wheels – 6•11, 6•12, 6•13
Buying spare parts – 0•11

C

Cables
  clutch – 1•9, 2•26
  lubricant – 1•2, 1•12
  speedometer – 8•12
  throttle – 1•8, 4•15
Caliper – 6•4
  slider pins lubricant – 1•2
Cam chain tensioner – 2•9, 2•32
Camshaft – 2•10
Catalytic converter – 4•17
Centrestand – 5•5
Chain – 0•14, 1•5, 6•17
  lubricant – 1•2
Charging – 8•4
  system testing – 8•18
Clutch – 2•22
  cable – 1•9, 2•26
  lever pivot lubricant – 1•2
  switch – 8•15
Coil (HT) – 3•2
Compression check – 2•5
Connecting rod – 2•36
Continuity checks – 8•2
Conversion factors – REF•26
Crankcase breather – 1•12
Crankcases – 2•35
  separation and reassembly – 2•33
Crankshaft – 2•36
  position sensor – 3•3
Cylinder – 2•16
  compression check – 2•5
Cylinder head
  overhaul – 2•13
  removal and installation – 2•12

D

Disc brake – 1•7, 6•6
Drive chain – 0•14, 1•5, 6•17
  lubricant – 1•2
Drum brake – 1•7, 6•10

E

Earth (ground) checks – 8•3
ECM – 4•12
Electrical system 8•1 *et seq*
  alternator – 8•19
  battery – 8•4
  brake light – 8•6, 8•8, 8•10
  charging system – 8•4, 8•18
  clutch switch – 8•15
  continuity checks – 8•2
  earth (ground) checks – 8•3
  fault finding – 8•2
  fuel gauge – 8•12
  fuses – 8•5
  general information – 8•2
  handlebar switches – 8•13
  headlight – 8•6, 8•7
  horn – 8•13
  ignition safety interlock circuit – 8•14
  ignition switch – 8•12
  instrument cluster – 8•10
  instrument light bulbs – 8•12
  lighting system check – 8•5
  neutral switch – 8•14
  regulator/rectifier – 8•19
  relay – 8•8
  sidelight – 8•6, 8•7
  sidestand switch – 8•14
  speedometer and cable – 8•12
  starter motor – 8•16
  starter relay – 8•15
  starter safety circuit diode – 8•15
  switch continuity checks – 8•3
  tachometer – 8•12
  tail light – 8•6, 8•8
  turn signals – 8•8, 8•9
  voltage checks – 8•3
  warning light bulbs – 8•12
  wiring continuity checks – 8•3
  wiring diagram – 8•20 *et seq*

Index

E

Engine management system – 4•1 et seq
  air filter – 4•5
  catalytic converter – 4•17
  components – 4•9
  ECM – 4•12
  engine management system – 4•7, 4•8, 4•9
  engine oil temperature (EOT) sensor – 4•9
  exhaust system – 4•16
  fault diagnosis – 4•8
  FI warning light – 4•7
  fuel injector – 4•10, 4•14
  fuel level sensor – 4•6
  fuel pressure and delivery check – 4•4
  fuel pump – 4•4
  fuel system – 4•2
  fuel tank – 4•3
  general information – 4•2
  idle air control valve (IACV) – 4•11
  intake air temperature (IAT) sensor – 4•10
  manifold absolute pressure (MAP) sensor – 4•9
  oxygen sensor – 4•10
  throttle body – 4•9, 4•12
  throttle cable – 4•15
  throttle position (TP) sensor – 4•10
  tip over (TO) sensor – 4•11
  warning light – 4•7
Engine numbers – 0•10
Engine oil – 1•2
  change – 1•11
  circulation – 2•6
  level – 0•13
  strainer and filter – 1•16
  temperature sensor – 4•9
Engine wear assessment – 2•5
Engine, clutch and transmission – 2•1 et seq
  cam chain tensioner – 2•9, 2•32
  camshaft and rocker arms – 2•10
  clutch – 2•22, 2•26
  component access – 2•5
  compression check – 2•5
  connecting rod – 2•36
  crankcase – 2•33, 2•35
  crankshaft – 2•36
  cylinder – 2•16
  cylinder head – 2•12, 2•13
  engine wear assessment – 2•5
  gearchange mechanism – 2•27
  general information – 2•5
  input shaft – 2•40
  main bearings – 2•35
  oil circulation – 2•6
  oil pump – 2•20
  operations requiring engine removal – 2•5
  operations with the engine in the frame – 2•5
  output shaft – 2•41
  overhaul – general information – 2•8
  piston – 2•17
  piston rings – 2•19
  primary drive gear – 2•28
  removal and installation – 2•6
  rocker arms – 2•10
  running-in procedure – 2•44
  selector drum and forks – 2•37
  starter clutch and gears – 2•28
  transmission shafts and bearings – 2•38, 2•40
  valve cover – 2•8
  valves – 2•13
Exhaust system – 4•16

F

Fairing panels – 7•4
Fault finding – REF•35 et seq
  engine management system – 4•8
  engine oil temperature (EOT) sensor – 4•9
  intake air temperature (IAT) sensor – 4•10
  manifold absolute pressure (MAP) sensor – 4•9
  throttle body sensor unit – 4•9
  throttle position (TP) sensor – 4•10
  electrical system – 8•2
FI warning light check – 4•7
Filter
  air – 1•17, 4•5
  engine oil – 1•16
Fluids – 1•2
Footrests – 5•2
  pivots lubricant – 1•2
Forks
  oil – 5•1
  oil change – 1•14, 5•8
  overhaul – 5•9
  removal and installation – 5•7
Frame and engine numbers – 0•10
Frame and suspension – 5•1 et seq
  brake pedal assembly – 5•2
  centrestand – 5•5
  footrests – 5•2
  fork oil – 5•1
  forks – 5•7, 5•8, 5•9
  frame – 5•2
  gearchange lever assembly – 5•3
  general information – 5•2
  handlebars – 5•5
  levers – 5•7
  shock absorbers – 5•14
  sidestand – 5•4
  steering head bearings – 5•13
  steering stem – 5•11
  swingarm – 5•15
Fuel system – 0•15, 1•11, 4•2
  delivery check – 4•4
  gauge – 8•12
  injector – 4•10, 4•14
  level sensor – 4•6
  pressure check – 4•4
  pump – 4•4
  tank – 4•3
Fuses – 8•5

G

Gearchange mechanism – 2•27
  lever assembly – 5•3
  lever lubricant – 1•2
  selector drum and forks – 2•37

H

Handlebars – 5•5
  switches – 8•13
Headlight – 8•6, 8•7
  aim – 8•7
  bulbs – 8•6
Horn – 8•13
Hoses and fittings – 6•9
HT coil – 3•2

I

Identification numbers – 0•10
Idle air control valve (IACV) – 4•11
Idle speed – 1•12
Ignition safety interlock circuit – 8•14
Ignition system – 3•1 et seq
  crankshaft position sensor – 3•3
  general information – 3•2
  HT coil – 3•2
  ignition switch – 8•12
  spark plug – 1•2
  system check – 3•2
  timing – 3•4
Injector – 4•10, 4•14
Input shaft – 2•40
Instrument cluster – 8•10
  light bulbs – 8•12
Intake air temperature (IAT) sensor – 4•10
Introduction – 0•4

L

Legal – 0•15
Levers – 5•7
  lubricant – 1•2, 1•13
Lighting and signalling – 0•15
  system check – 8•5
Lubricants and fluids – 1•2, REF•23 et seq

M

Main bearings – 2•35
Maintenance schedule – 1•3
Manifold absolute pressure (MAP) sensor – 4•9
Master cylinder – 6•6
Mirrors – 7•3
Model development – 0•9
MOT test checks – REF•27 et seq
Mudguards
  front – 7•6
  rear – 7•8

N

Neutral switch – 8•14
Nuts – 1•16

Index

O

Oil
  engine – 0•13, 1•2, 1•11, 1•16, 2•6
  fork – 1•14, 5•1
Oil pump – 2•20
Oil strainer/filter – 1•16
Oil temperature sensor – 4•9
Output shaft – 2•41
Oxygen sensor – 4•10

P

Pads – 6•2
Parts – 0•11
Pedal (brake) – 5•2
  lubricant – 1•2
  freeplay check and adjustment – 1.7
Piston – 2•17
Piston rings – 2•19
Pre-ride checks – 0•13 et seq
Primary drive gear – 2•28

R

Regulator/rectifier – 8•19
Relays
  circuit check – 8•16
  starter – 8•15
  turn signal – 8•8
Rocker arms – 2•10
Routine maintenance and servicing – 1•1 et seq
  air filter – 1•17
  bolts – 1•16
  brake fluid – 1•8
  brake system – 1•7
  cables – 1•8, 1•9, 1•12
  chain and sprockets – 1•5
  clutch cable – 1•9
  component locations – 1•4
  crankcase breather – 1•12
  disc brake – 1•7
  drive chain and sprockets – 1•5
  drum brake – 1•7
  engine oil – 1•11
  engine oil strainer and filter – 1•16
  fluids – 1•2
  fork oil – 1•14
  fuel system – 1•11
  idle speed – 1•12
  lever pivots lubrication – 1•13
  lubricants and fluids – 1•2
  maintenance schedule – 1•3
  nuts and bolts – 1•16
  oil strainer and filter – 1•16
  plugs – 1•8
  sidestand and starter safety circuit – 1•13
  spark plugs – 1•8
  sprockets – 1•5
  stand and lever pivots lubrication – 1•13
  starter safety circuit – 1•13
  steering head bearings – 1•15
  suspension – 1•13, 1•14
  throttle cable – 1•8
  valve clearances – 1•10
  wheels and wheel bearings – 1•14
Running-in procedure – 2•44

S

Safety First! – 0•12, 0•15
Seal lips lubricant – 1•2
Seats – 7•2
  cowling – 7•6
Security – REF•20 et seq
Selector drum and forks – 2•37
Self-tapping screws – 7•1
Shock absorbers – 5•14
Side panels – 7•3
Sidelight – 8•6
  bulbs – 8•7
Sidestand – 5•4
  safety circuit – 1•13
  switch – 8•14
Signalling – 0•15
Spare parts – 0•11
Spark plug – 1•2, 1•8
Speedometer and cable – 8•12
Sprockets – 1•5, 6•18
  coupling bearing – 6•16
  coupling dampers – 6•19
Stands – 5•4
  pivots lubricant – 1•2, 1•13
Starter clutch and gears – 2•28
Starter motor
  overhaul – 8•16
  removal and installation – 8•16
  relay – 8•15
  safety circuit – 1•13, 8•15
Steering – 0•14
Steering head bearings – 1•15, 5•13
  lubricant – 1•2
Steering stem – 5•11
Storage – REF•32 et seq
Suspension – 0•14, 1•13
Swingarm – 5•15
Switches
  brake light – 8•10
  clutch – 8•15
  continuity checks – 8•3
  handlebar – 8•13
  ignition – 8•12
  neutral – 8•14
  sidestand – 8•14

T

Tachometer – 8•12
Tail light – 8•6, 8•8
  bulb – 8•8
Technical terms explained – REF•44 et seq
Throttle body – 4•12
  sensor unit – 4•9
Throttle cable – 1•8, 4•15
Throttle position (TP) sensor – 4•10
Throttle twistgrip lubricant – 1•2
Timing (ignition) – 3•4
Tip over (TO) sensor – 4•11
Tools and working tips – REF•2 et seq
Transmission shafts and bearings – 2•38
  overhaul – 2•40
Turn signal assemblies – 8•9
  bulbs – 8•9
  circuit check – 8•8
Twistgrip lubricant – 1•2
Tyres – 6•16
  care – 0•15
  pressures – 0•15
  tread depth – 0•15

V

Valves
  clearances – 1•2, 1•10
  overhaul – 2•13
Valve cover – 2•8
Voltage checks – 8•3

W

Warning light
  bulbs – 8•12
  check – 4•7
Wellnuts – 7•1
Wheels – 1•14
  alignment – 6•11
  bearings – 1•15, 6•14
  front – 6•12
  inspection and repair – 6•11
  rear – 6•13
Windshield – 7•4
Wiring continuity checks – 8•3
Wiring diagram – 8•20 et seq

Haynes Motorcycle Manuals – The Complete List

Title		Book No
APRILIA RS50 (99 – 06) & RS125 (93 – 06)		4298
Aprilia RSV1000 Mille (98 – 03)	♦	4255
Aprilia SR50		4755
BMW 2-valve Twins (70 -96)	♦	0249
BMW F650	♦	4761
BMW K100 & 75 2-valve models (83 - 96)	♦	1373
BMW F800 (F650) Twins (06 – 10)	♦	4872
BMW R850, 1100 & 1150 4-valve Twins (93 – 06)	♦	3466
BMW R1200 (04 – 09)	♦	4598
BMW R1200 dohc Twins (10 – 12)	♦	4925
BSA Bantam (48 – 71)		0117
BSA Unit Singles (58 – 72)		0127
BSA Pre-unit Singles (54 – 61)		0326
BSA A7 & A10 Twins (47 – 62)		0121
BSA A50 & A65 Twins (62 – 73)		0155
CHINESE, Taiwanese & Korean Scooters		4768
Chinese, Taiwanese & Korean 125cc motorcycles		4781
Pulse/Pioneer Adrenaline, Sinnis Apache, Superbyke RMR (07 – 14)	◇♦	5750
DUCATI 600, 620, 750 & 900 2-valve V-twins (91 – 05)	♦	3290
Ducati Mk III & Desmo singles (69 – 76)	◇	0445
Ducati 748, 916 & 996 4-valve V-twins (94 – 01)	♦	3756
GILERA Runner, DNA, Ice & SKP/Stalker (97 – 11)		4163
HARLEY-DAVIDSON Sportsters (70 – 10)	♦	2534
Harley-Davidson Shovelhead & Evolution Big Twins (70 -99)	♦	2536
Harley-Davidson Twin Cam 88, 96 & 103 models (99 – 10)	♦	2478
HONDA NB, ND, NP & NS50 Melody (81 -85)	◇	0622
Honda NE/NB50 Vision & SA50 Vision Met-in (85-95)	◇	1278
Honda MB, MBX, MT & MTX50 (80 – 93)		0731
Honda C50, C70 & C90 (67 – 03)		0324
Honda XR50/70/80/100R & CRF50/70/80/100F (85 – 07)		2218
Honda XL/XR 80, 100, 125, 185 & 200 2-valve models (78 – 87)		0566
Honda H100 & H100S Singles (80 – 92)	◇	0734
Honda 125 Scooters (00 – 09)		4873
Honda ANF125 Innova Scooters (03 -12)	♦	4926
Honda CB/CD125T & CM125C Twins (77 – 88)	◇	0571
Honda CBF125 (09 – 14)	♦	5540
Honda CG125 (76 – 07)	◇	0433
Honda NS125 (86 – 93)	◇	3056
Honda CBR125R (04 – 10)		4620
Honda CBR125R, CBR250R & CRF250L/M (11 – 14)	♦	5919
Honda MBX/MTX125 & MTX200 (83 – 93)	◇	1132
Honda XL125V & VT125C (99 – 11)		4899
Honda CD/CM185 200T & CM250C 2-valve Twins (77 – 85)		0572
Honda CMX250 Rebel & CB250 Nighthawk Twins (85 – 09)	◇	2756
Honda XL/XR 250 & 500 (78 – 84)		0567
Honda XR250L, XR250R & XR400R (86 – 04)		2219
Honda CB250 & CB400N Super Dreams (78 – 84)	◇	0540
Honda CR Motocross Bikes (86 – 07)		2222
Honda CRF250 & CRF450 (02 – 06)		2630
Honda CBR400RR Fours (88 – 99)	◇♦	3552
Honda VFR400 (NC30) & RVF400 (NC35) V-Fours (89 – 98)	◇♦	3496
Honda CB500 (93 – 02) & CBF500 (03 – 08)	◇	3753
Honda CB400 & CB550 Fours (73 – 77)		0262
Honda CX/GL500 & 650 V-Twins (78 – 86)		0442
Honda CBX550 Four (82 – 86)	◇	0940
Honda XL600R & XR600R (83 – 08)	♦	2183
Honda XL600/650V Transalp & XRV750 Africa Twin (87 – 07)	♦	3919
Honda CB600 Hornet, CBF600 & CBR600F (07 – 12)	♦	5572
Honda CBR600F1 & 1000F Fours (87 – 96)	♦	1730
Honda CBR600F2 & F3 Fours (91 – 98)	♦	2070
Honda CBR600F4 (99 – 06)	♦	3911
Honda CB600F Hornet & CBF600 (98 – 06)	◇♦	3915
Honda CBR600RR (03 – 06)	♦	4590
Honda CBR600RR (07 -12)	♦	4795
Honda CB650 sohc Fours (78 – 84)		0665
Honda NTV600 Revere, NTV650 & NT650V Deauville (88 – 05)	◇♦	3243
Honda Shadow VT600 & 750 (USA) (88 – 09)		2312
Honda NT700V Deauville & XL700V Transalp (06 -13)	♦	5541
Honda CB750 sohc Four (69 – 79)		0131
Honda V45/65 Sabre & Magna (82 – 88)		0820
Honda VFR750 & 700 V-Fours (86 – 97)	♦	2101
Honda VFR800 V-Fours (97 – 01)	♦	3703
Honda VFR800 V-Tec V-Fours (02 – 09)	♦	4196
Honda CB750 & CB900 dohc Fours (78 – 84)		0535
Honda CBF1000 (06 -10) & CB1000R (08 – 11)	♦	4927
Honda VTR1000 Firestorm, Super Hawk & XL1000V Varadero (97 – 08)	♦	3744
Honda CBR900RR Fireblade (92 – 99)	♦	2161
Honda CBR900RR Fireblade (00 – 03)	♦	4060
Honda CBR1000RR Fireblade (04 – 07)	♦	4604
Honda CBR1000RR Fireblade (08 – 13)	♦	5688
Honda CBR1100XX Super Blackbird (97 – 07)	♦	3901
Honda ST1100 Pan European V-Fours (90 – 02)	♦	3384
Honda ST1300 Pan European (02 -11)	♦	4908
Honda Shadow VT1100 (USA) (85 – 07)		2313

Title		Book No
Honda GL1000 Gold Wing (75 – 79)		0309
Honda GL1100 Gold Wing (79 – 81)		0669
Honda Gold Wing 1200 (USA) (84 - 87)		2199
Honda Gold Wing 1500 (USA) (88 – 00)		2225
Honda Goldwing GL1800	♦	2787
KAWASAKI AE/AR 50 & 80 (81 – 95)		1007
Kawasaki KC, KE & KH100 (75 – 99)		1371
Kawasaki KMX125 & 200 (86 – 02)	◇	3046
Kawasaki 250, 350 & 400 Triples (72 – 79)		0134
Kawasaki 400 & 440 Twins (74 – 81)		0281
Kawasaki 400, 500 & 550 Fours (79 – 91)		0910
Kawasaki EN450 & 500 Twins (Ltd/Vulcan) (85 – 07)		2053
Kawasaki ER-6F & ER-6N (06 -10)	♦	4874
Kawasaki EX500 (GPZ500S) & ER500 (ER-5) (87 – 08)	♦	2052
Kawasaki ZX600 (ZZ-R600 & Ninja ZX-6) (90 – 06)	♦	2146
Kawasaki ZX-6R Ninja Fours (95 – 02)	♦	3451
Kawasaki ZX-6R (03 – 06)	♦	4742
Kawasaki ZX600 (GPZ600R, GPX600R, Ninja 600R & RX) & ZX750 (GPX750R, Ninja 750R) (85 – 97)	♦	1780
Kawasaki 650 Four (76 – 78)		0373
Kawasaki Vulcan 700/750 & 800 (85 – 04)	♦	2457
Kawasaki Vulcan 1500 & 1600 (87 – 08)	♦	4913
Kawasaki 750 Air-cooled Fours		0574
Kawasaki ZR550 & 750 Zephyr Fours (90 – 97)	♦	3382
Kawasaki Z750 & Z1000 (03 – 08)	♦	4762
Kawasaki ZX750 (Ninja ZX-7 & ZXR750) Fours (89 – 96)	♦	2054
Kawasaki Ninja ZX-7R & ZX-9R (94 – 04)	♦	3721
Kawasaki 900 & 1000 Fours (73 – 77)		0222
Kawasaki ZX900, 1000 & 1100 Liquid-cooled Fours (83 – 97)	♦	1681
Kawasaki ZX-10R (04 – 10)	♦	5542
KTM EXC Enduro & SX Motocross (00 – 07)	♦	4629
LAMBRETTA Scooters (58 – 00)	♦	5573
MOTO GUZZI 750, 850 & 1000 V-Twins (74 – 78)		0339
MZ ETZ models (81 – 95)	◇	1680
NORTON 500, 600, 650 & 750 Twins (57 – 70)		0187
Norton Commando (68 – 77)		0125
PEUGEOT Speedfight, Trekker & Vivacity Scooters (96 – 08)	◇	3920
Peugeot V-Clic, Speedfight 3, Vivacity 3, Kisbee & Tweet (08 – 14)	◇♦	5751
PIAGGIO (Vespa) Scooters (91 – 09)	◇	3492
SUZUKI GT, ZR & TS50 (77 – 90)	◇	0799
Suzuki TS50X (84 – 00)	◇	1599
Suzuki 100, 125, 185 & 250 Air-cooled Trail bikes (79 – 89)		0797
Suzuki GP100 & 125 Singles (78 – 93)	◇	0576
Suzuki GS, GN, GZ & DR125 Singles (82 – 05)	◇	0888
Suzuki Burgman 250 & 400 (98 – 11)	♦	4909
Suzuki GSX-R600/750 (06 – 09)	♦	4790
Suzuki 250 & 350 Twins (68 – 78)		0120
Suzuki GT250X7, GT200X5 & SB200 Twins (78 – 83)	◇	0469
Suzuki DR-Z400 (00 – 10)	♦	2933
Suzuki GS/GSX250, 400 & 450 Twins (79 – 85)		0736
Suzuki GS500 Twin (89 – 08)	♦	3238
Suzuki GS550 (77 – 82) & GS750 Fours (76 – 79)		0363
Suzuki GS/GSX550 4-valve Fours (83 – 88)		1133
Suzuki SV650 & SV650S (99 – 08)	♦	3912
Suzuki DL650 V-Strom & SFV650 Gladius (04 – 13)	♦	5643
Suzuki GSX-R600 & 750 (96 – 00)	♦	3553
Suzuki GSX-R600 (01 – 03), GSX-R750 (00 – 03) & GSX-R1000 (01 – 02)	♦	3986
Suzuki GSX-R600/750 (04 – 05) & GSX-R1000 (03 – 06)	♦	4382
Suzuki GSF600, 650 & 1200 Bandit Fours (95 – 06)	♦	3367
Suzuki Intruder, Marauder, Volusia & Boulevard (85 – 09)	♦	2618
Suzuki GS850 Fours (78 – 88)		0536
Suzuki GS1000 Four (77 – 79)		0484
Suzuki GSX-R750, GSX-R1100 (85 – 92) GSX600F, GSX750F, GSX1100F (Katana) Fours (88 – 96)	♦	2055
Suzuki GSX600/750F & GSX750 (98 – 02)	♦	3987
Suzuki GS/GSX1000, 1100 & 1150 4-valve Fours (79 – 88)		0737
Suzuki TL1000S/R & DL V-Strom (97 – 04)	♦	4083
Suzuki GSF650/1250 Bandit & GSX650/1250F (07 – 14)	♦	4798
Suzuki GSX1300R Hayabusa (99 – 14)	♦	4184
Suzuki GSX1400 (02 – 08)	♦	4758
TRIUMPH Tiger Cub & Terrier (52 – 68)		0414
Triumph 350 & 500 Unit Twins (58 – 73)		0137
Triumph Pre-Unit Twins (47 – 62)		0251
Triumph 650 & 750 2-valve Unit Twins (63 – 83)		0122
Triumph 675 (06 – 10)	♦	4876
Triumph Tiger 800 (10 – 14)	♦	5752
Triumph 1050 Sprint, Speed Triple & Tiger (05 -13)	♦	4796
Triumph Trident & BSA Rocket 3 (69 – 75)		0136
Triumph Bonneville (01 – 12)	♦	4364
Triumph Daytona, Speed Triple, Sprint & Tiger (97 – 05)	♦	3755
Triumph Triples & Fours (carburettor engines) (91 – 04)	♦	2162
VESPA P/PX125, 150 & 200 Scooters (78 – 12)		0707
Vespa GTS125, 250 & 300 (05 – 10)		4898
Vespa Scooters (59 – 78)		0126

Title		Book No
YAMAHA DT50 & 80 Trail Bikes (78 – 95)	◇	0800
Yamaha T50 & 80 Townmate (83 – 95)	◇	1247
Yamaha YB100 Singles (73 – 91)	◇	0474
Yamaha RS/RXS 100 & 125 Singles (74 – 95)		0331
Yamaha RD & DT125LC (82 – 87)	◇	0887
Yamaha TZR125 (87 – 93) & DT125R (88 – 07)	◇	1655
Yamaha TY50, 80, 125 & 175 (74 – 84)	◇	0464
Yamaha XT & SR125 (82 – 03)	◇	1021
Yamaha YBR125 & XT125R/X (05 – 13)		4797
Yamaha YZF-R125 (08 – 11)	♦	5543
Yamaha Trail Bikes (81 – 03)		2350
Yamaha 2-stroke Motocross Bikes (86 – 06)		2662
Yamaha YZ & WR 4-stroke Motorcross Bikes (98 – 08)		2689
Yamaha 250 & 350 Twins (70 – 79)		0040
Yamaha XS250, 360 & 400 sohc Twins (75 – 84)		0378
Yamaha RD250 & 350LC Twins (80 – 82)		0803
Yamaha RD350 YPVS Twins (83 – 95)		1158
Yamaha RD400 Twin (75 – 79)		0333
Yamaha XT, TT & SR500 Singles (75 – 83)		0342
Yamaha XZ550 Vision V-Twins (82 – 85)		0821
Yamaha FJ, FX, XY & YX600 Radian (84 – 92)		2100
Yamaha XT660 & MT-03 (04 – 11)	♦	4910
Yamaha XJ600S (Diversion, Seca II) & XJ600N Fours (92 – 03)	♦	2145
Yamaha XJ6 & FZ6R (09 – 15)	♦	5889
Yamaha YZF600R Thundercat & FZS600 Fazer (96 – 03)	♦	3702
Yamaha FZ-6 Fazer (04 – 08)	♦	4751
Yamaha YZF-R6 (99 – 02)	♦	3900
Yamaha YZF-R6 (03 – 05)	♦	4601
Yamaha YZF-R6 (06 – 13)	♦	5544
Yamaha 650 Twins (70 – 83)		0341
Yamaha XJ650 & 750 Fours (80 – 84)		0738
Yamaha XS750 & 850 Triples (76 – 85)		0340
Yamaha TDM850, TRX850 & XTZ750 (89 – 99)	◇♦	3450
Yamaha YZF750R & YZF1000R Thunderace (93 – 00)	♦	3720
Yamaha FZR600, 750 & 1000 Fours (87 – 96)	♦	2056
Yamaha XV (Virago) V-Twins (81 – 03)	♦	0802
Yamaha XVS650 & 1100 Drag Star/V-Star (97 – 05)	♦	4195
Yamaha XJ900F Fours (83 – 94)	♦	3239
Yamaha XJ900S Diversion (94 – 01)	♦	3739
Yamaha YZF-R1 (98 – 03)	♦	3754
Yamaha YZF-R1 (04 – 06)	♦	4605
Yamaha FZS1000 Fazer (01 – 05)	♦	4287
Yamaha FJ1100 & 1200 Fours (84 – 96)	♦	2057
Yamaha FJR1300 (01 – 13)	♦	5607
Yamaha XJR1200 & 1300 (95 – 06)	♦	3981
Yamaha V-Max (85 – 03)	♦	4072
ATVs		
Honda ATC 70, 90, 110, 185 & 200 (71 – on)		0565
Honda Rancher, Recon & TRX250EX ATVs		2553
Honda TRX300 Shaft Drive ATVs (88 – 00)		2125
Honda Foreman (95 – 11)		2465
Honda TRX300EX, TRX400EX & TRX450R/ER ATVs (93 – 06)		2318
Kawasaki Bayou 220/250/300 & Prairie 300 ATVs (86 – 03)		2351
Polaris ATVs (85 – 97)		2302
Polaris ATVs (98 – 07)		2508
Suzuki/Kawasaki/Artic Cat ATVs (03 – 09)		2910
Yamaha YFS200 Blaster ATV (88 – 06)		2317
Yamaha YFM350 & YFM400 (ER & Big Bear) ATVs (87 – 09)		2126
Yamaha YFZ450 & YFZ450R (04 – 10)		2899
Yamaha Banshee and Warrior ATVs (87 – 10)		2314
Yamaha Kodiak and Grizzly ATVs (93 – 05)		2567
ATV Basics		10450
SCOOTERS		
Twist and Go (automatic transmission) Scooters Service and Repair Manual	◇	4082
TECHBOOK SERIES		
Motorcycle Basics Techbook (2nd edition)		3515
Motorcycle Electrical Techbook (3rd edition)		3471
Motorcycle Fuel Systems Techbook		3514
Motorcycle Maintenance Techbook		4071
Motorcycle Modifying		4272
Motorcycle Workshop Practice Techbook (2nd edition)		3470

◇ = not available in the USA ♦ = Superbike

The manuals on this page are available through good motorcycle dealers and accessory shops.
In case of difficulty, contact: **Haynes Publishing**
(UK) **+44 1963 442030** (USA) **+1 805 498 6703**
(SV) **+46 18 124016**
(Australia/New Zealand) **+61 2 8713 1400**

MCL 07.05.15

Preserving Our Motoring Heritage

The Model J Duesenberg Derham Tourster. Only eight of these magnificent cars were ever built – this is the only example to be found outside the United States of America

Almost every car you've ever loved, loathed or desired is gathered under one roof at the Haynes Motor Museum. Over 300 immaculately presented cars and motorbikes represent every aspect of our motoring heritage, from elegant reminders of bygone days, such as the superb Model J Duesenberg to curiosities like the bug-eyed BMW Isetta. There are also many old friends and flames. Perhaps you remember the 1959 Ford Popular that you did your courting in? The magnificent 'Red Collection' is a spectacle of classic sports cars including AC, Alfa Romeo, Austin Healey, Ferrari, Lamborghini, Maserati, MG, Riley, Porsche and Triumph.

A Perfect Day Out

Each and every vehicle at the Haynes Motor Museum has played its part in the history and culture of Motoring. Today, they make a wonderful spectacle and a great day out for all the family. Bring the kids, bring Mum and Dad, but above all bring your camera to capture those golden memories for ever. You will also find an impressive array of motoring memorabilia, a comfortable 70 seat video cinema and one of the most extensive transport book shops in Britain. The Pit Stop Cafe serves everything from a cup of tea to wholesome, home-made meals or, if you prefer, you can enjoy the large picnic area nestled in the beautiful rural surroundings of Somerset.

John Haynes O.B.E., Founder and Chairman of the museum at the wheel of a Haynes Light 12.

The 1936 490cc sohc-engined International Norton – well known for its racing success

The Museum is situated on the A359 Yeovil to Frome road at Sparkford, just off the A303 in Somerset. It is about 40 miles south of Bristol, and 25 minutes drive from the M5 intersection at Taunton.
Open 9.30am - 5.30pm (10.00am - 4.00pm Winter) 7 days a week, *except Christmas Day, Boxing Day and New Years Day*
Special rates available for schools, coach parties and outings   Charitable Trust No. 292048